LABOR:

Readings on

Major Issues

LABOR:

READINGS ON
MAJOR ISSUES

Richard A. Lester

CHAIRMAN, DEPARTMENT OF ECONOMICS

PRINCETON UNIVERSITY

RANDOM HOUSE

NEW YORK

PREFACE

This book of readings is designed to supplement a textbook for college courses in labor economics, labor problems, industrial relations, or collective bargaining. The introductory statements also facilitate its use as the basic reading material in short courses or programs for management or union groups.

To stimulate thought and discussion in the classroom, the book stresses analysis and major policy issues. The forty-odd selections have been chosen for their depth of treatment and their differences in approach and viewpoint. They include historical, institutional, and political analysis as well as various aspects of economic theory. A number of the selections are classics.

Most of the material in this book has been tested by classroom experience. For the past thirteen years the author has compiled a series of annual collections of reprints of important articles for use as supplementary reading in a one-term course in labor problems taken by approximately a hundred juniors and seniors and an advanced seminar in labor economics taken by fifteen to twenty seniors with special interests in the labor field. In both courses, some forty different articles and cases have been included in the assigned reading. In the introductory course, groups of eight to ten students ("precepts" in the Princeton terminology) meet each week with the instructor to discuss issues. These discussions help each student to prepare a short paper carefully analyzing the policies of the union that he selects from a list of some thirty national unions at the beginning of the term. In the seminar course, the articles provide a basis for critical oral and written reports by the students.

Special features of this book include: (1) concentration on a limited number of basic issues; (2) an ample introduction to each part in order to orient the reader and to point up the issues; (3) each part organized as a self-contained unit, permitting use in any order; (4) largely unabridged articles that enable the reader to appreciate the full range of the author's thought; (5) focus of the historical material on the period since 1900 and especially on the 1930's; (6) considerable attention to union development and to individual unions; (7) frequent application of economic analysis particularly in Parts IV, V, and VI; (8) extensive material on national manpower problems, including the President's 1964 manpower report; (9) a few well chosen cases, two of them providing sufficient detail to bring out the importance of personal, institutional, and historical factors as well as economic elements, especially at the plant level.

In a lively and controversial subject like labor, experience shows the need for a knowledge of various approaches, emphases, and insights. Truth in the labor field is not encased in a simple set of propositions or formulas. In a complex, many-faceted subject, eclecticism is not an intellectual offense. It is wiser to appreciate the limitations of approaches and conclusions than to be blindly doctrinaire, and to be approximately or conditionally correct than to be unqualifiedly and precisely wrong.

I wish to thank the hundreds of Princeton students whose comments on questionnaires and in oral discussion in seminars have served as a helpful guide in the selection of this set of readings. Thanks are also expressed to the publishers for permission to reprint, so that articles from a wide variety of sources can find more convenient access and added usefulness between the covers of a single book. From some of the articles, footnotes for acknowledgment or reference purposes have been omitted. Wherever any textual material has been excised, that fact has been indicated by the customary ellipsis.

This book will have achieved its purpose if it opens up new avenues of thought and stimulates a search for answers to the complex problems of labor in our highly specialized and technical society.

                                                                    R.A.L.

Princeton, N. J.

CONTENTS

PART IV. UNION ANALYSIS AND PRACTICE

PART V. WAGE THEORY, LABOR MARKETS, AND NATIONAL WAGE POLICY

PART VI. AUTOMATION AND JOB RIGHTS

PART VII. COLLECTIVE BARGAINING

PART VIII. PUBLIC POLICY AND LABOR RELATIONS LAW

PART IX. MANPOWER PLANNING

PART X. CASES

L A B O R :

Readings on

Major Issues

PART I

ASPECTS OF AMERICAN LABOR HISTORY

INTRODUCTION

Throughout the nineteenth and the first half of the twentieth centuries, industrial relations in the United States involved a struggle between two conflicting philosophies. The dominant elements in American management favored the view that stressed competition in labor, individualism, property rights, and freedom and authority for management, and assumed that management and worker interests were basically the same. On the other hand, proponents of labor organization and collective bargaining emphasized group action to negotiate and enforce job rights, protection of workers from competitive pressures and arbitrary management actions, the need to force consideration of the human costs of production, and the introduction of elements of democracy into life in factories.

Clashes between those two philosophies took place not only in industry but also in the legislatures and the courts throughout the nineteenth century. However, significant alterations in the position and power of management and labor began to occur, as Cyrus Ching points out in the first selection, only when labor was in short supply during World War I. The balance of power shifted much more in labor's direction with the upheavals of the Great Depression of the 1930's. As established patterns of life and thought were badly shaken and many workers, believing that they had been unfairly treated by management, flocked into unions as a means of redressing their grievances, labor won new rights at the bargaining table and in law.

Ching's experience spans the first half of the twentieth century and dramatically illustrates the conflict of labor philosophies in practice. He sets forth the "calloused indifference" of most managements toward employees, the wide use of labor spies and thugs as strikebreakers, and the rugged individualism prevalent in management circles, especially in large firms using immigrant labor. Ching then explains the "social awakening" which occurred as a result of economic conditions during World War I that stimulated the rise of modern industrial relations policies and practices. Some prominent industrial leaders began to show genuine interest in the welfare of their employees. This was evidenced by the establishment of industrial councils or employee representation plans in factories in the 1920's, when unionization of the mass production industries was simply not a possible alternative.

The second selection (excerpts from the 1937 report of the LaFollette Committee on industrial espionage) deals with the extent and effectiveness of hired spies in unions during the period about which Ching wrote—from 1900 until 1937, when the Wagner Act, which outlawed that practice, was declared constitutional by the Supreme Court. Widespread use of union spies by leading businesses showed how far American management was willing to go to prevent or destroy labor organization, and helps to explain the militant character of and violent episodes in American labor history prior to World War II.

Written late in 1937, the *Fortune* article, "Industrial Warfare," reveals the war-like character of management-union relations in much of American industry in the mid-1930's; the conflict of philosophies and the struggle for rights were bitterly and sometimes ruthlessly contested.

The last item in Part I, taken from the reports of the McClellan Committee, shows the use of violence and unscrupulous practices by some elements in organized labor in the 1950's, particularly in the Teamsters' union. It was such actions that led in part to the post-war shift in Federal policy toward organized labor. Under the Taft-Hartley Act (1947), curbs were placed on the uses of union power against management and the public. The Landrum-Griffin Act, adopted in 1959 following the McClellan Committee's revelations, seeks to prevent dictatorial control of unions and their use for corrupt purposes.

The half century beginning with World War I has witnessed great changes in the industrial relations policies of American management and in the activities and status of organized labor. Instead of treating employees with "calloused indifference" (a commodity-like concept of labor), management has generally followed an industrial relations philosophy that stresses employee welfare, two-way communication, and good human relations in the plant.

From an almost alien element in American culture, organized labor has developed into a major economic and political force in our society. It was favored by Congress and the public in the 1930's, but misuse of power by labor led to the adoption of legal curbs on abuses by and in unions two decades later. At the same time, unions were maturing in their aims and methods and becoming integrated into the American economy.

Although violence has been largely replaced by negotiation, arbitration, and legal settlement in American labor relations, basic philosophic differences remain. But management and organized labor have learned how to resolve conflicts of interest by practical adaptations. They have learned to live together, if not completely in industrial peace, at least in tolerance and often in cooperative problem-solving.

My Life in
Industrial Relations

CYRUS CHING

The year 1900, except as the beginning of a new century, was not particularly unusual or important in world or national history. But it was of especial importance to me. It was the year I left my native Prince Edward Island, a small piece of pasture and fir, shaped like a Scotty dog, off the coast of New Brunswick and Nova Scotia, in Canada. Wearied of the frugal farm life, I headed for the big town "down south," Boston. It was the thing to do among the adventurous young people of Canada—to go to the "States."

When I took the big step, Queen Victoria was still reigning over Britain, including little Prince Edward Island. It was the year of the Boxer Insurrection in China, the Galveston, Texas, hurricane in which thousands lost their lives. President McKinley was seeking re-election against the silver-tongued orator, William Jennings Bryan. Maude Adams, William Gillette, Sir Henry Irving and Maurice Barrymore were toasts of the theatrical set. In sports, James J. Jeffries held sway over the heavy-weight boxers, and a group of baseball "outlaws" were talking about organizing an "American League" as a rival to the long-established National.

It is hard now to tell people what things were like when I arrived in Boston in 1900 without my being accused of dreaming. There were no labor-management relations as we know them. A Socialist, Eugene B. Debs, was, in the language of the industrial leaders, still "trying to

Taken from Mr. Ching's book, Review and Reflection, A Half Century of Labor Relations *(New York: B. C. Forbes and Sons, 1953), Chapters 1 and 3, pp. 3–16 and 25–34. Reprinted with the permission of the publisher. At the time the book was written Ching had retired as director of the Federal Mediation and Conciliation Service and was in consulting practice.*

stir up trouble." The most respected man in the union ranks was Samuel Gompers. But even Mr. Gompers divided labor into two classes, the skilled, and the unskilled. And, outside of Mr. Gompers' own cigar-makers, some on the railroads, in the coal mines, the printing and building trades, there were comparatively few union members.

It was a period when the law of supply and demand governed labor relations. And the supply of labor, at least around Boston, ran ahead of the demand, with the still heavy flow of Europeans and Canadians into the country. Most of these immigrants were accustomed to little or nothing and they were willing to work for just that. They were handicapped by differences in language and customs. I was one of the "immigrants," but I was fortunate in having more of a community of interest with Americans than, for example, even some of my fellow Canadians, who spoke only French.

That is not to say that I was a particularly fortunate or attractive immigrant when I arrived in Boston. I had $31 in my pocket, Bryce's *American Commonwealth* in my bag, and no idea where, or how, I could earn more. Other than being unusually tall, six feet, seven inches, and unusually seedy, I had no personal distinctions. I wore ready-made clothes. There was some distance between my hands and the coat sleeves, and my pants averaged about six inches too short.

My early activities in this new country of the United States, needless to say, were limited by the size of my bankroll. But I made out until I found a job, living costs in 1900 being what they were. I found a $1-a-week room and a "perfect" eating place on Tremont Street in Boston. It had the best buy in food in town—a large plate of beans, two slices of bread, a big piece of apple pie and coffee, all for ten cents. I ate the same meal twice a day.

Aside from a kindredship with Americans in language and customs, I had another advantage over some immigrants. I had had quite a bit of schooling. I had attended Prince of Wales College in Prince Edward Island and also had taken a business course. So, it wasn't long before I landed a job as a motorman with the Boston Elevated. That is, I got the job and became a streetcar motorman after a little training.

I never had any ambition of conquering the world. In those days, I wanted to be a lawyer. About my only other ambition, and it drove me rather hard, was to get all of the book knowledge and practical knowledge that I could absorb. I had no idea of remaining with the Boston Elevated beyond the period of schooling. It was just a job to tide me over while I took a law course at night.

The hours were long. The pay was something short of handsome. I was on the so-called "extra list," and my average pay for the first few months was $7 per week. There was little time for social life. However, for several years I retained a $1 balcony seat at the Hollis Street Theater. I still vividly recall seeing Maude Adams in "Chanticleer," E. S. Willard in "The Cardinal," and Sir Henry Irving and Ellen Terry in "Macbeth."

My experience in the early 1900's with the working man and management was, of course, limited to the situations on the Boston Elevated Railroad. But I have learned since that conditions of employment on the Elevated were little different from those in most big companies of the country, regardless of the type of business in which they were engaged. The history of employee-employer relations of the company for which I worked was typical of national relations between management and the workers.

The working man, at the time my story begins, and for years afterward, was subjected to long hours, a bare subsistence wage, and terribly bad and hazardous working conditions. The average employer regarded his employees, particularly in the lower ranks, with a sort of calloused indifference to their plight which today almost defies comprehension. This was especially true of the larger companies. There were exceptions in the smaller outfits where the employers and their workers grew up together and enjoyed a closer relationship. The individual employee of the larger companies didn't count for much. Those were the days before the United States Supreme Court ruled that a worker was not a commodity, but a human being and must be treated as such. The worker was looked upon as just part of the machinery which kept the company operating and he was treated like that. If he were injured or totally incapacitated, even in line of duty, he was cast aside and replaced like a broken piece of equipment. There was no workmen's compensation to tide him over. And rare was the employer who gave a tinker's dam what happened to him. If a man was injured on the job, the only remedy he had at that time was recourse to the common law, and when such action was taken, it was met by the "contributory negligence" defense. This defense was, in most cases, very effective in preventing any very large awards being made.

The main objectives of managements in those days were to keep the surplus of manpower high and wages low. Even worse conditions in many foreign countries, coupled with an immigration policy in the United States which placed virtually no restriction on entry into the country, permitted managements to realize their objectives. There was a steady flow of manpower for the mills, factories, and railroads from other counties. Most people today do not realize that these conditions existed in this country; they were so much superior to the conditions existing in many of the countries from which immigrants came that most people were happy and well satisfied with their changed status in the new country.

Employers and politicians alike didn't have the concept then of the worker and the consumer being identical. They didn't realize, as most of us do now, that if you improve the lot of the working people, you increase the business of the country and improve the lot of all the people. In 1914, when Henry Ford established the $5-a-day minimum wage, it was considered by most people to be extreme radicalism, but it was the first time that the idea of the worker as a consumer began to take hold. There was no recognition or practice of the social sciences as we know them. The immigrants were brought in and dumped. Nothing was done to Americanize them, and many who spoke in foreign tongues never learned English. They lived apart from old-line Americans, most of whom were on management's side. This situation prevailed in most New England communities, and also in many other parts of the country.

The social awakening began only after this country became involved in World War I. And it resulted from an economic situation, rather than an improvement of conscience of employers. The war stopped importation of labor and quickened the wheels of American industry. The demand for labor increased. Soon the demand exceeded the supply. In order to retain their workers, employers were forced to raise wages, reduce hours and improve working conditions. This period really marked the beginning of the development of labor relations as we know the subject.

Union organizing is exceedingly difficult at a time of labor surplus even when the climate is otherwise favorable. In the early 1900's there existed every conceivable barrier to the growth of unions and the consequent improvement in the lot of workers. The idea of people banding together in organizations for improvement of their economic well-being was not accepted in most communities.

Elaborate and highly effective spy systems in most companies made it almost impossible for unions to get started. Company spies were strategically placed among the employees to report to their employers everything the workers did, almost every thought they expressed. If a couple of employees started talking union, they were fired forthwith. The employer then did not need, by today's standards, any really valid reason to discharge a worker. He could fire for "union activity" with impunity. Or, if the manager wished to be a little subtle about it, he would use some vague term such as "unsatisfactory service" as the reason. It was about this time that Louis Brandeis, who later became Justice of the Supreme Court of the United States, began to crusade for better employer-employee relationships, and for more consideration of the workers as individuals. He also believed strongly in the system of collective bargaining, but always emphasized the need for acceptance of responsibility on the part of those so engaged. The few unions which successfully ran the gauntlet of employer resistance, found their activities greatly restricted by governmental and court action. Strikes were readily broken by police action and court injunction.

I recall a big textile strike at Lawrence, Mass., in 1912, which the police ended by the un-American, though highly effective, method of shipping the strikers and their families out of town. It didn't cause much of a stir at the time because it wasn't very unusual. One of the people arrested and tossed into jail, for actively aiding the strike, was the little Scotsman, the late Robert Watt, who, many years later, was to become my good and highly respected friend. Mr. Watt rose to high rank in the AFL and was member of the National War Labor Board in World War II. He was looked upon by employers, government officials and labor leaders alike as a statesman in the field of labor relations.

Even where force was not used, striking unions and their leaders were so harassed by court injunctions and criminal indictments that they were soon compelled to give up the fight for recognition or improvement of wage or working conditions. Strike-breaking, through the importation of thugs and gunmen as replacements for the strikers, was a big business in the early 1900's and continued to be a big business for many years.

And, as I said earlier, about the only potent force in the union organizing line was represented by Samuel Gompers, the London-born cigar-maker, and his then numerically small American Federation of Labor. Mr. Gompers was interested in organizing only the aristocrats of the American labor force, the highly skilled of the building and metal trades. He regarded the semi-skilled and unskilled millions as either not worth organizing or too difficult to enroll. Unfortunately, it was this large group which felt the full force of the industrial policy of exploitation of labor, and was in most need of any help they might get through unionization.

Working conditions on the Boston Elevated were about as I have described when I went to work there. They had a very efficient company espionage system. There had been a strike a few years before. The strikers were fired and replaced, and the company officers were taking no chances of another union movement catching them by surprise.

Although always interested in people, their problems and interrelationships, I didn't choose the field of labor relations as my career, but drifted into it purely by accident and force of circumstances. As I said, my original plan was to be a lawyer.

In 1904, four years after I came to Boston, I had advanced from motorman to the position of trouble-shooter in the repair of electric railway equipment. This job was twelve hours a day, seven days a week, and the pay was $18.50 per week.

One warm day in August, the height of the afternoon rush hour found me working rather hurriedly to fix a loose shoe fuse on a stalled train. Standing on a dry board, I gripped a wire carrying 5,000 amperes and began to twist it off—a clear case of contributory negligence or recklessness. My clothes were wet with sweat, and while leaning over, my rump touched the damp wall of the tunnel. The initial shock threw me off balance. I slipped and grabbed a steel truss rod with my free hand. Then, the full power of the voltage flashed through my body, enveloping me in blue flame. It blew the circuit-breakers in the powerhouse and stopped the entire subway and elevated system.

When the police arrived, they found all my hair and my clothes burned off. My body was charred. They wrapped me in blankets and carried me to the nearest hospital in a horse-drawn ambulance.

Six days later I regained consciousness—in the DT ward. The doctors, not expecting me to live, had put me there to get me out of the way. They now gave me a chance to live, although they thought I would be permanently blinded. Actually, I was completely recovered in about four months. A rugged constitution plus kind attention of nurses and doctors worked miracles. My body still bears scars of the near electrocution, and the memory of it is still as vivid with me as though it happened yesterday.

As it turned out, that terrible experience did more to chart my career than anything else that ever happened. Some friends inquired and came to see me while I was recovering, in the hospital, but as far as I know, no one from the company ever called. From the minute the news of the accident came into company headquarters I was off the payroll. It was simple, and the truth, for them to say my negligence caused the accident. Although not very humanitarian, it was the practice of the times. I not only lost over four months' pay, but I had to foot the doctor bills. There was no recourse for me under the laws of those days.

While lying for months in the hospital, my thoughts centered on the queer, broad chasm between boss and worker, and I have been thinking about it ever since. It occurred to me then the system was wrong and somebody must do something about it, or one day there would be a terrific social explosion that would change the political complexion of the country.

On leaving the hospital, I returned to the employ of the company in another capacity, and later went back to the old job of trouble-shooting. Subsequently, I took another job which involved instructing motormen, conductors, and maintenance men on new electrical and air-brake equipment. It was a job on management's side of the fence. It was a job that gave me an opportunity to attempt to bridge the gap in relations between the employees and the company. I met a lot of people in the normal course of the new job, and went out of my way to meet more. Someone said later I could call 10,000 employees of the company by their first names, and it wasn't much of an exaggeration. I poked my nose into a lot of places not in my bailiwick and put in more hours than I had as a motorman.

During this period, I began to realize my life's ambition, entering Northeastern University Law School, and for four years I put in three nights a week at the University. When the schooling conflicted with my job, I paid someone to work for me. I was lucky during that period, what with work, school, and study, if I averaged five hours' sleep a night. After finishing the law course, I continued for another four years taking extension courses in philosophy, economics, public speaking. The economics as taught by Henry C. Metcalf had a sprinkling of what might be considered labor relations. He later became one of the outstanding teachers in the field of personnel management.

The Boston Elevated, like other companies at the time, had no employee relations or personnel department. After a man was hired and assigned a job, no one bothered about him as long as he did his work satisfactorily. The top rate for motormen and conductors was 22½ cents an hour. Some of the skilled people, who repaired and maintained equipment, got a bit more. No one was very happy about working for the utility.

For years there were rumblings of discontent among the workers, which became really serious in the spring of 1912. The company spy system turned up some talk about a union. The union turned out to be the Amalgamated Association of Street and Electric Railway Workers, AFL. It had won a toehold in some other cities and was trying to move into Boston. Those workers reported by spies as taking part in clandestine union meetings were summarily fired for "unsatisfactory service."

Altogether, about 170 people were discharged, most for union activity, but the movement among the employees to band together and do something about their lot had caught fire and the company couldn't stop it. More and more people began wearing union buttons, practically daring the company to fire them. There were too many of them for the management to cope with and maintain transit service.

The company, however, steadfastly refused to recognize the union or meet with its representatives, who had stored up an enormous number of grievances from individual employees. I was constantly advocating with my associates in management the idea that there must be something wrong in the relationships or we would not find ourselves in the position we were in. I was usually brushed off with the answer that possibly we could do something about it after the fuss had blown over. It soon became obvious that it was not the kind of fuss that was going to blow over very soon, and a strike was called by the union for June 12, 1912.

Some 7,000 employees of the Boston Elevated went on strike, including motormen, conductors and maintenance workers. The company engaged strike-breaking agencies, including the William J. Burns Detective Agency, Waddell & Mahon, Pinkerton, and others. Thugs, gunmen and other rough characters were employed and the cars continued to move, although not very regularly, as the strike spread. Then, the company began recruiting new people far and wide through the East and South as replacements for the professsional strike-breakers. A special school was set up to train them. There were dynamitings and other acts of violence.

Arrests and indictments alleging all sorts of real, and trumped-up offenses came thick and fast. One union business agent had 150 indictments against him when the strike finally was settled. Several of the railway superintendents were also indicted.

It was at this time I experienced my first taste of government intervention in a labor dispute, something I was to take part in hundreds of times in later years as an agent of government. The governor of Massachusetts at the time was Eugene Foss, and the mayor of Boston was John F. Fitzgerald, a colorful politician and father-in-law of Joseph P. Kennedy, who later was to hold many high Federal Government posts, including the Ambassadorship in London.

The striking union members had hired as their attorney a State senator, James H. Vahey, who, after entering the gubernatorial race against Foss, had withdrawn and thereby won the gratitude of the Governor.

At the suggestion of Attorney Vahey, Governor Foss called in William A. Bancroft, president of Boston Elevated, and, I understand, told him if he did not recognize the union he would investigate the activities of the company in the legislative field. The Governor's action did the trick and the company agreed to recognize the union, and the strike was over.

The first question to be settled involved company commitments to the new men hired from various parts of the country as replacements for the strikers. Arrangements were worked out to take back all the strikers and return the new people to their homes after paying them something for the inconvenience. This involved considerable expense to the company, but it paid dividends over the years in happier employee relations.

The violent strike, which lasted from early June to late August, had left our president, Mr. Bancroft, a nervous wreck. Someone had to meet the union and arrange terms for the strikers to come back, handle the many grievances, including the matter of what to do about the 170 people the company fired in its fruitless attempt to smash the union. A handful had been discharged for legitimate reasons, such as failure to register fares. But the only "crime" charged to most of the 170 was membership in the union, or so-called "unsatisfactory service." At the time, I was superintendent of instruction for operations and maintenance. Knowing no better, I volunteered, together with C. E. Learned, who was superintendent of inspection, to see what we could do in dealing with the union. Thus, I entered the labor relations business formally for the first time.

When our first meeting took place, we faced a union committee of 23 highly suspicious people who had every reason, nurtured in years of unhappy experience, not to trust company management or its agents. It was a new experience and a strange and uncomfortable situation. It had been a dirty strike. Both company and union had fought with every weapon at hand. The atmosphere was still bad. It was difficult to break the ice. I had some ideas on what to do, but they were untried and uncertain of success.

"What'll we talk about first?" the union chairman finally asked gruffly, "Reinstatement of the men?"

"No, I don't think that should come first," I answered after some thought, "I think first we should talk about how we are going to get along together."

Then I launched into a discourse on the company spy system, which, rightfully, was one of the sorest points with the employees. I told them there was no question that the company had spies all through the union, and, so far as I knew, there might be one in the room right at the moment. I said I knew the union also had spies. In fact, I continued, I knew there was a union spy down in my office. I had confronted the man and told him if he wished to continue working for me he would have to give up the extra activity. He blushed and asked to be allowed to stay.

"So long as I have anything to do about it," I told the union officers, "I will never tolerate any company spies in your union, and I do not want a spy of yours in our offices."

"I'm going to depend on you to tell me what goes on in your meetings that you feel I should know about. And there will be no company spying from now on." This policy had the backing of the management.

Rather accidentally, I had stumbled on the correct formula for better worker relations. Without intending to be boastful, my little talk did more to gain the confidence of the union people than anything else that happened.

With a new-born confidence in the air, and at least a basis for understanding, we were able to settle the cases of the discharged persons without too much difficulty. We agreed to take back those fired for union activity or "unsatisfactory service," and the union agreed to waive reinstatement claims of the few who were let go for "knocking fares" and other rule infractions.

The union then brought its demands for wage increases and improvement of working conditions. These, through mutual consent, were submitted to arbitration and, several months later, the union was awarded, among other things, a wage increase, as I recall it, of two or three cents an hour. The amount is practically nothing by present-day standards, but it seemed quite generous at the time.

Meanwhile, a change had taken place in the management of the company. A new president had taken over, a man who later became a very spectacular figure in Wall Street, Matthew C. Brush. He had the faculty of making friends, and had an extremely warm personality. He became quite friendly with William D. Mahon, who was then the international president of the Amalgamated Street and Electric Railway Workers. Due to the confidence that the employees of the company had in Mr. Brush, coupled with the confidence the union officials had in him, it helped very much in bringing about better relationships, and made the job less difficult in the attempts we were making to build up confidence and eliminate the suspicions that had existed for such a long time.

In the period 1912 to 1919, during which time I served as assistant to Mr. Brush, I learned the following principles and have adhered to them ever since:

1. Dealing with organized groups—unions—is not very different from dealing with individuals.

2. You must gain the confidence of the people you are dealing with, and that confidence must never be impaired or violated.

3. There must be a means of communication with all the workers, even those of the lowest rank. It must be a two-way system so that grievances can be spotted early and resolved quickly. A grievance, even a minor one, can become a major disturbance if allowed to fester unsettled.

Incidentally, the union on the Boston Elevated contributed indirectly to making Calvin Coolidge a national figure. It was the ambition of nearly every young man on the Boston Elevated who could pass the physical examination to get on the Boston police force. They were mostly of Irish and Maritime Canadian descent. Over a period of years, hundreds of our workers made the change. They had belonged to a labor union for years, so they carried the idea of unionization over to the police force. In 1919 wages on the "el" had caught up with police pay, which was held down by the city fathers. This outraged the policemen, who thought they had stepped up the social scale when they joined the force. So the police union, dominated by former "el" employees, struck. Whereupon Coolidge, then Governor of Massachusetts, quickly and before lawless elements could take over Boston, brought in the militia and smashed the strike. Coolidge, by his forthright handling of the very dangerous situation, gained nationwide fame and the Republican Vice Presidential nomination in 1920.

It was my firm conviction then, as it is now, that the action of Governor Coolidge on this occasion was the only action that a responsible officer of government could take, as I believe that those charged with the responsibility of law enforcement and the protection of the people should owe allegiance to no one but their government.

When the Boston Elevated passed from private hands to State ownershop, early in 1919, I looked around for another job. I thought I would be better off working for private enterprise than for the State. Naturally I leaned toward an industry which was expanding, and eventually decided on the rubber business. The Hood Rubber Company, Watertown, Massachusetts, offered me a job. I talked it over with Matthew C. Brush, who also had left the Elevated, and he advised connecting with a larger company like the United States Rubber Company.

I decided on a bold stroke, which I do not recommend, and probably would not use again. I sent a telegram to C. B. Seger, newly-elected president of U. S. Rubber, telling him I would be in his office in New York to see him at 10 o'clock the next morning. I had never met Mr. Seger, even casually. However, we soon discovered a common interest—railroading. He had had much more experience in that line than I. In fact, he had been president of the Union Pacific Railroad. We had a very pleasant chat, and I finally told him:

"I don't want a job. I want to help you run this company. My references are the motormen, conductors and directors of the Boston Elevated."

No one was as surprised as I when, a short time later, a message came from Mr. Seger, inviting me to New York to take a job. . . .

The decade from 1919 to the eve of the Great Depression . . . witnessed important advances in employers' recognition and understanding of worker problems. Our captains of industry may have buried their heads in the sand to the signs of economic collapse, but many of them gave a great deal of thought to labor-management relations, and actually, for the first time on any sizable scale, began doing something to improve those relations. This was true particularly of several of the big mass-production companies, although this may seem unbelievable in view of the bloody incidents that were to follow in the 1930's, accompanying the cio's drive to unionize the steel, automobile, rubber and other industries.

This birth of interest among industry leaders in the welfare of employees was not general. Like all great social movements, its beginnings were gradual among a comparatively few forward-thinking individuals. Their motivation may have been more practical and selfish than humanitarian. Regardless of motives, they were taking a long step forward from the time of calloused, and insensible, managerial indifference to the worker's plight, preceding World War I. And, as a result of this awakening of interest, a large number of wage-earners were removed from the old environment of the sweat shop.

I should make clear that the Boston Elevated Railroad, in the period following the 1912 strike, was far in front of the great majority of managements in its relations with employees. Our forced "awakening" came early. And I doubt seriously that our company would have seen the light had it not been for the strike intervention of Governor Foss.

There were several reasons why the industrial leaders began turning their attention to employee relations. The spectacle of the Bolshevist overturn of capitalism in Russia was jarring and, in some aspects, frightening. Lenin and his fellow-revolutionists were a far distance from our shores, but the basic theory of Marxism was one of world revolution, and already there were stirrings on this continent. One danger signal was in the activities of the International Workers of the World, the "Wobblies," as they were called. They were close kin of the Russian Bolsheviks. They had some toeholds in this country and in Canada. They paralyzed big cities by strikes.

Another reason was that more conservative unionism, as represented by the organizations of the American Federation of Labor, had made great strides during the war. The AFL, capitalizing on the ideal climate of low wages and high prices, made a drive and increased its membership from 1,900,000 in 1915 to over 4,000,000 in 1920. This was an alarming development to the industry people, many of whom pictured even an AFL organizer as a dangerous person, along with the IWW's. They associated unionism with collectivism. The objective of both, they thought, was the overturn of free enterprise. They had been jarred by abortive strikes in steel and other industries. They believed the unions had no business in their plants. They were determined, at all costs, to keep the unions out, and one way of doing it was to give better treatment to the employees.

A third reason, and an important one, for the awakening of management, was ultimately the realization among industrial leaders that good employee relations was good business which would pay off well in the long run in greater and more efficient production. This was manifested in the changed attitude on the part of many employers who began to treat their employees as people rather than as numbers on the payroll.

The sharply contrasting attitudes of the times toward the labor relations problem are illustrated by my experiences in the days following the war, after I had gone to work for the United States Rubber Company.

The name of Herbert Hoover has become synonymous and, I think, erroneously, with ultra-conservatism in this country. In his memoirs, Mr. Hoover pointed out that he, as early as 1908, recognized collective bargaining with organized labor, and in 1910 made a public statement urging that course. He felt that every effort should be made against the setting up of management and labor as separate classes. He believed they are both producers, and not classes. All through his public life, Mr. Hoover said, he supported the organization of labor and collective bargaining by representatives of labor's own choosing. But he was strongly opposed to a closed shop and "feather bedding" as denials of fundamental human freedom.

In 1920, Mr. Hoover made a proposal which, at the time, was regarded as "radical" by persons far less conservative than the frequenters of our Union League Clubs. At the time, Mr. Hoover was working on the Industrial Conference of 1920. It was some months before he was to be appointed Secretary of Commerce in the Harding Cabinet. In fact, he was regarded as Presidential material by both the Republicans and the Democrats.

Mr. Hoover was greatly concerned with the developments in the labor relations field, particularly with the activities of left-wing groups like Bolsheviks and "Wobblies," and the signs pointing to outright industrial war.

He had known Samuel Gompers well during World War I, from 1915 to 1919. Mr. Gompers and his American Federation of Labor co-operated with and aided Mr. Hoover in the Belgian Relief, the Food Administration, and the two served together on the American Delegation to the Peace Conference in Paris. He admired Mr. Gompers, particularly his staunch opposition to Socialism and the then emerging Communism.

In connection with his work on the Industrial Conference, Mr. Hoover called several meetings of businessmen, one of which I was privileged to attend. It was at the Metropolitan Club in New York. C. B. Seger, president of the United States Rubber Company, was invited, and he asked me to accompany him. I do not recall all of those present, but I do remember the group included A. C. Bedford, president of Standard Oil of New Jersey, C. J. Hicks, head of industrial relations for Standard, C. A. Coffin, Chairman of the Board of General Electric Company, and several others.

Mr. Hoover proposed, after some discussion of ways of improving relations with labor, that the big companies of the country establish liaison with Mr. Gompers and his AFL.

The idea got a very cold reception. In fact, it was given no consideration even by that audience which had been selected because its members held more advanced views toward employee relations.

The company officials couldn't conceive how Mr. Gompers could speak for their employees unless the employees were members of Mr. Gompers' unions. And none of us was ready to ask our workers to join. We were thinking of other ways of keeping our employees satisfied; of achieving an understanding of their problems, and they of ours.

It is interesting to speculate how the Hoover plan might have changed the whole history of labor relations in this country had it met with the approval of a large segment of industry. Of course, it would have led to the immediate unionization of the companies accepting it. Would we have avoided the violence and bloodshed of the 1930's? . . .

Another incident which reveals the thinking of the times on management's relations with employees also took place in 1920 at a meeting of the National Metal Trades Council in New York's Astor Hotel. I was one of the early speakers at the meeting on the general problems of industry. Another speaker was Arthur H. Young, then in charge of industrial relations of the International Harvester Company, the job corresponding to mine at U. S. Rubber. Both of us talked along the same line, of the need for developing a better understanding with employees. We suggested this might be done by establishment of some means of communication—for example, joint worker-management plant committees. We did not suggest anything so "radical" as unionization of the plants.

But, when Mr. Young and I had finished, the chairman of the meeting, a prominent industrialist who is still active, rose and said:

"Gentlemen, you have just heard two talks on Bolshevism. We will now proceed with the business of the meeting."

He was deadly serious, and I am sure his views were shared by a majority of the industrialists present.

Despite the attitude of the chairman and others at the Astor Hotel meeting, the idea of management and labor trying to solve long-standing problems by sitting down together in plant committees caught on. A large number of big companies established such committees. We called them "Factory Councils" at U. S. Rubber. At International Harvester they were known as "Industrial Councils," and Bethlehem Steel called the idea the "Employee Representation Plan."

There is no question that the factory council idea was responsible for a large part of the advancement in labor-management relations in the 1920's. It is noted that, as the idea spread through industry, the strength of organized labor, as represented by the AFL, declined. AFL membership dropped from over 4,000,000 in 1920 to 2,900,000 in 1929.

I am not advocating the factory council plan as a substitute for the labor unions. . . . There can be no substitute, in advancing the best interests of both workers and employers, for a democratically and intelligently run union, operating apart from the cloak of management.

But the factory council idea did fill a big need in the 1920's before many employers were ready to accept unions or the theory of collective bargaining. Under such plans, there was no union, no dues, no membership in anything. Elections were held on company property under company auspices and the workers chose certain of their associates to serve on various committees which discussed with the management grievances, production questions and other matters. They provided a stepping-stone to the collective bargaining stage of labor relations. And they were responsible, in no small way, for the comparative labor peace of the otherwise "Roaring Twenties."

The motivation for the advancement of the plant committee plan was a real desire on the part of the companies to improve the lot of their workers. I know from experience how the plans worked, and there was a very free exchange of information and ideas. The committees were set up on a local plant basis. The employee representatives were formally elected by the workers of the plant. Regular meetings were held to develop understandings on wages and other matters. There were no written contracts, but I know that, in our company at least, these oral agreements were as strictly regarded as though they had been signed and sealed. Later, when the CIO was organizing the mass-production industries, much unfounded propaganda was issued about the workings of employee councils. They were called "company unions" and finally were outlawed by the National Labor Relations Law (Wagner Act) of 1935. The idea had outlived its usefulness, but they were of great benefit to the country at the time before the infant, collective bargaining, was able to walk.

Among the men in the forefront of the movement to improve labor relations in the 1920's were A. C. Bedford and C. J. Hicks of Standard Oil; George W. Perkins, president of International Harvester, and A. H. Young, the company's labor relations head; Eugene Grace and Joseph Larkin of Bethlehem Steel; F. A. Seiberling and Paul Litchfield of Goodyear Tire and Rubber, C. B. Seger, president of U. S. Rubber; and E. K. Hall of American Telephone and Telegraph.

After I had left the Boston Elevated in 1919, and U. S. Rubber accepted my rather bold offer of service, Mr. Seger asked me what title I thought I should be given. I replied I was not interested in a title; in fact I said I hoped I could take six months to travel around to the various company plants and meet the people there.

My plans, however, for a leisurely trip among the rubber company's properties were short-lived. One of our plants in Canada developed serious labor trouble and I was dispatched to Montreal almost before knowing my way around the big New York headquarters.

The scene was the Canadian Consolidated Company, a Montreal subsidiary of the company which manufactured footwear, among other things. The man in charge of the operation was a company vice-president, a nice person, named William A. Eden. He told me labor troubles were all around, and that he didn't know anything about such things. I didn't tell him so, but I knew scarcely a thing about U. S. Rubber's labor policies at the time, having been with them so short a period.

But I did tell Bill Eden I was sure, if both of us worked together and used our heads, we would be able to do something about the situation.

There was one obvious reason for Mr. Eden's troubles. Although quite a few of the rubber workers were fairly highly skilled, the average hourly wage rate in the plant was below 30 cents, about the same as common laborers were getting in Montreal.

All signs pointed to a strike. The situation required very delicate handling to avoid a really bad disturbance because all through Canada the atmosphere regarding labor was tense. There were city-wide strikes in Toronto, Calgary, and Winnipeg, and an almost complete tie-up in Vancouver. The International Workers of the World, the "Wobblies," were involved in all.

The union in our Montreal plant was new. In fact, one of my difficulties was locating the union leaders so we could talk.

In those years, in both the United States and Canada, it was the usual practice of employers, when a strike occurred, to notify the employees they were no longer on the payroll, and if they wished to return to work they could come back as new employees at lower rates of pay and with loss of seniority. Even if the process worked to end the strike of the moment, it certainly was not conducive to smooth relations afterward, and could be counted on only to breed further disturbance.

Such a letter had been prepared in New York for the Montreal employees in event of a strike. The strike came quickly, before Mr. Eden and I had time to do anything to prevent it. But the usual letter never went out.

Instead, Mr. Eden and I worked all night in drafting another, quite different, kind of letter to the employees. In it we requested the workers to return to the job, and we guaranteed there would be no discrimination as a result of the strike. We told them we were willing and anxious to sit down with a committee of their choosing to talk wages and other issues. We requested them to select the committee and notify us of the time of meeting. We added something else that was almost unheard of at the time in either the United States or Canada. We said that, if an agreement couldn't be reached with the committee, we would submit the question of wages to arbitration. In the mass-production industries, at least, this whole approach was a new one.

Our letter was published in the Montreal morning newspapers, and before receiving an answer from the union we were in serious trouble. Homer E. Sawyer, executive vice-president of U. S. Rubber, arrived in town, very much disturbed. He virtually took me apart. He said that nothing like we had done—suggesting arbitration of strike differences—had ever taken place in the history of the company, and where was Eden? Mr. Eden had been in bed only a short while, but Mr. Sawyer woke him and dressed him down.

It appeared that both Mr. Eden and I were about to be fired. But, fortunately, Mr. Seger appeared on the scene. He had accompanied Mr. Sawyer to Montreal, though we didn't know it. Mr. Sawyer explained our action to the company chief in heated language. Then something happened I will never forget. Mr. Seger turned to the executive vice-president and said, simply:

"Sawyer, as long as I am its president, the United States Rubber Company will never refuse to arbitrate anything that comes up between the company and its employees."

The leadership of the new union was, at first, suspicious of us. But, within 24 hours after we sent our letter, they had picked a committee and we were meeting. Mr. Eden and I assured them of our good faith. They immediately ended the strike and we reached an agreement which brought a modest wage increase and settlement of other issues bothering the employees.

A union official later skipped town with all the money in the treasury and that ended the union. But the employees elected a committee to represent them with the management and we enjoyed good relations for a long time.

Feeling the need of a rest, even so early in my career with U. S. Rubber, I caught a train out of Montreal for my old family home in Prince Edward Island. But that vacation was never to come about. The train was flagged down by a stationmaster at a stop before I reached my destination. He handed me a telegram from Mr. Seger saying there was a strike on at a plant in Naugatuck, Connecticut, and for me to return at once.

I arrived at Naugatuck at 10 o'clock at night and found the company superintendent about ready to send the usual letter to the striking employees. It took me a week to ride that one out, but I did so with the help of Myron H. Clark, a very forward-thinking executive in charge of U. S. Rubber's footwear division. With another "assist" from Mr. Seger, we were able to kill the prepared letter and get out the kind we thought should be sent.

There was no union at the plant. We called a mass meeting of the employees. About 1,500 came out. I called for questions on their grievances, and then spent the next three-and-a-half hours standing and answering the flood of queries which followed from all sides. This marathon performance cleared the air and the employees agreed to select a committee to deal with us. The strike was settled and the committee arrangement worked peaceably for 15 years.

Within five years after the Naugatuck incident, employee committees had been established at all of our plants. Our formula for peace was an insistence on listening to all grievances of employees and being certain they understood our problems of management. We developed an effective system of communication and a mutual understanding which tempered the actions of both management and employees. We did not accede to their every request on wages and other matters. Far from it. But, always, we thoroughly threshed out those problems with the workers before giving an answer.

Like many other plans, this idea may not have been practical for all companies, but it worked well for U. S. Rubber as evidenced by the fact that there was no strike in the company for 22 years.

The Story of Industrial Espionage

LaFOLLETTE COMMITTEE

PURPOSE OF INDUSTRIAL ESPIONAGE

Since its inception in the 1870's labor espionage has spread throughout practically the whole of American industry. One national labor leader expressed it in these terms: "There is no gathering of union members large enough to be called a meeting that is small enough to exclude a spy." That statement from a labor leader is confirmed by spokesmen from industry itself. Herman L. Weckler, vice president and general manager of the De Soto Corporation (division of Chrysler Corporation) and himself a worker "up from the ranks" stated to the committee:

It (labor espionage) has been a practice that has been in existence for years. It is a practice we have grown up with.

J. H. Smith, president for almost forty years of the Corporations Auxiliary Co., largest espionage agency devoted solely to industrial work, testified that the nature of his business "has changed slightly, but not very much" in the last four decades.

Why has American industry resorted, during this period of its most active growth and consolidation of power, to a practice that every congressional and State inquiry has condemned since it came to public notice? Your committee can only conclude from its investigations that this practice is an infallible index of the stubborn and irreconcilable opposition of a considerable section of American industry to the recognition of labor's right to organize. The indefensible practices

Taken from Industrial Espionage, Violations of Free Speech and Rights of Labor, *Report of the Committee on Education and Labor pursuant to S. Res. 266, 75th Congress, 2nd session, Senate Report No. 46, Part 3, November 16, 1937, U. S. Government Printing Office, Washington, D.C., 1938, pp. 8–9, 20–23, 26–29, 44–47.*

assumed by industry in its opposition to labor's right to organize form a striking contrast to the growth of horizontal combinations in industry itself.

In addition to the increase in the size and strength of individual business units there has been a continual growth in the number of employer combinations. Today the Department of Commerce lists more than 7,000 associations of employers. Many of these associations, united primarily by common economic interests, are organized ostensibly to propagate lofty ideals of responsible business ethics, fellowship, and Americanism. Their business ethics do not countenance, as many of them testified, the introduction of spies, informers, and saboteurs in the ranks of their own organizations; yet countless members of these associations, citizens of repute, beset their own employees with paid spies. Their view of the responsibilities of management permits them, while proclaiming the virtues of American industry, to betray their workingmen. Neither their speeches nor their advertising label their products "made by spied-on labor."

Employer resistance to organization has taken many forms. These vary from company unions and other types of "welfare" organizations through blacklisting and espionage down to open displays of force. Espionage is the most efficient method known to management to prevent unions from forming, to weaken them if they secure a foothold, and to wreck them when they try their strength. Its use by management is an entirely "natural growth" in the long struggle to keep unions out of the shop.

But while management defends its antiunion "policy" openly—in fact, advertises it—it is less willing to defend or explain the "methods" by which unions are kept at bay. Even more sensitive and reluctant were the officials of the detective agencies appearing before the committee. As the hired help of industry, engaged in fighting unions, they made every effort to conceal that this was their true function. They went even further than management in inventing a variety of "reasons" for the employment of spies by industry. The odium attached to the practice made even the practitioners squirm.

The chief reasons advanced by employers and detective agency officials for the use of labor spies were: (1) Protecting industry against radicalism and Communism; (2) preventing sabotage (closely linked to the first); (3) detecting theft; (4) improving efficiency in methods and workers; merging into (5) improving relations between employers and workers, or "human engineering." These "legitimate" reasons for the employment of labor spies were strenuously advanced by officials of the detective agencies and, with diminished enthusiasm, by representatives of industry. These "reasons" were of so little merit that after examination by the committee they were repudiated by the same officials who advanced them. They are, however, interesting to examine for the light they shed on the actual motive. . . .

COMPANY SPY SYSTEMS

. . . [A] well-defined method of organized espionage is found in the company spy system, an entirely intramural organization solely responsive to the plant management.

The committee has as yet made no investigation of such private company spy systems. However, in the course of its investigations of the detective agencies the committee discovered that a growing number of corporations are turning from the detective agency to this method of organized espionage.

Certain factors operate to accelerate the tendency toward corporations setting up their own spy systems. First are the admitted shortcomings and untrustworthiness of operatives of the private detective agencies, many of them primarily interested in creating conditions which will perpetuate their jobs. In addition, the elaborate labor relations or personnel departments of certain corporations lend themselves to an extension into espionage very readily, particularly when in the past the major part of their duties was carried out in conjunction with operatives of the private detective agencies. Third, certain recent legislative requirements such as registration of all employees under the provisions of the Social Security Act, the Securities and Exchange regulations requiring statements of payments made, Federal and State labor relations acts, the work of this committee, and recent State legislation requiring registration of detective agency operatives, have all tended to hamper and impede the clandestine activities of the private detective agencies.

Finally, the odium associated with the employment of private detective agencies tends to influence certain corporations to set up their own systems. The abandonment of the private detective agencies in favor of a private espionage service is probably best illustrated in the testimony of Harry W. Anderson, labor-relations director of the General Motors Corporation. Mr. Anderson testified that the General Motors Corporation had recently discontinued the employment of the Pinkerton detective agency and had instituted its own plan. Although Mr. Anderson stated the new plan did not contemplate purchasing information from informants he indicated that the corporation had no intention of discontinuing securing the same kind of information through its own channels.

Senator LA FOLLETTE. In other words, your reason for discontinuing it was not the nature of the kind of service they were rendering, but you wanted to eliminate the third party; is that correct?

Mr. ANDERSON. That is right.

Senator LA FOLLETTE. And has any plan been made, or has any plan been put into operation to secure the same type of service and information through the organization itself?

Mr. ANDERSON. Yes, sir.

EXTENT OF ESPIONAGE IN INDUSTRY

A census of spies is impossible because the agencies' stock in trade lies in concealing from public gaze the extent of their activities.

Only in their private conversations with business leaders, when they are endeavoring to sell their services, do officials of the agencies reveal how well they cover American trade unions. One Burns agency operative of twenty years' experience relaxed his guard sufficiently before the committee to confess, "Senator, in my experience for the past twenty years I have found out there is stools in every union organization."

The questionnaires returned by the agencies are wholly misleading. They do not furnish any reliable evidence of the number of operatives or spies. The agencies whose responses admitted they engaged in espionage furnished approximately 685 spies to industries in the period 1933 to 1936. The number of spies reported in the questionnaires plus incomplete figures on the five agencies and the one employers' association which the committee examined yield the following totals for the period January 1, 1933, to July 1936, inclusive:

Agencies replying to questionnaires, 685 spies.

Railway Audit & Inspection Co., Inc., and affiliates (fragmentary records only), 313 spies.

National Corporation Service and affiliates, 437 spies.

National Metal Trades Association, 104 spies.

Corporations Auxiliary Companies, 677 spies.

Wm. J. Burns International Detective Agency, Inc., 440 spies.

Pinkerton's National Detective Agency, Inc., 1,228 spies.

The committee's known census of working spies for 1933 to 1936 totals 3,871 for the entire period. This census is far from complete. It does not consider the number of spies hired by company spy systems. It also neglects the number of spies hired by the 700 or more detective agencies which furnished no information to the committee. And it entirely omits the spies of the miscellaneous groups which send undercover agents into labor unions.

Further, these figures are deceptive if only because one spy may, and often does, work in several different plants in the course of a year. He may shift from one successful operation on a union to another in a different locality. Thus, E. C. Flynn, of the National Corporation Service, worked on at least three operations in 1934—for the Lake Erie Power & Light Co. at Bellevue, Ohio; the Val Decker Packing Co. at Piqua, Ohio; and the Hazel-Atlas Glass Co. at Washington, Pa. A spy may also work for two unions at once, as did Frank Shults, alias A. J. Wagner, a National Metal Trades Association operative who worked in Erie, Pa., and visited Paterson, N.J., locals to make special reports. The known "operative" may be a "hooker" who has under him a number of unidentified and designated "informants" in unions at the same time. The number of operations is therefore more reliable than the number of spies; but even these are not available and an operation may not disclose the number of spies at work for a single client. Another index of the extent of spying is the number of clients served by the detective agencies examined by the committee.

Pinkerton had 309 industrial clients in the years 1933 to 1936; Corporations Auxiliary Co., 499; National Corporation Service, 196; and Burns, 440. The committee secured a fragmentary list of Railway Audit & Inspection Co. clients totaling 165. The smaller agencies responding to questionnaires admitted to serving 497 clients. The National Metal Trades Association had spies in the plants of seventy-one member firms, but furnished information on labor organizing activities to practically its entire membership of 952. With the qualification that some firms have employed more than one of these agencies, the known total of business firms receiving spy services from these enumerated agencies is approximately 2,500. A single client may employ from 1 to 200 spies. The committee was unable to ascertain whether all clients of these detective agencies were receiving industrial espionage service. However, the evidence in the record makes the committee confident that these figures are accurate, save for a few minor exceptional cases. The names and distribution of these firms conclusively demonstrate the tenacious hold which the spying habit has on American business. From motion-picture producers to steel makers, from hookless fasteners to automobiles, from small units to giant enterprises—scarcely an industry that is not fully represented in the list of clients of the detective agencies. Large corporations rely on spies. No firm is too small to employ them. The habit has even infected the labor relations of noncommercial, philanthropic organizations—witness the employment of Railway Audit & Inspection Co. by the directors of the Brooklyn Jewish Hospital in New York City.

It is worth noting that many of the corporations appearing on the list have stubbornly fought the efforts of the National Labor Relations Board. Thus, both openly and secretly, they have opposed the organization of their employees into free associations.

The list as a whole reads like a blue book of American industry. The committee was impressed with the overwhelming power inherent in the size and wealth of these corporations opposed to the individual worker who is spied on. Thus, Pinkerton's largest single industrial client was the General Motors Corporation, a billion-dollar corporation with a gross income in 1936 of almost a billion and a half dollars. In that same year, General Motors employed 230,572 workers, not one of whom, it was evident from the records, was exempt from espionage. In the period January 1934 through July 1936, General Motors paid $994,855.68 to detective agencies for spy services. At times as many as 200 spies were reporting on the activities of its workers in the sixty-odd plants of the corporation. It provides a most convincing demonstration that no occupational group is free from the spy's constant surveillance—not miners deep in the earth, nor sailors at sea; neither cannery workers, skilled engineers, or nurses in hospitals.

It is obvious that with such widespread and imposing clientele detective agencies must do a lucrative business. In the years 1933 to 1936, inclusive, a list of selected corporations spent $9,440,132.15 for the coordinate arms of industrial warfare—spies, strikebreakers, and munitions.

A substantial portion of the foregoing expenditures found its way into the coffers of the detective agencies. That these incomes are largely if not wholly the result of industrial strife is convincingly demonstrated by the striking parallel between labor organizing activity and expenditures for agency service. During the period studied by the committee—1933 to 1936—there was a great increase in organizing activities and union membership throughout the country. But three fairly well-defined stages in this growth may be marked: (1) The rapid growth of union membership following the passage of the National Industrial Recovery Act and extending well into 1934; (2) the relative decline or quiescence throughout most of 1935 and into early 1936; and (3) the tremendous growth in power and size of unions throughout 1936 and 1937. Corresponding to this the committee found that expenditures by employers for detective agency services rose steadily throughout these four years, but that the rise was more pronounced in those periods when union activity was most intensive, such as the organizing drives of 1933 and 1936, and expenditures were greatest when strikes threatened or actually occurred.

One can chart the growth and activities of unions in various industries almost solely from the expenditures for spies in these industries. Thus, H. C. Parsons, secretary-treasurer of the Akron Employers' Association, which employed the Corporations Auxiliary Co. for 33 years to report on union activities among the rubber workers in Akron, admitted the close correlation between the growth of unionization among rubber workers and the employers' association's expenditures for spies. . . .

EXTENT OF ESPIONAGE AMONG UNIONS

Neither the numbers of spies at work, the huge sums of money spent for their services, nor the long lists of agency clients adequately conveys the intensity or effectiveness of industrial espionage. A consideration of the union affiliations and positions of the spies themselves is a true index of the extent of the power they wield over the American worker. This was the information which the agency and its client most closely guarded. After protracted—and in view of the results, understandable—delay, Pinkerton attorneys produced a list of its 1,228 industrial spies employed from January 1, 1933, through April 1937. This list indicates the union affiliations of all spies known by the agency.

This list is astonishing. Pinkerton operates in practically every union in the country, from aeronautic workers and Amalgamated Clothing Workers to the United Textile Workers and the Warehousemen's Union. Every important international union—many smaller and local unions—even company unions—whether American Federation of Labor, Committee for Industrial Organization, or independent, whether craft or industrial, has its quota of Pinkerton spies.

In the period from January 1934 to June 1937, 304 Pinkerton operatives were affiliated with 93 specific unions. Pinkerton also reported that 27 additional operatives were known to be members of some union, name unknown, and that it was without knowledge of the union affiliations, if any, of 37 more.

Thus, the Pinkerton detective agency contributed at least 331, possibly 368 members to American trade unions. The agency paid their dues and other expenses as union members.

Concentration of operatives in certain unions seems to depend on the intensity with which the Pinkerton clients are opposing organization. Thus, 52 operatives were concentrated in the highly important United Automobile Workers Union, reporting on the union drive in General Motors. At times this number of operatives within the union was vastly augmented by additional operatives working outside the union. Typical of their union affiliation known to the committee is a former president of a Chevrolet local in Flint and a former vice president of a Fisher Body local in Lansing. How many other important posts their 50 operatives held in this union is conjectural.

Pinkerton has 5 operatives in the United Mine Workers, chiefly concentrated in Pennsylvania, and 9 in the United Rubber Workers, chiefly in Cleveland; 17 in the United Textile Workers, 4 in the warehousemen's union, 4 in the Electrical and Radio Workers Union, 4 in the Sawmill Workers, 4 in the Printers' and Pressmen's Union, 13 in teamsters' unions, 16 in the International Brotherhood of Electrical Workers, 20 in the machinists' union, 12 in the Oil Field Workers Union, and 64 in the railway unions, 15 in the street railway workers union, and 7 in the Steel Workers Union, as well as dozens of spies in federal locals throughout the country.

These operatives report to Pinkerton officials in 27 cities. It is interesting to look for a moment at the geographical concentration of these spies.

Thus, in a typical industrial city like Indianapolis, Pinkerton had operatives in the Amalgamated Clothing Workers Union, in the Street Railways Union, in the American Federation of Hosiery Workers, in Brotherhood of Railway Shop Crafts, in the Brewery Workers Union, three operatives in the clerks union, and one in the glass blowers union, one in the Gas Station Attendants Union, in the grocery and warehouse employees union, two in the electrical workers brotherhood, two in the Pulp and Paper Mill Workers Union, two in the teamsters' union, one in the stereotypers', one in the molders' union, one in the United Automobile Workers' Union, one in the Electrical and Radio Workers' Union, and one in the Wire and Cable Workers' Federal Union.

In Cleveland, Pinkerton operatives were spying on workers in the Brotherhood of Railway Clerks, in several federal labor unions directly affiliated with the A.F. of L., two of them were at work in the International Association of Machinists, six in the teamsters and chauffeurs, one was a member of the painters' union, one was a hatter, four were members of the relatively small Mechanics Educational Society of America, one was in the Office Workers' Union, two were in the retail clerks' union, while eight were actively attempting to wreck the growing rubber workers' union, and two were in the textile workers' union.

On the West Coast, Pinkerton was paying the membership dues and expenses of four spies in the Warehousemen's Union, one in the shipping clerks' union, two in the Veneer Workers' Union, one in the Marine Cooks and Stewards' Union, two in the Mine, Mill, and Smelter Workers' Union, two in the International Longshoremen's Association, one in the machinists', two in the bottle blowers' union, one in the Brotherhood of Railway Trainmen, two in the Can Workers' Union, one in the Brotherhood of Railway Carmen, and a number in miscellaneous unions up and down the Pacific Coast.

The same story repeats itself in scores of American cities. The local or cross section coverage, enhanced by contact with other unions in the locality, plus the combined knowledge gained by Pinkerton about each international union through its vertical coverage, is an invaluable weapon in the hands of the agency. It enables the agency to peddle the information it gains about an international or local union to gain new clients in new localities.

It gives Pinkerton an opportunity to shift its spies from one locality to another, retaining membership in the international, or to push the spy up to higher and higher positions in the union with even greater coverage. But chiefly it gives the agency power and ability to frustrate the exercise by workers of fundamental constitutional and statutory rights. It is intolerable to permit such power to be wielded by any secret, irresponsible, and uncontrolled group in a democracy.

The committee's record makes clear the power that such a spy system controls. It places the employer in the very heart of the union councils from the outset of any organizing effort. News of organizers coming into a town, contacts the organizers make among his employees, the names of employees who show interest in the union, the names and addresses of employees who join the union, all organization plans, all activities of the union—these are as readily available to the employer as though he himself were running the union. When the union prepares terms for presentation to the employer, when grievance committees formulate their demands, when contracts are drawn, the employer knows beforehand everything that is to be known and can determine his own tactics accordingly. In the event a strike is called, the employer is forewarned. The strike plans, the strength of the union, its ability to hold out, its weaknesses are intimately known to the employer. Nor does the employer stop there with his uses of a spy service. When Government mediators attempt to settle the strike, they are subjected to constant scrutiny and their moves are reported to the employer. Every one of these practices is recounted in the sections which follow.

The power of these Pinkerton spies is increased tenfold by their official positions in unions. The Pinkerton list did not reveal the names of the unions in which their spies held offices. It did, however, inventory the offices themselves. Of the 304 Pinkerton industrial operatives who were acknowledged members of unions, 100, or almost a third, held offices of varying importance.

The offices held by these 100 spies were as follows:

National vice president	1
Local president	14
Local vice president	8
Local treasurer	2
Local secretary	20
Recording secretary	14
Trustee	14
Business agent	3
Organizer	3
Delegate to Central Labor Union	3
Chairman, shop committee	1
Committeemen	6
Financial secretary	4
Member, executive board	4
Division chairman	1
Local chairman	2

One Pinkerton operative had, through the years, achieved the position of national vice president of his union. Fourteen were presidents of their locals. Six were either treasurers or financial secretaries and 34 were secretaries of their local unions, which gave them ready access to the list of members and to the financial status of the unions. In addition to placing men in positions where they were the first to learn the names of new members, three Pinkerton spies were even acting as paid business agents and three as organizers of unions. Three of the spies were delegates to central labor bodies, and the remainder occupied various posts in the union from chairman of the shop committee to membership on the executive board. Pinkerton spies were even officers of company unions.

To anyone versed in the affairs of unions it is at once obvious how dangerous these spies can be. To take a comparable situation, if detective agencies had sent a number of operatives into business houses and one had become vice president of a large national corporation, others had become presidents of small firms and others had worked their way into positions of confidence and power of various kinds throughout the corporate set-up of the country, their capacity for wrecking would be practically limitless.

These two lists furnished by Pinkerton (its membership in unions and the offices their operatives hold) explain fully the obdurate refusal of Pinkerton and the other agencies to identify its operatives. Pinkerton is not protecting the operatives; it is hiding rather the history of their union-wrecking activities. For complete revelation would provoke a storm of protest, and more practically, all but destroy the agency's ability to capitalize upon the positions attained by spies.

The presence of these spies in so many unions and the offices they hold raise serious problems. Spies are members of unions in name only. Their oath to support and uphold the union is meaningless. They reveal union secrets, they steal union records, they aid in blacklisting their own fellows. They incite to untimely strikes, they precipitate violence. Their allegiance is to the detective agencies and their clients, not to the union.

The committee has followed through this one far-flung network largely because the information available, sparse and scattered as it is, is still more complete on Pinkerton than on other agencies. But similar, if not more effective spy networks—sometimes more dangerous—are the property of every agency.

Not only is the worker's freedom of association nullified by the employers' spies, but his freedom of action, of speech, and of assembly is completely destroyed. Fear harries his every footstep, caution muffles his words. He is in no sense any longer a free American. In a constitutional sense his very position reflects the mockery and contempt those who demand constitutional rights for themselves deny to others. Government, therefore, must overcome this spying practice which faces the average American worker or the spy and his reports, "the background on which we built our whole structure," will destroy every vestige of right which for 150 years we have thought our Constitution guarantees the average individual. The right to work means nothing if it is at the expense of more important rights. . . .

EFFECT OF ESPIONAGE ON EMPLOYERS

The surreptitious nature of the relations between the employers and the agency relieves the latter from responsibility to account for its activities. Since the two deal with each other in the obscurity of falsified records and clandestinely destroyed documents, the employer has little opportunity to control the activities of the spies he has unleashed upon his employees. His fear of genuine collective bargaining causes him to surrender to a group of unknown adventurers an increasing responsibility in his relations with his employees. The security of his employees is placed in the hands of men who stand to profit by a maximum of labor trouble and strife. In addition, the employer has admitted into his plant and exposed his business secrets to a class of persons whose loyalty he has every reason to suspect.

While spy agencies charge all that the traffic will bear their approach is usually gradual. The manager of the New York office of the Railway Audit & Inspection Co., Foster Strader, wrote to W. B. Groves, the vice president of the agency and commented: "This is a new client, so we do not want too big a bill at first." But eventually the agency gets as much out of its client as it possibly can.

To encourage sales of spy service, solicitors are placed upon a percentage basis. W. H. Gray, solicitor for the Railway Audit & Inspection Co., was paid on the basis of the number of spies he was able to place. The arrangement under which Mr. Gray worked is stated in a memorandum from the vice president of the agency, L. D. Rice, to the manager of the Atlanta office, G. E. Ivey:

> His compensation will be $150.00 a month, no commission on the first two operatives, and 50¢ a day thereafter on that all we can bill and collect for.

Gray was thus in the position of having to place two spies in a plant before he began to get his commission. He admitted that it was "certainly" to his interest to sell all the spies he could.

The spying habit, however, is not acquired all at once. At first the employer is likely to look upon the employment of spies as a "luxury." But once a client has been exposed to spy reports he can be frightened into spending an increasing amount of money for the service.

The superintendent of the Atlanta office of the Pinkerton Detective Agency, Joseph Littlejohn, instructed one of his spies who was working on the General Motors Corporation account that it was up to him to "pull the investigation along." Littlejohn told the spy that if he "made the reports longer and put more meat into them, that the Detroit offices would carry them along quite a while longer than they ordinarily would run. The agency makes it quite clear to the spy that his own job depends upon reporting matters which will keep the employer apprehensive about his labor relations. In a letter to the Atlanta office of the Railway Audit and Inspection Co., W. H. Gray described the lecture he gave to "E. E. M.," a spy:

I told him that he has got to keep right behind it, and get some material in the reports, and get them in more regular, as he has got a pension and does not know it, he seemed to be so anxious when I located him last fall and put him on that job, I guess that he has got all of the rinkles out of his belly now, and does not think so much about it, however I think that I woke him up when I told him that he was liable to be cut off.

When the spy is unable to find any information to send in with his report he can always turn to his imagination. C. M. ("Red") Kuhl, formerly with the National Corporation Service, stated that the spies are urged to make their reports interesting. He testified that if the—

client does not seem to think he is receiving enough information, why you go out and get hold of these "ops" and tell them; come right out and tell them flat turkey, "It is your job, too, so maybe you better use your imagination a little and write something in here that is of interest to the client."

The editing of spy reports affords the spy agency an excellent opportunity to extend its services. The practice of rewriting spy reports in such a way as to inflame the imagination of the employer and cause him to hire more and more spies is conceded to be a natural development in the espionage business. O. R. Abbott, of the National Metal Trades Association, claimed that the cooperative nonprofit system of espionage practiced by the association eliminated this otherwise uniform practice. He testified that the reports of the association's spies "are not built up in any way because we are not selling the service for profit." A similar argument was used by the solicitors for the association in attempting to take away business from spy agencies. A booklet prepared by the association for its solicitors suggested as an argument against the use of spy agencies—

Without asking what service is being used, it is reasonably safe to say that their income and profit is greatest when labor difficulties are at a maximum.

With spies in a plant, with the espionage system shrouded in mystery and concealed in a hundred ways, with the employers' apprehension excited by colored reports and inflamed by high-pressure sales methods, it is no wonder that the craving for spy information increases. It results in fear, in loss of judgment, and undermines the morale of management itself. The example of the General Motors Corporation is amazing and terrifying in the picture it presents of management caught in a hopeless maze of corruption and distrust.

Without exception, every plant manager of the General Motors Corporation engaged private-detective service. This did not suffice. The personnel directors of the Fisher Body and Chevrolet divisions of the corporation also felt the need for spy service. They did not rely on the reports received by their plant managers, but made independent contracts for detective service directly under their control. Thus a superstructure of espionage was spread over the basic plant-espionage network in these two divisions.

The end, however, was not reached. Still another superstructure of spy service was created. The labor-relations division of the executive offices of the General Motors Corporation, responsible directly to the president, did not rely either on the plant detective service or on the division detective service. A separate contract was entered into with the Pinkerton agency to provide for a spy service responsible directly to the labor-relations division, under Merle C. Hale and his successor, Harry W. Anderson. This contract was separate from the other contracts entered into by other branches of the corporation, and was even concealed from the plant managers themselves. A weird framework of spies among spies was created that bewildered even the Pinkerton officials.

The irresistible logic of espionage reached its final stages when the General Motors Corporation used the Pinkerton agency to spy upon its own Corporations Auxiliary Co. spies. The corporation found itself a victim of its own devices. In order to spy upon its workers and its officials it had admitted into its employment and exposed its business secrets to a swarm of unscrupulous men whose trade was corruption and deceit. The corporation had reason to believe a leak had occurred and that its confidential trade secrets had been betrayed to a competitor. Not unnaturally, suspicion fell upon the spies hired by the various branches of the corporation. Using spies to ferret out the misdeeds of other spies, however, was a method of solving its problem which displayed the folly into which the management of the corporation had fallen.

Industrial Warfare in the 1930's

FORTUNE MAGAZINE

To progressive sociologists it is axiomatic that the United States, most advanced of the industrial nations, has had the least developed philosophy of labor. These people contend that until the [Roosevelt] Administration took office, labor legislation in the United States, despite innumerable laws and commissions, resulted in little essential change in organized labor's standing. They especially emphasize such significant facts as that before the current [1937] United States union drive, no more than 18 per cent of United States nonagricultural labor was organized into trade unions, compared with over 35 per cent in Britain and more than 75 per cent in Sweden. And on the basis of these figures and various supplementary observations that we need not develop here, they hold that United States labor has lagged behind United States industry in the matter of self-fulfillment.

The United States businessman does not admit that his labor philosophy is backward. It is of course impossible to speak for all businessmen, and in attempting to speak for even a few one runs into insuperable difficulties in social terminology. . . . Here we can only say that in general, as the businessman sees it, this is a free country, with jobs open to all who can get them and the rights of private property; provided he can hire and fire as he sees fit; provided his individual employees can work when they want to; provided, that is to say, that traditional labor relations are not materially changed. If an "advanced" labor philosophy presumes the existence of national labor unions that curtail this familiar freedom of action, then the average

Taken from "The Industrial War," Fortune, XVI (November 1937), 105–10, 156, 158, 160, 166. Reprinted with the permission of the publisher.

American businessman does not want an advanced philosophy. Confronted with the possibility, or the threat, he takes his position upon the sturdy democratic tradition bequeathed to him by his forefathers, thus placing all those who are opposed to him in the awkward predicament of seeming to oppose that tradition. So that they become what Al Smith calls Communists.

Now whether you believe that this philosophy is backward, or whether you believe that it is the best that any democracy has so far devised, depends roughly upon which side of the private-property line your lot is cast. And as between those two irreconcilable extremes it is not the province of this article to choose. We are not here concerned with theory but with fact; the fact, namely, that for the past four and a half years the United States has been in the throes of a major labor upheaval, which can fairly be described as one of the greatest mass movements in our history. If one bars the irrepressible conflict of the Sixties, the only historical phenomenon comparable to the labor movement is the great trek westward, beginning in the Mississippi Valley and ending on the Pacific Coast. And if that classic American migration looms up to our generation as something far more permanent and vast it is well to remind ourselves that the labor movement likewise has a history. There has been labor unrest ever since there was a factory system, but the movement referred to here can properly be traced back to 1886–87, a period of open warfare characterized for the first time by a series of important strikes on the issue of the right to organize and bargain collectively through nationwide unions. The claim to that right, now widely conceded in Britain and the European democracies but still resisted in the United States, is the keystone of the American labor movement—is indeed what dignifies it as a movement rather than an intermittent and aimless war. Not that employers by and large are opposed to collective bargaining in principle. If they are involved in conflict, even as deeply involved as Mr. Tom M. Girdler [Chairman of Republic Steel Corporation], it is with national unions as instruments for achieving it. The various local unions and independent unions that many employers prefer are in themselves—since the passage of the Wagner Act—an important aspect of the industrial war; but we are here concerned with labor's longer attempt to achieve collective bargaining through nationwide unions such as are organized into the A.F. of L. and the C.I.O.

The history of that struggle can be had from any textbook and need not detain us here. At present we are considering its most modern phase—a phase that, corresponding roughly with the Roosevelt

Administration, is in itself a compound affair illustrating an exceedingly rapid change. In the early days of the NRA there was no C.I.O., there was no Wagner Act, there was no La Follette Committee, and no Mohawk Valley Formula; Big Steel had not yet "sold out" to labor; a sitdown strike had never been heard of in lay circles; and the American automobile was still for the most part innocent of unionized hands. Those things and those events were part of an evolution that was in its turn a part of the long labor movement above referred to. Not to understand this is to miss the point of every major event, every tactical decision, every judgment or error in judgment in the current labor world.

As a medical diagnosis can be reached only by a study of the symptoms, so it is necessary in an analysis of industrial warfare to reach into the heart of the problem by way of the strikes. For the strike is the external manifestation of labor's unrest, the thing that happens when an irresistible force meets an immovable body. . . .

From May, 1933, to July, 1937, a period of a little more than four years, there were some 10,000 strikes drawing out no less than 5,600,000 workers. This was aside from all the thousands of quickies, sitdowns, and other protests that tied up industry during that period—a "strike," as defined by the Department of Labor and used in this article, being an affair involving at least six workers for at least one day. . . . And perhaps most significant of all, there has been a marked trend in the causes of labor disputes, with the emphasis increasingly on the issue of union recognition. A labor movement fighting merely for better wages might or might not be a "movement" in the profound sense: it might be a kind of guerrilla warfare, indicating unrest but without historical direction. On the other hand, when men strike for union recognition, they are striking for collective bargaining, which we have already described as the keystone of the American labor movement. This collective bargaining theme has not always been to the fore by any means. Of the great 1919 strikes, only about 24 per cent were fought chiefly on this issue, while 55 per cent were fought chiefly for wages and hours. (The balance were "miscellaneous.") Up through 1926, indeed, the organization issue never represented 25 per cent of the total. Thereafter there was an abrupt rise, stimulated partly by the general prosperity and by 1929 about 40 per cent of the strikes were fought for collective bargaining. Then, after declining during the depression, the curve proceeded upward, breaking through 40 per cent in 1934, and reaching 50 per cent in 1936 and 53 per cent for the first half of this year—which so far as the record goes is an all-time high. This can be expressed in another way.

In the fourteen-year period beginning with 1919 there were in round numbers 20,000 strikes. Of these, 5,000 were primarily for union recognition. But in four years beginning with 1933 there were some 7,000 strikes. Of these, 3,000 were primarily for union recognition. The fact that half of the 1936 strikes were fought for a principle, with the trend continuing into the stormy spring and summer of 1937, is of such significance that those who follow labor closely are inclined to doubt the comfortable theory, . . . to the effect that the current wave of strikes is just a normal postdepression phenomenon. Coupled with the prodigious growth of union membership, the increased percentage of strikes won and compromised, and the apparent trend toward quicker settlements, it would seem to indicate the recrudescence of a major mass movement with its roots far in the American past. One must, to be sure, make allowances for Roosevelt "prosperity," which has made it possible for the worker to afford to fight for principles. And one must make a big allowance for assistance rendered by the government. This latter element, however, is itself symptomatic of a real pressure, for the machinery of Washington, unpredictable as its motion may be, does not operate in a vacuum of pure idealism. Washington has strengthened labor's position, not just for the hell of it, but in response to forces that the depression stimulated and revitalized. . . .

As already stated, the modern phase of the labor movement, the post-NRA phase, represents a distinct evolution, and the progress of the evolution has been fraught with warfare of the most harrowing character. It is of course impossible to choose from the 10,000 strikes included in this phase any several that would give a complete evolutionary picture; but it is possible to choose a few strikes to illustrate the more important points. . . . They are presented herewith.

TEXTILES, 1934

Mushroom Unions

If you were a union worker in the southern cotton textile industry on September 1, 1934, your earnings were around $11 a week— and in general you could expect a wage of little more than half the national average for workers in manufacturing. You probably lived in a town of less than 10,000 people. Unlike the 100,000 weavers, spinners, loom fixers, card grinders, smash hands, slubber tenders, and other cotton textile workers of the North, you lived in a region where the traditions of organized labor were not strong. You were new to industry, and there was much you disliked about it. Your great complaint was what you called the stretch-out, for if, under the NRA cotton textile code, you worked a basic forty-hour week, you insisted that you produced more than formerly in fifty hours. For instance, you used to make 144 dozen bloomers in ten hours, but now in eight hours you turned out 200 dozen bloomers. You might complain of "docks," of fines, of cases where a week's work brought in $5.88. You were one unit in a vast, disorderly, depressed industry, made up of some 1,200 mills operated by some 850 companies. And, you were probably in a union for the first time in your life.

More immediately, since June your position had grown worse. In that month the cotton textile code authority had reduced production 25 per cent, which meant a sharp cut in your wages. There was a statewide textile strike in Alabama. The delegates of your local, meeting at the national convention of the United Textile Workers in August, had voted for an industry-wide strike, demanding a thirty-hour week with no wage reduction, more uniform wages in the North and South, establishment of maximum work loads, reinstatement of workers fired for union membership, and—which has most bearing on this article—recognition of the union. Francis Gorman, Fifth Vice President of the Union, had sent the demands to George Arthur Sloan, President of the Cotton Textile Institute and Chairman of the Cotton Textile Code Authority. He replied that no one could bargain for the entire industry and that the strike was a strike against the code. And the cotton textile code was no ordinary code. The first of all NRA codes under which average hourly wages increased 65 per cent in a year, it outlawed child labor, established a labor board to handle disputes, and was generally regarded as one of the most liberal, as Sloan himself was judged a liberal trade association head. But the union charged that 2,000 cases brought before the board brought no appreciable results. And after six weeks, on September 1, 1934, at 11:30 P.M., you, as a good union man, went on strike.

You were caught up, in fact, in the first surge of the strike wave already described in statistics—and your strike accounted for almost 400,000 of the 1,467,000 workers who were involved that year. Above all, it was a strike of a union that had increased its members enormously under the impetus of the NRA drive, the United Textile Workers having grown from some 15,000 before the NRA to claim 300,000 in cotton textiles alone.

The textile strike was a strike involving primarily workers new to organized labor, pitted against a bitterly depressed industry, which meant that it was violent and brief. Twelve strikers and one deputy were killed in the three weeks that it raged. It was also emotional. "God is with us," cried a southern organizer as the strike began, "He will not desert us in this just struggle for ourselves and our families." It was characterized by what liberal economists politely call "employer resistance to collective bargaining." "Mobs of hoodlums and thugs!" thundered the President of the Alabama Manufacturers' Association, after a clash in the mill town of Boaz, "producing something like civil war in the South!" And the New England trade journal *Fibre and Fabric* asserted: "A few hundred funerals will have a quieting influence." The strike was followed by a period of disillusionment with section 7A and the elaborate mediation apparatus of the New Deal. With consequences that will presently be examined.

Largely because of its mushroom growth, the union could not support a long-drawn-out struggle. Facing enormous expenses, it had less than $1,000,000 in the treasury, and the strike might involve 500,000 cotton textile workers—to say nothing of about 700,000 other workers in silk, wool, rayon, and other branches of the industry. It had four regional offices covering thirteen states and seventy organizers. When Gorman handed out his orders for simultaneous transmission to 500 locals of the unions, he knew that the strike could not last longer than three weeks—or, as time is measured during strikes, he had 500 hours in which to win or lose.

The picket lines of fresh recruits tightened around hundreds of the industry's mills, and they stopped production so effectively that textile trade papers reported, along with indignant accounts of violence, that the employers felt they had been outgeneraled by an "audacious and intelligent minority." In the South, during the first week of the strike, fifty flying squadrons of pickets, with from 200 to 650 men in each column of cars, were operating along a 110-mile front from Gastonia to Greenville in the Carolinas. At Trion, Georgia, a deputy sheriff, a picket, and a strike sympathizer were killed and fifteen strikers were wounded in a two-hour pitched battle; at Greenville another strike sympathizer was killed, and during the strike's course there were clashes between pickets, deputies, nonstrikers, and Guardsmen as far afield as Woonsocket, Rhode Island, Lancaster, Pennsylvania, and Augusta, Georgia, where three more strikers were shot, one fatally. At the gate of the Chiquola Manufacturing Company's plant at Honea Path, South Carolina, a group of armed men opposing the strike charged the picket line, firing, killing six pickets and wounding fifteen. The union said that the armed group were deputies; the employers said they were nonstriking workers. By the second week of the strike more than 15,000 National Guardsmen had been mobilized in seven states, and a concentration camp for pickets had been set up in Georgia.

The strike's violence created so much bitter controversy that its fundamental issues were obscured. The union's introduction of flying squadrons of pickets, a then relatively unfamiliar weapon that it took over from the coal miners, caused a furor in the press. The employers claimed that the use of these groups of strikers in automobiles, descending on towns suddenly and unexpectedly, was proof that the union had the support of only a minority of the employees in each plant.

For this charge the union's rejoinder ran roughly as follows: the employees in company towns, especially in the South, could not form picket lines because of armed guards employed by the companies. Nor could ordinary organizing procedure be followed. At Rockmart, Georgia, the president of the local was kidnaped and driven from town; at Winfield, Alabama, two union officials were caught by thirty-three armed guards of the Alabama Mills Company and ordered to leave the county. And so forth. Against such odds, the union said, the only way a picket line could be established was by means of a flying squadron. At Fitchburg, Massachusetts, for instance, Organizer Powers Hapgood led fifty pickets to the edge of town, but was turned back by police. Later he returned with a flying squadron of 500 recruits drawn from a number of striking mills and succeeded in establishing a picket line. Whereupon the plant in Fitchburg also came out.

But underlying this was the matter of a union with limited resources and a vastly increased membership, waging a strike over an enormous area and around hundreds of mills, unevenly organized within the industry, with inexperienced strikers to man its picket lines—picket lines, the union asserts, that were attacked with forces strong enough to demoralize the most seasoned of hard-bitten unionists. And when the Winant Board issued a report that was a moral victory for the textile workers (since it recognized their basic grievances as real) but was a practical defeat (since it made no provisions for immediate or specific relief), the union called the strike off. "The union has won an overwhelming victory," said Gorman, the union complaining three weeks later that 25,000 strikers had been blacklisted. By the next year the membership claim of the United Textile Workers declined by about two-thirds.

Thus, if you were an average textile worker who went on strike on September 1, 1934, you probably came out of it three weeks later burdened with considerable doubt as to the effectiveness of section 7A. You had been a part of a mushroom growth of unionism that came into being with the signing of the NRA and fell away soon after.

REMINGTON RAND: 1936

The Back-to-Work Movement Develops

If you were an aligner, say, in Remington Rand's ancient red brick Ilion plant your union experiences were of a far more complex character. As an aligner you were one of the most skilled workers in the complicated field of typewriter and business machine manufacture, but during the depression you may have earned as little as $350 a year, and girls in the factory got as little as 16 cents an hour. You probably owned your own home in Ilion, but it was mortgaged. In 1933, soon after the NRA was signed and while the textile workers were being organized, a federal union was chartered in the factory, the old craft unions expanded, and by intricate steps too numerous to be traced here, you presently found yourself in John Frey's Metal Trades Department of the A.F. of L., organized, along with the employees of the four—later six—Remington Rand plants, into a Joint Protective Board of Office Equipment Workers.

Your union went through some of the typical troubles of the new unions of that period. Mr. Rand would not recognize it as exclusive bargaining agent, and on May 9, 1934, you went on strike. After five weeks, the union was recognized as a bargaining agency for its members (it claimed 90 per cent of the production and maintenance workers).

But the troubles of your union were only beginning. Through the winter of 1936, as a good union man, you were worried at rumors that Remington Rand had bought a huge abandoned automobile factory at Elmira, New York, and planned to move operations there, developing a new typewriter known as the Madame X. The union was worried because of the contract with Rand, covering the employees of six Rand factories. Would the contract apply in the new Elmira plant? And was the plant at Ilion to close? With these questions agitating them, union officials tried to see Rand. They charged, and the Labor Board later upheld them, that Rand's refusal to see them was a violation of their right of collective bargaining. To the company their questions were an unwarranted intrusion into management and an attempt to find out plans that could not be announced without disclosures to competitors. Plant managers conferred with union people discussing other matters of the contract, but could give no satisfactory answer to the crucial question of what was going to happen at Elmira with Madame X. For these and other reasons a strike vote was taken on April 28, and by a vote of 3,200 to 568, union officers were empowered to call a strike if, in their opinion, "all other means have failed to bring about a satisfactory conclusion."

The union contract contained a confidential clause. It read: "It is understood and agreed that any discrimination or intimidation on the part of any employee toward any other employee shall be just cause for discharge." As the union understood it, this only confirmed the public clause of the contract, which pledged both parties to the maintenance of peace and harmony—"We were not to bother or harm the few scabs, and they were to keep their skirts clean," was the union's interpretation. But on May 21, three weeks after the union authorized the strike, this confidential agreement became the mainspring of action. All employees of Remington Rand had received ballots distributed by the management, reading: *Are you dissatisfied with present working conditions? Are you in favor of a strike?* In the Syracuse plant the union leaders stopped work until the balloting was called off. Whereupon the company closed the plant for two weeks. Rand informed the mayor that he would reopen after the sixteen union leaders had been discharged—the point being, he insisted, that they had violated the confidential agreement in preventing the balloting. In Ilion, Syracuse, Tonawanda, Middletown, and Norwood, the union prepared for a strike, sending a last wire asking Rand if he was not letting "anger instead of reason rule." There was no reply. The second Remington Rand strike began.

If you were a good union man in Ilion you probably went to the strike meeting at the Temple Theatre on the night of May 25, listened to the speeches and turned out on the picket line the next morning. You may have eaten a sandwich at strike headquarters nearby. You may have watched the thirty-odd newly hired guards of Foster's Detective Bureau arriving to patrol the plant interior. And then things began to happen—not only to you, but to the mayor, the chief of police, a number of small city businessmen, the employees of Remington Rand in other cities, and a number of professional guards. In Ilion a Citizens' Committee was started by Barney Allen, Ilion's retail dealer in General Electric supplies. He was afraid Remington Rand would move out of Ilion, taking the $12,000-a-day payroll that was the town's main income. An organization called the Ilion Typewriter Employees' Protective Association was started by Reginald Boote, a young aligner who opposed the strike. It opened an office and began signing up employees who wanted to go back to work. A "For Sale" sign appeared on the factory. There was one tense moment the second day, with a threatened riot arising out of a brief encounter between strikers and guards. The Citizens' Committee appealed to Governor Lehman to send state troopers to supplement Ilion's six regular officers. He refused, since there had been no violence. Failing, the Citizens' Committee demanded that the mayor appoint 300 special deputies. In an atmosphere of growing hysteria, the Citizens' Committee held a mass meeting; Barney Allen called upon the mayor to co-operate or resign; the mayor agreed to co-operate (but he refused to ring the fire bell to summon the volunteer firemen to be deputized); and 300 deputies were signed up.

On the morning of June 10 the streets near the plant were roped off. Tear gas guns were mounted in the factory windows. Across the street members of Reginald Boote's Ilion Typewriter Employees' Association gathered for an open meeting. There were a few skirmishes between strikers and nonstrikers, ending when tear gas bombs were fired. Then the members and sympathizers of the Ilion Typewriter Employees' Protective Association (500 says the union, 800 says Reginald Boote) entered the factory; the flag rose on the factory flagpole; the "For Sale" sign was taken down; and Rand arrived to address the returning employees. That night a state of emergency was declared in Ilion on the strength of rumors that a flying squadron of strikers from Syracuse was rushing to town to help the Ilion pickets. All roads were blocked. The union headquarters were padlocked. During the "siege of Ilion," as the strikers called it, Union Leader Harold Beer (who had worked for Remington Rand for twenty-five years) entered Ilion by going on foot through the woods that lie behind the town. And the siege ended when the strikers broke, more than 1,200 returning to work two days after the strike began.

If you were a union man in Remington Rand's Ilion plant in 1936 you were one atom in the working out of a new force, which, amid charges and countercharges, accusations of prejudice, partisanship, plotting, and worse, was to be analyzed and defined by the National Labor Relations Board as the Mohawk Valley Formula. The nine steps of the Mohawk Valley Formula it found to include: (1) conducting a forced balloting under the direction of foremen to misrepresent the strength of the union, calling strike leaders "agitators," forming a Citizens' Committee under threat to move the plant; (2) arousing the community by calling for "law and order" because of "wholly imagined violence"; (3) calling mass meetings of citizens; (4) calling for armed deputies; (5) starting a back-to-work movement; (6) setting a date for opening the plant; (7) staging the opening theatrically; (8) turning the "locality into a warlike camp"; (9) keeping up a campaign of publicity to convince the remaining strikers that the plant is in full operation.

Thus the Labor Board pictured Rand as a superstrategist of strikebreaking and the originator of a foolproof strikebreaking technique. It revealed that during the Remington Rand strike the company paid, in all, $25,800 to Pearl L. Bergoff for his services and the services of 200 guards and "missionaries," whose function it was to discourage the strikers, $30,000 more to Captain Foster of Foster's Industrial and Detective Bureau, and an additional $25,000 to Raymond J. Burns of the William J. Burns International Detective Agency, Inc., the latter two, according to the company, for protection because of the recurring violence of the strike, which in some of its six towns lasted longer and was more bitterly fought than at Ilion. The Labor Board found Rand guilty of unfair labor practices and ordered him to offer reinstatement to all strikers unemployed, the case going to the courts, where it still remains.[1] The Joint Committee of Remington Rand Employees' Associations (the Board called the one at Ilion "a puppet association . . . secretly organized by the employer") denounced the Board and said its conclusions were based on the false statements of disgruntled ex-employees. And Remington Rand, which had not called witnesses at the Labor Board hearings, called the Board's charges a slander.

In the history of the Wagner Act, and in the Remington Rand strike itself, these charges and countercharges are of primary significance. But in the wave of 10,000 strikes, of which the Remington Rand strike was only a part, they are of less importance than the trends the strike revealed. For the Remington Rand strike shows quite clearly what other strikes barely suggest—the mechanics of a modern back-to-work movement.

RUBBER, 1936

The Sitdown Begins

Some observer poised high above the class struggle about that time might have thought that capital now had all the advantage, with labor's enthusiasm for the NRA ended and the spectacular, coordinated, theatrical Mohawk Valley Formula presently to come into

---

[1] [The courts held that the company illegally refused to bargain. *Ed.*]

being as an instrument for breaking strikes almost as soon as they got under way. And it might have seemed that with some of the mushroom unions of the NRA period smashed in their attempt to achieve recognition (as in the textile industry) and others broken after they had achieved it (as in the Remington Rand strike), the strike wave was now due to shrink to the proportions of an episode in labor's uneven history.

Instead, out in Akron, Ohio, at three in the morning of February 14, 1936, something happened that sent the strike wave surging to a new high—although its results were not immediately apparent. A major strike began in the rubber industry, growing out of a tangle of accumulated grievances, but taking a form that gave it historical importance. The form it took may have been a natural development in a long chain of brief stay-in and slow-down strikes. But whatever the reason, on that night a group of tire builders in Goodyear Tire & Rubber Company's Plant II sat down on the job. Theirs was not the first sitdown. But theirs grew into the Goodyear rubber strike that lasted five weeks, involved 14,000 employees, saw an eleven-mile picket line, and was described by the Department of Labor as "characterized by a lack of violence." It gave the sitdown nationwide publicity, ended with partial recognition of the union, and launched a drive that swept Akron's rubber union membership from less than 2,000 to approximately 37,000, the United Rubber Workers of America from about 3,000 to an organization of 75,000 with 136 locals and the reputation of never having lost a strike.

But it did not begin impressively. On that stormy St. Valentine's Day in Akron, Goodyear's management distributed some unwelcome valentines to sixty-nine tire builders of Plant II—the pink slips that meant a layoff. (February sales had been bad, said the management.) The first three men who got them, according to the story, "swore and sat down." They and many others remained sitting down while production heads hurried to the factory. The later shifts coming to work elected committees to support them, and—most important—the conveyers leading to the department were filled and the hot and steamy curing department immediately beyond had no tires to prepare. At nine in the morning the first sitdowners left the plant. Later shifts intermittently worked and sat down. At nine-forty that night Goodyear's outraged management gave notice that anyone not back at work in forty minutes would be dropped from the payroll. At ten-thirty the foremen began handing out notices. One hundred and thirty-seven men were dismissed. Thereafter the progress of the strike becamc confused—over the issues involved (it grew out of the union's opposition to increased hours and the threat of a wage cut); over union politics (since the union was one of the mushroom unions of the A.F. of L. involved in the split with the C.I.O.); over a back-to-work movement that flourished briefly and died; and over the numerous settlements proposed to end the strike. In the rubber strike itself, in Akron politics, and in the struggle between the A.F. of L. and the C.I.O., these subtleties were of first importance. But in the wave of strikes the sitdowns in Goodyear rubber were consequential because they introduced one of labor's answers to the Mohawk Valley Formula or the less highly organized back-to-work movements of the other sde. In the auto strikes that came soon after the sitdown it was to make history on a grand scale. And in the strike in Little Steel, the Mohawk Valley Formula was (perhaps) to be applied on a scalc no less sweeping.

AUTOS, 1936–37

The Sitdown

By November, 1936, the strike wave we have been describing had added up to over 7,000 strikes. It had included at least six general strikes, the great maritime strikes of the East and West Coast, a nationwide miners' strike, and a multitude of small strikes that followed in the wake of the big ones. It had passed through two distinct stages, suggested by our accounts of the textile strike and the strike at Remington Rand. And it looked as if it were going to decline. The number of strikes had increased slightly through 1936 but the number of men involved had gone down—which meant that the strike wave was now reaching smaller plants, and the figures were swollen by the inclusion of later strikes, strikes of grocery clerks, even by a strike of the graveyard workers of Minneapolis.

Then—to set an arbitrary date for the beginning of the next surge—at eight-twenty-five on the sunny morning of November 18, 1936, five men in the trim department of General Motors' Fisher Body plant in Atlanta were laid off because they came to work wearing union buttons. To General Motors that was a violation of company rules. To the union their dismissal was part of a general attempt to smash the United Automobile Workers, and a sitdown strike occurred. If you were a member of the union and had observed it rise and fall, you probably believed that the systematic firing of union men was part of General Motors policy. You may have joined the auto workers union in 1934 when, as a skyrocketing federal union of the A.F. of L., it claimed 200,000, with 60,000 members in Detroit. You may have been with it in 1935 when it plummeted down to the point where William Green could complain: "Today, I am sorry to say, we have 35,000. A year ago there were more, but for different reasons they are not with us now." Among those reasons was one later revealed by the La Follette Committee: that General Motors had spent $839,000 in two and a half years on detective services, that a Lansing local had five members, all officers and all stool pigeons provided by a spy agency hired by the company.

If you were a rank-and-file union man among General Motors' 135,000 employees, your biggest grievance was the "speedup"—the most likely cause for a "conflagration in the automobile industry," the NRA's Research and Planning Division had reported. And as a union man, the subsequent months of that conflagration were the most important of your union experience. There was a strike at the Kansas City Fisher Body plant when a union man was fired for jumping over the assembly line. There were three sitdown strikes in the auto-parts industry: at Bendix in South Bend and at Midland Steel and Kelsey-Hayes in Detroit. In Cleveland and Norwood, Ohio, there were General Motors walkouts; at the General Motors Guide Lamp Plant in Anderson, Indiana, there was a sitdown involving 2,400; and in the long, rectangular, brick factories that house the Fisher Body plants of Flint, the strike was touching the heart of the General Motors empire.

Deep in the interior of Fisher I, about a mile away from the imposing group of factories in the central General Motors plant, a sitdown started on December 30. The union had presented a contract to the company a few days before, and now the strikers saw (or thought they saw, for the company says it never happened) preparations being made for removing the big dies from which turret-top bodies are made. [This], they assumed, must mean that the plant was being abandoned. Or that a scare was being thrown into Flint, 45,000 of whose 150,000 work for General Motors. At Fisher II, across Chevrolet Avenue from Chevrolet II, three inspectors who were union men were demoted to the assembly line. (Because they were union men, said the union; because they were supervisors, said the company, and supervisors could not belong to the union.) Workers sat down in both Fisher plants. During the rubber strike, the sit-downers left the plant, formed their picket lines outside. But at Flint several hundred strikers remained in Fisher I and II. The union listed eight demands, including a thirty-hour week, seniority rights, a national agreement, and joint determination of the speed of the line. The company replied that the plants had to be vacated before there could be any discussion. The stage was set for what motor makers still call Detroit's sociological nightmare.

Seen only in relation to Detroit, or to the state of Michigan (where for a period one person in every thirty-three was on strike), or to the automobile industry, the sitdown certainly assumed nightmarish proportions. And because during the General Motors strike there was dancing twenty-four hours a day in Flint at the strike headquarters at Pengelly Hall, plus ball games in the struck plants, plus food prepared for the strikers by a union chef formerly of Detroit's swank Athletic Club, the sitdowns seemed to take place in a nightmare world where the laws of capitalism, if they operated at all, worked the way the laws of gravity do in a dream. But if viewed in relation to the 1933–37 strike wave, the General Motors strike becomes part of a great pattern. It saw, for example, a back-to-work movement, as well as an injunction against the strikers. The injunction was defied, and the back-to-work movement collapsed, for reasons connected not only with the sitdown, but with the change in labor's tactics in general.

During the strike General Motors got an injunction to evict the sitdowners. But the injunction lost some of its authority when the union promptly disclosed that Judge Edward Black, who issued it, owned 1,000 shares of General Motors stock. Whereupon General Motors got another injunction from another judge. But the sheriff who went inside the plant to read it to the strikers was greeted with boos and catcalls. And Governor Murphy refused to order the National Guard to enforce the injunction until all peaceful means of settlement had been exhausted.

As for the back-to-work movement, in this case called the "Flint Alliance for Security of Our Jobs, Our Homes, and Our Community," it came to its own peculiar kind of grief. While it was growing to claim 12,000 and making preparations for a mass meeting, Governor Murphy was holding conferences with General Motors and the union. On January 11 there was an unexpected crisis: the sitdowners remaining in Fisher II thought an attempt was going to be made to evict them. Heat was cut down; the company guards who had previously handed food into the factory now refused to let it enter. But according to General Motors the strikers had for the first time prevented the office force from going to work, which was why the heat was turned off, and although the company guards would no longer hand food into the plant, they would permit it to be handed through the windows. Whatever the reason, the situation suddenly became ominous. By nightfall police had assembled around the plant. In the beginning of a battle that lasted for seven hours, the police broke a window in the plant and fired a tear gas shell inside; the strikers built a barricade of autos in the street, doused the tear gas bombs with water from a fire hose, and held their ground. On the third rush the police fired, and fourteen strikers were wounded. And the next day militia massed at Flint, the Fleetwood plant went on strike, while from Washington John Lewis announced that the auto strikers would have the full support of the c.i.o. and Homer Martin hurried to Washington to confer with him.

During the forty-eight crowded hours after the riot in Flint, the ascetic Governor Murphy (whose picture, labeled "Our Friend," looked sternly down on several hundred sitdowners) arranged the famous "Lansing Truce." By its terms the union agreed to evacuate the plants, General Motors agreed not to resume operations in the struck plants, and the union temporarily waived its sole bargaining demand. So it came about that on Saturday, January 16, the sitdowners left the Guide Lamp plant in Anderson, Cadillac and Fleetwood in Detroit. But in Flint a hitch occurred. Talkative ex-Mayor George Boysen, once a Buick paymaster, organizer of the Flint Alliance, told a reporter that at four o'clock Sunday afternoon General Motors would announce that it was going to deal with the Alliance. The sitdowners were scheduled to leave the plants at one o'clock. Informed of this, the union refused to evacuate Fisher I and Fisher II in Flint, and the General Motors strike flared up again.

Such happenings gave a good share of Michigan's population its conviction that law and order had collapsed. But seen in perspective against the strike wave, they illustrated how profoundly union tactics, as well as unions themselves, had changed in the period since the textile strike. Unlike the Remington Rand strikers, the auto strikers had successfully countered a back-to-work movement. They had developed a new organizing technique and a new strike strategy. But more profoundly, they had developed a new concept of strike action, which is nowhere better illustrated than in the story of the seizure of Chevvy IV. By the end of the first month of the strike union leaders wanted a bold stroke to bolster union morale. Half a dozen of them went to the bluff overlooking the seven plants on Chevrolet's eighty-acre tract and decided that they had to capture Plant IV, which assembles motors for all Chevrolet automobiles. If the union could get and hold that plant, they could give General Motors all the rest of its establishments and still stop enough production to count.

But a direct attack on Chevvy IV was out of the question. Hardly a hundred feet from this plant was the personnel building, which served as the headquarters and arsenal for the company police. It was too well guarded. Furthermore, the union was not very strong there. They decided to make a false attempt to take Chevrolet IX, a bearing plant on the other end of the tract. Not more than eight strike leaders knew the full details of the plan.

First, thirty-five shop stewards were called to a meeting. It was held after midnight in Fisher I, where the sitdown was in progress, to impress them with its importance and secrecy. Among them, by design, were men known by the organizers to be informers. They were told that an effort would be made to capture Chevrolet IX. This plan met with strong objection because the men knew that the bearing plant would be hard to take—and also that it was relatively unimportant to production because General Motors could get bearings elsewhere. Nevertheless, the program was decided on.

At 3:00 P.M. on February 1, a mass meeting was held in Pengelly Hall. At 3:20 a note was handed up to Bob Travis, chairman of the meeting, who then announced that there was trouble at Chevrolet IX and that everybody should go down there at once. Actually, nothing had yet happened at Chevrolet IX, but promptly at 3:30 at the change of shift the men refused to work, refused to leave the plant, and set up a terrific din. When the strikers from Pengelly Hall arrived at 3:35 the "trouble" at Chevrolet IX was in progress.

As had been expected, guards rushed to the plant. Meanwhile, at Chevrolet VI, far from the scene of the trouble, promptly at 3:35 a union steward named Ed Cronk sounded a siren, picked up an American flag, and started marching around the factory. He led the march to Chevrolet IV. But in his excitement he forgot to look around, discovering when he got to Chevrolet IV that he had only twenty-five men with him. He rushed back and marched around the factory again, carrying the flag, and this time collected more followers. Once in Chevvy IV the strikers quickly ejected foremen, plant officials, and nonunion workers and began to barricade all the doors. Fourteen minutes had elapsed between the time the commotion had started at Chevrolet IX and the time Chevrolet IV was barricaded.

Out of all the sensational news of the auto strike, the seizing of Chevvy IV was the high point. In terms of the auto strike alone it was either the final indignity offered outraged property rights—if you were on the side of the employers—or an illustration of labor's growing initiative—if you were not. But in terms of the 1933–37 strike wave its significance is of a different order. When you compare it with the moves made during the textile strike it serves as a landmark, measuring how far labor had traveled in less than three years and through some 4,000 strikes.

Improper Activities, Teamster Style

McCLELLAN COMMITTEE

LOCAL 107, INTERNATIONAL BROTHERHOOD OF TEAMSTERS, PHILADELPHIA, PA.

By the use of subterfuge, intimidation, threats, and physical violence the control of Pennsylvania's largest Teamster union went into the hands of a group of greedy and unscrupulous officers headed by Raymond Cohen. These men thereafter completely stifled the democratic processes of the union by terror and brute force and proceeded to drain the union treasury of large amounts of cash under the guise of legal expenditures. The findings of the committee in the underhanded dealings of Raymond Cohen, assisted (or directed) by his "fixer" Ben Lapensohn are more specifically enumerated hereafter.

1. Raymond Cohen in a conspiracy with Joe Grace, the long time president of local 107, set the stage and engineered a "rigged" election in November 1953 to put himself in office as secretary-treasurer of the union. This was strictly a travesty of normal democratic processes.

Competition was eliminated by the prevention of nominations. By this means Edward Crumbock, secretary-treasurer for 20 years, who had built the union from a small local to a membership of nearly 14,000, was preemptorily "dumped." The manner in which it was

Taken from Second Interim Report of the Select Committee on Improper Activities in the Labor or Management Field, *U.S. Senate, 86th Congress, 1st session, Senate Report No. 621, Part 2, October 23, 1959, pp. 513–17, and* Interim Report of the Select Committee on Improper Activities in the Labor or Management Field, *U.S. Senate, 85th Congress, 2nd session, Senate Report No. 1417, March 24, 1958, pp. 98–101.*

done clearly shows that the whole deal was carefully planned and completely "rigged" from start to finish.

2. Cohen's method of forcing himself into office was too brazen for even Dave Beck, the Teamsters' international president, to ignore. Beck placed the union under trusteeship and ordered that new nominations and a secret ballot election by the membership be held.

3. With apparently unlimited funds to work with, Cohen surrounded himself with a squad of hoodlums and ex-convicts whose job it was to stamp out all competition to Cohen in the coming election by fear, threats, and physical violence.

4. Cohen's methods, unconscionable and ruthless as they were, paid off with Cohen's election as secretary-treasurer in May 1954.

5. Immediately after assuming office in June 1954, Cohen instituted a spending program which amounted to nothing less than a looting of the local's treasury. The first week in office he withdrew $25,000 in cash from the union treasury to pay off his henchmen and backers in the election campaign. He then paid his attorney's fee retroactive to December 1, 1953; repaid nearly $5,000 which Teamster Local 169 had loaned to him personally for campaign expenses; paid to himself an expense account and salary increase of $11,962.10 retroactive to January 1, 1954—all from the dues money from the members of local 107.

6. Cohen "purged" all of the business agents who had been elected by the membership and replaced them with his own henchmen who had been prominent in getting him elected. Many of these appointed business agents had police records and one of them, Al Berman, had been prominent in the numbers racket in Philadelphia for many years.

7. In order to insure his control of the union, Cohen set up a "goon squad" made up largely of ex-convicts and men with extensive criminal records. These men he paid at the rate of $125 per week, plus expenses, disguising their salaries on the union books under the heading "lost time." No withholding tax was ever paid to the Bureau of Internal Revenue on the salaries of any of these men, none of whom listed their income on their 1956 tax returns. It was further noted that on the 1957 returns, the union paid the Federal income tax for each of them.

8. As a union leader, Raymond Cohen's only method of organizing involved violence, the threat of violence, beatings, destruction of property and a complete disregard of all standards of ethics and decency. As soon as Cohen took over as administrative trustee of local 596, that union launched a drive to organize the employees of

Pontiac automobile dealers in the Philadelphia area. No standard ethical union organizing methods were utilized, only violence, the threat of force, and criminal vandalism.

9. In connection with the organization activities of local 596, Ben Lapensohn, Cohen's "fixer," pulled an outright "shakedown" of garage owner Julius Wolfson.

10. The drive to organize the employees of the Horn & Hardart restaurant and bakery chain in Philadelphia was one of the worst examples of irresponsibility and criminal leadership of a union yet to come to the committee's attention. By the use of roving "goon squads," Cohen endeavored to enforce a secondary boycott against the company by wrecking trucks, burning trucks, obstructing deliveries, stealing trucks and dumping them in the river and the repeated beatings of truck drivers which were just short of actual murder. When a year of tyranny failed to bring the company to its knees and force its employees into the union the drive was called off.

In addition to the wholesale criminality of the entire affair the senseless and irresponsible union leadership of Cohen is made apparent by the fact that had the membership drive been a complete success the maximum new members the Teamsters could have expected from the Horn & Hardart Co. was less than 150. For this a reign of terror was conducted which cost the union and the employers together hundreds of thousands of dollars.

Although the evidence indicated the police commissioner of Philadelphia did his best to give the Horn & Hardart Co. and individual truck owners the protection to which they were entitled, it was noted that the police protection was inadequate to control the situation.

11. In regard to the union goons who were arrested for various acts of assault and destruction of property, the committee found that at the time of its hearings in April 1958, 2½ years after the arrests, none of the cases had come up for trial.

12. That shakedowns and extortion were a part of Cohen's organizing by terror is shown in the $1,500 payoff by garage owner Julius Wolfson to Cohen's "fixer," Ben Lapensohn; and by the $50,000 extortion attempt on the Horn & Hardart Co. by ex-convict "Shorty" Feldman, Cohen's longtime friend in Teamster activities.

13. The committee found that the practice of writing union checks for "cash" was a means for surreptitiously stealing from the union. The vouchers purportedly supporting disbursement of the cash were false. Union members recorded as receiving certain amounts either received a lesser amount or payments to them were completely fictitious. The total cash embezzled in this manner could not be deter-

mined but was obviously considerable, since the sum total of these checks to "cash" written by Cohen as secretary-treasurer of the union was over a quarter of a million dollars during the period covered by the committee's examination.

14. Outright forgery was another method used by Cohen to extract funds from the union treasury. A series of checks exceeding $10,000 overall, bearing forged endorsements and then cashed, were drawn by Cohen from the union treasury. In addition, checks to Samuel Kirsch totaled $8,500 and were falsely labeled "for return of election expense." Kirsch turned the proceeds of these checks directly over to union "fixer" Ben Lapensohn.

15. The committee also found a further gouging of the union treasury in a series of checks totaling more than $12,000, written to Ben Lapensohn for "personal services" over and above Lapensohn's regular salary of $10,000 a year. Further evidence of the illegality of these payments was established by the fact that someone had surreptitiously removed nine of these canceled checks from the union records.

16. The committee found further that shortly before the "personal service" checks were written to Lapensohn that Lapensohn furnished Cohen $17,000 for use as a downpayment on a new yacht in April 1955. The manner in which Lapensohn was repaid by Cohen, if he was repaid, is not known.

17. In addition to the large sums of money which he removed from the union treasury under various pretexts, the committee found that Cohen also imposed heavily on the dues-paying members by charging as legitimate union expenses such personal luxuries for himself as $135 suits and overcoats, $13.50 shirts, $10 neckties, an expensive camera, Christmas gifts, car expenses, and hotel bills, as well as 3 and 4 months all-expense vacations in Florida for himself and family and $125 per week pocket expense money.

18. It was established by the committee that Cohen was handling nearly all of his own personal finances in cash, even expenditures of many thousands of dollars. This was during the same period that the $250,000 in cash was being removed from the union treasury under various pretexts. It was found that Cohen spent during this time several thousands of dollars more than all his known sources of income, and, at the same time, increased his net worth by more than $46,000. Since Cohen and his henchman refused to offer any explanation, seeking refuge in the fifth amendment to all questions, no other conclusion could be left to the committee but that Cohen, with

the assistance of some of his appointees, was steadily taking from the union treasury by clandestine means.

19. It was found by the committee that Ben Lapensohn, a union "fixer" successfully operated the advertising sales of the Pennsylvania Federationist and the New York Federationist as strictly "shake-down" operations, using the threat of labor trouble and the promise of labor tranquillity as a means of extorting "donations" and advertisements from legitimate businesses.

20. Despite the extremely lucrative results of this method of operation, Lapensohn still could not satisfy his voracity and took large amounts from the proportionate shares of the New York Federation of Labor.

21. It was the opinion of the committee that Ben Lapensohn, although never a working union member, made a large fortune over a period of years by exploiting both sides in labor-management relations with a complete disregard for the welfare of either.

22. The Food Fair Co. received a large concession over its competitors from Raymond Cohen during the contract negotiations in 1954 by receiving the privilege of dropping trailers in unlimited numbers. This was accomplished by having the Food Fair attorney Samuel Blank, go to Raymond Cohen behind the back of the negotiating team of the Motor Transport Labor Relations. The committee found that despite the claims of the Food Fair officials to the contrary, the practice of dropping trailers in making freight deliveries is a substantial economic advantage.

23. The committee attached a special significance to the concession granted the Food Fair Co. by Raymond Cohen when it was established that shortly after these negotiations certain substantial stock transfers were made by Louis Stein, president of Food Fair, to "fixer" Ben Lapensohn of local 107. On one transfer of Dan River Mills stock made through an intermediary, Lapensohn was given a $5,000 "windfall." Stein admitted to the committee that he knew Lapensohn as an "adviser" to Raymond Cohen and admitted selling the stock at a premium to Lapensohn to "avoid incurring his ill will."

24. Lapensohn was the recipient of another gift from Food Fair, this time through Lapensohn's brother-in-law, Jack Shore. This involved Food Fair "rights" which were worth $3,000 permitting Lapensohn to purchase bond units for $10,000 which had an actual value of $14,000. Lapensohn was also permitted to purchase through his brother-in-law $2,000 worth of Food Fair stock at the time the stock had a value of $8,000.

25. The committee found that the Food Fair Co. was shamefully involved in the actual soliciting of key labor leaders to "get in on the ground floor" on the company's new stock issue. By this preferred treatment 20 prominent labor leaders, most of whom had direct labor dealings with the Food Fair Co., were given stocks and bonds worth $90,400 for a total investment on their part of only $42,100. This was not only unethical but in the opinion of the committee was an outright violation of the law. We strongly feel that the Department of Justice, to which this matter was referred, should have taken action by this time. The committee strongly renews its request to the Department of Justice to act in this case.

26. The committee finds that the Philadelphia Bar Association acted in a manner not in keeping with the stipulated high ethical standards of the legal profession. It is indeed saddening that leaders of a profession which should set the highest moral and ethical examples for the rest of our citizens should act as they did with relation to this case. After first advising Attorneys John Rogers Carroll and Richard Markowitz that there was nothing unethical about their simultaneous representation of the dues-paying members of local 107 and of officers accused of taking money from the treasury of the local, they then reversed their position and advised Carroll and Markowitz that such simultaneous representation would be unethical. As the hearings continued, however, Carroll, and to a lesser degree Markowitz, conducted themselves in a highly unethical manner requiring constant admonishment for constant coaching of the forty-six witnesses they represented, all of them invoking the fifth amendment. Despite a referral of the matter to the Philadelphia Bar Association by this committee, it did nothing to deal with this unethical conduct. . . .

A SCRANTON BAKERY

. . . The third case of Scranton violence scrutinized by the committee involved the stinkbombing of the Sonny Boy Bakery, a manufacturer of Italian bread and pizza. Although the bombing was the ultimate destructive act against the bakery, the case is also worth examining for the pattern of attrition which preceded it.

Arnold Schiavi, third generation of his family to operate the business, told the committee that in February 1953 he received a letter from the teamsters notifying him that the six drivers he employed had signed up for local 229, and inviting him to discuss a contract. He had two such discussions, he said, about a month apart, both with teamster chief John Durkin. The first seemed to Schiavi to go smoothly; at the second, however, Durkin, he said, raised some points about which Schiavi foresaw difficulties. One was the hiring of an extra man because of the 6-day week; another, more troubling, was that "anyone who drove a truck at our bakery must belong to local 229." That bothered Schiavi, he told the committee, because 30 percent of his trade was with outside distributors who drove their own trucks to the bakery to pick up their products. The same point also concerned him because he, himself, and his father, also occasionally drove trucks.

Nevertheless, Schiavi went on, "we still left with the impression that we could negotiate a contract."

In the following weeks, however, what Schiavi described as a "war of nerves" began. On three separate occasions his drivers were instructed not to place any orders. Each time he closed down the bakery, but each time the men came back and again placed orders.

In the wake of these disruptive tactics he received 6-hour notice to sign the contract or face a strike. When his outside distributors came around the next morning to pick up their products, his own drivers, aided by 12 pickets, boarded the distributors' trucks and "told them it was very unhealthy to buy their products there from that day on." Schiavi next attempted to service the distributors without their having to come to the bakery. One who did appear, John Genova, testified as to the unhappy result.

On the first day of the strike, Genova recalled, no one bothered him. On the second day, six men pulled the ignition key and tried to pull him from his truck. Undeterred, he returned a third day, got his bread, and had driven several miles away when, he said, he was stopped by Robert Hubshman, who stepped onto the running board, saw the door was locked, and "put his foot right through my window." By now Genova got the point, he reported, and stopped going to the bakery.

But apparently the feeling remained that the point had to be hammered home a little more. Genova received about 10 phone calls, which he described thus:

> Well, they would tell me not to go up there for bread anymore, that maybe some morning a big trailer would hit my truck and nobody would ever know what happened.

> Well, sometimes they would say, "Your garage is on fire" and it wouldn't be true.

MR. KENNEDY. That your garage was on fire?

MR. GENOVA. Yes. They would call me up about 10 or 11 o'clock at night and tell me my garage was on fire, which wasn't true. It was things like that. Everything was disturbing.

Schiavi's brother-in-law, Anthony Duchnowski, a draftsman for an instrument company, also ran into force of harassment when he tried to help out by driving a truck during the strike. After 2 days, he told the committee, he was at the bakery garage when:

Robert Hubshman yelled down the driveway that he would like to see me a minute. So I got out of the car, and I walked up the driveway, I had my hands in the pocket.

Then I surmised that there might be a little trouble, and I took the hands out of the pocket. I asked him what is it he wishes to discuss about. He didn't say anything. He said, "This, you so and so," and he swung a few times. I ducked and he caught me on the lip, and he busted my lip.

Duchnowski, too, got the point, and never drove the truck again.

The Schiavis, meanwhile, were also getting an education of sorts. Nightly phone calls to Arnold Schiavi's home reminded him that his children had to cross the street on their way to school, hinted at the planting of explosives and other violence, and hurled foul language freely. On top of that, milk and fuel oil deliveries to this home were stopped. It was, he said, "cold war all the way." His father, too, felt the brunt. Delivering bread to one of their customers, he came out to find his truck tipped over.

Finally came the climax, Schiavi told the committee:

. . . the following night I went up to the bakery and found the windows all shattered and a foul-smelling liquid was in the place. If it permeated the rest of the floor it would have ruined about 600 bags of flour. But the glass was scattered all over the troughs and the boxes.

MR. KENNEDY. What had happened?

MR. SCHIAVI. Somebody had thrown a bottleful of foul-smelling liquid in the bakery and hit the window, and the glass from the bakery and from the bottle was all over the equipment and went in some of the dough troughs and ruined some of the dough.

The events leading up to this disaster were filled in for the committee by Paul Bradshaw:

I was driving my car up Linden Street, and John Durkin, business agent for 229, was standing on the sidewalk talking to Robert Hubshman. John waved me down. I pulled over to the side. I went over to him, and he said, "Come on upstairs, Paul. I want you to drive Hubshman over to the south side."

We got upstairs. John Durkin got a bottle of stink-solution fluid from a little safe that they had in the office and handed it to Hubshman. It was a quart bottle. He said, "Drive Hubshman over there and Hubshman will throw this bottle through the window." We got in the car and went over as far as south side.

We got as far as the high school. I don't know if it was myself or Hubshman, but we figured a quart was maybe too much, so we threw half of the quart away and put the other half in small bottle, a pint bottle. We pulled up as far as the bakery. Hubshman got up, went up to the door, threw the bottle of stink solution through, got in the car, and we took off.

Hubshman himself took the fifth amendment before the committee. Helen Canfield, however, attested to his satisfaction over a job well done. She told the committee:

Bob, he said to me, "Wait until they try soap and water to clean that up," because he said, "Only ammonia will take it out and they will never think of ammonia. They will use soap and water and it will make it that much worse and it will go into the cellar and it will ruin all of the flour that is stored there." And he said, "Wait until they turn on the oven," he said, "Then they will be running outside and I would love to see it."

When he was telling me all of that I wanted to go up and take a look and I thought it would be fun really.

Queried on the Sonny Boy Bakery affair, John Durkin denied to the committee that he had talked to Schiavi by telephone and also categorically labeled Bradshaw's testimony false. Of the strike, he said:

That was a legitimate stoppage or a strike and his employees voted for a strike by a secret ballot and we executed the strike because we had the secret ballot and I always instruct all of our people who are on strike, there be no violence and no violence of any kind or any type.

MR KENNEDY. Can you explain why—

The CHAIRMAN. That is rather intriguing. Can you tell me why such violence occurred up there, if those are the instructions?

Mr. DURKIN. I cannot tell you.

Admitting that he had not pressed inquiry into the various acts of violence surrounding the Sonny Boy strike, Durkin explained:

I cannot properly police the whole rank and file as one individual.

Schiavi's troubles were not yet over with the stink-bombing. Attempting to carry on his business, he testified, he would make deliveries himself; but his own striking drivers would follow him, blowing their horns, and threatening his customers; he would be followed, too, by strangers, "fellows with dark glasses." He lost about 35 pounds, his wife about 25:

> We never ate a square meal. It was always a continuing going, going, going, trying to stay alive.

At length, Schiavi testified, he capitulated and signed a contract, and since then the Sonny Boy Bakery drivers have been in the Teamsters union.

The CHAIRMAN. You went in voluntarily, I assume?

MR. SCHIAVI. It wasn't a case of voluntary or involuntary. It was a case of survival.

Conflicts of sworn testimony in the Sonny Boy Bakery incident, as well as in the others studied by the committee, have been referred to the Department of Justice.

PART II

LABOR MOVEMENTS
AND UNION EVOLUTION

INTRODUCTION

The development of organized labor in America has been the subject of much speculation and analysis. As Kassalow explains in the first article in this section, unionism in the United States and Canada, compared with European labor movements, has been less class conscious, less doctrinaire, and less political in its orientation. Organized labor in North America has focused largely on collective bargaining. It has been job-centered, with stress on the negotiation of written agreements with employers and on day-to-day servicing of workers' grievances on the job.

Labor movements abroad, Kassalow points out, have tended to be Marxist or socialistic, at least in their early stages, and have generally been class-conscious movements. Looking largely to political action and legislation for employee benefits of various sorts, including paid vacations and holidays, European unions have been less active at the plant level in dealing with individual workers' grievances. They have put more stress on government-devised schemes for union participation in the control of industry.

Since World War II there has been a tendency for unionism in all free countries to develop a similar outlook and set of objectives, to confront common problems, and to seek to solve them in similar ways. Since the mid-1950's, European as well as American unionism has had to contend with such problems as the failure to expand in total membership, middle-class views generated by prolonged prosperity that reduce the appeal of trade unionism, the complaint that collective bargaining is responsible for wage-price inflation, and the claim that unrestricted collective bargaining is incompatible with a government program of economic planning for full employment.

Since the end of World War II, many countries have been wrestling with a difficult and many-sided question. To what extent can unions be permitted to use their full powers to negotiate either wage increases exceeding those compatible with the nation's economic program or wage differentials that work against the occupational, industrial, and geographic allocation of labor necessary for full employment? In addition, two related questions have received widespread attention. One is, if organized labor insists on the unlimited right to negotiate large economic gains and tight job protection for an ingroup with long seniority in the firm, will it lose its missionary purpose and general appeal? The second is, will strong unions become merely a self-centered group, promoting its own economic advantage at the expense of others, especially of the large numbers of youth entering the work force, by blocking the way to much desirable production employment through union-negotiated barriers?

A union that has faced up to this range of problems is the United Automobile, Aircraft, and Agricultural Implement Workers of America, headed since 1946 by Walter Reuther. As A. H. Raskin points out in the second article, the Auto Workers has been exceptional in its pioneering in collective bargaining, in the dynamic quality of its membership as well as its leadership, and in that union's ability to attract, rapidly promote, and inspire men with high intellectual and leadership qualities. More politically oriented than most American unions, the UAW's leadership recognizes that collective bargaining must take account of the general public interest and has, therefore, strongly supported national economic planning for full employment, even at the expense of complete freedom in collective bargaining.

To a considerable extent, the auto union has exhibited highly individual characteristics. Since the 1930's, many unions in the United

States have lost their youthful dynamism. Many have gradually changed into administrative agencies, subject to considerable bureaucratic routine, to various pressures for conformity, and to a high degree of centralization of policy and control in the national headquarters. The top leadership, usually old in office, has sought to preserve the organization along traditional lines and has resisted ideas for marked alterations in policy or program. In other words, many unions have shown signs of suffering from institutional conservatism, if not stagnation.

The third article on the International Ladies' Garment Workers Union by Paul Jacobs illustrates some features of institutional maturity and long continued one-man domination. The transformation is so pronounced because in the 1920's and 1930's, the ILGWU in the field of women's clothing and the Amalgamated Clothing Workers in the men's field were hailed as the promising progressive elements in organized labor, with their exceptional educational, recreational, and benefit programs. Of course, they were limited by the highly competitive nature of the women's and men's clothing industries. But who would have predicted before World War II that, by 1962, staff members would vote for a union to protect them from the top management of the ILGWU, namely President Dubinsky?

An attempt to assess the condition of the American labor movement, especially in manufacturing industries, is offered by George Strauss in the fourth article largely on the basis of a study made in a mid-western city of half a million inhabitants. Strauss finds that the paid union representatives and unpaid local officials have lost much of their idealistic motivation and have declined in quality since the 1930's. He ascribes the present weaknesses of the union movement in large part to increased sophistication and militancy of industrial management, the difficulty of formulating a clear union policy for meeting the problems of automation, and a significant decline in dedication to union objectives.

The labor movement's failure to organize white-collar and engineering workers and technicians is potentially its greatest weakness. Trends in labor force growth and composition clearly indicate that, unless white-collar workers are unionized at a much more rapid rate than in the 1950's and early 1960's, organized labor is doomed to be a declining proportion of the nation's total work force, as has been the case since 1953.

The article on white-collar unionization by Solomon and Burns clearly sets forth the magnitude of the organizing problem facing the labor movement. The authors discuss union structure, strategy, and appeal and the organizing personnel that would be necessary in order for the labor movement to organize large numbers of the expanding sections of the labor force. Along with economic, political, and social conditions favorable to white-collar unionization, changes within organized labor perhaps as radical as the development of the CIO in the 1930's would seem necessary if office and professional workers are to be well organized. The union "establishment," in the opinion of the authors, is likely to forestall any such reform and reorientation.

The Solomon-Burns article provides other material of considerable significance. It sets forth trends in the expanding and contracting sectors of the labor force. It presents figures for the white-collar membership of fifty-odd national unions. It discusses the prospects of individual unions—the Office Employees International Union, the Retail Clerks International Association, the American Federation of Teachers, and the American Federation of Technical Engineers—and examines them in detail. Considerable attention is given to the likelihood of the unionization of large numbers of engineers, scientists, and subprofessional technicians.

In recent years much has been written about "the crisis" in the labor movement.[1] Actually there has been no crisis in the sense of a critical juncture or turning point. But gradual loss of vigor and momentum, a willingness to continue in well-worn ruts, a failure to adapt sufficiently to changes taking place in the economy have occurred, and these developments are perceived as critical by many observers of the labor scene.

[1] See, for example, Solomon Barkin and Albert A. Blum (eds.), *The Crisis in the American Labor Movement*, 15 articles in *The Annals of the American Academy of Political and Social Science*, CCCL (November 1963).

The Development of
Western Labor Movements:
Some Comparative Considerations

EVERETT M. KASSALOW

As a means of making analysis of labor movements abroad more dramatic and vivid, let us first examine the special nature and character of the American labor movement. Needless to say, any brief survey of Western labor movements must necessarily be oversimplified at practically every stage.

SPECIAL INFLUENCES IN U.S.
LABOR MOVEMENT DEVELOPMENT

A number of special forces shaped the development of the American labor movement. In the United States the capitalist enterprise system did not have to contend with a previously existing feudalism and a rigid set of class attitudes and practices. There were some traces of a feudal land system in America, but these were relatively unimportant. Indeed, the free frontier tended to encourage the emergence of new landholders.

The absence of feudalism meant, of course, that the triumph of capitalism for this and other reasons was ultimately more widespread and more successful in the United States than anywhere else. There were none of the usual aristocratic inhibitions on willingness to work, nor any excessive preoccupation with leisure pursuits that characterized the ruling classes of Europe.

Adapted from a speech given by Professor Kassalow in October 1961. Many of the themes contained herein are more fully developed in a forthcoming book, to be published by Random House. Everett M. Kassalow is a professor of economics at the University of Wisconsin and former Director of Research of the Industrial Union Department of the AFL–CIO.

The lack of a feudal tradition also served to blur class lines from an early period in American history. When an explosive, dynamic capitalism was combined with this, social mobility—though perhaps exaggerated in some of our literature—was certainly greater in American life than in that anywhere in Europe. Again, as a consequence of these factors, there was less tendency for class lines and attitudes to develop in the lifelong pattern that they had in Europe. The special form of American capitalism with its great emphasis on internal markets early resulted in a relatively high standard of living for the great mass of people, further weakening the possibility of the emergence of persistent class attitudes. The heavy flow of immigration into America also made any "unity" of the working classes more unlikely.

Full citizenship and voting rights for the male, white, urban working class existed at a relatively early date in American history. This too made the workers feel they were full partners in the growing society.

The establishment of free public education for all citizens long before the Civil War helped complete the integration of American workers into their society. Illiteracy among the masses persisted in most of Western Europe well into the latter half of the nineteenth century and was certainly a factor in alienating workers from the newly developing social orders.

The possibility of a higher standard of living and the possibility of social mobility into managerial and entrepreneurial positions tended at a relatively early point to make the American labor movement a highly economically oriented institution. By the latter part of the nineteenth century its feet were rather firmly set on the road of wages, hours, and working conditions, all of which were to become institutionally contained within the framework of collective bargaining and written agreements. (Of course, there were syndicalist and socialist exceptions, but in retrospect they were just that—exceptions to the main pattern of development.)

All these factors tended to give what Bruce Millen has called an "exclusionist" character to the American trade union movement. Its concentration was upon benefits to members rather than any great interest in the economic fate of the working class as a whole. Finally, for a great part of its history the American movement largely confined its activities to a limited number of trades and industries. Since the rise of the mass unionism of the thirties, the horizon of American labor has broadened considerably; but even today it is a relatively narrower movement than those in other Western countries.

On the other hand, the lack of class feeling as well as powerful opposition from employers (and often from public authorities) made both the existence and the continuity of unionism difficult in the American environment. This in turn led the unions to lay great emphasis upon exclusive bargaining rights, closed and union shops, and other forms of union security. Since the limitations of space do not permit a return to this point, suffice it to note that European unions have almost never resorted to these forms. This is largely true because the cement of class attitude made this additional bond unnecessary for the permanent existence of unionism. Since, as we shall see below, the typical European union was ideologically committed, it also would have been somewhat contradictory to compel "non-believers" to join the union and pay dues to it.

EUROPEAN LABOR: A CLASS MOVEMENT

Let us now examine some broad contrasts with the labor movements which developed in Western Europe. In the first place the social and political background was considerably different in Europe. To an extent (though this is still argued among historians) some of the early unions were influenced by the medieval guild tradition. Feudalism was firmly intrenched, leaving rigid class lines and social and economic distinctions many of which still persist. By the same token, European capitalism was less successful in shattering older attitudes and practices, which also reinforced the tendency to develop or continue class distinctions and class attitudes. The idea of the "naturalness" of group activity and group recognition has deep and lasting roots in Europe.

Against this background the European labor movement emerged as part of the attempt of the European working classes to achieve broad social, economic, and political objectives. In keeping with other European class movements, it created or inherited a total ideology and *Weltanschauung*. The European working class, developed within a more rigid type of society than that of the United States, committed itself to the advancement of the entire working class. It bent to this task by radically transforming the entire society. Political democracy developed later in Western Europe than in the United States, and this too tended to consolidate a class attitude of opposition on the part of European workers toward their societies and governments. The working-class movements in most countries, in these earlier years, came to embrace Marxism and the doctrine of revolutionary change—though not necessarily by violent means. More generally, it was committed to replacing the system of capitalism and private property and production with socialism and production for use.

It is worth noting that the ideological aspects of the British Socialist Party and trade-union movement, however, differed from those of the continent. British socialism was colored by Britain's nonconformist religious tradition in much the same way that Marxism colored the continental movements. British socialist feeling was, however, no less intense because of its religious—as opposed to the continent's Marxist—background.

It should be clear immediately that all these movements were less exclusionist than the American labor movement. Basically they embarked upon a course of advancing the entire working class by transforming the total society, in contrast to the emphasis of the American movement on the immediate specifics of wages, hours, and working conditions for its members only.

The discussion that follows presents the main forms and programs the European working class movements took. However, what is described is not entirely true of any one movement, since generalizations are necessary. Even what is described as the general model is certainly more true of the United Kingdom, Scandinavia, Holland, Switzerland—and to an important extent Germany, Austria, and probably Belgium—than it is of France and Italy.

Typically, the European labor movement developed country by country as a two- or three-pronged affair. There were first of all the trade unions; second, the labor, political, or socialist movements; and third, workers' cooperative movements—both of the consumer and producer variety. Each of these parts of the over-all working-class movement was intended to play an important role in the transformation of the society, but we shall focus upon the trade unions and the political parties. The cooperative movements have tended to become a bit less important in Europe in the post-World War II decades as central state planning and the elaboration of social welfare programs have come to be the pivot of socialist economics. The cooperatives may therefore be less important than the trade unions or the political parties in today's socialist complex, but they should be kept in mind, since they do indicate the broad front behind which the work of European labor has operated to engage its members' lives, in contrast to the almost exclusively trade union form of the American movement.

Space limitations preclude detailed treatment of the institutions in which a European worker-unionist was caught up in the total network of relations through his union, his party, his cooperative, and his

various workers' clubs, but this description by Shell of the Workers
Movement in Austria gives a sense of the dimensions:

The Movement . . . produced a home, literally as well as metaphorically
for a considerable part of the Austrian working class. It comprised clubs
and associations whose scope and interests ranged from stamp collecting
to militant atheism. Each one of these organizations insisted on drawing
a clear class line between itself and the rest of society. Singing, hiking,
playing chess, all these were carried on in associations proudly affixing
the term "worker" to their title and maintaining affiliation with the
Social Democratic Party. Through the Children's Friends (*Kinder-
freunds*) and the Free School (*Freie Schule*) an attempt was made to
ensure that the public school system should not alienate the growing working class child from his proletarian background or indoctrinate
him with antisocialist ideology. Through a determined drive against
the use of alcohol, the workingman was to be rescued from this particular "opiate of the people." Through the organization of cultural activities—book clubs, theatres, libraries and concerts—he was to develop
a sense for the higher things in life; all this on the assumption that sober,
well read and cultured—these rational workingmen would become conscious of the political position of their class, and join the struggle for a
socialist society. . . .[1]

This total substitute society, which seemed to be the aim of the European labor movements, is so remote from American labor philosophy that it is hard to grasp.

This degree of penetration by the socialist movement into a worker's life was probably deeper in Austria than in most other European countries, but it is a useful description of the general pattern. It must be added, however, that in the past decade or so, some
of the traditional socialist hold on the worker's life has broken down
in most countries under the impact of the welfare state, the automobile, television, and similar forces.

PARTY–UNION RELATIONSHIPS

It is sometimes difficult for Americans, especially American trade
unionists, to understand the great emphasis European workers place
upon political movements and workers' political parties. In the eyes
of European workers, however, the party and the trade-union movement are of equal importance in the advancement of the working
class.

[1] Kurt L. Shell, *The Transformation of Austrian Socialism* (Albany, N.Y.: State
University of New York, 1962), p. 11.

Since this development of parallel movements, party and union, is of critical importance in the study of labor movements anywhere in the world—especially outside the United States—this aspect should be stressed. There is no simple formula which determines which will emerge first, the political or the industrial (or union) arm of the working class. In the United Kingdom, for example, the trade union movement and the Trades Union Congress (the British equivalent of the AFL–CIO) were well developed before the Labour Representation Committee, which ultimately evolved into the British Labour Party, came on the scene. In Sweden, on the other hand, the Social Democratic Party had emerged as a central party before the *Central Federation of Labor* (LO) was created, though individual unions were in existence. Indeed, in the later years of the nineteenth century in Sweden, "Party district executives served as central organizations for union activities. . . . It was to them that the local unions, and to some extent even the weaker national unions, turned for counsel and support. . . ."[2]

In most countries the socialist party emerged as the first *national* center of the working class movement. (Britain is an exception.) By World War I, the unions also had their own national centers or federations, equal in status to the parties; but the long early period of party leadership made a lasting impression upon union members.

With respect to the structural relationships between parties and unions in given countries, the French sociologist Maurice Duverger draws attention to the distinction between what he calls direct and indirect types of socialist or labor parties. In the indirect type, the broad base of membership in the political party is primarily a bloc affiliation of trade union or cooperative groups. In the direct type, membership is basically by direct individual subscription to the party itself.[3]

A classic example of the indirect type is to be found in the United Kingdom, where the trade unions actually helped create the British Labour Party. Today about 90 per cent of the Labour Party's financial support in election campaigns comes from direct contributions that are made from national union treasuries. In turn, the unions each have a large bloc vote at the Party Congress. It has been estimated that the unions account for five-sixths of the votes in the Labour Party Congress, but they do not necessarily vote together.

2 Donald J. Blake, "Swedish Trade Unions and the Social Democratic Party: The Formative Years," *The Scandinavian Economic History Review,* VIII, No. 1 (1960), p. 26.

3 Maurice Duverger, *Political Parties* (London: Methuen, 1955), pp. 1–17.

The French Socialist Party is one of the pure examples of the so-called direct-party type, with membership set on an individual-subscription basis.

Almost invariably when affiliation is on an indirect-bloc basis the union movement exercises a major and often predominant influence within the political party. The result, historically, has been to produce a party which is less dogmatic, less doctrinaire, and somewhat more concerned with day-to-day problems. In the case of direct-membership parties, as in France, there has been traditionally a tendency for the party to pursue more doctrinaire and purely ideological positions.

In general, it can be said that where the trade unions developed before the socialist party, they generally had a hand in organizing the party and tended to exercise great influence in it. The lack of universal suffrage in a number of countries gave the unions a priority in development.

The unions, as opposed to the parties, tended to be more pragmatic and less dogmatic or doctrinal than the parties. Inevitably, working in the day-to-day industrial sphere, the unions concentrated on more immediate gains, while the party was concentrating on a global program. This was particularly true before World War I, when the parties were remote from any day-to-day responsibilities in most countries and continued to expound a "purer" brand of socialism. However, membership and leadership in the unions and party were often intermixed, especially in the early days, and both subscribed broadly and equally to the general goal of a socialist society.

During the period from World War I to World War II a pattern tended to appear in which the union continued to be to the right and the socialist parties to the left of the combined labor movement. However, as the socialist parties began to approach and share governmental power to a modest extent in the twenties and the thirties almost everywhere in post-World War II Europe, the situation began to change. Confronted with the difficult problems of actually governing and the necessity to conciliate other forces, such as the farmers and the new white-collar groups, if they were to remain in power, the parties moved away from the old dogmas. Since World War II this tendency has been accelerated as socialist parties have, on occasion, governed either alone or in coalition in almost every European country. Today it is often the union wing of the labor movement which is out on the left expressing irritation with the excessive "statesmanship" and conciliatory tactics of the party leadership.

These are broad generalizations; no attempt has been made to set up any rigid rules for judging union–party relations. Moreover, it might be fairer to say that the parties and the unions are arms which perform different functions for the working class. As these functions and needs vary in the course of social evolution, each arm receives changing emphasis.

Returning to historical development, the important advances of the unions, the rise in living standards, the establishment of social security systems, the obviously effective and influential roles which most of the socialist parties have come to play within existing parliamentary systems—all of these factors have tended to cool the revolutionary ardor of most of the Western labor movements with the passage of time. Their very achievements and growing power helped to integrate these labor movements into their societies.

Most of the socialist parties, as already noted, started out under strong Marxist influence.[4] Today in Scandinavia, Austria, and The Netherlands (to choose some examples), Marxism has long since been overtaken by reformism, and there is only moderate interest in the nationalization of industry. The emphasis today tends to be more and more upon planning for full-employment and welfare programs.

The rather recent *formal* conversion of the German Social Democratic Party from Marxism to something like welfare-statism is a good case in point. (I emphasize the word formal here, for most European socialist parties long ago abandoned Marxism as a matter of practical operations.) At its 1959 Congress the German SPD made its "final break . . . with the fundamental tenets of Marxism. . . . The name of Karl Marx and the concept of Marxism are missing from the declaration of principles, . . . words like 'class' and 'class struggle' are also carefully avoided. . . . The notion that the working class . . . is destined, by overthrowing capitalist class-society, to bring about the classless society, . . . has now been thrown by the German Social Democrats on the scrap heap of social utopias. . . . The transfer of the means of production to common ownership, which has hitherto represented the essence of every socialist program, has been stripped of its overriding importance. . . . The SPD has dropped the idea that socialism requires the nationalisation of the whole of industry, not only 'for the time being' but as a matter of principle."[5]

The same kind of transition, for practical purposes, has been ac-

---

4 The British Labour Party is an important exception. Differences in class relationships, civil rights traditions, and the influence of non-conformist religion helped produce a non-Marxian socialism in England.

5 F. R. Allemann, "German SPD Party Abandons Marxism," *Forum-Service* (December 26, 1959).

complished by nearly all the socialist parties of Europe. Occasionally, however, some diehard traditionalists, as in Great Britain, have resisted formal changes in the official party program, and the theoretical commitment to extensive nationalization of industry lives on as a doctrine, if not a reality.

STRAINS OF ECONOMIC PLANNING ON PARTY–UNION RELATIONSHIPS

While each has its separate province, party and union sometimes encounter severe strains and some conflict of interest in their relationships. Particularly is this the case today in the face of the central economic planning for full employment that is being undertaken by some socialist governments. The reconciliation of such economic planning with the traditional freedom of unions to bargain freely for wage increases can present some severe problems for the labor movement. The Research Director of the Swedish Trade Union Federation has, for example, formulated this question in these terms.

The now already classical postwar conflict between national economic policies and trade union wage policies can be formulated by the following question: "How are trade unions, bargaining from their strength in a full-employment economy, to trim their wage demands to the avoidance of consequent currency devaluation?" In other words: "How can wage increases be kept within rational limits in relation to a total increase in productivity?"

The same problem is being posed for labor and management in some other European countries, even under more conservative governments.

Confronted with inflation and a constant, serious threat to workers' living standards, the Austrian Federation of Trade Unions (ÖGB) took the lead in 1953 in proposing formal machinery to regulate wages and prices at the national level by means of a joint council of union, employer associations, agricultural and consumer groups. In return for the government's acceptance of the proposal to regulate prices, the ÖGB agreed: "(a) to recommend to its negotiators to exercise considerable restraint in wage claims already put forward; (b) to have both the amount and the urgency of further wage claims considered by a joint council prior to the initiation of collective bargaining, the members of this joint council to be nominated by the central authorities of the employers' and workers' organizations." In the plan which was finally accepted, the joint council was actually given the authority to determine whether "collective bargaining is permissible" in particular wage-claim cases.[6]

In most countries where central bargaining or some form of wage restraint or both have developed, however, it has tended to be on a more voluntary basis, without formal machinery. This is true in Scandinavia, for example; on the other hand, rather formal central wage-setting institutions have existed in The Netherlands for much of the post-World War II period.

An almost classic example of the tension which can develop between the twin poles of party and union can be found in a description of the activities of Ernest Bevin in Alan Bullock's brilliant biography of that great British union leader. The first Labour government in Great Britain took office at the end of 1923. This period coincided with an economic upswing, and Bevin, on behalf of the dock and tramway workers, was anxious to make an effort to restore some wage cuts suffered in earlier years. He moved swiftly, and after a successful strike these unions won an impressive economic victory. Bevin was highly satisfied with the results. Bullock notes, however:

This satisfaction was not shared by the Labour Government. MacDonald, in particular, out of sympathy with down-to-earth trade-union demands and increasingly inclined to take a high line about national responsibilities, was greatly angered by the strikes and never forgave Bevin for the embarrassment he caused the Government. This did not worry Bevin. But there were others in the Labour Party besides MacDonald who felt that Bevin had behaved irresponsibly and shown less than the loyalty the unions owed to the first Labour Government ever to take office. This impression was strengthened by the aggressive manner in which Bevin asserted his independence and expressed his contempt for politicians as a race.

A controversy broke out in the Socialist press in which the economist J. A. Hobson accused the unions of following a "separatist" policy. Bevin had to deal with the question of whether or not it was incumbent upon the unions to wait for the government to set up some new machinery to settle the workers' wage claims or whether the unions' strike action was correct. He commented:

We are all too aware of the Government's difficulties and desire as much as anyone to assist in the success of Britain's first Labour Government. A policy of industrial truce would, in our view, even if it were

    [6] Anton Proksch, "The Austrian Joint Wage Price Council," *International Labor Review*, LXXXIII (March 1961), pp. 238–39.

possible, not be to the best interests of the Government. There is work to do on the industrial field as well as in the political arena. While it is true that the two are to some extent part of the same effort, we must not lose sight of the fact that governments may come and governments may go, but the workers' fight for betterment of conditions must go on all the time.

Bullock further notes:

Nor did the rank-and-file members of the Union disagree with Bevin. They had waited a long time to recover the wage cuts they had suffered and to see some practical benefit from the Union they supported. They saw no reason why, the first time they gained the advantage in a dispute, they should not press it home simply because a Labour Government was in office. If that fact made the employers more reluctant to fight it out, so much the better: what did they pay the political levy and support the Labour Party for, if not to secure such advantages? No one could say the employers were reluctant to take advantage of the Tories being in office to force wages down and use the power of the State to defeat the miners. It was too high a price to pay for office if the only way the Labour Government could retain the Parliamentary support of the Liberal Party was to take sides against the unions in the legitimate defence of their members' industrial interests.

There is, however, a postscript to this interesting interlude. When Labour came to power in 1945, it had gained a clear majority in Parliament, unlike the 1923 Labour government, which was a minority government dependent upon the votes of other groups if it was to stay in power. Then Bevin was willing to face the issue of the national responsibility of the labor movement, as opposed to the immediate sectional interests of the trade unions. During this period he came, as a member of the government, to recommend to the unions a policy of "wage restraint which placed a heavy strain on the loyalty and forbearance of the trade unions."[7]

In a sense we have here an illustration of the pressures in today's world which often tend to put the socialist party to the right of its trade union ally. From what has already been said, it is scarcely necessary to add at this point that although these movements are two- and three-pronged, the trade unions jealously guard their own independence. Americans sometimes have the feeling that these union and political movements are one and the same thing. This is simply not the case. The unions, for example, have their own inde-

---

[7] Alan Bullock, *The Life and Times of Ernest Bevin, Trade Union Leader, 1881–1940* (London: William Heinemann, Ltd., 1960), Vol. 1, pp. 242–45.

pendent financing, policy conventions, and officers. In terms of structure and finances, the unions are in some ways more clearly independent of the parties than are the parties from the unions. The parties frequently, as we have seen, are highly dependent upon the unions for financial support. Furthermore, it is quite common for a socialist party specifically to reserve a few seats on the party's executive committee for representatives of the trade union movement. The same is not true in the reverse.

Some American experts have tended to see this process as one in which the unions gradually "emancipate" themselves from the parties. This is also inaccurate. Rather, as one writer describes the situation in Sweden, the relationship is essentially "one of interdependence."[8] Functions and responsibilities vary as economic and political conditions change, but both arms continue to perform vital functions.

COLLECTIVE BARGAINING: SOME KEY DIFFERENCES

The unions then are independent and have as *their* main sphere *industrial action* and *representation* on behalf of the working class. In this sense, of course, they resemble American unions. Furthermore, in the broad structural sense, there are many similarities, such as the existence of national unions along industrial or craft lines or both, a central federation, and some form of local organization.[9]

It is fair to say, however, that in their bargaining and industrial activities they do have a different attitude toward government action and political action than do American unions. Typically, for example, in many of these countries the unions accept government legislation as the regulator of such items as paid vacations and paid holidays. They also look to the government almost exclusively for social security items such as pensions, health, and welfare in contrast to American unions which also bargain "privately" on many of these items. In some European countries such as France, Belgium, Austria, the system of shop stewards owes its existence not to union agreements but to a state-sponsored series of plant elections. The rights and functions of these stewards are generally defined by legislation and only occasionally supplemented by union agreements.

---

[8] Donald J. Blake, *op. cit.,* p. 43.

[9] In the matter of local organization in some countries there are patterns considerably different from ours, but space limitations preclude further discussion of this. Similarly, in Europe the central labor federations, or confederations as they are called (the equivalents of our own AFL–CIO), often exercise greater power and influence over the labor movement as a whole than does the AFL–CIO.

NEW TRENDS IN UNION BARGAINING
STRUCTURES AND POLICIES

With respect to wages and hours, bargaining in Western Europe is usually done by industry on a regional or even a national basis. Unlike the industrial-relations pattern in the United States, there is much less emphasis upon bargaining with particular employers and enterprises. Union devotion to ideals of class solidarity and class equality coupled with employers' traditions of operating through strong associations tend to deter bargaining at the plant or firm level. One of the concomitants of this has been that, in comparison with American unions, European unions are less influential and less active at the plant level.

The enormous industrial changes and the great growth of the European economies in the past decade are causing some changes in traditional European union bargaining attitudes and structure. Confronted with complex problems of automation, as well as with the opportunity for economic advances on a scale hitherto unknown, some European unions have found that nation-wide, industry-wide, or region-wide bargaining is not entirely adequate. Bargains struck this way tend to be set in terms of what the marginal or relatively less efficient producer in a given industry can afford to pay.

Actually, in a number of European countries, especially in the highly prosperous large metal companies, the wage rates and earnings of workers today are often far above the rates negotiated in industry-wide agreements on a national or regional basis. As a consequence, rate setting in many major firms in a few countries has passed largely into the hands of the employers.

The so-called shop stewards' revolt in Great Britain in the past decade stems in part from certain structural weaknesses in the British trade union movement and the need to exercise greater worker control over wages and working conditions at the plant level.

Some of the European unions are responding to these challenges by placing new emphasis upon bargaining at the plant and firm level. The old union notion of working-class solidarity is being distorted in the context of the European "economic miracle." These unions may, however, run up against the problem of reconciling more energetic wage bargaining with price stability in the face of the strong and sustained full employment, which most European countries have successfully achieved in the past decade.

EUROPEAN LABOR AND THE ISSUE OF WORKERS' CONTROL OF INDUSTRY

Most European unions have not been content to limit their plant objectives to wages, hours, and working conditions. Socialist influence and tradition have led most of the labor movements to inscribe high on their platforms the doctrine of workers' control over industry, in the sense of industrial decisions on production, investment, and marketing. On the other hand, the doctrine that workers must have a *share* and *co-responsibility* in the management of enterprise has also had firm standing in European Catholic social doctrine since the latter part of the nineteenth century.[10]

These two different streams of social doctrine, as Frederic Meyers has commented, led to the establishment by legislation of systems of worker "representation," or at least worker consultation in the management of enterprise in a number of European nations.[11] There has been considerable American interest in the operation of the German co-determination laws; but forms of worker participation in, or consultation with management also exist in some other countries in Europe.

To date these "experiments" have not had a serious impact. The real business of running the enterprise remains in management's hands. In some countries, however, these devices have helped to increase the workers' power to influence many of the working conditions that we normally take for granted as within the province of collective bargaining in the United States, as opposed to managing the enterprise in the broader sense of that term.

This tradition of workers' control and participation in management is, however, a deep one.

EVALUATING UNITED STATES AND EUROPEAN MOVEMENTS

What have been described are the main outlines of what might be called successful, continuing unionism in Western Europe. Before we turn to a study of some of the deviationist and less successful European types, some over-all evaluation is in order.

Sharp and direct comparisons between American unionism and the European labor movements are obviously impossible. Different

---

10 Syndicalist and guild socialist influences, which have since largely disappeared from Western Europe, also helped develop workers' interest in the issue of participating directly in management, around World War I.

11 Frederic Meyers, "Workers' Control of Industry in Europe," *Southwestern Social Science Quarterly* (September 1958).

conditions produce different movements. It can be said, however, that in some respects European movements have been more effective than our own. They have succeeded in building a greater degree of security on the part of European workers. This is reflected in more comprehensive social security and medical care systems, greater protection against layoff, longer paid vacations, and union cooperative travel and recreation programs which have tended to enlarge the lives of European workers. Workers' housing is commonly a product of union cooperatives. This whole range of activities tends to create unity and a sense of allegiance between workers and their movements which is much stronger than in the United States.

In contrast, however, the European movements are considerably weaker than the American at the factory floor or the enterprise level, and they have given workers much less control over their day-to-day working conditions. Again, while it is hard to generalize in terms of sheer economic achievement, the advantage must be given to the greater bargaining power of the American labor movement.

It cannot be denied, however, that a number of European labor movements (encompassing labor parties and unions) are a broader and more powerful social force in their own countries than the American labor movement. In some of these societies (for example, in the United Kingdom, Austria, the Low Countries, or Scandinavia) the European labor movement has even assumed a full or a large measure of national governmental power.

Some of the evolutionary forces at play in the United States and in Western Europe seem to be bending the respective lines of union development closer together. Note, for example, that whereas some European unions have had to take more action at the plant level, American labor finds itself drawn into a new government-sponsored national labor-management committee. Again, United States labor has also increased its political activities sharply in the past decade, as it has become painfully clear that the attainment of full employment and a more just society are to a considerable extent beyond the competence of collective bargaining, important as the latter is.

FRANCE AND ITALY: "LEFT" DEVIATIONS

The main line of development of European labor movements was described above. One must also try to deal with the forms of trade unionism which deviate substantially from this norm, especially the labor movements in France and Italy. These movements have been somewhat less successful than those of the rest of Western Europe.

From time to time they show flashes of great strength, but they generally have lacked the kind of continuing power enjoyed by other movements.

Generally, these movements have tended to be leftist in character. In these countries the working class never seems to have become fully integrated into the going democratic political structure of its own society. In both France and Italy, prior to World War I, anarcho-syndicalism, with an emphasis upon violent change and political strikes as opposed to the acceptance of reform methods, was quite prevalent. Following both world wars this leftism gradually took the form of heavy Communist penetration into the labor movements and the working class mentality in France and Italy.

Explaining these trends which seemed to deviate so sharply from the rest of Western Europe is a fascinating game. Here are a few of the forces at play. In the first place, in these countries we seem to be confronted with an incomplete democratic revolution. The persistence of aristocracy and aristocratic attitudes seems to be a more critical factor in France and Italy than in the rest of Western Europe. Employers, too, tend to be more adamant in resisting unionism and collective bargaining here than elsewhere.

In both of these countries political activities and goals have at times tended nearly to snuff out the purely union activities of the working class. This is explained, in part, in France by the fact that "universal suffrage allowed the working class to take part in politics at a time when the development of trade unionism was impeded by obstacles, legal or otherwise."[12] In France, too, the memory and myth of the glorious French Revolution as the "method of change," as Val Lorwin has suggested, has tended to give a legitimacy to revolutionary ideas, to underscore political action, and to deprecate other methods of change, such as trade unionism and collective bargaining.[13] The myth of cataclysmic revolutionary change helps account for the receptivity of France to the ideas of the cataclysmic Russian revolution and the ideology of communism.

The role of the Catholic church in the nineteenth century, when it was not fully accepting the democratic revolution, was one of the complicating forces in French and Italian societies. Church support for a more hierarchical type of society may have made it

---

[12] Duverger, *Political Parties*, p. 16.
[13] Val Lorwin, "Labor Organizations in Belgium and France," in E. M. Kassalow (ed.), *National Labor Movements in the Postwar World* (Evanston: Northwestern University Press, 1963).

more difficult to integrate the working class fully into the new industrial order in the earlier decades of the industrial revolution.

In Italy, deeply ingrained and commonly expressed attitudes of superiority and paternalism on the part of many employers help to keep alive a spirit of class reaction and hostility among the workers.

Economic development in France and Italy seems to have been more uneven than in most of Western Europe. The persistence of vast areas of low-level agricultural development leads to sharp discontinuities in political life. Note the important sources of Communist strength in southern Italy and certain parts of southern and central France where economic development has been slow. The continued strength of Communism in these areas seems to reinforce the power of leftism as a force in the society, even among the better-paid industrial workers in other parts of the country.

In both of these countries, too, the labor movement has been plagued by pluralism. Not only is there a struggle between the Socialist and Communist labor movements, but also there tend to be separate Christian or Catholic labor movements. In the past, the leftism of the free[14] labor unions served as a convincing rationale for the need to build Catholic unionism; in turn, this tended to siphon off the more moderate forces and to intensify the antichurch, traditionally socialist and leftist attitude of the nonreligious unions.[15] As part of this union pluralism, today, there are usually three or four different unions sharing in the bargaining process at a given work place.

Of course, this kind of plural unionism at the work place and the existence of important Christian unions (Protestant as well as Catholic) are not confined to France and Italy alone. They can be found in the Low Countries and Switzerland as well, and were also prevalent in prewar Austria and Germany. Such union separatism seems, however, to be a more divisive factor in France and Italy, where the presence of strong Communist unions makes plural unionism especially difficult to practice; the Communist unions can generally be relied upon to "outdemand" the other unions, thereby tending to force the other union federations toward the left in their demands and

14 In Europe the *Catholic* unions are distinguished from the *free* unions.

15 In Italy the Catholic-oriented labor federation formally shed its religious ties some years ago, but the image that it is still a Catholic movement persists in many workers' minds; moreover, many of its leaders continue ties with the Christian Democratic Party. In France the Catholic labor center stresses its nonconfessional character and supports a set of social doctrines not unlike the program of the free trade union center. In 1964 the French Catholic labor movement took steps to drop references to the words Christian or Catholic in its official title and doctrines.

posture. One of the results of this system in France has been to make collective bargaining less effective and consequently to throw the workers towards more reliance on political action.[16]

SUCCESSFUL TRADE UNIONS: REQUISITE FOR STABLE DEMOCRATIC INDUSTRIAL ORDER

In France and Italy the institutions of democracy have lacked stability during a large part of the twentieth century. Much of this instability is linked to the lack of development of a strong, *continuously effective* trade union movement in these countries.

This leads to the conclusion that a strong case can be made for the proposition that an effective trade-union movement, which gives workers a sense of integration and participation in the great industrial processes of their own society, is one of the essential parts of a modern stable, democratic industrial order. As one examines the few countries in the world where a stable democratic order has emerged he finds, in the words of a British writer, "a system of industrial relations which can fairly be called the industrial parallel of political democracy. It promotes the interests and protects the rights of workers in industry by means of collective bargaining between employers and managers on the one hand and, on the other, trade unions independent of government and of management. This could be called a system of *industrial democracy by consent,* or *pressure-group industrial democracy,* or *democracy through collective bargaining.*"[17]

---

[16] The existence of plural unionism, as such, so long as there is no significant communist or actively revolutionary labor movement present, need not necessarily seriously impair the effectiveness of a given country labor movement, as the post World War II experience of The Netherlands demonstrates.

[17] H. A. Clegg, *A New Approach to Industrial Democracy* (Oxford: Basil Blackwell, 1960), p. 131. Emphasis in the original.

Walter Reuther's Great Big Union

A. H. RASKIN

The United Automobile Workers is a union in search of a mission. What differentiates it from other unions in this respect is that, in the last few months, it has moved from lip service to action in acknowledging the necessity for a basic reassessment of labor's goals and how to reach them.

Most unions are so lost in self-admiration that even Colonel Blimp would find their smugness extreme. The UAW, while still inordinately disposed to regard itself as a solitary pillar of virtue in an economic swampland, is turning a searchlight on all its preconceptions to determine whether it has changed enough in the past quarter century to meet the needs of labor and of the nation in a transitional society.

The most interesting aspect of this effort to restore the giant auto union to its old primacy as a promoter of fresh ideas in collective bargaining, industrial democracy, and social betterment is that it is going forward without any of the fanfare usually associated with projects initiated by the union's highly articulate president, Walter P. Reuther, a man whose critics have accused him of almost everything but reticence.

In May the UAW opened a unique leadership study center on the grounds of Solidarity House, its modernistic international headquarters in Detroit. This is in the nature of a postgraduate school for all the union's organizers and paid officials, most of whom got their education on the picket line. They will spend three to twelve weeks studying subjects ranging from labor morality to the language of computers and trying to develop new perspectives on the union and society. As

Taken from Atlantic Monthly, *CCXII (October 1963), pp. 90–99. Reprinted with the permission of the author. A. H. Raskin is a member of the Editorial Board of the New York Times.*

Reuther told the twenty-three officials in the first class, "If you go back home and do everything the way you did before, this school will be a failure."

The center will not stop with an effort to unlock the minds of those already on the union payroll; it will also attempt to attract into the UAW more college-trained youngsters of the kind who became the mainstay of union technical staffs in the early years of the New Deal but who now turn to better-paid jobs in industry, government, universities, and foundations. To offset this drain of professional talent away from organized labor, the UAW plans to offer internships to five or six youths each year, with the choice to be made both from college seniors and from the union's own members. The interns would receive grants of $5000 to $7000 a year and would divide their time between work at the union (in such fields as research, law, social security, education, or publications) and graduate courses at one of Michigan's three state universities. The UAW is convinced that, even if in the end the interns decide to make careers outside labor, there will be lasting dividends in improved understanding from their association with the union.

The building that houses the leadership study center was once used by the Chrysler Corporation as an executive-training institute. However, the UAW has borrowed little from traditional techniques of management training except the idea that constant vigilance is essential to keep dry rot out of the mental processes of leaders at every level of responsibility.

A policy statement drafted before the center opened warned that insistence on a uniform viewpoint in all the teaching would stultify the whole experience. "The UAW must be prepared to welcome to the faculty persons who do not share the union's point of view on all subjects—who in fact may be critical, either from the right or the left, of the union's program," the policy declaration said.

Among those the center hopes to have as participants in its seminars are such men as David Riesman, Erich Fromm, Daniel Bell, Seymour Harris, Mortimer Adler, Richardson Dilworth, and Arthur Schlesinger, Jr. Representatives of management also will be invited periodically as lecturers, in the thought that both sides will learn from a candid exchange of opinions about how well they perform their duties.

Reuther and his colleagues on the twenty-six-member international executive board have not exempted themselves from the obligation they have imposed on their subordinates to sweep cobwebs out of their thinking. In June the board held a week-long meeting at Tamiment in the Poconos to talk about the union's long-range problems and its internal communications.

The aim was not to adopt resolutions—the UAW already has these in mountainous supply, covering every subject from administered prices to the creation of a National Planning Agency in Washington. Rather, the discussion at Tamiment was geared to stimulating thought on where the union was going and what kind of world it hoped to build. There was nothing parochial about its range. It even encompassed the issue of disarmament, with Norman Cousins of *Saturday Review* to exhort a greater membership involvement.

More such sessions will be held in settings similarly remote from day-to-day pressures. One skeptical member of the executive board came away from the Tamiment parley convinced that the union high command would benefit as much as the secondary leadership from exposure to the training center and to the other methods Reuther is using to bring the union abreast of automation's challenge.

"We're all getting older," is the way this board member expresses it. "You can't keep talking to a guy about what happened in the depression when he wasn't even born then. Why, we've got members who don't even know about World War Two. And how are you going to get through to them? One of the things we learned at Tamiment was that the average person spends more hours than he ought to watching television and only twenty minutes a day reading—that goes for newspapers, magazines, books, every kind of reading. If we don't take that into account in our communications to workers and the community, all we will be doing is talking to ourselves."

REUTHER VERSUS MEANY

The quietness with which the union is engineering its self-examination reflects the recognition that no magic carpet is going to carry the UAW over the hurdles that face all major unions in this automated era. Any tom-tom beating about "departures from familiar paths" could lead only to exaggerated expectations about how much could be accomplished how soon.

But beyond this realistic deterrent to self-advertisement may lie factors more intimately related to Reuther's estimate of his personal role as a shaper of the destiny of the UAW, of labor generally, and of the total society. Recognized as the possessor of one of the most fertile minds and eloquent tongues in any branch of American life, even by those who like him least, Reuther has found himself increasingly excluded in recent years from any position of real creativity and influence in the affairs of organized labor.

Much of the dynamism that carried him to the top rung of the auto union, over the opposition of the porkchoppers in the entrenched union bureaucracy and their allies in the union's pro-Communist wing, has been wasted in sterile power feuds inside the AFL–CIO. Relations between Reuther and George Meany, the federation's president, deteriorated sharply after the merger in 1955—a merger that never could have taken place if Reuther, as president of the old CIO, had not stepped aside to allow the chief post in the fused organization to go to Meany, his AFL opposite number.

Wrangles over the federation's failure to make significant headway toward its target of organizing the unorganized grew into a general indictment by the Reuther faction of stagnation and purposelessness in the AFL–CIO headquarters. The pro-Meany majority in the federation's executive council saw nothing in the record of the Industrial Union Department, under Reuther's leadership, that indicated it had a better formula for pinning union buttons on the millions of workers outside union ranks.

The net effect of the bickering was to convince Meany and his partisans that Reuther would never be content until he moved into the number one job, an ambition not at all to Meany's taste. The downward spiral of their relationship culminated in a schoolboylike series of jousts between the two leaders, almost all of which wound up badly for Reuther and none of which was calculated to contribute anything notable to the general advancement of labor.

The designation of a labor member of the United States delegation to the United Nations was a case in point. For many years organized labor had argued that the presence of a prominent trade unionist as a spokesman for this country in the UN General Assembly would do much to counteract Soviet charges that Wall Street controlled everything here. President Eisenhower finally accepted this point in 1957, and Meany was named the first delegate.

When Meany's year ended, Reuther, who is by far the best known of American unionists in the developing countries of Asia and Africa, hoped the AFL–CIO would recommend him for the following year. Instead, Meany proposed George M. Harrison, chairman of the federation's International Affairs Committee. A year later Meany took the post again, thus effectively continuing the Reuther freeze-out until the end of the Eisenhower term.

Soon after President Kennedy's inauguration, Meany learned secondhand that Reuther expected to be appointed to the post by Ambassador Stevenson. The AFL–CIO president sent discreet word to the White House that he would welcome reappointment. Confronted with the necessity for choosing between two of its most resolute political supporters, the Administration chose neither. It did away with the notion of having any labor member on the delegation; the precedent labor succeeded in establishing under a businessman's Administration was lost when labor's candidate took office. As a consolation prize, both Meany and Reuther were made special advisers to Stevenson—posts with no defined duties.

A similar contretemps developed over the designation of an Under Secretary of Labor to fill the vacancy created last year when W. Willard Wirtz moved up to succeed Arthur J. Goldberg as Secretary. Reuther began lobbying for Jack T. Conway, formerly his administrative assistant at the UAW, who had gone to Washington as deputy administrator of the Federal Housing and Home Financing Agency. Meany made no secret of his high regard for Conway and his conviction that Conway would be an excellent Under Secretary of Labor, but he felt it more important to demonstrate once again that there was only one head of the AFL–CIO and only one man entitled to speak officially for it at the White House.

Accordingly, he put into nomination as his candidate Thomas E. Harris, the federation's associate general counsel. Again the White House stepped away from the necessity for a choice. It persuaded Meany to come up with another name—that of John F. Henning of the California AFL–CIO, a virtual stranger to all union bigwigs in Washington. The upshot of this and several similar contests was a presidential decree that Meany was to be recognized as the federation's sole authorized ambassador to the United States government.

This still left Reuther plenty of access in his separate capacity as president of the UAW, but there was a perceptible dip in his prestige in the power-conscious upper echelons of both labor and government. One of the President's closest advisers suggested last spring that the best way to relieve the White House of the embarrassments created by the tug-of-war between Reuther and Meany would be to designate the auto union chief as ambassador to India. Another ranking Administration official summed up Reuther's status in the single word "pitiful."

Somewhere along the line the message seems to have got through to Reuther that there might be a more effective way to operate. Ever since spring he has been comporting himself with a blend of serenity and decisiveness that may signal the emergence of a new Reuther at age fifty-six. If the change denotes a recharge of imagination and industry, rather than the resignation of a frustrated man prepared to settle for frustration, it will be the best of good news for a labor movement groping for new directions.

AID TO UNIONS OVERSEAS

The UAW is the most zestful of America's big unions, the least sunk in bureaucratic detachment from its rank and file. Most of its qualities of excitement have stemmed not from its strikes or even its trailblazing exploits in collective bargaining and politics, but from the caliber of its officialdom. It has been less afflicted than most huge unions by the loss of good secondary leaders who leave their union jobs discouraged by the blocking off of channels for advancement. The average age of its executive board is just under fifty. This is at least ten years below the average in most other unions spawned by the NRA and the Wagner Act.

But Reuther is still the pivotal force in the UAW's affairs, its most prolific generator of ideas, its bridge to stronger rapport with the membership and the community. That is why his apparent decision to invest much more concentrated attention in the UAW is of profound importance. He has been talking inside the union's board of establishing a mandatory retirement age of sixty-five for all officials. That would leave him only nine years in which to fulfill all his dreams for labor and the country.

The global compass of these dreams was given tangible expression in the decision of the UAW convention last year to earmark the interest on the union's $50 million strike fund for aid in building free labor organizations and in reinforcing their drives to improve wages and working conditions. One of the early allocations from this worldwide Marshall Plan for labor was $25,000 in financial assistance for workers in France's nationalized coal mines when they were striking against General de Gaulle's restrictive wage policies last March. At the same time, $1000 went to striking metalworkers in Turkey.

The foundations for this drive are not all altruistic. They are predicated on a hardheaded realization that American labor standards cannot keep on advancing if sweatshop conditions continue to prevail in competitive industrial countries abroad. "You no longer work for American corporations; you work for world corporations." This is the credo Victor G. Reuther, director of the UAW's international affairs department, has been seeking to pound home at regional UAW conferences on the mission of the Free World Labor Defense Fund.

"All over the world, in the most remote parts of Asia, South Africa, throughout Latin America, General Motors has its plants," Victor Reuther declares. "Ford has its subsidiaries and Chrysler its associates; and so have International Harvester and thousands of other firms. This interlocking worldwide control which vast corporations have means that their policies—fiscal and otherwise, as they affect ·your jobs—are determined not in the light of what is best in your home community, what is best for the United States, but in terms of what is best for General Motors."

By way of making the message of interdependence even more explicit, the UAW's chief envoy to world labor asserts that when American corporations set up shop overseas "they don't act like American employers who know something about labor relations." Instead, he says, they suddenly acquire all the bad habits of the local employers and are quite happy to pay the lowest wages and enforce the longest hours.

Despite such grim warnings that the survival of free unions in the United States depends on the strengthening of their struggling counterparts in underdeveloped lands, the immediate problems of the UAW in collective bargaining and in its efforts to offset the job-killing impact of new technology on existing employment opportunities are quite remote from those of unions in Sierra Leone or Tanganyika.

MORE GAINS FOR FEWER WORKERS

The gravest danger for the UAW at the bargaining table is that it will find itself doing more and more for fewer and fewer workers, and thus engender a tremendous incubus of resentment among young people and others shut out of jobs. This danger is envisaged with special grimness by Leonard Woodcock, vice president of the auto union and director of its General Motors department.

"The automobile industry is in its second boom year, but it is meeting much of its additional production through overtime hours of the existing force simply because it is cheaper to do so," Woodcock told the Industrial Relations Research Association in Pittsburgh last winter. "The costs of pensions, insurance, vacations, holidays and supplementary unemployment benefits are all tied to the individual and not to the hours worked, which means that costs are reduced when overtime is worked by fewer individuals. Thus we have the callous spectacle of overtime and sharp unemployment existing side by side in America's booming automobile cities."

The forecast of trouble unless the UAW broadened its bargaining sights to provide more job opportunities for those on the outside looking in was made sharper still when Woodcock met with delegates representing the 338,000 hourly-rated workers at General Motors in June to take a forward look at preparations for the 1964 contract round. He noted that joblessness among young people was running at nearly triple the rate for older workers, and he warned of mass discontent among these dispossessed youngsters if they saw the UAW and other unions focusing their energies on protecting the job security of those who already had jobs.

"Whom did Hitler first mobilize?" Woodcock asked. "He mobilized the young men. The Storm Troopers, the Brown Shirts were made up of kids who had no hope in the German Republic in the late 1920s and the early 1930s. Who is going to exploit this dissatisfaction against the labor movement? It is going to be the extreme right, which is gathering political force in this country. It is going to be the Barry Goldwaters or probably somebody else whose name we have not yet heard who will mobilize the young people. And if to them the labor movement stands as a group of selfish people concerned only with themselves and not with their plight, then we are really going to get the business."

The seriousness with which the UAW regards the necessity for turning the bargaining table into an instrument for full employment was indicated in the letters it sent to all the major auto and agricultural implement manufacturers last March, requesting that joint study committees be set up a full year in advance to begin work on problems that would require solution in next year's contracts.

Even before expressing its general desire to provide greater security and higher standards for the existing work force, the union stressed the need for joint action to "make such contributions as we can to the creation of new job opportunities for younger workers, for older workers still too young to retire and for members of minority groups in the face of automation and accelerating technological advance."

BARGAINING WITHOUT A CRISIS

In the past the Big Three auto makers have shunned anything resembling year-round joint consultations with the Reuther union for fear that these might become an entering wedge for co-determination or some intermediate form of union encroachment on management prerogatives. The vigor with which Reuther has campaigned for a government board to conduct public hearings on proposed price increases in autos, steel, and other large industries has kept such fear alive, despite the cordial day-to-day working relationships that have long existed between the union and the corporations.

The companies would probably not have agreed to sit down with the union this year if the success of the Human Relations Committee, established in the steel industry after its disastrous 116-day strike in 1959, had not touched off what amounted to a tidal wave of support for experiments in continuous dialogue in other key industries. A refusal to accept the Reuther bid would have exposed the auto giants to pressure from President Kennedy and Secretary of Labor Wirtz, both strong advocates of year-round labor-management discussions. Rather than risk more government intrusion in the industry's affairs, the Big Three said yes, without any outside push.

Under the rules laid down for the joint study committees, all the proceedings are off the record and neither side is committed by anything that is said. However, Woodcock gave the GM union delegates a peek behind this curtain of secrecy when he reported on the initial session. He said GM had been most cautious about the subjects to be canvassed in the talks and had made it clear that it might reconsider its agreement to participate if it found itself led into areas that impinged on politics, rather than those in which decisions could be made directly by labor and management. The union's comeback was that its biggest worry involved jobs, and that obviously the answers to fuller employment lay partly in collective bargaining and partly in government policy. All of this lent point to the observation of one rank-and-file delegate at the GM conference that when the union called for the joint study, "the guys in the plant thought this was a wonderful proposal, but when GM accepted, they wondered what was the matter with it."

The wonder may grow even stronger if the UAW seriously endeavors to use the 1964 auto contracts as the vehicle for a basic assault on unemployment, with the primary focus on creating openings for those who now have no jobs rather than on additional security and benefits for those who do. This would mark a radical shift from the prevailing orientation in collective bargaining, which treats present jobholders as a preferred group to be shielded against technological displacement but does nothing directly for the hundreds of thousands of youngsters cascading into the job market or for the four million workers already idle. The unemployed are made wards of the general community while the union and the industry concentrate on protecting the ingroup.

Thus, the pioneering formula negotiated by the Kaiser Steel Corporation and the United Steelworkers of America for sharing the fruits of increased productivity at the company's plant in Fontana, California, starts with a guarantee that no worker will lose his job because of automation. The formula also provides that the workers are to get one third of all the money the company saves as a result of greater efficiency in steelmaking. The shortcoming in this plan, as the UAW sees it, is that it treats those already on the Kaiser payroll as a group with a vested interest and makes those who never have been hired the victims of the shrinkage in total job opportunities that comes from being able to make much more steel with many fewer men.

The auto union has not even begun to formulate the specific demands through which it will try to make itself a spokesman for the outs as well as the ins in the 1964 negotiations. But if it does draft a program that breaks dramatically with the isolationism of "we must take care of our own," it will mark a fresh crystallization of the line of fidelity to social responsibility that Reuther has always enunciated as the touchstone of his union philosophy.

His concept is that labor must go forward with the community, not at the expense of the community. It was on this basis that he insisted, when unions in steel and other key industries were cheerfully riding the wage-price spiral, that the auto workers wanted no wage increase that could not be supported without a price increase. On the same basis he urged that the companies couple price rebates for car buyers with higher wages for UAW members in a proposed profit-sharing plan five years ago.

This proposal proved no more popular with the Big Three than most of the other novelties Reuther has put on the negotiating table in the post-war period. But this has not stopped him from winning a good many more than he has lost—notably supplementary unemployment benefits, a markdown from his original project for a true guaranteed annual wage but nonetheless a long step forward in income security for laid-off workers.

THE PROFITS OF MANAGEMENT

One reason for the substantial gains the UAW has made since the days of the speedup and the sitdown strikes is the fantastic profitability of the auto industry. Unlike most unions, the UAW does not take the view that it should keep quiet about the prosperity of its employers. It says bluntly that it considers the profits of the auto makers too high for the country's good, and it has compiled some arresting statistics to support its charge that workers and consumers are not getting their fair share of the pie.

The parent union has sent to all its GM locals charts intended to show that if General Motors had been content with a profit rate equal to the average for all United States manufacturing corporations in the fifteen years from 1947 through 1962, it could have cut the retail price of all its cars by $205 and also raised the wages of all its hourly-rated workers by fifty-seven cents an hour.

Taking GM's record profit of $1,459,000,000 after taxes last year, the union asserts that the colossus of the Big Three could have cut the price of the 3,742,000 passenger cars produced in its United States plants by $100 each and still had a profit of 21 percent on its investment, or more than double the average for all manufacturers.

Still another chart is designed to contrast the relative rewards of working for GM or owning its stock. It notes that the average GM hourly employee would have earned $3009 if he worked fulltime in 1947. A GM stockholder would have received exactly the same amount in dividends if he had bought stock worth $52,846 at the beginning of that year. At the end of 1962 the cumulative dividends and capital gain on the stock would total $463,000. The worker's aggregate earnings in the same period, assuming that he had never been laid off and that he had got all the union-negotiated wage increases, would have been $78,800—roughly one sixth of the shareholder's gain.

Perhaps the most startling of all the UAW charts, and certainly the one most likely to irk General Motors top brass, sets the $15.7 million in salaries and bonuses received by 56 GM officers and directors last year against the combined salaries of $13.8 million paid to 606 top government officials. The men who ran General Motors got more for their efforts than all of these officials put together: the President, the Vice President, 100 United States senators, 435 members of the House of Representatives, the nine Supreme Court justices, the ten members of the Cabinet, and the governors of all fifty states.

One concrete moral the UAW has drawn from these figures is that a profit-sharing plan would mean a lot to its members in the major companies. The UAW negotiated its first such plan at American Motors two years ago, and the plan has worked so well that the union hopes it will be extended to GM and Ford next year. On the basis of last year's profits Reuther estimates that the American Motors "progress-sharing" formula would have meant an extra $915 a year in benefits and stocks for each GM worker and $845 for each worker at Ford. Woodcock put the prospect of extending the idea somewhat less circumspectly when he addressed the UAW National GM Council. "If we could get the profit-sharing formula from GM, it would be like getting the keys to Fort Knox after somebody had shot the guards," he said.

GRIEVANCES IN THE PLANT

But not all the task of running a union of 1.2 million members in a period of meteoric change is concerned with mass decisions. The main business of the UAW, and in many respects its principal reason for being, is in its administration of the grievance machinery that protects the worker against petty tyranny at the plant level. The desire for individual dignity and a collective voice in a vast corporation was the spur for the union's formation, and even with the enormous improvements that have occurred in personnel administration most UAW members have not lost their fear that "Once you let the boss start pushing, he'll never stop pushing."

UAW local newspapers are full of complaints about the irritations and frustrations of plant life. The correspondent at one Detroit factory in which management had appealed for teamwork to help the plant survive wrote this wistful comment on the results of the campaign:

"The Team, as the company puts it, set an all-time production of over 5 million pounds of copper tubing for the month of March. That, I would say, is a good Survival Team, but the Team became split up when it came to the celebration end of it. The hourly rate ate in the company garage off of chairs and the VIP's dined and were entertained at the Lee Plaza, the latter is a good way to cut costs. Your entire bargaining committee clocked out at 11 A.M. and had their lunch elsewhere clocked back in at 11:41 A.M. They were penalized for being late—what happened to THE TEAM—I wonder if the VIP's punched a time clock in and also out upon entering and leaving the Lee Plaza Hotel?"

At a GM Fisher Body plant in St. Louis, with only 2800 employees, a backlog of 3000 individual grievances piled up. Early this year the accumulation of complaints grew so oppressive to both management and the UAW that a special union task force was sent in from Detroit to work with GM officials in ending the pileup. Five hundred of the grievances involved charges that foremen had put on gloves and done production work in violation of the contract.

The GM contract contains six hundred pages, and there are three or four supplemental contracts for every GM plant. This is shop law—law the workers have participated in writing through their union. Yet the rules are so well established that fewer than forty cases a year have to go to arbitration for final settlement.

"We deal for more than 300,000 workers in GM," says Nat Weinberg, director of the union's special projects department, "but in negotiations we will fight, bleed and die for a word that won't affect more than three people—perhaps not even one in the whole life of the contract. That's what differentiates us from the corporations."

How important the workers consider the rules and conditions in their own plants was driven home to Reuther and the other international union chiefs rather rudely in the 1961 negotiations. They were repeatedly overridden in local revolts when they tried to steamroller through a national settlement without allowing full time for the adjustment of local issues. In retrospect, the leaders say the rebellions were a healthy reminder that even the best national contract is no good if festering sores are left untended in the plant.

As an expression of its own recognition that maximum protection for individual rights is as essential inside the union as it is inside a corporation, the union acted in 1957 to establish an unusual Public Review Board, to which its members could appeal as a court of last resort if they felt they had been denied justice by the union's internal machinery. The board consists of seven distinguished clergymen, educators, and jurists, and is completely free of any control by the UAW.

A study completed last year by Professor Jack Stieber, director of Michigan State University's School of Labor and Industrial Relations, showed that the board had upheld decisions of the union's executive board twice as often as it had upset them. Dr. Stieber said the board represented "the broadest grant of authority over its internal affairs ever given voluntarily by a labor organization—or any other organization—to an outside body."

In a report at the 1962 UAW convention the board's chairman, Rabbi Morris Adler of Detroit, declared that the union's adherence to high standards of ethical and democratic practice could not be measured solely by the cases submitted to the board for review. "We have had no cases of organized corruption," he told the delegates. "We have had no cases where an officialdom was in collusion with those who are enemies of the union. We have had no great instances at all of anything that was fundamentally undemocratic in the constitution in our structure."

WHITE-COLLAR MEMBERSHIP

The high levels of auto production in the last two years, plus the UAW's success in organizing scores of relatively small shops in many parts of the country, have brought its membership up nearly 200,000 from the low point of early 1961, when it slipped below the million mark. However, there is no prospect that it can keep climbing unless the UAW makes much more substantial progress than it has up to now in unionizing white-collar and engineering personnel.

In automotive plants the expectation in union circles is that it will be possible to make a million more cars by the end of the decade with 50,000 fewer workers than are now employed. In the missile and spacecraft plants, the dollar volume of contracts is higher than it was in the days of winged aircraft, but the number of production workers is a third of the old requirement in many plants. The union's defeat in union shop elections at two aerospace companies last year has not enhanced its organizing drive in that field.

The effort to recruit office and technical employees in the automobile industry has been put under the direction of Douglas A. Fraser, one of the UAW's most enterprising young international executive board members. He is making his greatest bid for workers in offices attached to strategic production units, where the union can use the strength of its blue-collar membership to maximum advantage in speeding company recognition. Five white-collar workers who served initially as volunteer organizers have been put on Fraser's staff, and he is casting about for engineers interested in taking recruiting assignments. The whole theme of the approach to the white-collar groups is "Your Needs Are Different," and stress is put on the distinctiveness of treatment they can expect as against that given hourly-rated employees.

No titanic forward thrust is in sight on this front, but the experiments now under way in year-round discussions with the Big Three, the inauguration of the leadership study center, and the importance of finding a key to white-collar organization present a sufficient challenge even for Reuther's restless mind. He is also seeking to animate the AFL-CIO Industrial Union Department, which has matched the federation itself for spectacular nonaccomplishment. Jack Conway, long Reuther's chief aide in Detroit, has been installed as the department's executive director, but he inherits a staff jaded by seven years of loud talk and little action, so the job of overcoming inertia will be monumental.

"The phones never ring," complains one veteran official. "No one has any sense of purpose. You can't have an effective staff without a leadership that is really on the move. Confidentially, I'm looking for another job—outside labor."

Politically, Reuther always can find plenty to do. His conception of the interrelatedness of union and political activity is much more fundamental than that of most bread-and-butter unionists, who reluctantly accepted the idea that labor ought to have its own political machinery after the Taft-Hartley Act made it obvious that what they gained at the bargaining table could be lost in the legislative chamber. The UAW has become a major political force not solely in Michigan but in every Midwest state. Its influence is growing rapidly in California, where it has a thirty-eight-year-old regional director, Paul Schrade, who looks like an Ivy Leaguer but is a prototype of the labor leader of the future. Intelligent, eager, dedicated, he has all the drive of the union pioneers, plus the sophistication of a young man who left a scholarship after his junior year as a chemistry student at Yale's Sheffield School because he wanted to acquire some field knowledge in economics.

He went to Los Angeles with the thought of spending a year working in the experimental division of North American Aviation. He joined the UAW and learned that his department was only one percent organized. He became a volunteer organizer, then editor of the local union paper, vice president of the local, and finally its president. Reuther made him his special assistant, and at the last convention Schrade was elected to the international executive board as regional director for seven Western states.

Reuther's ability to attract into his union and to move up to posts of authority men like Schrade is one of his distinctive attributes. A Reuther aide says, "Walter is a wholly moral man, a true believer. He makes countless compromises to serve his larger purposes, but he thinks of himself as a practical radical. In fact, he argues with European socialists that he is more radical than they."

A glimpse of this phase of the Reuther character shone through a sentimental talk he gave when Paul Sifton, the former playwright, newspaperman, and unemployment insurance administrator, retired as the union's Washington representative a few months ago. "Paul Sifton," he declared, "has too much of what the American labor movement has too little of—social idealism." Reuther told the last union convention, "A labor movement can get soft and flabby spiritually. It can make progress materially, and the soul of the union can die in the process."

The implementation of this spirit is found in the UAW's record of combating racial discrimination. It battled Jim Crow tendencies in its Southern locals at a time when most unions were giving lip service or no service at all to the principles of equal treatment. When President Kennedy called top unionists to the White House just before introducing his civil rights bill, Reuther cut through the Claghornlike speeches of many of his associates with a crisp declaration: "If we really wanted to do something about it, the men gathered in this room right now could do more for civil rights in one month than the whole government could in five years." He was the spearhead in making $160,000 in labor funds available to post bail for Negroes arrested in the Birmingham demonstrations.

Now that he has apparently decided to curb his impatience to become head of the AFL–CIO, his standing with the rest of labor's high command has improved markedly. When the sixty-nine-year-old Meany does leave his post, Reuther is the man most likely to succeed. But waiting for what may happen—if—is a poor occupation for a man whose talents can be applied so fruitfully in the UAW. Happily, the signs point to a more constructive application, in the best interests of Reuther, the labor movement, and the country.

David Dubinsky: Why His Throne Is Wobbling

PAUL JACOBS

Once or twice a year I fumble through a small metal box in my dresser drawer, searching for those elusive plastic tabs that slip into the collar of my evening shirt. As I push aside broken tie clips and useless keys, my fingers usually roll around a small red-and-white lapel badge. Embossed on it, in tiny letters, is "International Ladies' Garment Workers' Union." I have saved it for more than twenty years from the days when, as an organizer for the ILGWU, I wore it very proudly.

To be a union organizer was one dream of many young liberals and radicals during the 'thirties and early 'forties; to be an ILGWU organizer, almost more than could have been hoped for in even their wildest fantasies. And for me, organizing shops owned by employers who had fled from New York to escape the union was even more than a mission; the status that went with being an ILGWU organizer meant a lot to me at a time when my life was bedraggled and miserable.

Almost too vividly, I can remember the details of sudden, brutal fights on picket lines and the mole on the chin of a strikebreaker whose head I was smashing against the side of a truck. I can still conjure up the sense of terror that flooded me the evening I walked slowly down a country lane, an insane farmer prodding me in the back with a loaded shotgun because I had tried to sign up his daughter in the union.

Taken from Harper's Magazine, *CCXXV (December 1962), pp. 75–84. Reprinted with the permission of the author. Paul Jacobs is on the staff of the Institute of Industrial Relations of the University of California at Berkeley and Staff Director of the Study of the Trade Union for the Center for the Study of Democratic Institutions.*

But there are scores of more pleasant memories too—the huge breakfasts we organizers ate after early wintry morning leaflet distributions, warmed as much by camaraderie and kibitzing as by the hot coffee we slurped up from heavy mugs; the lazy afternoons playing snooker in grimy pool halls before we started on our nightly round of visits to workers' homes; the weekend drives back to New York singing Socialist and revolutionary songs, all of us bound together by a sense of crusade.

Something else important is buried deep in my experience and, I think, in that of everyone who has worked for the ILGWU—the mark left by our relations, no matter how brief or peripheral, with David Dubinsky, the union's leader since 1932 and one of the most formidable and publicly admired labor leaders in the country.

By 1940, when I was working for the union, Dubinsky was already a legendary figure. All of us knew and talked about his quarrels with John L. Lewis over the use of Communists as CIO organizers and about his disputes with Sidney Hillman over the American Labor party. We knew, too, that he drank Canadian Club whiskey, that his daughter's name was Jean, that he worked ten or twelve hours a day, and that he had a formidable secretary. Very quickly we learned that it was "D.D.," as he likes to be called, who made most of the decisions in the ILG—ranging from where an organizing campaign should be started to how much of a car allowance, if any, should be granted. And it only took a few weeks to discover that all his colleagues were really his subordinates and that the awe in which they held him was mixed with fear.

In my imagination, Dubinsky was twenty feet tall, so it was a shock to me when I met him the first time at a birthday party given for him in the union's old headquarters, a small, rather shabby building on Sixteenth Street, just off Fifth Avenue. He walked into the room, accepting with a negligent wave the congratulations being offered him, and I saw that he was short and stocky, almost stubby.

"Hallo," he said to me when we were introduced, in a heavy Yiddish accent about which he is very self-conscious. He offered me a limp hand. But, despite his flabby grip, there was never a doubt in the mind of any staff member that D.D. was the supreme authority of our union.

Now, twenty years later, Dubinsky, once the source of the ILGWU's great vigor, has become the symbol of the union's internal weakness. For something important has gone awry inside the ILGWU; a sickness has turned the union's leadership rancid and mean. During the past eighteen months [written in late 1962], the ILGWU, long idealized as a model of socially responsible and democratic unionism—one which President Kennedy said recently "deserves the heartiest commendations"—has been embroiled in two ugly quarrels which reveal deep dissatisfactions about the union.

The sickness of the ILGWU is not, however, a sudden one even though its public symptoms are so recent. It has been developing for many years.

EIGHT DAYS OF ANGER

Normally, Dubinsky is a volatile man, quick to flare up into shouting anger, but his temper was even edgier than usual during the May 1962 convention of the International Ladies' Garment Workers' Union. In a steady rage that seemed to last for the eight days of the convention, Dubinsky lashed out at those "enemies" of the union who, he shouted, wanted to "undermine us, degrade us," who used "sneaky ways" and "machinations" against the ILGWU. But it was not the employers, the garment manufacturers, at whom the seventy-year-old Dubinsky continually hurled his defiance; indeed, *they* were honored guests at the convention. No, the "traitors to our cause" were those members of the ILGWU staff, mostly business agents and organizers, who had organized a union of their own.

Why should the staff members of the ILGWU want to organize their own union? Their complaints are simple enough. Traditionally the union has paid them low salaries; they have to make demeaning personal appeals to their supervisors in order to get raises; often they must chisel on expense accounts to meet their legitimate needs. After years of grumbling, a small group of ILG organizers met secretly in the fall of 1959 to form a union to represent them, calling themselves the Federation of Union Representatives (FOUR). By December 1959, the FOUR group believed they represented a majority of the organizers, business agents, and educational directors in the union. But when they sent a telegram to Dubinsky asking for recognition, they were flatly turned down.

"We look upon [an organization like FOUR] as a violation of the traditional spirit of our union," Dubinsky's Executive Board replied. "We are convinced that such an organization would be an instrument of internal dissension and strife, bound to undermine the standards and welfare of the ILGWU and its members." The Board argued that it opposed unionization of the ILGWU business agents—who made up the bulk of FOUR's membership—because they have duties "directorial in nature" and are "spokesmen for the union."

With this, Dubinsky started using every legal, financial, and organizational resource of the ILGWU to smash FOUR, resisting all attempts by the National Labor Relations Board to give the new group a fair chance to establish itself as a union. When the NLRB ordered that an election be held to see how many staff members favored FOUR, the ILG unsuccessfully opposed the order. When it was determined that FOUR won the election, the ILGWU was ordered to bargain with it, but it has refused to do so and has been charged by the NLRB for refusal to bargain. Dubinsky has made it clear that he will drag FOUR through every court he can before recognizing it.

At the same time, he has conducted a massive campaign within the ILG itself. Members of FOUR have come under ugly pressures by their superiors to quit their union. A stream of editorials have denounced FOUR in *Justice,* the ILG's newspaper, and so have advertisements in the New York daily papers. Not long ago, one of the NRLB's most experienced examiners found the ILGWU guilty of unfair labor practices against FOUR, and the union was ordered to cease threatening staff members with reprisals for their activities on FOUR's behalf. Predictably, the ILGWU is appealing this verdict, just as it has the others.

There is nothing very surprising about the demand by the ILGWU staff to bargain with its employer. Many other unions have been faced with staff demands for some form of collective bargaining. Staff members of unions representing airline pilots, chemical workers, teachers, newspapermen, electrical workers, and the AFL-CIO itself have all negotiated agreements with their union leadership, although some were achieved in the face of considerable resistance. But no other union officials have reacted with the explosive violence of Dubinsky, who has made strident personal attacks on such men as Norman Thomas because they disagreed with him in the FOUR case.

The same choleric emotionalism displayed in Dubinsky's fight against FOUR has also been evident in the dispute between the ILGWU and the National Association for the Advancement of Colored People, which charges that "Negro and Puerto Rican members of the ILGWU are discriminated against both in terms of wages and other conditions of employment and in their status as members of the union."

This accusation reflects one of the fiercest dilemmas facing Dubinsky and his fellow leaders. They rose to power in the 'thirties when the ILGWU's strength was mainly drawn from Jewish and Italian immigrants. But now Negroes and Puerto Ricans make up one-quarter of the union's national membership of 400,000, and one-half of the membership in New York City. And it is particularly in New York where the NAACP claims that the Negroes and Puerto Ricans are getting a raw deal. In at least one case, the New York State Commission for Human Rights found "probable cause to credit the allegations [of discrimination]" which the NAACP had lodged against Dubinsky's own local of cutters in New York. (Only "probable" because, until recently, the local refused to supply the Commission with the information it requested.)

Last summer the charges of discrimination in the ILGWU became the subject of an inept Congressional investigation sparked by Adam Clayton Powell, the Negro Congressman from Harlem who is chairman of the House Education and Labor Committee. Dubinsky has repeatedly denied all charges of discrimination and maintains that the committee investigation of the ILGWU is a "spite probe"—"based on malice, on blackmail." During Powell's absence, the subcommittee hearings were conducted by Representative Herbert Zelenko, who had been denied ILGWU support in the primary in New York this year; and Dubinsky points out that Herbert Hill, the national labor secretary of the NAACP, was serving the committee as a paid consultant.

There seems, then, to be some justice in Dubinsky's criticism of the impartiality of these confused hearings. But politics cannot account for all the savage bitterness with which he and his top leadership have reacted both to FOUR's request for a staff union and to the charges of the NAACP. Dubinsky is so convinced that his union is far better than any other that it is intolerable for him to witness public display of the ILGWU's alleged shortcomings or any real or imagined slights to his leadership.

WHEN "POPPA" IS HURT

For the union is Dubinsky's real family, his only real life. He is, as he told the House subcommittee, the "Poppa" of the ILGWU, to whom all the union's officials must account, the man who can "put the fear of God into their hearts." He believes the careers of the staff members are his to control as he wishes. One explanation of his vindictive response to FOUR is simply that he felt like a father whose children had turned on him. What he did not understand is that the badly paid staff felt they had to organize their own union precisely because Dubinsky views himself as the head of a family group for which he insists on making *all* decisions.

This paternalism encompasses not only the union but the garment industry itself. And although this is unfortunate, it becomes more understandable when one examines the bizarre world of clothes manufacturing which still centers around lower Seventh Avenue in New York City.

"For God's sake, Cohen, make some kind of an offer to the union," a state mediator once said to a dress manufacturer facing a strike by the ILGWU. "Offer the union a penny an hour if that's all you can afford—but offer *something* so they'll know you're bargaining in good faith."

Absolutely bewildered, the employer stared at the mediator. "It doesn't make any difference how much I offer," he explained patiently. "They *know* I'm not acting in good faith."

Indeed, good faith is a very rare quality in the garment industry where some twelve thousand employers—most of them running very small shops—engage in notoriously ruthless competition. The capital investment is low; the profit from a dress or coat that "clicks" can be very high; and the employers search grimly for the slightest competitive edge. The average women's garment factory employs only thirty-six workers today—exactly one more than in 1900—and the annual death rate of garment firms is one of the highest in the country. Furthermore, about 80 per cent of the workers are women, and they come and go so rapidly that the union has had to sign up 200,000 new members in the last three years merely to hold its level of membership.

In this concrete jungle, the ILGWU is far more than a conventional bargaining agent. It has become a major regulatory force. If it were not strong enough to dominate the rapacious animals of the jungle, they might eat one another up, devouring thousands of jobs in the process. Thus the ILGWU is not concerned simply with obtaining better wages and conditions for a highly fluid work force (a force increasingly composed of Negroes and Puerto Ricans with so little organizational experience that the union leaders, correctly or not, doubt their ability to solve their own problems). It is also concerned with keeping the frequently rickety firms it deals with in—or out—of business. And this peculiar situation is directly linked to the ILGWU's contention that its business agents—who deal directly with the employers—should be barred from joining FOUR because their duties are more "directorial" than those of business agents in other unions.

But for all the union's power, competition in the industry is so fierce and the profit margin so low that the garment workers receive relatively low wages—often not more than the federal minimum rate. In the past fifteen years, average wages in the printing, rubber, auto, and building industries—among many others—have all risen much more swiftly than those of the ILGWU members.

Nor do the average wage figures tell the whole story. A comparatively small elite of skilled garment cutters and pressers do in fact earn fairly high wages, while the far more numerous union members who work as floorworkers, finishers, examiners, and bundlers receive a great deal less. One of the NAACP's major charges is that Negroes and Puerto Ricans who do this low-paid work are barred from admission to the locals which control the more highly skilled jobs.

Whether or not discrimination is widespread, one thing is clear: little real communication exists between the growing colored membership of the union and the present leadership. No Negro or Puerto Rican holds any high office in the ILGWU. Under Dubinsky's hardened autocratic control, the union's aging leaders still reflect the patterns of an earlier era.

"D. D." RISES TO POWER

When David Dubinsky, a young, energetic, and ambitious Yiddish Socialist, emigrated to the U. S. from Poland in 1911, the garment trade was in a churning state of flux. The older Scotch-Irish, and German-Jewish garment workers, who had made whole garments, were being replaced by the newer Jewish immigrants from Poland and Russia. These "greenhorns," unable to speak the language, were bound together by family ties, common European origin, and politics. Crowded together on the Lower East Side, they were forced to slave in ghastly sweatshops which sprang up throughout the slums. They worked for contractors and subcontractors who hired them to perform single operations on garments brought in bundles from the larger manufacturers—a single garment might travel by pushcart to three different factories before completion, just as it might today.

Many of the new immigrants who went into the needle trades were Socialists like Dubinsky who had been very active in the Bund, the vigorous Jewish Socialist movement in Eastern Europe. At fourteen Dubinsky was already secretary of the bakers' union in Lodz, Poland, and helped run a strike that shut down all the Jewish bakeries in the city, including the one owned by his father.

Within a few weeks after Dubinsky arrived in the U. S. at nineteen, he was actively participating in the vigorous Yiddish Socialist movements that had been transferred from Europe to the crowded East Side slums. Dubinsky throve in this atmosphere. In 1914 he married Emma Goldberg, a garment worker and Socialist from Lithuania, but the pattern of his life was basically unchanged, for his drives could only be fulfilled inside an organization.

"I remember Dubinsky when he was running a co-operative restaurant," recalls an ILGWU veteran, "and even then he was the manager while everybody else was just a waiter."

In New York, Dubinsky became a garment cutter instead of a baker. Then as now, the cutters were the aristocrats of the trade, for their skill in guiding a heavy cutting machine through many layers of cloth can mean the difference between profit and loss for the employer. The cutters' union was still a stronghold of the older garment workers, who were far more conservative than the young Socialists like Dubinsky.

Dubinsky had very little time to spare from Socialist party activity for union work during his first four or five years in this country but when the younger cutters in his local organized a caucus to take over the leadership, he began to play an active role. Within five years he had become not only the general manager of the cutters' local but its secretary-treasurer as well—a pattern of control he was to follow in the years to come. But while Dubinsky was consolidating his position within the cutters' local, the national ILGWU was being torn apart by internal factional fights and badly run strikes. An active Communist group had been exploiting the dissension and trying to take over.

Dubinsky threw himself into the fight against the Communists and was a decisive force in defeating them. But this battle was so traumatic that he and many other ILGWU leaders developed a fear of factionalism which remains irrationally alive today, thirty years after the original cause has disappeared. The residue can still be found in the ILGWU's constitution, which prohibits the formation of internal union caucuses and factions, except for brief preconvention periods; and in Dubinsky's technique of presenting only one slate of officers for election. Incredibly enough, the old experience with the Communists has been used to justify the charges of "factionalism" which are being made against FOUR today. Dubinsky has even used Socialist support of FOUR as an excuse to conjure up a "Trotskyist" plot against the union.

By 1932 Dubinsky was in so strong a position that he was asked to become president of the international ILGWU on his own terms. These were that he be given the secretary-treasurer job as well—at least temporarily, until the splits within the national ILGWU were healed. When he took over the shattered union, it had only 40,000 members, almost all of them in New York, and it was more than $750,000 in debt. Two years later he was able to report to the cheering delegates at the 1934 convention that the membership has quintupled to 200,000 and that the treasury held a surplus of $500,000.

No doubt the election of Roosevelt and the spreading crisis of the Depression all contributed to this astonishing revival. But it was Dubinsky who ran the organizing campaigns and the strikes that brought thousands of garment workers all over the country flocking to the ILGWU. It was inevitable that he be formally elected president of the ILGWU at the 1934 convention. And after eliminating the new aspirants to the job of secretary-treasurer by preconvention deals, he was elected to that post too, "for a temporary period of two years." (In fact, he held onto the job until 1959, when he finally turned it over to his trusted follower Louis Stulberg, another member of the cutters' local.)

SIGNED BUT NOT DATED

The 1930s were the most important years of the ILGWU's life. As the New Deal took hold, the old Socialist ideologies of the union's leaders became more and more diluted. If it wasn't possible to reorganize the world, the Wagner Act at least made it possible to organize more garment workers into union locals and clean up filthy sweatshops. But the leaders soon ran into trouble: they had to deal not only with the employers but with the industrial racketeering which had infiltrated their industry.

Originally, hoodlums and gangsters had been brought into the garment trade by some employers determined to keep out the unions. The racketeers quickly managed to gain effective control not only of some garment-manufacturing companies but some union locals as well. It was at this time that Dubinsky began to demand signed but undated resignations from elected and appointed ILGWU officials—a practice that still prevails today. ("It's conducive to keep your union clean, very conducive," is Dubinsky's justification of the practice.)

No one will ever be able to write a history of the wars between the ILGWU and the mobs. Although the casualty list was long, the battles were fought in complete silence. Because the mobsters controlled so much of New York's political life, the unions couldn't count on the police. And so they were forced, sometimes, to be as unscrupulous as the enemy, allying themselves with their own strong-arm gangs against the racketeers, with both sides using the same arms—guns, acid, knives, and stink bombs. Honest union officials and dishonest hoodlums were trampled to death in vacant lofts in the same way. Tragically, the mode of conspiracy that the union was forced to adopt in those days has lingered on, inevitably affecting the way in which the union leaders conduct their fight against FOUR.

But this face of the union very rarely showed in public. Even if it had, no accurate sense of what the ILGWU was all about would have been gained by it. For despite Dubinsky's growing vanity and his increasing control over the union machinery, the organization under his leadership was still suffused with an élan that was unique to it then. If the leaders were no longer Socialists, they understood better than most union people that broad and unprecedented social possibilities were opening up in America.

Certainly the ILGWU's public programs were admirable. For the members, a union-sponsored educational program was developed; health centers began to spring up; Unity House, the members' vacation resort in the Pocono Mountains of Pennsylvania, was expanded; and semi-independent political action started with the birth of the American Labor party in New York. Those were the years to which Dubinsky nostalgically returns today as the best years of his and the union's life; the years in which "Pins and Needles," the ILGWU's own musical revue (the first and last of its kind), ran for weeks in New York and even gave a performance for President Roosevelt at the White House. And the ILGWU could be counted on to support causes in which few other unions took any interest. Even though most of the union's leaders had emulated Dubinsky in leaving the Socialist party, the ILGWU was still a haven in those years for political nonconformists. Its devoted organizing and educational staffs included liberals and radicals from every section of the left except the Communists.

The salaries paid out to staff and officers in the 'thirties and early 'forties weren't especially important to them, for they were committed to the union as a social movement. As late as 1940 and 1941, when I was working for the ILG, an organizer's salary was still only around $40 per week—supplemented, if you worked outside of New York City, by a weekly expense allowance of $7.50. I can still remember having an expense account rejected because I had taken an upper berth. Coaches were good enough.

But although we complained a little about our low pay and expense accounts, our biggest griping was reserved for Dubinsky's domination of the union and his demand for unquestioning allegiance.

"Everybody holler, 'Hurray for Dubinsky!'" Dubinsky would shout from the top of a table during summer parties at Unity House. And all the residents of "Vice Presidents' Row"—the cottages set aside for the union officers—dutifully shouted back, "Hurray for

Dubinsky!" But neither the union officers who were dependent upon Dublnsky, nor those who felt they were part of a crusade in which he played a key role, would publicly complain about the internal management of the union. No member of the executive board revealed that Dubinsky enforced his demands upon them by threatening to resign if his policy wasn't adopted. No member of the staff even filed a public complaint about the donations they were pressured to make to causes Dubinsky favored. Those were family secrets to be kept from the outsiders.

So the public mystique of David Dubinsky and the ILGWU grew and flourished, aided considerably by a very skillful public-relations operation and a friendly press, especially in New York City, where Dubinsky was treated as a sacred figure. He was, after all, largely responsible for some excellent ILGWU policies: its publication of complete financial reports, long before the law required it; its public stand against racketeering in unions, taken long before the McClellan Committee revelations; its support of liberal causes; and its involvement in the creation of the CIO.

"HARD" AND "SOFT"

But now the family secrets are coming out. Some of the most significant disclosures have been made by the ILGWU officials themselves in NLRB hearings as they tried to argue that the union's business agents exercise such important authority that they must be considered as "representatives of management," ineligible to join a staff union like FOUR.

According to the ILGWU leaders, the business agent can deal with the employers in very different ways. He may use what is called a "hard" policy—if he feels that the employer does not "accept the union completely and wholeheartedly," he can exert pressure by invoking the union's contract at every opportunity. For example, he can bring every single discharge of a worker to arbitration, "even where the facts show that the case was with cause." On the other hand, the business agent may employ a "soft policy"—he may uphold the employer when a worker is discharged and "the worker's rights . . . end at that point." And he can accommodate the employer in other ways.

The same ambivalence applies outside the plant. As one ILGWU official testified at the hearings, local units of the union might support sit-in strikes by Negroes in some communities; but ". . . it's alto-

gether conceivable that a business agent for a Southern local might
participate in the deliberations of a White Citizens Council. . . ."

In such testimony, the ILGWU leaders reveal a dilemma they are
unable to solve. Privately they believe they must maintain their disciplinary power over their business agents if they are to wield power
effectively in the fragmented and risky garment industry, accommodating one employer with "soft" policy, disciplining another with
"hard," warring against those gangsters who are still operating
shops. But at the same time they tell their business agents that it
would be improper for them to belong to FOUR because a business
agent, as one leader put it, is in a category with a "priest or a rabbi or
a minister." Dubinsky, in short, wants his staff to live and behave as
if they were carrying out a crusading mission of the 'thirties. But the
staff members know that in these days of finely calculated "hard" and
"soft" policies, unions are no longer crusading organizations, except
perhaps in the nostalgic memories of their leaders as their limousines
cruise up the White House drive.

Nor does Dubinsky help matters by dismissing the FOUR sympathizers as "peanut politicians" who "feel that the president and vice
president live too long," as he did at the ILGWU convention. He was
probably referring here to those FOUR members who were graduates
of the union's own Training Institute, once described by the ILG as
"labor's West Point." Amid great fanfare, the Institute was established in 1951 to train dedicated union members and outsiders for a
career of service in the union. Today, less than 50 per cent of the 308
graduates are still on the union's staff.

Some of FOUR's most active members were graduates of the Institute. This may be one of the reasons why the school closed down in
1961, ostensibly because there were no more jobs to be filled, and
why Gus Tyler, the school's director—and once a bright star of political action in the Socialist and liberal movements—has single-
mindedly applied his skills to the task of fighting FOUR.

Very little evidence has been produced to substantiate charges that
FOUR is really a faction trying to give itself the protections of a union,
while directed by forces outside. But it's certainly possible that some
ambitious FOUR members would like either to get power themselves
or change the structure of the ILGWU—a structure in which family
connections are a considerable aid to advancement. Shelley Appleton,
Dubinsky's son-in-law, who became manager of a large ILGWU local
after he married the union president's only child, was elevated to a
vice-presidency at the last convention. And the fact that Appleton is
extremely competent does little to erase the cynicism of other staff

members not fortunate enough to have fathers or fathers-in-law who are ready to place them in what has become, in effect, a family business.

THE TIGHT HOLD OF THE PAST

The tragedy of the ILGWU is that its leaders do not understand the membership of "their" union. A far deeper cultural empathy and common tradition exist today between the Jewish ILGWU leaders and the Jewish employers—many of them former garment workers themselves—than exist between the leaders and the members.

As much as anything else, the union's financial report for January 1959–December 1961 reflects the tight hold of the past. Of the $651,939.53 domestic donations made by either the ILGWU General Office or by a joint fund of ILGWU affiliates and the General Office, approximately $18,000 was given to Negro groups and $750 to a Puerto Rican group. The Congress of Racial Equality, one of the most active forces battling Negro segregation, received only $200, half the amount given to the New York Press Photographers Association. But the Yiddish and Jewish organizations to which the union's leadership is still bound received nearly eight times as much—more than $140,000.

The union's contributions of $462,000 made during the three-year period show an even greater disparity: almost $300,000 went to organizations in Israel or to Jewish groups operating overseas and $60,000 was given to Italian groups. One donation niftily combined both the Jewish and Italian interest in a grand public-relations gesture: $25,000 was given to the Luigi Antonini Stadium in Haifa! (An additional $25,000 had been donated earlier to the stadium, named for an ILGWU vice-president.)

No one can reasonably object to the ILGWU's officers making contributions to what are, after all, very worthy causes. But the large sums given to Jewish groups and the comparatively tiny amounts given to Negro, Puerto Rican, and Mexican groups illustrate the inability of Dubinsky to adjust to reality just as much as does his fight against FOUR. The money belongs not to Dubinsky but to the union members, most of them no longer either Jewish or Italian, and the amounts expended to keep alive the past are all out of proportion to the needs of the present.

Through the use of ILGWU funds, Dubinsky is able to dominate whole areas of New York life. His control of the Liberal party, the political action arm of the ILGWU, which was formed after the American Labor party split on the Communist issue, is another example of paternalistic ILG leadership. The Liberal party has become, not the independent party it was originally conceived to be, but instead the political organ of Dubinsky and of Alex Rose of the Hatters' union, used by them for the support of the candidates they choose. It was power politics, not principle, that gave Robert Wagner a blank-check endorsement for Mayor from the Liberal party before he had decided on either his running mates or platform. And it is power politics, not principle, that frequently determines whom the Liberal party shall support for a judgeship. Dubinsky's choices are questioned as rarely in the Liberal party as they are in the ILGWU.

"Well, what do you want, Jacobs?" is a legitimate question. "Haven't you changed, too, since those days when you were an ILGWU organizer out on the picket lines?"

Yes, indeed, I've changed. The plastic tabs I go looking for in the box with my ILGWU button fit into an evening shirt, and it has been a very long time since I smashed anybody's head against the side of a truck. But what is so deeply disturbing about the American trade unions today is not that they have changed, but rather that they haven't.

What are unions doing to develop cadres of new leadership? To confront the baffling problems of fast technological change? To help disadvantaged groups learn new skills and gain a foothold in the economy? To assess the basic function of unions in the coming decades? Such questions are barely touched upon in the AFL–CIO today. And that is why the tragedy of David Dubinsky is not unique, even though his empire is ruptured in its own distinctive way. As with many another union leader, Dubinsky's success has led to his failure. The question now is where new leadership can come from to redeem the responsibilities that union officers ought to fulfill, but very rarely do.

Union Maturity and Management Strength

GEORGE STRAUSS

Recent years have seen a noticeable shift in the balance of power in labor-management relations. Unions are getting weaker and management is getting stronger. Wage increases, particularly in manufacturing industry, have begun to level off. Industrial unions are clearly on the defensive. The most serious strikes in recent years have involved efforts to protect members' jobs against automation and technological change.

Why this reversal? Is the trend bound to continue? The paper which follows seeks to guess answers to these difficult questions. For the most part, my comments are based on research in one heavy-industry-dominated community.[1] These findings seem to be fairly applicable to manufacturing generally but not to the Teamsters and building-trades unions, groups which have lost little of their power.

I propose first to look at causes of the decline in union strength and then at the reasons for management's increase in power. I will center my attention on day-to-day labor relations at the plant level, both because my research has been concentrated in this area and because developments at this level contribute to the more headline-getting developments such as strikes and contract negotiations.

UNION WEAKNESS

It is generally agreed that the union movement is no longer a *movement*—that it has lost its forward direction. One author comments

This article appeared under the title, "Union Bargaining Strength: Goliath or Paper Tiger," in the Annals *of the American Academy of Political and Social Science, CCCL (November 1963), pp. 87–94. Reprinted with the permission of the author and publisher. George Strauss is Professor of Industrial Relations and Research Economist in the Institute of Industrial Relations at the University of California at Berkeley.*

[1] See George Strauss, "The Shifting Power Balance in the Plant," *Industrial Relations,* I (May 1962), pp. 65–96.

that the union member seems to have lost his "Messianic fervor to help fellow workers; complacency and self-satisfaction have taken its place, and the workers look upon the labor movement with boredom."[2] Labor's very success, it is argued, has tended to make unions less necessary: increased wages have given workers middle-class standards, while better human relations have eliminated many of the frustrations due to tyranny on the job. Consequently, traditional union objectives have become outmoded.

This point of view may easily be exaggerated. It is undoubtedly true that many union leaders have lost their sense of missionary zeal; like most Americans, unionists show little sense of moral urgency in this year 1963. In part, this was inevitable; the fever pitch of the 1930's, labor's heroic era, was impossible to maintain indefinitely. Yet workers may need their unions more than ever during a period of rapid technological change and widespread unemployment.

Unions are also weaker economically. Union organizing drives have petered out. Technological change has steadily reduced the proportion of the labor force working in the factory. Overcapacity in many lines of industry has made management less reluctant to take a strike, and foreign competition and reduced profit margins have stiffened its resistance to granting wage increases.

Both developments have weakened unions. Let us examine three vital union groups: (1) paid staff representatives—appointed by the international in most industrial unions; (2) unpaid local officers, and (3) the rank and file.

Staff Representatives

The average age of staff representatives is going up. The men who founded the industrial unions during the "heroic" days of the 1930's —when they themselves were in the twenty-five to forty-five age bracket—are today in their fifties and sixties. Age is taking its toll: these men have been through more than usual strain in their lives; quite a number suffer from ulcers and circulatory ailments, which, though not necessarily disabling, force them to limit their exertions.

Although the representatives' energy may have declined, the demands on their time have, if anything, become greater. Representatives today must handle the myriad details connected with Landrum-Griffin, supplemental unemployment benefits, hospitalization benefits,

2 Oscar Ornati, "The Current Crisis: A Challenge to Organized Labor," *Antioch Review*, XX (Spring 1960), p. 42. There is reason to doubt, though, if there *ever* was much "messianic fervor" on the part of most rank-and-file members.

and so on. Grievances are becoming increasingly complex: the very fact that collective-bargaining relations are getting older and more established means that simple questions of morality are much less common than subtle questions of interpreting contract language or past practices. Political and community activities also make increasing demands on already heavy schedules.

As a consequence, both personnel directors and union leaders have observed that unions are often badly understaffed. "Our representative has to handle so many situations he can't give adequate time to ours," commented one personnel director. "I seriously believe our situation would be better if he could give our local more guidance." Further, arbitrators and personnel directors have noted that in recent years it has not been uncommon for representatives to enter arbitration with only the sketchiest of preparation.

Representatives seem to have lost some of their idealistic motivation, which made them so effective in the thirties and forties. Men who were once inspired leaders have at times taken on the hardened cynicism of political ward bosses. Although most representatives are subtle bargaining tacticians and skillful picket-line organizers, many lack the flexibility to adjust to management's new strategy. With significant exceptions, they go through the same old motions, sometimes rousing themselves to their former greatness, but normally showing little creative zest.

In addition, unions are finding it difficult to recruit adequate replacements for the men who retire or die. Dedicated, energetic, and highly competent men were responsible for the rise of mass unionism during the thirties. Except for the Depression, many of these men would have been promoted into management or have gone to college and eventually have become professionals. For them, the union was an outlet for blocked aspirations—a chance both to express themselves and to serve an idealistic cause. There are fewer men of this sort among the ranks of hourly paid workers today, and many of the best of these are offered management positions as soon as they show ability as union officers.

Many of the more able leaders of the thirties received their basic training and idealistic orientation from Socialist and Communist movements; such movements are not important sources of union leadership today—Catholic labor schools and Negro action groups are, to a degree, playing such a role, however. Recent recruits have somewhat the same motivations as ward politicians: they look upon the union as a career rather than a cause. Although college men are often hired as union technicians—research and education directors or lawyers—they are rarely appointed to line policy-making positions. Because unions are political organizations, they must recruit their leadership from within their own ranks. Although such appointees typically have considerable skill in dealing with people and handling grievances, they have neither formal training nor breadth of experience. True, union educational departments are doing an increasingly effective job in training both paid and unpaid officers, but such technical training cannot make up for lack of idealistic motivation or the union's inability to select men on the basis of competence rather than politics.

Local Officers

The heart of the union is its local officers—local presidents, stewards, and grievance men who are in the plant and represent the men on the job. These are the noncoms who hold the organization together, process the bulk of the grievances, and set the tone of day-to-day relations.

The change, at this level, from even ten years ago, is brought out dramatically at routine local meetings which are attended chiefly by the active leadership. Gone are the factional maneuvers, the burning issues, the long-winded speeches, and the parliamentary rigmarole which kept meetings in some unions going for three to five hours. For the hard-core activist, the meeting is now primarily a social event. Even economic interest groups find it hard to muster enthusiasm for their own special pleadings.

In recent years, there have been significant changes in the role of local officers. In the first place, as the representative's available time declines, the local officers must take more responsibility for handling grievances and negotiating contracts. Secondly, local officers are less willing to give time to the union. Twenty years ago, it was not uncommon for local officers to spend as many as three nights a week at membership and executive committee meetings, all without compensation. Today, a growing number of unions pay their officers to attend meetings. Thirdly, there is considerable evidence of petty corruption, such as expense-account padding, misuse of "lost time" allowances, and kickbacks on purchases of union supplies.

Just as in the case of paid staff representatives, it is hard to recruit well-qualified individuals to take unpaid union office. Many of those who are active today look upon the union as an interesting hobby rather than a cause. Others run for office solely to bring themselves to management's attention as potential supervisors, to win superseniority and protection against layoffs, or to represent the special interests of their *own* work group as against that of others.

Rank-and-File Members

The attitude of rank-and-file members seems to be ambivalent. Most members feel that the union offers them a necessary form of protection, and many feel that this protection is still more important today, now that automation threatens their jobs; yet, except in periods of crisis, they look upon their unions as "they" rather than "we" and are rather mistrustful of their officers. As one officer told us, "A lot of members think every officer is a Hoffa." In contrast to the 1940's, when workers gave 90 to 95 per cent support to their unions in union-shop elections, recent union-shop elections in West Coast aerospace plants have gone rather badly for unions, with voter support ranging from 54 to 74 per cent.[3] General Electric was able to break a strike organized against it in 1960 by the International Union of Electrical, Radio and Machine Workers (IUE). On the other side, to take a more typical example, there was no back-to-work movement during the long steel strikes of 1959–1960. In general, members stand behind their unions, though with less enthusiasm than they did fifteen to twenty-five years ago. Three reasons partly explain this loss of enthusiasm:

(1) For the generation of union members who joined during the thirties, union membership was a voluntary act. These members participated in the great battles which led to union recognition. They remember personally the often tyrannical forms of supervision which proceeded unionism. They fought and suffered for the union on the picket line and experienced the thrill of victory. By contrast, many younger union members today are forced to join by the union shop.

(2) A new generation of supervisors is coming along. Many of these men are college graduates, others are former union members. Although the change may be exaggerated, these men are more sophisticated in the ways of human relations and much less likely to engage in activities which outrage a worker's sense of justice. Thus, there are fewer easily dramatized grievances.

(3) The threat of automation has thrown unions on the defensive. And the automation issue is one about which it is difficult to formulate a clear union policy or to arouse united membership support. The

---

[3] It should be noted that this is a fairly special situation. Turnover in these plants is exceptionally high and the typical worker is a fairly specialized technician who undoubtedly thinks of himself as being more white-collar than blue-collar.

impact of automation varies widely. (We shall use the term broadly and inaccurately—as most workers do—to mean all forms of labor-saving technological advance.) A few plants have been unaffected. In others, the level of employment has dropped substantially and the fear that unemployment will spread has had an almost numbing effect on employee attitudes. To quote a typical comment: "We've lost one third of our men, but we are producing as much as we did in 1955. Our youngest [least senior] man came in 1950. Everyone is scared that automation will hit him next. Sure, wages are high, but what good do these do when you are out in the street? And for a man of forty, finding a good job isn't easy these days."

This spread of automation has made work rules into a major issue. As new processes are introduced, fewer men are needed; the individuals concerned try to protect their jobs, and the battle is joined. When these issues are dramatized as matters of principle, as they were in the 1959–1960 steel strike, high emotional feeling is inevitable. Slogans like "featherbedding," "speed-up," "managerial prerogatives," "protection of job right," and all the rest are heard.

Surprisingly, when questions of principle are not involved, the union leaders' position in regard to automation is often fairly ambiguous. Naturally they are under great pressure from members whose jobs are threatened. Yet the leaders involved—particularly the international representatives who take a broader view of the problem—are far from sure what action they should take. Often they feel automation to be inevitable. "As I look at the plants I deal with, it's the ones who have the least automation which have lost the most jobs," one representative commented. "The companies must automate to stay in business, the ones which have kept the same processes for fifty years are losing men day by day."

Few unions are making an all-out effort today to stop technological change—the railroad case is something of an exception. Instead, industrial unions are seeking to *cushion* the impact of displacement through contractual demands for broader seniority, opportunities for retraining, severance pay, and automation funds. In a sense, unions are seeking to transform job rights into property rights and then selling these rights to management at the highest obtainable price. Yet, not until recently were unions able to win membership support behind even these proposals. Automation is a creeping phenomenon. Normally it hits only a few members at a time—here is where the railway firemen's case is exceptional. The workers' strong and understandable desire to hold on to what they have encourages a certain amount of selfishness and makes unity behind job-protection measures difficult to achieve. "The members are divided on the basis of seniority," one steward explained. "The high seniority men are sitting pretty and don't pay much attention to the fact that men with lesser seniority are being laid off. They seem to say 'it is not happening to me' and they close their eyes to what is happening." Thus, automation greatly aggravates internal differences, and a shrewd management can take advantage of this.

On the whole, then, unions have been able to do relatively little to protect their members against automation. Many officers reported that their members felt that their union had let them down, that it is not doing an effective job of protecting their economic interests. As one steward commented:

We're rapidly moving away from the crusading spirit of the thirties. . . . In 1953 we had one of the most militant unions in the labor movement. We had wildcat strikes, direct job action, and the contract permitted us to refuse to work if we thought the jobs were unsafe. (It still does—but we don't use it anymore.) Today there is much less of this. People no longer file grievances because they think it is no use.

THE NEW MANAGEMENT MILITANCY

Management has taken advantage of union weakness to go on the offensive. This new militancy is most dramatically evident when nationwide contracts are being negotiated, but it has also had an impact on day-to-day administration of contracts. Three closely interrelated factors seem to be involved: (1) *economics*—the cost-price squeeze, in particular, has made management anxious to save every penny of labor it can; (2) *ideology*—management is finding a new sense of purpose in dealing with unions; and (3) *personnel*—professionally oriented industrial-relations men, many with advanced degrees, are taking over industrial-relations offices.

Economic pressures undoubtedly have done much to encourage management to adopt a firmer line, and to make this firmer line successful. Indeed, management is able to maintain its firmness only when economic conditions are favorable. In the seller's market of fifteen years ago, the stress was on maintaining output rather than reducing costs. Faced with wildcat strikes, top management would often order the industrial-relations department to "get the men back to work" regardless of the cost in terms of undesirable industrial-relations precedents.

The economic climate today is very different. Many companies are selling a larger volume with a lower profit, and some have had to cut

costs to survive. "Management is showing increased cost consciousness," an active union reported. "When the industry was going full
blast there was not much pressure and the company would make
concessions. Now you can almost feel the pressure." But even where
there is no economic crisis, modern accounting control procedures
place heavy pressure on plant managements to cut labor costs.
Hourly rates are set by the union contract, but there are other techniques of gaining savings, such as reducing the amount of time spent
on grievances, bypassing strict seniority, increasing work loads, and
eliminating wildcat strikes.

Recent years have also seen substantial changes in the prevailing
management philosophy towards industrial relations. Top management is showing a new sense of firmness and purpose in dealing with
unions. Its emphasis is no longer on "getting along with the union"
but on fighting back to win some of the rights which it lost in the past.
"Back in the forties we fought like cats and dogs to keep the union
out," one executive put it. "But when it did come in we tried to buy it
off by giving everything it asked. We found that appeasement didn't
work, so the point came where we had to stand up for our rights if we
were to keep the company in business."

Particularly before the steel strike of 1959–1960, there was a good
deal of talk of "rolling the union back."[4] Employers are increasingly
trying to make bargaining a two-way street. They put forth demands
of their own, seek to eliminate restrictive contractual provisions, join
with other employers in a united front against the union, and often
engage in strenuous public-relations campaigns to demonstrate the
moral rightness of their cause to their employees and to the public
generally.

During the last ten years, industrial-relations departments have
grown in size and are more fully accepted in the management structure. More important, a whole generation of college-trained men has
taken over, displacing the old-timers who had moved up through the
ranks. Some of these new men have master's degrees in industrial
relations; almost all of them take a professional point of view toward
their job. Men are no longer selected for labor-relations work purely
because they can get along with people or because they are not useful

---

[4] Very recent developments—such as the 1963 steel settlement—suggest that union-
management tensions are relaxing once again. The current era of good feeling seems
to be the result of a recognition by unions that their weak bargaining position makes
it impossible for them to win substantial new gains rather than of any loss of firmness
on management's part. In my 1962 article, I suggested, "If unions accept their
weakened power position, as they are almost forced to do, then a new accommodation
is possible." (*Op. cit.,* p. 96). This new accommodation now seems to be in sight—
antediluvian cases like the railroads or the New York Typographers notwithstanding.

elsewhere. Less emphasis is being placed on "making friends and influencing people," much more on ability to bargain and engage in power politics.

There was a time when one had the feeling in negotiations and arbitration proceedings that the union representatives were skillful and better prepared than their management counterparts. Today, this is rarely the case. In sharp contrast with ten or fifteen years ago, today it is the management men who possess the greater flexibility, sensitivity, and ability to adjust to changing circumstances; it is the management men who give the sense of knowing where they are going, rather than of just drifting with the tide. Ten years ago, many industrial-relations directors looked upon themselves as mediators between union and management; privately, many conceded that their hardest job was to persuade foremen to get along with the union. Today, it increasingly is the industrial-relations department which is urging line management to be tough.

Management Tactics

Personnel directors generally agree that winning back management's prerogatives requires patience and long-range planning. They feel that lack of long-range planning in the past led to "crisis bargaining" where management made seemingly minor concessions which eventually eroded management's rights. Much closer attention is now being given to the interrelationships between contract negotiation, contract administration, and internal union politics. In effect, personnel men are following rules such as: "Don't make concessions between contracts for which you will not be given credit when a new contract is negotiated. Always save something at one negotiation which you can give at the next one. Do not introduce technological changes during negotiations, just before union elections, or when a wildcat strike would be exceptionally hard to bear." On the whole, the new approach seeks to avoid major tests of strength—or to make sure that such tests are confined to issues which management is sure to win. One personnel director explained that, before his time, "The union made all its gains through 'creeping,' establishing all the precedents they could. Now we are making the contract creep for us; if nothing prevents us from changing a condition in our favor, we will change it."

In the typical company throughout the 1945–1955 period, there developed a whole series of informal relations between union and management. Grievances were often handled on a "problem-solving" basis without much reference to the specific terms of the contract. Foremen and stewards, superintendents and committeemen were permitted to reach private unwritten understandings, or "bootleg agreements," which, in effect, modified the contract. Without question, unions learned to use this flexibility to their advantage. This sort of flexibility continues in some companies, but most of the newer personnel directors are prepared to make strenuous efforts to restrict unofficial bargaining and to confine employee protests to the rigid structure of the grievance procedure. They seek to formalize procedures, to follow the contract to the letter, and to cut down sharply on the freedom of union stewards to circulate and to collect grievances.

Many personnel directors make a special effort to discourage the union from using the higher stages of the grievance procedure. In the ideal situation, if management's case is weak, a concession is made at the first step of the grievance procedure without further haggling, preferably before a formal grievance is filed; but if a reasonably airtight case can be developed, then the grievance will be fought all the way through arbitration. Hopefully, under these circumstances, the union decides that appeal is useless. Of course, this "ideal" state is not often reached; yet, in many instances, the proportion of cases won by the union has fallen off sharply.

Ten years ago, wildcat strikes were fairly common through industry. Few companies were willing to take firm measures against such strikes, and many capitulated quickly, particularly when delivery schedules were tight. Workers learned that the wildcat was a quick and effective way of getting action. No wonder many personnel directors have given high priority to the prevention of wildcats, have refused to make concessions in the face of such strikes, and have insisted that those who take part be disciplined. Similarly, firm stands have been taken to eliminate the customs, which have arisen in some companies, for men to refuse to carry out orders to work under conditions which they believed to violate the contract.

Industrial-relations men show signs of giving increasing importance to the role of subordinate line management in dealing with unions. In the past, the tendency has been to bypass foremen and to negotiate directly with the union regarding grievances. Some foremen reacted to the slighting of their authority by becoming frustrated or apathetic, at times even giving up trying to control their department. Others, feeling that they were abandoned by top management, tried to make the best possible accommodation with the union and so established undesirable precedents. The trend today is to bring line management more and more into the picture. The typical program consists of one or more of the following parts: (1) elimination of bypassing, so that foremen participate in the first step of the grievance procedure; (2) training in the meaning of the contract, so that foremen will interpret the contract and handle grievances in a consistent manner; and (3) training in human relations in the hope that this will reduce some of the discontent which leads to grievances. In addition, many companies are taking steps to raise the foreman's overall authority and status in management through such techniques as bringing foremen into management conferences.

The net effect of these moves has been to make it easier for management to exercise its prerogatives, to eliminate the necessity for constant bargaining with the union, and to permit management to make decisions unilaterally, subject to check only if the union can prove that the contract was violated.

CONCLUSION

To return to the main question of this paper: how strong are unions today? Certainly, economic factors—automation in particular—have tended to shift the balance of power toward management's side, and the balance has switched most radically where economic pressures have been greatest. In addition, unions have lost much of their vitality and forward motion; they are playing an essentially conservative role in the plant community, seeking to preserve what they have rather than to make gains. Few officers or members look upon the union as a cause any more. Burning issues which unite the membership are rare, and neither officers nor members know how to deal with automation. Cynicism has paved the way for petty corruption. The "founding fathers" of unionism are close to retirement, but replacements are hard to find. The change in ideological climate means that there are not many *dedicated* younger members, and economic conditions mean that *able* young men are less likely to look for factory employment in the first place.

But it would be wrong to exaggerate this tendency. The General Electric and aerospace examples notwithstanding, most members stand by their unions; for example, few would consider walking through a picket line. And, when an issue is properly dramatized, the members give not only their support but also their enthusiasm. The union may not be a goliath today—it never was—but it is surely not a paper tiger. Indeed, its role as a constructive force is seen today perhaps more vividly than ever before as it struggles to insure that automation is introduced in an orderly fashion and with a regard for human, rather than purely economic, values.

Unionization of White-Collar Employees

BENJAMIN SOLOMON AND
ROBERT K. BURNS

In recent re-examinations and "agonizing reappraisals" of the status and "decline of the labor movement,"[1] the possibility of unionization of white-collar workers is being given increasing attention. This article will present a detailed quantitative picture of the growing white-collar work force, the pattern of union penetration in this field, and certain implications for unionism in the future.

A summary, based on data from the decennial Census and a union-by-union survey, is presented of the organized and unorganized parts of the white-collar union potential (defined as that part of the work force falling within the scope of trade unionism). In 1960, the overall union potential totaled 47 million, of which 20.8 million, or 44 per cent, were white-collar employees and 26.2 million, or 56 per cent, were blue-collar employees. Of the white-collar workers, an estimated 2.7 million, or 13 per cent, are union members. These comprise 15 per cent of all union members in the United States. Other data classify unions by proportion of white-collar membership and show the occupational and industrial distributions of this membership, as well as their concentration in a few unions.

This article entitled, "Unionization of White-Collar Employees: Extent, Potential, and Implications," has been reprinted from The Journal of Business, XXVI (April 1963), pp. 141–65, with the permission of the University of Chicago Press. Copyright 1963 by the University of Chicago. Some tables and footnotes have been omitted. Benjamin Solomon is Research Associate in the Industrial Relations Center at the University of Chicago, and Robert K. Burns is the Executive Officer of the Industrial Relations Center and Professor of Business Administration in the Graduate School of Business at the Universiy of Chicago.

[1] E.g., see Solomon Barkin, The Decline of the Labor Movement and What Can Be Done about It. Center for the Study of Democratic Institutions, Santa Barbara, Calif., 1961.

Unionization in the heterogeneous white-collar sector is characterized by multiple contenders, including manual unions, in some key fields. Most unionization has taken place among "peripheral groups," as compared with the proportion in the more "pure" white-collar occupations. Here the potential is largely untapped, organizing resources are few, and major concentrations, such as office workers in downtown business districts, are left untouched. Finally, structural problems are analyzed in two key fields, office workers and engineers and scientists. Present structural patterns are found to be unpromising from the union standpoint, nor are there discerned any easy paths toward more effective patterns.

The term "white-collar employee" (or its European equivalent "salaried employee") covers a heterogeneous array of occupations. Arbitrariness will necessarily enter into any drawing of occupational boundary lines to reflect the notion of "white collar." The term itself is a popular and not a scientific one, and its popular meaning and application have suffered from the continuous changes in the occupational structure to which it refers.

Broadly, white-collar occupations are those characterized by non-manual work. Such work derives directly from, or is closely related to, business and administrative functions or is based on specialized bodies of formal knowledge or on the higher creative techniques.

Since white-collar work is essentially non-manual in character, the Bureau of Labor Statistics includes managers and proprietors as part of the white-collar classification. However, we exclude these groups from our consideration because they clearly are not a part of the union potential. In short, we include in the white-collar category all employees who perform white-collar work and who could be considered part of the union potential. Specifically, this analysis covers the following Census major occupational groups: clerical and kindred workers; professional, technical, and kindred workers; and sales workers. First-line supervisory officials, such as foremen, are also included.

CHANGES IN UNION POTENTIAL: WHITE COLLAR AND BLUE COLLAR

The over-all sweep of white-collar expansion for the ninety-year period from 1870 to 1960 is shown in Table 1. Over these nine decades, the three major white-collar occupational groups underwent a 2,800 per cent increase as compared to a 400 per cent increase for the work force as a whole. The white-collar sector grew from 0.74

TABLE 1

TOTAL LABOR FORCE AND WHITE-COLLAR COMPONENTS, 1870–1960*

	1870		1910		1950		1960		PER CENT INCREASE	
	Gainful Workers (000's)	Per Cent of Total	Gainful Workers (000's)	Per Cent of Total	Employed (000's)	Per Cent of Total	Employed (000's)	Per Cent of Total	1870–1960	1950–60
Total labor force..	12,925	100.0	36,720	100.0	56,225	100.0	64,639	100.0	400	15.0
Total white collar†	740	5.7	5,515	15.0	15,730	28.0	21,178	32.8	2,762	34.6
Professional, technical, and kindred	341	2.6	1,698	4.6	4,909	8.7	7,232	11.2	2,021	47.3
Clerical and kindred..........	98	0.8	2,016	5.5	6,894	12.3	9,307	14.4	9,397	35.0
Sales	302	2.3	1,800	4.9	3,927	7.0	4,639	7.2	1,436	18.1

* Source: Adapted from Census decennial data.
† The professional and sales groups include a number of self-employed (as, e.g., fee-practicing doctors or many real estate agents). The proportion declines in later years. In 1950, 13.3 per cent of the professional and technical group and 10.9 per cent of the sales workers were self-employed.

million to 21 million persons, increasing its proportion in the work force from 5.7 per cent to 32.8 per cent. The gain for the clerical group was the largest—from about 100,000 to over 9 million persons.[2]

More closely linked to our analysis of white-collar unionism are the 1950 and 1960 figures for union potential in both white-collar and blue-collar sectors (Table 2). The notes to the table explain the composition of the three categories—the union potential in the white-collar area, in the blue-collar area, and the remainder listed as "outside the union potential." The white-collar union potential differs slightly from the white-collar totals in the historical series (Table 1) because of the elimination of self-employed persons and the addition of the "foremen" category.

The white-collar sector makes up a substantial and an increasing proportion of the union potential, as shown in Table 2. In 1960, the total union potential amounted to 47 million workers, a little under three-quarters of the employed work force. Of this total the white-collar groups accounted for 44 per cent, as compared with 39 per cent in 1950. The rate of growth of the white-collar union potential from 1950 to 1960 was 35.2 per cent, more than four times as great as the 8.3 per cent growth of the blue-collar union potential. The white-collar sector contributed 5.4 million, or 73 per cent, of the gain in the total union potential in this decade.

A breakdown of the white-collar union potential by major occupational groups for 1950 and 1960 is presented in Table 3. The most dynamic group was professional, technical, and kindred workers, which grew by 2.25 million, or 53.6 per cent, over the decade. The largest of the major white-collar groups, clerical and kindred workers, increased by 2.3 million, for a growth rate of 35 per cent. By 1960, one out of seven members of the work force was in the clerical union potential; one out of ten was in the professional and technical union potential; and one out of sixteen was in the sales-worker union potential. All told, almost one out of three persons in the work force was part of the over-all white-collar potential that confronts the American labor movement.

The occupational base of blue-collar unionism is, as shown in the above data, becoming relatively smaller while the white-collar fields continue to grow at a rapid rate. Not only is the blue-collar propor-

2 The relatively high female composition of the white-collar force should also be noted. Slightly over half the white-collar sector in 1960 was female as compared to a little under one-third for the work force as a whole. For major groups, the percentages of females are: clerical, 67.6; professional and technical, 38.1; and sales, 35.8 (from 1960 Census data).

TABLE 2

APPROXIMATE UNION POTENTIAL, WHITE COLLAR AND BLUE COLLAR, 1950 AND 1960*

	1950			1960			1950 TO 1960			
	No. in Group (000's)	Per Cent of Union Potential	Per Cent of Work Force	No. in Group (000's)	Per Cent of Union Potential	Per Cent of Work Force	Amount of Gain (000's)	Distribution of Gain in Union Potential	Distribution of Gain in Work Force	Rate of Gain 1950–60
White-collar groups†§	15,384	38.8	27.4	20,806	44.2	32.2	5,422	73.1	64.4	35.2
Blue-collar groups‡§	24,242	61.2	43.1	26,242	55.8	40.6	2,000	26.9	23.8	8.3
Union potential—total	39,626	100.0	70.5	47,048	100.0	72.8	7,422	100.0	88.2	18.7
Groups outside the union potential§‖	16,599	......	29.5	17,591	......	27.2	992	......	11.8	6.0
Employed work force—total	56,225	100.0	100.0	64,639	100.0	100.0	8,414	......	100.0	15.0

* Source: Adapted from Census decennial data.
† White-collar groups include: professional, technical, and kindred workers; clerical and kindred workers; sales workers; foremen; and officers, pilots, pursers, and engineers, ship, and postmasters. The small number of white-collar workers in agriculture are excluded.
‡ Blue-collar groups include: craftsmen, foremen, and kindred workers (less foremen); operatives and kindred workers; service workers; except private household; laborers, except farm and mine.
§ Self-employed and unpaid family workers were deducted from the union potential groups and shifted to "outside the union potential."
‖ Those outside the union potential include: farmers and farm managers; managers, officials, and proprietors, excluding farm (less deductions noted in n. †); private household workers; farm laborers and foremen; self-employed and unpaid family workers in agriculture; and occupation not reported.

TABLE 3
WHITE-COLLAR UNION POTENTIAL BY OCCUPATIONAL GROUPS, 1950 AND 1960*

	1950		1960		RATE OF GAIN, 1950–60
	No. in Group (000's)	Per Cent of White-Collar Union Potential	No. in Group (000's)	Per Cent of White-Collar Union Potential	
Professional, technical, and kindred workers	4,207	27.3	6,460	31.0	53.6
Clerical and kindred workers	6,770	44.0	9,103	43.8	34.5
Sales workers	3,490	22.7	4,000	19.2	14.6
Foremen†	917	6.0	1,243	6.0	35.1
Total white-collar union potential	15,384	100.0	20,806	100.0	35.2

* Source: See Table 2, including nn. † and §.
† Includes the following: foremen (n.e.c.); officers, pilots, pursers, and engineers, ship, and postmasters.

TABLE 4
WHITE-COLLAR MEMBERSHIP OF AMERICAN TRADE UNIONS, LATE 1961

Union*	Estimated White-Collar Membership	Union*	Estimated White-Collar Membership
Retail Clerks International Association	388,000	American Federation of Technical Engineers	14,000
American Federation of Musicians	269,000	National Alliance of Postal Employees	12,600
Brotherhood of Railway and Steamship Clerks	200,000	National Marine Engineers' Beneficial Association	11,000
Communications Workers of America	192,000	International Organization of Masters, Mates and Pilots	10,000
United Federation of Postal Clerks	140,000	American Communications Association (Ind.)	8,000
National Association of Letter Carriers	138,000	Oil, Chemical & Atomic Workers International Union	7,600
United Steelworkers of America	130,000	United Mine Workers of America (Dist. 50)	7,110
International Brotherhood of Teamsters (Ind.)	88,000	Transport Workers Union of America	7,000
American Federation of Teachers	70,000	United Electrical, Radio and Machine Workers of America (Ind.)	6,400
International Brotherhood of Electrical Workers	70,000	Railway and Airline Supervisors Association	6,311
Office Employes International Union	65,000	National Broadcast Employees and Technicians	6,000
Retail, Wholesale and Department Store Union	64,000	Theatrical Stage Employees and Moving Picture Machine Operators	5,000
American Federation of State, County and Municipal Employees	63,000	Railroad Yardmasters of America	4,500
American Federation of Government Employees	60,000	International Chemical Workers Union	4,000
Associated Actors and Artistes of America	55,000	American Train Dispatchers Association	3,500
The Order of Railroad Telegraphers	53,000	Directors Guild of America, Incorporated (Ind.)	2,140
United Automobile Workers ...	50,000	International Union of Life Insurance Agents (Ind.)	2,000
Building Service Employees' International Union	50,000	The National Association of Special Delivery Messengers	2,000
Alliance of Independent Telephone Unions (Ind.)	50,000	Writers Guild of America, West (Ind.)	1,868
National Rural Letter Carriers Association (Ind.)	38,500	Railroad Yardmasters of North America Inc. (Ind.)	1,450
National Postal Union (Ind.) ..	38,000	Writers Guild of America, East (Ind.)	1,200
International Union of Electrical, Radio and Machine Workers .	32,500	American Radio Association ...	1,000
American Newspaper Guild	31,500	Technical Engineers Association (Ind.)	700
The Commercial Telegraphers' Union	31,000	Air Line Dispatchers Association	650
International Association of Machinists	30,000	26 blue-collar unions with white-collar membership estimates of less than 4,000 each	21,152
National Federation of Federal Employees (Ind.)	30,000		
Amalgamated Meat Cutters and Butcher Workmen	28,200	All national and international unions	2,709,081†
Amalgamated Clothing Workers	27,000	Unaffiliated local and single-employer unions	118,434‡
National Association of Postal Supervisors (Ind.)	26,000		
Insurance Workers International Union	25,000	Total—all unions	2,827,515
International Air Line Pilots Association	14,800		
National League of Postmasters of the United States (Ind.) ..	14,400		

tion of the work force declining, but the absolute increase in the number of manual workers in the union potential may be coming to an end, as indicated by the small increase from 1950 to 1960.

It should be noted that the trends shown here are in terms of the standard occupational categories and their accepted meanings. Underneath the quantitative changes mentioned above may be basic changes in job content and climate that will make less meaningful the line drawn between important segments of blue-collar and white-collar workers. This article will not attempt, however, to deal with these intriguing qualitative changes. They are mentioned to emphasize the fact that the figures cited earlier reflect a basic change in society. The core of life in modern society revolves around occupation and industry. The trends shown above summarize profound shifts that have taken place in this core. The data clearly indicate that, if the union movement is to be successful in the future, it must organize white-collar employees as well as blue-collar workers.

WHITE-COLLAR MEMBERSHIP IN AMERICAN TRADE UNIONS

White-collar membership lags numerically far behind that of blue-collar unionization. Nevertheless, there is enough of a base, in numbers and in variety of occupations, industries, and unions, to permit an assessment of its present importance and future potential.

The basic data cover size and distribution of white-collar membership in national, international, and unaffiliated local unions. These membership estimates by union are shown in Table 4. The major part of this table is a list of national or international unions arranged by order of size of *white-collar* membership.[3] All white-collar unions are shown, no matter how small the membership, but blue-collar unions with estimated white-collar membership of less than 4,000 are

[3] The basic list of national and international unions is found in Bureau of Labor Statistics, *Directory of National and International Labor Unions in the United States and Canada, 1961* (Washington, D.C.: Government Printing Office, 1962). These unions will sometimes be referred to hereinafter as the *"Directory* unions."

---

* Unions that are wholly or predominantly white collar are in italics (see text). All unions are members of the AFL–CIO except those labeled "(Ind.)," for "independent."

† The BLS in its 1961 *Directory* reported 2.2 million white-collar members in eighty-four national or internatonal unions for the year 1960. The BLS white-collar membership figures are not published by individual unions. A variety of factors account for the difference between the authors' figures and those of the BLS: differences in what occupations are considered "white collar," in the survey responses of unions and in the estimates for non-reporting unions, and in the year covered.

‡ Based primarily on Harry P. Cohany and H. James Neary, "Unaffiliated Local and Single-Employer Unions in the United States, 1961," *Monthly Labor Review,* September, 1961.

grouped at the end of the list. *Directory* unions that do not appear on the list are assumed to have negligible or no white-collar membership. The last entry in the table is a figure for total white-collar membership in unaffiliated local or single-employer unions.

Basic data for the *Directory* unions were derived from a questionnaire survey, made by the authors in early 1962, which asked for total white-collar membership and distribution of major white-collar occupational groups for 1961 or the "most recent period." A number of replying unions requested that the source of information they supplied be held confidential. Close to 84 per cent of the 2.7 million white-collar membership total for *Directory* unions shown in Table 4 is based on information secured from union sources; 6 per cent represents 1960 membership figures in the BLS Directory for non-replying unions that are clearly white collar; and 10 per cent represents estimates based on a study of available data for other non-replying unions.

It is generally recognized that available union membership figures may be subject to some degree of inaccuracy for a variety of reasons. Estimates of white-collar membership made by union officials in response to the authors' questionnaire were in many cases not based on any actual membership count but represent judgments based on individual knowledge of the union. *Total* union membership figures given later in this article are those published by the Bureau of Labor Statistics.[4]

OTHER ORGANIZATIONS OF WHITE-COLLAR EMPLOYEES

Mention should be made of certain types of occupational organizations whose membership consists of white-collar employees but that do not appear in Table 4. These include state and local public employee associations and professional associations.

A recent study of state public employee associations showed that they have nearly 400,000 members.[5] It may be surmised that a high proportion are in white-collar work. These associations, as organizations concerned with job interests of their members, appear to vary somewhat in their objectives, assumptions, policies, and methods. As far as can be determined from the evidence, they are not organized

    4 In its latest *Directory*, the BLS notes the possibilities for research arising out of the union financial reports required by the Landrum-Griffin Act and adds that it "hopes to explore the relationship between annual per capita receipts . . . and membership totals before its next survey" (p. 45).
    5 Joseph Krislov, "The Independent Public Employee Association: Characteristics and Functions," *Industrial and Labor Relations Review*, XV (July 1962), 510–20.

and operated in a manner comparable to trade unions. The same conclusion can probably be applied to the unknown number of local government employee associations.

Many or all of the members of professional associations such as the National Education Association, the American Association of University Professors, the American Nurses Association, or the National Society of Professional Engineers are salaried employees. In one way or another, such associations have become involved in the problems of earnings and employment conditions affecting their salaried employee members. Nevertheless, these organizations usually not only oppose unionism in their professional fields but also reject a policy of collective bargaining on their part with employers. A notable exception is the American Nurses Association whose "Economic Security" program is based on the attainment of collective bargaining for professional nurses.

WHITE-COLLAR MEMBERSHIP

The Union Potential

We estimate that there are currently 2.8 million white-collar union members (Table 4), comprising 15 per cent of the 18.6 million total union membership in national and international unions and unaffiliated local unions.[6] Taking national and international unions alone, the white-collar membership estimate is 2.7 million, which is 15 per cent of the 18.1 million total membership of these unions for 1960 as reported in the BLS *Directory*.[7] Turning now to the much smaller, unaffiliated local union sector, white-collar membership is estimated at 118,000, or one-fourth of the total membership (over 450,000) of this class of unions as reported in a recent study by the BLS.

As stated in the first section, white-collar groups make up an important part, 44 per cent, of the total union potential of 47 million persons in the United States work force. With a total of 17.5 million union members in the United States *alone* (after subtracting 1.1 million members of international unions who live outside the United States), the proportion of the over-all union potential that is organized is 37 per cent.

The proportion of the *white-collar* union potential who are union

---

[6] Bureau of Labor Statistics, *op. cit.*, p. 46. Included are 1.1 million members of international unions outside the United States, mainly in Canada.

[7] *Ibid.* Some 80,000 members of federal labor unions and local industrial unions affiliated with the AFL–CIO are included in this total.

members is much smaller, 13 per cent, or 2.7 million members out of a white-collar potential of 20.8 million.[8] In the blue-collar sector, over one-half, or 56 per cent, of its union potential is organized. The total *unorganized* union potential is 29.6 million, of which white-collar workers make up 61 per cent and blue-collar workers, 39 per cent.

Concentration and Classification—
National and International Unions

White-collar membership is concentrated in a number of larger unions, which is typical of the union movement generally. The seven unions with over 100,000 white-collar members each have about half (1.4 million) of the total number of organized white-collar workers. These unions are illustrative of the heterogeneity of the white-collar field. Six are white-collar (or predominantly white-collar) unions in the following fields—retail trade, musicians, railway clerks, telephone-industry office workers and telephone operators, post office clerks, and post office letter carriers. The seventh union (United Steel Workers) is an industrial union that has organized many office workers and plant clerical workers.

Most national or international unions with white-collar members are affiliated with the AFL–CIO. The only exceptions worth mentioning are the several independent organizations in the federal government field, the Independent Telephone Alliance, and the Teamsters.

Of the eighty-two national or international unions with some white-collar membership, thirty-nine are wholly or predominantly white-collar in character. These are unions in which 60 per cent or more of all members are white-collar workers. The remaining forty-three are manual or predominantly manual unions with some white-collar membership. Among large unions in the white-collar category with 60 to 70 per cent of their total membership white collar are: National Federation of Federal Employees, American Federation of Government Employees, Brotherhood of Railway Clerks, and Communications Workers of America. Other unions in the white-collar category are almost wholly white collar. The white-collar membership of the thirty-nine wholly or predominantly white-collar unions totals 2 million, about 75 per cent of the total number of white-collar unionists in the *Directory* unions.

8 The blue-collar and white-collar components were adjusted downward to account for Canadian membership by the same ratio as the total figure for national and international unions.

On the other hand, seventeen national unions, predominantly blue collar but with estimated white-collar memberships of 4,000 or more, have among them a total of about 670,000 white-collar members. Two of the unions classified here as predominantly blue collar are worth special notice because they are usually thought of as "white-collar" unions. One of these, the American Federation of State, County and Municipal Employees, appears to have a membership that is only 30 per cent white collar. The membership of the second union, the Retail, Wholesale, and Department Store Union, is estimated to be 45 per cent white collar. The important section of this union that is concentrated in New York City is predominantly white collar, but the reverse appears to be true outside of New York where the union has organized to a great extent in light manufacturing and the food-processing industries. These unions probably should be characterized as "mixed."

The United Steelworkers have the largest white-collar membership among manual unions. Of a total of 130,000 white-collar members, 45,000 are in salaried units and 85,000 in production and maintenance units. Ten other blue-collar unions have over 25,000 white-collar members. All told, these eleven unions had a total membership of over 7 million in 1960, of whom more than 600,000, or 9 per cent, are estimated to be white-collar workers.

Membership of Local, Unaffiliated Unions

Of the 2.8 million white-collar union members, 118,000 are in unaffiliated local or single-employer unions. The Bureau of Labor Statistics, in a 1961 survey of independent local unionism in nongovernmental areas, found that 113,000 out of 452,000 members in the local nonaffiliated unions were from white-collar occupations. These 113,000 white-collar members were in 375 local unions, of which 150 were between 90 and 100 per cent white-collar. An additional, 400 white-collar members are accounted for by local unions in the government sector.

Professional nurses, telephone operators and office workers, and engineers and scientists, each with about one-fifth of the total white-collar membership in unaffiliated local unions, comprise the most important occupational sectors in this white-collar union area (see Table 5). Only 11,000 of the 25,000 professional nurses, it should be noted, work in units with collective bargaining agreements. About 11,000 of the engineers and scientists are in sizable units at four West Coast aerospace companies—General Dynamics, Douglas, Boeing, and Lockheed.

TABLE 5

WHITE-COLLAR MEMBERSHIP IN UNAFFILIATED
LOCAL AND SINGLE-EMPLOYER UNIONS, 1961*

	White-Collar Members (000's)	Per Cent of Total White Collar
White-collar membership	118.4	100.0
Professional nurses†	25.0	21.1
Telephone employees†	22.6	19.1
Engineers and scientists‡	21.5	18.1

* Source: Cohany and Neary, *op. cit.*, Tables 1 and 4, which reports on a survey of local unions in the non-governmental sector and accounts for 113,000 of the above total. An additional 5,400 white-collar members of unaffiliated, local unions in the government sector have been added by the authors.
† Supplied by Bureau of Labor Statistics.
‡ Adapted from National Society of Professional Engineers, *op. cit.*

About two-thirds of the white-collar members of unaffiliated local and single-employer unions work in non-manufacturing and about 30 per cent in manufacturing. As already suggested, the largest concentrations are in the hospital and telephone fields. The largest single-firm independent union appears to be the Federation of Westinghouse Salaried Employees, with 16,000 members in fifty-one locals. Forty per cent of the membership are engineers and technical personnel while 60 per cent are clerical employees.

Occupational Distribution

The largest number of white-collar union members are in the clerical and kindred occupations, where 1.6 million are organized. This represents also the highest proportion of union potential organized in the major white-collar occupational fields—namely, 18 per cent of the clerical potential. In terms of the *total* white-collar membership of unions, 57 per cent of all white-collar union members are in clerical and kindred occupations; 21 per cent in professional and technical occupations; 18 per cent in sales occupations; and the remaining 4 per cent in supervisory positions. . . .The occupations included for various theoretical and practical reasons in our classification of "white collar" represent a rather broad continuum. Some are clearly more central while others are more peripheral to the concept of "white collar." The Census Bureau implies this, for example, in using the category "clerical and kindred" to cover the variety of occupations listed under that heading. Among those who might be considered "kindred" to the clerical field arc telephone operators, telegraphers, and letter carriers. A further distinction must be made regarding clerical workers themselves. Those employed in the central or separate offices of manufacturing and other industries, in insurance companies and banks, and in government offices are ordinarily accepted as being "office workers" and as being in the mainstream of the concept of "white collar." On the other hand, clerical workers such as postal clerks, many railway clerks, cashiers in restaurants, and various clerical workers inside factories and warehouses work in circumstances which place them somewhat on the fringes of the central idea of "office worker."

We estimate that as high as two out of three of the 1.6 million unionized "clerical and kindred" workers fall into *kindred and peripheral* occupations, whose work situations vary considerably from that of typical office employment and who are somewhat less white collar in character. This has important implications in viewing the status and prospects of white-collar unionism, since the "office worker" sector is of central significance, both numerically and conceptually, for the white-collar field.

The largest numbers of union members among "professional, technical, and kindred workers" are the musicians and entertainers. These are clearly professional people, yet because of historic reasons and rather special employment contexts, they have a somewhat less white-collar aspect about themselves than do other large professional groups such as engineers, scientists, and teachers. A similar situation is found in the retail sales field where, as indicated in the next section, a large part of existing unionization is in what may be termed a peripheral area.

A high degree of organization has been achieved by a limited number of specialized unions that cater to persons in numerically small yet distinctive occupations. Examples are airline pilots, railroad yardmasters, directors, writers, and newspaper reporters. These add substantially to the number of white-collar unions, though the combined membership is not large. Their existence reflects, in part, the variety of white-collar occupations (particularly in the professional and technical field), though many similar specialized occupations, such as social workers and librarians, do not have unions.

Industrial Distribution

The great proportion of white-collar union members are concentrated in six industries. Taken together they comprise 85 per cent of the total 2.8 million white-collar union membership. These are as follows: retail trade, post office, manufacturing, transportation, communications, and entertainment services. With the exception of manufacturing and post office, one or two unions account for the bulk of the membership in each of these industrial fields.

A major part of the unorganized union potential is to be found in a number of industrial fields where relatively few white-collar employees are unionized. The "other services" category, which includes professional, business and repair, and personal services, shows only 2 per cent unionized out of a total of over 3.3 million white-collar employees. Similarly, in the finance, insurance, and real estate fields, with 1.8 million salaried employees, less than 2 per cent are unionized. Finally, in the field of public education, only about 4 per cent of 2 million white-collar employees are union members.

Large unorganized numbers of white-collar workers are also to be found in two of the six industrial fields noted above which contained the bulk of white-collar unionization, namely, manufacturing and retail trade. In the remaining four of the six industrial fields—transportation, communications, entertainment, and postal service—the proportion organized runs quite high. The abnormally high total for union membership in the entertainment field derives in part from the fact that many union card-holders among musicians and actors work at these occupations on a part-time and supplementary basis and are listed in the Census under another occupational heading. Also many performers hold memberships in more than one of the entertainment unions.

UNION ORGANIZING PATTERNS IN WHITE-COLLAR OCCUPATIONAL-INDUSTRIAL FIELDS

. . . Approximately 5.4 million of the 9.1 million clerical and kindred workers in the 1960 union potential are "office workers" as contrasted with peripheral and kindred groups such as railroad clerks, letter carriers, telephone operators, clerical workers in plants and warehouses, and the like, who account for the remaining 3.7 million. Of the 5.4 million office workers, about 70 per cent, or 3.8 million, are estimated to be located in urbanized areas (central cities and their fringes). A major part of the office workers in urbanized areas are concentrated in central business districts or outlying business or manufacturing districts.

Office workers are the largest of the white-collar groups and represent perhaps the most widely accepted image of the white-collar employee. It is interesting to note, therefore, that the number organized is probably no more than 500,000, less than 10 per cent of the total. There is little apparent concentration of organization, whether by union, by geographical location (such as the central business district of a large city), or by industry. The union with the primary jurisdiction in the field, the Office Employees International Union, had only 65,000 members in early 1962. A more substantial segment is held by a number of industrial unions in manufacturing fields and by unions in the telephone industry. In important fields such as finance, insurance, and real estate (with some 1.2 million office employees in 1960), there has been little organization of office workers by any union. The unions operating in the government field (not including post office) are estimated to have less than one-sixth of government office employees in their ranks.

In the peripheral and kindred groups, the several postal unions have a high degree of organization of the clerical workers in post offices. The same is true for unions among railway clerks, railway telegraphers, and commercial telegraphers. There is substantial organization of telephone operators. Industrial unions have organized some significant numbers (though not large proportions) of plant clerical workers. The retail unions and the Teamsters have organized small sections of the clerical employees in stores, warehouses, and mail-order houses. All told, the peripheral and kindred group account for about two-thirds (or about 1.1 million) of the total union membership among the 9.1 million clerical and kindred workers.

Professional, Technical, and Kindred Workers

Professional workers in the entertainment services are highly organized, and there is substantial unionization in the smaller fields comprised of reporters, air pilots, and technicians in radio communication. Important unionization efforts exist in two large fields, engineers and scientists and schoolteachers, but on a scale that is small compared to the size of these fields. There is limited organizing activity in the professional nursing field. Beyond this, there are a variety of professional or technical occupations, mostly of medium or small size, for which there is no union whose major jurisdiction is in the field, though one or more unions may organize some of the members of the occupation.

Unionization of engineers and scientists by the American Federation of Technical Engineers (AFTE), which has the AFL–CIO jurisdiction among engineers, is negligible. In 1960, there were over 1 million engineers and scientists, of whom some 850,000 were in private employment. Of those in private employment, 70 per cent were in manufacturing, with concentrations in electrical equipment, aerospace and ordinance, and chemicals. A good part of the small membership of the AFTE is at subprofessional levels and is in the state and local government, construction and railroad fields. The largest share of organization among engineers and scientists is that held by the local, non-affiliated unions, with the major concentration of these in the West Coast aerospace industry. Some of the large industrial unions affiliated with the AFL–CIO have sought to organize engineers and scientists in their respective jurisdictions but with limited results so far.

Out of a total of 1.8 million schoolteachers in 1961, almost 1.5 million worked in public elementary and secondary schools in 31,700 school districts. An estimated 600,000 of the public school teachers are concentrated in 800 to 900 school districts in cities of about 25,000 or more population. The American Federation of Teachers (AFT), the chief union in this large occupation, had a membership of 70,000 in early 1962.

Though the jurisdiction is vast, the future extension of unionism among teachers will be decisively influenced by the headway the AFT is able to make in a small number of large city school systems. A high proportion of AFT membership has historically been concentrated in the large northern and western cities, but most of these locals have not been able to win a majority of teachers as members. While the union has gained steadily during the post–World War II years, its progress has been slow despite the favorable climate for new organization provided by inflationary pressures and demand-and-supply conditions. However, the winning of collective bargaining rights for the 40,000 teachers in the New York City schools following a brief strike in 1961 may provide a new impetus for AFT growth.

The new fluidity in teacher unionization arising from the possibility that other school boards may be persuaded to grant collective bargaining may also affect the policies and tactics of the AFT's traditional rival, the National Educational Assocation. The NEA, by vigorously advocating the doctrine that teacher unionism is unprofessional, has been a major force in limiting the progress of the AFT. But with the growing likelihood of the spread of collective representation and negotiations, the role of the NEA and its state affiliates may undergo significant change in the coming years. It appears likely that the NEA, while still eschewing unionism, will strive to develop approaches that it can describe as "professional" and that will enable it to establish itself as the representative of teachers in negotiating salaries and working conditions with school boards.[9]

Sales Workers

Of the total union potential of 4 million in the sales occupations, 2.6 million, or 65 per cent, are retail sales workers. The largest single retail group, totaling 0.5 million, are in the food lines, while the remaining 2.1 million are in the various other retail merchandise lines. Some 1.4 million sales workers are in non-retail fields, such as insurance, advertising, or selling at the wholesale and manufacturing levels.

The major base of sales-worker unionization is in the retail sector. The Retail Clerks, by far the strongest union in the retail field, has about half its strength among food supermarkets and the other half among the other retail lines. The much smaller holdings of the Retail, Wholesale and Department Store Union include department stores and specialty lines such as shoe and drug stores, mainly in New York City. In some sectors the Meat Cutters have extended their organization to the grocery departments of supermarkets, while the Clothing Workers have some retail strength in men's clothing stores and, more recently, in discount stores. The Teamsters have established something of a foothold through their organization of a large part of Montgomery Ward.

As with other major white-collar fields, such as office employees or schoolteachers, the focus of organization has been in the urban areas and large cities. Points of concentration are food chains, mail order chains, large department stores and department store chains, and chain systems in other retail lines. On a geographic basis, the downtown shopping districts of large cities, neighborhood shopping districts, and suburban shopping centers offer concentration of retail salespeople. Most organization is along trade lines within a particular city or larger region.

The organization of retail sales personnel has moved forward steadily as indicated by the approximate doubling in membership since 1949 of the leading union in the field, the Retail Clerks. However, the greater part of the jurisdiction still remains unorganized. Progress in the last decade has been slow among department stores, a sector of both numerical and strategic importance. A little under one-

[9] See, e.g., *Addresses and Proceedings,* 100th Annual Meeting, July 1–6, 1962 (Washington, D.C.: National Education Association, 1962), pp. 46–52, 142–50, and 174–84; Martha Ware, *Professional Negotiation* (Washington, D.C.: Urban Project, National Education Association, 1962).

half of white-collar retail union membership consists of supermarket employees. From the standpoint of the amount of salesmanship required by grocery sales clerks in supermarkets, these employees can best be viewed as a peripheral white-collar group.

Organization among wholesale salesmen is minor and is practically nonexistent in other sales lines such as manufacturing salesmen, real estate agents, or advertising salesmen. In the insurance field, there is strong organization among only one category of insurance agent, the sellers of industrial insurance.

Supervisory Employees

The notion of unionism among first line supervisors or even high management levels has made much less headway in the United States than in some western European countries. The wave of foremen unionism in manufacturing that appeared with amazing suddenness during World War II seems to have died out, leaving but little residue of organization. Certain categories in rail, air, and water transportation that are classified as supervisory are strongly organized. In the post office, supervisors and postmasters, respectively, have national organizations, both of them non-affiliated.

SOME IMPLICATIONS FOR FURTHER EXPANSION AND FUTURE CHARACTER

The data and discussion have brought out major structural characteristics of present-day white-collar unionism. Though strong in a few fields, unionization of white-collar employees on an over-all basis has made small headway in major sections of this vast, sprawling potential. The strongly organized fields and the large white-collar unions tend to be found in the peripheral instead of the core white-collar fields. Many blue-collar unions have some white-collar members, and a number of these unions are relatively important contenders in key, though still lightly organized, white-collar fields.

Thus, while a union foothold of some significance has developed among the white-collar occupations, it nevertheless represents an uncertain point of departure for what is perhaps the greatest challenge before the American labor movement—the organization of the growing white-collar potential. Four key occupational groups stand out in considering the prospects for union growth in this potential—office workers, engineers and scientists, retail sales employees, and schoolteachers. Together these comprise about one-half of the total white-collar union potential.

The bearing of union structure or pattern on the chances for further unionization is a factor of considerable importance for two of these areas, office workers and engineers and scientists, but is of less importance among retail sales employees and schoolteachers, where union organization is likely to be mainly by white-collar unions. In these two fields occupation and industry coincide and the respective white-collar occupations are the dominant ones in their industries. In contrast, office workers and engineers and scientists are cross-industry occupations and thus are exposed to multi-union organization. Possible alternative union structures exist, the main contrasting forms being that of occupational (craft) unionism, on the one hand, and inclusion of the white-collar occupations in industrial unions, on the other. The question is: *What implications do these (and other) structural patterns hold for the chances of union expansion in the office and professional-technical worker fields?*

In discussing this question particular attention will be given to the relationship between structure and the subjective attitudes that white-collar people have toward unionism. Their outlook on unionism may be viewed as the most pervasive factor characterizing the heterogeneous occupations included under the designation "white collar." A number of elements enter into the making of a common attitude toward unionism by white-collar workers, such as: (1) occupational origins substantially different from blue-collar groups, (2) a tradition of being apart from, and of higher status than, blue-collar workers, and (3) a relatively strong reluctance among white-collar employees (though with certain exceptions) to adopt collective action based on a concept of conflict of interest with employers. Thus, their subjective attitude toward trade unionism may be subsumed under the rubric "non-union tradition." Existence of the non-union tradition may influence decisions about the structure of union organization to the extent that structure is believed to affect, one way or another, the subjective outlook of white-collar people. For example, is a particular structural pattern likely to reinforce the non-union tradition among white-collar workers? Or is it likely to leave this outlook unaffected? Or might it aid in weakening the non-union tradition, thus allowing a greater acceptance of the notion of unionism?

It is somewhat hazardous to assess the significance of alternative structural patterns of unionism, including those in existence today, on possible white-collar expansion in the future. One reason is that the larger part of the central white-collar occupations are unorganized and there is no compelling evidence to indicate that they ever will be organized. Indeed, some might hold that the most realistic prediction is negligible further growth of white-collar unionism, no matter what the structure or pattern.

Alternative Union Structures

Office employee unionization.—The major concentrations of office workers are in the business districts of the large cities. The test of office unionism, therefore, is its capacity to create a technique of business district organization and to achieve a breakthrough in one or more large cities that would generate a favorable orientation toward unionism among office workers in other cities.

The current structure of unionization among office workers, as noted in the previous section, is dominated by a number of industrial unions. The Office Employees International Union, the union with the formal jurisdiction for office workers, has only a toehold in this vast field. Its protests over infringements of its jurisdiction by other unions have been ignored. The OEIU approach consists of an opportunism dictated by its general lack of resources—namely, the pursuit of organizing leads in widely scattered locations.

If the present pattern for unionizing office workers were to be projected into a major business district, we would have a welter of unions—blue-collar, non-office white-collar, and the OEIU—all striving in an unco-ordinated and often competitive fashion to unionize the area. They would face determined and experienced employer resistance, with very little likelihood of any appreciable support by the unorganized office employees themselves. Thus present union structure offers little basis for headway in the decisive areas of office employee concentration.

Two other possible structural patterns of office unionization are worth discussing. The first is a co-ordinated multi-union approach which is a variant of the present pattern. The second is the "pure" occupational structural form, fully developed in terms of recognition and support in the union movement.

Under the co-ordinated multi-union pattern, those unions with established interests in office employees would have to agree on jurisdiction and methods of organization. The major jurisdictional settlement would undoubtedly require acknowledgment by the OEIU of the established interests of a large number of blue-collar and white-collar unions in office employees. The OEIU would, in effect, be compelled to accept the residual of industries in which other unions did not operate—such as banking, brokerage and exchanges, real estate offices, various other business services, and miscellaneous offices.

Several strengths of a combined approach could be cited. The resources of numerous unions, including the stronger industrial unions, would be brought to bear in a decisive area of white-collar potential—the office workers. If the orientation and identification of office workers primarily follow company and industrial lines, the co-ordinated union approach might allow for the most natural lines of union organization. Moreover, advantage could often be taken of existing collective bargaining relationships with blue-collar workers. Further, the impression of strength conveyed to office workers by the combination of unions would provide the maximum possible reinforcement of the union appeal. The OEIU, too weak to undertake a major campaign by itself, could benefit from the combination of such resources. Its residual jurisdiction would still be a substantial one, and it would be able to organize more office employees than it ever could by itself.

Criticism of the co-ordinated multi-union approach, as stated by advocates of the "pure" occupational strategy, would include the claims that the unions would not work well together over an adequate period of time, that recurrent strife or public unpopularity affecting one or more of the participating unions would disrupt the over-all organizing effort, and that blue-collar unions do not have the personnel or experience to work effectively in downtown business districts. Perhaps the most basic criticism would be that the combined campaign of many unions would present a confusing, blurred, and still alien image of unionism to office employees, an image not likely to induce a change in attitudes favorable toward unionism.

An occupational union, it might be argued, could make a much stronger appeal to the office employees in the business district. It could more effectively take advantage of their concentration in the business district to stimulate interaction among them and to create a community of interest around economic and career issues. Such a union might be better able to conduct an effective campaign. It would understand the need for a consistent effort and appeal over a long period of time, for the buildup of knowledge and a network of relationships, and for the careful cultivation of a positive image of office unionism. An occupational union, moreover, could get favorable attention and acceptance by office workers on the basis of legitimate identification with their interests. It could involve itself naturally and responsibly in their affairs and speak and act authoritatively as their representative.

Since office worker unionism has the grim task of proceeding from city to city, another important consideration is the possible effects on the attitudes of office employees in other cities of success achieved in any one city. The occupational proponents would argue that there would be a more effective countering of the non-union tradition in other cities if the initial union breakthrough were achieved by a distinctive occupational organization than if it were achieved through the more blurred and alien image of a multi-union approach. If successful, the occupational approach could result in an office employee union of formidable size, with its organization strength stemming from the business heartlands of many important American cities.

The case for the co-ordinated, multi-union approach can, of course, be applied against the validity of the "pure" occupational organizing pattern just described. Moreover, an effective occupational approach would require acknowledgment by the union movement of the pre-eminent jurisdiction of the OEIU and contribution to it of considerable resources. Satisfaction of these conditions (or, for that matter, of the conditions for the combined union pattern) would represent an unusual degree of unity for the present union movement. Finally, even if organized labor rallied behind whatever it felt to be the best structure, there is no certainty in the foreseeable future that the formidable resistances to office unionization which exist in the business districts of our major cities would be overcome.

Unionization of engineers and scientists.—The strategic concentrations that define the organization task among the engineers and scientists are primarily in large companies and a number of industries. Geographic distribution is of lesser importance, with the possible exception of the concentration of the aerospace industry on the West Coast.

Local, independent unions with about 21,000 members are the dominant factor in the current pattern of unionism among engineers and scientists. Many of these were once members of a loose federation, the Engineers and Scientists of America (ESA). This organization went out of existence at the end of 1960, following a factional split in 1957 and reverses encountered by important member units. Industrial unions such as the International Union of Electrical Workers and the United Auto Workers have shown a continuing interest in professional technical workers in their industries but have been unable to organize more than a few thousand. The American Federation of Technical Engineers, the AFL–CIO union whose formal jurisdiction covers professional engineers (and subprofessional technical categories), is a small union whose membership is primarily comprised of technicians.[10] All told, unionization among engineers and scientists is no more than 2.5–3.0 per cent of the potential.

A projection of the present structure of unionization of engineers and scientists into a future possible expansion in this field would show the following: (1) substantial numbers of engineers and scientists organized as members of local, independent unions, (2) some, but still small, gains by industrial unions in their respective industries, and (3) a relatively insignificant group in the AFTE. This is hardly a very convincing picture of expansion, since it implies an indefinite, spontaneous increase of local, independent unions without any effort to federate and without any help from a central body.

There are three other structural possibilities worth discussing, namely, a new independent national union, a new national union for engineers and scientists within the AFL–CIO and new organizing thrusts by industrial unions. The first of these, a new independent national union to federate local, independent unions, might be successful with a more experienced and unified leadership than that of the late ESA. Conceivably it could take advantage of any opportunity to achieve a somewhat stronger base for engineering unionism. Any such initial breakthrough might then set in motion changes in attitudes and the organizing dynamics that would bring other concentrations of engineers and scientists into its fold. Where the required resources would come from to support such an organization or whether any favorable and decisive organizing opportunity would ever appear remain unanswered questions.

A second structural alternative is a new national union within the AFL–CIO having jurisdiction over professional engineers and scientists and based on the existing, non-affiliated, local unions. To become a reality, jurisdictional accommodation would have to be obtained from both the industrial unions, and the AFTE and the non-affiliated unions would have to be persuaded to join. This structure would require, therefore, a considerable realignment within the AFL–CIO and among the independents. Its advantages would include the formation of a national organization; the co-operation of the industrial unions; and the availability of substantial resources (on the presumption that this would be part of the over-all arrangements). On the basis of the rather impressive record of rejection by engineers and scientists of affiliation with the regular labor movement, the for-

---

[10] Unions in the federal, state, and local government fields also have organized some engineers and scientists.

mation of a new union might have a negligible or even a negative effect on the attitudes of the professional people. From the AFL–CIO standpoint, however, such a structure would represent its strongest possible bid to engineers and scientists.

The third possible pattern is organization by industrial unions of substantial numbers of engineers and scientists in their jurisdictions as a result of more intensive organizing effort. Presumably, the professional technical workers would take their places within these unions in separate departments and separate locals, following the structural practices inaugurated in recent years. As already noted, the recent experience of unions such as the IUE and UAW has not indicated that engineers and scientists would join with their manual or even with their lower level white-collar fellow employees in industrial unions. Yet the possibility of some future change in the situation must not be entirely ruled out, given the resources of the large unions and their growing interest in engineers and scientists. It should also be noted that, on the basis of the experience of the 1940's, the actual effect of a strong industrial union campaign might be to galvanize a new movement toward either local, non-affiliated unions or a national non-affiliated union.

To summarize, the current pattern of unionization among professional technical employees does not seem to satisfy the structural requirements for organizing the unorganized potential. Other structural forms, which might be more effective, are not likely to come into being in the near future, given the conditions that must be satisfied for their formation. By and large, if unionization of engineers and scientists should expand to substantial proportions, the probabilities are that the expansion will be through an occupational union rather than through inclusion in primarily blue-collar industrial unions. The latter would seem less likely because of the fact that the occupational images and ties of engineers and scientists are comparatively strong and extend beyond the company and industry of employment. While this observation supports the probability of occupational as against industrial unionism, it also raises doubts about the possibility of any substantial increase of unionization at all. The occupational images of professional technical employees are bound up with the concept of professionalism and with the existence of strong, anti-union professional associations. The National Society of Professional Engineers, in particular, has developed an effective, comprehensive program for counteracting unionism.[11]

11 For a report on the NSPE program and philosophy, as well as an account of engineering unionism, see its recent study, *The Engineer in Industry in the 1960's* (Washington: National Society of Professional Engineers, 1961).

Perspective on Structure in the Two Key Fields

We have analyzed structure as an important (though by itself far from a sufficient) condition for union growth. A major conclusion from our analysis in two key white-collar fields is that the structural patterns emerging at this stage of white-collar unionism do not appear to be geared to the structural requirements for future union growth. At the same time, it would seem to be very difficult for the unions concerned to take the required steps to shift to new and perhaps more effective structural patterns, nor is there agreement on the best alternative pattern.

Our analysis also included references to the bearing of structure on subjective views about unionism among white-collar people. With respect to engineers and scientists, it would appear that if unions are to make headway with this group, the structural forms that are adopted must in some way satisfy this group's strong professional identification. The problem with respect to office workers is more difficult to define. Office workers, it seems clear, generally reflect the non-union tradition. It is not so evident, however, that they possess images and ties that bind them together and provide a basis for any kind of group action along occupational lines. The task, then, of union leadership might be defined as that of supplanting a relatively weak and diffuse occupational consciousness with a stronger one, one which involves a sense of being a group with a responsible role in helping to shape its own destiny in society. One major difficulty in viewing this task is to determine along what union structural lines occupational consciousness can be most naturally developed.

PART III

UNION DEMOCRACY

INTRODUCTION

One of the principal objectives of unions has been to introduce democratic practice into industry. Traditionally, they have also professed to aim at being democratic in their internal government. Nevertheless, many national unions have been subject more to dictatorial than to democratic control, and doubts have been expressed by scholars as to whether democracy is a practical goal for effective union government.

The authors of the three articles that follow express somewhat differing views on the desirability and practicability of union democracy. Also, they seem to favor different tests for the existence of democratic government in unions.

Seidman thinks that national unions have tended to sacrifice democracy too much for internal discipline and, writing in 1958, he favored action by government and the labor movement to strengthen democratic procedures and controls in unions. That ostensibly was the main objective of the Landrum-Griffin Act of 1959. It had been argued that the Federal Government under the Taft-Hartley Act certifies a union as the sole bargaining agent with which the employer must deal exclusively; and therefore, the Government has an obligation to see to it that a union given such a monopoly of bargaining rights is subject to democratic checks and procedures.

On the other hand, Stein maintains that effective collective bargaining requires leadership authority to act and that the usual forms of democracy do not seem very appropriate for large unions dealing with complex and technical issues. Therefore, visions of a really workable union democracy "are doomed to disappointment." Stein explains that the more responsive a labor leader is to rank-and-file sentiment, the less will he pursue "statesmanlike goals" in the interest of the general public. Only an entrenched leadership enjoying some dictatorial powers can be sufficiently independent to take an enlightened and long-range view not confined to the direct interest of a majority of the membership.

It has frequently been assumed that the building trades unions are rather undemocratic because the power to call strikes and to allocate employment is concentrated in the hands of a business agent. However, Strauss points out that a business agent generally is responsive to the members' demands and that there are many pressures and checks on his actions. One should not judge union democracy just by actions at union meetings. As Strauss explains, expression of members' views on the job or informally on other occasions may be an effective means of democratic participation in union policy determination. Form may be less significant than informal communication.

Strauss indicates that management may also influence the degree of dictatorship or democracy in the union with which it deals. Managements are often ambivalent as to whether they prefer democratic or undemocratic control of the union. While theoretically they may favor full control by the membership, as a practical matter they may prefer well-disciplined, "responsible" unions with a strong leadership in control. A management can make a "deal" with such a union without fear that it will be upset by shifts in rank-and-file sentiment.

In their analyses, the three authors raise questions concerning the basis for determining how democratic unions are or should be. A standard or test that can be used to distinguish between democratic and dictatorial control may be difficult to devise and apply, as the articles on the UAW and the ILGWU in the preceding section indicate. The authors recognize that the criterion or test may vary with the size of a local union and may be different for national unions than for locals. Small units can have more direct membership participation than large ones, which must rely more heavily on elected representatives and delegates.

Among the possible criteria for judging the existence of union democracy are: (1) regular rank-and-file participation in policy-making at meetings of the union; (2) direct and indirect control by the rank-and-file over vital decisions of the union on special occasions; (3) reliance on officials to run the union but with adequate membership checks on their actions; (4) leadership control that is responsive to membership demands as expressed formally and informally; (5) leadership control based on what the leadership presumes are the desires of the membership.

There are varying degrees of union democracy and various means of achieving it. Political democracy, we assume, requires for its proper functioning at least the following: (a) open and honest elections to assure majority representation; (b) a free press to provide sufficient information and critical comment for the voters to form intelligent opinions; and (c) an independent judiciary to protect individual and minority rights from arbitrary or improper executive or legislative action; and (d) the existence of a genuine two-party or multi-party system.

Unions generally lack two-party competition and an independent judiciary in their systems of internal government. The union press is usually the organ of the administration, financed by the union with the editor serving at the pleasure of the executive.

How much would union democracy be improved by an independent judiciary along the lines of the Public Review Board of the UAW? How much by a free and independently operated union press? A two-party system? And how much would each of those measures serve to reduce the effectiveness of a union as a collective bargaining agency that may need to call and pursue strikes to a successful conclusion?

With respect to open and honest elections, the Landrum-Griffin Act of 1959 requires standards for unions that are more strict than those for public office. This act was passed amid great debate concerning exactly how democratic large unions can and should be and how much union democracy can be promoted by Federal law. That debate still continues. The act was designed to promote democratic procedures in the conduct of union affairs. Its other aims include safeguarding the individual rights of union members under a "bill of rights," assurance of honest handling of union funds, and protections against unwarranted use by union administrations of the trusteeship or receivership device which suspends democratic procedures. Enforcement is largely by the Secretary of Labor who, upon complaint, investigates and arranges for prosecution of apparent violations, with ultimate determination, of course, by the Federal courts.

Some Requirements for Union Democracy

JOEL SEIDMAN

What concept of democracy is appropriate in a trade-union context? If it means the determination of policy directly by a rank-and-file majority, democracy is to be found only in small local unions; various types of authority must be entrusted to officers in large organizations and it is rare for the majority to participate actively, except during crises or when the organization is new. If the test of democracy is the power of the rank and file to control vital decisions either directly or else through the election of officers, then most local unions in this country are democratic and most national unions are not, for reasons that will be discussed later. If, however, the definition of democracy is responsiveness by the leaders to the presumed desires of the membership, then most unions are democratic, at the national as well as the local level. If membership approval of leader performance is the test of democracy, the United Mine Workers are democratic, although the key officers of two-thirds of the districts have long been appointed by Lewis and are subject to removal at his will.[1]

At the other extreme is the International Typographical Union, which has had a well-developed two-party system for the past half century. Here the internal political system resembles that to which we are accustomed in our national political life: permanent parties, regular contests, opportunity for the electorate to become acquainted with opposing platforms, and recognition on the part of all that opposition

Taken from American Economic Review, *XLVII* (*May 1958 Proceedings Number*), *pp. 35–43. Reprinted with the permission of the author and the publisher. Joel Seidman is Professor of Industrial Relations at the University of Chicago.*

1 [In 1964 the Justice Department, on behalf of the Secretary of Labor, brought suit against the United Mine Workers, charging that six of its districts are being managed as trusteeships in violation of the Landrum-Griffin Act of 1959. *Ed.*]

is legitimate.[2] If these are considered the conditions of union democracy, however, only one national union in this country is democratic. Some hold that democracy in unions is secondary to considerations of efficiency or discipline. John L. Lewis, for example, has denied that the issue of district autonomy in the UMW involved a fundamental principle, asserting that the question was one of business expediency and administrative policy.[3] A somewhat related view, emphasizing fighting ability as exhibited in strikes as vital to collective bargaining success, places primary reliance on strong leadership and discipline. Here the psychology is much like that of a nation at war, fearful lest internal division give an advantage to the enemy. To those holding such views, union democracy, which emphasizes the issues upon which union members disagree, is a weakening influence. It is thirty years since A. J. Muste called attention to the dual nature of the trade-union, which tried to combine the social structure of the town meeting with that of the army.[4] Which is the more important objective: democracy with its recognition of internal differences or discipline at the price of enforced internal unity?

It is even asserted that considerations of democracy are irrelevant in an appraisal of the labor movement. To the British writer V. L. Allen, for example, a union is a service organization created to perform collective bargaining and related functions; not interested in self-government, workers cast their effective votes by joining a union and paying dues or by dropping their membership, thereby putting an unsatisfactory union out of business. Yet Allen points out that this view is possible only where freedom of movement in or out of a union exists; therefore it is not applicable where union security clauses, as in this country, are in widespread use.[5]

My own feeling is that national unions have tended to err on the side of discipline, sacrificing far more in the way of democracy than is desirable. It must be granted, however, that some discipline is necessary to permit effective functioning; that unrestrained democracy borders on anarchy, just as excessive discipline results in dictatorship;

2 For an able analysis of the two-party system within the ITU and the factors that made it possible, see Seymour Martin Lipset, Martin A. Trow, and James S. Coleman, *Union Democracy: The Internal Politics of the International Typographical Union* (Glencoe, Ill.: The Free Press, 1956).

3 See, for example, *Proceedings of the Thirty-fourth Constitutional Convention of the United Mine Workers of America*, 1936, p. 122. See also the discussion in Bernard Karsh and Jack London, "The Coal Miners: A Study of Union Control," *Quarterly Journal of Economics*, LXVIII (August 1954), pp. 415–36.

4 A. J. Muste, "Factional Fights in Trade Unions," in J. B. S. Hardman, editor, *American Labor Dynamics* (New York: Harcourt, Brace, 1928), pp. 332–33.

5 V. L. Allen, *Power in Trade Unions* (London: Longmans, Green, 1954), pp. 10–11, 15.

and that there is a border area where the values of discipline, efficiency of administration, or collective bargaining effectiveness appear to conflict with democracy. I would suspect, however, that the conflict is more often apparent than real, in that a democratic organization has resources of membership loyalty vital to its survival. Yet in some cases it may be true that factionalism has weakened union bargaining effectiveness; where this happens it is part of the price paid for democracy.

Granted that authority must be vested in leaders if contracts are to be negotiated and union affairs administered, democracy is achieved if the members can make their will felt, if they can replace the leaders and change the policies that they dislike. Their ability to do this, however, is diminished by the low level of membership participation found in most local unions.[6]

In all of this, the position of the union leader is an interesting one. He has a vested interest in preferring discipline to democracy, in order to ensure his own tenure of office. Yet his reputation as a labor leader in his own union, as elsewhere, depends largely upon his ability to match, if not exceed, the collective bargaining gains obtained by rival unions. If he fails in this, his own members will become dissatisfied and are likely to support an opposition candidate or become an easy prey to rival unions, while his organizers can expect little success in enrolling new members. His own interests, therefore, drive him in the direction of wage and related gains for his members—most of whom are likely to care far more for such advances than for the exercise of abstract democratic rights.

It should be noted that union posts vary enormously in their appeal, with their material benefits as well as psychological rewards increasing as one mounts the scale. At the local level, the unpaid posts of steward may be difficult to fill, because of the unrewarding nature of the steward's duties, combined with the lack of compensation. At the level of the local-wide officers, headed by the president, the prestige and power that go with the office make the posts attractive, even where no money or only a nominal sum is involved. Such unpaid jobs, however, tend to turn over frequently even where there is widespread satisfaction with the incumbent. The duties crowd into

---

6 Most studies have shown union meeting attendance at rather low levels. Sayles and Strauss, for example, found attendance usually ranging between 2 and 6 per cent in a group of industrial locals of medium size. Leonard R. Sayles and George Strauss, *The Local Union: Its Place in the Industrial Plant* (New York: Harper, 1953), p. 173. A recent estimate places typical branch (local union) attendance in Britain between 3 and 15 per cent, with a heavy concentration between 4 and 7. B. C. Roberts, *Trade Union Government and Administration in Great Britain* (Cambridge: Harvard University Press, 1956), p. 95.

his spare time, disrupt his family life, and after a time he usually prefers to leave both the prestige and the headaches of the office to someone else.

The situation of the full-time, paid local union officer is entirely different. He does not superimpose additional duties on a working day in the plant or at the trade. Instead, he leads an entirely different style of life; he dresses in a business suit, works at a desk like any other executive, and enjoys a larger income than he could earn in the shop. It rarely, if ever, happens that one gives up all these advantages voluntarily to return to the trade. These rewards, both in economic and psychological terms, are enormously increased as one moves up to the important jobs at the national union level. Measured by any test—salary, economic power, political influence, or publicity—the heads of the important national unions are part of the power elite of the nation. Only men with great personal drive are likely to win their way to such posts, and only rarely does one relinquish his office voluntarily. The question, rather, is why so few aspirants contest for such desirable posts, why the heads of important unions tend to be re-elected for successive terms without opposition.[7]

The political advantages of the holder of union office may be divided into three groups: (1) control over channels of communication, (2) opportunity to build a political machine, and (3) elements of power over the rank and file. In a small local union the incumbent has little advantage in terms of communication. The larger the local, however, the greater advantage he enjoys over any challenger. Particularly is this true where members work on scattered jobs, as in building or many service industries. Here the business agent is known to all on the jobs he services and forms the communications link between the member and the organization.

In the national union, however, these advantages are vastly increased. The publicity that an important national head receives in the daily press, the union journal that functions as a press organ for him, the flow of communications in his name to all the local unions, the spotlight that plays on him at the national convention, the expense account that permits him to visit locals throughout the country—all these are political advantages of the first order, impossible of matching by a rival candidate. Best of all, these activities, so vital to a re election campaign, are carried on throughout his term of office and at the union's expense.

7 See Chap. 2, "Opposition in Union Elections," in Philip Taft, *The Structure and Government of Labor Unions* (Cambridge: Harvard University Press, 1954), pp. 35–64.

An opposition candidate, in contrast, needs large sums of money just to bring his name and program to the attention of the membership. It is a rare union, such as the International Typographical Union, that allots him space in its paper for this purpose. One would never have known, by reading the pre-election issue of *Steel Labor*, that Donald C. Rarick was opposing David J. McDonald for the presidency of the United Steelworkers in the February, 1957, election. In many unions, moreover, constitutional provisions hamper an opposition campaign. The constitution of the United Mine Workers punishes the circulation or the reading of a statement that wrongfully condemns the decision of an officer and outlaws the contribution of funds to promote candidacy for office. In other unions, such as the Railroad Trainmen, the permission of the international president is required before a circular may be sent generally throughout the union. At the extreme, an opposition caucus may be outlawed as a dual union.

Supplementing his control over communication is the power of the union head to build a political machine. The head of a small local union has few favors at his disposal, other than his support to a candidate for lesser office or committee or other appointments that confer limited prestige. If the local is large enough to support several paid officers, these become political plums worth striving for. The question there is whether the head of the organization has enough influence with the membership to carry to election those whom he puts upon his slate. It is highly unlikely that an independent candidate will outvote any of the business agents and other officers who run as a slate for re-election; and the ambitious member is more likely to bide his time, support the incumbent group, and hope for a place on the slate when a vacancy occurs.

The head of a large national union, of course, typically has dozens of desirable positions, most of them appointive, around which a political machine can be built. Posts of organizer or international union representative, usually at the disposal of the union president or under his effective control, can be used to reward supporters or to placate ambitious men heading large locals who might otherwise seek high elective office. If the international vice-presidents or general executive board members are elected by majority vote of the convention rather than by a caucus of delegates from the area each serves, then the head of the union who enjoys the support of most of the delegates may control the entire election, insuring the success of each candidate given a place on his slate. Ambitious men therefore tend to wait their turn for administration support, meanwhile showing their faithfulness and value to the head and building up popular support in their own right so that they will bring strength to the administration slate.

Executive board members may be dependent upon the officers in other ways. In the United Mine Workers, as earlier observed, a majority of the board members were appointed by Lewis and hold office at his pleasure. In the Amalgamated Meat Cutters and Butcher Workmen, executive board members, by virtue of their election to that office, do not draw salaries from the national union office. They may, however, be assigned to duties for the International by the executive officers, who then fix their compensation. Between conventions the general executive board, in theory, serves as a check upon the power of the officers. Obviously its members cannot serve this function if they are dependent upon the leading officer for their jobs or their salaries.

The more desirable the union post, the more effective it is as a reward for political support and, by the same token, the more its threatened loss is an effective punishment. Here the crucial factor is the desirability of the union post in financial as well as psychological terms, as compared with working at the trade. In professional and some white-collar occupations, where work is interesting, fairly well paid, and of prestige value in the community, the union job is of no great value and its loss is relatively unimportant. In the skilled trades, except for the printers, the difference both in terms of pay and prestige is greater, and consequently the union job is the foundation of the political machine. In less skilled work it is even more effective; it is very rare for the factory worker who loses his union post to return to his old occupation. The result is not only that the political machine is built and kept intact but that the former official is not back in the plant and in the union to provide experienced leadership to an opposition group.

In addition to all these advantages, the union head often possesses power over rank-and-file members that may be used to crush dissent. Every union needs to establish and enforce appropriate rules of behavior for members; employers, indeed, would insist upon this before entering into collective bargaining relations. The most careful students of the problem have shown that this power is not generally abused;[8] they have also shown, however, that the machinery is faulty,

---

[8] Clyde Summers, "Disciplinary Powers of Unions," *Industrial and Labor Relations Review* (July 1950), pp. 483–513, and "Disciplinary Procedures of Unions," *Ind. and Labor Rela. Review* (October 1950), pp. 15–32; Chapter 4, "Discipline and Appeals in Labor Unions," in Taft, *op. cit.*, pp. 117–80.

precisely at the point where the political process within the union is involved.

The chief weaknesses of the judicial process from this point of view are four in number: (1) members may be subject to charges based on vague provisions in the union constitution, such as "disturbing the harmony of meetings," "conduct unbecoming a member," "creating dissension," "improper conduct," or "insubordination or just and sufficient cause"; (2) the union executive and judicial machinery typically are merged, so that officers sit in judgment on or review cases in which their factional opponents are defendants; (3) the right of appeal to a disinterested body of judges is available only in several unions, such as the Upholsterers' International Union and the United Automobile Workers, both of which have established review boards of leading citizens; and (4) many unions permit too easy revocation of the charters of locals, without any requirement for the re-establishment of autonomous rights within a specified period of time. . . .[9]

One problem is that many unions grant far too much power to their national officers. The president of the Teamsters, for example, appoints International organizers and the chairmen of the four powerful regional conferences; he approves the bylaws of local unions and joint councils; he approves or disapproves of strikes by subordinate units; he interprets the constitution and laws of the International and decides all questions of law under them; he removes local officers where warranted and appoints trustees without time limit for the trusteeship.[10] The head of the International Brotherhood of Electrical Workers enjoys a similarly broad grant of authority, as do some other union heads. The president of the American Federation of Musicians has the remarkable power to set aside provisions of the union's constitution and bylaws, except those dealing with finances, and substitute others of his own making when in his judgment this is necessary to protect the interests of the union. Philip Taft found that 51 international unions out of 115 that he studied granted extensive power to the chief executive.[11] British unions make no comparable grants of authority to their heads; and the former CIO unions, along with many of the old AFL unions, have built effective unions without any such concentrations of authority in the hands of officers.

9 [The Landrum-Griffin Act limits such trusteeships in various ways. *Ed.*]
10 [The Landrum-Griffin Act limits such trusteeships to eighteen months unless further extension can be clearly justified. *Ed.*]
11 [The "bill of rights" of the Landrum-Griffin Act provides for a full and fair trial in union discipline cases. *Ed.*]

If union officers abuse their authority, why do union members submit? The answer is, I think, twofold: (1) the great majority, concerned with economic benefits rather than with internal union political life, tend to support an administration that produces wage gains and other benefits; and (2) the sanctions that can be imposed upon recalcitrants are very effective. Expulsion from a union where a union shop clause exists resulted in the loss of one's job until the Taft-Hartley Act effected a modification. In industries such as the building trades where jobs are typically of short duration and where, to all practical purposes, the closed shop still operates, loss of union membership means banishment from the unionized portion of the industry. Where jobs are filled under a hiring hall or other employment system under union control, political opponents may be discriminated against without depriving them of union membership. Even where a threat to one's job is not involved, loss of union membership may cost a worker a pension, insurance, rights under a health or welfare plan, or other important benefits.[12] As a result, workers submit, except where dissatisfaction is so widespread that they can replace the disliked union with another—provided that their jobs are not lost in the process.

There have been extreme cases, of course, in which the rights of the membership have been crushed and political dissent—or even the asking of questions—punished by violence. The inquiry in recent years into the affairs of the International Longshoremen's Association disclosed that one local of that organization in New York City had gone thirty years without electing officers. Earlier the Tobacco Workers' International Union went without a convention from 1900 until a court order in 1939 forced the officers to call one. While these cases are exceptional, they show that union democracy cannot be taken for granted and that the heads of national unions as well as the officers of locals may be the ones at fault.

Because of all the political advantages possessed by national union heads, the political life of the national union tends to develop at best into a one-party political structure and, at worst, into a personal dictatorship. Indeed, the argument has been advanced that the growth of bureaucracy at the expense of democracy is rooted in the nature of the union in particular and of organization in general.[13] A functioning democracy, as opposed to a single political machine or a benevo-

---

12 Philip Taft, "The Constitutional Power of the Chief Officer in American Labor Unions," *Quarterly Journal of Economics*, LXII (May 1948), pp. 459, 464.

13 See, for example, Will Herberg, "Bureaucracy and Democracy in Labor Unions," *Antioch Review* (Fall 1943), pp. 405–17.

lent dictatorship, is likely to emerge in a large organization only where the formation and activity of opposition political groups are considered legitimate. For such activity to be effective, in turn, non-administration groups must be able to meet, raise funds, print literature, and reach the membership by circularizing the locals and by having space in the union publications. All of this will far from equal the political advantages of the administration; in their absence these advantages will prove insurmountable.

. . . The type of action that I would support, by government as well as by the labor movement, would be designed to strengthen democratic procedures and controls without injuring collective bargaining effectiveness. Indeed, it is possible that strengthening of internal democracy, by improving morale, may increase membership loyalty and therefore bargaining strength.

Control by the Membership in Building Trades Unions

GEORGE STRAUSS

A common stereotype among industrial relations students is that building trades local unions are undemocratic and their business agents highhanded and often corrupt. In part this impression is based on lurid cases which have reached the courts and investigating committees. Unfortunately, to date there has been little research on the internal dynamics of these unions.[1] Yet the problems they face and their means of solving them obviously differ from those in the industrial unions, which have recently received the bulk of academic attention.

This article reports on a thirty-month study of thirteen building trades unions in a community of approximately 400,000.[2] How typical these unions are of building trades unions elsewhere is matter for further research.[3] By ordinary definitions the locals here were

---

This article has been reprinted from the American Journal of Sociology, LXI (May 1956), pp. 527–35, with the permission of the University of Chicago Press. Copyright 1956 by the University of Chicago. George Strauss is Professor of Industrial Relations and Research Economist at the Institute of Industrial Relations of the University of California at Berkeley.

[1] A relevant and important article is Richard R. Meyers, "Interpersonal Relations in the Building Industry," Applied Anthropolgy, V, No. 2 (1946), pp. 1–13. For an analysis of industrial locals similar to those given here for building trades unions see Leonard R. Sayles and George Strauss, The Local Union (New York: Harper, 1953).

[2] For a general discussion of research technique see Sayles and Strauss, op. cit., pp. 259–63. Much of the data for this study was gathered by riding with business agents on their daily rounds.

[3] The majority of the locals had between 400 and 1,000 members, the largest having about 2,700. The community is characterized by stable employment and a high degree of homeownership and civic pride. Manufacturing is only partly organized. The building trades unions control large-scale construction but have only a foothold in housebuilding. Employment has been generally high since the war. Management has been fairly aggressive in resisting union demands.

democratic. Business agents faced opposition at election time; re-election was never automatic. Members had considerable opportunity to express their points of view and, in so far as has been observed, were not subject to retaliation. Meetings were well attended when matters of general concern were considered, and officers' decisions frequently were reversed. Business agents were interested in and responsive to members' demands. At the time there was no evidence or serious charge of corruption in any of the locals, although this had not always been true. There were important differences between the locals, but, at the same time, there was a great contrast between all these unions and industrial unions—enough to make generalization possible.

THE KEY POSITION OF THE BUSINESS AGENT

Any analysis of local unionism in the building trades must center on the business agent. Normally he exercises far more power than any single officer in an industrial union. The reasons are many. First, he is a full-time official. Second, in contrast to industrial locals whose unpaid officers can usually get together on the job, at lunch, or immediately after work, it is difficult for members of construction locals to keep in touch with one another. They work on widely scattered projects. Third, in many instances building tradesmen are dependent on their business agents for jobs. Fourth, collective bargaining in the building trades is highly informal, and special adjustments are often required. This makes it more difficult for the rank and file to check on the business agent's actions. Finally, the short duration of building projects makes quick action necessary; the business agent cannot wait until he has received the executive board's approval for everything he does. Further, it should be noted that collective bargaining in the building trades is normally on the local level and that the international exercises only limited controls.

However, in spite of their great authority, business agents in the community studied were not dictators. Instead, as we shall see, the internal politics of building trades unions can be likened to a system in equilibrium. The arbitrary discretion of the business agents is checked by pressures from other union officers, the international, employers, the general public, and, above all, the rank and file.

The locals in this community were probably more democratic than most. In the absence of similar studies in other communities, one can only guess why this should be so, and the hypothesis is advanced that it is in part due to the small size of the local. This makes it possible for the members to keep in communication with one another and thus check up on the activities of the business agent and organize a political life independent of his control.

In this article we will look first for external evidences of democracy in elections and meetings and then examine some of the internal pressures which keep the business agent responsive.

ELECTIONS

The elections observed were conducted with democratic safeguards, including secret ballots or voting machines. Participation ranged from 7 to 60 per cent, with the higher interest naturally being shown in the smaller locals and when the contest was close.

In the most recent elections seven out of fourteen full-time business agents faced opposition, and one was defeated. Over the last six years six had been either defeated or forced to retire in face of membership pressure. At the time this study was made, business agents had been in office for an average of 7.5 years—yet none felt completely secure. Elections were never taken lightly, and for some the prospect of being defeated was a source of constant and often neurotic worry. For executive board positions opposition and turnover was even more common.

Election issues varied. At times the business agent was charged with being insufficiently militant in protecting the members' legitimate rights or so militant as to jeopardize their chances of employment (and sometimes of both faults at the same time by different factions). Often personal ambition or Irish-Italian-Negro rivalry was the primary motivation. But the agent's power was most seriously challenged when the opposition could charge him with inefficiency. One agent told how he won an election:

Old Jim had been business agent for fifteen years. When he started out, he was bright, aggressive, and able. But gradually he took to the bottle. . . . In meetings he would yell at the people to sit down and shout abuse at them. . . . There were times when you just couldn't find him when you had a problem. . . . His books were in miserable shape.

Three years ago he was elected by a thirteen-vote majority. A lot of the men voted for him just out of loyalty. They didn't like the old man to lose his job. . . . Well, in the last election I knew that someone was going to beat him. I just had to run.

Almost identical stories could be told in two other locals. Even where alcohol was not a problem, elections were often close.

MEETINGS

Attendance at meetings was higher than in industrial locals of the same size. A turnout of from 5 to 10 per cent was typical of meetings without special business. Perhaps 20–25 per cent showed up to vote on dues increases or contract demands or to authorize a strike. Over half might attend when the contract was finally presented for ratification. Since many of the members lived from twenty to fifty miles from town, this high attendance requires explanation. To some extent members reasoned that if they attended meetings the business agent would see them and thus be more likely to give them jobs. More important, the meeting was a social event which gave old friends who were working on different projects a chance to see one another.

Discussion was often vigorous. Name-calling and displays of temper were common. Local presidents were largely selected on their ability to keep order during the meeting.

More commonly than in industrial locals, discussion on the meeting floor was centered on policy questions (with the business agent often refusing to make recommendations); details and implementation of policy, on the whole, were left to the business agent and the executive board. Parliamentary rules were largely ignored, and the parliamentary maneuvering which often paralyzes the meetings of industrial unions was almost entirely absent. Since every member did the same kind of work, most problems were of interest to all, and discussion was much more fruitful.

Although a majority of meetings were dull and uninteresting, on many occasions they got out of hand, at least from the business agent's point of view. Among the questions giving rise to most controversy were: What should be done to limit the number of members in face of possibly declining job opportunities? How militant should the union be in coming wage negotiations? Should the union fight for fringe benefits or settle for straight wage increase? On each of these issues meetings were observed in which the business agents' proposals were emphatically rejected after long discussion. In three instances contracts were rejected and strikes called, contrary to their advice.

EXECUTIVE BOARDS

Although to the general public, the employers, and even to the membership the business agent is the union's spokesman, the executive boards—which consist of the unpaid officers—played an important role behind the scenes and significantly limited his power. In most local important decisions were made only with their approval, and in all cases members could appeal to them from business agents' decisions.

Antagonistic boards could hamstring a business agent by a number of means: refusing to punish men who had violated his instructions, disapproving items of expense, overruling his decision on important cases, and (in two incidents observed) actually calling a strike of which he disapproved.

EXAMPLES OF DEMOCRACY

It may be instructive to look at four representative locals more closely.

Local A.—The business agent had been in office for almost ten years. On two occasions his re-election met with opposition; both times he won by a landslide vote. However, political enemies have sat on his executive board. Perhaps the strongest opposition came from a lower-paid minority subcraft. (Subcrafts were in opposition in a number of trades. Their opposition was more vocal and more effective where they were of higher status.)

Attendance at ordinary meetings ranged from 5 to 10 per cent of the members. When the last contract was presented for ratification, 85 per cent of the affected members attended, the debate lasted for two hours, and, when the final vote was taken, almost 40 per cent were still in opposition. On another occasion a proposal dear to the business agent's heart—to fight for fringe benefits instead of a larger wage increase—was defeated by a close vote. (Since the research was completed the members turned down a contract recommended by the business agent and went on a lengthy strike.)

Local B.—The business agent had been re-elected annually for twenty years, but on a majority of occasions he had faced determined opposition. This local had a well-developed two-party system based largely on the question of whether men should be allowed to obtain jobs on their own or through the agent. Frequently the opposition controlled the executive board.

Attendance at meetings dropped fairly low, but even a relatively minor dispute could raise it to 20 per cent. Proceedings were turbulent, and some members went merely to "see if we can get him [the business agent] mad tonight."

Local C.—The business agent had held office for over ten years, and in recent elections he was unopposed. Although as a rule, there were contests for executive board positions, the agent normally remained neutral. In the last election he mildly opposed one man, who was elected anyway.

The business agent was careful to sound out members of the executive board before making any proposals which might be rejected. Attendance at local meetings was low; in one instance the agent was forced to use parliamentary maneuvering to prevent a vote on a motion which might have been approved by those present but was certainly not in the interest of the vast majority of the members.

Meetings of subcrafts were frequent and well attended. Here the business agent frequently revised his proposals in face of opposition.

Local D.—Politics in this local were quite turbulent. The business agent had been in office for about three years and had faced determined opposition every election. His predecessor was asked to resign by the executive board for inefficiency. The business agent and the president are rivals, and the business agent's recommendations are often upset by the executive board. When this happens, the agent appeals to the local meeting. (In an election held since this research was completed, the former president took over the business agent's job.)

Meetings are exciting, although not always well attended. This local is noteworthy for the number of its wildcat strikes and the tendency of the membership to disregard completely the business agent's instructions.

All four of these locals were democratic. Yet they differed widely in the relationship which existed between the business agent and the membership.[4] The agent of Local C had perhaps the firmest control over his local, but he retained it only by keeping his ear closely attuned to union public opinion. The business agents of Locals B and D were more likely to make decisions on their own—but there was a strong opposition ready to trip them up when they made mistakes.

This suggests that it may well be worth while to examine the techniques of control which business agents use and the pressures to which they are subject. Particular attention will be paid to the pattern of relationship between business agents and members. In this we shall see the principle of mutual dependency or exchange of favors which characterizes building trades' life.

Business agents and members meet on the job, during membership and executive board meetings, and in the union office. With this in

---

4 Originally it was hoped to study why some locals were democratic and others not. However, it turned out to be impossible to distinguish between degrees of democracy: different locals were democratic in different ways. Further research should be done in locals which are clearly undemocratic.

mind we can divide union business into three main areas: (1) relations with employers; (2) internal administration of the union; and (3) distribution of jobs and admission of new members. We will consider each in turn.

ON THE JOB

One of the most important of the functions of the business agent is that of inspecting building projects under his jurisdiction to make sure that the union's contract and customary working rules are being respected. Often business agents and employers entertain contrasting interpretations of custom. Although the contract calls for arbitration, in almost every instance the problems are informally adjusted, the agent using as a club his power to shut down the job.

Business agents cannot police every job in their jurisdiction. They must rely upon the members to report violations of union conditions. Where the workers are in league with the employers, the business agents' hands are tied. For instance, individual members may agree with an employer to work overtime without premium pay, if they know that otherwise they would not get the extra work at all.

Furthermore, business agents depend to a considerable extent upon "spontaneous militancy" from their members. When this is lacking, the position of the business agent is considerably weaker. As two business agents put it:

> Sometimes all you've got to do is wink an eye, and the men are out. Other times you have to put up a picket, and even then there are some people who want to work.
> When the men walk off by themselves, then you're really in the driver's seat. If you have to push them out, things aren't so good.

A good part of meeting time is taken up by the business agent's "educational" campaign to get the members to take action by themselves; for example:

> MEMBER: The raincoats that [employer] is giving us are so old the water goes right through them. What are you going to do about that?
> BUSINESS AGENT: What are *you* going to do about it? Your business agent can't go around testing every raincoat in the county. If he gives you a bad raincoat, tell him you're not going to work until he gives you a good one. If enough of you get together, he won't fool around with you.

Many seemingly spontaneous strikes are instigated by the business agent or have his benevolent approval. However, on occasion members can be too militant. Really unauthorized wildcat strikes can be very embarrassing and are one of the most dramatic and effective ways the members have available to show their disapproval of union policies. If a business agent cannot control his members, employers will ignore him and bargain individually with their men.

On the other hand, when the members show little spontaneous militancy, they are largely dependent on the business agent for maintaining good working conditions. Individual members are often hesitant to stand up for their rights against the employer. Since they do not have seniority protection, it is easy to lose one's job and be informally blacklisted by the other employers. Unless all the members on the project display a united front, it is much easier to get in touch with the business agent in secret and have him handle the problem than to deal directly with the employers.

Naturally this adds to the business agent's power. If a political opponent calls for help, he can always be too "busy" to visit the project (although in most cases observed business agents tried to give just as good service to their enemies as to their friends). Thus, ironically, where members are apathetic, the internal power of the business agent is considerably greater, even though he may be weaker vis-à-vis the employer. Actually there is a three-way relationship on every project, and the employer plays an important role. For instance, through paying extra-high wages, he may induce his men to work Sundays without reporting this to the agent, in violation of union rules. When this happens, the agent can do little. On the other hand, when his relations with employers are good, the agent is in a much stronger political position. He has no need to test his economic strength by calling strikes, and the employer can support him by punishing his enemies and give the better jobs to his friends. Indeed, when relations are too good, the temptation is strong to enter into a conspiracy in which both parties combine to reduce competition.

In communities where such combinations exist the employers keep the business agent's political enemies in check, and he keeps down the number of new contractors entering the field. Together they keep the men from causing "trouble." The employer gains lush profits; the business agent wins firm control of his union and perhaps a little "protection money" on the side. The customer pays the bill.

There was no evidence of this in the community studied, among other reasons perhaps because the small size of the locals made rank-and-file supervision possible, and the partially organized condition of the industry created the ever present possibility that nonunion firms might take away part of the work.

178 UNION DEMOCRACY

In summary, business agents rely upon the support of their members for the enforcement of union rules and the protection of the union generally. However, as relations with employers improve, they become less dependent upon the membership. On the other hand, where the members are likely to show "spontaneous militancy," the business agent's internal political power is weaker, even if the union's economic power is stronger. Therefore, a hypothesis for future research might be that there is a tendency toward an inverse relationship between democracy in building trades unions and labor-management peace.[5]

IN INTERNAL UNION POLITICS

Just as the position of the business agent is strengthened if he has a series of mutually supportive two-way relationships with employers and the rank and file, so he is also dependent upon his stewards, executive board members, and active members, and they in turn depend on him.

Take stewards, for instance. Their chief function is to deal with grievances which arise on the job. The business agent cannot cover all jobs at once, and the stewards are his "eyes and ears." Without their co-operation his job becomes much harder. In addition, as the "noncoms," so to speak, of the union, they are important in internal politics as well as in collective bargaining. When an election or important meeting approaches, the business agent makes sure that they bring their men to the meeting hall.

Stewards are appointed by the business agent. Yet his freedom of choice is often restricted. If the steward he appoints is not popular on the job, the men will not follow him in either economic or political activity. The union will be weaker on that job in case of a strike—and "spontaneous militancy" becomes more difficult to achieve. In fact, an unpopular appointment may mean that the business agent himself will lose votes in the next election.

The relations of the business agent with his executive board provide an acid test of his political ability. Board members, of course, are elected by the entire membership. On many boards there is factionalism and backbiting. As long as the members fight each other to win the business agent's favor, he is secure. When men start attacking him, his position is obviously more difficult. Yet it is not uncommon for business agents to work with boards a majority of whose members are

[5] For a discussion of this thesis in relationship to industrial unions see Sayles and Strauss, *op. cit.*, chap. xvi.

hostile. Even a single member of the opposition can cause trouble, since as a board member he becomes acquainted with the intricacies of union business and commands a receptive hearing from the members when he reports on alleged mismanagement.

On the other hand, the business agent has weapons of his own to hold the board members in line. Many of them are personally dependent on him for being placed on good jobs. Also he commands minor forms of patronage, such as being sent to conventions and being put on the union payroll for odd jobs. More important, he has a natural advantage at election time. He can do his campaigning on the job. He can contact the entire membership. Opposition candidates normally see only those who attend meetings or who work on their own jobs. If the business agent is re-elected, he can, in most cases, carry the rest of his slate along with him.

In most instances business agents live in harmony with their boards, although this harmony is often achieved at the cost of considerable effort. Often it is obtained through sounding out members in advance of meetings and avoiding contests of strength. One business agent gave as the secret of his success the fact that he allowed his board plenty of freedom to decide little things; once the members had exhausted themselves arguing about trivia, he was able to win acceptance of major proposals without too much debate.

In theory, the union meeting includes the entire membership, but, in fact, normally only a minority attends. Yet this minority determines policy for the entire union. The steady attenders are often older men—men particularly dependent upon the business agent for work. They can embarrass him, and he can embarrass them.

Furthermore, the business agent cannot be sure to what extent those who speak at meetings represent the rank and file as a whole. If he follows the dictates of the vocal few, he risks losing the support of the passive majority. Yet, in the end, these vocal few may be able to swing the majority along with them. This means that he cannot ignore their wishes. Instead, he must adjust himself to pressure—and in return exert as much pressure as he can to keep the dissidents from causing trouble. Usually he is careful to see how the wind blows before he commits himself. As long as the bulk of the membership is satisfied with what the business agent does, attendance remains low. However, once he starts making mistakes, the word spreads from project to project (often through social contacts at night), and attendance increases.

All in all, the most secure business agents, politically, are those who campaign twelve months a year. Their constant contacts with

members on the job and at meetings serve the dual purpose of reveal-
ing what the members want and of advertising the effectiveness of
their own leadership.

One of the main purposes of the business agent's regular round of
projects is, as one commented, "just to show my face—if they don't
see me around, they think I am lying down on the job." Normally, he
spends most of his time with the steward, maintaining his contacts
there, but before leaving he is sure to walk around the project, talking
to some of the members and letting others know "I've been there."
(Only a small proportion of the construction teamsters may be on a
project at a given time, but the business agent of their local advertises
his activities by insistently honking his horn at all construction trucks
he passes.)

IN THE DISTRIBUTION OF JOBS AND
ADMISSION OF NEW MEMBERS

A business agent's power and prestige are in part determined by the
number of those who come to him for help. One told how the men
living outside the central city were "more loyal and more militant"
because they could not find jobs for themselves and had to depend
upon the union office.

In some locals employers were required to hire all their men
through the union hall; in others, members were free to find work
themselves. Yet, even when not so required, employers often asked
the business agent to provide them men. Naturally, this control over
jobs gave him considerable opportunity to show favoritism. In theory
men who were out of work longest received first priority on new jobs.
However, the lists could be easily manipulated. If they wished, business agents could discriminate between friends and enemies both
among employers and among union members.

Interestingly, political factionalism was as great in those unions in
which the business agent had absolute control over placement as in
those where the men could find their own jobs and sometimes even
greater. Control of jobs did not make the business agents into dictators. Instead it increased the members' interest in internal politics.

Business agents were also able to exercise considerable choice in
recommending candidates for membership or apprenticeship, and political considerations could well play an important part in their decisions. Yet most locals required candidates to appear before an examining board or apprenticeship committee. Of course, a business
agent might fill a board with political allies—but each board was a
potential check on his powers.

In distributing jobs, business agents operate under terrific pressure which substantially reduces their freedom to make arbitrary decisions. In the office, on the jobs, at home, or even during social affairs, they are constantly besieged by members who are looking for favors and who often complain that unfair advantages have been given to others. For instance, if for good reason a member is sent on the job without regard to the out-of-work list, the other members who are out of work soon hear about it and object. Several business agents said frankly that one of the chief reasons for not giving favors was that, "for every friend you make, you make several enemies." As one business agent put it:

My trouble is that the men are always watching me. For instance, I put one man on a job, and another will come to me and say, "Why didn't you give me the job?"

I'll say, "Well, your name wasn't on top of the list; his was."

He'll say, "I thought you were a friend of mine. You didn't have to tell him." And so it goes. It would save me a lot of time, bother, and worry if everyone found a job by himself.

The business agent can satisfy only a few of the demands made upon him. In self-defense against these pressures he has two alternatives. The first is to establish a set, formal system of distributing job opportunities and other advantages. (This is often called "going by the book" and corresponds to the formalized system of considering grievances utilized in some industrial unions.) The second alternative is to engage in out-and-out favoritism, to give the best plums to your friends, and to leave the crumbs for the rank and file. This is possible only when the agent has already strongly solidified his control of the union and has little fear of being kicked out. None of the business agents studied enjoyed such power.

Thus, it would seem that, in unions which are already democratic, there are strong pressures on the business agent to act impartially— and thus help keep the union democratic. In those which are undemocratic, he can employ favoritism to strengthen his position.

OTHER PRESSURES

Naturally, business agents are subject to numerous other pressures, only two of which will be mentioned here. In theory, if the business agents act in a dictatorial way, the dissatisfied members may appeal to the international. In some instances the international may even put the local in "receivership." However, as long as the business agent does not publicly embarrass the union or weaken the economic position of other locals, the international will not care to intervene. Indeed, the international officers often depend upon the business agents of the various locals to provide them with votes for their re-election.

Union leaders are naturally concerned with public relations. In general they try to avoid unfavorable mention in the press and on radio and television. Most agree that participation in community affairs has a favorable effect upon public relations. In part, this is merely an indication of the normal human desire to be "thought well of"; in part, union leaders realize that their task will be more difficult if the general public and, in particular, government officials are antagonistic.

WHY WERE THESE UNIONS DEMOCRATIC?

Obviously, the degree of democracy in a building trades union depends largely upon the position of the business agent. Democracy in these unions can be measured not only in terms of turnover of business agents but also by the amount of adjustment which they must make to avoid turnover. If the agent is firmly in power and has no need to react to rank-and-file pressures, then the union is undemocratic.

As we have seen, relations between business agent, members, and employers are complex and interrelated. In a way the business agent's power is cumulative. If he is strong, he has no need to depend on rank-and-file support on the job. He can dominate his executive board and the members' meeting, and he can play favorites with impunity. In other words, he can run an undemocratic union.

It is probably safe to say that, compared with members of industrial unions generally, building tradesmen have a greater interest in the affairs of their union. The union usually gets them their jobs. Furthermore, their identification is greater, since typically they belong to the union all their lives, while working for many employers. Indeed, the union offers fraternal needs and prestige, which industrial unions rarely provide.

When they take little risks in doing so, members will be more likely to participate in union activities. However, where the business agent can retaliate against those who oppose him, few members are willing to take the risk. This would suggest that the range of democracy in building trades unions will be greater than in industrial unions.

We are still left with the question: Why were the business agents in this community so responsive to their membership? Only partial explanations can be given. One is that, since the construction industry there was only partially unionized, employers could show greater independence and that the business agents were more dependent on rank-and-file support. Another is that the unions were less closely connected with the local political organization than is apparently true elsewhere.

Perhaps the effect of size was even more important. Joel Seidman explains why craft unions in large metropolises are undemocratic as follows:

> In a typical craft union situation the opportunity for informal upward communication is even less than in industrial unions. Here the workers are typically scattered among a great many employing units, each of very small size, with jobs often of short duration. In a large local a large staff of full-time business agents is needed to police these jobs, and inevitably they are given authority over the jobs and over the members. There is no informal shop society of which the business agent is a member and to which he is responsive. . . . Entry into the union and expulsion were controlled by the business agent or union head, who might be as far removed from the worker, for purposes of political control, if not communication, as the head of a large corporation.[6]

The difference between this community and the situation described by Seidman is this: here there was a definite "shop society." To a greater extent than in industrial locals the author has studied, the members knew each other. They had all done the same sort of work for years. Most of them mingled at work; most of them had seen each other at union meetings or waiting in the union office for jobs. In addition, there were ethnic and family ties which bound them together even closer. The business agent was *not* far removed from the worker.

CONCLUSION

1. The locals in this community were democratic, to the extent that the business agents were forced to be responsive to the desires of the members—with defeat looming if they were not. The degree of mem-

[6] "Discussion: Leadership and Communication in Companies and Trade Unions," *Proceedings of the Fifth Annual Meeting of the Industrial Relations Research Association, 1952,* p. 154. See also Joseph Kovner and Herbert J. Lahne, "Shop Society and the Union," *Industrial and Labor Relations Review,* VII, No. 1 (October 1953), pp. 3–14. For a more general analysis of union democracy see Sayles and Strauss, *op. cit.,* chap. xiii.

bership participation and interest was higher than is common in industrial unions of the same size.

2. Hypothetically, it is proposed that the effectiveness of the membership controls was to some extent a function of the locals' small size and cohesiveness.

The Dilemma of Union Democracy

EMANUEL STEIN

Underlying much of the recent writing on American trade-union government are assumptions which, through insistent repetition, have come to be widely regarded as self-evident truths and as sound guides to policy. These assumptions which are often implicit rather than articulate, run something like this: the trade union is philosophically and traditionally a democratic institution which differs from other types of association, notably the business corporation, in the degree to which it emphasizes internal democracy; it is highly desirable for both internal and external considerations that unions should be democratic; through a variety of circumstances—especially the apathy of large segments of the membership and the self-aggrandizement of power-hungry leaders—power and authority have progressively been transferred from the rank and file to the leaders; this has led to many abuses which would be eliminated by the restoration of democratic government, which, in turn, can be achieved by the institution of various structural devices, statutory proscription of certain conduct, and education of the membership.

Insofar as these assumptions individually purport to describe a fact situation, it may be conceded that they contain a large and uncomfortable amount of truth. As explanations of developments in the basic character of union government, however, they are often dubious or irrelevant. Indeed, because of their stress upon behavioral excesses, they may hinder a correct assessment of the state of union government and of the factors which condition it. Stated briefly, the

Taken from Annals of the American Academy of Political and Social Science, CCCL (*November 1963*), *pp. 46–54. Reprinted with the permission of the author and publisher. Emanuel Stein is Professor of Economics and Head of the Department of Economics at New York University.*

theme of this paper is that the lessening of union democracy is inextricably and inevitably interwoven with the large growth of the individual union, that the prospects for the recreation of literal democracy diminish as the size of the union is increased, and that the problems of union government, if they are to be dealt with successfully, must be approached in other ways.

If we measure democracy by the extent and vigor of member participation, it is evident that most unions are less democratic than they used to be. Even where the leadership strives to attain what it believes to be the members' objectives, members are free to exercise their civil rights within the organization even to the point of forming opposition parties, and the leaders give regular and detailed accounts of their stewardship—in short, even where there are present within a union the elements commonly regarded as essentials of democracy,[1] the plain fact is that control has increasingly devolved upon small groups of leaders and their retinues. To an ever-larger extent, government has become the business of a more-or-less full-time officialdom, with the membership occupying mainly a ceremonial or ritualistic role.

The much greater membership participation in the early days of a union is far less the product of a philosophical commitment to democratic principles than of the circumstances attending organization. Apart from personal grievances which impel them to join a union, when workers are solicited individually or in small groups in the face of employer hostility, and are thus invited in effect to become targets of retaliatory measures, it is scarcely surprising that they should assume a prominent role in the affairs of the organization. But unions are not established to illustrate the theory of democracy; their function is to advance the economic interests of the members. In the circumstances of our times, the performance of this function induces, if it does not compel, a transfer of power from the membership to the leaders. Of course, the organization will be stronger, other things being equal, if the members identify themselves with it actively and continuously. It is also true that persons interested in the self-organization of workers are likely to be much more firmly committed than the general run of the population to democratic principles. However, the link between democracy and the trade union cannot withstand the pressure exerted by the needs of the organization in its principal areas of activity.

[1] C. P. Magrath, "Democracy in Overalls," *Industrial and Labor Relations Review*, XII, No. 4 (July 1959), pp. 504–05.

Unions are not alone in having to face issues of democratic government. Senator Fulbright, speaking of the political community, said recently:[2]

. . . government by the people is possible but highly improbable. The difficulties of self-government are manifest throughout the world.

The history of political thought in the last century and a half is largely one of qualification, modification, and outright repudiation of the heady democratic optimism of the eighteenth century. . . .

The case for government by elites is irrefutable insofar as it rests on the need for expert and specialized knowledge. The average citizen is no more qualified for the detailed administration of government than the average politician is qualified to practice medicine or to split an atom. But in the choice of basic goals, the fundamental moral judgments that shape the life of a society, the judgment of trained elites is no more valid than the judgment of an educated people. The knowledge of the navigator is essential to the conduct of a voyage, but his special skills have no relevance to the choice of whether to take the voyage and where we wish to go.

The distinction of course is between means and ends. The experience of modern times shows us that when the passengers take over the navigation of the ship it is likely to go on the rocks. This does not mean that their chosen destination is the wrong one or that an expert would have made a better choice, but only that they are unlikely to get there without the navigator's guidance.

EXIGENCIES OF UNION FUNCTION

How is the distinction between means and ends to be made in a union? In contrast to the state, the union is a single- or, at most, limited-purpose institution.[3] As to the general goals—improvements in wages and conditions of work—there would certainly be no disagreement. But who is to determine whether, in a particular year, wage increases should be sought and of what size? Whether a strike should be called? How much shall be given up in wages in return for paid vacations or holidays? Whether the union shall consent to a program of automation, notwithstanding substantial reductions in employment, in exchange for enlarged benefits to those remaining at work? Of course, these and similar crucial questions are generally submitted to the membership, but such submission comes as a request for ratification of action taken by the leadership, and the consultation

2 J. W. Fulbright and Others, *The Elite and the Electorate* (New York: Fund for the Republic, 1963), pp. 3–5.
3 Magrath, *loc. cit.*, pp. 506–07.

of the membership is mostly an empty formality. There is no basic difficulty in having the membership decide such peripheral matters as whether the union should establish a bank, a home for its "senior citizens," or scholarships for the children of its members. However, in the central area of union function—collective bargaining—the leadership must have the authority to act if it is to be effective. Successful collective bargaining today calls for a great deal of specialized knowledge and for experience in utilizing that knowledge. It is utterly unrealistic to expect that the membership will be able to pass informed judgment upon the mass of economic, actuarial, and technological considerations underlying a collective-bargaining agreement. Hence, the membership is obliged to rely upon the recommendations of the leaders; in substance, therefore, in most unions, the power to make collective-bargaining agreements has been effectively concentrated in the hands of the leaders, notwithstanding that the rituals of formal ratification by the membership have, for the most part, been scrupulously preserved.

Even if the membership possessed the expertise necessary for collective bargaining or if it were felt that, nevertheless, the membership should retain effective power to act, it is plain that the facts of economic life would still entail the transfer of power to the leadership. Given the "business unionism" characteristic of the American scene, the locus of power within a union is going to be found at the point where the collective bargaining takes place, and this in turn is determined by market considerations. If, in many unions, locals have become mere administrative subdivisions of the national, the operative factor has been the nature of the product or factor market. As the markets have widened, the area covered by the individual collective-bargaining agreement has also widened. It would be absurd to have a single local in a multiplant company negotiate an agreement for itself on wages and conditions without regard to what sister locals in other plants were doing. It would be no less absurd for one local dealing with one employer in a competitive industry to ignore the actions of the locals dealing with the other employers. The necessities of the situation thus produce centralized bargaining which enhances the power and prestige of the bargainers and diminishes the importance of the locals for whom the bargaining is being done. It follows that the ability of the membership to participate effectively is likewise diminished. I am not suggesting that the leadership has played a wholly passive role in the process of acquiring power or that it has not sought to add to that which was dictated by market forces. However, it seems to me that the personal ambitions of leaders have been far less significant in the building of their power than the market factors over which they have no control. For, where the markets have remained local, power has not tended to gravitate to the national to any material extent. Leaders of unions have thus been in the position of having power thrust upon them, power which they could not have seized in the absence of a propitious market situation.

I have no intention of making light of labor racketeering or similar malpractices, but these are not materially different from racketeering and corruption in other segments of the community and are susceptible of control through the application of the criminal law. Moreover, we cannot equate undemocratic unions with corrupt unions; corrupt unions are almost certain to be undemocratic, but many undemocratic unions are the embodiment of financial integrity. Nor do I minimize the extent or significance of infringements upon the civil rights of members—denial of the right to speak at union meetings, or to run for office, or to be consulted on matters required to be submitted to the membership, or protection against the unwarranted imposition of discipline. While such abuses are not easily dealt with, promising efforts at control have been commenced both within the unions—for example, through the public review boards—and by statutory enactment. However, it seems to me that the most rigid emphasis upon civil rights would not produce widespread and effective participation by members as long as the size of the union and the complexity of its affairs compel the concentration of power in the hands of the leadership.

Many writers have pointed out that there tends to be more democracy at the local level than at the national. I agree that this is so and think it is to be attributed to the relatively small size of the local. Where the membership of a local is numbered in the thousands, we find the same forces operating as in the nationals to make membership participation difficult, if not impossible. Of course the membership is apathetic, as has been so often observed![4] Having so little of consequence to do, what reason is there for attending union meetings? Hence, as George Brooks has said, members exercise "their inalienable right to be indifferent" and to leave the affairs of the organization to the small number who control it.

---

4 G. W. Brooks, *The Sources of Vitality in the American Labor Movement* (Ithaca: New York State School of Industrial and Labor Relations, 1960), pp. 5–6. See also George Strauss, "The Shifting Power Balance in the Plant," *Industrial Relations*, I, No. 3 (May 1962), pp. 74–75.

THE CORPORATION ANALOGY

The many significant differences between business corporations and trade unions argue against the validity of comparisons between them. Yet, it seems to me that the history of the government of corporations does provide insights which may be valuable for the study of union government. Despite many assertions to the contrary, the corporation is based upon assumptions of democratic government *in relation to its stockholders*. Early corporations were free associations of investors for agreed-upon purposes. Corporate functions and powers were limited by charter; stockholders elected directors as their representatives in the conduct of the enterprise, and the directors in turn appointed the officers. Power and authority vested in directors by statute were predicated upon the view that the directors were, in fact as well as in law, responsible to the stockholders for the proper performance of their duties. In the small, closely held corporation, it is true even today that stockholders have an effective voice. But, in the large, publicly held corporation, it has long been apparent that the stockholder has been substantially disfranchised. Studies made over a generation ago by Brandeis, Ripley, and Berle pointed to the separation of ownership of the corporation and its control. Then, the trends in corporate government were obscured by the emphasis placed upon malpractice, including the looting of corporations, the mulcting of stockholders, and the building of vast personal empires. As time has gone on, however, it has become increasingly apparent that malpractice has very little to do with the matter but that size has everything to do with it. As corporate assets mount into the hundreds of millions or billions of dollars and their stockholders are counted by the tens or hundreds of thousands, control of the enterprise passes securely and irrevocably from the owners to the insiders. These may be men of the most punctilious integrity with an unswerving dedication to the welfare of the business, but their ownership interest is typically minuscule.

Now, determined efforts are made to preserve some vestigial remains of stockholder democracy. The New York Stock Exchange refuses to list nonvoting common shares; the Securities and Exchange Commission requires detailed proxies; annual reports are distributed; stockholders are solicited to attend meetings; at the meetings, stockholders—the tiny number who attend—may speak freely and criticize the management, vote for directors, and pass upon a variety of proposals. However, the most exacting observance of the ritual of consulting the stockholders cannot conceal their almost total lack of power. Indeed, the wide publicity accorded the upheaval in which incumbent management is ousted is eloquent testimony to the rarity of the event.

To describe what has happened is not to pass judgment upon its desirability. Doubtless, considerable support would be forthcoming for the proposition asserted by some corporate managers that the corporation must serve, in addition to the interests of stockholders, the interests of its suppliers, its employees, its customers, and the community generally. A recent study has argued that the traditional view of the corporation as solely a money-making enterprise is no longer adequate and that "the directors of large corporate enterprises are in need of more substantial doctrine than legal and economic theory has provided as a rationale for the powers they must exercise."[5] In any event, I do not think it can be successfully disputed that the managers of our large corporations do not have quite the same philosophy and do not respond to quite the same motivations as their stockholders or the managers of small corporations and that in some instances the differences are very large. The professional managers tend, I suggest, to develop institutional and personal goals which vary, in greater or lesser degree, from those the corporation would pursue if the stockholders could participate effectively in the enterprise.

THE MEMBERSHIP-LEADERSHIP GAP

As in the corporation, so in the union! When membership increases to the point that full-time officials are required and can be afforded, a gulf between the members and the leaders begins to appear, a gulf which widens progressively with the growth of the union. It is not only that the official's salary is greater than that of the man at the bench and that, in the case of important officials, the difference may be quite substantial, though it is plain that the living standards would almost certainly be higher. Nor is it only the fact that the official has power both within and outside the union, though this, too, has obvious significance. It is, rather, that the men at the top and those at the bottom seem to live in different spheres, to concern themselves with different problems, and to respond to different motivations. The head of a large union—for example a Reuther or a Dubinsky—may continue to live in a modest home in a working-class district; he may talk wistfully of "the old days in the shop" and may exchange social

<hr>

[5] Richard Eels, *The Government of Corporations* (New York: The Free Press of Glencoe, 1962), p. 11.

visits with former fellow workers. But there is no blinking the fact of the vast separation. In innumerable ways—some subtle, some obvious—this separation makes itself felt: in living standards, in travel, in community activities, in power vis-à-vis the employer, in political influence, in publicity. And the greater the tenure of office, the deeper and more unbridgeable the separation, so that one is tempted to ask what there is really in common between the man in the shop and the national president of his union.

One must not conclude that leaders are not sensitive to the sentiments of the rank and file concerning such matters as dues and collective-bargaining gains. Quite the contrary is true! If nothing else, a prudent regard for the security and continued enjoyment of his own position would compel a leader to strive to "bring home the bacon," in which lies ultimate immunity from successful revolt. Of course, there is more—much more. I do not for a moment doubt that the overwhelming majority of union leaders have a sense of genuine loyalty to their constituents, a real desire to secure economic gains for them, and a conviction that the cause is just. And I suspect that a kind of "instinct of workmanship" would operate to induce a drive for achievements which would compare favorably with those of their "opposite numbers" in other unions. Yet, doing *for* the members is not the same as doing *with* them. A union is not democratic because it has made impressive gains in wages and conditions; even the most selfless dedication to his constituents does not indicate that the leader is acting democratically. J. B. S. Hardman made the point tellingly long ago in his discussion of the stakes of leadership, distinguishing between a "leader of labor"—a democrat in a democratic union— and a "labor leader"—a professional skilled in the arts of manipulation and in selling the labor power of his members at advantageous rates.[6]

The gap between the membership and the leadership is manifested at numerous points. To the individual member, the most important considerations are income and job security; his loyalty to the union is apt to reflect faithfully the degree to which he believes the union has "delivered the goods." The leader, too, is interested in the wages and conditions of his constituents, but his primary allegiance is to the union; it is the union, as an institution, which must at all costs be preserved. Often, of course, both sets of interests may be served simultaneously and harmoniously, but there are times when the in-

---

6 "XYZ Has It Out With His Younger Self," in J. B. S. Hardman (ed.), *American Labor Dynamics* (New York: Harcourt, Brace, 1928).

terests diverge. Shall a concession be made on wages in return for a provision on union security? How much is a checkoff worth? How much shall be given up in potential gains in order to create a public image of a responsible and restrained union or to accommodate the wishes of a president or governor whose good will may be viewed as important to the union and its leaders?

It has been fashionable in some circles to criticize union leaders for not being statesmen, for being unmindful of the public interest or long-range economic considerations. In other words, they are taken to task for pressing too vigorously for what are held to be excessive adjustments in the terms of employment. Of course, the real pressure for wage increases comes from the rank and file, and the more responsive the leader is to rank-and-file sentiment, the more persistent his efforts towards the so-called "unstatesmanlike goals."

Criticism has come also from quarters friendlier to unions. This has taken the form of assertions that "business unionism" can no longer serve as adequate trade-union philosophy, that unions need a "new look," possibly in the form of "social unionism" which will serve the whole community and contribute to the realization of democratic ideals generally. Assuming that union leaders were to set out on such a course, one wonders to what extent the membership would approve and follow.

We cannot have it both ways! Realistically, if the membership is to determine union policy, directly or indirectly, it follows inevitably that the policy will express primarily the traditional objectives of increased income and enhanced job security for the individual to be obtained through the traditional medium of collective bargaining. Public-policy considerations and the interests of other segments of the community, including other groups of organized workers, will play a distinctly secondary role. It is only as the leadership acquires a measure of independence from the membership that it is able to have a broader perspective. In time, the situation may change, and the rank and file may moderate its emphasis upon historic business-union objectives, but such a change is, putting it mildly, not imminent. If anything, the pressure upon leaders to win bargaining concessions is increasing. One newspaper account, entitled "Union Men's Rising Defiance over Contracts Imperils Labor Leaders and Managements,"[7] pointing to a marked increase in members' rejection of collective bargaining agreements negotiated by their leaders, says in part:

[7] *The Wall Street Journal,* June 3, 1963, p. 26.

. . . Hampered at the bargaining table by high unemployment, the threat of greater job-cutting because of automation and a more skilled and determined management opposition, union officials are finding it harder to get the comfortable contract concessions they once won.

This has aroused a certain amount of dissatisfaction among workers against their leaders. "In some cases this failure is because the leaders know they aren't strong enough to get what they'd like," says one union aide, "but it's also true that some of the chiefs have lost close touch with the wants of the Indians." Whatever the reason, the result has been that union dissidents have found it easier to mobilize opposition to their leaders' wishes. . . .

To some union men, the solution to the contract-rejection problem is simple: "Get more (in benefits) and the members will have less to beef about."

I think it would be generally agreed that union leaders, for whatever reasons, are far more willing to go along with the notion of noninflationary wage adjustments than their members are with the collective-bargaining agreements embodying such adjustments. Further, it has often been remarked that, in recent years, unions have not, for the most part, fought technological change with anything like the intensity of earlier times; on the contrary, many leaders have expressly approved automation and have sought only to cushion its impact. One wonders whether the longshoreman who has been automated out of a job by the so-called "containerization" has quite the same attitude toward the technological change as the officers of his union. However desirable moderation in wage policy and cooperation in technological progress, to cite only two illustrations, may be from the standpoint of the public interest, it is to be doubted that unions would act as they have acted on these matters if the rank and file could exert real influence.

PROSPECTS

If we evaluate union government in terms of its consequences and impact upon public economic policy, we may quite properly conclude that the outlook is not at all bad, for union leaders have broader perspectives and better understanding than their predecessors and than their constituents. On their own, or under the tutelage of their economic advisers, they talk easily about gross national product, economic growth, and the requisites for sound domestic and foreign economic policies. So viewed, it becomes a matter of concern if the leaders are unable to deliver the vote—that is, unable to get their constituents to endorse a collective bargaining agreement based upon "sound" economic ideas. And it is not utterly fantastic to suppose that, if a number of outstanding unions should, as it were, become "runaways" and insist upon maximizing the gains to their members without regard for public policy, we might witness a reimposition of public wage controls.

However, if we evaluate union government as *process,* I think we must conclude that the prospects for effective mass participation are very dim—not because of member apathy, nor because of the ambition or cupidity of the leaders, but simply because the size of the union and the complexity of its functions make such participation substantially impossible. It is regrettable, but nonetheless true, that visions of a really workable trade-union democracy are doomed to disappointment. This does not mean that the civil rights of members cannot be effectively protected or that they should be ignored. I think that unions have made encouraging progress on these civil rights and that the delinquents can be reached by legislation. Nor does it mean that corruption and racketeering cannot and should not be brought under workable control. It does mean, however, that we may have to revise our notions as to what is possible in trade-union government. We may be compelled to recognize that the preservation of the *forms* of democratic government, important as it may be for sentimental reasons as well as to safeguard the ultimate right of revolution by the members, may not be a sufficient answer to the challenges posed by union structure and function in a highly integrated economy. We may have to invent new concepts and devices which will permit a viable balancing of the competing interests in light of the realities of contemporary unionism.

PART IV

UNION ANALYSIS AND PRACTICE

INTRODUCTION

American unionism has been subject to a variety of interpretations. To some, the labor movement has seemed radical, threatening basic elements in the free enterprise system. Others have considered it to be a conservative force, serving to preserve American capitalism from revolutionary changes.

The label that one pins on trade unionism in America partly depends on one's concept of the enterprise system and the conditions deemed necessary for its satisfactory functioning. Whether one views unions with apprehension or equanimity depends, in part, also on one's model of union behavior and one's assumptions regarding the basic aims of organized labor.

This section deals with concepts of American unionism, and throws light on a number of critical questions. Does a common purpose guide union policies? Does one principle control the variety of activities of organized labor? Do all unions try to maximize the wage and benefit income of the membership? Or do unions and their leaders also have nonmonetary objectives (social and political missions) that may conflict with the largest possible income for the present membership of a union? Are labor organizations in their operations and aims largely economic or political? And, to the extent that unions differ in their motivation, what is the typical or standard model of union behavior?

In analyzing union policy, Simons, in the first article, considers unionism inimical to democratic government and the American enterprise system. That conclusion logically follows from his concept of the ideal society and his concept of the union. Writing in 1941, Simons analyzed unions in terms of monopoly theory. Therefore, he saw no reason why a union should not consistently seek to maximize the income of the original members on a lifetime basis, squeezing the firm or industry so that declining employment and membership do not exceed the attrition by death and retirement of the original members. Although the leaders might want increased membership, Simons assumed that the members' insistence on the highest possible wage rates would win out in the determination of union policy.

A markedly different concept of the union is presented by Ross in the second article. He rejects monopoly theory and dollar maximization for the members as misleading determinants of union behavior. In his view, the union's survival and growth usually take precedence over membership wishes which, generally, are so diverse and conflicting that the leadership must work out a compromise that is equitable, obtainable, and acceptable to a majority. Thus, Ross has largely a political explanation of union decisions, but recognizes that they are restricted by economic circumstances. The decisions are the results of various political pressures exerted on the leadership by interest groups within the union and by outside factors (other parts of organized labor, employers, and government).

These two hypotheses concerning union policy are, to some extent, tested by the Raskin article on Hoffa and the Teamsters and by Levinson's article on the wage policy of the Auto Workers. Those two unions are far apart in the labor philosophy of their leaders and in the breadth of their programs. They tend to represent the opposite extremes in the range of union variation.

In part, Hoffa and the Teamsters seem to conform to Simons' concept of unionism. Hoffa views unions as a business; the labor leader's job "is to sell his members' labor" for the highest possible price. For that purpose the union's strategic position is used to apply economic pressure (monopoly power?) on the industry at higher costs to the consumer. However, the evidence does not indicate that Hoffa would place the income interest of the membership ahead of growth of the union as an institution, in case those two objectives were to conflict.

Levinson's article specifically tests alternative hypotheses about union wage policy. It analyzes conformity with and deviation from the auto pattern settlements in eighty-five Detroit firms negotiating with the UAW during the period from 1946 to 1957. The results do not support Simons' notion that unions, taking account of the elasticity of demand for the members' labor, seek to maximize the lifetime income of an exclusive membership along the lines of monopoly theory.

Levinson's findings partly support and partly conflict with Ross' "political" theory of union wage policy. Generally, the UAW's policy was consistent with Ross' views up to the point where a further increase in labor costs would be likely to force the firm out of business; then economic considerations of members' employment became paramount. Except in that sort of situation, political pressures stressing wage equity were usually dominant. Levinson concludes that a combination of "political" and "economic" viewpoints is required for a full explanation of union wage policy.

As the articles in this and the preceding sections indicate, unions are complex institutions. Most of them are part of a movement with international ties and interests. They must work with and make their gains through employers. They are active in local, state, and national politics. Consequently, it is difficult to uncover one goal that guides all of their various activities, or to devise a single measure of union success. But the effort to do so sharpens one's understanding of the essence of American unionism and the factors that account for differences of policy in individual unions.

Some Reflections on Syndicalism

HENRY C. SIMONS

Questioning the virtues of the organized labor movement is like attacking religion, monogamy, motherhood, or the home. Among the modern intelligentsia any doubts about collective bargaining admit of explanation only in terms of insanity, knavery, or subservience to "the interests." Discussion of skeptical views runs almost entirely in terms of how one came by such persuasions, as though they were symptoms of disease. One simply cannot argue that organization is injurious to labor; one is either for labor or against it, and the test is one's attitude toward unionism. But let me indicate from the outset that my central interest, and the criterion in terms of which I wish to argue, is a maximizing of aggregate labor income and a minimizing of inequality. If unionism were good for labor as a whole, that would be the end of the issue for me, since the community whose welfare concerns us is composed overwhelmingly of laborers.

Our problem here, at bottom, is one of broad political philosophy. Advocates of trade-unionism are, I think, obligated morally and intellectually to present a clear picture of the total political-economic system toward which they would have us move. For my part, I simply cannot conceive of any tolerable or enduring order in which there exists widespread organization of workers along occupational, industrial, functional lines. Sentimentalists view such developments merely as a contest between workers who earn too little and enterprises which earn too much; and, unfortunately, there has been enough monopsony in labor markets to make this view superficially plausible,

The article has been reprinted from the Journal of Political Economy, *LII* (*March 1944*), *pp. 1–19, with the permission of the University of Chicago Press. The last 6 pages of the article are omitted. The manuscript of this article was prepared in 1941. At the time he wrote this article Henry C. Simons was an Associate Professor of Economics at the University of Chicago.*

though not enough to make it descriptively important. What we generally fail to see is the identity of interest between the whole community and enterprises seeking to keep down costs. Where enterprise is competitive—and substantial, enduring restraint of competition in product markets is rare—enterprisers represent the community interest effectively; indeed, they are merely intermediaries between consumers of goods and sellers of services. Thus we commonly overlook the conflict of interest between every large organized group of laborers and the community as a whole. What I want to ask is how this conflict can be reconciled, how the power of strongly organized sellers can be limited out of regard for the general welfare. No insuperable problem arises so long as organization is partial and precarious, so long as most unions face substantial nonunion competition, or so long as they must exercise monopoly powers sparingly because of organizational insecurity. Weak unions have no large monopoly powers. But how does a democratic community limit the demands and exactions of strong, secure organizations? Looking at the typographers, the railway brotherhoods, and metropolitan building trades, among others, one answers simply: "It doesn't!"

In an economy of intricate division of labor, every large organized group is in a position at any time to disrupt or to stop the whole flow of social income; and the system must soon break down if groups persist in exercising that power or if they must continuously be bribed to forgo its disastrous exercise. There is no means, save internal competition, to protect the whole community against organized labor minorities and, indeed, no other means to protect the common interests of organized groups themselves. The dilemma here is not peculiar to our present economic order; it must appear in any kind of system. This minority-monopoly problem would be quite as serious for a democratic socialism as it is for the mixed individualist-collectivist system of the present. It is the rock on which our present system is most likely to crack up; and it is the rock on which democratic socialism would be destroyed if it could ever come into being at all.

All the grosser mistakes in economic policy, if not most manifestations of democratic corruption, arise from focusing upon the interests of people as producers rather than upon their interests as consumers, i.e., from acting on behalf of producer minorities rather than on behalf of the whole community as sellers of services and buyers of products. One gets the right answers usually by regarding simply the interests of consumers, since we are all consumers; and the answers reached by this approach are presumably the correct ones for laborers as a whole. But one doesn't get elected by approaching issues in this way! People seldom vote in terms of their common interests, whether as sellers or as buyers. There is no means for protecting the common interest save in terms of rules of policy; and it is only in terms of general rules or principles that democracy, which is government by free, intelligent discussion, can function tolerably or endure. Its nemesis is racketeering—tariffs, other subsidies, and patronage dispensations generally and, outside of government, monopoly, which in its basic aspect is impairment of the state's monopoly of coercive power.

Trade-unionism may be attacked as a threat to order under any kind of system. The case against it is crystal clear if one thinks in terms of purer types of systems like democratic collectivism. A socialist government, faced with numerous functional minorities each organized to disrupt the whole production process unless its demands are met, would be exactly in the position of recent Chinese governments faced with great bandit armies continuously collecting ransom from the nominal sovereign. It would either deprive such minorities of the power to act as units in withholding services or be displaced by a nondemocratic authority which could and would restore monopoly of violence. There is no place for collective bargaining, or for the right to strike, or for effective occupational organization in the socialist state, save in the sense that revolution against established authority is an undeniable privilege and violent chaos always an imminent possibility; and every intelligent socialist, whatever his public utterances, knows as much.

I am arguing, however, not as a socialist, but as an advocate of the elaborate mixed system of traditional economic liberalism. The essence of this practical political philosophy is a distrust of all concentrations of power. No individual may be trusted with much power, no organization, and no institution save the state itself. The state or sovereign must, of course, possess great reserves of power, if only to prevent other organizations from threatening or usurping its monopoly of violence. But the exercise of power inherent in government must be rigidly economized. Decentralization of government is essential. Indeed, the proper purpose of all large-scale organization or federation—as should be obvious to people facing the problem of world order—is that of dispersing power.

Let me remark in passing that highly centralized nationalisms are peculiarly inimical to sound political order. Federalism or informal union of states has everything to commend it if the central government confines itself largely to preserving order and free trade among constituent states, and to providing a stable, common currency. But federal governments like our own and the great powers abroad have become a great obstacle to world order. Originating largely as customs unions or agencies for securing free trade within their boundaries, they were rapidly exploited by minorities to provide subsidies via restraints upon external trade; they have undertaken all kinds of internal policies which must be abandoned if freer world trade is to be achieved; and, finally, they have been largely utilized to restrict trade among their own constituent states or sections. These monsters of nationalism and mercantilism must be dismantled, both to preserve world order and to protect internal peace. Their powers to wage war and to restrict world trade must be sacrificed to some supra-national state or league of nations. Their other powers and functions must be diminished in favor of states, provinces, and, in Europe, small nations.

Along these lines we may reconstruct a total political system in which organization becomes progressively looser and functions increasingly narrow and negative as one moves from local government (counties?) to states, to nations, and to supra-national agencies. The good political order is one in which small nations and governments on the scale of American states are protected in their autonomy against neighbors and protected against federalisms or unions which appropriate their powers, take positive government farther from the people, and systematically subordinate common to special interests.

The great sins against world order, by way of trade restraint and military activity, are those of great, not small, nations. In spite of popular impressions to the contrary, the worst breaches of political morality, the worst patronage corruption, and the most glaring weakness against organized minorities are characteristic of great national or federal governments far more than of smaller units—and of our federal government, with all its "respectability" and "efficiency," especially.

Governments can be trusted to exercise large power, broad functions, and extensive control only at levels of small units like American states and under the limitations imposed by freedom of external trade. Especially in the higher levels or larger units of government, action must follow broad general rules or principles. Only by adherence to "constitutional" principles of policy can the common interest be protected against minorities, patronage, and logrolling; and only in terms of issues of broad principle can government by free, intelligent discussion (democracy) prevail. Most important here are the presumptions in favor of free trade and against dispensations to producer minorities. Constitutional principles or accepted norms are also peculiarly important, and lacking, in fiscal (monetary, budgetary) policy.

Other implications of this older liberalism may be mentioned briefly. The government must not tolerate erection of great private corporate empires or cartel organizations which suppress competition and rival in power great governmental units themselves. (In Germany the great cartels, and the great banks especially, attained to power which no private bodies can enjoy under a sound democracy.) It must guard its powers jealously both against the combination of numerous pressure groups and against powerful lobbies like the present federal lobby of landowners. (The case of German democracy and the Junker interests is again excellently in point.) It must hold in check organizations designed for raiding the Treasury (witness the history of pension legislation and the political power of veterans' organizations). Finally, and most important for the future, it must guard its powers against great trade-unions, both as pressure groups in government and as monopolists outside.

The danger here is now most ominous, in the very nature of such agencies and also because the danger is least well recognized and commonly denied entirely. In other areas we are, if diffident and careless, at least on our guard; nothing is likely to happen that cannot be undone if we will; but labor monopolies and labor "states" may readily become a problem which democracy simply cannot solve at all. There must be effective limitations upon their powers; but I do not see how they can be disciplined democratically save by internal competition or how that discipline can be effected without breaking down organization itself. Here, possibly, is an awful dilemma: democracy cannot live with tight occupational monopolies; and it cannot destroy them, once they attain great power, without destroying itself in the process. If democratic governments cannot suppress organized extortion and preserve their monopoly of violence, they will be superseded by other kinds of government. Organized economic warfare is like organized banditry and, if allowed to spread, must lead to total revolution, which will, on very hard terms, restore some order and enable us to maintain some real income instead of fighting interminably over its division among minorities.

A community which fails to preserve the discipline of competition exposes itself to the discipline of absolute authority. Preserving the former discipline, we may govern ourselves and look forward to a peaceful world order; without it, we must submit to arbitrary authority and to hopeless disorder internationally. And, let me suggest again, the problem is quite as critical for democratic socialism as for the decentralized system of orthodox liberalism. An obvious danger in collectivism is that the vast powers of government would be abused in favoritism to particular producer groups, organized to demand favors as the price of maintaining peace, and available to support established authorities against political opposition. Adherence to competitive, productivity norms is, now or under socialism, a means for avoiding arbitrariness and, to my mind, the only feasible means. . . .

Every organized group of sellers is typically in a position to gain by raising prices and restricting sales; the popular notion that they commonly are more exploitative than their own interests would dictate (that we need only more enlightened price and wage policies by organized groups) is simply mistaken, for inadequacy of monopoly power usually leaves them far short of ideal monopoly restriction. When organization becomes widespread, however, the common interest in increased production may greatly outweigh particular interests in restriction, even for those practicing restriction; but, I repeat, the common interest may be implemented only by competition or by authoritarian dictation. There is little hope that mass organizations with monopoly power will submit to competitive prices for their services while they retain their organization and power. No one and no group can be trusted with much power; and it is merely silly to complain because groups exercise power selfishly. The mistake lies simply in permitting them to have it.

Monopoly power must be abused. It has no use save abuse. Some people evidently have believed that labor organizations should have monopoly powers and be trusted not to use them. Collective bargaining, for the Webbs, was evidently a scheme whereby labor monopolies were to raise wages to competitive levels, merely counteracting monopsony among buyers, but eschewing further exercise of organizational powers. A trade-unionism, affecting wages and working rules only within such limits, and doing all the many other good things that unions can do, would be a blessing all around.[1] No one could seri-

1 It has seemed best in this essay simply to recognize that unions perform many useful functions and render many valuable services besides those having to do with wage rates, labor costs, restrictive practices, and monopoly or bargaining power—without attempting to detail or to appraise the salutary activities or aspects of activities. This deliberate omission implies no inclination to question or to minimize the good things of unionism, but merely a disposition to emphasize considerations and

ously question its merits in the abstract. But monopsony in the labor market is, I think, very unsubstantial or transitory; and it is romantic and unreasonable to expect organizations to exercise powers only within limits consistent with the common interest. All bargaining power is monopoly power. Such power, once attained, will be used as fully as its conservation permits and also used continuously for its own accretion and consolidation. The skin disease of monopsony is certainly a poor excuse for stopping the peaceful and productive game of free enterprise and free exchange in favor of the violent contest of organized producer-minorities.

I do not assert that our only monopoly problems lie in the labor market. Save for the monopolies which government is promoting in agriculture, however, no others seem comparably important for the future. It is shameful to have permitted the growth of vast corporate empires, the collusive restraint of trade by trade associations, and the gross abuse of patent privilege for extortion, exclusion, and output restriction. But enterprise monopoly is also a skin disease, easy to correct when and if we will, and usually moderate in its abuses, since its powers are necessarily small, and since the danger of political reckoning is never very remote. Enterprise monopoly, enjoying very limited access to violence and facing heavy penalties for unfair methods against rivals, is always plagued by competition, actual and potential, and must always operate against a deeply hostile, if lethargic, attitude of courts, legislatures, and the public. In exceptional cases it has acquired vast power and sustained power over long periods. In many cases it has transformed salutary price-competition into perverse and wasteful "competition" in merchandising and advertising. But, to repeat, the proper remedies here are not very difficult technically or politically.[2]

Labor monopolies are, now or potentially, a different kind of animal. If much violence has been used against them as they struggled into existence, this should not obscure the fact that, once established,

---

aspects which are the proper and special business of economists as such. To stress those things which are especially amenable to quantitative or abstract analysis is not to imply that others are unimportant.

I wish I could honestly and tactfully propose that large unions be protected and fostered in their good functions and deprived of their socially bad ones (monopoly power). Like others, I can *wish* for this solution, but, also like others, I cannot honestly propose it, for I have no notion *how* it could be done.

2 It is difficult to focus attention upon the potentially greater problem of labor monopoly without seeming to underestimate the corresponding and complementary problem of enterprise monopoly. My best defense against this charge may be found elsewhere, e.g., in "Postwar Economic Policy: Some Traditional-Liberal Proposals," *American Economic Review,* Suppl. (March 1943), pp. 431–45.

they enjoy an access to violence which is unparalleled in other monopolies. If governments have tolerated flagrant violations of law by employers, they are nearly impotent to enforce laws against mass minorities even if majority opinion permitted it. Thus, unions may deal with scabs in ways which make even Rockefeller's early methods seem polite and legitimate. They have little to fear from chiselers in their own midst; and they have now little to fear from Congress or the courts.

Patently restrictive practices are now commonly deplored and, perhaps because unnecessary, seem somewhat on the wane. But there have been many cases of severe limitations upon entry—high initiation fees, excessive periods of apprenticeship and restrictions upon numbers of apprentices, barriers to movement between related trades, and, of course, make-work restrictions, cost-increasing working rules, and prohibition of cost-reducing innovations, notably in the building trades—not to mention racial and sex discriminations against which effective competition in labor markets is probably a necessary, if not a sufficient, protection.

It is not commonly recognized, however, that control of wage rates *is* control of entry, especially where seniority rules are in force and, even failing such rules, where qualitative selection is important and turnover itself very costly to firms. If able to enforce standard rates, experienced, established workers can insulate themselves from the competition of new workers merely by making their cost excessive, i.e., by establishing labor costs and wage-expectations which preclude expansion of production or employment in their field. New and displaced workers typically migrate, not to high-wage occupations but to places where employment opportunities exist; high wages are less attractive if jobs cannot be had. Wage control, determining a major element in operating cost, also determines the rate at which a whole industry will expand or, more likely, with strong organization, the rate of contraction.

Frankly, I can see no reason why strongly organized workers, in an industry where huge investment is already sunk in highly durable assets, should ever permit a return on investment sufficient to attract new capital or even to induce full maintenance of existing capital. If I were running a union and were managing it faithfully in the interest of the majority of its numbers, I should consistently demand wage rates which offered to existing firms no real net earnings but only the chance of getting back part of their sunk investment at the cost of the replacement outlays necessary to provide employment for most of my constituents during their own lifetimes as workers. In other words, I should plan gradually to exterminate the industry by excessive labor costs, taking care only to prevent employment from contracting more rapidly than my original constituents disappeared by death and voluntary retirement.

If I were operating, as labor leader, without the valuable hostages of large sunk investment, I should be obliged to behave more moderately. But I should still seek, controlling prices via labor costs, to restrict production as rapidly as consistent with decline of my membership by death and retirement and, while permitting some return to investors, should try always to induce only as much employment and production as my original constituents could take care of without new members. If investors disliked my high wages, they would like the high prices which I could assure them by excluding lower-wage competitors. In both cases I should, of course, not serve my constituents well toward the end unless I utilized the opportunity of permitting some newcomers, by payment of heavy tribute, to enter, to acquire skill and experience, and to become established with my older cronies; for the initiation fees would contribute handsomely to our retirement annuities.

The situation is more complicated, of course, where unions do permit and facilitate entry, i.e., where work is shared equally between newcomers and others. Here the advantages of high wages are dissipated by the sharing of unemployment; and annual wages may even drop below a competitive level, if workers value leisure highly or are usually able to find other remunerative work during their periods of layoff. The outcome resembles that of the pure cartel among enterprises, where price is fixed by voluntary agreement, output divided by quotas, and newcomers admitted freely and granted quotas on the same basis as old firms. No one gains, and everybody as consumer loses. There is great social wastage of resources, of labor in one case, of investment in the other; and the two wastes are likely to occur together, as in coal-mining.

But free entry and division of work are not likely to characterize unionism of the future and have rarely prevailed in the past. Employees increasingly seek seniority rights; employers prefer to exercise qualitative selection; and the demands from both sides are roughly consistent, especially in large established firms where workers are carefully selected in the first place and experience is important. Some conflict arises, fortunately, between the rank and file, who want the highest possible wage rates, and labor leaders, whose power and influence, in government and in labor circles, depends on the number of their constituents; but this conflict will usually be reconciled in favor of the interests of the rank and file or avoided via organizational imperialism (jurisdictional conquests). Sentimentalists will urge that strong unions should moderate wage demands, recognizing an obligation to permit entry of young workers and workers displaced in decadent industries; but I should not expect them to behave so or blame them for using power, if they have it, in their own interest; and I see no way to avoid severely restrictive policies save by depriving them of control over wages, i.e., of bargaining power.

Union Wage Policy

ARTHUR M. ROSS

INTRODUCTION

In 1928 an eminent English economist complained that ". . . *all*
existing wage theories appear to ignore a phenomenon which has
completely changed the whole condition of the labour market . . .
namely the rise to power of trade unionism, with all its consequences."[1] Eighteen years later, an eminent American economist remarked that "little is known about the determinants of union wage
policies."[2]

As a matter of fact, there is a considerable body of literature on
wage rates which recognizes the existence of unionism, but it suffers
from a conception of the union as a decision-making organism which
is both inadequate and incomplete. Research on the determinants of
union wage policies is currently in progress at a number of universities, but there is danger that a similar misconception will defeat the
purpose of these efforts. Analysis of institutional policy must begin
with an understanding of the institution itself.

Sympathetic authors often conceive of the union as a primitive,
undifferentiated protest group governed by town-meeting democracy:
the union becomes synonymous with its members. Hostile critics tend
to portray it as a dictatorship governed by an official bureaucracy:
the union here becomes synonymous with its leaders. Economic
theorists are prone to regard it as a monopolistic seller of labor

Taken from American Economic Review, *XXXVII* (*September 1947*), *pp. 566–88,
under the title, "The Trade Union as a Wage-Fixing Institution." Reprinted with the
permission of the author and the publisher. Arthur M. Ross is Professor of Industrial
Relations at the University of California at Berkeley.*

[1] J. W. F. Rowe, *Wages in Practice and Theory* (London, 1928), p. 194.
[2] Sumner H. Slichter, "Wage-Price Policy and Employment," *American Economic
Review,* XXXVI, No. 2 (May 1946), p. 305.

governed by a maximization principle; the union thus becomes analogous to a business firm marketing a commodity.

None of these images is sufficiently accurate to provide a suitable basis for an analysis of trade union policy. To be sure, any theoretical model must abstract from "the richness and complexity of behavior."[3] Abstraction becomes falsification, however, when it so oversimplifies human behavior as to leave it unrecognizable and unexplained.

The nature of the union as a representative political agency should be no mystery. If nothing had been written on the subject since the Webbs' classic description of nineteenth century British unions,[4] much would be known. Bakke's penetrating monograph, *Mutual Survival*,[5] is the latest addition to an already substantial body of literature. The difficulty is that, like dwellers in a metropolitan area, political analysis and economic analysis have long occupied adjoining apartments but have never become well acquainted with one another.

The Webbs dealt with wage rates, but employed a primitive concept of union wage policy principally defined as the maintenance of a "standard rate." Some of the monographs in the Johns Hopkins University studies made a promising beginning two or three decades ago, but then the road came to a fork—one branch leading toward empirical surveys, and the other toward deductive speculation. Mr. Slichter's *Union Policies and Industrial Management* is based on careful study of union structure and function, but deals primarily with nonwage aspects of the collective agreement.

Mr. Dunlop almost takes the plunge. He points out that the union is a decision-making unit, and that its choices do not necessarily represent the sum of the preferences of individual members.[6] He recognizes a group of "non-income objectives" of trade union wage policy—promoting membership, encouraging an equitable division of work opportunities, controlling the rate of technological innovation and attaining desired working conditions. Apparently, however, these are considered as incidental aberrations which need not be integrated into the theoretical model. The model of the union is essentially a business enterprise selling labor services to the employer, and arriving at wage decisions in the light of its "wage-membership function" and the employer's "wage-employment function."

3 John T. Dunlop, *Wage Determination under Trade Unions* (New York, 1944), p. 5.
4 Sidney and Beatrice Webb, *Industrial Democracy* (London, 1902).
5 E. Wight Bakke, *Mutual Survival—the Goal of Unions and Management* (New Haven, 1946).
6 "The institutionalized form of collective action may introduce new preferences . . . ." Dunlop, *op. cit.*, p. 31.

Dunlop argues that for theoretical purposes a union must be assumed to maximize something. This is doubtless true in the sense that speculation about the union's behavior must be oriented to some central objective. He concludes, however, that the central objective of the union must have a dollar dimension: the total wage bill, or the total wage bill of those employed (which would seem to be identical with the first), or the total wage bill minus the union's out-of-work benefits, or some similar quantitative object of maximization. Among the various possibilities, Dunlop selects total wage bill as the most appropriate for a model of union behavior.[7]

This formulation of the central aim has one remarkable implication. If, as many authors argue, it is true that the demand for labor in a single segment of the economy is often quite elastic, then we would expect to see unions insisting on wage cuts, even to the point of striking.[8]

But a more fundamental objection can be raised against the adequacy of any postulated central objective with a dollar dimension. The union is not a business enterprise selling labor. It is a political institution representing the sellers of labor, and there is no necessary reason to assume that it will automatically or mechanically behave in the same fashion as a profit-maximizing business enterprise.

DISTINCTION BETWEEN THE UNION AND ITS MEMBERS

Every institution has a formal purpose, a stated intention, an official rationale. For the Church, it is the promise of spiritual salvation; for the State, the provision of common defense, the protection of domestic tranquility, etc.; for an economic system, the production of goods and services. The formal purpose is always a statement of the benefit which the institution provides for its rank-and-file. Ordinarily, the members of the institution must feel that it satisfies the formal purpose as an incident to its activities; otherwise, it is not likely to survive.

When an organization feels the need for justification, it will refer its activities to the formal purpose, and assert that every decision has contributed to this purpose—at least in the long run. The Church will argue that lay functions are necessary guarantees of spiritual salvation. The State will contend that an imperialist venture is necessary for the common defense of its citizens. Perhaps these claims are valid.

7 "Probably the most generalized assumption respecting actual aims of trade unions would be the maximization of the wage bill." *Ibid*, p. 119.
8 This assumes that union leaders are aware of the true elasticity of demand.

But the student of ecclesiastical or international policy will hardly care to accept them at face value.

As an institution expands in strength and status, it outgrows its formal purpose. It experiences its own needs; it develops its own ambitions and it faces its own problems. These become differentiated from the needs, ambitions and problems of its rank-and-file. The trade union is no exception.

It is the beginning of wisdom in the study of industrial relations to understand that the union, as an organization, is not identical with its members, as individuals. This becomes more true as the union becomes better established and more "responsible."

Experienced employer representatives are accustomed to emphasize the distinction between the union and its members. Therefore, they sometimes say that there are three parties to a collective bargaining agreement. So long as this remains true, there will be two aspects of "industrial relations"—the worker-management relation and the union-management relation; and there will be two techniques for the handling of industrial relations—personnel administration and collective bargaining.

Union members often realize that the organization has its own needs and problems, apart from their own, and has a claim on their loyalty even where self-interest is not evident. There is something similar to national patriotism—the memory of the grievances that were suffered, the pride in the battles that were won, the enjoyment of fellowship and solidarity. If the union is effectively organized, the members will adopt its institutional needs as their own when mobilized for combat.

It is for these reasons precisely that the editorial writers of the nation, and some scholars as well, have been so wide of the mark in their pursuit of the increasingly popular pastime of counting the workers' losses in a strike. The arithmetic which demonstrates that it will take two years and eight months to recoup the difference between wages lost in a strike and the wage increase gained is generally exact. But unfortunately it is irrelevant. A patriotic citizenry does not count the cost of a war unless the war is lost.[9]

[9] In bilateral monopoly theory, the "lower limit" of the wage bargain is often described as the wage rate below which workers will prefer to transfer to another industry. This might be the lower limit of an individual bargain between an employer and an unorganized worker, but in a successful union the members simply do not think in these terms. The lowest wage they will accept is the lowest wage which the union will accept. A disastrous strike will demoralize them much as a military debacle will demoralize the citizens of a nation; but short of such a catastrophe, the putative "lower limit" of bilateral monopoly theory has no place in their calculations. In the event of such a catastrophe, it is no longer a situation of bilateral monopoly.

THE TRADE UNION AND THE BUSINESS FIRM

In economic literature, as mentioned above, the union is often conceived of as analogous to the monopolist in a commodity market; the comparison is made in order to utilize modes of analysis which have proven useful in theorizing about price and output decisions. A far greater amount of study has been given to the determinants of business behavior than of union behavior. Moreover, as Bakke points out, unions are expected to conform to the code of business morality, and the typical union leader wishes to behave in a businesslike fashion— to be "a fellow you can do business with." For these reasons, it is instructive to consider the points of similarity and dissimilarity between the trade union and the business firm.

The two institutions do have certain features in common. In either case, there is a formal purpose or official rationale, which is represented by textbook authors as the sole determinant of policy. The rationale of the business firm is to maximize the profits of stockholders; and of the union, to maximize the economic welfare of members.

Even at the formal level, there is an element of vagueness about the official rationale. The profit to be maximized is anticipated profit, not merely in the current production period but over the life of the enterprise. The economic welfare to be maximized is a vague bundle of benefits relating to "wages, hours, and conditions of work," again over some indeterminate period. There is obviously scope for interpretation, and need for it, in either case.

Therefore, the formal purposes must be interpreted and applied to the problems at hand by leadership groups—corporate management and union officialdom. They must constantly decide whether this or that course of action is likely to contribute toward the maximization of profit, on the one hand, and the augmentation of group welfare, on the other. It is here that the intangible attributes of leadership are brought into play—judgment, experience and moral authority.

It is here also that a battery of political pressures comes to focus on the leadership. Each pressure emanates from some interest group which is concerned that the formal purpose of the institution be interpreted in a manner favorable to itself.

Corporate management is surrounded by stockholders, bondholders, bankers, suppliers, customers, employees, the union and the agencies of government. Each group realizes that management has considerable latitude in making decisions, and endeavors to dominate relevant decisions in its own interest. All feasible means of persuasion are used; at the level of argument, it is typically asserted that the favored course of action will contribute, at least in the long run, to the total profit of the enterprise.

Union leadership is surrounded by a similar configuration—the rank and file, the employers, the officials at higher or lower levels of organization, the other unions, and again the agencies of government. Each of these will endeavor to prove that the course of action which happens to be in its own interest will also contribute to the welfare of the rank and file.

The task of corporate management and union leadership is to reconcile these pressures. This is the central core of the managerial function. It is at this point that the formal purpose of the organization is supplanted by a more vital force, the necessity of survival and the impulse toward growth as an institution. In many cases, of course, the decision which is most clearly related to the formal purpose will also best serve the institutional objectives. Where there is a conflict, however, a healthy institution will look to its own necessities. Therefore, pressures are reconciled in the manner which seems most conducive to the survival and growth of the organization.

Suppose, for example, that the managers of a flourishing and currently profitable corporation should become persuaded that the formal objective of "maximizing profits over the life of the enterprise" could best be served by dissolving the corporation immediately, as an alternative to making certain capital commitments which otherwise would be necessary. Suppose that the leaders of a successful union should become convinced that the members could improve their economic welfare by transferring in a body to some other industry or some other union. Would either organization put itself out of business under these circumstances? It is the normal rather than the exceptional case in which conflict between a formal rationale and a vital institutional need is resolved in favor of the latter.

In stating that the institutional objective is foremost in the normal state of organizational health, one assumes that the leaders have been able and willing to achieve more or less complete identification with the institution—that the corporate manager is wholeheartedly a "company man" and the union official wholeheartedly a "union man." When this is not true, the situation becomes more complicated, and a third type of motivation is introduced. In the failure of voluntary identification, and the absence of social controls requiring compulsory identification, the leaders are governed by their own survival needs and their own ambitions, which are at variance with those of the organization. The wrecking of organizations in pursuit of personal advantage is not unknown either in the corporation world or the union world.

Thus, in comparing the motivating impulses of the business firm and the union, we have encountered three kinds of objectives: (1) the formal purpose or rationale, representing the benefit accruing to the rank and file (stockholders and members); (2) the institutional objective—survival and growth of the organization; and (3) the personal ambitions of the leadership. Ultimately the human animal is selfish. In the absence of identification, personal ambitions will come first; but in the normal case, the leader advances himself by advancing his organization. The formal purpose must be accomplished, to a greater or lesser extent, if the organization is to stay alive, but when in conflict with institutional objectives, it is forced to give way.

DISSIMILARITIES BETWEEN THE UNION AND THE FIRM

So far the comparison holds together fairly well. There are, however, significant points of difference. An understanding of these points should help in appraising the value of the analogy, and illuminating the relationship between the union official and his rank and file.

The formal purpose of the union is vaguer than that of the business firm. Profit can be measured in one dimension. "Economic welfare" is a congeries of discrete phenomena—wages, with a dollar dimension; hours of work, with a time dimension; physical working conditions, economic security, protection against managerial abuse and various rights of self-determination, with no measurable dimension at all. Therefore, the union leader has considerably more discretion in interpreting the formal purpose. If he is able to convince the rank and file that his own interpretation is correct, there is no one else with the moral authority to contradict him successfully; but a corporate manager would find it difficult to convince his stockholders that a $2.00 dividend was really $3.00. The inherent difficulty of measuring "economic welfare" is obvious whenever one union official attempts to persuade another that he has negotiated the better contract.

Corporate managers must operate under the surveillance of cost accountants, finance committees, etc., who have the function of navigating leadership activities toward the accomplishment of the formal purpose of the enterprise. Corresponding agencies in a rudimentary form are sometimes found in union organization, but they are probably less of a "drag" upon the leadership (and offer less help in the formulation of policy), because the formal purpose of the union is less capable of measurement. In many unions, constitutional provision is made for the election of trustees, whose formal function is to serve as watchdogs of the rank-and-file interest but whose chief activity, in practice, is to guard the petty cash account against misappropriation.

The business firm sells goods or services, but the union does not sell labor. It participates in the establishment of the price of labor, but the sale is made between the worker and the employer. The union is not mechanically or automatically concerned with the "quantity of labor sold"—that is, in the number of workers employed in the branch of the economy over which it asserts jurisdiction. It is vitally concerned with the size of union membership, but this is not the same as the number of workers employed, except in the case where the industry is "100 per cent organized" and the union has no desire to expand its jurisdiction. This would be the apex of institutional maturity, a position in which the only way to increase membership is by increasing employment. But in the present stage of development of the labor movement, the "employment effect" will frequently differ from the "membership effect" and may even move in the opposite direction. An upward wage adjustment may bring in new members, even though the employer is reducing personnel. A downward wage adjustment may bring about a wave of resignations even though the employer should add to his personnel. Inasmuch as the "membership effect" is more closely related to the growth and survival of the organization than is the "employment effect," it will necessarily take precedence when the two are in conflict. The union as a wage-fixing agency is clearly not the same as the conjectural monopolist of bilateral monopoly theory.

The relationship between the union and its members is very different from the relationship between the corporation and its stockholders. Union members are not satisfied with a stabilized rate of return. The corporate stockholder is not constantly called upon to ratify operating decisions. Stockholders are widely dispersed and exceedingly inarticulate.

Further, the stockholder's dividend from a single company is usually only a minor share of his total income, while the employee's wage is the predominant source of income. When dissatisfied stockholders sell their equity, there is no diminution in the amount of capital under control of the enterprise; but when dissatisfied employees resign from the union or transfer to another industry, the size and strength of the union are correspondingly lessened. Moreover, the corporation has alternative means of raising capital. Stockholders and bondholders constitute a rather homogeneous electorate, differentiated only on the basis of propensity for assuming risk; while union membership is often heterogeneous in the extreme.

Lastly, there is an essential difference in the survival problems of the union and the business enterprise. The basic threat to the survival of the enterprise is that capital will not be replaced if the operations are unprofitable. An intermediate danger is the possibility of proxy fights and declining security prices. The most immediate peril is the loss of customers.

It might be argued that the survival problems of the union, although political rather than economic, are equal and parallel: dissolution of the union corresponds to the non-replacement of capital; disaffection of members corresponds to disaffection of stockholders; and loss of jobs corresponds to loss of customers. The analogy is valid in a formal sense; but as it appears to the union leader, the peril is more complicated. He would distinguish at least four types of survival problems.

1. The first is the characteristic apathy of the American worker, who, up to the present at least, has not been a firm unionist by nature. As Perlman states, "The overshadowing problem of the American labor movement has always been the problem of staying organized. No other labor movement has ever had to contend with the fragility so characteristic of American labor organizations."[10] Corporation stockholders are also notoriously apathetic, but with vastly different consequences. Their apathy is a blessing to those who lead them, rather than a curse.

2. The union must survive against the actual or potential hostility of the employer. To be sure, some of the most powerful weapons have been removed from the arsenal of the anti-union employer, such as the yellow-dog contract and the right of discriminatory discharge; and a large number of employers are tolerant or sympathetic toward the participation of the union in the control of employment conditions. Nevertheless, there is still ample room for anti-union strategy within the law; and even when the employer is not seriously concerned with breaking the union, he may well be desirous of weakening its hold on rank-and-file employees. In many industries, there is a running controversy over the proper status of the union. To be sure, it is possible for sellers in a commodity market to put buyers out of business, but ordinarily they do not have the same interest in doing so as powerful buyers of labor have had in putting unions out of busi-

---

[10] Selig Perlman and Philip Taft, *History of Labor in the United States, 1896–1932* (New York: Macmillan, 1935), p. 7.

ness. The ordinary business contract does not require the same sacrifice of prerogatives as does the collective bargaining contract, and is not resisted in the same way.

3. The union must endeavor to survive against the threatened encroachment of rival unions into its jurisdiction. The problem is not limited to the traditional jurisdictional dispute over the "right to the job" as a property right attaching to particular crafts. It results also from differences in union structure (particularly the conflicting claims of craft and industrial unions over the right to organize groups of skilled workers); from dual unionism (such as competing maritime, longshore, automobile, electrical and street railway unions in the A. F. of L. and the C.I.O.); and from the expansionism which is characteristic of vigorous and successful organizations of any kind and which is by no means limited to the well-known jurisdictional claims of District 50, United Mine Workers of America. It may be pointed out in rebuttal that the business firm must survive against the encroachment of rival enterprises. This is true, of course, but the difference is that the encroachment generally takes the form of gradual infiltration into the market, rather than a mass political overturn engineered by a *coup de main*.

4. The union faces the threat of repressive labor legislation. Antiunion proposals are always in the wind, but occasionally they gather into a cloud, as they did in 1947. Whether or not the Taft-Hartley Act will have consequences as far-reaching as union leaders claim, it is clearly an attack upon the degree of security which unions had previously attained. There can hardly be doubt that trade union wage policy was dominated, in the early months of the year, by the desire to avoid repressive legislation. Here again, the objection will be raised that the corporation also faces the threat of repressive legislation and will take this into account in formulating its price policy. Surely there is a large difference in degree, however. The corporation has never had to face such a sustained hostility on the part of a substantial proportion of voters and legislators as the union faces. Business enterprise is the dominant institution of economic life, while the union is not yet fully recognized as legitimate.

The elected union official has his own survival problem as well—re-election and advancement. This is particularly true at the local level of organization. Dependent on the continued support of the rank and file below him, he is in a fundamentally different position from the corporation official, who must cultivate and maintain the approval of executives above him. An official hierarchy which is built up from the bottom by popular election is not the same as one which is built down from the top by executive appointment. Officials in either type of organization are required to exercise political strategy in order to safeguard their status, but the second type permits a greater degree of personal security than the first. Keeping one's fences mended with a few superior officers is vastly less complicated than holding the allegiance of a large and heterogeneous electorate, which is often receptive to the blandishments of rival leaders and would-be leaders. In consequence, it is more difficult for the local union official to achieve complete identification with the institution. Merely because the union survives, it does not follow that he will survive. And if he does not survive, there is often no alternative but to return to the shop—an unpleasant alternative indeed, despite the avowals of willingness which are frequently heard.

It is true that, with respect to the tenure of local union officials, there are considerable variations vetween the old and the new union, between the dictatorial and the democratic union, and between the homogeneous and the heterogeneous union. It is also true that there is a striking difference between lower and upper strata of organization. The tenure of a local union official may hang by a thread, but when he becomes an international representative, he has arrived (unless the international union is badly factionalized). International union executives tend to have unlimited tenure in office, except in the case of a major debacle. They enjoy a degree of security which is probably not less than that of company officials.

Employers and economists generally consider international officers to be more reasonable and responsible than local officers. This is variously attributed to their maturity, greater experience, better knowledge of the industry, etc. Actually, the most important reason is that they are better insulated from rank-and-file pressure. Democracy in the union, like competition in the product market, is universally the object of reverential obeisance, but is not especially enjoyable to those on the receiving end.

HETEROGENEITY OF MEMBERSHIP

It has been shown in the preceding sections that the formal purpose of the trade union must be interpreted and applied by the leaders in such a manner as to ensure its survival and growth and to fulfill their own professional ambitions. This requires that attention be paid to a complex group of political relationships, some inside the organization and some extending to the employers, to other unions, and to the government. Inside the union, the major political problems are those created by the heterogeneity of membership, by the need for division of labor and balance of power between the local and the international, and by the machinery for rank-and-file participation in the making of decisions.

A trade union is never a homogeneous group. The ordinary "craft" union includes a number of skilled occupations as well as apprentices and helpers, and the occupational composition of an industrial union is, of course, even more heterogeneous. Most unions are represented in a number of industries; craft union organization follows an occupation, a process or a material, wherever found. The "industrial" union is more often multi-industrial; for example, the United Steelworkers of America have organized a multitude of distinct industries, blanketed informally by the omnibus designation of "miscellaneous steel," whose only common demominator is the fact that all are engaged in the fabrication of a common raw material. The wage income of the union membership may account for widely different proportions of total cost in their respective industries. Even within a single industry, there are the employees of profitable and unprofitable firms, and the employees residing in high-wage and low-wage areas. Moreover, there are young and old workers, fast and slow workers, male and female workers, married and single workers, employed and unemployed workers.

Non-homogeneity of membership often gives rise to conflicts of interest. It is one of the most delicate political tasks of the union leadership to reconcile these conflicts in the course of formulating its wage program. The ultimate resolution depends upon (1) the effective political pressure generated by the various interest groups, and (2) the political skill of the leadership.

Justice is guaranteed to no man. If the interest group is not aware of the conflict, if it has no articulate spokesmen, and if it has no bargaining power inside the organization, it cannot generate any effective political pressure. Many union wage scales show discrimination against female members, either by providing for "men's rates" and "women's rates" or else by assigning abnormally low rates to the occupations in which females predominate. Trade union wage policy in a depression may be dominated by the employed members, particularly when the unemployed cease paying dues and drift away from active participation in the union. According to Shister, the unemployed members of the Hosiery Workers and the "substitute" or non-steady workers in the typographical unions were in favor of wage cuts in 1937, but were overruled by those with regular employment.[11] But God helps him who helps himself. Across-the-board wage increases gained by the United Automobile Workers between 1937 and 1942 had the result of flattening the rate structure of the industry. The rate differential between a sweeper and a toolmaker was reduced from about 120 per cent to about 40 per cent. In 1944, a number of articulate spokesmen began to agitate the skilled workers. The Mechanics' Educational Society of America (an independent union centered in Toledo) became more active in Detroit and aroused considerable interest among tool and die workers. There was some possibility that carpenters, electricians and other maintenance men would transfer to various A.F. of L. unions. The result was a five cent increase for all apprenticeable occupations in the automobile industry. (Convincing the National War Labor Board that it might legitimately order the increase under stabilization rules was a spectacular political achievement in itself.)

Political ineptitude on the part of the leadership may lead to disastrous results. The unity of the organization disintegrates. Off at one side instead of at the center, the officials are no longer in a position to stem the tide of subversive influences. The disaffected element may overturn the leadership; it may desert to a rival organization; it may become disgruntled about unionism in general; and it may even "scab" on union members.

An important aspect of the leadership function is reasonably to ensure that every interest group which can exercise effective political pressure is represented in the bargaining process. In a multi-craft union, the important crafts will be represented; in a multi-industrial union, the different branches of trade; and in regional or national negotiations, the various geographical units of the organization.

If it is not feasible to engineer a single settlement, it may be necessary to differentiate the bargaining structure so that the different interest groups can bargain separately under specialized leadership. Despite its emphasis on industrial unionism, the Amalgamated Clothing Workers has a differentiated local structure in certain areas; the cutters' locals in New York and Boston, which were organized prior to the Amalgamated, have remained virtually independent of the Joint Boards. The Building Service Union has ten locals in San Francisco—a department store local, an apartment and office building local, a theater local, etc. Similarly, the Teamster's Union has a

---

[11] Joseph Shister, "The Theory of Union Wage Rigidity," *Quarterly Journal of Economics*, LVII (August 1943), p. 523.

draymen's local, a milk drivers' local, a warehouse local, and others. But there are no administrative devices which will entirely eliminate the need for careful management of the wage bargain so as to hold the organization together. The union must decide not only what demands will be pressed upon the employer, but also what form the benefits should take. Suppose, for example, that the employer is willing to grant a ten per cent wage increase, but is relatively indifferent as to the distribution of the gain. All occupational rates might be advanced ten per cent—one type of "across-the-board" increase. Assuming that the present weighted average rate is $1.20 per hour, all occupational rates might be advanced 12 cents—another type of "across-the-board" increase. The common labor rate might be increased 18 cents, and higher rates by progressively smaller amounts, in order to "eliminate excessive differentials." The higher rates might be increased by larger percentages, in order to "restore historical relationships." Low-wage plants in outlying areas might be levelled up to high-wage plants in metropolitan areas so as to provide "equal pay for equal work." Some kind of distribution among various occupations might be effected for the purpose of "ironing out inequities" in the rate structure. A combination of two or more of these possibilities might be devised, such as eight per cent across the board and two per cent distributed here and there to eliminate inequities. Each of the forms in which the wage increase might be taken involves a different distribution of the total gain. The union's problem in apportioning the gain is similar to the problem of the 80th Congress in apportioning the proposed income-tax reduction.

DISTRIBUTION OF AUTHORITY BETWEEN THE LOCAL AND THE INTERNATIONAL

Observers of the wage-bargaining process invariably note that there are great differences between one union and another in the locus of decision-making power, ranging all the way from unrestricted local autonomy to rigid centralization.

The level of organization at which a decision is made is primarily affected, of course, by the scope of the decision. A master bargain covering the entire membership of the union will be made at the top level. Subordinate units will participate in the process, by being represented in a consultative policy committee or even on the negotiating committee; but in the end the decision is made for the organization as a whole. Similarly, a regional bargain will be made at the regional level, or higher.

The more interesting question is the extent to which the international union participates in a decision covering a single local union, company or plant. There are several devices available to the international union. It may require that locally negotiated contracts be approved by the regional or national office. It may furnish negotiators, attorneys and research personnel. It may establish standards from which the local union is not permitted to deviate. It may require that the local secure the permission of the parent body before striking.

Variations in the extent of international union control over local decisions can be illustrated by three unions in the San Francisco Bay area—the Building Service Workers, the Teamsters and the Steelworkers.

At one extreme are the Building Service Workers, showing almost complete decentralization. There is no intervention from the parent organization in collective bargaining, and nothing which might be called a national wage policy. Most of the locals have accumulated sizeable strike funds, and are not dependent on the international even in the case of a strike.

At the other extreme are the Steelworkers, who are governed by the "wage policy" of the international union. This takes the form of a uniform "across-the-board" increase in cents per hour (although the Steelworkers, like the Auto Workers, are formally on record in favor of nation-wide equalization). The pattern is set by annual negotiations between the top officers of the union and the U.S. Steel Corporation. Control over local negotiations is assured by the requirement that local contracts be approved by the international union, and by the participation of international representatives. As the president of the Northern California Council of Steelworkers stated in January, 1947, "We're all acting together in this business, with no one going off on any sidelines of his own."[12]

The Teamsters negotiate locally, ordinarily without the participation of the International Brotherhood. Local contracts must be approved by the Brotherhood, but in practice this is only a *pro forma* requirement. The real control is in the constitutional provision that a local union cannot strike without permission of the Brotherhood. The national and regional offices are anxious to build up their reputation for responsible business unionism, and to use the strike weapon only as a last resort. They will insist on the protection of institutional security, but will equally insist that a wage agreement be attained in a peaceful manner. Local leaders must take account of several possi-

[12] *Labor Herald,* Vol. X, January 17, 1947.

bilities: if they apply for permission to strike, the Brotherhood may refuse; if they go on strike without permission, the Brotherhood may order them back; and if they refuse to terminate the strike, the Brotherhood may "move in and take over."

There are several factors which influence the degree of control exercised by the international union over the local wage bargain. Unions organized in local-market industries can, and do, permit more local autonomy than those organized in national-market industries. Unions which have grown from the top down, such as the Steelworkers, are more centralized than those which have grown from the bottom up, such as the Clothing Workers. Personal characteristics and historical accidents undoubtedly play a role. . . .

There has been considerable discussion of the virtues and vices of intervention by higher officers in local bargaining. It is generally approved by employers and economists, although there is an element of ambivalence in the thinking of both.

Employers believe that international representatives are more farsighted, better acquainted with industry problems, and farther removed from rank-and-file pressures. Yet on specific occasions they often object to the intrusion of outsiders who have no personal interest in the enterprise, and to the introduction of "extraneous" demands which are based upon international union policy. Actually, the international union may either play up or play down the demands of the local union. In a particular case, the employer's attitude will depend upon whether the international officers act as a moderating or aggravating influence (from his own standpoint).

Shister concludes that the intervention of the national office has "a decidedly beneficial effect" on the local wage bargain. Since the national officers understand the problems of the industry, because of "longer and more intimate contact with the management group," the wage bargain "is bound to have less detrimental effects on costs, and, therefore, on employment opportunities."[13] In other words, the wage rate is bound to be lower. But in the same paragraph he adds that "national representatives are often able to obtain greater concessions for the local than the latter could by itself."

Whether good or bad, the drift is unmistakable. Moreover, it is only part of a more general tendency toward centralization and con-

---

[13] Shister, *op. cit.*, p. 525. Some economists seem to believe that a "farsighted" union leader is one who foregoes a wage increase during a period of prosperity, in order to prevent inflation, and accepts a wage decrease during a period of depression, in order to reduce the cost of production.

solidation in the wage-bargaining process. Multi-employer, multi-union and multi-area agreements are evidence of formal integration of bargaining structure. As the orbit of comparison widens, unions and employers become increasingly dependent on patterns of adjustment; shadows from the outside are thrown across the bargaining table, and the isolated or "atomistic" wage determination becomes more and more of a rarity. In this way, as in so many other ways, developments in union policy are only a reflection of corresponding changes in almost every sphere of economic activity.

THE ROLE OF THE RANK AND FILE

Prevalent opinion on the desirability of rank-and-file participation in the wage bargain is curiously divided. Devotion to the ideal of union democracy is quite genuine; it cannot be written off as mere lip service. The bargaining process is commonly described as a means of attaining industrial democracy wherein the individual wage earner can define the terms under which he supplies his labor. On the other hand, it is widely recognized that a considerable measure of discretion in the hands of the leadership is an indispensable condition for a sound and business-like settlement. . . . The underlying issue is whether trade union wage policy should represent the wishes of the rank and file, as expressed by the rank and file; or the interests of the rank and file, as interpreted by the leadership.

In addition, there is a preliminary question of fact. To what extent *is* trade union wage policy (as represented in the contract proposal, the approval or disapproval of the employer's offer, the decision to strike, etc.) determined by the membership? Here again, an atmosphere of unreality surrounds the standard treatment of the question. The difficulty is that the answers are based almost entirely on formal constitutional provisions and parliamentary procedures. This kind of analysis is seldom reliable; in the U.S.S.R., the "most democratic constitution in the world" is not incompatible with a great centralization of political power.

The membership may formulate the demand; in the case of a local wage bargain, it ordinarily does. It may designate the bargaining committee. It may listen to periodic reports on the progress of negotiations, and express its opinion as to proper strategy. It may vote on whether the union should strike, and whether a strike should be terminated. It may be called upon to accept or reject the employer's offer, and to ratify a tentative agreement, either in meeting or through a referendum. It may select its delegates to the annual or biennial convention of the union, where the general policies of the organization and the conduct of its leaders are submitted to review. There are few institutions in the economic or social life of the nation with so many channels of communication between the rank and file and the leadership.

It does not follow, however, that trade union wage policy is actually made up of rank-and-file decisions, in any real sense. And in point of fact, the rank and file is extremely dependent on the leadership for guidance on what is equitable, what is possible, and what is acceptable. The most important business of meetings and conventions is to permit the officers to communicate with the members. The essential function of the strike vote and the referendum is to demonstrate the solidarity of the union in support of its leaders. The wage policy of a union, like the foreign policy of a nation, is a matter poorly suited to the methods of primitive democracy.

This is not to argue that the rank and file is only a passive tool. It does have a temper, apathetic or militant; it does have a propensity or disinclination to strike; it is highly susceptible to the appeals of rival leaders or would-be leaders. The relationship with the rank and file remains the most important in the horizon of the union official.

The rank and file always wants more. There are two circumstances under which the pressure is likely to be imperative. One is a strain upon established standards of living brought about by an inflation in the price level or a reduction in take-home pay. When these occur simultaneously, as they did in 1945–46, the pressure is particularly great. The other is an invidious comparison with the wages, or wage increases, of other groups of workers. This comparison originates more often over the clothesline than over the lunchbox. These are the sources of labor unionism at the grass roots, because they jeopardize the worker's way of life and damage his self-respect. When the refrigerator is repossessed by the dealer, and when the neighbor's wife begins to put on airs, the worker feels a deep and abiding sense of injustice. Other considerations, such as the percentage of profit earned by the employer and the increase in output per man-hour, are infinitely more remote, but they are seized upon as supporting arguments once the original feeling of injustice is created.

The union must deliver; that is clear. But *how much?* The individual member is not in a position to decide how much the union must deliver in order to hold his fealty. Within wide limits, this must be decided for him.

How much is equitable? Among the profusion of occupations and industries in economic life, among the variety of methods of payment

and non-wage benefits, and among the multiplicity of equitable criteria, the "square deal" becomes a complicated and technical matter.
The individual member may know how much he would like to have,
and his wife may know how much he really deserves, but both are
aware that this is not a world of perfect justice. What he ought to
receive as a condition of provisional satisfaction is another question
altogether. The individual member is not equipped to answer the
question with moral certainty. He needs the technical knowledge of a
trusted leader.

How much is obtainable? Here the individual is even more at sea.
He cannot say what the employer can afford to pay. More important,
he is not versed in the diplomatic and military strategy which is the
key to the problem. The member wants all that can be obtained, but
the guidance of experienced leadership is absolutely indispensable on
these points. To expect a rank-and-file determination of bargaining
strategy is about as plausible as to expect the government of the
United States to conduct its foreign policy through a monthly plebi-
scite of registered voters.

How much is acceptable? In the end, the result is frequently disappointing to the rank and file, because the original demand is almost
always subject to shrinkage. What seemed equitable and obtainable at
the outset of negotiations is not in the cards when the chips are down.
At some point or other, it is wise to conclude negotiations (or terminate hostilities) and sign a treaty for another year. This is another
strategic decision which the rank and file is not equipped to make.

Thus, trade union wage policy is inevitably a leadership function.
The reason is not that the leadership has wrested dictatorial power
from the rank and file but that it alone is in possession of the necessary knowledge, experience, and skill to perform the function adequately.

This analysis applies to the normal condition of organizational
health, where the rank and file has trust in its leaders and is willing to
follow them. There are occasions, to be sure, in which the rank and
file appear to revolt. They insist on striking against the advice of the
officials, or they stay at work in the face of an order to strike. They
reject a tentative agreement which is vigorously supported by the
officials. This is not so much a sign of vigorous democracy as an
indication of internal demoralization. The membership believes it has
been sold down the river; it has lost faith in the leadership. Moreover,
a rank-and-file revolt during a period of mobilization or a state of
hostilities is almost positive evidence that rival leaders are at work—

a dissident faction with its own candidates for union office, or else organizers and sympathizers for a rival union. The truly spontaneous rank-and-file revolt is largely a myth, like the spontaneous strike and the pitchfork rebellion.

In addition to gauging the intensity of rank-and-file pressure, the union leader must take into consideration two other factors—the degree of inclination to strike and the degree of danger from rival leadership.

The inclination to go on strike is the net result of many positive and negative influences, including the *mores* of the workers' community, the financial resources of the rank and file, the probable duration of the strike, the condition of the weather, and the length of time since the last strike. It is ordinarily not feasible to ask a group of workers to undergo a prolonged strike more than once every four or five years, just as it is not feasible to conduct a major war more than once every generation.[14] In conducting wage negotiations, the union official must take into account the current propensity to strike. For example, the propensity to strike was very great in 1946, and very slight in 1947. This is a partial explanation for the infrequency of strikes and the small size of wage increases in major manufacturing industries during 1947.

Rival leadership may threaten from inside or outside the organization. Some leaders, such as the late Sidney Hillman, enjoy the virtually undivided loyalty of the membership, and command a faithful and disciplined political machine. Others . . . must contend with a bitter factionalism. Since the opposition will seize upon any opportunity to deprecate their effectiveness, they must take care that a wage settlement is not vulnerable to partisan attack. Some unions, such as the Teamsters in most localities, occupy a secure territory; they may be annoyed by border skirmishes, but the main centers of the organization are well fortified against assault. Others, such as the three unions in the meat-packing industry, are constantly required to beat back each other's forces of invasion. Any wage settlement is subjected to scorn and ridicule in the periodicals and pamphlets of the opposing unions; the advantages of the settlement are minimized; the leaders are excoriated as piecards, Commies, or company stooges; the membership is commiserated for having been sold down the river.

---

14 The coal miners must be noted as an exception. Many of the commercial mines would shut down during the spring or summer in any event, because of the seasonality of demand for coal. In addition, the frequency of prolonged strikes in the coal industry can be explained by the social isolation of the miners, their exceptionally bitter sense of injustice, and the rigors of underground work.

In arriving at a settlement, it is obviously important to guard against these accusations, and to ensure that they will not be persuasive to the rank and file.

There has already been occasion to observe that the provisions of trade union constitutions and by-laws are ordinarily as democratic as any advocate of popular government could desire. But an apparatus, no matter how carefully designed, cannot guarantee the objective it seeks. It is not proof against the need for technical knowledge and tactical skill, a need which constantly enlarges the scope and authority of leadership and limits the role of the rank and file. It is interesting to observe how the procedures for rank-and-file participation in the wage bargain have increasingly become tools for the use of leadership. Originally intended to implement the final authority of the rank and file, they have gradually undergone a subtle metamorphosis, until they have become a means of conditioning the membership, communicating indirectly with the employer, and guarding the flank against rival leadership.

The rank and file is assembled to formulate a wage demand. Knowing what seems obtainable, sensing the temper of the membership, and bearing in mind the strategic possibilities of the situation (from the standpoint of the union's institutional objectives), the officials must decide whether to "play it up" or "play it down." They can emphasize the employer's exorbitant profits, or his high costs of production and difficult marketing problems. They can point to the rapid advance in the cost of living, or they can argue that the price level shows definite signs of receding. In calling attention to the wages, and wage increases, of other groups of workers, they have a wide field of selection. They can praise the employer's cooperative attitude, or condemn his lack of good faith. In other words, they can elect to play the role of militant fighters, or cautious advisers. They must take care not to overrun the limits of discretion; but between these limits, the range of choice is quite considerable.

Negotiations proceed unsatisfactorily, and the rank and file is asked to take a strike vote. This is a ritual affirmation of solidarity, a symbolic gesture to impress the employer. To vote "no" would be equivalent to a complete nullification of the union's bargaining power, an act of total disarmament during a crisis in foreign relations. An affirmative strike vote does not necessarily mean that the membership is desirous of striking; as a matter of fact, in the great majority of cases, an affirmative vote is not succeeded by a strike. The strike vote is merely a vote of confidence in the leadership, taken at a time when it can hardly be denied.

It is for this reason that the strike-vote procedure of the Smith-Connally Act proved so ineffective. The procedure was based on the illusory hope of driving a wedge between the rank and file and the leadership. Many thousands of strike votes have been conducted by the National Labor Relations Board; although statistics are not available, one may venture to guess that more than 95 per cent have been affirmative. The only effect of the provision was to instill the habit of securing an affirmative vote at the outset of negotiations, a solemn ceremony which occasioned no end of merriment among union and employer representatives.

The membership is asked whether it wishes to approve or reject the employer's offer, which the union officials may have tentatively accepted, subject to ratification. On this occasion, much depends upon the manner in which the offer or tentative agreement is presented. The rank and file wishes to know whether it is the best obtainable. Somehow, the officials must communicate an answer. They may point out the flaws in the offer, in which case it will surely be rejected. They may present it without recommendation, in which case it has no more than a 10 per cent chance of acceptance. Only when they give it vigorous support is it likely to be ratified. If it matches the expectations of the rank and file, it will be described as "the best contract in the industry." If it falls short of their expectations, it will be characterized as "a down payment on our just demands." In either case, vigorous support will result in ratification—that is, unless the officials have grossly misjudged the temper of the membership or the union is factionalized.

Rank-and-file approval is useful to the officials because it affords some measure of protection against rival leadership. The members have participated in the bargaining process; any attack upon the settlement is a reflection on themselves as well as their leaders.

From time to time, prudence may also require the vigorous prosecution of lost causes. A group of workers may feel strongly about some fancied grievance, or a grass-roots wage demand, which from any impartial view must be judged unfounded or unwarranted. Notwithstanding the virtual certainty of defeat, the issue may be militantly pressed in collective bargaining. Employers frequently understand that union officials are required to support improbable demands, and develop a spirit of tolerance toward the practice if it is not carried too far. If it is politically impossible for the officials to accept a refusal, the issue may be carried to arbitration, again without expectation of success. All of these procedures are part of the equipment of successful trade union leaders. The improbable demand has important functions;

it permits a periodic display of militance and devotion to rank-and-file interests; it is useful as a symbol of the employer's intransigeance and the arbitrator's prejudice. The moral which emerges is useful and pointed. If the employer is callous and the arbitrator prejudiced, the only recourse a worker has is to a union strong enough to enforce his just demands.

SUMMARY

The trade union is a political institution which participates in the establishment of wage rates. To conceive of the union as a seller of labor attempting to maximize some measurable object (such as the wage bill) is a highly misleading formulation. Although comparable with a business firm in some respects, it is so dissimilar in other respects that the analogy is of questionable value.

The formal rationale of the union is to augment the economic welfare of its members; but a more vital institutional objective—survival and growth of the organization—will take precedence whenever it comes into conflict with the formal purpose.

Trade union wage policy is a function of the leadership. It is expressed in the various operating decisions which officials are required to make in the course of wage bargaining. In making these decisions, the officials must harmonize a variety of pressures which are focussed upon them in the bargaining process. These pressures emanate from a complex of political relationships surrounding the officials; relationships with the rank and file, with the employers, with other organizational levels of the union, with the rest of the labor movement, and with the government. In the normal state of organizational health, the officials identify their own personal aims with the institutional objectives of the union. Therefore, they attempt to reconcile the pressures in such a manner as to contribute most to the survival and growth of the organization.

The relationship between the leadership and the rank and file of the union has been explored in some detail in the present article. Trade union membership is ordinarily quite heterogeneous; differences in occupation, age, sex, seniority, employment status, product, process, and place of employment give rise to conflicts of interest within the organization. It is one of the most delicate political tasks of union leadership to reconcile these conflicts in the course of administering its wage program; political ineptitude will disintegrate the coalition.

Despite the elaborate formal procedures for membership control of the wage bargain, the rank and file is extremely dependent upon the officials for guidance as to what is equitable, obtainable, and acceptable, as well as the indispensable tactical wisdom which only they possess. In consequence, the procedures originally designed to guarantee control *by* the rank and file have become devices for control *of* the rank and file. With respect to its wage policy, a union is no more a primitive democracy than a monopolistic seller of labor.

A theory of trade union wage policy must address itself to the essential character of the union as a decision-making institution, and achieve a perspective more intimate than is ordinarily provided by formal economic analysis. At the level of normative judgment, there is no point in exhorting unions to behave in a manner incompatible with their survival and growth; if we want them to follow a certain course of action, we must make it consistent with their institutional aims. We must make a choice, or at least strike a balance, between the ideal that the union be operated as a pure democracy, and the desire that its leaders conform with the canons of business morality. And we must give up, once and for all, the notion that unions can be made more responsible by making them less secure.

The Power of James R. Hoffa

A. H. RASKIN

The International Brotherhood of Teamsters, the nation's biggest, strongest, and most investigated union, is a monument to the sweet uses of adversity, a testimonial to the proposition that nothing succeeds like bad publicity. For nearly seven years all the awesome powers of the federal government, reinforced by every instrument of mass communication, have been focused on the destruction of the union's iron-fisted president, James R. Hoffa. Yet both Hoffa and the Teamsters have prospered, while the AFL–CIO, which cast them out as a disgrace to organized labor, is sunk in bureaucratic torpor.

True, this inverted morality play is not over, and the implacable resolve of Attorney General Kennedy to "get Hoffa" creates a better-than-even chance that the cocky Teamster chief will eventually wind up in jail—an ambition to which Mr. Kennedy's brother, the President, dedicated himself in the 1960 campaign. But, whatever the position of the players when the final curtain comes down, the factors that have enabled the union led by Hoffa to grow bigger and vastly more powerful in the face of the most sustained, most widespread public hostility ever concentrated on a single labor organization provide an insight into the power structure of our economic society that is as disturbing as it is illuminating.

The 20,432 pages of testimony about labor-management malpractices gathered by the McClellan Committee in its three years of televised hearings contribute only foggily to this insight, even though they, and the criminal proceedings against Hoffa they engendered, represent the start and finish of most evaluations of the Teamsters as a social force.

The important thing about the Teamsters is not Hoffa's web of

Taken from Atlantic Monthly, *CCXIII (January 1964), pp. 39–45. Reprinted with the permission of the author and the publisher. A. H. Raskin is a member of the Editorial Board of the* New York Times.

underworld associations or his contempt for conventional standards of union ethics, but the extent to which his code is accepted uncomplainingly, even enthusiastically, by the members of his union and the great bulk of the employers in his industry, to say nothing of many leaders of the federation, which has labeled him a pariah. Of parallel importance—and more menacing still in their economic implications—are the strategic command that the union's 1,500,000 members give Hoffa over the country's distribution lifeline and the influence he is thus in a position to exert over most other unions and industries.

This year Hoffa confidently looks forward to putting the capstone on an edifice he has been building, brick by brick, for nearly a quarter century—the achievement of the first nationwide trucking contract. This, as his enemies never tire of pointing out, would put him in position to stop a million local and long-distance trucks with a single strike order. But Hoffa ridicules such fears. His success in using divide-and-conquer tactics to play the selfish interests of one group of truck owners against those of another has left him sublimely sure that he can always get what he wants without paralyzing the nation.

There is nothing vainglorious about this belief, nor does it represent the zenith of Hoffa's ambitions. On the contrary, the projected national trucking agreement is merely the underpinning for a far more pretentious structure of interrelated industry-wide union contracts— all of which would expire at the same time—through which the Teamsters could extend their economic leverage into the domain of unions in every field dependent on trucking.

Since there is nothing, from baby's milk to rockets for Project Apollo, that does not move at some stage by truck, the range of potential alliances is as broad as the economy. No farm, factory, store, or warehouse would be untouched. In a period when automation is circumscribing the size of most other unions and the effectiveness of their strike weapon, many are likely to find singularly appealing the opportunity to have their bargaining objectives underwritten by the Teamsters' undiminished economic muscle. The price of partnership in sacrifice of autonomy may be high, but not too high for unionists who feel disarmed by the inadequacy of their defenses against the job-killing impact of changing technology.

The dream of such a labor superfederation, with the Teamsters as its sparkplug, is Hoffa's dream, but the power on which it is based is the Teamsters' power, and it would not evaporate if the restless, ruthless Hoffa were swept out of the driver's seat and into a federal penitentiary. The idea and the machinery to implement it would remain as Hoffa's legacy, a testament to a brain as cunning and resourceful as that of any builder of our gigantic corporate complexes in public utilities, railroads, or manufacturing.

To make sense out of the Humpty-Dumpty version of the Horatio Alger story that is the career of Jimmy Hoffa, it is instructive to look back thirty years into the history of both Hoffa and his union. Hoffa called his first strike when he was eighteen years old, a tough kid who had to quit school after the ninth grade. He was unloading freight cars on the platform of the Kroger grocery warehouse in Detroit. It was 1932, the depth of the Depression, and the pay was thirty-two cents an hour—when there were cars to unload. "The rest of the time you just sat around, waiting for more boxcars to come in."

Detroit was a citadel of the open shop. There was no United Auto Workers at General Motors or Ford or anywhere else. Talking union was a sure way to lose your job and be blacklisted for any other. But Hoffa did not scare easy, then or now. "I got interested in unions because we were getting kicked around. We started talking about it on the sly. We got four other people together who agreed to be leaders, and we talked it up."

The instinct for the jugular that has always been the foundation of Hoffa's economic strategy manifested itself in his first engagement with Kroger. He decided that timing had to be the key for a successful strike, one that would be over almost before it began. His moment came when a carload of strawberries rolled up to the warehouse. The workers folded their arms, and Hoffa notified management that the workers had formed an independent union and would not go back to work until it was recognized. The company wilted before the strawberries did. The strike was over in less than an hour, and the strawberries became Hoffa's launching pad to the top rung of unionism.

It was a rough ascent, and long before he reached the top, Hoffa had developed a cynical conviction that nothing in our society was fair, least of all the forces of law and order. "The police would beat your brains in for even talking union," he recalls. "The cops harassed us every day. If you went on strike, you got your head broken."

When he took over Detroit's two puny, debt-encumbered locals of the Teamsters Union, the truck owners sent goons to smash his office furniture, to plant dynamite in his car, and to rough him up. "There was only one way to survive—fight back. And we used to slug it out on the streets. They found out we didn't scare."

Not all his battles were with the employers and the police. His bellicose ways did not endear him to the deadhead leaders of the international union in the Midwest, they turned a deaf ear to his appeals for organizational and strike support. Out of it all came the central guiding principle of Hoffa's life: You get what you take. Nobody gives you anything except what you fight for.

But Hoffa never would have climbed very far in his ascent to power if he had confined his concept of fighting to the rule of club and claw. His fists were, and have remained, a prized part of his arsenal; musclemen have always been prominent in his entourage. But with this reliance on brute force has gone an extraordinary deftness in the manipulation of power. He has played employer against employer, union against union, with a sense of *realpolitik* equaled only by the most accomplished of world diplomats.

Characteristically, he took as mentor in evolving his anatomy of power a unionist whose ideas of the end uses of power were 180 degrees removed from his own. Farrell Dobbs, a Minneapolis Teamster leader in the turbulent years when Hoffa was slugging his way up in Detroit, was the author of the centralized bargaining strategy so successfully employed by Hoffa to consolidate power in his hands.

An exquisite irony, worthy of extended study in a graduate school of political science, is embodied in Hoffa's emergence as the implementer and perpetuator of the Dobbs economic theories. Dobbs was a political idealist, so devoted to the precepts of proletarian revolution preached by Leon Trotsky that he quit the union at the peak of his prestige and four times made the forlorn race as presidential candidate of the Socialist Workers Party. Hoffa, whose bleak view of idealistic motivation is summed up in the observation, "everybody has his price," has always put politicians in the forefront of the "for sale" category. His scorn for "longhairs" and "save-the-world" types is unreserved.

The distinctive new element that Dobbs and his Trotskyite associates in Minneapolis—Vince, Miles, and Grant Dunne—introduced into Teamster tactics was the organization of long-distance truck drivers as the integrating element in bringing all trucking in the Midwest under standard union agreements. The concept of area-wide negotiations was alien to Teamster tradition in that period. The union was a relatively loose confederation of local baronies, each sovereign unto itself. Daniel Tobin, then the union's president, was a man of substance at the White House and in the councils of the American Federation of Labor. He was closer than any other labor leader to President Franklin D. Roosevelt, and he bossed William Green, the Milquetoast head of the AFL, with shameless arrogance. But he walked softly in the presence of the men who exercised imperial rule over the big Teamster units in New York, Chicago, and other major cities.

They operated in a dog-eat-dog industry, with thousands of small employers devoting much of their energy to trying to steal business from one another. Some of the fleet owners were former rumrunners and hijackers forced to go legitimate—but not very—by the repeal of the Volstead Act. Under-the-table agreements to get an edge on labor costs were frequent. So were payoffs to everyone from union business agents to the cop on the beat. No one paid much attention to unionizing over-the-road drivers; the great bulk of long-haul freight still moved by rail, and the union hierarchy, from Tobin down, viewed the highway drivers and the fly-by-night truckers for whom they worked as riffraff unworthy of enrollment under the Teamster banner.

Not so the politically oriented Dobbs and the Dunne brothers. They had used the technique of the general strike to obtain total domination of the trucking industry in Minneapolis; they counted on the over-the-road drivers to serve as evangels of their brand of unionism through a much broader area. The initial reaction from the parent union was frosty; it sent in strong-arm squads to discourage the expansionist move of the Minneapolis local.

Whether Hoffa came as enemy or ally in the first instance is lost in the haze of history, written and rewritten. Paul Jacobs, director of the trade-union study project of the Center for the Study of Democratic Institutions, who was a young Trotskyite on the fringes of the Dobbs-Dunne organization in the mid-thirties, recalls Hoffa as a member of a goon squad sent in by Teamster headquarters to help smash the Trotskyite hold on the local. Hoffa's own version, as told to Ralph and Estelle James of the University of California's Institute of Industrial Relations, is that he came as the most junior of a little band of Midwestern Teamster officials that gave the Dobbs enterprise support from the start.

In any event, Hoffa was quick to grasp the potentialities of the network Dobbs was threading together. The Minneapolis leader got a somewhat flickering green light from Tobin in 1937 to organize over-the-road drivers, and he speedily formed a central council to seek uniform wages, hours, and working conditions throughout the Middle West. Adroit use of the leverage afforded him by the weakness of the employer associations in the industry, the vulnerability of individual companies to selective strikes in their unionized terminals, and the necessity for "interlining" transcontinental shipments from one regional carrier to another brought Dobbs a whirlwind victory—at the cost of only one serious strike, in Nebraska.

By the end of 1939 he had cemented his hold on the Central States and was reaching out for new territories in the Southwest to bring under the umbrella of the standardized agreement. But victory had lost its savor for Dobbs. His mind was on the war clouds gathering over Europe. Spurning Tobin's proffer of a post as international vice president, he resigned to devote all his energies to the Socialist Workers Party and to keeping this country out of war.

His heir, after a brief interregnum, was Jimmy Hoffa, and the Central States Drivers Council has become Hoffa's chariot to power, the generator of the national contract through which he hopes to unify the standards of 400,000 drivers from coast to coast this year.[1] The freewheeling adjustments he has made in the Dobbs pattern have been detailed by Professor James and his wife in two remarkable articles published last year in *Industrial Relations,* a University of California journal.

Hoffa gave them an access, more direct than any other outsiders have been allowed, to the inner workings of the negotiating and grievance machinery on which he relies to dominate both industry and union. They set forth their findings with the clinical detachment of medical researchers describing the spread of cancer through a body. There is none of the melodrama of the McClellan hearings, no moral preachments, no excoriation; yet the totality of their recital is even more chillingly depressing than the Senate record in the inexorableness with which it points to one overriding fact: Each limitation Congress has sought to clamp on Hoffa's power has been negated by the dexterity with which he and his legal battery have refashioned and reinforced the instruments of his rule.

Some of his techniques for exerting an economic squeeze on balky employers have become so subterranean that even a James Bond would find it impossible to trace the secret telephone calls and manipulations through which one layer of pressure is carefully placed atop a second layer and perhaps a third or fourth until the trucker decides to capitulate. A manufacturer may find his goods subjected to "unavoidable" delays or delivered to the wrong address until he builds a bonfire under his trucking company to go along with Hoffa. But usually such subtlety is superfluous.

Hoffa's most dependable allies in breaking the will to fight of holdout truckers are a handful of giant transcontinental haulers. Again and again they have been his stalking horses in areas where smaller operators showed signs of standing together against regional com-

[1] [A nation-wide contract was negotiated in 1964. *Ed.*]

pacts. Hoffa lets the objectors know that he is prepared to sign separate agreements with their big competitors and thus put them in a position to get even bigger while the little fellows are shut down by a strike. In the affairs of the American Trucking Association, which has periodically talked about establishing a national system of strike insurance or some other mutual-assistance program to guard its members against Hoffa's brand of industrial cannibalism, it is the big companies that customarily are most active in making sure that the protective devices never get past the talking stage.

Even more startling as a prop for the Hoffa throne is a grievance structure ideally gaited to serve as a device for rewarding his friends and punishing his enemies on either the company or union side. Most unions and employers have taken both favoritism and conflict out of the grievance procedure by leaving the final decision to an arbitrator if no direct settlement is reached. But Hoffa derides arbitrators as expensive haggle-masters, more interested in avoiding offense to either side than in dispensing justice.

Under the Teamster procedure the union is free to strike if a grievance is not settled—a powerful whip over the employer. Hoffa, always a take-charge guy, sits in the joint appeals committee in what amounts to the role of chief justice and chief executioner. An uncooperative employer is likely to get hints that the union will "throw the book" at him. An obstinate business agent can be made to lose face with his rank and file by being sent back the loser in case after case. No systematic record of past decisions is kept, so it is virtually impossible for anyone to complain that the balance has been unfairly tipped against him.

But to concentrate on all these appurtenances of power—and a dozen others equally calculated to make him master in the Teamsters' glass and marble palace a few hundred yards from the Capitol—is to overlook the essence of Hoffa. He is not head of the Teamsters Union because the constitution—rewritten by a committee he chaired and passed by a convention over which he presided—gives him more centralized authority than any other union chief in America. He is president of the country's most strategic union because he has the overwhelming backing of its million and a half members.

This says something for Hoffa. And it says something for his members, exposed as they have been to seven years of charges that their leader has turned the union into a hoodlums' paradise and has used his vast power in ways that his Senate critics called "tragic for the Teamsters Union and dangerous for the country at large." It is, of course, fashionable to dismiss the Teamster rank and file as members of a subculture so accustomed to the notion that "everybody steals" that they are content to forgive Hoffa any trespass so long as he keeps delivering them fatter paychecks and more generous welfare benefits every year. But to one who has spoken to many hundreds of individual Teamsters at terminals and loading docks in a half-dozen major cities since 1957, the idea that they are a special breed, untypical of Americans generally, is foolish.

They give no sense of being callous or sunk in cynicism. They do not live in a world apart, as do coal miners, whose manhood is stripped away when the mine closes for good. They differ little from auto workers or steel workers in the urges and satisfactions to which they respond. Many are churchgoers, heads of families, war veterans, a few even college graduates. If they lack polish, that is hardly a surprise. As Joseph McDonald, a moonfaced, barrel-bellied driver in Hoffa's home local in Detroit, put it, "We didn't build our union in this tough industry in a town this size with feather pillows."

When Ann Landers, the advice-to-the-lovelorn columnist, ran a letter from a girl who did not want to invite her fiancé's friends to their wedding because they were truck drivers, a torrent of angry replies cascaded in from truck drivers' wives. The one Miss Landers chose to print came from a college graduate who cited some of the joys of being wed to a Teamster:

We have three bright children, own a comfortable home, take a three-week vacation every year (twice to Europe since '56) and I have a beautiful nine-stripe beaver coat with a mink collar. The girl who wrote that letter must be living in the Dark Ages. Today truck drivers make a handsome living. Many of our friends who are professional people and executives of large companies are struggling to get by, but not us. I am proud to be married to a Knight of the Road. SHE should have it so good.

The closest Hoffa ever gets to sentimentality is when he is talking about Teamsters. "Our members are different from anybody else," he says. "The people in our union know the guys they work for wouldn't give 'em a cracker without the union. You can walk on any dock and blow the whistle. They'll all go out and never ask why. They'll figure there must be a reason."

He says it almost reverently. It is the secret of his power, and he never forgets it. So long as the men at the wheel and on the loading dock are behind him, he can thumb his nose at his detractors and say, "Hoffa don't need nobody. Hoffa can do this job alone." The $75,000-a-year salary and the years of good living have not separated him from "the guys that made me." A month away from his fifty-first birthday, he still looks like a guy ready to climb over the tail gate of a truck, and he seems most alive when he climbs into the cab of a forty-foot rig and gabs with the driver about four-banger engines and how to hold the mark on the clock while going from fourth overdrive into fifth.

He is tireless, the embodiment of Jimmy Higgins, the legendary rank-and-filer who never stops working. When the AFL–CIO moved into Philadelphia to "bury Hoffa," after an insurgent faction in the big Teamster local there had come close to toppling Ray Cohen, one of the gamiest of Hoffa's lieutenants, the Teamster head took personal command of the rescue party. He spent fifteen weeks in the City of Brotherly Love, talking personally to every member of the local he could reach. By the time the National Labor Relations Board ran a second election last April, he had convinced enough of the eight thousand unionists to give the Teamsters a two-to-one margin. In the process he learned a lot about Cohen's own deficiencies, a subject on which he had exhibited a totally closed mind when Cohen invoked the Fifth Amendment ninety-seven times before the McClellan Committee or when he was subsequently cited for looting the local treasury. The end result was Cohen's resignation in October.

But there are no signs that his departure means a general exodus of the rogues' gallery of Teamster bigwigs whose presence in positions of influence prompted the AFL–CIO Ethical Practices Committee to recommend that the union be expelled in 1957. Since Hoffa's name led the list of those the federation considered unacceptable, the purge could scarcely be complete enough to satisfy George Meany, in any event.

Meany, just re-elected at the age of sixty-nine to a new two-year term as the federation's president, stands as a granitelike bar to the readmission of the Hoffa-led Teamsters. Without his opposition the demand for taking the truck union back would be irresistible. The ethical practices drive, proudest adornment of the merger compact in 1955, was tucked away in mothballs when Congress passed the Landrum-Griffin Labor Reform Act of 1959 in the delusive hope that it would cut Hoffa down to his five-foot-five-and-a-half-inch size.

Meany's coldness toward Hoffa is as unrelenting as Bobby Kennedy's. And Hoffa's feeling toward both of them is no less icy. He considers the Attorney General a spoiled brat, determined to bend everyone to his will. "Something is happening in this country by the name of Bobby Kennedy," he told a convention of Pittsburgh transportation executives last February. "Today it is me. You may be next." Of Meany, he says, "When you're old and decrepit on top of being stupid, you're in trouble. Some day the man is going to come to the door and tell you you're out of business. He's blocking us now, but he can't live forever."

The same divide-and-conquer tactics Hoffa has invoked so often to split employer fronts are being applied to cause rifts in the AFL–CIO —a task that requires little outside stimulation. In a four-hour tape-recorded interview with *Playboy* magazine last November, Hoffa solemnly proclaimed his belief that when Meany died the one right man to succeed him would be Walter P. Reuther.

"I don't always agree with what Reuther is doing or how he operates," said Hoffa, "but I recognize the fact that he runs a successful union, that he's a hard worker, a smart fella, he knows his business, he's currently up to date on the problems of the country, and he's trying to do something about them, and that's more than I can say for most people."

Reuther, for all the impatience he has exhibited at periodic stages to move into labor's number one spot, has shown no eagerness to make Hoffa chairman of his fan club. The UAW head is the high priest of austerity in top union office, and it is not so long ago that Hoffa was mocking him before Hoffa's own local for spouting socialism and one-worldism, instead of talking a language the workers understand. Hoffa, then as now, viewed unionism as a business, with the leader's job to sell his members' labor "at the highest buck we can get." To Reuther this reduces unionism to the level of a cash register or a slot machine. But such ideological refinements are of no concern to Hoffa when he is in the market for a marriage of convenience.

He is as full of bounce as ever, and as audacious. He made that clear a few weeks ago when he unveiled his initial asking price in his push for a nationwide trucking pact. The fleet operators, who had expected a modest bill the first time around to soften some of the public outcry against the "arrogance" of the basic power grab Hoffa was engineering, gulped when they read the figure on the package— $600 million for a three-year agreement. Just to make the whole thing more irritating to all, Hoffa rushed to point out that the employers could not expect to foot the cost out of their own profit margins and would have to pass it on in higher freight rates. This was another way of saying the increase—more than double any that would fit within the present Administration's guidelines for wage-price stability—would filter through the economy and wind up, with appropriate markups for every way station in the distribution network, as an extra charge on the consumer.

Pattern Bargaining: A Case Study
of the Automobile Workers

HAROLD M. LEVINSON

During the past several years, increasing attention has been directed toward the nature and impact of strong collective bargaining on the operations of the economy. As part of this broader concern, economists and others have attempted to develop a better understanding of the nature of trade union wage policy and of the major environmental factors which affect it. Within this context, the present article is designed (1) to present the findings of an empirical study of "pattern bargaining" by the United Automobile Workers, (2) to describe and evaluate the major variables affecting the union's wage policy, and (3) to explore the significance of these variables within the framework of the major alternative hypotheses which have been developed regarding the nature of trade union wage policy.

THE EMPIRICAL FINDINGS

The data which are presented in Table I are based upon a field study which was concerned with the nature and extent of pattern bargaining by the United Automobile Workers with firms in the Detroit metropolitan area, excluding the three major vehicle producers. The figures were obtained from a detailed analysis of the collective bargaining agreements negotiated with eighty-five firms over the period from 1946 to 1957. Only companies unionized throughout all, or nearly all, that period were included; also, the eighty-five concerns were

Taken from Quarterly Journal of Economics, LXXIV (May 1960), pp. 296–317. Some of the tables have been omitted. Reprinted with the permission of the author and the publisher. Harold M. Levinson is Professor of Economics at the University of Michigan.

selected so as to provide reasonably good diversification with regard to size, type of product, financial strength, etc.[1] In addition, the contract data were supplemented by extensive personal interviews with the union officials who were most directly familiar with the negotiations in the plants involved.

Despite the widespread use and apparent acceptance of the term "pattern bargaining," several conceptual problems are involved in defining the "pattern," quite aside from the statistical problems involved in measuring it. Of considerable importance is the matter of whether it is to be considered as the same *absolute* level of wage-fringe benefits as exists in the "key" company or the same *change* in level as is negotiated in the "key" bargain; clearly, these become identical only if absolute levels are the same in the beginning. Ideally, it would be desirable to measure both. As a practical matter, however, any attempt to compare absolute levels among varied firms raises extremely difficult problems of differences in employee-mix, differences in incentive versus hourly earnings, differences in the job content of similar job classifications, and a host of others. Consequently, the term "pattern" is here used to denote the major *changes* in wage-fringe benefits negotiated by the UAW with one of the large automobile firms and incorporated into the "key" bargain. To the extent that some companies began the period under review with different absolute rates than prevailed in the "Big Three," deviations from the pattern could represent, up to some point at least, movements toward the same absolute level.[2]

Several related questions also arise because of the widespread introduction of various fringe benefits after 1950. When the key bargain is multidimensional, is the pattern to be defined in terms of the exact form of the key bargain, or in terms of an equivalent total "package"? How many fringe items are to be included in the package? Is the pattern to be measured in terms of equivalent costs or in terms of an equivalent value of benefits (since, as between firms, equal costs may buy different benefits or equal benefits involve different costs)? These questions have been dealt with in this analysis by

[1] While it is not possible to obtain exact figures, it is estimated that the eighty-five units comprised approximately 25 per cent of the total firms and 70 per cent of the total union membership outside the "Big Three" and unionized throughout the entire period under review.

[2] Though empirical data could not be obtained, there was general agreement that this had occurred to some extent. It was not until after the war that "rounds," and "patterns," became an accepted part of the bargaining procedures, and attention was focused on "area rates" or "Big Three rates" as criteria. Up to that point, bargaining was more an individual affair, so that some concerns did enter the postwar period with rates different from (usually above) the Big Three level.

defining the pattern broadly so as to include both the "exact" and "equivalent" package; by including within the pattern the following items—general wage adjustments, paid holidays, pension and welfare plans, and SUB[3] plans; and by measuring the pattern in terms of the value of equivalent benefits rather than actual costs.[4]

A general summary of the results of the study for the entire eleven-year period and for three major subperiods is provided in Table I. Considering the period as a whole for all firms in the sample, it is clear that deviations from the pattern were considerable; furthermore, these deviations became increasingly prevalent over time. Over the entire eleven years, only 26 per cent of the companies, employing 40 per cent of the employees in the sample, followed the pattern (including both exact and equivalent settlements).[5] Comparing the sub-period 1946–49 with 1955–57, the proportion of companies adopting the pattern declined from 58 to 30 per cent; while the proportion of employees declined from 83 to 40 per cent. Furthermore, the data show a very marked shift away from the exact toward the equivalent pattern, particularly after 1950. The figures for below-pattern agreements reflect in large part, of course, the opposite side of these trends, with both the per cent of companies and of employees covered by below-pattern contracts rising consistently during the period.

As might be expected, above-pattern settlements were of much less importance. Nine firms, comprising 11 per cent of the bargaining

3 [Supplemental unemployment benefits, provided by the company and added to the weekly State unemployment compensation. *Ed.*]

4 These procedures were determined partly by the nature of the available data and partly by what I felt was the most meaningful approach in terms of the hypotheses being evaluated. The specific items included represented the most important changes negotiated during the period; while the total "package" of *benefits* was preferred because (1) benefit data were usually directly available in the collective agreement, whereas cost information was very difficult to obtain, and (2) the employee, the union and the employer usually judge the acceptability of a settlement in terms of equivalent benefits rather than equivalent costs.

Another definitional variable which, with one exception, will not be considered here, is the matter of timing. A concern may "meet" the pattern with a lag, or it may negotiate a below-pattern agreement at one time and an above-pattern agreement later, thus bringing it "into line" for the period as a whole. A close analysis of the data for the entire period indicated that a more refined statistical technique designed to introduce timing as a variable would have yielded no significant changes in the general results of the study, but would have made the analysis much more cumbersome. The only exception which will be noted in the discussion occurred in 1955, when the importance of the deferred SUB plan made it desirable to recognize it separately in the statistics.

5 It should be noted, however, that an additional four concerns, employing another 38 per cent of the employees, deviated from the pattern only to the extent of a deferred SUB plan in 1955.

TABLE I

NUMBER AND PER CENT OF COMPANIES AND EMPLOYEES COVERED BY VARIOUS
TYPES OF COLLECTIVE BARGAINING AGREEMENTS, 1946–1957

Type of Agreement	1946–1949	1950–1955	1955–1957	1946–1957
Above-Pattern:				
Number of Companies	6	15	6	9
Per Cent of Companies	7%	18%	8%	11%
Number of Employees	10,800	26,000	1,300	1,800
Per Cent of Employees	9%	22%	1%	2%
Exact-Pattern:				
Number of Companies	46	14	11	8
Per Cent of Companies	54%	16%	14%	10%
Number of Employees	96,500	54,000	30,700	24,100
Per Cent of Employees	82%	46%	32%	26%
Equivalent-Pattern:				
Number of Companies	3	19	13	13
Per Cent of Companies	4%	22%	16%	16%
Number of Employees	900	16,900	8,000	13,600
Per Cent of Employees	1%	14%	8%	14%
Below-Pattern:				
Number of Companies	30	37	49 (7)*	49 (4)*
Per Cent of Companies	35%	44%	62% (9%)	62% (5%)
Number of Employees	10,100	21,400	54,500 (37,350)	55,000 (36,100)
Per Cent of Employees	9%	18%	58% (40%)	58% (58%)
Total Companies	85	85	79†	79†
Total Employees	118,300	118,300	94,500	94,500

* All figures in parentheses refer to companies and employees covered by agreements
which were below the pattern only to the extent of a deferred SUB plan in 1955.
† Six companies included in the sample up to 1955 were excluded after that time
either because of shutdowns or because of a considerable change-over in production which
prevented any comparison of wage-fringe benefits.

units and employing only 2 per cent of the employees, had negotiated
benefits greater in value than those incorporated into the key bargains
over the entire 1946–57 period. The trend here has also tended to
be downward, at least in terms of employees covered, except for a
very substantial rise in 1950–55. A close analysis of this rise, however,
indicated that it was very largely due to "make-up" provisions, designed to compensate wholly or in part for below-pattern agreements
negotiated during the prior period from 1946–49. By 1955–57, the
downward pressures again became stronger, so that only six small
plants remained in the above-pattern category.

A more detailed breakdown of the data clearly indicates a close
relationship of pattern settlements to the size of firm, and to the
relationship of the firm to the automobile industry. The size intervals

chosen were based primarily on the need to obtain a reasonably good representation of concerns in each category. The criterion for considering a company as auto or nonauto was simply the proportion of its production or sales represented by motor vehicles or sold to vehicle producers, with the dividing line at 50 per cent. The great majority of firms, however, fell clearly at the one extreme or the other.

The data show a consistently stronger tendency for the large firms to follow the pattern, both for the entire period and for each of the subperiods. As between the medium and small units, the relationship was still strong, though not as consistently so. Large concerns more commonly adopted the exact pattern, whereas the medium-small plants were more inclined to shift to an equivalent package. The above-pattern figures, however, are perhaps surprising in reflecting a fairly clear inverse relationship with size, at least with respect to the large versus the medium-small companies. Over the entire period, none of the large concerns exceeded the pattern, as contrasted with 18 per cent of the medium-small units which employed over 20 per cent of the workers in those size categories.

Considering the period as a whole, . . . 38 per cent of the automotive firms, employing 44 per cent of automobile employees, had negotiated pattern agreements as compared with only 11 per cent and 15 per cent, respectively, in the nonauto sector. This relationship was also evident within each size group except "under 100 [employees]," where over 85 per cent of both auto and nonauto concerns did not meet the pattern; apparently the small size of these units was such as to overcome the influence of the type of product involved. These same general relationships appeared, though somewhat less consistently, in the pattern and below-pattern contracts for each subperiod. The main exceptions occurred in the 1950–55 period and were accounted for mainly by the large number of above-pattern contracts negotiated during that period. Over the entire 1946–57 period, however, above-pattern agreements bore no apparent relationship to the automobile industry.

Both size and relationship to the automobile industry, therefore, were clearly of importance in explaining the incidence of the pattern. The role of these variables in the formation of the union's wage policy will be analyzed in the following section. As will be seen, two other major variables were also important—viz, the financial and employment conditions in the firm, and considerations of equity and organizational strength among union members. These latter two variables, however, did not lend themselves as well to quantitative measurement[6] and will require a more qualitative evaluation.

THE ROLE OF THE MAJOR VARIABLES

We turn now to a discussion of the role of these major variables in the union's wage policy and to an analysis of their relative strength in differing situations. In doing so, it will be helpful to establish a frame of reference which distinguishes three different levels of wage-fringe benefits which were of significance in the formulation of union policy: (1) the pattern level, defined as that *change* in the total value of benefits which is equal to that negotiated in the key automobile bargain; (2) the crisis level, defined as that level beyond which the union fears that a further increase in costs will force the firm out of business; and (3) the competitive level, defined as that level at which the union judges the company to be meeting the labor standards of its major competitors.

In any given situation, these three levels may occur in all possible orders, although there are often important relationships between them. For automobile plants, the competitive and pattern levels tended to coincide, though this was not always the case; for non-automotive units, they often diverged, sometimes by considerable amounts. The crisis level of a particular concern may lie above or below its competitive level and above or below the pattern level, depending largely on its productivity, its product market characteristics, and other factors affecting its profit position. Finally, it is possible that no competitive level exists for monopolistic firms or that it may be very difficult to identify for multiproduct firms.

One further point before proceeding. The fact that we are concerned here with the union's formulation of policy should not be taken to mean that the employer plays no part in it. The history of his relationship with the union and with his employees, his skill in convincing the union of the nature of the economic condition of the firm, his willingness to take a strike (or to make the union believe he is willing to take it), and other elements of this type can be of considerable importance in affecting the union's final policy. In effect, we are simply taking these factors as given and evaluating the union's reaction to them.

6 Adequate data were not available to measure the profitability or employment experience of most concerns in the sample. The analysis, therefore, is based primarily upon interviews with union representatives.

Wage Policy up to the Crisis or Pattern Level

We can simplify the problem of analysis to some extent by confining this portion of the discussion to plants producing a majority of their output for the automobile industry and by examining first the restraints which may be imposed upon the union as it considers the desirability of pushing wage-fringe benefits up to the pattern level. The most immediate possible restraint, of course, is the potential reduction in the volume of employment in the firm—i.e., the elasticity of demand for labor. On this issue, there was overwhelming agreement among union negotiators that wage-employment relationships were given virtually *no* consideration *up to* either the crisis or pattern level, whichever was the lower. Unless either of these levels was being approached, the unequivocal position of the union was that it did not concern itself with price-quantity relationships.[7]

Two explanations of this approach were given by union spokesmen. First, that the relationship between changes in wages and changes in employment was too uncertain, short of a crisis situation, to be used as a basis for agreeing to pattern concessions. Second, that so long as a company was not at a crisis level, those who were employed should not, as a matter of equity, be asked to forego "justified"—i.e., pattern—increases in order to assist those who were or might be unemployed, even if the employment effects were reasonably predictable.

Wage Policy in a Crisis Situation

With rare exceptions, therefore, the only point at which the union gave serious consideration to a below-pattern settlement arose when a crisis was threatened. Whether or not a crisis did in fact exist was, of course, a matter of judgment on the part of the union leadership; for this reason, it is impossible to define it with precision. In formulating such a judgment, the union often attempted to obtain a "look at the books"; another more compelling type of evidence was the existence of a substantial amount of unemployment among the company's work force. Clearly, the crisis concept is basically a reflection of the union's judgment of the financial-employment conditions in the firm. These

[7] For the record, a very small number of exceptions to this generalization should be noted. In these instances, a one or two cent concession on the pattern was made in large automotive concerns having no immediate financial difficulty in order to permit them to bid on or retain orders which represented a considerable amount of employment. It is interesting to note that in these instances, the major other bidders were not automobile firms.

conditions became relevant, however, only in a situation in which the union believed there was a "clear and present danger" of the firm's closing down. In the absence of some evidence of a "true" crisis of this sort, the company's case was usually considered to be less than persuasive.

It was only within the context of a crisis situation, therefore, that the wage-employment relationship became a factor in the union's wage policy. In effect, the belief that a crisis existed acted as a catalyst by making the relationship between *further* wage adjustments and *future* unemployment appear both more determinate and highly elastic within the individual bargaining unit involved. Thus the crisis represented an important link between the economic environment and the decision-making process within the union.

The belief that a crisis situation existed, however, while almost always a necessary condition to the union being *willing* to consider a below-pattern settlement was not in itself a sufficient condition to induce such a settlement. *Even when a clear crisis situation threatened,* two other general barriers to a below-pattern agreement existed. These barriers were strongly related to the size of the firm and to its relationship to the automobile industry. Thus they provide a large part of the explanation for the considerably greater prevalence of pattern settlements among the larger firms, particularly those producing most of their output for automobile production.[8]

The importance of these two variables stemmed primarily from the crucial role which the large automobile concerns played in the union's over-all bargaining tactics. Once the key bargain was negotiated, the union was then vitally concerned with establishing it firmly as the "competitive" standard for the automobile industry, at least in the Detroit area. To do this, it was important that exact or equivalent contracts be signed with other automotive concerns of sufficient size to have achieved a recognized "status" in the industry. These agreements represented, in effect, "transmission belts" by which the pattern became standardized and accepted by other firms in the automobile industry. After completing this phase of its bargaining, the

8 In addition to these generally applicable considerations, several factors unique to the particular firm involved entered into the union's estimate of the situation—such factors as the past relationship between the union and the company, the availability of alternative employment opportunities, the value of seniority or other rights which depended on the continued operation of the plant, the extent to which management inefficiencies were considered to be an imporant contributing factor, the extent to which any "feasible" concession would provide the concern with a reasonable chance of recovery, etc. These added considerations did not necessarily represent further barriers to concessions; more commonly, in fact, they tended to reinforce a more moderate policy, particularly during the latter years of the period under review.

union entered the final stage of negotiating contracts with the hundreds of remaining smaller units. It is clear that under these circumstances, any important downward modification of the pattern in a large automobile company could present a very serious threat to the union's ability to establish the pattern as the standard for the industry, since other firms would press strongly for similar concessions.[9]

In formulating its wage policy, therefore, the union took into account not only the potential adverse effects of a pattern settlement in the particular firms faced with a crisis, but also the potential *indirect* implications of a below-pattern settlement on the union's over-all bargaining strategy. But these latter problems of indirect influence became much less serious as the firm became smaller and less closely tied into the automobile industry; consequently, the much greater prevalence of below-pattern agreements among those firms.[10]

In view of these rather strong barriers to below-pattern settlements in the large auto concerns, were concessions in fact made in these firms? The answer is yes, in two ways. First, *direct* pattern concessions—i.e., wage or fringe adjustments below those incorporated into the key bargain—were made in at least some instances. Direct modifications of this type, however, were usually quantitatively quite small and were negotiated only after lengthy periods of financial crises.

A second important method of adjusting to the needs of large auto

---

[9] A more sophisticated version of this facet of the union's policy, as expressed by some union spokesmen, was that for firms in the automobile industry, concessions based upon an elastic demand for labor in one company, even if predictable because of a crisis, would result very largely in a mere shift of employment away from more efficient unionized firms rather than in any net increase in employment over-all. For given the fact that the key bargain had been established among the "Big Three" vehicle producers, and given the nature of competition in the product market, it follows that elasticity of demand for labor in the industry as a whole, including suppliers, would be very low for any specific wage concession below the pattern. This indicates nothing, of course, as to the extent to which the union may have considered the *aggregate* elasticity of demand for labor when negotiating the key bargain.

The indirect implications of current wage concessions was also extended by some union representatives to include potential effects on the bargaining position of the union in future negotiations with the same company. The long strike over a one-cent difference between the "pattern" and the company's offer can be explained as a rational "economic" decision on the basis of either type of indirect influence.

[10] The president of a large amalgamated local, who has had considerable experience in dealing with relatively small supplier plants, took strong exception to this assertion that indirect influences were less compelling in the smaller automobile units. It was his belief that the greater incidence of below-pattern agreements in the smaller auto companies was primarily due to the closer employer-employee relationships in these firms, so that the worker was more able to see and more willing to accept the fact that the concern was in financial difficulty. The majority of union spokesmen felt, however, that size played an important role in the bargaining strategy itself.

It should also be stressed that it was size *per se* which was the important variable, since the fact that the firm was large was what made it important in he union's thinking. Thus size is not to be considered as a substitute for profitability or for other variables possibly associated with size.

concerns faced with a crisis was through concessions in the form of efficiency adjustments.[11] These took various forms, including raising production standards, reducing time allowances for washing up, rest periods, etc. Adjustments of this type permitted greater flexibility in holding down unit labor costs, while giving the union greater protection of its over-all bargaining strategy, since the contract itself did not reflect any pattern modifications.

It was extremely difficult to ascertain with any degree of certainty the number of instances in which this type of adjustment had actually occurred. Union representatives indicated that approximately 20 per cent of the concerns in the sample (both auto and nonauto) had been faced, at one time or another, with the problem of a *relatively* low general level of efficiency.[12] These situations had developed, of course, largely as a result of the strong sellers' market which prevailed during the war and postwar years. During these periods, management was relatively unconcerned about costs and was quite willing—indeed, anxious—to attract and hold labor by whatever means were at hand. In this environment, poor efficiency was inevitable. With the return of increasingly severe competition on the selling side of the market, several of these firms found themselves in mounting financial difficulty.

In general, the upper and middle levels of union representatives were well aware of the problem and were quite willing to "back up" the management in trying to correct it. This was always a long and difficult process, however, since the prevailing practices had become accepted as proper over a long period of years, and because the union itself has had a long history of strong opposition to the "speed up." Under these circumstances, it is not surprising that out of a total of close to twenty firms admittedly faced with this problem, the "efficiency" approach resulted in "substantial" improvement in only five or six cases, in "some" improvement in three more, and in very little or no change in the remainder. What is of considerable importance, however, is that this approach was tried much more commonly in the larger firms, for reasons already noted. To the degree that it was successful, therefore, it introduced an added dimension of flexibility

11 The term "efficiency" is used here to denote physical effort, speed, or other factors which depend mainly on the worker himself, as contrasted with "productivity" which is affected by several variables outside the individual worker's control.

12 It should be stressed that I am here referring to efficiency which is *relatively* low as compared with a company's competitors and that no judgment is being made regarding the appropriateness of the *absolute* standards involved. It also follows that, as in the case of some of the "direct" below-pattern contracts, these efficiency adjustments were designed to bring these plants *into line* with industry standards rather than to increase them.

into the union's policy, particularly in the large automobile firms. Considering all the automotive concerns in the sample, it is clear that pattern modifications of one type or another were by no means the exception.

This raises the question of the role of the final major variable relating to the union's wage policy—viz., considerations of equity among union members and of the organizational strength of the union itself. These considerations, commonly referred to as "political" in nature, refer to pressures exerted on the union leadership to obtain at least as much in negotiations as have other union leaders in order to satisfy the demands of the membership for "equity," to preserve the strength of the union as an institution, and to retain the political allegiance of its members. These "political" factors, then, were usually oriented *toward* a pattern agreement.

The fairly common incidence of below-pattern agreements indicates, however, that the union leadership was not so concerned about their potential adverse political repercussions as this hypothesis suggests. For while the union officials were certainly responsive to the needs and preferences of the membership for "equitable" treatment, they were also often willing to adopt a more "responsible" approach to bargaining by recommending concessions on the pattern where economic conditions required it.[13]

The willingness of union officials to support a moderate point of view, despite its political overtones, stemmed largely from the organizational structure and collective bargaining arrangements in the UAW. Under this structure, the major responsibility for the conduct of negotiations and the formulation and presentation of recommendations to the membership was usually placed in the hands of a union official whose political security was not dependent *solely* upon the support of the membership in any one bargaining unit which he represented. Rather, his support was usually on a much broader political base so that he could, in effect, recommend a more moderate approach to any one unit (or to several) without facing the threat of immediate political repercussions.

In almost all of the smaller plants in Detroit and in several of the large concerns as well, the negotiating team was made up of a shop committee, elected directly by the members in the unit, plus an international representative or an amalgamated local union official; the primary responsibility for negotiations, however, usually rested with

---

[13] Here again, the caveat must be pointed out that this discussion provides no insight into the role which political considerations may play in the negotiations of the key bargain.

the latter. The international representative was appointed by the regional director, who was in turn elected at the biennial convention by delegates from all the locals within the region. The amalgamated union official, on the other hand, was elected directly by the entire membership in the local; however, this usually included a large number of separate bargaining units, so that again his political base was much broader than any one unit. In these circumstances, the top union official, who usually led the negotiating team, was more able than were the local shop committee members to point out to the membership the economic realities of the company's position and to recommend acceptance of a below-pattern agreement to them.[14] The ultimate decision, of course, rested with the membership in the bargaining unit.[15]

Wage Policy When the Crisis Level Exceeds the Pattern Level

We are left with the final situation in which the crisis level lay above the pattern level; that is, in which the company could meet the pattern without serious financial difficulty. As would be expected, the very great majority of instances of this type resulted in a straight pattern approach—deviations from the pattern in either direction were rare. Where below-pattern settlements did occur, the explanation was usually to be found in the unwillingness of the membership to strike. For the period as a whole, this circumstance arose in only about 5 per cent of the firms in the sample (both auto and nonauto). In these cases, of course, the top union officials would have preferred to be more aggressive than the membership, but were forced to settle for less than what they felt could and should have been obtained.[16]

14 This does not mean, of course, that the local shop committee did not agree with the recommendations of the top official or that they did not play an important role in the formulations of policy. In fact, agreement was usually reached by the entire negotiating team prior to their making any recommendation to the membership. The international representative or amalgamated local officer, however, was commonly the moderating influence on the team. Often, the shop committee agreed privately with the moderate approach, but preferred to have the top official "carry the ball" in the membership meeting, because he was in a better political position to do so.

15 This evaluation of the role of political pressures within the union is also consistent with the fact that the incidence of pattern contracts varied directly with size. For the logic of this argument clearly suggests that political considerations would carry greater weight in the largest bargaining units, both because of their relative voting strength and because more responsibility often was given to the representatives elected directly by the bargaining unit itself. Union spokesmen, however, placed considerably greater stress on the economic implications of size already discussed above— i.e., the repercussions of indirect influence.

16 Actually, this 5 per cent figure overstates the number of instances which are relevant in this context, since it includes not only instances in which a pattern settle-

The very few "pattern-plus" cases in the automotive sector also require some comment; only four companies were involved, all of medium or small size. The small number of instances is partly due, of course, to the fact that a large portion of the auto concerns in the sample simply did not have a sufficiently high margin of profit (i.e., the crisis level was too close to the pattern level) to permit an above-pattern settlement. Beyond that, however, was the fact that once the pattern had been met, management's resistance to further concessions increased greatly, while the willingness of the membership to strike for such additional concessions markedly declined. It is interesting to note, however, that three of the four auto concerns which did sign pattern-plus agreements specialized in the production of items in which they were extremely efficient and hence less subject to "normal" competitive pressures. This high degree of specialization on particular items may also account for their smaller size.

Union Policy in Nonautomobile Companies

It is now possible to analyze briefly the union's policies in non-automobile firms, utilizing the framework developed above. Two important differences can be immediately noted. First, the "pattern" level (automobile) was no longer closely identified with the "competitive" level,[17] and second, the considerations of indirect influence of below-pattern agreements on the union's over-all bargaining strategy became much less crucial. Consequently, the economic pressures for a pattern contract were greatly reduced and the union could be more flexible when faced with a crisis situation. In addition, it was frequently not possible for the union to determine with even moderate accuracy what the competitive level of a particular company was. In about 25 per cent of the cases, the competitive standard could be identified with a key bargain negotiated by another union in the industry in which the UAW-organized plant competed. In perhaps another fourth of the nonauto firms, no key bargain existed, but the prevailing standards of the concern's major competitors were easily known. In the remaining situations, however, no well-defined competi-

---

ment would have been feasible (in the judgment of the union official), but also instances in which a below-pattern agreement would have occurred in any case. In the latter situations, the unwillingness to strike resulted in the final contract being further below the pattern than otherwise.

[17] The reader will recall that the competitive level was defined as that level at which the union judges the company to be meeting the labor standards of its major competitors.

tive level was available, primarily because the firm produced a range of items for diversified markets, or, in a few instances, because it held a monopolistic or semimonopolistic market position.

Where a clearly established competitive level was available and economic conditions were permissive (i.e., no crisis was threatened), the union normally pressed for a contract based at least upon that competitive standard. This was most easily accomplished if there were a key bargain in the industry in which the nonautomobile firm competed, to provide a guide. In two instances, this resulted in an above-pattern settlement as compared with automobile standards; in most cases, however, the result was a below-pattern contract. There was also a tendency, in firms making profits, for the union to push for a settlement somewhat above the competitive level of the industry in which the plant was operating, but closer to the pattern level of the auto industry.[18] This approach was carried through with caution, however, because of the continuing recognition that a *potential* crisis might result if the firm were too far "out of line."

On the other hand, in those nonauto situations in which the crisis level lay below an identifiable competitive level, and in the large number of instances in which no clear competitive standard existed, the union's primary objective was to adjust to the crisis levels involved, or (for highly profitable firms with no competitive level) as close to the crisis level as the union's bargaining power would permit. Most commonly, the resulting wage-fringe adjustments were below the automobile pattern, particularly overtime. Three of the above-pattern firms, however, were among those having high profits, steady employment and no clearly defined competitive level, largely because of patent controls or other market advantages.

It is clear that these policies in the nonautomotive sector are generally consistent with the analysis already developed. For one thing, the automobile pattern, particularly overtime. Three of the above- of the union's bargaining policy;[19] where an alternative competitive level existed, it was the more dominant criterion for a contract settlement, so long as no crisis was threatened. Where a crisis situation did exist, however, concessions on these alternative "patterns" were made more readily by the union than was true in automobile plants.

18 This was sometimes justified on the ground that the automobile key bargain was as much an area as an automobile pattern. An over-all view of the union's policies gives more support, however, to the position that industry standards were more important than area standards.

19 It was standard practice, of course, to include the entire UAW "package" in the presentation of the original demands of the union. This was usually more a matter of form than substance, however.

THE RELATIONSHIP BETWEEN THE MAJOR VARIABLES AND THE THEORY OF UNION WAGE POLICY

In general, the major variables discussed in the preceding section represent various facets of the two major alternative hypotheses relating to the nature of trade union wage policy. These hypotheses, usually identified with the names of Arthur Ross and John Dunlop, are widely known and need not be expanded here.[20] . . . In essence, [Ross] views the union's wage policy as the resultant of various group pressures, among the most important of which is the feeling among union members that they *should* obtain the "pattern" as a matter of equity. Dunlop's "economic" approach, on the other hand, considers the union's policy as being primarily oriented toward maximizing some income variable, most logically the total wage-fringe bill. In doing so, the union is primarily concerned with the potential "employment effects" of its wage policy, that is, with the relationship between changes in wages and changes in employment.

It is clear from the preceding analysis that the available evidence does not provide unqualified support for either of these points of view. For wage increases *up to* the crisis or pattern level, the union's policy was quite consistent with the Ross point of view. Until that level was approached, the union considered the relationship between changes in wages and changes in employment to be sufficiently uncertain, and the demand of the union's membership for an "equitable" settlement sufficiently important, that the possible employment effects were largely ignored.

In general, the union's policy in situations in which the crisis level lay above the pattern level also gave greater support to the Ross hypothesis. In these instances, of course, a pattern settlement could fully satisfy the political pressures on the union leadership while posing no threat to the union's over-all bargaining strategy. But the fact that above-pattern agreements were so rare even among quite profitable firms suggests that the political pressures stressing equity were again dominant, while economic considerations designed to maximize total income by discriminating among buyers became secondary.[21]

---

[20] The original discussions can be found in Ross, *Trade Union Wage Policy* (Berkeley: University of California Press, 1953), and in Dunlop, *Wage Determination Under Trade Unions* (New York: Macmillan, 1944). For some critical evaluations, see especially M. W. Reder, "The Theory of Union Wage Policy," *The Review of Economics and Statistics*, XXXIV (February 1952) and Albert Rees, "Union Wage Policies," in *Interpreting the Labor Movement* (Industrial Relations Research Association, Publication No. 9, 1952).

[21] It may be argued that the dominance of the pattern under these conditions can still be considered as an economic decision, taking into account the potential costs of

The major point at which the conflict between the economic and political hypotheses came into sharpest focus, however, was in a crisis situation. Here the record gives considerably stronger support to the economic point of view; considering the entire sample of companies over the entire postwar period, pattern concessions of one type or another have been more the rule than the exception. In addition, there was considerable evidence to indicate that union leaders were not so concerned with the political repercussions of a moderate approach to bargaining that they insisted upon a pattern contract even in the face of adverse economic conditions.[22] These general findings are the more striking in view of the fact that the situation analyzed here was probably most conducive to a strong pattern emphasis—a militant union operating in the center of production of an industry virtually 100 per cent unionized. It should be noted again, however, that the importance attached to the "employment effect" arose only within a quite narrow range of possible wage settlements, and did not reflect a policy of considering a broad range of potential wage-employment relationships.

SUMMARY

To recapitulate briefly, the essential points brought out by this analysis of the bargaining policies of the UAW have been the following:

First, there has been a considerable degree of flexibility in the union's approach to "pattern bargaining." The qualification has been noted, however, that in some degree, deviations from the pattern have represented movements toward the same absolute level of labor costs. In addition, some downward adjustments from the automobile pattern have been a reflection of the acceptance of an alternative industry pattern as a basis for settlement.

Second, the most important variables affecting the union's wage policy were the size of firm, its relationship to the automobile industry, its financial-employment condition, and the desires of the union

---

and benefits from a strike under conditions of increased management resistance and decreased employee willingness to strike. This was not the position stressed by the union, however. There was much more emphasis on a pattern settlement being "equitable" to all parties concerned.

22 It is interesting to note in this connection that the two major empirical studies in which "employment effects" were found to be an important element in the union's policy were largely based on cases which fell into this crisis category. See George Seltzer, "Pattern Bargaining and the United Steelworkers," *Journal of Political Economy*, LIX (August 1951) and G. P. Shultz and C. A. Myers, "Union Wage Decisions and Employment," *American Economic Review*, XL (June 1950).

membership and leadership to obtain an "equitable" settlement. It was also suggested that the interplay of these forces came into sharpest focus for the formulation of union policy at three possible levels of wage-fringe adjustments—a crisis level, a competitive level, and a pattern level.

Third, the analysis indicated that neither the "economic" nor the "political" hypothesis alone provides an adequate frame of reference for understanding the union's policies. On the one hand, union leaders were not as affected by political considerations as Ross suggests; on the other, the employment effects stressed by Dunlop arose only in crisis or near crisis situations. Thus a synthesis of these two points of view was necessary in order to describe more fully the nature of trade union wage policy.

PART V

WAGE THEORY, LABOR MARKETS, AND NATIONAL WAGE POLICY

INTRODUCTION

Wages and salaries are part of the daily experience of most Americans. They constitute about three-quarters of the national income. But commonplace as it is, compensation for work can be quite complex and difficult to explain in all of its aspects—the relative level of pay for particular jobs, the variety and size of fringe benefits, and the manner in which wage differentials, benefit differentials, and the level of wages and benefits change over time.

The classical explanation of wages, as Pierson indicates ("An Evaluation of Wage Theory"), was in terms of the competitive hypothesis. Wages were the resultant of competition of employers for workers and of workers for jobs. Employers hire labor to the extent that it is profitable for them to do so; workers seek out and select jobs to maximize net advantage or satisfaction. Demand and supply forces are brought into balance at an equilibrium wage. It sounds simple, and would be if wages and employment operated the way that the traditional theory assumes.

As Kerr points out ("Labor Markets: Their Character and Consequences"), there is not just one type of market for labor services, but a number of markedly different market situations. Generally speaking, actual employment conditions during recent decades have moved farther and farther away from the labor market concept of classical theory. Outside of agriculture and other kinds of casual employment, it is difficult to find examples which approach the classicial model in practice. As industry becomes increasingly subject to institutional controls and collective influences, and as the wage-determining and job-allocating factors become more independent of each other, the idea of a "competitive labor market" resulting in an equilibrating "competitive wage" becomes less and less useful, especially for analysis of wage behavior over short-run periods. Consequently, traditional wage theory seems too abstract and narrow to provide much help in solving the mysteries of money wages and employee benefits in particular industries, occupations, and firms.

Monopoly theory likewise is too abstract and unrealistic to throw much light on the major features of wage-setting behavior in large firms under either union or nonunion conditions. The purchase and sale of labor (employment) typically does not occur under conditions approaching pure competition, monopoly, or bilateral monopoly. Therefore, the framework of analysis for wage determination must take account of developments in industrial relations, and particularly in wage and employment practice. That is part of the point of Kerr's development of five different models of labor markets.

With regard to governmental wage policy, it is interesting to note that Federal intervention is not based on competitive or monopolistic theory. Instead of stressing demand and supply or the marginal value contribution of individual workers, the Federal Government has developed a "wage guidepost" program, based largely on a nonmarket criterion—that of the trend in physical productivity per work hour for the nation as a whole.

In part that standard was selected because of the effort to combat wage-price inflation in advanced industrial countries during the postwar period. Government wage policy has been part of a program of economic planning for full employment and price-level stability, with the analysis developed in terms of national aggregates rather than individual markets and firms.

The problems of formulating and enforcing a national wage policy are examined by Douty and Rees in their respective articles. Douty points out the difficult analytical issues involved in government programs of wage restraint. Rees' article, preceded by a statement of the wage-price guidepost policy by the Council of Economic Advisers, specifically criticizes that policy. Not only is Rees skeptical of any program that ties wages to productivity, but he and Douty both hold that collective bargaining in the United States is largely decentralized, that much of the economy is not subject to collective bargaining, and that the general guidepost (the national productivity trend) has no direct relation to the circumstances surrounding particular negotiations. Nevertheless, the Council states that permitted exceptions, which do allow for particular circumstances including market forces in individual cases, are to apply in only a relatively few instances in any one year.

Many labor economists believe that the wage guidepost policy is not well conceived and is practically unenforceable without government controls. It is perhaps worth noting that the OEEC committee of six economists, upon whose report Douty comments, contained no economist specializing in the labor field. Experience indicates that governmental attempts at wage restraint in peacetime are at best effective for only short periods of time. That is because the impotence of government admonition soon becomes apparent, unless it is backed up by the threat of punitive action and the power to impose penalties.

The Council of Economic Advisers considers its wage-price policy a needed safeguard in the program to eliminate excessive unemployment without causing significant yearly increases in the commodity price level. The main reliance for expansion has been on a large Federal income tax cut and a policy of relatively easy money. A manpower program of training and mobility, as discussed in Part IX, would aid in avoiding labor shortages in particular occupations and areas and thus in forestalling labor-supply pressures for wage increases leading to price increases. Whether, in addition, a government program of wage restraint in key collective bargains is necessary or desirable on a continued basis without an emergency appeal (such as a serious balance-of-payments deficit), is a nice question on which distinguished economists disagree. Some, like Rees, are concerned that Federal intervention in wage negotiations may be arbitrary and uneven and begin to threaten the bases of a free enterprise system.

An Evaluation of Wage Theory

FRANK C. PIERSON

In contrast to developments in the field of wage-setting techniques, little progress has been made of late in our understanding of wage-setting fundamentals. Today employers and labor representatives can draw on an impressive fund of knowledge concerning such matters as how to run a community wage survey, establish a job-evaluation plan, or install an incentive system, but on broader issues of principle, wage analysis commands surprisingly little esteem—probably less now than it did fifty or a hundred years ago.

The dangers attending this state of affairs need no elaboration. The wage question is too important, its ramifications too numerous, to be dealt with by piecemeal or opportunistic means. The fact that wage decisions often have to be made under rapidly changing conditions, with consequences which can be only dimly foreseen, helps explain but does not justify this lack of an acceptable conceptual framework.

Deductive versus Inductive Analysis

One factor contributing to the muddled state of wage economics is the gap which has come to exist between deductive and inductive wage analysis. An axiom of all scientific endeavor is that these two methods of inquiry should closely parallel one another, each enriching and forwarding the other. The study of wage phenomena, however, is marked by no such mutuality. Theorists frequently appear to be dealing with one subject, empiricists with another, the work of each suffering as a result.

Taken from George W. Taylor and Frank C. Pierson (eds.), New Concepts in Wage Determination (New York: McGraw-Hill Book Company, 1957), pp. 3–31. Reprinted with the permission of the publisher. Frank C. Pierson is Professor of Economics at Swarthmore College.

There are a number of reasons for the unhealthy cleavage which has developed between these two approaches to the field. As in other areas, the training and temperament of the investigator are bound to be reflected in the way he looks at his subject. More important, the nature of the subject itself makes this sharp dichotomy quite understandable. The "price" for labor in a given market at a given time or over a given period is notoriously hard to pin down and any number of pitfalls exist to trap the investigator. For some, this suggests that little is to be gained by inductive studies and that deductive analysis is the only route left open. For others, these difficulties are taken as further evidence that the essence of the subject lies in its variety and detail, underscoring the need for intensive inductive investigations.

The major reason for the sharp division in this field, however, grows out of a difference in viewpoint or vision. Fundamentally, interest in deductive work has centered on how the buying and selling of labor's services fits into the workings of the economy as a whole. The assumptions made about how employers and workers, either individually or collectively, approach their dealings with one another are the same as those made about purchases and sales in all other spheres of economic life. The conception of the entire system, as it were, comes first, and each of the individual parts, including the determination of wages, is fitted into the general framework wherever or however the logic of the system dictates. Thus, at the outset of his analysis of wages, Alfred Marshall stated: [1]

> The nominal value of everything, whether it be a particular kind of labour or capital or anything else, rests, like the keystone of an arch, balanced in equilibrium between the contending pressures of its two opposing sides; the forces of demand press on the one side, and those of supply on the other.

J. B. Clark put the matter in these words: [2]

> Looking at the transactions between employers and employed, can we see in them anything that causes wages to fluctuate about a standard which is more or less akin to the natural prices of goods? We shall at once find that there is a similarity between what the classical economists distinguished as the market price of goods and the market rate of wages. . . . We shall find that it [the wage rate] is fixed in a way akin to that in which the immediate selling prices of goods are determined. Later we shall find that, in both cases, the market rates fluctuate about permanent standards.

[1] Alfred Marshall, *Principles of Economics*, 8th ed. (New York: St. Martin's, 1920), p. 526.
[2] *The Distribution of Wealth* (New York: Macmillan, 1902), pp. 81–82.

It need hardly be pointed out that an analysis of wages along these lines must proceed at a high level of abstraction. Differences tend to drop from view; details about how wage rates behave in individual firms, industries, or regions are likely to be swallowed up in broad averages, long-term trends, or vague references to differences in efficiency and in the net advantages of the terms of employment. Thus, out of the myriad forces and changes continuously at work in the wage field, deductive analysis singles out only the barest number deemed to be of controlling importance. The *method* is deliberately designed to remove many elements of the real world, but the *results* are said to reveal underlying forces which shape wage relations.[3]

The parallelism between this view and the attitude of many employers toward wage questions is striking. For management, labor is but one of a number of essential elements in the production-selling process. The nature of the market for the firm's product and the nature of the firm's relation to its principal customers on the one hand and to its principal rivals on the other largely dictate the amount of labor and other productive elements which can be employed. As to the terms on which labor is hired, employers tend to think of labor's price as being set "by the market" in much the same way as the price of raw materials, of equipment, or of any other factor of production. Phrases like "meeting our competitors' wage" and "paying what the market demands" are not mere euphemisms; they are part of the cost-price calculus which employers use to appraise every transaction and contract into which they enter. In point of fact, the compulsions to which employers are subject in the hire of labor cannot be limited to market forces; and especially in large companies, there is likely to be considerable latitude in the choice of a firm's wage policy. Employer thinking in this area, however, generally appears to proceed from the opposite set of premises.

The parallelism between the deductive approach to wages and the attitude of employers is hardly accidental. The individual employer stands at the center of the economic theorist's world, and the greater part of the latter's work consists of translating into precise (some might say unintelligible) language, the principles which underlie business management's actions and decisions. Similarly, in emphasizing the influence of broad, impersonal market forces on wages as well as on all other transactions, the theorist and the businessman are inclined to stress the futility or danger of any efforts to deflect these forces

---

[3] J. R. Hicks, *The Theory of Wages* (New York: St. Martin's, 1932), pp. 4–5. Deductive or theoretical analysis can be thought of merely as a tool of inquiry or as a set of generalizations about actual behavior; the term is used in the latter sense here.

through government or trade union means. By no means all theorists, nor all businessmen for that matter, have subscribed to this view. Two of the greatest economists who wrote in the classical tradition, Marshall and Pigou, were far from doctrinaire on the question, but the tone of their writings, as with most of the better-known theorists, was hostile to direct government-union efforts to raise wages.

Marshall's temperate viewpoint on the issue is indicated in the following passage:[4]

> The power of Unions to raise general wages by direct means is never great; it is never sufficient to contend successfully with the general economic forces of the age, when their drift is against a rise of wages. But yet it is sufficient materially to benefit the worker, when it is so directed as to cooperate with and to strengthen those general agencies, which are tending to improve his position morally and economically.

A. C. Pigou, in his *The Economics of Welfare,* takes essentially the same position as Marshall; nonetheless, he deals at considerable length with cases in which wages are "unfair" and in which interference to raise pay levels is justified and desirable.[5]

By contrast, the work of empiricists reflects a rather deep-seated skepticism about the notion that dealings between employers and workers are subject to the same principles or "laws" as are transactions in other spheres. While a certain surface similarity may be said to exist, empiricists tend to regard this notion as a source of much mischief. In their view, the essence of wage relationships is to be found in the details of individual firm, industry, or regional experience. While simplifying assumptions have to be made in order to keep the analysis manageable, it is felt they should be kept as close as possible to the particular class of cases under investigation. Broad propositions about wages and how they are related to the economic system as a whole are not stressed. To writers of this school, "it seems questionable in fact whether there can be one all-embracing theory of wages, which will sufficiently satisfy our sense of reality, and stand the test of historical experience."[6]

In a number of respects the viewpoint of empiricists toward wages is in accord with the general approach of trade union spokesmen. Both underscore the variability of wage relationships and the essential difference between labor and commodity markets. Both emphasize

---

4 *Elements of Economics of Industry* (New York: St. Martin's, 1892), p. 408.
5 A. C. Pigou, *The Economics of Welfare,* 4th ed. (New York: St. Martin's, 1932), chaps. 14–17.
6 J. W. F. Rowe, *Wages in Practice and Theory* (London: Routledge, 1928), p. 192.

the latitude which employers frequently enjoy in adapting themselves to wage changes and the new dimensions which are added to wage setting when competing firms bargain as a single group. Both tend to distrust any analysis which reduces dealings in the labor field to a single rule of behavior, especially when such reasoning is applied to worker-union decisions to offer or withhold labor. Since empiricists stress the scope which the parties often enjoy in deciding wage questions, it is hardly surprising that their approach has proved congenial to trade unionists.

The limitations of these two methods of inquiry when pursued independently of one another are obvious. The weakness of deductive analysis in the wage field is that its findings are impossible to prove or disprove by appeal to the facts. The marginal-productivity theory of wages, for example, was arrived at almost wholly by deductive means many years ago; yet to this day it lacks any solid factual underpinnings, since it embodies concepts which defy empirical verification.[7] In this connection one cannot help being struck by the rigor with which writers of a theoretical bent analyze wage relationships deductively in contrast to the extremely casual, unscientific methods they employ in checking their findings against the facts.

The besetting weakness of inductive work, on the other hand, is its inability to link its conclusions together in some kind of unified whole. Indeed, the results of this work to date have been too limited, too pluralistic, and too loosely related to one another to justify being characterized as a body of principles at all. It would appear that if theorists have been too daring in drawing broad implications from their materials, empiricists have been too timid. Thus whatever pre-eminence equilibrium-wage theory still enjoys seems largely attributable to the fact that no alternative system of thought has been developed to replace it.

The need, then, is for fashioning concepts which will facilitate both deductive and inductive work—concepts which will prove general enough to provide a framework for more intensive analysis, yet flexible enough to allow for major differences in observed behavior. This, in turn, appears to call for a careful review of the wage field at a level of inquiry considerably nearer to day-to-day experience than the more traditional deductive analysis makes possible. . . .

7 As a theorist who stoutly defends the marginal-productivity theory of wages, Fritz Machlup's observations on this point are particularly interesting; see Machlup, "Marginal Analysis and Empirical Research," *American Economic Review,* XXXVI (September 1946), pp. 519–54.

CONTEMPORARY THEORETICAL ISSUES

In canvassing the possibilities for bringing deductive and inductive wage analysis more closely together, consideration must first be given to the general role which a theory of wages can be expected to play. The answer turns on what are the most pressing questions currently being asked about wages, since these are the issues on which theory is expected to throw light. As the philosopher Ernest Nagel has said:[8]

It turns out that questions of the *truth* of theories (in the sense in which theories of truth have been traditionally discussed) are of little concern to those who actually use theories. Reflective inquiry is instituted for the sake of settling a *specific* problem, whether it be practical or theoretical, and inquiry terminates when a resolution of the problem is obtained.

Our initial task, then, is to determine what questions in this field call for intensive examination at the present time.

To help in the task of finding answers to these central questions, wage theory need not include many of the details of observed behavior; in fact, the essence of theory is that it simplifies, i.e., abstracts from reality so that the essential can be distinguished from the nonessential. On the other hand, the theory need not be so abstract as to exclude all differences of detail either. The nature of the field or the present extent of knowledge about it may mean that a less generalized and perhaps less precise theory might well be more useful. As one writer puts the matter:[9]

In the theoretically advanced stages of science these two aspects of concept formation [empirical and theoretical] are inseparably connected; for, as we saw, the interpretation of a system of constructs presupposes a network of theoretical statements in which those constructs occur. In the initial stages of research, however, which are characterized by a largely observational vocabulary and by a low level of generalization, it is possible to separate the questions of empirical and of systematic import; and to do so explicitly may be helpful for a clarification of some rather important methodological issues.

The wage field seems to be in this in-between position. Understanding of the subject is still in a rather primitive state. The field is broken

8 Ernest Nagel, "Principles of the Theory of Probability," in *International Encyclopedia of Unified Science*, I, no. 6 (Chicago: University of Chicago Press, 1939), p. 74.

9 Carl G. Hempel, "Fundamentals of Concept Formation in Empirical Science," in *International Encyclopedia of Unified Science*, II, no. 7 (Chicago: University of Chicago Press, 1952), p. 46.

up into a number of quite different and isolated parts. At this stage, the most that can be expected is a theory that reduces the bewildering variety of cases to a manageable number of broad categories and provides a general framework for studying the relationships between them. If there are ultimate principles which can be said to underlie these relationships, their formulation can wait until this interim kind of theorizing is more advanced.

Issues of Primary Interest: Three Questions

Speaking broadly, the wage issues commanding most interest today center around questions of wage-rate *levels* and wage-rate *structures,* i.e., questions concerning the level of wage rates in the plant or firm, industry, region or nation, and the spread of wage rates around these different levels.[10] Interest in each of these four areas, in turn, can be said to fall under three broad headings: (1) how choices in the determination of wages mesh with related choices or activities of worker and employer organizations: (2) why different kinds of wage relationships assume particular forms of patterns: and (3) what effects follow from changes in wage relationships.

These three parts of the subject are closely linked. An understanding of how wage-determination choices are related to a broad complex of employer-union-worker activities is essential to an understanding of why various wage patterns emerge and what their major effects appear to be; similarly, it is impossible to go very far in analyzing the determinants of wage levels and structures without considering how wage-setting choices are related to other aspects of employee-employer behavior or what repercussions follow from wage changes. In each instance, attention is focused on the particular factors deemed to be critical, but in reality these three parts of the subject are merely different aspects of a single whole. . . .

A decision about wage rates in a given situation has to be reconciled with a variety of other, often rather remote, considerations. Such matters as when wage rates should be changed and by how much, how they should be distributed among different employees, and what firms should be covered affect a wide range of personal and organizational interests. Disputes between employers and unions over wages are often part and parcel of conflicts over such diversified questions as union recognition, the closed shop, or the relative stand-

---

10 Unless otherwise indicated, the discussion refers to straight-line hourly rates (or earnings in the case of pieceworkers) plus the value of so-called "fringe benefits" in cents per hour.

ing of rival union leaders. What is deemed a "good" wage settlement by one party or the other may depend on such considerations as what improvements in labor efficiency now become possible, what wage gains have been secured by other workers in nearby plants, or whether lower-wage competitors will be brought into line. A somewhat "higher-than-average" wage increase can work to the advantage of a particular company or employer group if it fits in with special recruiting requirements, enhances the firm's reputation as a good employer, or is a logical counterpart of a broad program for improving industrial relations. Similarly, a somewhat "lower-than-average" wage increase can work to the advantage of a particular group of workers or union if it means avoiding a prolonged strike, winning certain safeguards over discharges, or improving job prospects for certain skills. The fact that such terms as "average increase" and employer or worker "advantage" are difficult to define is itself an indication of the variety of objectives that a given wage change is likely to reflect.

Implicit in the foregoing is the view that the parties to wage settlements typically confront a rather wide range of choices and that the final outcome in a given case depends on how much weight they elect to give to a number of varying and perhaps conflicting considerations. Do these circumstances apply to less important wage adjustments as well as to the so-called "pace-setting" or key wage bargains? With certain modifications, the answer appears to be in the affirmative. If attention is focused solely on a few strategic rates, many pace-following settlements appear to be wholly mechanical in nature; this is especially likely to be true in highly inflationary periods, such as existed in the years immediately following World War II. If account is taken, however, of changes in the whole structure of a firm's rates, in such important "nonrate" elements in labor costs as shift premiums, pension contributions, etc., and in the way a company's wage structure is administered in terms of overtime premiums, promotions, and job-duty assignments, the parties typically exercise a considerable element of choice even in pace-following situations. Indeed, the very fact that there is some type of a pattern settlement to which it has been decided particular firms should adhere is itself evidence of conscious design and deliberate choice.

Thus, a major task of wage theory is to help explain what alternatives confront parties to wage settlements and what considerations enter into making one choice or combination of choices rather than another. In this connection, there is a temptation to speculate about the "ultimate" objectives of employers, unions, and workers, but it is difficult to believe that anything very solid can be developed in this direction. Rather than try to pierce the inner recesses of the human or "collective" mind it would probably be more rewarding to find out what kinds of choices have been made in actual practice.

Closely related to these matters is the broad question of the determinants of wage relationships. As in the analysis of how choices are reconciled in the wage field, highly simplified theorizing is likely to prove of little help. At the outset, it is important to make clear what kind of wage-rate relationship is under consideration—whether wages are being studied on a plant, industry, regional, or national level—since the controlling influences in each case are likely to differ. Attention must be given to the nature of wage-decision-making bodies—their size, degree of centralization, internal and external rivalries, etc.—to get an understanding of different traditions and customary attitudes that have developed in individual firms or industries; what is considered a "fair wage," for example, cannot be understood without probing into the different employer-worker groups' attitudes on such matters. As one writer has observed: [11]

> In a hierarchical society such as ours, large issues of social status are involved in wage and salary scales. Pay and prestige are closely linked. . . . Once this rule is admitted as a factor in its own right, it is remarkable how effectively it explains much that, on a purely economic hypothesis, has to be explained away.

Thus, in some contexts, the standards and mores of a particular locality or region can have an important bearing on wage-rate relationships. In others, the chief controlling influence may be a gradual or sudden change in technology, in sources of labor supply, in the firm's competitive standing, or in the general sales-and-profits prospect of the industry.

The task of theory is to help reduce this bewildering array of influences to some kind of order without allowing the crucial elements in the wage-setting process to be lost from sight. Indeed, the test to apply is whether a given theory, in simplifying wage relationships, helps bring out the most significant features of the wage-setting process. It is easy enough, on the one hand, to catalogue all the conceivable factors that impinge on different wage-rate levels and structures or, on the other, to set up a model from which almost all the complexities of the subject have been removed. The more difficult and important job is to develop generalizations that show how these determinants of wage-rate levels and structures are interrelated and

---

[11] Barbara Wootton, *The Social Foundations of Wage Policy* (New York: Norton, 1955), p. 68.

what significance should be attached to each in different classes of cases.

Analysis of the effects following wage-rate adjustments at the plant, industry, regional, or national level is subject to much the same type of difficulty. Mention has already been made of the fact that the parties can materially alter the effects of a given wage change simply by the way wage systems are administered. One of the most elusive but important aspects of the matter is the effect of a wage change on the productiveness of workers and on the managerial efficiency of employers. A hardly less complex issue is the relation between wage-rate changes and shifts in labor *supply* between firms, industries, or regions, and the impact of wage changes on employer *demand* for different labor skills or for machine substitutes.

These matters call, in turn, for analysis of a wide range of subjects—the impact of wage changes on costs, prices, profits, and even employer-consumer expectations—the study of any one of which is beset with many difficulties and pitfalls. Beneath these issues lie such important but imponderable questions as the effect of wage changes on the growth or strength of unions, the development of employer bargaining associations, the competitive product positions of different firms and industries, and the level and distribution of new capital expenditures, savings, and national income.

These issues pose a dilemma even more baffling than that encountered in the analysis of choices and determinants: If in the interest of clarity a narrow framework is used, many important elements of the subject will doubtless be excluded; if in the interest of realism a broad framework is used, anything like definite conclusions will be put completely out of reach. Again, there seems to be no other recourse than to pick one's way between these two extremes, using theoretical constructs or hypotheses which are neither unduly simplifying nor hopelessly complicating. As before, the most fruitful approach would appear to be to formulate and test generalizations about the effects of wage changes in terms of a number of classes of cases, . . .

To a considerable degree, the results derived from analyzing wage relationships in terms of choices, determinants, and effects depend on what concept of time is used. The results will differ, of course, depending on whether a very short or a very long period is assumed, since adjustments can be made under the latter circumstances that are ruled out under the former. In any given period, however, the investigator has to ask himself the more basic question: whether the different sources of change are to be studied singly, the remaining changes being held constant, or whether attention is to be centered on the interrelationships between changes occurring in given situations. In short, the investigator must choose between a predominantly static and a predominantly dynamic kind of analysis. Under static analysis, the adjustments which follow a given change yield a precise result; under dynamic analysis, a variety of results becomes possible. Under static analysis, a given wage adjustment is viewed as occurring within a system of unchanging relationships in which a delicate balancing of counteracting forces is continuously being realized; under dynamic analysis, the system of relationships within which wage adjustments occur is itself changing, the outcome being very possibly a cumulative, rather than a self-correcting, change. . . .

POSTULATES OF EQUILIBRIUM WAGE THEORY

Wage theory consists of two quite different branches: partial- and general-equilibrium analysis. Theorists customarily use partial analysis to explain the wage levels of individual firms or industries and, until recently, they have used the same framework to analyze the national wage level and labor's share in the national income. Today, the approach to wages in this latter area has been greatly altered by Keynesian general-equilibrium analysis, although many economists still use the traditional approach in explaining labor's income share.[12] Moreover, the fact that there is a basic similarity between these two ways of analyzing wage issues should not be overlooked. Both use essentially the same method of investigation; both proceed on the same underlying assumptions about individual economic behavior; and while the results of the two approaches *may* be interpreted as mutually contradictory, logical necessity does not require it.

As in other aspects of economics, the foundations of partial- and general-equilibrium wage analysis consist of three main elements: the concept of maximization, the method of static analysis, and the conditions of equilibrium. As to the first, the notion that buyers and sellers of labor's services seek to maximize some magnitude (profits, real income, net satisfactions, etc.) is considered essential, since in the absence of some such assumption there would be no rational basis for expecting one wage rate to prevail rather than some other. The maximizing calculations are assumed to relate to the price paid for labor; that is, it is assumed that the changes which buyers and sellers

12 The term "general equilibrium" as used here refers to the Keynesian theory of national-income determination, not to the general-equilibrium system of pre-Keynesian economists like Leon Walras.

are constantly making to achieve maximum gains result from, and are reflected in, changes in the wage rate for the labor in question. It is assumed that a wage increase, for example, will lead employers to recalculate how much labor should be hired in order to maximize profits, while workers will be led to recalculate how much labor or labor effort should be expended in order to maximize the net benefits from their work. This same highly simplified view of employer-worker motivations has been carried over into general-equilibrium analysis, although in the latter, attention is focused on aggregate, not individual-firm, equilibrium conditions.

The second characteristic of theoretical work in the wage field is the use of static or stationary analysis. According to this method, certain severely limiting conditions are set up which are assumed to remain unchanged for the period under examination, while the effects of altering one variable in the system are traced through various paths of adjustment. Later, the limiting conditions may be relaxed in order to bring the analysis closer to reality. Thus, in order to isolate the effects of a change in wage rates on a particular group of firms, the assumption is made in partial-equilibrium analysis that all other conditions affecting the firms' revenues and costs, such as consumers' tastes, the level and distribution of national income, the techniques of production, and the number of competitors in both the product and labor market, remain the same. If the period of time under study is very short, it is postulated that the amount of capital invested cannot be changed and that there will be no opportunity for firms to enter or leave the industry. If a longer period is involved, shifts in the so-called fixed factors can be allowed for. The essential feature of this method of inquiry is that the various limiting conditions are relaxed one at a time, so that the effect of each change can be made clear as the analysis is brought closer to reality.

In general-equilibrium analysis this same procedure is followed, although the relationships which explain the national income level and the national wage level are, of course, not the same as those involved in the theory of the firm. According to so-called Keynesian theory, the determinants of national income can be reduced to a few simple relationships, and if certain assumptions are made about the nature of the supply of labor and of other factors of production, these same determinants also control the nation's real-wage level. As before, the analysis consists of changing one of the determinants, the others being assumed to remain the same, and tracing the effects through different channels. If, as in dynamic analysis, the other determinants are not assumed to remain unchanged, the effects of altering a given variable become less predictable and the results less precise.

The third element in the approach which theorists have taken to wage determination, the notion of equilibrium, is a logical counterpart of the two points just discussed. If the market for a given type of labor is assumed to be subject to a specified set of conditions and all buyers and sellers are assumed to be seeking to maximize some definable magnitude, then a change in any one of the specified conditions will call forth certain adjustments until maximum gains of all parties are once again realized. This holds true for analysis of national income levels as well as of individual firms or industries. The channels through which the equilibrating forces move are different, but the notion that the system is essentially self-balancing or self-correcting underlies both approaches. On the other hand, dynamic treatments stress the possibility that the adjustments may, at least within certain limits, assume a cumulative character.

Weaknesses of Stationary-equilibrium Analysis

A number of questions, as noted below, can be asked about the appropriateness of an analysis of wage relationships based on these three elements. The single point emphasized here is that stationary-equilibrium analysis puts wage issues into a frame of reference which can be considered as either highly restricting or extremely broad; especially is this true of partial-, as opposed to general-, equilibrium formulations.

Consider for example, the notion of maximizing behavior on which the entire structure of partial-equilibrium theory rests. If this notion is given specific content, as when it is said that employers seek to maximize profits, other hardly less important objectives are lost from view. If it is broadened to allow, say, for differences in the net satisfactions or aspirations of different workers or worker groups, the notion can be said to explain everything—and at the same time nothing. Or take the concept of stationary equilibrium as a way of getting at the major forces shaping wage relationships. An essential aspect of the subject is that these forces, either as determinants or effects, do not refer to the same point of time but are continually changing and interacting with one another over periods of time. Thus, some part of any one decision made by buyers and sellers of labor depends on decisions made in prior periods under conditions probably quite different from those now in existence; another part depends on expectations of future conditions regarding prices, costs, output, employment, and the like. Stationary-equilibrium analysis, as such, precludes attention to these all-important facets of market behavior and any observations which theorists may make about these matters must rest on grounds which lie wholly outside their system of thought.

This rather harsh judgment is somewhat modified, but not fundamentally changed, when the principles of stationary-equilibrium wage theory are examined more directly and in somewhat greater detail. These principles can be grouped under three headings: competitive, noncompetitive, and general-equilibrium theory. Attention is now turned to an evaluation of theoretical work in these three areas.

COMPETITIVE THEORY

The three postulates of stationary-equilibrium theory just discussed, when combined with the assumption that labor is bought and sold under conditions of pure competition, form the core of traditional wage theory. This view of the major forces controlling wage relationships, commonly referred to as the marginal-productivity theory, envisages a world of many individual buyers and sellers, so many that no one of them can affect the prevailing wage; a world in which all buyers and sellers are seeking to maximize their satisfactions (i.e., their "returns" over "costs") and in which the effects on total costs and returns resulting from small (marginal) changes in the amounts of labor offered or demanded can be determined; a world in which the units of labor in question are perfectly homogeneous and the workers supplying this labor are perfectly mobile; finally, and most importantly, a world of stationary equilibrium in which all other conditions—including the prices of products, technological conditions, and the flow of money purchasing power through the economic system—remain unchanged.

Under these conditions the only wage rate that will satisfy the conditions of equilibrium is the one at which each buyer and seller is receiving a money return for an added unit of product which just covers the amount of expenditures or sacrifice incurred in producing such additional output. Various demand and supply configurations can be assumed, notably those associated with different time dimensions, different ratios of variable to fixed costs, and different technological data, but the essential element in all cases is that added output (and thus added input) will eventually entail more cost or sacrifice than is gained in the way of added revenue or benefit. If every buyer and seller has reached a position where the addition of another unit of output will entail more in the way of cost than in revenue, there will be no incentive for anyone to move or change his scale of operations, and a condition of equilibrium will have been achieved.[13]

Bearing of Competitive Theory on Three Main Questions

How does this view of wages answer the three main questions with which contemporary wage theory is concerned—how choices among alternative wage policies are made, what determinants shape wage relationships, and what effects follow from wage changes? The answer in each case is essentially the same—any change in conditions on either the supply side or the demand side of the market for labor will touch off a series of adjustments which will automatically bring about a new equilibrium position. The competitive theory of wages says nothing about policy choices among alternatives, because in a perfectly competitive market, buyers and sellers must either sell on the same terms as rivals or be excluded altogether. The theory does not explain in any detail what the determinants of wages are—only that the sole basis for every increase or decrease in wages is a change in labor's marginal product and that whenever such a change occurs, the buyers and sellers of labor automatically adjust themselves to the new situation.

Nor does the theory throw much light on the manifold effects that are likely to follow from wage changes beyond the proposition that individual employers and employees must meet the "terms of sale" prevailing in the market or suffer displacement. Wages under competitive conditions are extremely, if not perfectly, flexible and the amounts of labor demanded by employers and offered by workers under these conditions are extremely, if not perfectly, responsive, or elastic, with reference to such changes. Accordingly, a rise in the relative wage level of a particular firm, industry, or region will cause the quantities of labor being bought and sold to change until equilibrium is regained.[14] In short, the competitive hypothesis is about the simplest, most straightforward view of wage determination imaginable, with all the advantages and disadvantages associated with highly abstract formulations of this type.

[13] If allowance is made for effects of general wage increases on either the efficiency or supply of labor, more than one equilibrium position is possible, but this involves going outside the assumptions of stationary analysis.

[14] Strictly speaking, the purely competitive hypothesis assumes that the individual firm is able to expand its labor force by any desired amount without raising wages, because its size is small relative to the total number of buyers. An entire industry could hardly be assumed to do so without attracting labor from other uses, which in turn would entail raising the industry's relative wage level; thus, the industry's supply curve of labor is generally assumed to be upward sloping.

When viewed against the complex and shifting network of relationships involved in the wage-determination process, discussed above, competitive theory seems completely out of touch with the world of actuality. Except in a very loose or general sense, this hypothesis affords a poor basis for explaining wage relationships; when combined with the other assumptions of partial-equilibrium analysis it provides too limited a framework for analyzing the issues which command greatest interest in the wage field today.

Useful Aspects of Competitive Theory

While the hypothesis of pure competition does not provide much help in analyzing wage relationships, it should certainly not be lost sight of entirely. Three aspects deserve particular attention in this connection:

1. The notion of a purely competitive labor market is frequently used to provide "bench marks" for studying contrasting market situations. There can be no objection to this procedure on analytical grounds as long as it is made perfectly clear that the bench marks have no more than a theoretical or expositional significance. One may still question whether, in view of the impossibility of determining how far a particular wage deviates from the competitive norm, this procedure has any value, but this is quite different from saying that the competitive hypothesis is invalid.

The same holds for the view that, regardless of how wages are set in practice, pure competition is the standard or ideal that *should* be followed as closely as possible. Just what the economic world would be like if all firms and unions were small enough and numerous enough even to approximate the conditions of pure competition is difficult to say; the proposal involves such broad questions of social policy that a dogmatic conclusion one way or the other seems out of the question. Nonetheless, the case for competition is a powerful one because it generally coincides with consumers' interests. Wherever active competition exists, employers and workers alike must be prepared to meet the terms of innumerable rivals or fall by the wayside. Wherever employers or workers combine to withhold the benefits of such rivalry from consumers, the major purpose of economic activity is defeated. One may quarrel with the notion that combinations in the labor field actually have this effect, but the possibility certainly exists and much is to be said for an analysis which makes the nature of this danger clear.

2. The competitive hypothesis is useful in explaining general, long-

term trends in wage relationships. As has frequently been noted, the economists of the nineteenth century tended to view the wage problem in these terms, with particular reference to the question of labor's share in the nation's total output. For such questions as the relative wage position of general categories of labor in different regions or countries over long periods, the competitive hypothesis is useful in directing attention to certain important influences which have been at work. Difficulty comes when it is also used to explain the more detailed aspects of wage experience in particular industries or localities over shorter periods of time—the kinds of questions commanding most interest today.

3. Even in the latter area, the role played by competitive forces should not be entirely lost sight of. The variety of choices facing the parties to wage bargains and the multiplicity of channels along which both the determinant influences and the impact effects of wage adjustments move have already been mentioned. These circumstances underscore the possibility that competitive pressures may be exerted indirectly or by roundabout means, even though the immediate conditions surrounding the buying and selling of labor seem anything but competitive. The crux of the matter is the availability of alternatives or substitutes. If conditions on the supply side are such that workers, whether unionized or not, have alternative job openings to which they can readily turn, powerful competitive pressures will be brought to bear on individual firms to meet prevailing standards of wages, working conditions, etc. Where alternative job openings do not exist, as in periods of widespread unemployment, pressures in the opposite direction will begin to assert themselves as employers, both large and small, seek out different means for trimming costs and defending sales positions. These stratagems will vary, depending on which give promise of most gain for least cost. They may be confined to shifts in product lines, changes in production methods, or elimination of unproductive labor; as such, they may not involve changes in basic wage rates at all. The results, however, are no less important for the workers in terms of total rewards derived from the job and for the employers in terms of costs and revenues. As a broad but pervasive influence continually impinging on employer-worker relationships, competition must still be accorded an important role in the theory of wages.

NONCOMPETITIVE THEORY

In view of the limitations which mark theorizing about wages on the assumption of pure competition, it is not surprising that economists have long given attention to formulations based on the noncompetitive hypothesis. The simplest construct, pure monopoly, stands at the other extreme from pure competition, and it has the advantages as well as the disadvantages of any polar case. In a pure selling monopoly, a single organization controls all the supply, and buyers (in this case, employers) have no alternative sources or substitutes to draw on; in a pure buying monopoly, or monopsony, there is only one buyer, and sellers have no opportunity to sell their services elsewhere. In either case, the wage is set at whatever level the party enjoying the monopoly advantage decides will yield him the best possible results. The theory should not be interpreted as meaning that the monopolist can adjust the wage to any degree without suffering adverse effects but only that within a given range he suffers no adverse effects from rival sellers or buyers offering more attractive conditions of sale. Moreover, within this range he need have no concern about possible rivals invading his private domain in the future; in fact, he can count on receiving a supernormal level of returns indefinitely.

It need hardly be pointed out that this conception of wage setting is quite as far removed from the real world as that of pure competition, a complete monopoly in which there is only one buyer or seller of labor being rarely, if ever, found in practice. Few types of labor are sold to only one employer or even to one closely knit employer group. Few unions have been able to cut off employers from *all* sources of substitute labor or methods of production for any considerable length of time. There may be some instances in which local skilled-worker groups have achieved this measure of power for rather long periods, but there is no evidence to suggest that employers in such situations are incapable of forming their own "countermonopoly" bargaining organizations.

More importantly, both monopoly and competitive theory use essentially the same narrow frame of reference based on the same highly restrictive postulates of partial-equilibrium analysis. The notions that an employer monopoly seeks to maximize some definite magnitude, such as short-run or long-run profits, that regardless of its size it can act as a monopolist and still keep within the *ceteris paribus* bounds of partial-equilibrium analysis, and that any disturbance pushing a monopolist away from its equilibrium position sets in motion forces tending to restore this position again—these notions are hard to vest with much meaning. When conditions permit the employer a considerable range of discretion in choosing between various wage policies, hiring practices, and the like, differences between choices, not their common elements, become the center of interest.

As for its applicability to trade union activities, monopoly theory can easily become downright misleading. Without the anchor of maximum profits, what becomes of the theory? If union wage rates move together throughout an industry or group of industries, what is left of the *ceteris paribus* assumption? In what sense can it be said that the wage for a particular class of union labor is in equilibrium but for another class it is not? It would seem that the concepts of monopoly theory, which of course were originally designed to explain a certain type of commodity market, throw very little light on the major aspects of wage-setting behavior.

Main Contribution of Monopoly Theory

The principal contribution of monopoly theory to the wage field is the general direction it has given to the study of the subject. The essential characteristic of monopoly is absence of competition, in the sense that a seller or buyer is insulated against compelling or exacting pressures from rivals. This is also a common characteristic of labor markets. In describing the determinants and consequences of wage changes, labor economists repeatedly stress the numerous barriers to the operation of competitive adjustments in this area, both on the side of employees and employers. If workers are attached to a particular firm, area, or industry in such a way that a decrease in their wage will have little or no effect on the amount of labor supplied, the employers can act as monopsonists and can lower rates without losing workers. If the employers, on the other hand, continue to hire the same amount of labor even when wages go up, a union representing all the workers involved can act like a monopolist and raise wages without losing job opportunities. The fact that they do not always do so or that conditions in the real world are not so clear-cut as the foregoing suggests should not be allowed to obscure the substantial element of truth which monopoly theory contains.

If the theory is modified to include different degrees of monopolistic or noncompetitive control, the concept becomes somewhat blurred, but its essence remains. Thus some of the most important advances in wage theory in recent years have been built around formulations of this type. That wage rates are typically rigid rather than flexible, that wage rates in different markets frequently move together, that wage-rate differences persist indefinitely among workers doing the same work at the same level of efficiency in the same industry or area—these are facts which can hardly be reconciled with the competitive hypothesis but which the non-competitive hypothesis can readily explain.

Bilateral Monopoly View of Wage Theory

One type of noncompetitive market deserving special mention is bilateral monopoly. Roughly speaking, this type of monopoly obtains whenever a union can raise the wage level of a firm or industry within a certain range without causing any adverse effects on the demand for labor and whenever employers can reduce the wage level without any adverse effects on the supply of labor. More precisely, the upper limit is the point at which the wage (and amount of labor employed) would be set if all the monopoly advantage were on the side of the union and, similarly, the lower limit is the wage that would be set if all the monopoly advantage were on the side of the employer. In a bilateral monopoly situation, the wage and amount of labor hired would usually fall somewhere between these upper and lower limits. Note, however, that above the "no-reaction" range, there is virtually no labor demanded at all and that below it, hardly any supplied. If the top and bottom limits are very close to one another, the parties have little latitude for bargaining, but in many situations this is not the case and the resulting wage will depend on such vague considerations as the type of leaders involved, public pressures to reach agreement, and relative bargaining strengths. Each party can be said to enjoy a certain advantage by reason of its monopoly position, but each likewise suffers a certain disadvantage by reason of the other's monopoly power.

This view of wage determination deserves serious consideration for at least three reasons:

1. Experience in many bargaining situations indicates that relative to wages for comparable work elsewhere, there is a considerable range within which wage levels can be adjusted up and down without any observable effects on employment, methods of production, amounts of labor supplied, etc., but that outside this range further adjustments cause serious repercussions.

2. By directing attention to the limits within which wage adjustments can be made, this view highlights one of the most critical elements in wage determination. Objective circumstances such as the cost levels of competing producers, the availability and substitutability of other factors of production, consumer resistance to higher prices, and actual and prospective profit margins may mean that there is a fairly well-defined ceiling to possible wage increases. If there are other job opportunities to which the workers can readily turn, conditions of labor supply may even mean that there is something like a specific floor below which wage levels cannot fall. But in either case,

estimates by the parties of what the other will probably do, what their own constituents will insist upon, and how their customers, suppliers, and rivals may react will also affect judgments as to how far a change in wages can be allowed to go.

3. In explaining when a particular wage or wage change falls within a given range, this view leaves room for a wide variety of influences which lie outside the usual frame of reference of equilibrium analysis. As noted earlier, objectives and strategies in wage determination can vary from industry to industry and from period to period, so even at the loss of a certain precision and clarity, theory must allow for this diversity of behavior. The major weakness of the competitive hypothesis, it will be recalled, is the extremely simple framework it employs for analyzing wage relationships. Formulations built around the notion of bilateral monopoly, on the other hand, set the stage for a more meaningful kind of analysis.

Most of the work in the latter direction has been kept within the severe limitations of partial-equilibrium theory and cannot be said to have added significantly to our understanding of wage principles. Some noteworthy attempts have been made, however, to go beyond the usual bounds of theory and in some cases they have already yielded important insights. One such, which has received a great deal of attention, introduces "political" as well as "economic" influences into the explanation of wage relationships.[15] Another approach treats wage determination as but one element in a broad bargaining process in which two or more organized groups, with quite different goals and subject to quite different pressures, explore the costs and benefits of reaching or failing to reach agreement.

Some writers have even tried to apply the principles of game theory to wage-setting problems, but it is too early to say whether this particular approach will prove of any real value. All of these formulations have two elements in common: They involve a sharp departure from the purely competitive model, and they go outside the major assumptions usually employed in noncompetitive analysis. . . .

GENERAL-EQUILIBRIUM THEORY

To the nineteenth century economist, the wage question was largely one of analyzing the real share of the nation's product going to labor. In one sense, this entailed a quite different approach to the study of wages from that involved in partial-equilibrium analysis, since it

---

[15] Arthur M. Ross, *Trade Union Wage Policy* (Berkeley: University of California Press, 1948).

meant that labor was treated as a single homogeneous factor, differences among workers in particular areas, industries, and skill categories being disregarded. Attention was focused on the nation's total output rather than on outputs of individual firms or industries and on the real income position of the laboring class as a whole over long periods of time.

In a more fundamental sense, however, the approach in both partial- and general-equilibrium analysis was the same. National demand for labor was simply viewed as the sum of the offers made by all the firms in the country; national labor supply as the sum of the offers of all the workers at different wage levels—all expressed in real terms. If the real-wage level was reduced, other things being equal, more labor would be hired. The intersection of the two schedules gave both the national wage level and the total volume of employment, the product of wage times employment giving labor's total income for the period in question. The same reasoning was followed to explain the price and income paid to the other factors of production, of which the most important was payment for the use of capital.

This view of the relationships governing real wages in the country considered as a single market is wholly analogous to the approach taken by classical economists to the study of wages in individual submarkets or industries. The concepts that individual buyers and sellers are maximizing a definable magnitude, such as net profits, that certain conditions such as consumer tastes and the state of technology remain unchanged, and that a variation on the side of either demand or supply will set in motion certain equilibrating adjustments—these concepts underlie the reasoning in both cases. As in partial-equilibrium analysis, the system as a whole is viewed as tending toward a position in which labor everywhere is employed in such a way that value of added output equals added cost. Employers and workers in the aggregate behave just as they do in individual markets; the same analysis governing their choices among alternatives, the determinants of wages, and the effects following wage changes holds true for both.

Pure Competition or Pure Monopoly?

In line with this view, one of the crucial questions is whether the buying and selling of labor are done typically under conditions approaching pure competition or pure monopoly. If the former, the real-wage level and the total amount of labor employed can be said to be the result of countless transactions entered into by individuals, no one of whom can affect the wage prevailing in a given market. Every employer will continue to hire additional workers at the prevailing wage until the value of any one worker's contribution to the firm's output falls below the added or marginal cost involved in hiring him. Accordingly, workers everywhere will receive a wage equal to the value of their marginal products. Moreover, involuntary unemployment will be no more than a limited or transitory phenomenon, since wages will automatically fall until all those seeking work find jobs. Just as in any one submarket, labor and capital will continue to shift throughout the country until net returns derived from utilizing small increments of each factor are made everywhere the same.

If labor is bought and sold typically under conditions approaching pure monopoly, however, the real-wage level does not adjust itself automatically in such a way as to bring about full employment, nor is labor allocated everywhere in such a way that workers receive wages equal to the value of their marginal physical products.[16] If employers generally possess a monopoly advantage in their dealings with employees, both the national wage level and the level of employment will tend to be less for a given number of workers than would be the case under pure competition, since employers will find it to their interest to restrict employment below what it would otherwise be. If the monopoly advantage, through unionism, lies on the workers' side, the real-wage level for those who remain employed will tend to be higher than under purely competitive conditions; on the other hand, employment of labor generally will tend to be less since the labor organizations will find it to their advantage to restrict the amounts of labor offered in order to keep the wage for employed workers above the level it would otherwise be. It follows that neither full employment nor optimum allocation of labor will be realized if the buying and selling of labor are carried on under noncompetitive conditions.

Extended evaluation of this approach to the study of the national wage level, and of labor's share in the national product, is unnecessary, since it is subject to many of the same criticisms already noted in connection with partial-equilibrium analysis. The notion of an average wage level for all labor throughout the economy is so all-inclusive as to be devoid of much meaning. The competitive hypothesis makes it possible to speak of a normal or equilibrium wage level in some highly abstract sense, but if the noncompetitive hypothesis is used (and realism seems to require it), the notion of equilibrium

16 Wages should still equal marginal-revenue products, however—the difference being that, under monopoly, changes in outputs of individual firms affect product prices, while under monopsony, changes in amount of labor hired by individual firms affect wages.

becomes considerably less precise. The principal value of this formulation is realized when it is applied to labor's long-term real-wage position in different industries, regions, or countries. Clearly, the relatively high real-wage level in a country like the United States is tied, in a general way, to the value of labor's marginal product in this country. Moreover, broadly speaking, the shares of the national income going to labor and capital in a particular region or country reflect the relative abundance or scarcity of these two factors of production.

Perhaps the main lesson to be learned from classical wage theory is that, at any given moment of time, a rise in the money-wage level is unlikely to entail a rise in the real-wage level, and if it does, the increase in the money- and real-wage level is even less likely to entail an increase in labor's total real income. Over a period of time, however, classical doctrine teaches us that the entire marginal-product schedule of labor may shift upward as mechanical methods of production or other improvements in efficiency are introduced on a widening scale; under these conditions, a rise in the real-wage level, in labor's total real income, and, conceivably, in labor's share in total output becomes possible. When stated in these broad terms, which are almost in the category of homely truths, few economists would take exception to the classical formulation, and in this sense it still appears to afford the best frame of reference for getting at long-term influences bearing on the nation's real-wage level.

MODERN INCOME THEORY

In modern income theory, in contrast to the classical system, the question of the level of aggregate demand comes to the forefront of attention. According to this view, even a country with a well-trained work force, an elaborate money and credit structure, a large stock of capital equipment, and a highly competitive business system may suffer from a low real-wage level and considerable unemployment. This anomalous result (the paradox of poverty in the midst of plenty) follows from the fact that there is no assurance that the principal spending propensities in the private sector—the propensity to consume, the propensity to lend, and the propensity to borrow (or invest)—will yield a total volume of expenditure which will fully utilize the country's physical and human resources. If these propensities—or, more strictly, the relationships among them—are such as to discourage spending, it follows that aggregate output, employment, and income will settle at a point well below the full-employment potential and that the real-wage, as well as the money-wage, bill will be reduced. If, on the other hand, the spending propensities are favorable, all the advantages flowing from a full utilization of the nation's resources will be realized and the real-wage bill will be correspondingly greater. Once full employment is attained, moreover, the important considerations become the same as those stressed by the classicists in explaining long-run changes in real wages.

Bearing of Income Theory on Three Main Questions

The difference between the modern and classical approach to national-wage-level questions is most clearly seen in their implications for policy. According to the classicists, any general surplus in the supply of labor relative to demand could be (and, under conditions of pure competition, would be) corrected simply through adjustments in the money- and hence the real-wage level; any adverse effect that an all-around decrease in wages might have on aggregate demand was not taken into account. According to modern income theory, a reduction in money wages may lead to a corresponding reduction in prices and thus produce no change in the real-wage level at all. What is more significant, even if real wages were to fall, there is no assurance that the effects, on balance, would lead to a rise in aggregate demand and hence in employment. In the first place, the decline in money wages and the lesser decline in prices may involve some redistribution of income away from wage earners (and, to a lesser extent, from profit recipients) toward fixed-income receivers; this in turn will involve a shift in income toward groups with a relatively high propensity to save. In the second place, a cut in real wages will mean a lowering of costs, which may stimulate investment, particularly since the decline in wages and prices would reduce the amount of cash needed for business transactions, thus leading to a lowering of interest rates. When, in addition to these conflicting influences, allowance is made for changes in expectations of consumers, borrowers, and lenders, the net effects of wage cuts on aggregate demand become rather hard to predict. However, the prevailing view among economists is that a policy of wage reductions would probably intensify rather than alleviate any condition of general unemployment.

Enough has been said to indicate the new perspective on the effects of general wage changes brought about by modern income analysis. What light does this analysis throw on the determinants of the national wage level? As in the case of effects, the question of determinants depends on the interactions between the spending propensities and, through them, on the level of national income. Consider, for example, the effects of a general rise in the profitability of new investment on the money-wage level. If the money supply remains unchanged or the liquidity-preference schedule increases or the proportion of additional income consumed falls, the net effects may be nil; if the opposite conditions are assumed, the money-wage level (and the general price level) may rise.

But this is only half the story, for the results will differ in accordance with the assumptions made about the behavior of output and returns, and here real factors intrude. If supplies of labor and of the other factors are highly elastic (as they tend to be in periods of general unemployment), an increase in returns on new investment may well result in a substantial rise in the real-wage level but little or no rise in the money-wage level. If supply conditions for the various factors are highly inelastic (as in periods of full employment), just the reverse result is likely to obtain. Income theory, in short, yields few definite conclusions as to the determinants of the general wage level, whether in real or money terms. All that can be said at this juncture is that income theory has helped in formulating issues, in asking important questions, and in suggesting fruitful lines for further inquiry.

While modern income theory has put analysis of the national wage level in a wholly new light, it suffers from certain limitations or weaknesses which deserve mention.

1. The theory is couched in broad aggregative terms. The consumption function, the marginal efficiency of capital, and the liquidity-preference schedule (to use Keynesian jargon) embody relationships of a most general character, and in applying these concepts it is easy to overlook important differences among consuming and investing groups. The analysis has been especially criticized for losing sight of the importance of cost-price relationships, differences in supply elasticities among industries, and variations in the sales-profit positions of different firms—considerations which are handled with considerable facility in partial-equilibrium analysis. This criticism seems justified, although it is more applicable to the way in which modern income theory has sometimes been applied than to the validity of the theory itself.

2. Income theory, strictly speaking, deals only in static, short-run relationships. In this respect, the theory is subject to the same weaknesses as the earlier formulations based on partial-equilibrium analysis; in fact, by concentrating on short-run conditions, one could argue, it is even more open to censure on this score. For many

economists it is hard to attach much meaning to the notion that if a change occurs in one of the key determinants of national income, a series of adjustments will follow which will restore the balance of the system again. On the other hand, if the determinants are assumed to vary over time and if the relationships between the different spending categories are treated as cumulative within limits rather than self-limiting, the analysis is greatly complicated. Once again, theory seems to be faced with almost a Hobson's choice: to be either simple and meaningless or extremely complex and relevant.

3. Income theory has not yet successfully bridged the gap between money values and real values. As long as the analysis is confined to one basis or the other, this problem does not arise, but when the two sets of values are combined within a single system of relationships, serious difficulties occur. This was clearly evident in the comments already made concerning the determinants of the national wage level, when the leap was made from money terms to real terms.

4. As the foregoing suggests, the theory has been no more success-ful than any of its predecessors in dealing with the supply of labor. In order to close the system, some kind of supply curve of labor has to be introduced, but lacking a better means for handling the matter, a supply curve of labor has simply been assumed. In other words, the forces determining the national wage level are treated as lying largely outside the system of income relationships. A first order of business for those working in the wage field is to try to fill this void.

In the perspective of subsequent developments, the greatest con-tribution of modern income analysis has come primarily as a by-product, for while the theory is essentially static in conception, it has given an enormous impetus to the study of dynamic relationships. The analysis of wages has as yet received little benefit from this new development in economics, but it can be confidently predicted that it will do so in the future.

CONCLUSIONS

In this brief review of wage theory, emphasis has been put on those features of deductive analysis which have added most to our under-standing of contemporary wage issues. Broadly speaking, partial- and general-equilibrium theory have been found to provide an unsatisfac-tory framework for analyzing wage relationships in terms of choices, determinants, and effects—the three questions of major interest to-day. On the other hand, the direction in which recent work in these two areas has been moving shows considerable promise. In the area of partial-equilibrium analysis, theorists are putting less emphasis on the rather simple, almost mechanical view of wage determination based on the hypothesis of pure competition and developed in its most elaborate form in the theory of marginal productivity. Increasing attention is being given to formulations based on the noncompetitive hypothesis, such as bilateral monopoly, and on the interplay between competitive and noncompetitive influences. Thus, while contemporary theorists (quite properly, it seems) still use the competitive or marginal-productivity hypothesis to explain wage movements of a broad, long-term nature, they tend to approach the study of structural wage differences and short-term wage movements in terms of the noncompetitive hypothesis.

This accords with the view that influences other than the compulsions of competitive markets play a large role in shaping wage relationships. An understanding of these other influences calls particularly for an analysis of salient aspects of industrial relations: how managements and unions approach their wage bargains, how the prospect of nonagreement affects their dealings, how various intra- and interplant wage structures emerge, and the like.

Our critique of general-equilibrium theory has yielded somewhat similar findings. Except for explanations of long-term movements, modern theorists no longer use the marginal-productivity framework in analyzing the general wage level. The controlling forces emphasized today are those associated with modern income analysis. This analysis, however, yields rather fuzzy results; it is impossible to speak with much definiteness about the relationships between changes in the general wage level and the other elements of national income determination. Again, the way is open for further work which will help fill the gap that modern theory has exposed.

The principal conclusion to which this critique has come is that in both branches of deductive analysis, theorists are now saying that wage determination cannot be reduced to a single rule of behavior, that in so far as economic influences as such are concerned, there is an element of uncertainty or even indeterminateness in wage setting, which earlier economists were inclined to minimize. This accords with the main line of development in empirical work, suggesting that it is in this direction that deductive and inductive wage analysis may yet be able to reach common ground.

Labor Markets: Their Character
and Consequences

CLARK KERR

A double life has developed for the term "labor market" and this has been the source of much confusion. Some economists employ the term in one sense; some in the other; and some in both at the same time without realizing or acknowledging the actual or potentially different meanings.

THE WAGE MARKET AND THE JOB MARKET

Two processes, among others, are going on all the time in our economy: wage rates are changing and individuals are moving among jobs. The two processes may or may not be closely connected. It is out of their changing degree of association that the confusion develops.

Conventionally, in wage analysis, the labor market is the totality of jobs for which, given the achievement of equilibrium and an allowance for "other advantages,"[1] the same wage is paid. It is the area within which the single price pertains. Local labor markets are separated by costs of movement, which result in price variations. Granting that some imperfections exist, the labor market is the area within which the single price would exist if the imperfections did not interfere. The labor market sets the price. This is the economists' traditional view.

Taken from American Economic Review, XL (May 1950 Proceedings Number), pp. 278–91. Reprinted with the permission of the publisher. Clark Kerr is President of the University of California.

[1] J. R. Hicks, The Theory of Wages (London: Macmillan, 1935), p. 7.

There is another sense in which the term is used, more particularly by employer, union, and government administrators but also by economists. The labor market is the area, defined occupationally, industrially, and geographically, within which workers are willing to move and do move comparatively freely from one job to another. Movement within the area is fairly easy and customary; and migration into it or out of it is less frequent and more difficult. The market is defined by resistance points on the scale of mobility. There are a multitude of markets and more than a single price may be paid in each; and a single price may cover more than one market, although each of such markets may be otherwise quite different. The market is the mechanism which distributes jobs.

In this discussion, whenever a distinction is made, the first will be designated as the "wage market" and the second as the "job market"; and the two need not encompass in each instance the identical composite of jobs. In fact, it is out of their potential and frequently actual separateness that some of the more interesting and important problems evolve.

MODELS OF THE MARKET

The markets with which we are concerned may and do vary almost infinitely in structure and dynamics. Five general models or ideal types represent, but do not fully describe, the differences which are in kind as well as in degree.

1. *The Perfect Market.* This model is the accepted measuring device of economists. A "market place," in the historical sense, exists as a result of free entry and exit, complete knowledge, a sufficiency of relatively small and undifferentiated buyers and sellers, and the absence of collusion. Perfection is achieved if the product market also displays these characteristics; and the consumer reigns supreme in the allocation of resources and the determination of the rewards to individuals.

Under these circumstances, the dichotomy of the wage market and the job market does not exist. Physical movement of workers and the wage setting process are inextricably interwoven. The single price prevails and the market is cleared.[2]

Wages . . . tend to that level where demand and supply are equal. If supply exceeds demand, some men will be unemployed, and in their efforts to regain employment they will reduce the wages they ask to that level which makes it just worth while for employers to take them on. If

2 *Ibid.,* pp. 4–5.

demand exceeds supply, employers will be unable to obtain all the labour they require, and will therefore offer higher wages in order to attract labour from elsewhere.

2. *The Neoclassical Market.* Hicks considered the above "a good simplified model of the labor market. . . . Wages do turn out on the whole very much as if they were determined in this manner."[3] It is, however, a "simplified model" and some minor amendments to it have often been deemed necessary in order to approach reality more closely. The "neoclassical market" emerges. It departs from perfection but still performs its economic tasks adequately.

This was the market as seen by Alfred Marshall.[4] The supply of skilled workers is inelastic because of the extended period of time involved in acquiring skill. Unskilled workers are at a disadvantage because of the perishability of the service they have to sell. Unions exist but they are only sufficiently strong to offset market imperfections introduced by combinations, formal or informal, of employers. Workers do differ from one another.

Yet, all in all, the market is the main determinant of wages. Workers have sufficient knowledge of alternative opportunities and do, despite some inertia, move quite readily in the direction of net economic advantage. Wages may for a time be above or below the "competitive level" but over time they tend toward equality for workers of equal qualifications. Resource allocation approaches the optimum in the long run. While neither the product nor the labor market is perfect, the consumer retains his sovereignty. Adjustments, while not delicately made, are amply pleasing: all is for the best in the best of all possible worlds.

This model has frequently been held to be a fairly accurate description of reality:[5]

. . . for the general tendency for the wages of labourers of equal efficiency to become equalized in different occupations (allowance being made for the advantages and disadvantages of employment) has been a commonplace of economics since the days of Adam Smith. . . . The movement of labour from one occupation to another, which brings it about, is certainly a slow one; but there is no need to question its reality.

3. *The Natural Market.* Abundant evidence now testifies that it would, in the absence of collusion, be almost more correct to say that

---

3 *Ibid.,* p. 5.
4 Alfred Marshall, *Principles of Economics,* 8th ed. (London: Macmillan, 1938). See particularly pages 525–79.
5 Hicks, *op. cit.,* p. 3.

wages tend to be unequal rather than the other way around. The avalanche of wage data by occupations and by localities during World War II at first bewildered and later convinced War Labor Board economists. Occupational wage rates, locality by locality, in the absence of collective bargaining displayed no single "going rate" but a wide dispersion. Absence of a single price was found to be the general rule.[6] A sure sign of collusion, not of the working of market forces, came to be the existence of a uniform rate. The market, it seemed, set rather wide limits and within these limits employers could develop policies as high-, medium-, or low-paid firms, and workers could accept high, medium, or low rates. Nonwage conditions of employment, such as welfare provisions, sick leave with pay, and so forth, were found to reinforce rather than offset the rate inequalities.

The explanation of the prevalence of this type of market behavior is, in part, the two constrasting views of the market of the economist and the worker. To the economist, the job market is an objective fact. It consists of those jobs among which the workers could pick and choose and move without substantial cost for retraining or physical transference. To the worker, the market is much more ill-defined and subjectively described. It may consist only of other jobs within his own plant, or, more likely, those jobs about which he has information, largely from friends, and which fit his own conception of himself as to trade and income level. The worker operates within the market as he sees it, and his view is limited by lack of knowledge and a restricted conception of himself (particularly as to occupation).

Although the majority of the workers are vaguely conscious of the job market, they cannot be said to be actively in it. They are sufficiently satisfied with their current jobs or fearful of the uncertainties to be encountered in movement so that they are not weighing the advantages of other jobs as against their own. Unless ejected from their current jobs they are only passive participants in the market. Not only by choice but also by necessity is this the case, for many employers, as demonstrated by a current study of employer hiring practices in the San Francisco Bay Area, prefer not to hire persons employed elsewhere. From the point of view of the smooth functioning of the job market, they are the hard core of the employed. Some persons, however, are aggressively in the market—largely the unemployed and the otherwise unsettled workers (mostly the young). Their numbers are not normally sufficiently great or their conception

6 Allowance, of course, had to be made for the lack of identity of job specifications and worker performance, but rate discrepancies were too great to be explained away by these considerations.

of the market adequate enough to provide such volume of movement as would equalize net economic advantage.

The natural market may thus be defined as one in which the average worker has a narrowly confined view of the market and, in addition, is not an alert participant in it. Unions do not exist. Employers, while not formally organized, either because of smallness of number or informal co-operation (the "tacit, but constant and uniform combination, not to raise the wages of labour above their actual rate" of which Adam Smith spoke[7]), can exercise some monopsonistic influence in the labor market. Sovereignty is jointly held by the consumer and the employer. Wages are not set uniformly at the competitive level, and resources are not utilized to the best advantage. The operation of the job market does not determine wages but, rather, sets the limits within which they are fixed and influences the specific levels within these limits.

4. *The Institutional Market.* The institutional market is distinguished by the substitution of institutional rules for frictons as the principal delineator of job market limits; of institutional and leadership comparisons for physical movement as the main basis for the interrelatedness of wage markets; and of policies of unions, employers, and government for the traditional action of market forces as the more significant source of wage movements. Strong unions interested in policy and capable of having policies range alongside of large employers and employers' associations likewise interested in policy and capable of having policies. The purpose of these policies is, in fact, to curtail the free operation of supply and demand. The pertinent policies relate to the definition of job markets, the determination of rules affecting entry into, movement within, and exit from these markets, and the setting of wage rates. Formal rules, consciously selected, supplant informal practices determined by market conditions. Nor are policies solely developed by the private governments of industry and organized labor, but also by public government which may intervene to assure that monopoly encroachments do not entirely eliminate competition from the market, that wages do not fall below a given level, and that employment be maintained at acceptable levels.

This is, in its full-blown development, a relatively new kind of market in the United States and has assumed large-scale importance only within the past two decades. The wage market and the job market are substantially disjointed and can and sometimes do go their quite separate ways. For many kinds of labor there are no spatial

7 Adam Smith, *An Inquiry Into the Nature and Causes of the Wealth of Nations* (New York: Modern Library Edition, Random House, 1937), p. 66.

boundaries within which it can be said that supply and demand considerations determine wages. Men find and lose employment within a restricted job market but the wage market is an orbit—"an orbit of coercive comparison."[8] This orbit frequently is spatially quite unlimited. It is the sphere of influence of organizations, policies, and concepts of equity. The job market area and the orbit of wage influencing considerations become quite distinct entities.

The job market no longer alone sets the upper and lower bargaining limits for wage determination. Its operation generally widens these limits, for institutional policies often make it harder for labor, and sometimes capital, to migrate and thus lower the minimum workers will accept and raise the maximum employers will offer since withdrawal is less possible. Customarily the more significant limits are set by the danger points at which the survival of leaders and associations and coalitions is threatened. Bargaining limits are fixed as much by political as by economic inducements.

Within these limits, it is not economic bargaining power by itself which concludes the settlement but also such largely noneconomic considerations as "patterns" and commonly accepted principles of equity. It is not so much what can be done economically which is important but what must be done politically—on both sides. Employers' associations and large corporations, as well as trade unions, have a political life which claims attention just as do the economic goals.

The wage rate under conditions of bilateral monopoly and bilateral oligopoly is economically indeterminate. "The theory of the determination of wages" is no longer, as Hicks said, "simply a special case of the general theory of value," for the "free market" no longer exists.[9] If wages should be set at the competitive level, it would be by chance and not by virtue of any economic law.

The single price does usually exist but as a consequence of policy and not the operation of market forces. Its existence proves that market forces have been supplanted by institutional controls. This single rate may not clear the market, and, if it does, this may result from control over entry rather than the achievement of a competitive equilibrium position. Supply and demand do adjust and can be adjusted to the wage rate rather than wages adjusting to supply and demand. This is not to say that supply and demand have no effect on price, but only that their influence is often both indirect and muted. If the market is cleared, it is more likely to be the result of other

---

[8] Arthur M. Ross, *Trade Union Wage Policy* (Berkeley: University of California Press, 1948), p. 53.
[9] Hicks, *op. cit.*, p. 1.

factors, such as the policies of government and of private investors, than of wage adjustments.

Consumer sovereignty has now been supplanted by producer-consumer sovereignty. The policies of unions and employer groups as well as the choices of consumers affect the distribution of resources and the assignment of rewards.

5. *The Managed Market.* Economists, in the past, most commonly viewed the labor market as sufficiently perfect; but a number of them, more recently, have deemed it unsupportably imperfect. A major shift has taken place from defense to attack. Some form of managed market is offered as the solution for the shortcomings. One group favors a return to competition—to "compulsory individualism"; another group favors a step farther toward positive participation by the state. In either event state control should replace, in part or in whole, private control.

a) *Compulsory Individualism.* Henry Simons favored the abolition of trade unions since they seek to destroy free labor markets: "I simply cannot conceive of any tolerable or enduring order in which there exists widespread organization of workers along occupational, industrial, functional lines . . ."[10] since "unionism . . . enables an aristocracy of labor to build fences around its occupations, restricting entry, raising arbitrarily the costs and prices of its products, and lowering the wages and incomes of those outside, and of the poor particularly."[11] Along with limitations on trade unions, he favored antitrust prosecutions to increase competition in the product market. Hayek, apparently, favors the same approach.[12]

b) *Collective Determination.* Meade sees the same problem— "trade unions are monopolistic bodies with power and the incentive to rig the market"[13]—but basically a different solution. In addition to enforced competition in the product market, or, lacking that, socialization, he proposes consideration of two solutions: limitation of single bargains to employees of a single employer; and government fixation of individual wage rates so as to equalize supply and demand.[14] Beveridge sees a somewhat different problem and supports a more specific program which includes government control of prices;

10 Henry C. Simons, *Economic Policy for a Free Society* (Chicago: University of Chicago Press, 1948), pp. 121–22.

11 *Ibid.*, p. 138.

12 Frederick A. Hayek, *The Road to Serfdom* (Chicago: University of Chicago Press, 1944). See particularly p. 36.

13 James Edward Meade, *Planning and the Price Mechanism* (London: Allen and Unwin, 1948), p. 68.

14 *Ibid.*, p. 76.

limitation of wage increases through employer resistance, the action of arbitration tribunals, and the self-discipline of the trade unions; the planned location of factories; and "organized mobility" through the greater willingness of workers to change place and occupation, the dropping by the unions of restrictive rules, and the greater and perhaps compulsory use of the government employment service to guide movement.[15]

Lindblom, who seems unsettled as between compulsory individualism and collective determination, believes that "unionism and the private enterprise economy are incompatible."[16] Despite doubts as to feasibility, he considers certain measures necessary: (1) the breaking of the monopoly power of unions by prohibiting strikes over wage issues, (2) the reviewing of wage changes or the direct fixation of wages by public authority, and (3) the prohibition of all joint collusive activities of unions and employers.[17]

The managed market, particularly as suggested by Simons, Meade, and Lindblom, would, through government intervention, seek to tie wage setting and worker movement more closely together. Wages, so far as possible, would, through enforcement of competition or government fixation, be set at the competitive rate and labor resources would be properly utilized. Producer control would be limited and consumer supremacy restored.

REALISTIC ALTERNATIVES

Among these five models, the first, the perfect market, is truly a "labor market," since worker movement and wage movement interact precisely. The second (the neoclassical market) and the last (the managed market) are, by customary standards, sufficiently satisfactory wage setting and labor distributing mechanisms. In the former case this is due to natural forces and in the latter to government intervention. The two remaining models (the natural market and the institutional market) are usually counted the least satisfactory, since they operate so imprecisely in allocating resources to their most efficient uses and in setting wages—yet they are and have been by all odds the most common types.

Regardless of the alternatives with which one might choose to be

---

[15] William H. Beveridge, *Full Employment in a Free Society* (New York: W. W. Norton, 1945), pp. 166–75 and 198–203.
[16] Charles E. Lindblom, *Unions and Capitalism* (New Haven: Yale University Press, 1949), p. v.
[17] *Ibid.*, pp. 243–45.

faced, the perfect market and the neoclassical market are not currently obtainable in the United States. The natural market, while still the most ordinary occurrence, is on the wane. The growth of unions, of large enterprises, and of employers' associations is reducing its prevalence. The trend is against it. The managed market, though adumbrated by federal and state bans on the closed shop, cannot conceivably be fully introduced at the present time: (1) unions will not be destroyed or strikes over wages prohibited, as suggested by Simons and Lindblom; nor (2) will wages be fixed or reviewed by the government, plants be located by government decree, or hiring of any or all workers be forced through the employment service, as suggested by Meade and Beveridge. The economist's usual version of a satisfactory market, if it ever existed, is not going to be put together soon again in the United States, either by enforced atomistic competition or government wage fixing. The first is impossible of achievement and the second, while possible, would not, because of private pressures, lack of knowledge, lags in obtaining information and making adjustments, and difficulties of enforcement, be reasonably effective in obtaining the desired result. The institutional market will, instead, gain in importance. In the United States, the near future, at least, is on the side of stronger private governments. The consequences of institutional markets, consequently, warrant particular attention.

TESTS OF PERFORMANCE

No single test of the ability of wage and job markets to execute appropriate functions is sufficient. Wage and job markets serve more than one purpose and their effective working capacity needs to be evaluated against more than a single criterion. Nor should a perfect record on any test be expected. Human relations seldom lend themselves to the divine attribute of complete excellence. The degree of satisfaction of the minimum requirements of society is a more realistic if less consummate test than of the maximum desires of economists. The operational impacts of institutional wage and job markets will be matched against certain of these societal requisites.

1. *The Wage Structure.* Ideally the occupational and industrial wage structure should reflect alike the disutility flowing from the work and the utility of the service rendered. For closely similar work and workers, closely similar rates should be paid; and rates should be dissimilar in proportion to the dissimilarity of work and workers. There is no evidence that such a Utopian wage structure has ever

fully existed. It is a useful norm for theoretical speculations but an unusable departure point for empirical studies. Such studies must compare, unsatisfactory as this comparison may be, developments where institutional controls (more specifically collective bargaining) are applied with developments in areas not responding directly to such controls, although these areas need not display "the competitive level" of wages.

One consequence of contemporary institutional controls in the labor market is evident. They conduce to the single rate within the craft or industrial field which they cover. The best, although not thoroughly convincing, evidence now indicates they have surprisingly little effect, however, on interindustry differentials, confirming the conclusions of Paul Douglas of a quarter of a century ago.[18] Whether this is because other forces such as productivity, comparative changes in employment, governmental policy, and product market configurations far outweigh unionism, or because collective bargaining while strengthening the power of the workers also leads to an offsetting augmentation of the strength of employers, or because union rates pull nonunion rates after them, or for some other reason, it seems to be a fact that collective bargaining has much less of an ensuing result on interindustry differentials than commonly supposed.

Sir Henry Clay has noted that in England before World War I, "wages, it may fairly be said, constituted a system, since there were well-understood rates for most occupations; the relations between these were stable and generally accepted, and a change in any one rate would prompt demands for a change in other rates."[19] This "system" resulted, in part, from commonly accepted rules of equity and from institutional controls. Both militate against economic forces which tend to pull the "system" apart. As institutional controls spread and deepen, the "system" may become increasingly formalized with "historical relations" and "patterns" taking the place more and more of supply and demand. Widely pervasive political interrelationships instead of physical movement of workers will tie the wage structure together. It may eventually appear that the "system of wages" will have to be regarded by economists as an independent variable, rather than a dependent variable at the mercy of a myriad of economic causes.

By and large, the wage structure has not been distorted from its pre-

[18] Paul H. Douglas, *Real Wages in the United States, 1890–1926* (Boston: Houghton Mifflin, 1930), p. 562.
[19] Henry Clay, *The Problem of Industrial Relations* (London: Macmillan, 1929), p. 74.

existing mold as one would expect if unions were exploiting to the full their economic monopoly power. But then unions are not primarily economic monopolies but political organizations. The political test of meeting workers' notions of equity has more of an impact on wage policy than the economic test of income maximization.

If collective bargaining has had no revolutionary effect on the wage structure except to bring the single rate within the industry and within the craft, then, by means of wage influences, it seems likely its impact on the allocation of resources has often been exaggerated.[20] This does not mean that the wage structure under collective bargaining is ideally designed to allocate resources, but only that it has not been changed so greatly from its "natural" state, bad as that may have been.

There is some real question how effective a wage structure can be in distributing labor in any event. Wages are only one of several important considerations which repel workers from some jobs and attract them to others. The push of unemployment, for example, is often more effective than the pull of higher wages.

If institutional controls change the wage structure surprisingly little from its former conformations, it remains to be asked whether governmental wage fixing would bring it any closer to the competitive norm. No definitive answer is, of course, possible. It may be suggested, however, that much the same equitable considerations, albeit more uniformly applied, and equivalent pressures, though emanating even more from political incentives and less from the market, would leave their mark and we should be as far as ever from the flexible, equilibrating wage structure.

The institutional market does bring the single rate within the industry and craft, although by a different process. In adjusting inter-industry and intercraft rates it may represent an economy of means.

---

20 Collective bargaining can have three principal impacts on wage rates: (1) on intraindustry and intracraft relationships, (2) on interindustry and intercraft differentials, and (3) on the general level of money wages as distinct from the structure (to which the next section of this paper refers); and in these three principal ways, through wage influences, can change the allocation of resources. Most attention is normally paid to the second (impact on interindustry differentials); but the first (impact on intraindustry and intracraft relationships) and the third (impact on the general level of wages) may be the more significant. Equalizing rates within the industry and craft and raising the general level of wages can substantially affect resource allocation, even if interindustry differentials are not much changed. Equalizing rates can affect, for example, which firms survive and the relative profitability of those which do; and raising the general level, for example, can affect the relative proportions of labor and capital utilized and relative amounts of final products and services demanded since the demand for some is affected more than for others when prices rise in response to higher costs. In general, however, it seems that resource allocation may be less affected and in somewhat different ways than is often stated.

The market can be tested and the wage structure adjusted more quickly and with less physical movement than would be the case in the natural market.

2. *The General Level of Wages.* The institutional market undoubtedly causes the general level of money wages to behave differently than it otherwise would, and a large literature has developed around this point. Here again, however, there may be a tendency to view with too much alarm. Wages always rise under conditions of full employment. The upward movement appears more spectacular under conditions of collective bargaining but possibly may not be as great as in its absence. At least the case for the opposite view is by no means clear. During World War II, nonunion wages on the average must have risen as fast or faster than union wages, although many other factors were at work aside from unionization. Wage levels in unorganized areas generally went up more than in such highly organized areas as Seattle and San Francisco, although here again other forces serve as explanations, too. Experience in other democratic capitalistic nations also indicates that a high level of institutional controls has not been associated with abnormal wage advances but rather the opposite.

Unionism is not normally introduced into a society under conditions of *ceteris paribus.* Employers coalesce, also, and formally or informally have policies, too; and the government, through settlement of labor disputes, if in no other fashion, becomes involved. The new force of unionism is met by increased countervailing force. The problem of undue wage increases under full employment is more the result of full employment than of unionism.

Institutional controls while conceivably dampening the upward surge of wages during full employment certainly retard their downward tendency during depression; and thus the over-all effect may well be to raise the general level of wages. Given reasonable resort to other methods than wage control of achieving price stability, a continued growth of employers' associations, a further bureaucratization of trade unions, a continued rise in man-hour output, and a volume of employment not overly full, the impact of unionism on the over-all level of labor costs and purchasing power may be quite tolerable.

3. *The Distribution of Job Opportunities.* Under our system we depend on the choice of individuals to allocate human resources. But it is not alone resources which are being allocated but also job opportunities. The economic goal of efficient utilization of manpower is at least matched in importance by the political goal of equality of opportunity.

Institutional rules, in a sense, create markets—markets with specific occupational, industrial, and geographical boundaries and with rules affecting entry, movement within, and exit. Both unions and employers have policies affecting these dimensions and processes, but those of the former at their fullest development tend to be the more precise and restrictive. Selig Perlman's term, "job territory,"[21] well conveys the emphasis on citizenship and noncitizenship, immigration restrictions and quotas, and passports.

Instead of ill-defined markets existing most significantly as subjective impressions of workers and employment managers, markets become a finite entity. This is especially true of the hiring hall which is a market place, a bourse. Balkanization of job markets results, and these Balkanized markets operate differently internally and in their external relations than "natural markets." Internally, wages and conditions are more uniform, knowledge more complete, and movement is according to more formalized guides for conduct, such as seniority. Among markets, movement is both reduced in totality and redirected.

Union policies variously control, guide, and influence market processes. Control is illustrated by closed shop arrangements where access to the market is solely through union channels; guidance by the practices in the garment trades, for example, where the unions actively distribute work and workers but lack full control; and influence by the mass-production industries where union rights, such as seniority, and union membership by itself, identify the individual worker more closely with the company and the industry. Both the recently completed New Haven labor market study[22] and the current Oakland study[23] demonstrate that, for whatever reason, union members are less mobile. Formal policies of employers and employers' associations also effectively influence hiring and movement from job to job within the company.

These institutional policies affect less importantly the number of jobs available and the adequacy of supply to match them than they do the selection of those workers to whom individual opportunities are open. In addition to qualifications related to job performance, other attributes precedent to employment are frequently required. Perhaps the most socially questionable impact of institutional controls is on the availability of free access to jobs. This prompts the

21 Selig Perlman, *A Theory of the Labor Movement* (New York: Macmillan, 1928), p. 273.

22 Lloyd G. Reynolds and Joseph Shister, *Job Horizons* (New York: Harper, 1949), p. 48.

23 Conducted by the Institute of Industrial Relations, University of California (Berkeley).

suggestion that the admission policies of unions and employers are of key importance in the operation of institutional markets.

4. *Freedom of Competition and Freedom of Association.* All forms of freedom are not fully compatible. Freedom of competition, a most laudable objective, and freedom of association often run counter to each other. Economic groups most frequently associate for the purpose of reducing or eliminating competition. Yet freedom of association is as basic a political right as freedom of competition is an economic blessing. Freedom of competition can only be assured in job markets by destruction of freedom of association, since freedom of association leads directly to institutional controls. The first can only be completely obtained by the complete elimination of the latter; and complete fulfillment of the latter can lead to the destruction of the former. Since it is not likely, nor proper, that either freedom should thoroughly supplant the other, a compromise of their claims is in order. Since associations are the aggressor, it is proper public policy to see that none becomes too strong as against any other, against the state, or against the individual, and that they be required to act responsibly. There will be some cost to freedom of competition, but then the policy of Simons is not without its different and greater costs. Both the causes of political freedom and economic efficiency must be served. The achievement of J. M. Clark's goal of "responsible individuals in responsible groups"[24] is, however, no simple task.

5. *Consumer and Producer Sovereignty.* Economists historically have favored consumer sovereignty, and there is no adequate substitute for it in a free society. Institutional controls cause this sovereignty to be shared with producer groups. While this most frequently reduces economic well-being, decisions of producer groups can display some wisdom as well; and producers can have some minimum demands for security and recompense which they can properly assert against the wishes of consumers.

6. *Preservation of Law and Order.* Some job markets make more of a contribution to industrial stability than others. Institutional controls are generally accepted or tolerated. With all their faults, they lend a certain order and discipline to industrial life. Destruction of unions and presumably of employers' associations, as suggested by Simons, or prohibitions of strikes over wages, as suggested by Lindblom, or government wage fixing, as suggested by Lindblom and Meade, would be lacking in that minimum voluntary approval which is indispensable to enforcement in a democracy.

---

[24] John Maurice Clark, *Alternative to Serfdom* (New York: Knopf, 1948), chap. V.

CONCLUSION

Among the five models of the labor market which we have set forth, the trend is unmistakably toward the institutional market. It will always miss high excellence but it can be an adequate economic mechanism. It probably has rather less of an impact on the wage structure and the general level of wages than is frequently assumed, while reflecting freedom of association, allowing expression of a measure of producer concern, and contributing to over-all public tranquility. Such a market requires, however, particularly careful scrutiny of the efficiency and equality with which it distributes jobs. It is more likely to lack as a job distributing market than as a wage setting market, although it is the latter aspect which more often generates the greater concern.

Compulsory atomization and compulsory wage fixation should both be rejected and institutional markets accepted as the best alternative (although far from the best theoretical market form), and such modifications in them should be attempted as are deemed necessary to the protection of the legitimate welfare of individuals, groups, and the economy at large.

Most economists in the past have been too little critical of labor markets; some now are too much so. In an effort to achieve what is perfect, they would lose what is acceptable.

Some Problems of Wage Policy

HARRY M. DOUTY

It has become commonplace to argue that pressure on the general level of prices from the side of wages and salaries would be removed if money wage increases, on the average, conformed to the secular gain in national productivity.[1] The achievement of such a result would eliminate one of the primary sources of cost inflation. The other major source is represented by profits above the competitive level that reflect the exercise of market power by employers. The fact that this article, except for incidental references, is concerned only with the question of wages and salaries is not intended to suggest that the problem of administered prices is unimportant.

Since wages should perform an allocative function in the labor market, a wage policy geared to the secular increase in productivity does not, in its usual formulation, provide for uniform (percentage) increases throughout industry. On the contrary, as the Council of Economic Advisers suggested most recently in its annual report, wage increases should vary from the average in a downward direction in industries in which labor, assuming reasonably full employment in the economy, is redundant, and in an upward direction in industries in which labor is in short supply.[2] The Council proposed an additional criterion. It suggested that wage increases above the average would be appropriate in industries in which comparative wages are exceptionally low "because the bargaining position of workers has been weak,"

Taken from Monthly Labor Review, *LXXXV (July 1962), pp. 733–41. Harry M. Douty is Assistant Commissioner of Labor Statistics for Wages and Industrial Relations and for Business Labor Statistics.*

[1] Money wage increases should be understood to include employer expenditures on fringe benefits.

[2] *Economic Report of the President, Transmitted to the Congress January 1962, Together With the Annual Report of the Council of Economic Advisers* (1962), pp. 185–90.

and should fall short of the average where wages, reflecting strong bargaining positions, are exceptionally high.

The Council's statement, issued in the form of guidelines to wage negotiators, is a reasonably explicit formulation of a national wage policy. This article attempts, first, to indicate the factors underlying the announcement of such a policy; and, second, to present some analysis of the policy in terms of the ends that are sought and of the major institutional factors that may affect its implementation.

UNIONS, FULL EMPLOYMENT, AND WAGES

It was conceded, in simpler times, that unions in particular crafts or industries might succeed in raising wages above the "competitive" level. This could be accomplished primarily through restrictions on entry or other regulation of the labor supply. This meant, in turn, that the workers denied access to the unionized trades would seek other employment, thus lowering wages in the nonunion sector. On balance, therefore, the general level of wages would not be affected by union action.

By the end of World War II, three factors had changed this perspective. The first was the revolution in economic thought by Keynes and his interpreters, in particular the role assigned to fiscal and monetary policy in maintaining high levels of output and employment. The second was the political acceptance of full employment as a major goal of public policy. The third was the rise of trade union power in many strategic sectors of the economy under the protection, in the United States, of law guaranteeing to workers the right to organize and imposing upon employers the duty to bargain. It was the conjuncture of these developments, which could not fail to have a profound effect on the labor market, that produced present-day concern with wage pressure on the price level.

Indeed, some concepts of full employment, if realized in practice, inevitably would produce cost inflation even if trade unionism were nonexistent. Thus, Beveridge defined full employment to mean that there are "always more vacant jobs than unemployed men, not slightly fewer jobs" or, in different words, that "the labor market should always be a seller's market rather than a buyer's market."[3] But if the demand for labor is always greater than the supply, wages, and hence prices, will show a continual tendency to rise. As Robbins puts it, "there can be few ways of defining an inflationary situation

3 William H. Beveridge, *Full Employment in a Free Society* (New York: W. W. Norton, 1945), pp. 18–19.

more precise than a definition which runs in terms of Lord Beveridge's objective."[4]

It should be noted that full employment, even in the Beveridgian sense, makes allowance for some unemployment of a seasonal and frictional nature, averaging perhaps 3 per cent of the labor force annually. Such unemployment, largely short-term and unavoidable, would not represent deficiency of demand for labor. Taking seasonal and transitional factors into account, the aim of full employment policy might well be equality in the supply of and the demand for labor at current wage rates. This would avoid pressure on the general level of wages from the side of demand. At the same time, however, it would represent a labor market situation in which institutional pressures could be exerted with substantial hope of success. In fact, strongly organized worker groups appear capable of exercising market power under less favorable circumstances.

The theoreticians of full employment were certainly not unaware of the problem of wages. Beveridge noted that "there is a real danger that sectional wage bargaining, pursued without regard to its effects on prices, may lead to a vicious spiral of inflation, with money wages chasing prices and without any gain in real wages for the working class as a whole."[5] Hansen remarked that, "If stability is to be achieved along with full employment, wages and prices cannot be left wholly to automatic forces."[6] Kalecki pointed out that under full employment, "the bargaining power of trade unions will be very strongly enhanced. Thus there may be a spontaneous tendency for money wage rates to increase which leads to a rise in prices and the cost of living; this in turn leads to a secondary rise in wages and so on."[7] Keynes did not deal at any length with the question of wages in relation to full employment, but he clearly recognized the problem. In an article in 1943, he wrote that "some people argue that a capitalist country is doomed to failure [in preserving stability of internal prices] because it will be found impossible in conditions of full employment to prevent a progressive increase of wages. According to this view, severe slumps and recurrent periods of unemployment have been hitherto the only effective means of holding efficiency wages

---

[4] Lionel Robbins, *The Economist in the Twentieth Century* (London: Macmillan, 1954), p. 22.

[5] Beveridge, *op. cit.*, p. 199.

[6] Alvin H. Hansen, *Economic Policy and Full Employment* (New York: McGraw-Hill, 1947), p. 240.

[7] M. Kalecki, "Three Ways to Full Employment," in Oxford University, Institute of Statistics, *The Economics of Full Employment* (Oxford: Basil Blackwell, 1948), pp. 43–44.

[wages per unit of output] within a reasonably stable range. Whether this is so remains to be seen. The more conscious we are of this problem, the likelier shall we be to surmount it."[8]

As we shall see at a later point, the nature of the problem was more clearly perceived than its solution.

THE MECHANISM OF COST INFLATION

Inflation can result from pressure on prices from the side of demand or from the side of costs, or it may, in modern industrial societies with democratic institutions, contain a mixture of demand and cost elements. Historically, most inflationary movements appear clearly to have resulted from conditions of excess demand. . . . The rise in the level of prices in the United States during World War II and the immediate postwar years was demand-induced. . . .

Demand inflation is not difficult in principle to understand, although mild doses, as from an investment boom in an industrially advanced country, may not be readily diagnosed. On the other hand, cost inflation (wages or administered prices) presents a greater challenge to analysis. For one thing, it is not ever likely, by itself, to result in a dramatic upsurge of the price level. It tends rather to produce a slow upward movement in prices (which can, however, be cumulatively important), and even this movement may be obscured during some periods by contrary movement in one or more components of the price index (e.g., agricultural products). Moreover, persistent cost inflation must, at some point, find support in demand if output and employment are to be maintained. Thus cost and demand factors tend to become entangled, and the cause of an inflationary episode often becomes obscure and the subject of controversy.

Perhaps the most useful schema for the analysis of inflation is that suggested in a recent article by Professor Machlup.[9] He points out, first, that "an inflation of effective demand is a necessary condition not only for a demand-pull inflation of consumer prices but also for a cost-push inflation. Without an expansion of demand, the cost boost would result in less production and less employment, not in a continuing rise in the level of consumer prices." As the following diagram indicates, expansion of demand can be autonomous, in the sense that it is not linked to previous or expected cost increases.

8 John Maynard Keynes, "The Objective of International Price Stability," *Economic Journal* (June–September 1943), p. 187.
9 Fritz Machlup, "Another View of Cost-Push and Demand-Pull Inflation," *The Review of Economics and Statistics* (May 1960), pp. 125–39.

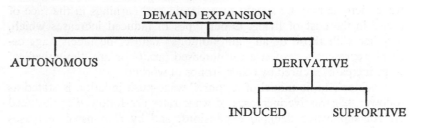

This is the source (assuming reasonably full employment of resources) of pure demand inflation. But expansion in demand can also be a derivative of cost increases; that is, the expansion follows and is a consequence of increases in wages or other costs. "Induced" expansion, in Machlup's terminology, would occur, for example, when industrial firms utilize cash reserves or borrow from banks to finance a wage increase granted under union pressure. A "supportive" expansion would occur when the monetary or fiscal authorities act to increase demand in order to reduce or prevent unemployment arising from wage or other cost advances.

The anatomy of cost increases is more complicated. In terms of the following diagram, "responsive" increases (e.g., in wages) are those that are demand-induced; that is, they reflect conditions in the labor market that would have led, in any case, to higher wages.

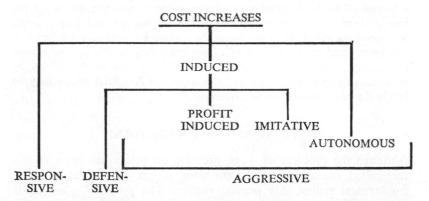

At the extreme right of the diagram are cost increases that are "autonomous" in nature; that is, they reflect purely the exercise of market power by unions or employers. Machlup designates certain types of increases as neither strictly responsive nor autonomous, but as "induced" by changes in the economic situation. Thus, a "defensive"

wage increase may be sought to maintain real earnings in the face of a rise in the cost of living. Other types of induced increases which, together with those of an "autonomous" nature, he labels "aggressive," represent a response to increased profits or are "imitative" of wage increases secured by other groups of workers.

Machlup's basic model of a "pure" wage-push inflation is stated as follows: "Aggressive increases of wage rates are followed by induced and/or supportive demand expansions, and by responsive increases of material prices and other wage rates." The Machlup formulation has the merit of suggesting not only the elements and sequence of cost inflation but also the great difficulty in the real world of determining its causation in concrete situations. Nevertheless, given the existence of strong trade unions in strategic sectors of the economy, and government policy calculated to support employment at a high level, the process of wage determination can plainly exert secular pressure on the price level. The result, if not in some way counteracted, may well frustrate such basic goals as high employment and economic growth. It has been forcefully pointed out, for example, that:

. . . it may prove to be an arduous task to maintain full employment when the cost-price system has become ossified through group control over wages and prices. As the economy loses its suppleness, the need for compensatory spending rises. Yet additional expenditures, whether 'injected' by the government or generated within the private sector, may be siphoned off in the form of higher incomes for groups already employed, before there is an opportunity to expand production and employment. Whenever the government intervenes to reverse a contractive tendency, it will be haunted by the specter of a forward policy on the part of organized groups. Sequences of income generation may be swallowed up by advances in wages and prices, and the hoped-for beneficial effects may be lost in the cumulative upward movement.[10]

THE SEARCH FOR A WAGE POLICY

Although the problem of wage pressure on prices has been widely recognized, the answer to the problem, within the context of a full employment policy, has proved elusive. The problem often tends simply to be brushed aside. Thus, Kaldor, writing with particular reference to the British situation, states: "All that is necessary is to recognize that the proper way of dealing with inflation is to damp down, or restrain, the rate of increase in money wages *as such*, in-

[10] James R. Schlesinger, "The Role of Monetary Environment in Cost-Inflation," *Southern Economic Journal* (July 1957), p. 24.

stead of damping down the demand for goods and services. . . . Measures restricting the cost-push inflation coming from the side of the unions, unlike measures restricting the demand for goods, do not necessarily interfere with the real rate of growth of the economy."[11] But Professor Kaldor fails to tell us how this end can be accomplished. In fact, his only suggestion is for the introduction of the long-term (2-year) contract in Great Britain, on the debatable ground that "the biennial round of wage increases would be bound to be less than twice the annual round."[12]

In his pioneering work on full employment, Beveridge, again with British conditions particularly in view, was able only to suggest that the unions attempt to develop a unified wage policy, and that employers and the unions resort to arbitration when they failed to agree.[13] As it turned out, compulsory arbitration, but not a unified wage policy, was a feature of British postwar industrial relations.[14] In the United States, Hansen's thoughts also turned to arbitration; he argued that, to keep wages in line, "adequate provision for a permanent system of Federal mediation and arbitration of wage disputes is imperative."[15] Unfortunately, a system of arbitration can be a procedure for wage determination, but not in any sense a substitute for a wage policy.

As the postwar period advanced, more and more attention in the United States and elsewhere tended to center on productivity—in the sense of output per man-hour in the economy as a whole—as the substantive key to national policy on wages. Since productivity experience typically varies from one year to another, emphasis has been placed on the long-term trend in man-hour output. Aside from technical problems of productivity measurement, and the question of the appropriate period over which to compute secular change, the productivity standard appeared to offer a framework within which wage movements could be judged in terms of their impact on costs and prices.

The argument, simply stated, is approximately as follows. If monetary and fiscal policy, given reasonably full employment, can prevent pressure on prices from the side of demand, then the annual gain in real output per hour can be realized in the form of higher money

---

11 Nicholas Kaldor, "Economic Growth and the Problem of Inflation," *Economica* (November 1959), p. 296.
12 *Ibid.*, p. 297.
13 Beveridge, *op. cit.*, pp. 200–01.
14 Until March 1, 1959, when the Industrial Disputes Order ceased to be in effect. The revocation of the order was opposed by the unions but supported by the employers.
15 Hansen, *op. cit.*, p. 240.

wages, salaries, and profits without a secular rise in the general level of prices. This will be possible if, from the wage side, the average gain in money wages conforms to the secular rise in productivity, and provided also that price decreases in high productivity industries, where unit costs are falling, roughly balance price increases in low productivity industries.

In a more or less explicit form, the elements of a productivity-based wage and price policy may be found in the Economic Reports of the President throughout the postwar period. In the 1947 midyear Economic Report, for example, note was made (p. 3) of certain special circumstances justifying wage increases. Aside from these special circumstances, the report continued, "wage increases should be related to general trends in productivity and not made on a basis which forces price increases or prevents price reductions needed to assure sales of increasing supplies." The 1953 Report of the Council of Economic Advisers (p. 114) suggests that "since wages constitute the bulk of personal income, the preferable general formula—once wages, prices, and profits are in a workable relationship—is for money wages to increase with productivity trends in the whole economy." The 1957 Economic Report (pp. iii-iv) pointed out that business managements must "recognize the broad public interest in the prices set on their products and services." Both management and labor were urged "to reach agreements on wages and other labor benefits that are consistent with productivity prospects and with the maintenance of a stable dollar." The 1960 Economic Report (p. iv) argued that "the achievement of inflation-free economic growth . . . requires a blending of suitable private actions and public policies." The Report (p. 8) pointed out that wage increases "are the major means in our free economy by which labor shares in the fruits of industrial progress. But improvements in compensation rates must, on the average, remain within the limits of general productivity gains if reasonable stability of prices is to be achieved and maintained."

Impetus to the more explicit formulation of wage-price policy in terms of the productivity criterion may have been given by the publication in the spring of 1961, under the auspices of the Organization for European Economic Cooperation (OEEC), of a study of the problem of inflation by six distinguished economists.[16] The report contended that, "from an economic standpoint, wage increases can be considered an independent causal factor of price increases only when they are determined by negotiations between organized labor groups

16 William Fellner and Others, *The Problem of Rising Prices* (Paris: Organization for European Economic Cooperation, 1961).

and employers (or raised by government decree). In such circumstances, the average increase in wages is not necessarily that which would have resulted in a freely competitive market."[17] For the period under review (1953–60), the study concluded that "excessive wage increase constituted both an important and independent inflationary force" in the United States, the United Kingdom, and certain other countries.[18] On these points, there was agreement among the six authors.

On the question of a solution to the problem, however, the group split. The majority position was that governments should adopt a wage policy, the elements of which were stated as follows:

> By having a wages policy, we mean, first of all, that the authorities themselves must have a reasonably precise view, estimated by the best means which they can devise, of the average increase in wages that is appropriate to the economic situation and consistent with stability of the price level. This view will necessarily depend primarily on experience and expectations regarding the longer run rate of productivity in the economy. But it may also have to take into account various aspects of the current economic situation, such as the phase of the trade cycle and the state of the balance of payments. Having such a view, getting it known by the interested parties, and mobilizing support for it as an objective towards which to work, is the essence of having a wages policy.[19]

With respect to the implementation of policy, the majority view at first seemed unexceptional, with statements to the effect that the problem was one involving the art of the National Government in reconciling divergent economic interests; that recognition of the problem and the enunciation of a wage policy would in itself constitute an enormous step forward; and that the establishment of a norm for wage increases should create a situation in which the burden of proof would be upon any labor or management group that wished to deviate from it. But beyond these homiletic prescriptions, the majority suggested an institutional role for government in the following words:

> As the aim of wages policy is to set a norm for the increase in wages, there must be a center of authority in the public services charged with this function and machinery for appropriate consultation with representatives of the broad parties at interest. Furthermore, it might be of benefit to arrange for the governmental authorities to be represented at important wage negotiations—not simply as mediators but as a party at interest to represent the general public's stake in the outcome. It is not reasonable

17 *Ibid.*, p. 45.
18 *Ibid.*, p. 46.
19 *Ibid.*, pp. 57–58.

that this function should be neglected, or at best left vaguely to the press and public opinion.[20]

The majority also urged that governments develop wage policy for their own employees, especially to avoid wage and salary lags that subsequently must be corrected by sharp upward adjustments. Finally, it was suggested, without specific recommendations, that the machinery for wage negotiation in the private sector of the economy might need review and change.

Clearly the guidelines set forth in the 1962 Economic Report of the President, and summarized in the first section of this article, meet the criterion of a wage policy as defined in the OEEC study. Notably in the basic steel situation, the governmental authorities made the intent of this policy clear to the parties at interest,[21] and it appears to be the intention of the Government to continue to do so in other situations.[22] What follows represents an effort briefly to appraise certain aspects of the policy and the circumstances under which it must operate.

ASPECTS OF WAGE POLICY

1. A Federal Reserve Board study in 1946 concluded: "The fact is that collective bargaining with strong unions, price stability, and full employment are incompatible. We can have any two of these but not all three. So long as union power is not dampened down by unemployment, there is no apparent power in the State strong enough to check a parallel upward sweep of wages and prices."[23] The basic aim of wage policy is to resolve this dilemma by asserting, in a variety of ways, a public interest in the magnitude of wage settlements. In essence, the aim of policy is to stabilize the level of efficiency wages, not the level of money wages or real wages. It should be observed

20 *Ibid.*, p. 59.

21 At his press conference on April 18, 1962, the President stated: ". . . we worked very closely with the steel union in an attempt to persuade them that it was in their interest and the country's interest to meet the standards set by the Council of Economic Advisers, and it was done. That is why this matter [of steel prices] came particularly in sharp focus last week."

22 The fact must be emphasized, however, that general responsibility for wage decisions will continue to rest with the parties. In his address to the convention of the United Automobile Workers, May 8, 1962, the President declared: "We are neither able nor willing to substitute our judgment for the judgment of those who sit at the local bargaining tables across the country. We can suggest guidelines for the economy, but we cannot fix a single pattern for every plant and every industry."

23 Charles O. Hardy, "Prospects of Inflation in the Transition Period," in *Prices, Wages, and Employment* (Washington: Board of Governors, Federal Reserve System, 1946), p. 24.

that the Federal Reserve Board conclusion was drawn at the height of the postwar demand inflation. Conditions are now considerably different. Judgment must be reserved with respect to the "power of the State," under present-day economic circumstances, to influence the terms of wage bargains.

2. The achievement of a stable price level would prevent the erosion of real income among those groups (e.g., annuitants) whose incomes are fixed in money terms; it would mean, however, that such groups would be precluded from sharing in the gains from technical progress. This latter result could be avoided only if the aim of policy were a long-term decline in the price level (perhaps creeping deflation), which would involve a decline in efficiency wages and other costs. Such a policy has its advocates.[24] But for both technical and institutional reasons, price level stability rather than decline appears to represent a more feasible goal of policy. It should be recognized, however, that such a policy implies some shift in income (in both money and real terms) in the direction of those groups, primarily wage and salaried workers, equity shareholders, and independent entrepreneurs, whose incomes have upward flexibility.

3. A wage policy of the type here under discussion would not alter the relative share of wages and salaries in national income. Both labor and nonlabor income would grow, but at the same relative rates. It is sometimes thought that labor would obtain the entire gain in output under a productivity-based wage policy, but this would not be the case. If wages, salaries, and supplementary compensation represented 70 per cent of costs in the economy, then roughly 70 per cent of the gain in man-hour output would accrue to labor in the form of higher wages and benefits. The remaining 30 per cent would augment non-labor income. There is, indeed, little evidence to suggest that collective bargaining is a powerful instrument for altering income shares in a direction favorable to the working class as a whole. A broad scale effort in this direction would almost inevitably produce a round of price increases, as business sought to protect its income position. Conversely, if business, in response to a favorable demand situation, sought to improve its income share through general upward price adjustment, a reaction from the side of wages would undoubtedly occur. A wage-price or price-wage spiral is essentially a struggle over income distribution.

24 For example, see Council on Prices, Productivity, and Incomes *First Report* (London: H. M. Stationery Office, 1958), pp. 32–33. The council reported that "we have been impressed by the apparently widespread revival of interest in the idea of falling prices" and raised the question of whether "a gently falling price level" should not be considered as a goal of policy.

4. A wage policy involving an announced permissible average annual increase in wages might have an inflationary effect of its own. Thus, the British Council on Prices, Productivity, and Incomes has suggested that there would be "a real danger that the prescribed average would always become a minimum, and the process of wage inflation therefore [would be] built into the system."[25] In Machlup's model of the mechanism of cost inflation, this would occur through "responsive" reactions to "aggressive" wage increases in some sectors of the economy. The guideline approach does tend to reenforce expectations of annual wage advances that have grown up during the postwar period. On the other hand, even in the immediate postwar years, when demand inflation was at its height, there was by no means uniformity of response in terms of wage settlements, and the notion of pervasive "patterns" of adjustment, except within the orbits of certain industries or employments, has little current substance. Conditions affecting particular firms and industries should continue to play an important role in differentiating wage settlements.

5. Nevertheless, the preceding consideration does lead to one of the critical questions relating to the guideline type of wage policy. A policy prescribing that annual wage increases, on the average, shall not exceed the long-term gain in man-hour output inevitably means that some increases should fall short, and others should exceed, the average. The principal reasons for divergence from the average are clearly indicated in the statement of the Council of Economic Advisers. In industries or employments where labor is in excess supply, the increase should fall below the average or perhaps, in a given year, be skipped altogether. But given a union capable of exercising market power, how is this result to be achieved? Would not such a union strive to attain at least the average increase sanctioned by the wage policy? There is, after all, no central power on the trade union side that might assist in the allocation of the permissible annual wage increase among constituent unions. Indeed, the practice and tradition of autonomy in the American trade union movement is so strong that relinquishment by individual unions of control over collective bargaining policy and tactics would represent an extraordinary development. It is perfectly natural that any organized group should consider itself the best interpreter of the needs of its constituency.[26]

---

25 *Ibid.*, p. 45.
26 At its 1961 convention, the AFL–CIO, in its resolution on collective bargaining, decried "efforts to bind bargaining by national formulas, by ceilings, and other constraints." The resolution continued, in part: "The 'public interest' is the announced justification for such efforts. The public interest is multifaceted. The overall and long-run public interest cannot be served in a democratic society by throttling genuine

This attitude does not mean, of course, that unions or employers can overlook the existence of a wage policy or of governmental efforts to implement it. These factors add new dimensions to the bargaining process. They may well have to be taken into account, at least in key situations, in the formulation and rationalization of demands, and in bargaining strategy. The crucial question, in fact, revolves about the role of government, and it was fundamentally this issue that gave rise to dissent to the majority OEEC position on wage policy. The minority among the six OEEC economists stated their position as follows:

The majority of the group assumes that governmental guidelines (or "norms") relating to the supportable average rate of money wage increases could contribute importantly to the solution of the problem. We have at best moderate hopes in this regard. Hence we believe that the rather ineffective steps, against which we have no particular misgivings as long as governments do not go beyond them, would have to be followed by more specific measures if governments were to make a real effort to put into effect a national wages policy. Wage negotiations and pricing practices relate not to average wage rates and prices but to wages and prices in specific industries. Where wage-push inflation tends to develop, governments committed to a national wages policy would, in our opinion, have to become involved in rather extensive regulations relating to individual wages and prices. In such circumstances, political considerations and the usual group pressures would exert a very significant influence on the wage and price structure and also on the general wage and price level. We are opposed to moving in this direction.[27]

It is, of course, much too early to gage the extent to which Government in the United States might have to intervene in the labor market (or the product market) to make a guideline wage (and price) policy effective. If, again to use Machlup's terminology, potentially "aggressive" wage actions were confined to a limited number of sectors in the economy, then the power of Government admonition and public opinion might produce the desired result. Even in such circumstances, however, the question arises of whether, with time, admonition would lose its effectiveness.

---

and unshackled collective bargaining. Responsible management, we believe, will resent any alteration of the fundamentally free character of collective bargaining because the disadvantages of such change would far outweigh any seeming or short-run advantages of 'orderliness' or 'industrial peace,'." See AFL–CIO Resolutions Committee, Report No. 2, pp. 65–67.

[27] William Fellner and others, *op. cit.*, p. 63.

6. Finally, there is the intractable fact of the labor market, that immensely complex mechanism through which the wage level is determined by thousands upon thousands of collective and individual bargains and employer personnel actions. On the institutional side, there are in our system few bargains that have a national impact, in the sense that they tend to determine wages and conditions of work for the employees of entire industries. We operate, indeed, under a comparatively decentralized system in which the locus of bargaining for most industries and employments is the individual plant or company, associations of similar employers within particular labor markets, or, more rarely, industry associations on a broader geographic basis. For large sectors of employment, including some in which wages and salaries are advancing rapidly, compensation is not determined through formal collective bargaining procedures at all. This general system has many advantages. For one thing, it permits account to be taken of the economic circumstances of individual firms and of the interests of particular groups of workers; it tends to encourage novelty and innovation in the terms of employment.

However, the system may not be well adapted to the application of a national wage policy of the guideline type. To use some obvious examples: Average annual employment in the contract construction industry, where bargaining is predominantly on a local basis, is more than four times as great as employment in basic steel where, in essence, national bargaining occurs; employment in food stores, a single segment of retail trade, is almost twice as great as in the manufacture of automobiles and parts; and a union such as the International Association of Machinists has bargaining agreements in numerous industries, ranging from automobile repair to aircraft-missiles, but its bargaining is primarily with individual companies or local employer associations. Some bargains admittedly are vastly more important than others; it may be argued that these "key" bargains set the tone for wage determination in broad areas of the economy and that the crucial problem is to keep these in line with policy. But the relationship between the "key" bargains and the tens of thousands of "non-key" bargains may not be as great as one might suppose, and the cumulative effect of the latter may be substantial.

Underlying the institutional mechanisms for wage determination are demand-supply conditions in the labor market at any given time and over periods of time. These fundamental factors help powerfully to determine the pattern of wage change; in many situations, the impulses of the market are simply transmitted through the collective bargaining process. It is bound to be difficult in many cases to judge the extent to which, if at all, unions have exerted market power, in the sense that settlements are greater than they would otherwise have been. Within the manufacturing sector, a great deal of information is available on the structure of wage settlements during 1960. In that year, which was one of recession, approximately 11.4 million factory workers were employed in establishments with a policy of making general wage adjustments.[28] General wage increases were received by about four-fifths (9.1 million) of these workers, with the increases ranging from less than 1 per cent to 10 per cent or more. Increases of 3 per cent or more were received by three-fourths of the workers for whom upward adjustments were made. The average (median) increase, including in the calculation those who received no increases, was between 3 and 3.5 per cent. Fringe benefit improvements were made for a substantial proportion of the workers whose wage rates were advanced. However, it is not possible to tell how the distribution of general wage increases would have been altered if increases in expenditures on fringe benefits could have been included with the wage rate changes.[29]

These data throw some light on the pervasiveness of wage pressures under conditions of less than full employment. But the main point for this discussion is the diversity of the adjustments suggested by the data. Clearly there would be immense difficulties in external judgment of the validity of these adjustments within the framework of a wage policy. Adjustments of, say, 5 or 6 per cent may be completely justifiable on labor market grounds in some instances, and adjustments of 2 per cent not justifiable in others. Put differently, an increase of 6 per cent in certain circumstances, may simply reflect labor market pressures rather than union power. It may be observed, by way of illustration, that increases in the average annual salaries of college and university teachers, who are largely untouched by unionism, have equaled or exceeded 6 per cent in each of the past 6 academic years.[30] These increases may well reflect excess demand for academic personnel; they do not reflect institutional pressure in the labor market.

[28] The remaining workers, about 1.3 million, were in establishments where pay adjustments were made on an individual rather than on a general basis.
[29] See "Wage Developments in Manufacturing During 1960," *Monthly Labor Review* (August 1961), pp. 846–50.
[30] *Salaries Paid and Salary Practices in Universities, Colleges, and Junior Colleges, 1961–62* (Washington, D.C.: National Education Association, 1962), p. 25, table 22.

CONCLUSION

The United States is by no means alone in grappling with the problem of peacetime wage policy in the context of policies relating to full employment, price stability, and economic growth. In Great Britain, for example, the Government in July 1961 called for a "pay pause" to permit productivity to catch up with incomes and to "mark the beginning of a new long-term policy."[31] A subsequent White Paper declared that the "objective must be to keep the rate of increase of incomes within the long-term rate of growth of national production."[32] A National Economic Development Council, with a permanent staff, has been established to provide guidance on national economic development. Even West Germany, with its postwar miracle of economic growth, has not escaped the problem. In a speech on March 21, 1962, Minister of Economics Erhard proposed setting up a council, which he thought should be "more scientific and technical than administrative," to advise industry on the adjustment of wages to costs and prices.

This article has attempted to indicate the circumstances giving rise to the quest for a wage policy, the nature of the policy that appears to be emerging, and some of its implications and difficulties. The problem is real, the objectives of policy are important, and the implementation of any type of policy is immensely difficult. The objective, in brief, is to keep the rise of national money income, including wages and salaries as its major component, in line with the rise in national output. Real incomes will thus advance within a framework of price stability. To achieve this end without sacrificing the great advantages of freedom in the labor market (or, on the price side, in the product market) is one of the challenges of our time. The aim is for responsibility and restraint within the field of private decision-making, and not for state planning of private actions. The more deeply and widely the nature of the problem is understood, the more likely we are to work out a viable approach.

---

[31] Statement of the Chancellor of the Exchequer in the House of Commons, July 25, 1961. The pay pause ended on March 31, 1962.
[32] *Incomes Policy: The Next Step* (London: H. M. Stationery Office, Cmnd. 1626, February 1962), p. 4.

The Wage-Price Guideposts

COUNCIL OF ECONOMIC ADVISERS

Government policies can only provide an environment conducive to responsible private price and wage decision making. By choice, our Government can advise, inform, and bring to bear the pressure of public opinion—but it cannot direct.

With so much at stake, however, the Government's opportunity to advise and inform the public is one it must seize. In the Kennedy Administration, general advice as to the pattern of private price-wage decision making that would take account of the public's interest in avoiding market-power inflation was first formally set forth in the Economic Report of January 1962. The "guideposts" therein described—and repeated in the 1963 Report—offered standards by which union and business leaders themselves—along with the general public—could appraise particular wage and price decisions. They are restated here.

The guideposts contain two key propositions. The first—the general guidepost for wages—says that, in a particular firm or industry, the appropriate noninflationary standard for annual percentage increases in total employee compensation per man-hour (not just in straight-time hourly rates) is the annual increase in *national trend* output per man-hour. The standard is not the productivity trend in the particular firm or industry in question. Nor is it the particular year's productivity change, which can be influenced by short-run transitory factors.

The general guidepost for prices specifies that when an industry's trend productivity is growing less rapidly than the national trend,

Taken from Economic Report of the President Together With the Annual Report of the Council of Economic Advisers, *transmitted to the Congress January 1964, U.S. Government Printing Office, Washington, D.C., 1964, pp. 118–20.*

prices can appropriately rise enough to accommodate the labor cost increases indicated by the general wage guidepost. Similarly, in an industry whose trend productivity is growing more rapidly than the national average, product prices should be lowered enough to distribute to the industry's customers the labor-cost savings it would make under the general wage guidepost.

It should be emphasized that the general price guidepost does not counsel against price changes per se in a particular firm or industry. On the contrary, it contemplates changes in specific prices—downward in industries with high rates of productivity gain, as well as upward in industries with lower-than-average productivity gains.

Adherence to these general guideposts not only would make for over-all price stability but would be generally consistent with the tendencies of competitive labor and product markets. The principles established by the guideposts do not imply that the entire gains from productivity improvement should go either to labor or to capital. Rather, they suggest a proportionate sharing of average national productivity gains among labor, capital, and the other related factors of production throughout the economy.

The general guideposts can cover the vast majority of wage and price decisions, but cannot provide for all of the adjustments the economy requires, especially over an extended period. Hence, the guideposts, as originally expounded in 1962, appropriately included a set of exceptions that reflected certain considerations of equity and resource allocation.

On the wage side, it was suggested that exceptions might be made to adjust for labor supply conditions and for wages that are exceptionally high or low compared with the average for comparable work. Price exceptions took into consideration capital requirements, nonlabor costs, and profits based on excessive market power.

The original formulation of the guideposts in the January 1962 Report of the Council of Economic Advisers also noted that ". . . Although output per man-hour rises mainly in response to improvements in the quantity and quality of capital goods with which employees are equipped, employees are often able to improve their performance by means within their own control. It is obviously in the public interest that incentives be preserved which would reward employees for such efforts."

These modifications of the general guideposts still apply, but it must be emphasized that they are intended to apply to only a relatively few cases. Particularly at a time when our national capabilities for responsible price and wage making may undergo a more serious test than in recent years, the most constructive private policy in the great majority of situations would be to arrive at price decisions and wage bargains consistent with the general guideposts.

Two other comments on the guideposts seem appropriate this year. First, it is not the purpose of these advisory policies permanently to freeze the labor and nonlabor shares of total industrial income, as would a rigorous, unrelieved application of the general guideposts. The 1962 Report noted that "The proportions in which labor and nonlabor income shares the product of industry have not been immutable throughout history . . ." It went on to point out that bargaining over the shares is consistent with the guideposts if it is conducted "within the bounds of noninflationary price behavior." Specifically, this means that it is consistent with the guideposts for wage and profit shares to be bid up or down in a particular industry *so long as price behavior in that industry remains consistent with the general price guidepost indicated above.*

Second, it is appropriate to focus special attention this year on *price reductions.* The guideposts call for reductions in those industries whose trend productivity gains exceed the national trend. It is fair to say that large industrial enterprises thus far have not widely heeded this advice. And yet, as noted earlier, there will be ample room for such price reductions in 1964. If they are not forthcoming, over-all price stability will be rendered more difficult, since price increases are likely in industries that are progressing at a less-than-average rate. Moreover, in industries whose trend of productivity rises faster than the national average, if wages conform more nearly to national than to industry productivity trends (as the guideposts would have them do), failure to follow the general price guide will cause profits to pile up. Such profits become highly visible to the public and constitute a lure for strongly intensified wage demands.

Such circumstances pose a most unattractive dilemma from the viewpoint of the public interest. On the one hand, extra increases in wages or fringe benefits might tend to spread to other industries, creating a general cost-push from the wage side. On the other hand, there is no justification, on either economic or equity grounds, for distributing above-average gains in productivity exclusively through the profits channel. The real way out of this dilemma is for the firms involved to remove its cause by reducing prices.

In 1964, a year of still ample unused resources and a year in which both after-tax profits and labor incomes promise to rise substantially, there is no occasion for actions that result in substantial price increases. The public, quite properly, will be intolerant of any major businesses or unions whose short-sighted actions tend to set inflation in motion. To discharge its own responsibility, the Administration is taking steps to follow emerging price and wage developments with great care and to assemble data that will illuminate the price- and wage-making situations in particular industries. It will not hesitate to call public attention to major private decisions—by either business or labor—that seriously overstep noninflationary price and wage standards.

Certainly it is reasonable to hope, however, that such instances will be rare and that 1964 will be recorded as another year when American private price and wage makers demonstrated their capacity for responsible action.

Productivity, Wages, and Prices

ALBERT REES

I should like to [discuss] the relationship between wages and productivity. . . .

Perhaps I should begin by defining some of the terms that I will be using. Let me start with wages, which I will use as a kind of shorthand to mean gross average hourly earnings plus fringe benefits. It is the entire compensation of the worker and not just the wage element of it. This becomes increasingly important because a large part of total compensation now consists of fringe benefits.

When I talk about productivity, I will mean an old-fashioned and familiar productivity concept, namely, output per man-hour. There are a lot of alternative productivity concepts that could be used, and some of them are more relevant for certain purposes, but, for the purpose of discussing wages, output per man-hour is as good as any. . . .

An increase in wages can come from one of two places fundamentally. It can come from increased production—that is, increased output per man-hour—or it can come from some redistribution of the existing output.

Increased output per man-hour is frequently called "labor productivity" simply because it has man-hours of work in the denominator rather than units of capital, or units of all inputs taken together. But any factor of production can be responsible for an increase in output per man-hour. This increase is not something uniquely attributable to labor.

One may get increased output per man-hour because workers are

This article appeared as Selected Papers No. 1 of the Graduate School of Business, University of Chicago, 1962. Reprinted with the permission of the publisher. Albert Rees is Professor of Economics at the University of Chicago.

working harder or because workers are more skilled. But one may also get it for totally different reasons. One can get it through using a better quality of raw materials, if we are thinking about this at the level of the plant or firm. And, finally, one can get it through technological change. Technological change, often incorporated into investment, is, of course, the outstanding source of increases in output per man-hour.

Therefore, when we talk about rising output per man-hour, we do not mean in any way to prejudge the issue of claims against, or shares in, this rising output. Any one of the factors of production could have a part in causing this increase, and usually more than one factor will be involved.

If we set aside for a moment the possibility of changing shares; if we assume that somehow the shares of labor and capital in output have been fixed, then a policy tying wages to output per man-hour has one obvious merit—and it is this obvious merit that has made the policy so popular. For this makes it possible to have a stable level of prices of final products. If wages go up only in line with productivity, unit labor costs do not go up, and, therefore, there is no cost-push pressure on prices.

I think it is this very simple relationship that has led so many people to suggest we ought to have a policy that somehow ties productivity and wages together.

I am going to take a skeptical view of such a policy, and I might as well confess at the outset that I am in a very small minority of economists by doing so. The great majority of the people in my profession feel that a tie between productivity and wages is a very desirable kind of relationship to have.

There are two or three different ways of tying productivity and wages together. One way would be to do it industry by industry, or firm by firm, or even plant by plant—to measure output per man-hour, let us say, in the steel industry and let the wages of the steelworkers be related to output per man-hour in the industry. This will produce the result that we desire. There will be no changes in unit cost of labor in the industry, and, therefore, no cost pressure on prices. What could be nicer? The same pleasing result will occur if we choose the firm or the plant as our unit.

But, when you start to inquire into this, you find there are some difficulties. Productivity changes take place very unevenly among industries, among firms, among occupations or sectors of the economy.

The ultimate result of tying wages to productivity industry by industry or firm by firm would be to develop tremendous disparities between wages of people doing similar work in different places. A man might get $1.00 an hour if he were a janitor for the public schools and $5.00 an hour if he were a janitor in a missile factory. This would impress us all, of course, as being inequitable. It would not only impress management as being inequitable, particularly the managers of missile factories, it would also impress the trade unions as being inequitable because, after all, they believe in equal pay for equal work.

Suppose that we had the policy in, let us say, the television-manufacturing industry of tying wages to output per man-hour, and suppose that we had commenced this policy in 1946, when the television industry was in its infancy.

If wages had been tied to output per man-hour back in 1946, workers would be getting fantastic wages in the industry today because it is an industry which was growing very rapidly, which was making rapid technological progress, and in which the output per man-hour was obviously going up much more than the average. However, we would also find the price of television sets much higher now than it actually is, because the great bulk of this increase in output per man-hour has actually been used, not to raise wages, but to lower the price of the product. That, of course, is as it should be, and that is the reason for objecting to the policy of tying wages to productivity at the industry level.

If we have an industry whose output per man-hour is rising very much more rapidly than average, and if our goal for the economy as a whole is a stable price level, then, in that industry, prices should be falling—not just relatively but absolutely. There should be dollars-and-cents price reductions in that kind of industry, and, there have been very substantial ones in black-and-white television. This same reasoning will apply to color television. I do not think we want to say that the people who make color-television sets should have their wages tied to their productivity because, as volume expands, their productivity is going to go up very rapidly, and their jobs may actually become simpler rather than more difficult.

Take the other side; take my job. I am a teacher. There is a lot of talk about teaching machines, but as yet they are not widely used. If we measure productivity as we usually do, then the only measure that we would have for teachers would be something like pupils taught per year. That seems to be going down, as we feel a preference for smaller and smaller classes. So, of course, the type of policy we have been discussing would mean that we should give dollars-and-cents pay cuts to teachers because the number of pupils taught per teacher per year is falling. It would be very difficult to hold people in the teaching profession under that kind of a policy.

If there is an industry or occupation that is valuable to society and that, nevertheless, has measured productivity increases lower than the average for the economy as a whole, then in that industry wages and salaries will have to go up faster than output per man-hour in order to hold labor in the industry. Again I think that this is as it should be.

Therefore, this seemingly attractive policy of tying wages to productivity at the industry, occupation, or firm level, were it to continue through any long period of time, would lead to an intolerable mess—and the policy therefore has to be rejected.

We very often see arguments in the press, or hear discussion between union and management people, about whether productivity or wages has been going up faster in a particular industry. In my judgment, this is of no relevance at all for wage policy. If somebody attempts to say something about wage policy this way, the best thing to do is not to argue about the figures and say, "Well, you are not measuring productivity correctly or you are not measuring wages correctly," but to say, instead, "It really doesn't matter and, therefore, why dispute it?"

This brings me to a policy which is not so easy to dispose of—the policy of tying wages to productivity at the national level. This policy says that wages in each industry, in each occupation, should rise in the same amount as productivity in the economy as a whole. That is a very popular policy these days.

I suppose the start of it, more than any other one thing, was the United Auto Workers–General Motors agreement of 1948, in which there was negotiated (more or less at the instigation of the company) the so-called annual improvement factor. This said that over and above the increase in the cost of living, which was also covered in the contract by an escalator clause, the workers at General Motors were to get an annual real wage increase. The clause has been continued right down to the present day. In the current contract it is a stated number of cents per hour, or 2½ per cent per year, whichever is larger.

Two and a half per cent is just about in the middle of the range of estimates of the long-term increase in output per man-hour for the economy as a whole, and so the figures are related. Also, in arguing in favor of this arrangement, both the company and the union have made the statement that this provision has something to do with productivity increases.

Similar contract provisions are contained in the labor agreements in many other collective-bargaining situations. However, in industries that do not bargain with the United Auto Workers, it is much less common to call such provisions something like an annual improvement factor or to talk about them in terms of productivity. They are generally just a built-in wage increase, stated in the contract as so many cents per hour, and there is no sort of intellectual rationale offered for them.

In addition to its use in collective bargaining, we find this kind of policy advocated at very high levels in the federal government. One might say that this has been a non-partisan policy in the federal government.

To my knowledge, the first strong plea for tying wage increases to national increases in productivity was made during the Eisenhower administration, when the Council of Economic Advisers put a strong plea of this kind in Mr. Eisenhower's report. You will find it again this year in Mr. Kennedy's economic report, written, I presume, by his Council of Economic Advisers.

When the Joint Economic Committee held hearings on Mr. Kennedy's report, two members of the preceding Republican Council of Economic Advisers testified on it, and both said they thought this part of the report was just fine. I am going to criticize this policy, one which has had the full approval of both the Eisenhower and Kennedy administrations, . . .

Why is it that there are weaknesses in this policy? Let me come back again to a point in my earlier remarks. The policy has the effect of freezing labor's share of income, especially if you define wages as I have done, to include fringe benefits. The slices of the pie would always remain exactly the same number of degrees, if you like, as they were when the policy was first inaugurated.

Now, I have no particular reason to think that labor's share of income is either too large or too small right at the moment. On the other hand, I have no reason to think that it is exactly right.

And I certainly see no reason to assume that the same shares will always be appropriate despite changes in future conditions, whatever those future conditions might happen to be.

It is sometimes said that labor's share of income has been stable in the past and that, therefore, it should be stable in the future. I think that a careful examination of the historical record will show this has not been true. A very good article by Irving Kravis, of the University of Pennsylvania, appeared in *American Economic Review* about two years ago, in which he measured labor's share of income in a variety of ways and showed, in any way he measured it, that it had been increasing slowly with time.

Of course, the position of the union on this is that labor's share should continue to increase. Indeed, that is what they are in business to do. And the United Auto Workers, who helped to start the whole thing in the first place (if my history is correct), have never accepted the implication that labor's share should be frozen. Not only that, but they have not accepted it in practice. They have not been content simply to collect their annual improvement factor. Every time that the contract has been opened for renegotiation, they have negotiated improvements in fringe benefits. They have negotiated pension plans, they have negotiated supplementary unemployment benefits, they have negotiated guaranteed work weeks—and all this over and above the annual improvement factor. Therefore, it is quite clear that labor has not been content to live by this policy. And, indeed, the managements involved in the automobile, agricultural implement, and aircraft industry contracts—those covered by UAW contracts—have *agreed* to improve the wage-earner's share of the total income generated in those industries.

I will say in defense of the Economic Report of the President for January, 1962, the first Kennedy report, that it is the first such report to point out the income-share implications of this policy and to express some concern over them. Its answer to this problem is that any company and union wanting to rebargain their shares should be free to do so—but within the framework of constant prices. Of course, it may be a little bit more difficult to bargain shares that way, but then at least the problem has been admitted, and I think this is progress.

The second difficulty is that, if every industry and every firm increases its wages in proportion to average productivity in the nation as a whole, there is no room for taking into account in the bargaining process, or the wage-determination process, the peculiar circumstances of the local labor market, of the company or of the plant; and I believe that these are all relevant to wage determination.

Again, the current report of the Council of Economic Advisers (and I distinguish this from the President's report because they are now two separate reports) represents a step forward on this point. I believe that the person who first started talking about this was Professor Abba P. Lerner of Michigan State University.

In his original statement, made in the late forties, he provided for special increases and decreases in wages to be added to or subtracted from the national formula according to the state of the local labor market. That kind of thinking has now gotten into the report of the

Council of Economic Advisers, which states very clearly that, where there is a shortage of labor in the market in an occupation or an industry, then the wage increase should be more than the national increase in productivity; where there is surplus of labor in the market, then it should be less. It also states what may boil down in many cases to about the same thing—that where unions have in the past been very successful and have had a great deal of bargaining power so that wages at the initial date are very high, future wage increases should be less than the average called for in the formula. In the reverse situation, where unions have been weak and had little bargaining power and therefore wages are low, the increase should be more than the average called for in the formula.

In its report the Council of Economic Advisers was able to do something which worked very nicely—they were able to state what the economists would accept as valid, general principles and to state them in a form and at a time when they produced the result that was desired in the collective-bargaining negotiation immediately confronting the Council, namely, that between the steel industry and the United Steelworkers. There is an excess of labor in the steel industry—there are many people unemployed and laid off who have substantial amounts of seniority and whose prospects for re-employment at the moment are not good.

It was through having a very strong union that the workers in the steel industry had made very substantial gains in the past—much more than those of other comparable unions. Therefore, the Council's policy could certainly be used to argue that the steelworkers should not get more than the national average increase in productivity.

The government, as you know, intervened rather directly and forcibly in those negotiations. Arthur Goldberg, who knew the negotiations intimately because he had participated in them for many years as attorney for the Steelworkers, participated in them this year for the first time as the Secretary of Labor. He was able to get a settlement that appeared to be consistent with this formula, and he was able to get it without a strike. On the face of it, this was not only a notable achievement, and one that Secretary Goldberg and President Kennedy could be proud of, but also one which the industry could be proud of.

However, when we start digging deeper, one wonders whether the settlement was all in all consistent with the formula as modified in the fine print in the back of the report. It is true that we have a settlement calling for labor-cost increases smaller than those in previous steel settlements. From that point of view, it is what the President has termed a "non-inflationary" settlement. However, the fine print in the formula called for special consideration of circumstances of labor surplus and for special consideration of very large past union gains.

The formula taken as a whole could have been used to argue either that the steelworkers were not entitled to any economic improvements in their current contract or, if they were entitled to improvements, that these should have been substantially less than those represented by the average increase in productivity in the economy as a whole. That, of course, was not the result. If we look into it more carefully, we find that the administration did not really make the formula stick—not if we read the formula together with the qualifying clauses and the ramifications.

I am somewhat uneasy about this formula, despite the success of the administration in getting a steel settlement without a strike and at a relatively modest figure compared to past settlements. It is very easy for the government to bring pressure to bear on the steel industry. The steel industry has one set of negotiations covering eleven firms and representing the bulk of employment in the industry. Put pressure on this settlement, and you have it made. It is all there in one spot. You know who the people are—you can call them all up on the telephone. It is very amenable to control from the city of Washington.

However, our whole economy is not like the steel industry. We have, for example, the building trades, where there are literally thousands of local settlements taking place all over the country. We have the trucking industry and related industries, represented by the largest trade union in the United States—the International Brotherhood of Teamsters—with the toughest and most aggressive labor leader in the United States (now that John L. Lewis has mellowed) in the person of James Hoffa. It is not going to be easy to apply these formulas to James Hoffa or to the building trades. You are not going to know where to find the points at which to apply pressure. I suspect the danger resulting from this, over a period of time, will be that those industries that are amenable to control from Washington are going to be controlled and a lot of others are going to be uncontrolled because you cannot get to them. Therefore, if we go that route, we will eventually develop an inequitable wage structure.

If we set up some machinery that would control the building trades and similar industries, it would mean peacetime wage-and-salary controls—a peacetime counterpart of the War Labor Board. This would scare me even more, because I think that then you get the widespread development of formulas that do not take into account local circumstances, the market forces that do get reflected at the bargaining table. One of the virtues of our decentralized system of wage determination is that it does take these into account.

I have talked about the difficulty of applying the formula to the strong unions. It also has some disadvantages in connection with the weak unions, especially if the objective of the policy is to hold down wages, as I am sure it is.

Where you find a weak union, one that has unemployment among its membership or where, for one reason or another, the members are reluctant to take a strike, that union is very often willing to make a settlement that calls for no increase or for a very modest one.

I have heard reports originating from people in the Federal Mediation and Conciliation Service indicating that the formula has made their job more difficult, especially when a weak union is involved. Where previously management and the union might have agreed that it was not in the cards to have a wage increase at this particular time in this firm or industry, the union now says: "Well, the President says that we are entitled to a wage increase equal to the average increase in output per man-hour in the economy. Are you as the employer going to tell us that we cannot even get what the President of the United States says we are entitled to?"

This is something that may make collective bargaining with the weak unions more difficult and more expensive, and it could lead to more strikes in those situations.

I should like to conclude by touching on some broader considerations.

I think one has to worry about the whole question of how much the government ought to participate in setting wages and prices, at least during peacetime, in a free-enterprise economy. We can have a series of decisions, each of which may look sensible and may be very popular at the time it is made, and, yet, in the long run, the impact of a series of such decisions and interventions could be to undermine the kind of economic system that we have had, . . .

Therefore, I get a little bit scared about some of these interventions. And I get a bit more scared when they seem to be highly successful and highly popular than when they are unsuccessful and unpopular.

I think, too, that we want to be very, very careful about justifying this kind of thing in the name of the balance of payments. We are perilously close to an economy where we are letting the tail—foreign trade—wag the dog, which is the domestic economy. If our problem is gold outflow, then I do not really think we should be dealing with this through employment policy, through wage policy, through price policy. I do not think that it should become the determining factor in every economic decision that needs to be made.

There is nothing sacred about the price of gold being thirty-five dollars a fine ounce. That is the one economic policy decision that nobody ever thinks of talking about—the policy decision about what the price of gold should be—something which has been the same for close to thirty years and which we, therefore, do not think of as a policy variable. But it is a policy variable, and maybe we would do better to have a free market in gold. This would also permit us to have freer markets in steel, wheat, and some of the other commodities and also in labor services.

PART VI

AUTOMATION
AND JOB RIGHTS

INTRODUCTION

Automation has become a "scare" word. People stand in awe when servomechanisms automatically correct other machines in production lines and computers run by tape instruct batteries of machines and insist that they perform as programmed. With automatic equipment eliminating hundreds of thousands of jobs each year, it is easy to conjure up a vision of machines at work by themselves while millions of idle people bang on factory gates demanding work, and Walter Reuther keeps pointing out to Congressmen that machines do not go to stores and buy the articles that they are producing.

Gardner Ackley ("Automation: Threat and Promise") points out that such fears are not well founded. He maintains that technological change has been destroying jobs for centuries; that some European countries, which experienced more rapid mechanization than we did in the decade ending in 1964, nevertheless had more job vacancies than unemployed workers; and that technological change may create as many jobs as (or more jobs than) it destroys. There is no assurance, however, that over the short-run the job-creating forces will match the job-displacing effects of mechanization. Indeed, they are not likely to do so in the same industry or area, so that workers must change occupations, industries, and geographic location in order to adapt to technological and economic changes.

Considerable controversy has arisen over how much unemployment is due to deficient demand and how much arises from mismatching due to structural difficulties (demand shifts and lack of supply adjustability). Neither Ackley nor Sultan and Prasow ("The Skill Impact of Automation") attempt an answer. Sultan and Prasow point out that a definite theory of structural unemployment (of which automation presumably explains a part) is lacking. Without one, a well-designed test of the thesis that structural unemployment has been an increasing proportion of total unemployment is not possible.

A related issue concerns the effects of automation on job skill requirements. Sultan and Prasow indicate that many studies, including their own, cast doubt on the thesis that automation per se results in a significant increase in the skill requirements for the nation's work force. Also, they find that high or low wages are not a major factor in management's decisions to automate; rather, the important pressure usually comes from the competition of rival firms which are gaining from the advantages of automation.

Clearly, there may be serious human problems of adjustment arising from automation. Partly, the individual firm can minimize them by advance planning so that its loss of employment can be offset by attrition (quits, discharges, and retirements). Where workers lose their jobs from technological change, questions of compensation and readjustment, such as relocation or retraining, arise. For workers, rapid technological and economic changes mean more rapid job and occupational shifts and, therefore, more emphasis on good career guidance and well-directed retraining programs. As Sultan and Prasow explain, such guidance and training should be based on better analytical information about current and prospective job opportunities than is now available. Adjustment of the nation's manpower resources to developing labor requirements is more fully considered in Part IX.

The problem of compensation for job loss is presented in a new light in Gomberg's article. He proposes that a worker's job (or employment) connection be considered a property right and that the cost of worker obsolescence from industrial and economic change be assessed on employers. Severance pay could be calculated by capitalizing the earning power that the worker loses when he is deprived of his "job property." Thus, the amount of the compensation would be related to factors such as his age and prospects for other employment.

Gomberg's proposal raises a number of interesting questions. Exactly how would the capitalized value of job property rights be fixed for particular individuals? How much would the determination hinge on speculation about future employment opportunities in the nation and in particular localities? How much would such job property rights affect labor mobility and the willingness of individual workers to adjust to changing job requirements? Would such a program hamper economic change and employment expansion, by raising the penalty costs of disemployment? How would it affect the structure of industry and company programs of on-the-job training? Would the rationale of the proposal weaken with a long period of full employment?

Such questions are most pertinent because in some industries there has been a movement in the direction which Gomberg indicates. Severance pay programs have been applied in the airlines and railroads that have involved amounts of compensation to individuals as large as $25,000 and $30,000. Consequently, if intelligent decisions are to be made, the answers to those questions should be known.

Automation: Threat and Promise

GARDNER ACKLEY

Unemployment in America is, and has been for six years, excessive and distressing. Some people say it is the project of a new force in our economy—automation—and that this kind of unemployment is impossible to eradicate without new and drastic remedies. Against this, I will argue that the effects of automation on employment are nothing new; that any employment problems created by automation can be solved if we adopt the right policies, and that as we solve these problems, automation will prove a blessing, not a threat.

Engineers define automation as "the transference of control functions from human beings to computers and servomechanisms." To the economist, its meaning is much simpler—it reduces the number of workers needed to produce a given quantity of goods and services. In that sense, there can be no doubt that automation destroys jobs, but there is nothing particularly new about that. Technological change has been destroying jobs since the beginning of civilization—faster and faster since the Industrial Revolution—and yet the *total* number of jobs has, with occasional interruptions, risen continually.

For example, this year it will take about 2 million fewer workers than were needed last year to produce the same total output (just as last year, the previous year's output could have been produced with about 2 million fewer workers). Yet, last year, total employment rose by about a million jobs, and we expect a rise of perhaps 1.4 million jobs this year. This means that about 3 million *new* jobs were created last year, and nearly 3.5 million new jobs will be created this year.

Taken from New York Times Magazine, *March 22, 1964, pp. 16, 52, 54, and 57. Copyright © 1964 by The New York Times Company. Reprinted by permission. Gardner Ackley is chairman of the Council of Economic Advisers on leave from the University of Michigan where he is Professor of Economics.*

It is clearly one-sided, therefore, to concentrate on the job-*destroying* effects of automation without considering the job-*creating* ability of our economy as a whole.

Popular concern with "technological unemployment" has always varied over the years. We heard a tremendous amount about it during the nineteen-thirties, when unemployment was epidemic. But during World War II and the first postwar decade, when jobs were readily available despite radical changes in productive methods, it was seldom mentioned. Since 1957, however, unemployment has averaged 6 per cent of the labor force, and in no month has it fallen below 5 per cent. Once again some people have decided that technological change—called automation this time—is the primary cause of unemployment. In that regard, Europe's experience is instructive. There, the postwar technological revolution has been far more dramatic than here (because European industry started so far behind ours and has largely caught up). But full employment has been maintained and very little has been heard about the technological displacement of labor.

From the history of our economy, it is clear that technological change has always created more new jobs than it has destroyed. Our technologically progressive economy has continually offered more and better jobs and incomes, more and better goods and services for most of us to enjoy, and more leisure time in which to enjoy them. We are employing half again as many workers as we did in 1929. We are producing almost three times as much. And average earnings of employes and the self-employed have more than doubled—from $2,522 in 1929 to $5,224 today, in terms of present buying power.

But the fact that past technological gains have proved entirely consistent with rising total employment and increasing individual welfare does not make us satisfied with our present excessive unemployment. To get the unemployment rate down to 4 per cent by the end of 1965, we would need to create about 9 million new jobs during 1964 and 1965—about 4 million to offset productivity gains and 5 million to take care of the unemployed and those who will enter the labor force. Finding that many new jobs is our most challenging piece of domestic business. How can we do it?

Demand is the crucial factor. When it expands as fast as "potential output" (the output we *could* produce with *full* employment of both men and machines), then automotion means more goods sold rather than fewer jobs—and we congratulate ourselves on the wonders of technological progress.

There are several ways in which technological change itself directly stimulates the demand for goods and services, and hence creates as well as destroys jobs. In the first place, greater productivity means higher incomes for the workingman and the owner of a business, and with their higher incomes they buy more goods and services. In each of the years 1949 to 1963, American families spent between 92 and 94 per cent of their after-tax incomes on goods and services. Over this period, both the purchasing power of the average family and the actual quantity of goods and services bought by the average family rose by one-third. And since the number of families increased by one-fifth, total consumer spending, at constant prices, rose about 60 per cent.

Second, technological change stimulates consumer buying. It not only reduces the cost of existing products, but also creates new products. Without TV sets, air conditioners, dishwashers, "miracle fabrics" and many other innovations, it is possible that the percentage of incomes spent in consumer markets might well have slipped over the years.

Then again, new technologies provide a powerful incentive to business spending on new plants, machinery and equipment. Expenditure on automation alone—to replace older but still usable equipment—has in itself recently constituted a significant part of the total demand for goods and services.

Yet it is clear that, since 1957, over-all demand has not been growing as fast as our potential output. Those who fear automation say this shows that our productive powers are now outstripping our wants, that the public is satiated, that our private and public needs have been met so adequately that from now on it will be hard for demand to keep pace with productive capacity.

But there seems little evidence to support this view. The fact that American families have been spending a constant proportion of their after-tax incomes on goods and services at a time when average family incomes have been continually expanding hardly suggests satiation. Very few families indeed seem to have much of a problem deciding how to spend another $1,000 a year. Even in our affluent society, the average family income is still only about $6,000 annually —and one family in five gets less than $3,000. In my view, no conceivable rate of technical progress, and of associated gains in personal incomes, could lead to consumer satiation in our lifetime. Give consumers the incomes they could earn with full employment and they will find plenty of ways to spend them.

As I see it, our problem of insufficient demand has arisen from a tax "brake" that has kept consumer and business purchasing power from moving up at the same rate as our potential output. The present tax system is a legacy from the days when postwar backlogs of consumer and business demand, together with the requirements of the Korean conflict, kept our men and machines fully employed.

If, today, the economy were operating at only a 4 per cent level of unemployment, the Federal Government's tax receipts would exceed its expenditures by some $8 billion. The Federal budget has thus been exerting a strong restraining influence on private demand—which could only be justified if private and public demand together were sufficient to maintain full employment—a condition not seen since 1957.

The slack markets and high unemployment of today are thus neither new nor mysterious—and a major part of the cure is now at hand. The $11.5 billion tax-reduction program will turn the Federal budget from a restraining into an expansionary influence. Releasing the tax brake will permit the economy to respond fully to the opportunities provided by automation by creating a high and growing demand for goods and services and thus an adequate growth in the number of jobs.

These new jobs will not always appear in the same industries in which jobs are destroyed. Sometimes they do. In the nineteen-twenties, for instance, cost-reducing innovations in the automobile industry stimulated national demand for cars, gasoline products and highway construction and greatly expanded the number of jobs in these areas. In other cases, however, productivity gains can cause a loss of jobs in an industry, because demand for its products does not keep in step. Striking productivity gains in farming and mining, for example, have not been matched by a rising consumption of wheat and coal.

A progressive, growing economy thus often requires a shift of workers from declining to growing industries, and the uneven impact of automation may increase the need for this migration. Moreover, automation, like all other technological changes, demands different kinds and degrees of skills, increasing the risk of mismatching between the qualifications sought by employers and those offered by workers.

The design, construction and installation of automated equipment require highly trained specialists. And the use of such equipment reduces our relative need for unskilled and semiskilled workers. But changes in job requirements are generally paralleled by the evolution of appropriate skills among the labor force.

Each year, the working population contains more and more highly trained—often college-trained—workers. Just since 1941, the average number of school years completed by adult male workers has risen by 50 per cent. New recruits to the labor force are considerably better educated than those leaving it. By 1970, 30 per cent of it will consist of persons who entered the job market after 1960—and their training will be readily adaptable to the demands of new technology.

But while the skill requirements of automation can be, and are being, met, there is no room for complacency. There are far too many high-school dropouts. There are far too many high-school graduates whose intellectual capacity would permit them to complete college, but who do not for lack of money or lack of motivation. And our graduate and professional schools—even though growing more rapidly than any other part of our educational system—must grow still faster.

Moreover, it is not only academic education that is important. We also need better vocational training, and, particularly, better vocational *retraining* programs; improved labor-market information; and better guidance and placement services.

The human cost of rapid technological change has always been high, but we can reduce it by helping workers to adjust effectively to change. With the affluence technological change has brought us, we can also afford to do more than we have in the past to alleviate the plight of those too old, too limited in education or otherwise unable to share in it.

To meet the challenge of automation, then, we need, first, policies to maintain a strong and growing demand for goods and services, and thus a sufficient over-all demand for labor; and, second, policies to help workers adjust to change. The first will be primarily monetary and fiscal measures; the second, "labor-market" or "structural" policies.

This complementary approach can not only meet the challenge of automation, but convert it from a threat to jobs to a source of strength and well-being for us all. Properly harnessed, automation can also make a major contribution to solving our balance-of-payments problem in world trade. Lower costs of production, and the rapid introduction of new and better products, will improve our competitive position and help end the drain on our gold supply.

Automation is not our enemy. On the contrary, like all past technological change, it can confer the blessings of higher incomes and better living, and more leisure to enjoy them, if we but pursue the proper policies.

The Skill Impact of Automation

PAUL SULTAN AND PAUL PRASOW

Much of the present diagnosis of current unemployment has tended to polarize on two explanations: Unemployment is said to reflect either the inadequacy of demand or the inadequacy of labor force adjustments to "adequate" demand. That distinction, in effect, attempts to attribute unemployment to dislocations on either the demand or the supply side of the labor market, or to establish the labor market's more important cutting edge. While that dichotomy draws attention to the complexities of the employment problem to be found on both sides of the market, and is obviously a crucial distinction in any discussion of remedial action, it does more to encompass than transcend traditional explanations for unemployment. As a consequence, it has somewhat inhibited the full consideration of the wisdom found in existing employment theories, simply because in much of traditional analysis, demand and supply are not usually regarded as competing or mutually exclusive determinants of employment. The purpose of this paper is to review some aspects of employment analysis rooted in supply considerations, and more particularly the range of opinion regarding the impact of automation when consideration is given, not to the amount of labor demanded, but to the quality of labor that must be supplied.

Unemployment that is not explained by a lack of demand is labeled structural unemployment, and since this category is pressed into

Taken from Exploring the Dimensions of the Manpower Revolution, *compiled for the Subcommittee on Employment and Manpower of the Committee on Labor and Public Welfare of the U.S. Senate, Vol. 1 of Selected Readings in Employment and Manpower, Committee Print, 88th Congress, 2nd session, U.S. Government Printing Office, Washington, D. C., 1964, pp. 542–58. Paul Sultan is Professor of Economics at the Claremont Graduate School and Paul Prasow is Lecturer in Personnel Management and Industrial Relations at the University of California at Los Angeles.*

service to explain everything not explained by a lack of demand, it is not surprising that confusion and uncertainty surround its meaning and cause. It is said to be unemployment not quite synonymous with technological, frictional, or even hard-core forms. Indeed, much of the conjecture on structural unemployment suggests that it involves something more than a reclassification of conventional doctrines. Rather, it categorizes a form of unemployment that is quite distinctive in substance from anything we have faced in the past.[1]

There are several reasons for the current attention given to the supply side of the labor market, or, more specifically, to the structural unemployment explained by these supply considerations. First, the collective bargaining process has been increasingly involved with adjustments to automation, or the adjustments of labor supply to the "uncontrollable" shifts in labor demand. But while the levels of aggregate, industry, or corporate demand usually appear well beyond the influence of the parties to the bargaining process, contract terms designed to cushion labor from the impact of technology are not; these are now emerging as the "gut" issues of collective bargaining. There is growing evidence of employer willingness to collaborate with unions on setting up early warning systems, to implement programs for labor relocation and retraining, to phase the introduction of technology in a manner designed to minimize human hardship. A consensus has emerged that every effort must now be extended to increase the volume and improve the distribution of economic intelligence on job vacancies, to encourage the mobility of labor, to undertake the task of upgrading labor skills. And where corporate, union, and personal resources appear insufficient to meet the cost of the adjustment process, there seems to be less resistance to the use of

---

[1] Concepts of unemployment may be developed within the framework of a particular economic theory or, as a pragmatic alternative, to categorize available unemployment data. The "structural" designation has both causal and descriptive pretensions. It is said to be caused by pronounced shifts in the direction of consumer expenditure, technical changes that involve a radical alteration in the form and location of production functions, "administered" wage and price adjustments, and impediments or delays in labor adjustment to labor-market requirements. Since structural unemployment reflects the lag of supply adjustments to demand, it is "identified" by its very persistence. It is further isolated by the heavy incidence of unemployment in those industries, occupations, and regions most affected by change, and by the increasing incidence of unemployment for those components of the labor force with particular age, skill, educational, race, and sex characteristics least willing or able to accommodate themselves to change. It is not surprising that a "theory" of structural unemployment that would encompass the complex of forces affecting the quality and quantity of labor supply, as well as the quality and location of labor demand, has yet to be developed. For discussion, see *"Unemployment: Terminology, Measurement, and Analysis,"* Subcommittee on Economic Statistics of the Joint Economic Committee, 87th Congress, 1st session (1961).

public funds designed to speed the reeducation, retraining, and relocation process.[2]

The hope of reducing unemployment by adjustments in the quality and location of labor supply has been further nurtured by the growing volume of statistical evidence pointing up the high correlation between education, job skill, income, and job security. Such evidence, together with the eloquence of those with a vested interest in extending our investment in human capital, gives further authority to the hypothesis that we can expand employment by upgrading labor skills.

America's balance-of-payments crisis is also relevant to the structural unemployment issue. The efforts of fiscal and monetary authorities to sustain the buoyancy of an economy constantly overloaded with upward cost-price adjustments now seem to be weakening. As we appear to be running aground on the reef of foreign competition, few feel it is prudent to raise the keel of exchange rate stability and even fewer are willing to see the Nation jettison additional amounts of domestic employment. It is not surprising, then, that hope has developed that we can contrive those structural alterations in the ship of state that would allow for both stability and buoyancy. Ironically, the confidence we now have in the capacity of the Government to provide full employment emerges at a time when these fiscal instruments to stimulate demand and employment must be employed cautiously. Barred (to employ the Keynesian analogy) from moving the piano stool to the piano, we are now involved in the tedious task of moving the piano itself. Or, to put the case more directly, the constraints represented by our balance-of-payments require that we give attention to adjustments of labor supply rather than to problem adjustments of labor demand.

Further attention to structural unemployment has developed by those who see cost-push inflation as the cause of cost-push unem-

---

2 Unions, of course, have strongly favored such programs. There was striking evidence of agreement at the American Assembly Conference on Automation, Palm Springs, Nov. 8–11, 1962, when both union and management representatives gave full support to the retraining principle. A dispute developed, however, when two educators took issue over the relative importance of the liberal versus the applied programs offered by the schools they represented. A unionist quipped: "Why don't these fellows settle their jurisdictional dispute elsewhere?" Emerson P. Schmidt of the U.S. Chamber of Commerce testified to a congressional committee: "We suspect that a dollar spent on retraining has many times the impact of a dollar spent on loans and grants for industrial or community facilities. We would not be surprised if the $5 million appropriated for retraining in the depressed areas measure approved by the House does more good than the rest of the appropriations combined." *Impact of Automation on Employment,* hearings before the Subcommittee on Unemployment and the Impact of Automation of the House Committee on Education and Labor, 87th Congress, 1st session (1961), p. 472.

ployment.[3] In this view, the increase of labor costs has compelled some labor displacement in the short run, and as it encourages the substitution of capital for labor in the long run, it compels even further labor displacement then. The resulting unemployment is said to be structural inasmuch as it reflects the pressure of structural blocs pushing for gains that cannot be supported by industry.

The designation of unemployment arising from this source as "structural" has not inhibited union use of the same term. But in the union view, structural unemployment reflects structural flaws in the pricing mechanism, and more specifically the insensitivity of prices to expanding capacity and expanding labor productivity.[4] Price rigidity denies that stimulus to market demand necessary to absorb expanding supply. Structural unemployment emerges because of malfunctions in the pricing mechanism, because of the structure of product market concentration, or even because of the capital-intensive innovations that provide dramatic economies in the use of labor.

Although the usefulness of this category of unemployment is weakened when it becomes a term meaning all things to all people, or when a single label is used to explain conflicting or contradictory causes of unemployment, that confusion does not allow us to retreat from the full examination of remedies for unemployment that can be located in the supply side of the market.

In approaching the employment problem from the supply side, one would expect to be confronted immediately with proposals to reduce wages, or to alter the location of the labor supply schedule so that it might intersect the labor demand schedule where higher levels of

---

[3] L. E. Gallaway finds only limited statistical support for the structural unemployment argument, but he is unwilling to surrender to the lack-of-demand alternative. "Rather the findings at the microeconomic level offer the possibility that the impact of union market power may be disrupting the labor-market allocative process at the interfactor level; i.e., that the relative price of labor in general has been increased by the actions of labor unions to a level that generates widespread unemployment." "Labor Mobility and Structural Unemployment." *American Economic Review*, LIII, no. 4 (September 1963), pp. 714–15. Harold Demsetz concludes his statistical analysis: "Minimum-wage laws and union wage rates make it impossible or difficult for a growing component of our labor force to offer its services at wage rates sufficiently low to be employed." "Structural Unemployment: A Reconsideration of the Evidence and the Theory," *Journal of Law and Economics,* IV (October 1961), p. 90.

[4] Solomon Barkin contends that price-setters in administered-price industries are confident that governmental monetary and fiscal action will support their decisions to raise prices; they are subject to no compelling pressure to lower prices. In his view, this explains the "chronic imbalance between productive capacity and consumption." *Impact of Automation on Employment, op. cit.,* p. 196. In more technical analysis, Sylos-Labini attributes price rigidity and its byproduct of economic stagnation to technological discontinuities within oligopolistic industries, contending that the alternative to prices that allow large firms substantial profits is sheer chaos. *Oligopoly and Technical Progress* (Cambridge: Harvard University Press, 1962).

employment can be obtained. While there is today general support for the proposition that wage adjustments must somehow be kept within the limits of labor productivity, the hypothesis that wage reductions can encourage employment, or even inhibit the pace of capital-intensive innovation, has not yet received much support. But the attention usually reserved for the cost of labor is now given over to the quality of labor.

Even though wage policy and skill upgrading programs are in no sense identical, both can be analyzed in terms of their influence on the labor supply, or, to put the case more directly, in terms of the employability of labor. Policies of wage reduction or skill upgrading are somewhat analogous in their employment generating consequences, for both are presumed to lower unit labor costs. In the first case, the reduction of hourly wage rates, with labor productivity unchanged, obviously reduces unit labor costs; in the second case, increases of labor productivity, with hourly wage rates unchanged, have a similar effect. And so long as we admit some measure of elasticity in the demand for labor, the reduction of unit labor costs by either device should encourage the employment of labor. In the thirties, Keynes offered a convincing rationale for reducing the "real" cost of labor by increases in prices rather than through the painful struggle to reduce money wages. In the sixties, we still hope to bypass the hostile reception that would follow any exhortation that money wages be cut, by programs to increase labor's productivity or skill. Inhibited as we are—and for good reasons—from tinkering with money wage levels, and inhibited further by the discipline of foreign competition from adopting an overt inflationary policy, it is not surprising that we should turn hopefully to the remaining expedient: devices that would increase the employability of labor through the upgrading of labor's skill. There is, therefore, an analogy between the hope of the thirties that everyone might be reemployed if wages (or prices) were set at levels that would allow for their profitable employment and the hope widespread in this decade that everyone might be employed if skill levels were so upgraded that employers could not resist the utilization of such talent.

What, then, are the prospects for minimizing unemployment by speeding labor's accommodation to the requirements of industry, by upgrading labor's skill levels? The range of responses to this question is indicated in charts I, II, and III.

In chart I, frequency distribution A represents a hypothetical skill mix possessed by the existing labor force. In order to preserve the distinction between lack-of-demand and structural arguments, we

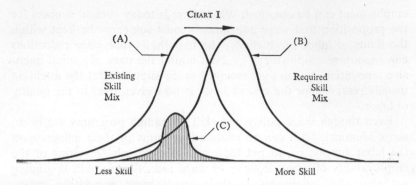

CHART I

(A)   (B)

Existing   Required
Skill   Skill
Mix   Mix

(C)

Less Skill   More Skill

shall arbitrarily assume that automation does nothing to reduce the number of job opportunities in industry. In other words, to focus on the skill issue alone we shall isolate our analysis from conjecture that automation reduces the total number of job opportunities (viz., reduces employment to the shaded distribution C in chart I). So long as parity is preserved between the total of job opportunities and the number in the labor force, unemployment reflects the problem of matching the specific qualities of labor demand with the specific attributes of labor supply.

How are the skill requirements of industry affected by automation? In the conventional view, automation involves a substantial upgrading of labor skills, and upgrading that can be represented in chart I with the hypothetical skill distribution B. There is no lack of testimony to support such conjecture on the skill impact of automation. Drucker, for example, avows that automation will bring with it ". . . the greatest upgrading of the labor force ever seen."[5] In this situation, the unemployed are not involved in a demoralizing search for jobs that do not exist; rather, unemployment reflects only labor's delay in acquiring the location and skill attributes required by industry.

A chilling shadow has been cast on the optimism in the skill distribution of chart I, mainly because of the very persistence of unemployment. Not all who are fully aware of the seriousness of the problem reject the contention that automation involves an upgrading of skill; some suggest, however, that we have not yet fully comprehended or absorbed the intensity of the changes taking place. Their anxiety is reflected in chart II by the wide, and widening, chasm

5 Peter F. Drucker, "Integration of People and Planning," *Harvard Business Review* (May–June 1955), p. 38; see also John Diebold, *Automation: The Advent of the Automatic Factory* (New York: Van Nostrand, 1956), p. 164.

CHART II

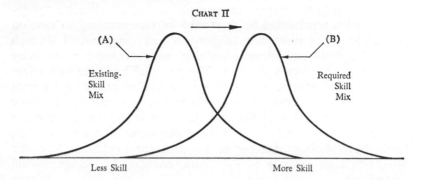

(A)

Existing·
Skill
Mix

(B)

Required
Skill
Mix

Less Skill   More Skill

between labor's existing skill mix (A) and that mix (B) now required by industry. What are the specific sources of such anxiety?

There is a distressing variety of considerations advanced to explain the persistence of this skill gap. To some, the increasing tempo of change is the prime difficulty, a problem reflected in a recent New Yorker cartoon in which the personnel manager's handshake with the new job applicant is interrupted by the production manager: "Hold it, Frank; that job's been replaced by a machine." In brief, the acceleration in the pace of technology makes less certain the form and application of future innovation, and less reliable the estimates of the labor coefficient required for future production functions. How, then, can we establish now the appropriate educational program to meet the unspecified manpower requirements of the future? Deficiencies of current educational programs seem obvious enough when it is realized that two-thirds of all young labor force entrants have neither college nor vocational training.[6] But can we be certain that the attention now given to the expansion of vocational training will also encourage the development of multipurpose skills necessary for the "revolving" nature of future job requirements? In computer automation, for example, we are told that the use of magnetized tape is eliminating the need for keypunch operators, and that the use of microwaves will eliminate the need for those who punch magnetized tapes.[7] Obviously workers with single-purpose skills will be poor candidates for the adaptations that such continuing innovations require. Technical change alters the skill mix required by industry; but rapid change makes the analysis of the ingredients in that unstable mix both difficult and tentative.

[6] Sar A. Levitan, *Vocational Education and Federal Policy* (Kalamazoo: W. E. Upjohn Institute for Employment Research, May 1963), p. 1.
[7] Testimony of Howard Couglin, president, Office of Employes International Union, in *Impact of Automation on Employment, op. cit.,* p. 407.

In addition to this "tempo of change" barrier, we witness a "gestation" barrier, represented by the length of time required to develop skills. The talent most eagerly pursued today is acquired through years of rigorous and intensive training, not provided in a retraining program of a few weeks' duration. The pressures to obtain such talent today may, unfortunately, complicate the task of providing for such talent tomorrow. Many teachers able to impart knowledge to those students who would meet the skill shortages in the future are being lured away from teaching to private employment. As a case in point, Louis N. Ridenour, director of research for Lockheed Aircraft's Missile Systems Division in Palo Alto, confided to a congressional committee:

I paid last year Federal income tax in an amount slightly greater than my total salary as dean of the Graduate College at the University of Illinois, 5 years before.[8]

Financial and motivational barriers operate at the student level too. Only 7 out of 10 high school graduates in the genius class—those with IQ's of 163 and above—go on to college. Half of the dropouts do not continue studies for alleged financial reasons.[9] Furthermore, only 45 percent of the top 30 percent of the ability distribution of society graduate from college.[10] Estimates further indicate that in this decade some 7½ million young people—over one-half of the net increase in the labor force—will be persons who have dropped out of high school. A sample study of the Office of Education of such dropouts indicates that only a small percentage within this group lack the mental competence to "make it academically."[11] But even for those who continue their education, it is not certain that incentives are adequate to encourage their registration in the "hard" programs that technical and scientific training requires. Only 4 percent of American high school students study elementary physics, 7 percent chemistry, 27 percent algebra, and 13 percent geometry.[12]

8 *Instrumentation and Automation,* hearings before the Subcommittee on Economic Stabilization of the Joint Economic Committee, 84th Congress, 2d session (1957), p. 163. For purposes of this discussion "skill" is defined very broadly to include all levels of competence, professional as well as technical.

9 Testimony of Erick A. Walker, president, Pennsylvania State College, in *Instrumentation and Automation, op. cit.,* p. 118.

10 Cited by D. W. Wolfle, executive director, American Association for the Advancement of Science, in *Manpower Problems,* hearings before the Subcommittee on Employment and Manpower of the Senate Committee on Labor and Public Welfare, 86th Congress, 2d session (1960), p. 46.

11 Testimony of Seymour Wolfbein, in *Manpower Problems, op. cit.,* p. 29.

12 Statistics cited by Arnold O. Beckman, in *Instrumentation and Automation, op. cit.,* p. 27.

While the incentives to acquire an education may be lacking for some with ability to learn, it has been pointed out that the ability to learn is missing in some who are eager to learn. Emerson P. Schmidt of the Chamber of Commerce testified:

In a typical population, roughly 23 percent have IQ's of less than 90; most of these cannot expect to become highly skilled or to be entrusted with responsible jobs; 7.3 percent have IQ's below 80; most of these are at best marginally employable. And 2.7 percent have IQ's below 70; most of these latter are strictly unemployable. Every indication we have of the shape of the future shows rising requirements of employability, and therefore a growing percentage of any age group which is unemployable.[13]

Whatever the impediments to the upgrading process—whether lack of ability, lack of financial incentive, lack of enthusiasm for difficult courses, lack of instructional programs, or lack of appropriate counseling—the skill gap between supply and demand postulated in chart II is not likely to diminish in the near future. In this decade, for example, it is estimated that the demand for professional and technical labor will increase by 40 percent, whereas the demand for unskilled labor is not expected to increase at all.[14] The outlook for those 7½ million entering the labor market without completing high school, and for those 2½ million who will not complete their elementary schooling appears bleak indeed.

But if the task of defining and undertaking the appropriate investment in youth necessary to meet future labor-market requirements is perplexing, the problem of retraining displaced workers is even more so. For example, Henry Winthrop wonders if those unskilled and semiskilled workers who have been content to work for years below their "latent" ability would be motivated to undertake retraining programs. But more important, he contends that all talk of extensive upgrading may be "so much poppycock" when the development of electronics and engineering talent calls into play ". . . intellectual abilities only sparsely distributed among the semiskilled and unskilled. . . ."[15] Even if the basic ability estimates offered by Schmidt and Winthrop are discounted, the 1960 census reveals that over 11 million Americans 24 years of age and older have less than 6 years of schooling, while 2½ million adults are unable to read or

13 *Impact of Automation on Employment, op. cit.,* p. 473.
14 *Manpower: Challenge of the Sixties,* U.S. Department of Labor (1960), pp. 11, 16.
15 Some Psychological and Economic Assumptions Underlying Automation," *American Journal of Economics and Sociology,* XVII, no. 4 (July 1958), p. 401.

write.[16] Since unemployment hits the less educated workers severely, the task of imparting labor skills to some in this group may also require programs to improve their basic literacy.

The efforts to relocate displaced Armour employees have frequently been cited to illustrate the problems of retraining. Of 400 workers laid off by the closing of the Armour plant in Oklahoma City, 170 took advantage of the employment tests and counseling offered by the Oklahoma Employment Service. Of these 170, only 60 gave evidence of being able to benefit from additional training; 58 enrolled for training, and 7 found work at their new skills.[17] Even the skilled worker may be a poor candidate for retraining, particularly if his existing skills draw upon a narrow range of his abilities and have a low degree of transferability. For retraining purposes, he too may have to be treated as an unskilled worker.

There are, of course, several institutional impediments to labor adjustment which may reinforce the ability barriers analyzed above. For example, wage structures may not be sufficiently sensitive to the relative scarcities and surpluses of labor in various markets, and thus may not serve as an effective allocator of labor. The employee who has accumulated considerable seniority is likely to believe that the value of the "certain" income stream of his present job is greater than the value of the uncertain income stream of alternative jobs, wage disparities notwithstanding. That conviction does not readily evaporate, even with the loss of his job; the uncertain prospect of gaining work elsewhere reinforces the hope that he will be rehired at his old job. It is not surprising, then, that prolonged unemployment exists in those geographic areas suffering a pronounced sag, if not collapse, of general labor demand. An employer interviewed in the course of this research explained the force behind the "social barrier" to adjustment operating in such areas:

Look at it this way: Most workers are apprehensive about changing an employer, or even taking on a new job with an old employer. But now we expect some men to make three or four major shifts simultaneously; to shift to a new job, to a new employer, to a new industry, and perhaps to a new community. How many are willing to do that?

He was not optimistic that those who were confronted with such a coincidence of adjustment demands would rise to the challenge, par-

16 *Adult Basic Education,* hearings before the General Subcommittee on Labor and the Select Subcommittee on Education of the House Committee on Education and Labor, on H.R. 10143 and H.R. 10191, 87th Congress, 2d session (1962), pp. 9, 86.

17 *Manpower Utilization and Training,* hearings before the Subcommittee on Unemployment and the Impact of Automation of the House Committee on Education and Labor, on H.R. 7373, 87th Congress, 1st session (1961), p. 20.

ticularly in view of the self-doubts that displaced workers so often develop about their basic abilities. Unfortunately the defeatism that corrodes the moral and economic status of the unemployed in depressed areas may not be fully reflected in existing unemployment data, for persons not looking for work (nor volunteering information as to why this is the case) are excluded from the ranks of both the labor force and the unemployed.

And finally, there is the "informational" barrier to adjustment. No systematic collection of data on job vacancies has yet been undertaken and much of the information available in employment offices may not be reaching all unemployed persons searching for work.

The discussion to this point has emphasized problems related to the skill-upgrading requirement that automation involves. But it should not be concluded that automation involves only the upgrading of skills. Indeed, there is some evidence to support the contention that the skill impact follows the contours found in the bimodal distribution of skills (B) in chart III.

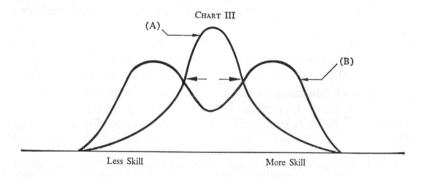

CHART III

(A)

(B)

Less Skill   More Skill

This prospect can serve to minimize the pessimism of those who fear we cannot overcome the ability barriers alluded to above, for an intensive investment in human capital is not required of those who will be performing "diluted" job functions represented by the left hump of distribution (B). But this impact creates immediate problems for employees confronted with the downgrading rather than the upgrading of their work functions. Skilled artisans are likely to be sensitive to transfers into such catchall job classifications as an "automation equipment handler." If such adjustments involve not only a loss of pay and status, but also a shift to a new employer, industry, or labor market, the sources of resistance and discontent are self-evident.

The more important issue, however, is not whether some jobs are downgraded by automation but rather the relative incidence of the upgrading and downgrading process. James R. Bright has concluded that we have given excessive attention to the way automation may upgrade skills.[18] Skill dilution is, in his view, a function of the stage of automation achieved; he employs both logic and field study analysis to support the contention that once a certain level of mechanization has been achieved, less rather than much more operator skill is required. Employers, as well as employees, are prone to exaggerate their skill requirements, a delusion that can involve an extravagant overinvestment in manpower by the corporation. . . .

There are some persuasive arguments for giving much more weight to the engineering analysis offered by Bright than to the more numerous lyrical projections of skill requirements that too frequently rest on mere assertion alone. Modern automation challenges almost every skill that the human agent offers to the production process. Those human capacities—including such senses as touch, sight, smell, hearing, the facility for calculating, remembering, learning, the capacity to exercise discretion—are attributes now challenged by the astonishing capacities of new mechanisms. The integration of information and production technology represents the essence of this innovation, a process that draws attention to the limitations of the human agent, now more than ever dismissed as the badly designed single-purpose machine tool. Machines have been taught to oil themselves, to adjust their worn parts, to replace their own cutting edges, to preserve through feedback mechanisms a uniformity and quality of product hitherto unknown to mass production. But more than this, automated

18 James R. Bright, "Does Automation Raise Skill Requirements?" *Harvard Business Review*, XXXVI (July–August 1958). William A. Faunce, testifying on his field study of automation in the auto industry, explained: "There is a higher proportion of skilled people because there are fewer people who are unskilled and semiskilled. . . . for the machine operators in this plant, there was no retraining program at all. They were simply transferred in, and the estimates of the workers themselves regarding how long it took them to learn their job indicated that very little new skill was required. . . . I am not saying that there are no new skills called for, but rather that the number of jobs created is small. *Impact of Automation on Employment, op. cit.*, pp. 326–27. Corrobative evidence was provided by Malcolm L. Denise, vice president of labor relations, Ford Motor Co. In introducing new technology in Ford plants, he indicated, on-the-job instruction was "quite adequate in training our production workers to operate new equipment." Formal and detailed training programs were not often necessary for that purpose. Further, he was not certain "generalized training programs" represented a fruitful solution to the unemployment problem. He agreed that from time to time particular skills—such as diemakers to staff a new stamping plant—were difficult to locate, but recruiting such talent from "far afield" was not often necessary. In analyzing the "really valuable skills" he explained: "You are talking about something that you do not pick up in 6 or 8 weeks." *Impact of Automation on Employment, op. cit.*, pp. 530, 550, 551.

machines are conversing with each other both to adjust the pace of production and to vary the product mix in the light of the inventory and other market data speedily digested by computers. The skill impact is suggested by labor's designation of its new job: "Now we're the babysitters for machines."

There is a possibility, too, that we may exaggerate the skill upgrading involved in the steady growth in the proportions of indirect labor to direct labor. The rapid expansion of computer technology promises substantial economies in the use of clerical, supervisory, and even middle-management personnel. While our analysis is arbitrarily bypassing the reduction of job opportunities that automation may involve, its quantitative effects are relevant to the skill issue. To take a hypothetical case, let us say that the distribution between the unskilled and the skilled labor force for a firm is 70 and 30, respectively, for the total of 100 employees. Following automation let us assume that the ratio is reversed to 3 to 7, now favoring the skilled employee, but with only 10 workers employed. Certainly the skill level within the firm has been increased, but the upgrading of job requirements for 7 employees must be set against the displacement of 67 unskilled workers and 23 skilled employees. The Bureau of Labor Statistics studies of office automation indicate that the application of computers in offices does involve an upgrading of the skill level of office personnel, but that upgrading is achieved more by the less extensive use of unskilled than by any numerically significant increase in skilled workers employed to program and operate the computers.[19]

There is some possibility that a distorted view of skill requirements can develop from the recruitment efforts of defense and aerospace industries for college graduates. Where cost-plus contracts are operative, the marginal revenue product or demand for such labor is not only above, but also rises more rapidly than, the marginal cost for such labor. Riding up these schedules need not jeopardize the competitive position of any one firm so long as it does not get "out of line" in making that advance, and so long as the urgency given to the delivery of hardware is not subject to precise or binding budget constraints. Such arrangements reflect, of course, genuine scarcities of technical manpower skills arising because of the "crash" character of many aerospace projects.

In market where demand shifts are more intensive than supply shifts, equilibrium is obtained by rising prices. One suspects, how-

19 *Adjustments to the Introduction of Office Automation*, U.S. Department of Labor, Bulletin no. 1276 (May 1960), pp. 30–37.

ever, that the salary adjustments offered engineering personnel already in the industry have not risen sufficiently to provide that equilibrium. But market pressures are not to be denied, and the excess of demand over supply at existing prices is manifest in the intense competition for engineering talent between firms. Such competition gives an upward lift to the salary structure not otherwise allowed by salary policies for labor within the firm. Substantial pay increases follow the promotions given those willing to shift from company to company. Firms intent on preserving existing levels of manpower must undertake a heavy recruitment effort to obtain new workers, for in this way they can fill the vacancies inevitably arising when their own employees respond to the attractions of employment offered by other firms. From the macroview, however, the energy expended in such recruitment does more to influence the present location of such talent than to increase its present overall supply. The upgrading of rewards for such skills does, of course, serve its genuine economic function in encouraging the expansion of the long-run supply, but equilibrating the market in the short run by advertising and turnover may not only be a rather poor device, considering the disruption this involves for production, but also creates the impression that massive armies of technical talent could be absorbed in the industry today.

There may be, too, some misallocation of high-level talent within the industry, particularly when the collection of an imposing inventory of manpower skills is an important consideration in awarding contracts. There is also the possibility that the chances of receiving a contract are improved if it can be demonstrated that such talent is not being fully utilized.

Further, there is a danger of describing the overall scarcity of creative engineering talent in terms of technical facilities that have yet to be created or perhaps even conceived. We must distinguish actual present and future needs from the conjecture that hypothetical technical talent—if it existed—would create hypothetical innovations that would require for their operation a hypothetical army of technicians.

These considerations, while in no sense exhaustive, give credence to the Bright hypothesis. Automation can surely involve both the job enrichment and the job dilution of demand and require both upward and downward adjustments of labor supply. . . .

Because of the profound impact automation has on manpower, the Institute of Industrial Relations of the University of California, Los Angeles, has embarked upon a field study of manpower changes induced by technical change, a field study of actual manpower problems and policies of individual firms undertaking technological changes of any kind. Twenty-five firms in the southern California area have cooperated with this institute project to review the changes undertaken and their implications for their own work force. These firms represent a wide range of industries, including the food processing, electronics, banking, motion picture, publishing, shipping, transportation, automotive, chemical processing, manufacturing, food and drug distribution, and aerospace industries. Information has been collected covering a wide range of issues, including the inducements for labor-saving innovation, labor problems involved with the change in production methods, warning systems and other collaborative procedures found useful in introducing change, and the various rewards, anticipated and unanticipated, arising from new production methods. Data have also been collected on the impact of change upon total employment, and on the details of relocation and retraining programs with particular emphasis on the characteristics of labor upgraded and relocated. The generous investment of time given this project by senior corporate officials and personnel directors in the frontline of change attests to the significance attached to analysis of the manpower issue. While the survey is broad in scope and is still in its early stages, the information gathered to this date provides several promising clues on the impact of change on job design. Even the process of data gathering has proved instructive, for it has pointed up the problem of isolating the manpower impact of technical change from other concurrent economic influences, such as swings in the level of product demand. It has revealed, too, the complexities involved in efforts to "lay your bare hands" on the skill issue. One suspects that the "factual desert" regarding the impact of technology on job design reflects neither the insignificance of the issue nor the indifference of students to it, but the illusive nature of skill itself.

Firms cooperating with this venture had an advantage in manpower planning not available to all firms; they were located in growth industries or in a growth area and were thus able to absorb the displacement caused by engineered economies in unit labor requirements through the employment required to support additional production. In only one firm were substantial layoffs reported, but this firm operated within an industry that had bought out union resistance to automation, an industry making payments to the union stabilization fund to cushion employees from such displacement. The absence of layoffs was so uniformly reported that it seemed difficult to reconcile with the current concern over unemployment.

Several procedures were found useful in minimizing necessary manpower adjustments where the output increases alluded to above were not sufficient to absorb displaced labor. First, the average lead-time in introducing change was approximately 1½ years; firms relied heavily on the "A. & P." (attrition and pregnancy) solution to reduce manpower needs in that interval. Second, changes were introduced, where possible, during an upswing in the cycle of economic activity. Third, changes that affected only a portion of corporate operations gave the firm the opportunity to relocate surplus labor in unaffected areas. Contractual commitments promising no reductions in force were more the exceptions than the rule, although it was made clear, through the plant newspaper, bulletin-board announcements, special meetings, and newsletters, that every effort would be made to preserve the job and income levels of present employees. In almost every case collaboration with the union and workers proved effective in minimizing formal resistance to change. One company that had agreed contractually not to reduce its labor force because of technological improvements conceded that hiring now involved a much more judicial scrutiny of new job applicants and company manpower needs. The obligations created for the company when new workers had worked beyond the 3-month period to be eligible for such security were not taken casually. This same company reported a backlog of technical changes in the blueprint stage; their introduction was being phased to pace the anticipated attrition of its labor force, an attrition that, ironically, appeared to be dampened because of the company's enlightened manpower policies. The determined efforts of cooperating companies to preserve the job rights of existing employees suggested, however, that any adverse employment effects were more likely to fall upon the young worker seeking his first job.[20]

The gap between existing and required labor skills hypothesized in charts I, II, and III appears rather tenuous in the light of collected evidence. There was little evidence that substantial numbers of highly skilled personnel would be absorbed, if available, because of unmet manpower needs in automated sections of the plant. Certainly there was no evidence of new technology idled because of manpower bottlenecks.

Only one firm spoke of the problem of securing labor sufficiently competent to assure the smooth running of automated equipment. In planning for the change in production method, it appeared that as much attention was given to manpower as to technical requirements involved. Retraining programs were undertaken well in advance of

[20] Testifying on the incidence of unemployment, Abraham Ribicoff indicated that of 5 million unemployed, about one-third were under 22 years of age, and one-half of those had not held a job since leaving school. *Manpower Problems, op. cit.,* p. 105.

changes, staffed by company personnel with experience or briefing on the mechanisms, or by the staff of the computer manufacturer. Tests were employed to determine employees most suitable for the retraining programs. However, companies were not generally swamped with applicants eager to participate in retraining programs. Some employees were reported to be apprehensive about their capacity to score well on the tests and about their ability to hold down the new job. What seemed more important, they worried about the reliability of the new mechanism and their job status should the new operation prove unworkable. A broad variation in time, ranging from 2 hours to 4 years, was reported in this retraining effort. Most programs were conducted on the job. For those who did not complete such retraining programs, physiological deficiencies such as lack of mechanical or motor coordination, or lack of depth perception, appeared more important than the lack of ability to comprehend the tasks related to the new job.

But if the inability to locate skilled labor did not appear as a barrier, either to the introduction of the new method or to its subsequent operation, were not the "deficiencies" of labor, including the burden of wage costs, considerations that encouraged the introduction of change? Surprisingly, wage levels were not assigned a central role in the testimony regarding the impulse for automation, although reference was made to the problem of labor turnover, particularly by firms using computers to reduce reliance on the services of unmarried girls who made up a substantial part of their clerical staff. When, at an American assembly conference, a corporate official described how such labor turnover encouraged his firm to pioneer in the development of automated equipment, a labor economist asked why the company had not experimented instead with wage increases to determine if this would reduce the turnover. The economist reversed the usual capital substitution argument by suggesting the possibility that, in such a situation, if wage policies justified automation it was not because wages were too high, but because wages might be too low.

There was no evidence of general and persistent manpower scarcities, but evidence was provided on the efforts of workers to obtain jobs. One personnel officer pointed to a stack of applications many times greater than the anticipated employment expansion, applications made as a result of the decision to "confide" to existing employees that employment might expand in the near future. He described the skill level of the applicants in this way: "I never have seen so many gas station attendants in my life."

Apart from the cost related to labor turnover, there was some evidence to suggest that labor may have been a neutral or passive element in the decision to change production methods. Stress was given to the role of intensified competition, domestic and international, actual or impending. In some cases it was clear that the decision to automate was not made by comparing the marginal productivities and costs of capital and of labor, but rather by comparing the marginal productivities and costs of existing capital with those of a new technology soon to be adopted by competitors. Some respondents indicated they had no choice but to automate. While the advantages of automating were not altogether clear before the fact, there seemed little doubt in their minds about the risks of not automating.

Beyond this, the random nature of forces that encouraged new production methods was indicated by one respondent who described the revolution in technology that followed the hiring of two Harvard Business School graduates. Company operations had been profitable even though technology had been unchanged for 20 years, but the new employees labored with uncontained energy to introduce innovations in production methods that were proving highly successful. In another case, an industrial engineer described the radical production change he had pioneered as simply a "routine" function; it was his job to exercise an unrelenting curiosity about ways to improve the efficiency of every job.

The pressure didn't come from the top. In fact, it worked the other way. My biggest job was to sell the idea, to prove the equipment would pay for itself in 3 years.

These considerations do not, of course, allow the conclusion that wage costs and manpower problems were irrelevant to the decision to alter the capital structure or capital-labor inputs, even though wage costs and manpower problems were not identified as the immediate or prime causes for change.

The companies were generally successful in preserving wage standards for relocated labor even if the skill requirements of their new jobs were not sustained. It is this process that unions have labeled as "horizontal downgrading." There was evidence that the jobs involving the use of automated equipment drew upon a different order of skill than many conventional functions, frequently giving priority to attentiveness, concentration, and accuracy, while reducing the arduous elements of the job. Grievances reflected the contention that income increases did not match the worker's enhanced stream of output. Seniority disputes were common when new work groups were carved out of old units. One company official described their difficulties as a classic example of what not to do:

Before the precise nature of the change had been specified and the manpower requirements detailed, foremen had sought to placate anxious workers by making informal assurances to them. Most employees considered these as firm commitments by the company, and the results proved explosive when the company found it could not deliver on all the "promises" thought to have been made. It required the authority of the international to restore order within the local, and to assist the company in mediating the disputes between factions within the work force bitterly competing for job interests.

The respondents were not reluctant to stress that these innovations often involved job simplification; while there was added responsibility attached to some jobs in the sense that labor operated with intricate equipment, worker anxieties reflected the initial adjustment problems. When the rhythms of the new industrial operation were established, they felt workers were much more content with the new rather than the old production methods. One respondent described the demise of an old craftsman whose function was to mix the ingredients for the industrial product, an intuitive skill with a long and noble tradition. That function had been taken over by instrumentation, providing a sharp increase in the quality and uniformity of the product.

On the matter of education, one official humorously described his company as "nuts on the subject," adding that he had just returned from Stanford where he had attended an executive session involving the use of computers in corporate decisionmaking. He explained that education served as a standard in recruiting labor at all levels of the company operation:

If we needed 3 men, we would review, shall we say, the current 20 applications on hand, and if everything else was equal, pick the 3 with the most education. If we needed more men, we would just keep digging deeper and deeper into the barrel.

This analysis suggests why correlations between education and employment should be interpreted cautiously. Unless we can be certain that the quality of the 20 job applicants determined whether more than 3 would be hired, it is possible that education may determine the incidence of employment and not its cause. Certainly education or even skill should not be treated as the single, independent, and sufficient determinant of the "employability" of all labor.

The emphasis on education was obvious in all field studies with one exception. One corporate official explained that recently graduated high school students were poor candidates for their apprenticeship program.

Now we look for the high school graduate who has been pushing a broom for a year or so; perhaps a fellow who is married and with a child. He sees the world pretty clearly from the end of a broom.

This sampling of collected testimony is in no sense definitive, but is offered to illustrate some of the dimensions of the manpower problems we face even in expanding labor markets. The absence of reported manpower bottlenecks in the automated areas of company operations represents a sobering consideration when skill upgrading is so frequently identified with the automation process. Needless to say, the benefits of automation that involve increased leisure and improved living standards can set in motion new activities with their own separate mix of manpower and skill requirements. Such activities have not been the focal point for this study.

This analysis suggests, too, that the complete solution to structural unemployment is not likely to be realized by measures that would upgrade labor skills. The nature of unemployment is sufficiently severe to require bold and expanded pressures on both the supply and the demand side of the market. Labor relocation and skill upgrading may well be a vital necessary step for labor reabsorption, but it is hardly a sufficient step. The bromide offered in the 1920's by Foster and Catchings may have some relevance to the structural employment problem of our decade: "A willing buyer doesn't have to wait long; a willing seller may have to wait forever." Unless skill upgrading programs are general, they may do more to redistribute the incidence than to remedy the cause of labor displacement; they may draw a tighter line around those willing sellers of labor service who have already been waiting some time for a job.

The Work Rule Problem and Property Rights in the Job

WILLIAM GOMBERG

The question of work rules must plague any dynamic society. Technological stagnation would put an end to the work rule problem or, perhaps better yet, the problem would never arise. Innovation subverts the stability of the management-labor relationship; carefully worked out job descriptions and established property rights in jobs disappear overnight and are replaced by new job descriptions requiring a reworking of new relationships in the presence of contenders who are refugees from the old technological climate. No sooner are the new sets of rules developed than a restless management again subverts the new relationship with new innovations and new fights replace old ones. The radical unionist fights conservatively to hold on to his old job while the conservative manager never stays in one place long enough to let the dust settle.

THE PROPERTY RIGHT CONCEPT

Practically all discussions of work rule problems have proceeded upon a set of implicit assumptions. Management has implied that it is entitled to a volume of work that calls for the full exertion of the worker just short of his physiological and psychological limits. The trade unions have never openly rebelled against this concept. They have, therefore, adapted their arguments to this assumption and usually couched discussions about rules in terms of health and safety. In

Taken from Monthly Labor Review, *LXXXIV (June 1961), pp. 595–96. William Gomberg is Professor of Industry in the Wharton School of Finance and Commerce at the University of Pennsylvania.*

the back of the mind of the trade unionist is an emerging property right which he is attempting to assert. The rituals of our society are not yet ready to accommodate this new concept, and so he conservatively attempts to secure his objective through indirection by complying with the conventional rituals.

Many of the work rules define an emerging property right of the worker in his job. For example, a jurisdictional claim of a yard worker that he and he alone can handle a train in the yard, and the corresponding claim of a road worker that he and he alone can handle a train on the road, stem from a property right of each craft in the particular job area. The equivalent of the worker's property deed is the collective agreement.

It would be silly and pointless to deny that work in many cases could be performed more cheaply if these property rights and the penalties for their violation did not exist. In a democracy, however, other values than those of productivity receive equivalent attention from the community.

Work rules are insistently treated as a separate question in collective bargaining, but are they, in fact, unrelated to the other issues of bargaining? The history of negotiations is an extremely complex story of the comparative weighting of different objectives. How many demands for additional increases in wages were sacrificed in exchange for a work rule? Any program to undertake the revision of work rules must always keep these considerations in the background.

CASES IN POINT

Excellent examples of what we are talking about are provided by the recent conflicts over contracting out between the crafts and industrial unions. The maritime industry, the railroad industry, and the steel industry provide more classic kinds of examples.

The Pacific Coast longshoremen and the employers were able to reach an agreement without third party intervention. The setting up of the railroad commission represents an effort to make a new use of neutrals in collective bargaining. The[ir] recommendations . . . are not compulsory.

Suppose, despite their best efforts at achieving a consensus, despite heroic efforts to mediate the demands of the parties, they are unable to gain an agreement, what then? The strike is still open, but largely as a ceremonial weapon rather than an operational tool. Certainly the railroad unions learned this lesson during the general strike of the Locomotive Engineers during the Truman administration. Is compulsory arbitration the answer? The stock answers are readily available with all of the examples of why, where, and how it has not worked in the past. Suppose, however, we set up a tribunal on the basis of a fundamental acknowledgment of the worker's property right in his job; that it is not for the tribunal to decide whether or not the job exists, but whether or not the job deserves to be continued and if it deserves not to be continued, what is the surrender of the property right in the job worth? In other words, assign to the tribunal the equivalent of the power of eminent domain for the job area. Defining the procedure and frame of reference for a compulsory arbitration tribunal of this nature may lead to a more real acceptance of its authority rather than a wide-open tribunal that creates its own frame of reference and its own sense of equity to suit itself.

IS THE OBSOLETE WORKER A CAPITAL CHARGE?

The cost of obsolete workers should be viewed as being as rational a charge on industry as the cost of obsolete machinery. There is no reason why an enterprise should expect to create a depreciation reserve or an obsolescence reserve for hardware and at the same time be free of any similar obligation for human ware. At present, the costs of worker obsolescence are undertaken by the community by the socialization of the charge through unemployment insurance and by community relief when the unemployment insurance period has expired. Unemployment insurance has been supplemented of late through supplemental insurance benefits negotiated through collective bargaining.

It is a truism that the more we keep our economic decisions decentralized and out of the State sphere, the more we will break up unhealthy combinations of power concentration with their ultimate political consequences. The movements for severance pay are an attempt to move in the direction of localized reserves for human obsolescence. New experimentation with collective bargaining devices at the local level can lead to a rational procedure which will capitalize the earning power of a worker who is deprived of his job property.

Payments can be related to criteria such as worker age, prospective transferability of the worker to other occupations, and earning opportunities. In a sense, it becomes the obligation of the private enterprise manager to treat labor as a capital charge rather than a variable charge on the enterprise. Top management personnel is treated this way now; it is merely a matter of extending this attitude toward labor obligations down the plant hierarchy on the assumption that a worker develops an equity in his job in a property sense. To be sure this does not exclude the State from many functions that can only be socialized, like minimum standards of unemployment insurance and social security. However, an acceptance by management of the job property principle would lead to diversity in handling the problem at the local level that can be treated by decentralized decisionmaking. This would be in accord with our unique cultural pluralism, characteristic of the West.

A PLEA FOR EXPERIMENTATION

It has become clear that collective bargaining is rapidly approaching an impasse. If it is to survive, experiments with new institutions become necessary. In a sense, this echoes a development that took place when collective bargaining agreements began to break down administratively over the process of grievance solving. The clothing workers' unions then pioneered the concept of a permanent umpire, with a thorough knowledge of the industry, who could propose equitable solutions. The previously employed system of ad hoc arbitration of grievances had become increasingly unsatisfactory: arbitrators, ignorant of all the intricacies of union-management relationships in the complex industry, often rendered decisions that were judicially equitable but operationally impossible. The ad hoc arbitrator had to become a professional member of the family—albeit one with a professional obligation to the public.

Today, increasing dissatisfaction with ad hoc governmental intervention at the climax of negotiations for new contracts has led to a similar experiment, again making use of "members of the family" with a professional obligation to protect the public interest. But this time, the experiment is applied not merely to the settlement of grievances but to the actual formulation of contracts.

PART VII

COLLECTIVE BARGAINING

INTRODUCTION

Collective bargaining between unions and managements is a process for jointly considering and resolving industrial problems. It is a practice with an extensive history in all free, industrialized countries. Its particular features usually differ somewhat from country to country, and even from industry to industry within a country, depending on economic circumstances, institutional characteristics, negotiators' personalities, and past relationships between the parties.

As a process of mutual accommodation between two institutions (a union and a company) or groups of institutions (with multi-union and multi-employer negotiations), collective bargaining is a mixture of opposing views and mutual interests, of institutional rivalry and union-management cooperation, of industrial conflict and industrial self-government. Basically, its aim is to achieve acceptance of the terms and conditions of employment over a future period. It covers not only wages but also work rules, work conditions, employee benefits, employee and management rights, and a procedure for handling complaints with respect to the interpretation and application of negotiated agreements. Through the daily handling of such complaints under grievance procedures, collective bargaining may come to be viewed as a more or less continuous process or relationship.

In recent years in certain industries, collective bargaining has involved an increase in informal communication and reconciliation of differences, occurring outside the grievance procedure and formal negotiating sessions. As Simkin explains ("The Trend Toward Maturity in Industrial Relations"), joint study committees established in steel and other industries have facilitated a relaxed exploration of complex issues prior to any formal confrontation at the bargaining table. In that way, the parties have at times been able to accommodate differences in interests and desires without any threat of economic pressure.

The "Panel Discussion of Joint Study Committees" examines the important ingredients for success in such prebargaining meetings. Both management and union leaders point out that joint study committees are no panacea. They do not eliminate the fact that unions and companies are institutions with different methods of operation, separate internal problems, and divergent goals. The union is a vehicle for furthering and protecting the interests of workers as a group. It is not surprising, therefore, to find a union pressing for shorter hours *collectively* while many of its members seek longer hours *individually*. The company, on the other hand, is in business to expand sales and to make good profits; it is not aimed solely at satisfying the desires of the employees as a group. Consequently, joint study committees must recognize that the interests of management and managed workers will diverge and conflict in some respects, despite wide areas of mutual interest in problem-solving.

The possibilities of conflict between management and union viewpoints are indicated in Northrup's article on General Electric's labor program, popularly known as "Boulwarism." The G.E. management attempts to maintain the initiative and the dominant position in labor matters in that company. Through an aggressive program of communications with the individual employees, G.E. seeks to demonstrate that the plant workers' long-run interests are best promoted and protected by the company and that certain union demands are "unsound" and will continue to be rejected by the management regardless of strike threats or the length of any strike. Such tactics, of course, tend to deny the union much credit for employee gains. The National Labor Relations Board has held that they do not constitute bargaining in good faith as required by the Taft-Hartley Act, even though the company did agree to special joint committees to explore contract language and other problems in advance of formal negotiations with two unions with which it bargains on a multi-plant basis.

The Northrup article clearly indicates that certain special conditions are necessary for the success of a Boulware type of program. What some of those conditions are can be appreciated if one asks how successfully Boulwarism could be practiced by one of the big automobile, steel, rubber, or trucking companies. For example, at G.E. about half of the production employees are unorganized, and the organized section is split up among 15 unions. A high degree of product diversification and plant independence, moreover, eliminate any threat that a strike in one location or a few plants (as in autos) could soon close down most of the rest of the company's operations.

Although Boulwarism *per se* has not been adopted by a significant number of companies for fairly obvious reasons, Blum ("Management Paternalism and Collective Bargaining") points out that it is part of an industrial relations philosophy that is still widely prevalent in American industry. Many company personnel programs assume that management knows what is in the best interest of its production employees and that union leaders are more interested in labor politics than they are in the welfare of the workers in an individual company. Where such views prevail, collective bargaining is likely to be mainly a contest, characterized by sharp clashes of opinion.

On the basis of more than a dozen years of experience in the labor movement, Brooks ("The Case for Decentralized Collective Bargaining") is deeply concerned about recent trends in collective bargaining. He believes that multi-plant and multi-company bargaining are leading to excessive centralization of decisions in both unions and management. Such centralization has contributed to a loss of vitality in local unions, to a feeling by the members that at the plant level they have lost much of the power of policy determination and local self-government. Because both industrial relations executives and national union leaders generally favor the uniformity of top-level decisions and pattern-following, Brooks is not optimistic that the centralizing trend can be reversed, but he does suggest some specific steps to halt the drift.

Three industries in which collective bargaining has broken down badly at times and which have required a considerable amount of Federal intervention to help straighten out their labor problems, have been maritime shipping, the railroads, and the airlines. Shils in the final article of the section sets forth the union complexities and rivalries that help to explain why collective bargaining has frequently failed to solve industrial relations problems in those industries except at the expense of the general public. The disappointing results of collective bargaining in maritime shipping, railroads, airlines and trucking have led to strong support for compulsory arbitration in place of collective bargaining in those industries. After over four years of failure to achieve settlement by negotiation, Congress in August 1963, did legislate compulsory arbitration for a two-year period for two railroad issues—elimination of firemen's jobs in yard and freight operations and the proper size of train crews.

The Trend to Maturity
in Industrial Relations

WILLIAM E. SIMKIN

When the events of our current era are fitted into the perspective of the history books one of the commentaries likely to be made is that collective bargaining came of age. If we will only try to avoid the plight of the man who "couldn't see the forest for the trees," we will discover considerable evidence that labor-management relations are gradually attaining promising new levels of maturity.

A dramatic shift is under way in the pattern of collective bargaining:

1. In a growing number of bargaining relationships labor and management are no longer waiting until the eleventh hour to begin serious consideration of major problems. There is increasing experimentation with factual studies and frequent informal meetings during the contract term to outline and attempt to solve the complex matters confronting both sides.

2. There is an expanding awareness and acceptance of the concept of the public interest in the bargaining relationship. Those at the bargaining table are coming to realize they are in the process of making decisions that, to some degree at least, will affect the national welfare, and that failures and prolonged strikes will hurt not only themselves but their community and their country.

3. Finally, it seems to me there is an increasing tendency to come up with contract terms that are more in consonance with economic justice than with "what the market will bear," or what one side can beat out of the other. Unions and management pay more attention in

Taken from Industrial Relations, *III (February 1964), pp. 1–4. Reprinted with the permission of the publisher. William E. Simkin is Director of the Federal Mediation and Conciliation Service.*

their discussions these days to matters such as how the product is selling, what the competition is doing, future plans for expansion and contraction, and employment prospects—in short, the common welfare of the operation and its employees.

While it is true these new practices and attitudes have not as yet been embraced generally in the industrial community, they have been adopted by a significant fraction. More and more managements and unions are at least considering the abandonment of horse-and-buggy bargaining methods in favor of a more meaningful problem-solving approach.

EXPERIMENTATION IN PROBLEM-SOLVING

Fortunately, bergaining is a creative process, susceptible to change and never static. Its practitioners are always eager to glean from the frequent seminars and journals of the trade that which is novel, ingenious, and adaptable to their own labor relations problems. Thus I would like to urge employers and labor organizations at least to try new mechanisms that may aid the problem-solving process.

Some may ask, "Why rock the boat and get into a continuing nonnegotiating relationship when you don't know where it will lead?" To the skeptics I urge, "Give it a try." Opposite numbers at the bargaining table certainly can start out in a modest way by examining issues on an off-the-record basis, with complete understanding that there is no commitment to continue nor obligation to reach any agreement. With the proper advance safeguards, simply trying out calm, unhampered discussion will cost nothing.

Our mediators in the Federal Mediation and Conciliation Service are actively engaged in many instances in helping employers and unions establish various types of such new consultive relationships.

It is a wonder to me how often labor and management find they have a great deal in common if they will only talk a little. R. Heath Larry of the U. S. Steel Corporation, one of the management members of the steel industry's highly successful Human Relations Committee, has this to say regarding that Committee's experiences:

> The mechanism will remain only as good as the parties together make it and want to make it. Attitude is paramount.
>
> It will not, nor is it intended to, turn a union into a "company union," i.e., it does not in any way alter the respective loyalties or institutional roles of the parties; but it can provide enough joint understanding of the problems of the companies, the unions and the employees so that each

new solution comes closer to a "best fit" of accommodating the respective interests. . . .

Perfect answers have not been the result thus far and, no doubt, will not be in the future. But there has been progress—considerable progress. Settlements have increasingly recognized a reflection of the economic realities of the companies in the steel industry and of the needs of the employees. Such progress can and, we believe, will continue.[1]

Naturally the Human Relations Committee approach could not be recommended for every bargaining relationship. The objective should be to devise a prebargaining program tailored to the needs of the particular parties, the one which seems likely to work best and which can be altered as experience dictates. The purpose, however, should always be the same, or as Mr. Larry puts it, to "considerably narrow the areas of difference and lay a foundation of confidence and understanding."

It really should not be too surprising that this new bargaining maturity is developing in steel and other industries. It has been only a little more than a quarter century since Congress officially adopted collective bargaining as a national policy. Comparatively speaking, it is a process barely out of its teens and scarcely accustomed to being an adult. So it is just about time that bargaining did a little growing up.

THE ADMINISTRATION'S ROLE

This maturing process has been quietly but persistently encouraged by the present and last administrations. The act of bringing clearly to the attention of all citizens our common responsibility for keeping the nation strong and competitive, increasing foreign trade, maintaining a favorable balance of payments, and assuring steady growth in the domestic economy without incurring inflation, has helped stimulate national purpose and resolve in bargaining as well as in other areas.

The much-debated economic "guideposts" put forth in early 1962 by the President's Council of Economic Advisers were intended to cultivate particularly a sense of industrial statesmanship. Although submitted as a "contribution . . . to discussion," the guideposts were treated in some critical quarters as an alleged new stabilization formula for wages and prices.

Others have commented at length on the merits or demerits of the guideposts. I only note that President Kennedy stated that he had no

[1] *Steelways* (September 1963).

intention of seeking to control either wages or prices. What the guides amounted to was a statement of a goal and, whether the statement had any contributing effect or not, the fact remains that we have continued to enjoy substantial economic stability.

CURRENT STATUS OF BARGAINING

What I have said up to this point is not intended in any way to claim that all is finally peaceful on the labor relations front. It would be foolish to suggest that collective bargaining is without problems. Argument and dissension are the peculiar trademarks of the bargaining system. Controversy is the very nature of the business. Let us hope it will always be so, for it is our way of self-government in the industrial world.

The bargaining system, despite its detractors, is working extremely well in the face of the serious current tensions engendered by substantial unemployment and the effects of automation. Individual employers and labor organizations cannot on their own solve these substantial nation-wide economic problems, but they can and are succeeding in large measure in their attempts to negotiate the necessary accommodations which will permit both adopting the efficiencies and easing the burdens of technological change.

Those who claim that bargaining is a dying institution and has somehow outlived its usefulness are guilty, I think, of taking a worm's eye view and looking at only a selected part rather than the over-all situation. They do not make a very realistic appraisal.

We know, for example, that at the same time that we were experiencing troubles in the railroad, maritime, newspaper, and airline industries, we were chalking up settlements in the steel, aerospace, rubber, and electrical manufacturing industries. The peaceful settlements failed to get the same attention as the bargaining breakdowns, with the result that the public got the distorted view that bargaining was collapsing in chaos.

Without any effort to excuse the bargaining lapses, the facts are that when the level of labor peace is measured by working time lost due to strikes the recent record has been excellent. For several years now working time strike losses have remained at the lowest point since World War II. They have remained low on a sustained basis, without the ups and downs which characterized prior periods.

Actual strike losses are down to the point where for every day an employee is on strike he works for 700 days without a strike. This is a fairly remarkable achievement in view of the unusually tense problems involved in current claims of workers for greater job security and demands of employers for improved production economy and efficiency.

I have taken pains to try to put the bargaining picture into perspective because there is a danger that repeated exaggeration of shortcomings could court disaster. By that I mean it is possible to talk up a storm. A colleague of mine calls this the "self-fulfilling prophecy"— that is, if enough people become convinced that the free bargaining process is becoming obsolete their predictions will make it so.

We often hear the claim that bargaining is in a crisis or "on trial." This is because in such an arena of conflicting economic ideas and goals there is always going to be controversy, and there will always be people who are impatient when solutions don't always come so easily. These are the people of little faith with the worm's eye view discussed earlier.

In my view free collective bargaining is a valuable institution that is worth defending. No better method has yet been devised to permit the resolution of differences between labor and management within the tradition of a free society.

A Panel Discussion of
the Joint Study Approach

In a conference held in 1964 the human relations committee or joint study approach to the problems of collective bargaining was discussed and analyzed. The edited observations of the panel are presented below. The panelists were:

MALCOLM L. DENISE, *Vice President-Labor Relations,* Ford Motor Company.

JOHN S. HARRISON, *Executive Vice President,* Aluminum Company of America.

JAMES J. HEALY, *Professor of Industrial Relations,* Harvard Business School.

R. HEATH LARRY, *Administrative Vice President, Personnel Services,* United States Steel Corporation.

MARVIN J. MILLER, *Assistant to the President,* United Steelworkers of America, AFL–CIO.

W. BOYD OWEN, *Vice President-Personnel Administration,* Owens-Illinois Glass Company, chairman.

MR. OWEN: The human relations committee approach to collective bargaining has attracted considerable interest because of the way it has developed in the steel industry in the last few years. It would be helpful to begin this discussion by getting some insight into the ra-

This panel discussion appeared in The Conference Board Record, *I (May 1964), pp. 22–31 under the title, "The Human Relations Committee—A Breakthrough in Collective Bargaining." Reprinted with the permission of the National Industrial Conference Board.*

tionale that underlies the steel committee's operations, and as Heath Larry and Marvin Miller are both members of the committee, we have a rare opportunity to do so. Marvin, could you start off?

MR. MILLER: In considering the human relations committee in the steel industry you must go back to the unenviable labor relations record both sides had in the post-World War II period. You will recall that there were nationwide strikes in 1946, 1949, 1952, 1956, and 1959—the last continuing for 116 days. With this as the background it became quite clear to all of us that almost any change in our procedures would have to be an improvement.

FUNCTION OF THE STEEL COMMITTEE

The steelworker-management committee was created in January, 1960, under the settlement that ended the 1959 strike. Its function was to study specific problems listed in the settlement. These included such things as medical care, the job-classification program, incentives, and seniority. The committee was to work out joint solutions to such specific problems, if possible, and submit them to the principals in the form of recommendations. To do this kind of work was the committee's job then and it is now.

Perhaps one of the best ways to indicate what the committee is would be to indicate what it is not. It must be understood at the outset that the committee is neither a negotiating committee nor a grievance committee. The committee operation is not basically an attempt to reconcile two points of view. It has done so in some cases, but our four-year experience has shown that there are certain areas in which there aren't two points of view because there are really no points of view—areas in which neither side has the answer to a problem.

In other words, we have come to realize that there are areas in which neither of us has the answer, areas in which joint exploration is required. We have realized, in essence, that to adopt and cling to preconceived, opposing notions about an issue without studying it thoroughly can prove not only damaging but unnecessary—that it can be fruitful to study problems instead of squabbling over issues.

I would like to emphasize, however, that the committee in steel was not set up, as some people have thought, to deal with philosophical principles. The over-all committee exists to review the experience and work of subcommittees that are assigned to study the specific problems stated in the contracts. The committee itself receives periodic reports; we attempt to help the subcommittees through difficult areas;

we make suggestions. But the groundwork and the structural work are done by the subcommittees. Now, this does not mean that we never get into generalized concepts. We do. I think that any committee like this is bound to, but it is not our primary function. I can certainly say that generalizations have absorbed only a small amount of our time.

MR. LARRY: Marvin has broadly outlined what our human relations committee is and what it is not. I would like to add something about its mechanism.

MORE ABOUT THE MECHANISM

The steel committee has two co-chairmen, Mr. Cooper [R. Conrad Cooper, executive vice president, personnel services, United States Steel Corporation] and Mr. McDonald [David J. McDonald, president of the United Steelworkers of America AFL–CIO]. Each created what seemed to be a kind of guaranteed-work year for Marvin and myself by assigning us to be co-ordinators for the union and the companies, respectively. This means that one part of our job with respect to the human relations committee is to round up the small, knowledgeable subcommittees. These comprise people selected from various places within the union, and from the various echelons within the companies, who have knowledge and experience concerning the particular subjects to be studied. We also develop the approach to the studies and the agendas, and in addition determine when meetings should be held.

The experience of the committee has demonstrated, I believe, that four ingredients are vital to its operation. These may not all be found in other approaches, they may not be absolutely necessary for everybody, but I think that each has contributed importantly to whatever success we have had.

I believe that the first and all-important element is the joint will to attack a problem in a problem-solving atmosphere—to want to find the means to avoid the kind of recurring conflicts we have suffered. It has been frequently suggested that this will was created by our unhappy experience in the 116-day strike, but I suspect there were really many causes. It is probably most accurate to say that all elements in our past experience contributed. Increased knowledge and increased understanding of economic circumstances on the part of both sides possibly had an effect. Bills submitted in Washington that in essence threatened collective bargaining possibly had an effect. In any event, a will to solve our problems did emerge.

I was disturbed not long ago to read a suggestion that was made because our committee's work with respect to the last two steel agreements appeared to have value. The suggestion was to amend the national labor law to make the committee approach a requirement for good faith bargaining everywhere. I think that to do this would be about as successful as taking two people at random and telling them they have to fall in love. It won't work that way. Both parties must have the desire.

The second requisite involves the ground rules. In the committee and subcommittees we are not bargaining. Our job is to do the essential groundwork, and it soon became apparent that the type of discussion involved in a study requires a new approach. Past negotiations had to contend with what is probably the universal experience of having every infinitive you split held against you. Any time a position was taken by either side there could be no retreat. You had to try to move ahead from the point at which you found yourself. There was no flexibility. So we decided that our committee meetings should involve no records, no bad faith charges, no accusations if a position was changed, and no public statements that might induce rigid positions and controversy. There had to be complete flexibility for both sides if objective exploration was to be possible. Pressure to hold back because a tentative or not overly thoughtful suggestion might bounce back and haunt you had to be eliminated. Unfortunately, I can't report on the minutiae of our subcommittee meetings because to do so would violate these rules of ours. I am happy to say that I know of no violation. The honor concept is respected.

The third element of real importance is that both sides must have competent and sophisticated staffs. We faced a very competent steelworkers staff. This really is the best kind to work with.

The fourth major element also involves flexibility—flexibility in time. I would question whether our efforts to feel our way along in advance of negotiations would have been as productive as they were in 1962 and 1963 if we had faced a preset no contract-no work deadline. It was mutually understood, however, that the termination-date option officially established for both sides in our contract would not be exercised automatically. We all appreciated that our study programs require flexibility with respect to time—that trying to solve extremely complex problems with a deadline pressing in on you can reduce chances for success.

The 1962 settlement was reached before notice of termination, which would have had the effect of setting a strike deadline, was permissible. Termination notice was delayed in 1963. In some quarters it was said that to have such a delay would mean that nothing would be accomplished. This isn't necessarily so, of course. The potential for serving notice and setting a termination date always exists. The fact, however, is that it has been possible for us to work constructively in the absence of an automatic termination date that is set months in advance and cannot be based on full knowledge of the circumstances that may exist when it arrives.

I think that in every case these four basic ingredients helped us to gain a healthier knowledge about what the real facts were and what the real motivations of the parties were. You must take cognizance of the facts and motivations when you are trying to solve a specific problem.

Looking at our procedure in still another way, you might liken it to a fail-safe mechanism. I am now sure that as long as we maintain this type of joint study mechanism we will not have accidental wars. We'll plumb the depths for opportunities to solve the problems that are creating differences, and we will know that any problem that does not succumb is a really basic, institutional problem.

PROBLEMS HAVE CHANGED

MR. HEALY: Marvin and Heath certainly make clear why the joint study approach has gained widespread interest and is stimulating various industries and companies to engage in creative collective bargaining. It is that labor relations problems confronting both sides in collective bargaining these days are far more complex than they have been traditionally. We're dealing with problems that just cannot be resolved intelligently in the traditional 30-day or 60-day bargaining period that precedes the traditional strike deadline, problems that are aggravated by the tension that accompanies the setting of such a deadline.

For example, if we were to think into the future we might speculate that many companies and unions will be ridding themselves of incentive pay systems, which are apparently becoming less useful than they were in the past. Dissolution of an incentive system, of course, presents deep problems. It would be risky, to say the least, to do as one company and union did. They agreed shortly before a strike deadline that, effective the following Monday, the incentive system was to be abolished. You don't handle such a problem in so cursory a way. Many companies and unions have come to the practical realization that many of the traditional characteristics of collective bargaining that have prevailed for the past 50 or 60 years just do not contribute much to intelligent resolution of complex subjects.

As Heath and Marvin have indicated, the human relations committee approach, or comparable approaches, require an orientation toward problem solving. I can report that a study by graduate students at the Harvard Business School has turned up many cases of companies and unions that are quietly and yet very constructively evolving new and imaginative approaches. They appear to be making real headway along the same lines, or similar lines, as those developed in the steel industry.

MR. OWEN: What is the situation in your industry, Malcolm?

THE SITUATION IN THE AUTO INDUSTRY

MR. DENISE: An important difference in the background and approach of the automobile and steel industries, I believe, is that in auto we have had a relatively good record in collective bargaining since, say, about 1950. The major settlements have been reached without major strikes, although we have had brief company-wide strikes and some local stoppages over local issues. It is true that the public is usually alarmed by the shouting, but despite the shouting peace generally has prevailed.

Last year in the automobile industry, as you know, we agreed with the United Auto Workers to set up joint study committees. Each of the automobile companies has a separate committee, and some of the farm implement manufacturers have formed similar committees with the UAW. Because of our ground rules, I can't talk about the details of what we are doing. Generally, however, it is the function of a joint study committee in auto to talk about matters that may become issues in the negotiations this year [1964]. This is spelled out in the agreement creating it. The agreement also states that within this broad framework we will mutually agree as to specific subjects to be studied as we go along, and furnish such data as we mutually agree are appropriate. There is no commitment other than to make a start down this road and see where it gets us. We hope that the committee deliberations will help in our negotiations. I think such a committee approach can be a very sound and useful device if supported with the proper spirit.

I would also like to note that, apart from such formal committees, there is a lot of informal communication between management and the union which receives little public notice. It is not conducted through the medium of a committee or anything else that is spelled out in capital letters, but in one form or another it has been carried on over the years. This has been constructive. It has always been our feeling that communication is a vital ingredient of good labor-management relations, even though it doesn't guarantee them.

The essential fact, as Heath has emphasized, is that establishing a committee of one type or another is not going to assure fruitful communication. A positive attitude on the part of both sides is the really important ingredient. If the will exists, the mechanism can be found, and its form is not of major importance.

IN THE ALUMINUM INDUSTRY

MR. HARRISON: As in the automobile industry, we do not bargain as a group in the aluminum business. We bargain by individual company, although all companies bargain at the same time. This is one important difference between our approach and that of the steel industry. The other is that we have no formal committees of the human relations type. In this we differ from auto as well as steel. However, there has been a significant parallel between us and the steel industry in at least one respect. In our last two major negotiations with the steel union in 1962 and 1963, top-level, informal discussions and informal joint decisions preceded our formal negotiations. We reviewed what seemed to be the urgent matters that needed attention. The ground rules for these informal meetings were similar to those already mentioned here. There were no commitments, no negotiations, nothing said that couldn't be withdrawn, nothing indicated that couldn't be modified, and indeed there was nothing said at all so far as disclosing details of what went on in the meetings was concerned.

This points up, as Malcolm has indicated, that what we are basically talking about are improved methods of communication, improved ways of establishing areas of understanding. This appears to be in an early stage of development. All of us seem to agree that our own specific procedure is no panacea, that none of us has a formula that others must use if they are to be successful, that there is not just one way to get the job done.

MR. MILLER: The approach that has developed between the steel union and the aluminum companies appears to me to be a very sensible one in view of our history. While the agreement negotiated in steel is not followed precisely by Alcoa and the other aluminum companies, it has always provided a framework for those negotiations. In view of this history it would probably not make good sense to have separate aluminum study committees functioning at the same time as those in the steel industry. What has evolved in aluminum is a variation that is activated soon after a settlement in steel. What we and the aluminum companies do is to come together informally in individual meetings and see which parts of the steel settlement meet our joint problems, which do not, and determine what we must do to work out appropriate variations.

MR. OWEN: In the glass industry we have been negotiating on an industry-wide basis for about 50 years. And since 1954 we have been meeting informally with the union about two or three times a year, not to negotiate, but to exchange information in an effort to learn about each other's problems so that when we do negotiate we understand one another better.

We regard our meetings as a communications medium. We and the union discuss the state of business, what the order backlog is, developments in competitive industries, what the union can do to help us become more competitive, what our plant problems are, and so on. We believe this has helped reduce the chances of crisis bargaining of the kind we see in the railroad, longshore and automobile industries, and which used to characterize steel.

MR. DENISE: I am certainly not intrigued with the crisis type of bargaining we have gone through. I think a good deal of it is rather senseless on the part of mature people. There ought to be a better way in terms of time, in terms of approach, in terms of less propaganda. I think a vast improvement can be made and that it is worth a real effort to try and make it through the joint study committee. I feel, however, that there is a little bit of a problem, in that expectations may be raised higher than they ought to be raised. People may assume that a committee working in good faith implies an early settlement, a quiet settlement, or a modest settlement.

I see nothing to insure this in the things that are occurring in the automobile industry in reference to the 1964 bargaining—I am talking now not about what is happening in the committees, but about other developments that are public knowledge. They indicate that the UAW is proceeding: toward a convention at which it will formulate its propositions with the usual fanfare, toward giving the usual kind of termination notice along about the first of July, and toward bargaining up to the contract expiration date. If there are any union plans different from this, such plans have not yet become evident.

However, if the sequence of events unfolds this way, as indicated, one should not assume that the joint study committees were just window dressing or were a failure. The objective of the committees, according to the concept on which they are based, is to provide a product to be considered by the parties when they reach the bargaining stage, a product that may help in the negotiations. This must be remembered.

WHEN ONE PARTY HAS MISGIVINGS

MR. HEALY: I think there is a question that must be in the mind of many people as it is in mine. How can a worthwhile joint study committee of the kind we are discussing be created if only one of the parties wants to improve what has been an arm's-length relationship, and at the same time the other party has misgivings about the committee approach? Do you have to go through a traumatic experience such as that in the steel industry in 1959 before the reluctant party becomes interested? Whether the approach is in the form of a human relations committee or another mechanism, or even if it is quite informal, how can you achieve the necessary ingredient, the will and attitude, that Heath referred to?

MR. LARRY: Unfortunately, I don't think there is any pat answer that would be applicable generally. Any answer would have to be tied to the specific case and the history of the relationship. It might be that the persistence of a situation that was very bad might itself move one of the parties to find a remedy, and might make it easier for the other to go along with it, at least in the sense of giving it a try. It might be that public pressure great enough to threaten the structure in which both sides exist will make them see the light. It might be that you must just wait for the passage of time to bring maturity.

MR. MILLER: I believe that an essential ingredient is not necessarily a bad experience in the past but a feeling that if you keep doing what you are doing there is going to be a pretty damaging experience in the future. I think you may need one or the other, possibly both.

MR. OWEN: How about the many labor relations problem areas in which we already have practices that are workable but which fall short of being really satisfactory? I would imagine, for instance, that a really satisfactory seniority clause has never been written.

MR. MILLER: Well, not for all time.

MR. OWEN: How about some of the other problem areas?

MR. LARRY: I am sure Marvin would agree that there is one area about which we might comment generally. I am referring to the subject of overtime.

Before President Johnson got involved in this question, the local officials of the steelworkers had given the international officers the impression that there was a rather massive overtime problem in the steel industry, that there was a great deal of voluntary use of overtime in lieu of recalling people. As a result, we spent a lot of time in subcommittee accumulating all the relevant statistics we could get hold of. We studied these figures and had a series of meetings with a lot of local management and union people. They were brought in from the plants to tell us specifically what was going on with respect to overtime and what was on their minds.

The statistics and the talks ultimately made two things apparent. One was that the overtime problem was not nearly as much of a problem as had been thought. The second was that overtime was not necessarily general in any one plant. At various times and at various places questions about overtime arose because of what appeared to be a lack of understanding of why the overtime was required. I think this illustrates that it is much easier to deal with a question in detailed, tangible form than in the form of a broad allegation about which neither side has all the facts.

MR. OWEN: If there was a wildcat strike in some plant, would the committee discuss it and try to settle it?

MR. MILLER: This is not a function of the committee. I can conceive of a situation which might end up in the committee if all other procedures failed, but this certainly would not happen in the beginning.

"HRC WILL HANDLE IT"

MR. LARRY: As was noted before, it is fundamental that the committee was not created to be a grievance-settling medium. There seemed to be a slight tendency at the beginning, however, for unit management and local union people to shrug off problems in areas to be considered by the committee. It was as if they had said: "Let's not bother too much about this. The HRC will handle it someday."

We quickly discovered what was happening in these few instances and made clear that the contract procedure for resolving grievances was to be observed, that the committee was not created to deal with such matters.

MR. MILLER: That is correct. Yet we have had a situation that might be described as in the middle ground.

We had negotiated the extremely complex extended vacation plan, which became effective January 1 of this year. Not long before this date, as a result of what was happening at the plants, we realized that we had made an error in one aspect of the plan. We had created a situation that, in my opinion, prevented local management and local unions from properly scheduling vacations, and therefore, they were unable to properly implement the new program.

Now, this unexpected problem was brought to our attention by what you might call grievances—complaints at the plant level. It was clear, however, that it was a universal problem. It wasn't just a particular grievance at a particular place.

The committee met quickly. (It occurred to me some time later how efficient it was. This sounds like I am patting us on the back, but it really was.) In a matter of a day or so we reactivated the same subcommittee that had done all the groundwork on the extended vacation plan. It sat down to resolve a problem that was industry wide, and it succeeded in a very brief period.

So in a sense we were handling a grievance, but it was what might be called a universal grievance, and it certainly was an exceptional case.

MR. OWEN: This illustration certainly underscores the value of having a positive attitude and a mechanism that permits quick and efficient action. How about a situation in which a difficult problem, but not a strike issue, can't be resolved satisfactorily in negotiations?

SOLVING NONSTRIKE PROBLEMS

MR. MILLER: I don't know why, but there has been some misunderstanding about this. The fact is, of course, that not every problem is solved in our negotiations. In 1962, for instance, there were many problems left over. Also, new problems come up. Our contracts provide for further study of carry-over problems by the committee. The contracts also list new problems to be studied, and, hopefully, solutions will be recommended at the time of the next negotiations. For example, the 1962 contract said the committee would try to develop recommendations for such problems as contracting out, overtime, scheduling vacations, and creating employment opportunities, perhaps by arranging for longer vacations. The contract went even further and included our respective points of view concerning these problems.

The companies stated, in part, that the scheduling of vacations and duration of vacations have significant bearing on the operating efficiency of the business. The union stated that expansion of employment opportunities requires shorter worktime and that a practical method of approaching this goal is to provide longer vacations.

The human relations committee had to study these matters to determine whether changes could be made that would be consistent with the respective interests of the parties. So there was a direct mandate to the committee to study and come up with a recommendation, which it did, and this, of course, became a part of the 1963 settlement.

MR. LARRY: It might be added that the contracts include a rather general clause enabling the committee, if advisable, to consider subjects in addition to those that are specifically listed. We have done this in several cases.

MR. HEALY: By way of contrast, one case of stalemate over a complex issue that I know about involved an eleventh-hour bargaining struggle over subcontracting rights. In the agonizing period immediately before the deadline, both sides did what unfortunately happens all too often. They deliberately wrote a completely ambiguous clause that would make it possible for each side to say its view had prevailed. Privately, they acknowledged that it was an ambiguous clause. The upshot, of course, was that arbitrators began to make interpretations that were appalling to the union and equally impossible for the company.

What did they do? As a result of their traumatic experience they appointed a special *ad hoc* committee whose sole job was to study the details and implications of the subcontracting problem. That committee worked a full year, and when the next negotiations took place the committee presented its report. Many, though not all, of its recommendations were adopted and incorporated in the agreement.

This is but one illustration, and a footnote can be added to it. As a result of that experience the company and union have created another *ad hoc* committee to review the seniority system as it applies to layoffs. I think this example indicates another path by which the joint study approach can get under way.

MR. DENISE: There is a gamut of possibilities with respect to what these joint study committees may be assigned to do. There are also instances, of course, in which committees, ostensibly of this type, really have no positive function whatsoever. They are provided for in a contract to become a graveyard, at least a temporary graveyard, if you will permit the contradiction, for matters that are tacitly regarded as too sticky to handle. I suppose, however, that it could be argued that even this is a function of sorts.

MR. HARRISON: I believe we all have to remember that the human relations approach, using the term generically, is not going to do away with the fact that a union and a company are different kinds of institutions. Heath touched on this. Unions, I am sure, are going to do what they feel they must do for their members, and this will conflict with what management thinks it must do to prevent unnecessary increases in labor costs and prices. I don't think any of us should hide behind these joint study techniques and pretend that they will eliminate organic differences. I believe that while communications may be enhanced by the approaches we are talking about and that one of their effects will be to reduce the possibility of what was called an "accidental war," we are still going to have conflicts. I worry, though, that the government doesn't want us to have wars, meaning strikes.

AN IMPORTANT NEW ELEMENT

MR. MILLER: A good relationship under a human relations committee will not eliminate the possibility of strikes, but I think the existence of such a mechanism and sincerity in its application will by itself tend to reduce chances for major strikes.

Let me explain. Consider that the steel committee has now functioned successfully through two sets of negotiations. Under our current contracts a strike cannot occur before May 1, 1965. This will add up to more than five years without an over-all strike in the basic steel industry. It will be by far the longest strike-free period in the labor-management history of the industry. Having accomplished this, let us suppose that some time in the future, certainly not necessarily in 1965, we become involved in a basic impasse of the type indicated by Jack Harrison. Let us say we have a steel strike—quite a long strike, as has usually been the case with us. In such an event, I submit, there would be a very good possibility, even a probability, that the human relations committee approach in the steel industry would be wrecked. There would be a good chance that one could not simply shrug off such a strike by saying: "Well, the human relations committee has a certain function, and if it carries that out and there is a strike anyway, well then, you will eventually settle the strike and go back to the old committee approach." I doubt this would happen.

If I am right, I think it follows that a new element has entered the picture: it is that we have a situation not unlike that of nations worrying about war. I am using the term "war" here in the sense of something after which things will never be quite the same again. I think this factor is one which both parties to a human relations approach have to be aware of. I think it is a good factor, and an important one. If getting involved in a strike can wreck the joint study approach, and the positive spirit on which it is based, it seems to me that the prospect of such a strike will be weighed more seriously than ever by both sides.

MR. HEALY: I fully agree with you, Marvin, that there is an inherent risk. If there is a strike in situations in which these joint study efforts exist, it is going to be difficult to move back to the prestrike situation. It will mean going a couple of steps backward and starting over again, and hoping that the will can be reborn.

MR. OWEN: We tend to talk about a strike as if it were a dirty word, and yet I believe that a strike, under certain circumstances, can be healthy. I don't think you can tell whether strikes are going to be good or bad before they get under way, but I believe that they sometimes have their positive aspects.

MR. HEALY: A strike is obviously undesirable if it is an outgrowth of ignorance or a position anchored in unreasonable stubbornness, or if it results from unnecessary misunderstanding that might qualify it to be termed an "accidental war." But I also belong to the old-fashioned school with respect to strikes, a school that believes that an economic strike is an integral part of collective bargaining. Despite having been involved in a variety of government assignments, I deplore what until recently was an excessive desire by government to put out any and all fires, wherever they occurred.

I am convinced that many companies in the United States and many of their unions could have avoided very prolonged and extremely painful strikes had they faced up to the issues at an earlier date, when the issues might have been resolved by shorter strikes. Unfortunately, in the case of a strong union and a weak management, what too many companies did was put up a show of resisting union demands before yielding at the last minute. But the time may come when you must undo the damage this has done or go out of business. Then you have a long, painful strike to try to correct the damage caused by what might be described as too much peace over the years.

What I am saying, of course, is not an indorsement of strikes. Obviously, strikes can be avoided—and soundly avoided—by methods the panelists have been describing. But all the effects of a possible strike, both long and short term, should be weighed carefully by the parties.

MR. DENISE: This ties in with what has been described as too much of a tendency to judge collective bargaining on its strike record. It probably should be judged to a greater degree on its accomplishment or lack of accomplishment with respect to whether the agreement is an economically sound and appropriate solution to a problem, and whether it is consistent with the economic needs and best interests of the country. As has been noted, the existence of the strike option is what makes collective bargaining work on a voluntary basis. It is the responsibility of people in government to recognize this.

QUESTION: Was the steel human relations committee responsible for the early steel settlements in 1962 and 1963, or would early settlements have been negotiated anyway?

MR. LARRY: I suppose early settlements might have been negotiated without the human relations committee. Anything is possible. But the committee contributed immeasurably.

MR. MILLER: I don't see how it would have been possible to develop the 1962 or 1963 settlement without some mechanism to provide the opportunity and time for joint studies of the problems involved. I am thinking, for example, of our seniority problems in 1962. They required months of review. We brought in local union people and local plant management and got their views.

A meaningful settlement of an issue like this without advance preparation would have been impossible. This was equally true in 1963 with respect to the extended vacation plan and the contracting-out and overtime issues. Reading the very complex extended vacation plan, for instance, will clearly indicate the problems involved and the time required to develop ways to cope with them.

QUESTION: Mr. Healy, you mentioned a research study of many cases in which human relations committees or devices comparable to them are being used. Have you discovered that certain conditions must pre-exist if such an approach is to be successful? For instance, must the union be paramount in its industry and not seriously challenged by another union? Must it be one whose leaders are not being challenged from within? Must it be a union that is free of communist influence and/or racketeering elements? Must the company be one that is not out to break the union?

MR. HEALY: If these circumstances did not prevail, the chances for success would be reduced. A measure of success might be attained, but better results would be likely if the union's leadership was secure and not confronted by continuing attacks from rival unions. Also, an attacking union might try to convert a joint study approach, which involves a cooperative attitude, into a weapon in its campaign against the recognized union. And if there are ideological concepts that conflict with joint exploration of problems, they could impair chances for success. They certainly would reduce confidence in success.

On the management side, there is a factor in addition to a "get-the-union" attitude that would probably frustrate a joint study approach. It is this. I doubt that joint study programs can be successful if there is overabsorption by management in what I would call a rather false notion about management prerogatives. I do not mean issues involving substantive managerial rights. I mean, in particular, notions having to do with disclosure of information. An essential ingredient in the successful operation of these joint programs is willingness to disclose information that will be useful and pertinent in resolving a problem intelligently. A considerable obstacle to success would be for a company to say to its employees and their union: "Why don't you understand our problems better?" and then, when the time arrives for going into the details of a problem, to say: "Wait a minute. This information is none of your business."

QUESTION: From what levels of the management and union organization do the people who serve on human relations subcommittees come from? Also, do they serve on a permanent basis or as their expertise is required?

MR. LARRY: With respect to management, we draw personnel from a spectrum of levels, depending on the nature of the specific problem being considered. It is not at all uncommon to have the subcommittees include one or more labor relations vice presidents from the 11 steel companies that participate in our bargaining. Neither is it uncommon to use people from the next level, or from one and two levels further down. We use specialists who regularly work in the area of the problem and who have particular experience and competence in that area. They are best qualified for detailed analysis. We have roamed widely among the management personnel of the 11 companies to pick our subcommittee staffs.

With respect to the time a subcommittee staff member devotes to its work, the answer is: as long as is necessary. If some problem requires full-time work our people work full time until the job is completed. Then they return to their regular work. On other occasions such constancy isn't necessary, and our subcommittee people devote time as required.

In connection with modifying the job classification program, for instance, members of the subcommittee worked full time for weeks on end to the exclusion of everything else. The subcommittee did not meet continually, however, because a lot of work might be required to make sure there would be something constructive to contribute at a meeting.

UNION LACKS FINANCES

MR. MILLER: We draw from all union levels also. The top human relations committee includes the steelworkers' three international officers, counsel, and myself. At the subcommittee level we have one or more of the international officers. Elected district directors of the union have served on subcommittees at times. So have field staff representatives and directors of various headquarters' staff departments, including the heads of the pension and insurance department, the wage incentive department, and so on. They do not devote full time to such work. The union simply does not have the financial and personnel resources to permit its staff to devote time exclusively to the human relations committee and not attend to their other responsibilities. In a number of cases the work of the committee could have been improved if we had people working on a particular problem full time.

QUESTION: Do you think that the human relations committee approach, with continuing discussions during the term of a contract, may result in a trend toward open-end contracts?

MR. DENISE: I would be very much surprised if this became the general practice, although it is possible that some open-end contracts will result. As always, there are two ways of looking at the question. There are people in the United States who see considerable virtue in an open-end contract. We also know that in some European countries, where open-end contracts have been traditional, there are industries and companies that look with envy on the definite-term contract that is common in the United States.

MR. LARRY: In steel I believe it will depend on the degree of maturity our joint study committee ultimately develops. I think Marvin would certainly agree that we are not ready for an open-end contract yet. It must be kept in mind, however, that we do not now have a one-date, definite-term contract in the sense that all of its programs and provisions are terminable at the identical time. The termination dates for some of our programs vary considerably, as you know.

MR. HARRISON: I don't think that maturity, sophistication and competence have developed sufficiently to make open-end contracts the general practice. I don't think it is practicable for us to accept contracts that substitute uncertainty for definite effective dates. To do so would raise very serious problems. As the situation exists today, considering political and economic factors of concern to both sides, I feel that if there is going to be a reopening there must be provision for a termination date.

MR. MILLER: We have not yet tested the open-end concept, of course. The human relations committee idea, however, includes provision for the parties to modify the contract at any time during its term if a solution to a problem they are studying is reached and if they both agree it is reasonable to adopt the recommendations regardless of the contract's formal effective date.

MR. LARRY: There has been what you might call a little bit of a test. We have negotiated adjustments during the term of the contract.

MR. MILLER: That's right. It involved writing in retroactivity for pensions. But this is a long way from an over-all, open-end contract, of course.

QUESTION: Apart from the joint study committees, what other procedures may foster better communications?

ALCOA'S APPROACH TO ARBITRATION

MR. HARRISON: There are many procedures that will help, of course, if they are wisely and efficiently administered. One that has helped Alcoa is our approach to arbitration.

In 1947, when we signed our first agreement with the steelworkers that included a permanent arbitration system, we decided to limit the scope of arbitration very carefully. In addition to making generally clear that the scope was limited, we said that not all grievances would be subject to arbitration. We specifically excluded a number of matters in the day-to-day work area, including work schedules, production standards, contracting out, and many other matters that we felt should be left to the operating judgment of our plant management. This is not novel, but we think it has developed some interesting ramifications.

It has required our management, particularly at lower levels, to recognize its responsibility in discussing grievances which under our contract may bring on a stoppage. (The union has the right to strike over nonarbitrable grievances if they are not resolved under the grievance procedure.) This means that the management has to be aware of its responsibilities rather than prerogatives. It must make the effort to obtain understanding and consent to the operating decisions from the people whose working lives and habits are affected by those decisions and who can resist them. While some strikes have occurred, this procedure has stimulated vital communication throughout the term of the contract. It is necessary to work out problems before they can fester, which, apart from possibly bringing on grievance strikes, may make terminal negotiations much more complicated.

These continuing discussions involve the international union as well as locals. Under our procedure a nonarbitrable grievance must be reviewed by top management and union representatives before a strike is permissible. This helps us learn at first hand what problems are really bothering people. We can determine if there are appropriate changes. Sometimes we can resolve these problems at this stage. Also, it is sometimes recognized that a question is too broad for immediate disposition and should be deferred until our major negotiations.

[The intraunion warfare preliminary to the February 1965 contest for the presidency of the United Steelworkers threatened the Human Relations Committee with mortal injury. Although both the challenger (I. W. Abel, the Secretary-Treasurer) and the incumbent (David J. McDonald) were members of the Committee, a significant element in the anti-administration attack by the Abel forces was the charge that the Committee had become a medium for "secret deals" at the national level in disregard of rank-and-file interests. Ed.]

The Case for Boulwarism

HERBERT R. NORTHRUP

The labor relations policies of the General Electric Company—popularly known as "Boulwarism"—have recently been condemned by a National Labor Relations Board trial examiner as "bargaining in bad faith."[1] This NLRB case has added to the already wide interest in the General Electric concept among management personnel. After a short analysis of the GE background, this article will explain what the concept is and how it works in practice. Final sections are devoted to analysis of the *Trial Examiner's Report,* and to the extent to which the GE concept may have general application.[1a]

THE COMPANY BACKGROUND

General Electric is one of the giants of U.S. business, with more than 250,000 employees, 165 plants, and sales in excess of $4.5 billion. It is also one of the most diversified companies in the world, involved in manufacturing almost every conceivable type of electrical product, from locomotives to transistors, turbines to lamp bulbs, refrigerators to tiny wires, and so on. In addition, GE is one of the country's leading chemical manufacturers, operates a glass company with nine plants, is one of the few manufacturers of large jet engines, and

Taken from Harvard Business Review, *XLI (September–October, 1963), pp. 86–97. Reprinted with the permission of the author and the publisher. Herbert R. Northrup is Professor of Industry in the Wharton School of Finance and Commerce at the University of Pennsylvania. Before becoming a professor at Pennsylvania in 1961, he was employee relations consultant at General Electric for three years.*

[1] NLRB Case No. 2-CA—7581 *et al., Trial Examiner's Report.* The 111-page *Trial Examiner's Report* is summarized in the *Daily Labor Report,* no. 64 (April 2, 1963), pp. AA 1–6.

[1a] [Following the article, a decision in this case by the National Labor Relations Board on December 16, 1964 is briefly reported. *Ed.*]

without doubt is one of the greatest research organizations in the world.

From the labor relations point of view, this diversification is highly significant. It is clearly impossible to shut down GE by striking a key plant, as the auto workers shut down Ford by striking a forge shop in 1953. There has been, too, a diversification of employee types and interests. The majority of employees in some plants are men; in others there is an 85% female majority. In some plants the workers are middle-aged and older; in others they are very young. And in GE, as elsewhere, this diversification has been accompanied by a steady reduction in the percentage of hourly employees, now less than half of the company total, and a failure of unions to organize the clerical and professional groups. Finally, as I will explain later, the organized employees in GE are widely split into competing unions.

GE as a "Good Employer"

From its earliest days, the GE management prided itself on being a good employer. Thus, it established its pension plan in 1912, and developed many other benefit programs at an early date. In the 1930's, it agreed without a struggle to bargaining elections, first under the labor boards of the NRA period, and then under the NLRB. By 1938, GE had signed a company-wide agreement with the newly formed UE, without strike or legal bickering. (All unions which are identified by an abbreviation in the text are listed in EXHIBIT I.)

War and Postwar

During World War II, the UE grew to a total membership of almost 500,000, and with its growth its policies tended more and more openly to line up with those espoused by the Communist Party. That a union so oriented should have an unobstructed communication track to GE employees caused great uneasiness among the company's management.

Added to this uneasiness was the feeling among GE management, as probably in the country generally, that during the war the power of the unions had been too greatly enhanced. The 1946 strike wave seemed to bear this out. UE made a $2 per day demand on General Electric, Westinghouse, and the electrical division of General Motors. When none agreed, a strike was authorized against all three, which began on January 15, 1946. General Electric, for its part, offered a 10%-per-hour increase with a minimum of 10¢ per hour, which the union rejected.

EXHIBIT I. PRINCIPAL UNIONS REPRESENTING GENERAL ELECTRIC
EMPLOYEES, 1963

Union	Approximate number represented
International Union of Electrical, Radio and Machine Workers (IUE)	65,000
United Electrical, Radio and Machine Workers of America (UE)	9,500
International Association of Machinists (IAM)	9,000
United Automobile, Aerospace and Agricultural Implement Workers of America (UAW)	5,500
Allied Industrial Workers of America (AIW)	4,000
International Brotherhood of Electrical Workers (IBEW)	2,500
Sheet Metal Workers International Association (SMW)	2,500*
American Federation of Technical Employees (AFTE)	2,000
International Brotherhood of Teamsters (IBT)	2,000
United Steelworkers of America (USW)	800

* Almost all at Hotpoint, Chicago; not certified there till 1962.

UE's strike at General Motors started after the automobile workers struck. It was ended by an 18½ ¢-per-hour increase about one month later. General Electric held firm to its original offer for another month before settling at the 18½ ¢ figure demanded by UE after the General Motors settlement, and Westinghouse capitulated after still another month.

BOULWARE AND HIS CONCEPT

The 1946 strike was followed by a reassessment of company employee relations policies. A new start was made when Lemuel R. Boulware was named to the new post of vice president for employee and community relations, and the "relations" function was put on a par with other key management functions—marketing, engineering, manufacturing, and finance.

To Boulware, GE's main shortcoming in employee relations was a failure in "marketing." In his colorful language, he expressed his belief that if the "misunderstanding and disapproval" of GE by employees and communities alike were to end, "General Electric management must set out with a firm resolve, first to begin to do *whatever was necessary* to achieve ultimately the same success in *job marketing* that we had accomplished in *product* marketing. In other words, we wanted *good* job customers and *satisfied* job customers."[2]

What seemed to be needed, therefore, was to apply the tools of marketing to employee relations—market research, product planning, market development, and merchandising. In following this program, General Electric developed its new concept of collective bargaining. Instead of offering less than it intends to give, then permitting the union to force (or often *appear* to force) it to grant more, GE, after its careful research, puts what it believes is proper on the table and changes this only on the basis of what it considers "new information." Though GE's "research" has always included a careful analysis of union demands, as publicized before negotiations and as discussed in negotiations prior to the offer (and although in every negotiation except one the dominant union has been able to develop sufficient "new information" to induce GE to alter its initial offer), the GE approach basically denies the union the political victory of appearing to force the company to accede to union demands, or at least to seek a compromise satisfactory to the union.

General Electric believes that this approach, by ending "haggling," puts negotiations on a more factual and less emotional basis. GE does not attempt to drive a bargain less favorable to employees than would be achieved by a different bargaining approach. As the labor editor of *The New York Times* noted after the 1960 strike, "Most of the emulators forget that GE puts a tempting dish on the bargaining table and does not confront unions with a long list of concessions calculated to give the union a fighting issue."[3] This "tempting dish" is aimed at meeting the aspirations and needs of the employees, including those expressed by the union officials. But because the dynamics of the situation derive from GE and because through its communication GE makes that point abundantly clear, union officials often see in the GE approach a threat to their security or, as the case may be, a convenient scapegoat for union failure.

Balanced Best Interests

Inherent also in the Boulware approach is the refusal to be moved toward unsound positions by force or threats of force. This means

2 "Year-End Review: Where We Were, Where We Are, Where We Are Trying to Go in Employee Plant Community and Union Relations," General Electric Company, *Employee Relations News Letter* (December 31, 1954), p. 2; this contains an excellent statement of "Boulwarism" in language obviously that of the man himself.

3 A. H. Raskin, "Showdown for Carey," *New York Times* (Oct. 23, 1960).

that if the management believes its position is correct, then the company should stand willing to take a strike rather than to accede to demands which it believes are unwise and unsound or, in the Boulwarian terminology, not in the "balanced best interests" of all "contributor-claimants" to the business—that is, employees, customers, shareholders, vendors, and "neighbors or public along with the government." To the charge that this gave management the right to "play God"—that is, to decide who receives what portion of the corporate pie—Boulware noted that if any contributor-claimant is not (*or thinks he is not*) being dealt with fairly in either the financial or nonfinancial areas, he will not do his part, and he and all the others will suffer. If there is any attempt to favor any *one* at the expense of another, the attempt is bound to damage "the interests of all."[4]

Management, GE reasoned, is charged with operating the business. Its job is to unite all factors with an optimum producing organization. Management is in the best position to allocate resources. The unions are obviously there to see that their members obtain their fair share, but management must also consider others. If management fails in its job, it too will lose. With Boulwarism came also company decentralization and the Cordiner doctrine that GE management was not to be mediocre and secure, but rather opportunity-minded, well-compensated, fully responsible for its decisions and hence "at risk."[5]

Communication

Just as effective salesmanship and advertising are basic to good marketing, so Boulware believed that communication was a *sine qua non* of effective employee and union relations. Henceforth, individual employees and "community neighbors" were to be kept fully informed about company plans, programs, and proposals. Although the company would not engage in a mudslinging contest with anyone, it would not hesitate to set the record straight if the occasion demanded.

General Electric maintained that its failure to communicate to its employees and to those living in communities where it had plants was a fundamental reason for the strike debacle of 1946. Unless the company communicates its point of view, Boulware reasoned, employees and the public—and even supervisors and middle manage-

4 "Year-End Review," *op. cit.*, p. 3.
5 See *Time* (January 12, 1959), p. 85; and GE's *Report of the 1957 Annual Meeting*, p. 13.

ment in a large diversified company—are likely to learn about events affecting their wages and working conditions only through union communications, or through rumor and the grapevine. Under such conditions, company actions, proposals, and viewpoints are not likely to be portrayed accurately.

Moreover, unions have fairly good natural communication lines. Through union newspapers, meetings, handouts, and pamphlets, the union viewpoint is portrayed. But most important from the union point of view is the shop steward or committeeman. He attends grievance and negotiation meetings, union strategy meetings, and other conferences. From the discussion at such gatherings, he learns both union and company proposals, strategy, and tactics. He is then in a unique position to bring his information back to the shop. In the absence of managerial communication, the union steward becomes the sole source of information, interpreting it as he sees fit and all too often even providing the foreman with the "inside dope."

Effective union communication (while management is either silent or ineffectual) can often provide the basis for managerial loss of control of the shop. It places management and supervision at a tremendous disadvantage, both in day-to-day relationships and in a time of crisis. Union positions and demands are communicated in terms and contexts which appear proper and logical to the man in the shop, and often to his supervisor as well. Restrictions on managerial freedom to manage, innovate, or change can be made to seem reasonable, fair, and constructively protective of employee interests unless rebutted by (a) the facts of economic and competititve needs and (b) the unvarnished truth that not to innovate and not to change means becoming high-cost and uncompetitive, with resultant loss of business and unemployment—obviously not in the employee interest.

Effective communication, GE has found, involves use of all the resources available, aimed at all the audiences involved. This includes communication with and through union committees. Boulware believed in doing this as much as any labor relations manager.

General Electric managers and employee relations specialists meet with numerous union committees, not only to discuss grievances, but also to exchange ideas on many things, such as the state of the particular business, prospects for employment, impending changes in production methods or technical developments, and other questions of mutual interest. Most of these meetings are on a local basis, because that is both where the problems are and where the bargaining takes place. In cases where bargaining is on a national basis—i.e., with the IUE, the UE, and the Pattern Makers League of North America—such informative meetings have occured nationally for many years.[6] Communication, however, is not in itself a program. It must be based upon, and reflect, performance. It must be truthful. Boulware stressed from the beginning that since GE had a long record as a "good employer" and "good community citizen," it must continue to "do right voluntarily" and make the fact known to employees and the public. But also it must admit its mistakes, correct its errors, and stick to the truth so that its credibility will be established.

Boulware also maintained that communication must be regular or even continuous to hold its audience. A company which stops advertising when its products are selling may well find that its frantic endeavors to capture sales later, when customers are dropping, suffer from lack of advertising readership. So, too, a company that communicates only when it needs its readers' help may find it difficult to reach its audience at a moment of crisis. Under Boulware, plants established or revamped papers, bulletins, and various types of oral and written communication media; and a central staff supplied some syndicated material to supplement local news. Over the years a lot of talent and effort went into making GE communication media readable and pertinent.

BOULWARISM IN PRACTICE

The Boulware regime at General Electric coincided with the beginnings of the UE crackup as a result of the Communist issue. In 1947, GE met the 15¢ industry pattern. Then, in 1948, the company made its offer, which was accepted by the UE without major or minor change—the only time this has occurred. The 1948 contract marked the beginning of direct communication to employees of the terms of an offer. Full-page advertisements explaining GE's position were placed in the press of all communities where GE had plants. The 1948 agreement ran for two years, with a wage reopening in 1949; but, in the latter year, the first postwar recession, GE declined to increase wages. The UE, on the verge of internal breakup, was in no position to risk a collision.

---

6 Thus GE and IUE, and GE and UE, established three special committees in April 1963 to explore contract language and other problems prior to the August commencement of bargaining for a new contract; similar committees were also set up prior to the 1955 negotiations.

The Carey Career

The crackup of the UE meant the return of its former president, James B. Carey. Since a concept like Boulwarism is shaped by its opponents as well as by its proponents, a brief examination of the career of Carey, Boulwarism's principal opponent, is pertinent.

After a very short work experience during the early 1930's as a tester and inspector in the Philadelphia radio laboratory of Philco, Carey helped to form a local union. Then, at the age of 21, he was elected president of the Radio and Allied Trades Council, which three years later joined with other independent and AFL locals to form the UE, again with Carey as president.[7]

From the beginning, Carey took only a minor part in the collective bargaining aspects of his job. He concentrated on organizing and public relations. As an attractive young man and a good speaker, he soon became quite capable at debating and moving crowds—qualities which distinguished him more than his abilities in administration and bargaining.

Carey's fellow high officers in the UE were James J. Matles, director of organization, and the late Julius Emspak, the secretary-treasurer. Matles controlled the appointment of organizers and other personnel; Emspak controlled the organization's finances and its paper. With this authority, combined with Carey's concentration on outside activities, it is clear that Matles and Emspak dominated the UE then just as Matles still does today. In 1948, Louis Budenz, managing editor of *The Daily Worker,* testified before Congress that the Communist Party considered Matles to be one of its ablest and most trusted comrades. Budenz also testified that Emspak was high in Communist Party circles and was known as Comrade Juniper. (When called before this committee, Matles and Emspak refused to state whether or not they were Communists.)[8]

In retrospect, it appears that the UE was set up in much the same way as were other labor organizations of the period which became CIO affiliates after John L. Lewis recruited organizers directly from the Communist Party. It was typical strategy to obtain the election of an attractive, respectable non-Communist (preferably a member of

7 For a history of this period and Carey's career, see Walter Galenson, *The* CIO *Challenge to the* AFL (Cambridge: Harvard University Press, 1960), pp. 239–65.

8 U.S. House of Representatives, 80th Congress, 2nd session, Committee on Education and Labor, *Investigation of Communist Infiltration of* UERMWA, 1948, pp. 351, 353–58, 112–14, 157–58; also Galenson, *op. cit.;* and U.S. Senate, 82nd Congress, 2nd session, Committee on Labor and Public Welfare, *Hearings on Communist Domination of Unions and National Security,* 1952.

the Catholic church) as president of the union, but to lodge all effective power in the hands of other officers who were Communists or who had close Communist connections. In time, however, the presidents of some of these labor organizations, like others who had mistakenly cooperated with Communists, realized that they were being used and broke with them. Carey was the first of these union presidents to make the break—a fact which led to his later loss of the presidency of the UE. Both Michael Quill of the Transport Workers Union of America and Joseph Curran of the National Maritime Union of America followed his lead in purging their organizations.

When Carey lost his UE presidency in 1941, it was to Albert Fitzgerald, another non-Communist. The issue was the Communist question, but other issues were lack of attention to union duties and lack of tact in dealing with local union officials. These alienated many non-Communists, including the leadership of the Lynn, Massachusetts, local of which Fitzgerald was president. The Lynn local supplied the difference against Carey.

Between 1941 and 1948, Carey continued his opposition to the Matles-Emspak faction, using his job as secretary-treasurer of the CIO to keep the issue alive, but the Matles-Emspak leadership was not severely challenged. Then, as the cold war grew colder, several locals seceded to other unions, Congress began an investigation of Communist control of the UE, and the CIO began moving toward a break with its Communist-controlled affiliates. At the CIO's 1949 convention, the UE withdrew (or was expelled) from the CIO; a new union, the IUE, was created by the CIO with Carey as its head; and the UE began to crumble. In a series of NLRB elections, the IUE of Carey clearly came out on top. In GE's largest plant, Schenectady, the UE retained power until Leo Jandreau, the business agent since the founding of the local, swung over to IUE in 1954.

Today, IUE is clearly the largest in the industry, but the UE is far from dead. In General Electric, UE represents less than 10,000 employees, a majority of whom are in Erie; IUE represents six times as many. But UE remains a threat with a large following at Lynn and Pittsfield, Massachusetts, as well as smaller factions at several other locations. EXHIBIT I shows the present status of representation by leading unions in the General Electric Company.

Boulwarism and IUE

Relations between the IUE and GE commenced on a stormy note because of Carey's demand for, and GE's refusal of, terms superior to

those negotiated with other unions. Carey promptly ordered a series
of strikes against the company, but these were less than fully effective
since the large Pittsfield local refused to join the strike at all. In a few
weeks, a contract was signed on terms close to the company offer.

Bargaining during the next few years with the IUE did not erupt in
major stoppages, although some local strikes occurred. IUE was
mainly on the defensive, as major locals and their officials refused to
sanction strike action to improve offers made by the company or to
gain such coveted union demands as the union shop. In 1953, the
company did substantially modify its original wage offer after General Motors acceded to the United Automobile Workers to make their
contract "livable." Carey called this a great victory over Boulwarism.
To GE, it merely demonstrated that the company would indeed
change its position when the facts indicated such a change to be in
order. The following year the company pretty much stuck to its guns
after its original offer was on the table—and, when it saw other
unions accept the offer, the IUE did, too.

The year 1955 saw negotiations conducted with considerably less
heat. Carey was ill during much of the negotiating period, and the
negotiations on the union side were led by local IUE officials anxious
for agreement. General Electric, desiring a long-term agreement
(since its starry-eyed market forecasters saw only a continuation of
great prosperity), put a generous five-year wage package on the table.
GE's offer included a 3%-per-year wage increase for three years,
3.48% for the fourth year, 3.46% for the fifth year, plus quarterly
cost-of-living adjustments if warranted; a checkoff revocable only
annually; a new comprehensive insurance program, as well as improvements in other fringe benefits; and a provision for a reopener in
1958 of the unemployment security issue. The latter item was a
concession to the IUE for accepting a contract without the latest
fringe, supplemental unemployment compensation. GE also agreed
informally not to launch any "resign from union" campaign during
withdrawal periods and has followed this policy.

The good feeling engendered by the 1955 agreement was short-
lived. Business did not keep pace with the company expansionist
projections, with heavy unemployment resulting in the older locations
where IUE membership is concentrated. Moreover, the cost of living
rose more rapidly than forecast, making the contract wage escalator
clause more expensive than the company had predicted. When the
1958 reopener came around, what Carey had termed "the splendid
settlement" of 1955 appeared considerably tarnished. The IUE demanded SUB (supplemental unemployment benefits); GE proposed

instead that the impending wage inciease be "rearranged" to establish an employee savings program. No agreement ensued, but again key local unions voted not to strike.

Quoted by *Steel* in mid-1959 as saying that he "owed" GE a strike,[9] Carey set out to make 1960 the year in which he would prevail over Boulwarism. Carey increased his power over the locals and the IUE–GE Conference Board (IUE organization of locals within one company), and the union's anti-GE propaganda intensified. The IUE also made an attempt to forge an alliance with other unions representing GE employees.

The main IUE demands were again SUB, union shop, and a substantial wage increase. General Electric offered a detailed retraining program, a 3% increase effective in 1960 with either a 4% increase or a wage reopener effective 18 months later, and various improvements in pensions, insurance, and so on. Many of these items were aimed especially at taking care of the security problems at the older plants where there existed considerable unemployment associated especially with the decline of the utility heavy apparatus business.

After more negotiations, GE made several modifications in its offer, including improvements in the medical insurance, changes in retraining, and a further option to the second wage offer which provided a 3% increase, an eighth holiday, and a four-week vacation after 25 years. The four-week vacation and eighth holiday option were first offered to the IUE as a whole, and later proposed on a local option basis, in order to prevent a new plant–old plant option split within the IUE. No agreement was reached, however, and the strike began on October 2, 1960, despite the fact that several large plants voted not to walk out. (Locals at Schenectady, Pittsfield, Bridgeport, and Syracuse voted against the strike. By the IUE's own count, only 30,000 of the 65,000 members which it represented actually voted to strike.)

Except for a few locals of AFTE and one of IAM, no other union representing GE employees joined the strike. As the strike began, key locals of IAM and UAW signed agreements on terms which were basically identical to those rejected by the IUE. The UE continued to bargain without striking.

Nor was Carey able to rally complete support within the IUE ranks. The Schenectady local, largest in the IUE, which had voted in secret ballot overwhelmingly against a strike, refused at first to join the strike. But under intense pressure, Jandreau authorized a walkout a few days later, only to approve a return to work in less than ten

9 John R. Botzum, "Interview with James B. Carey," *Steel* (July 27, 1959), p. 71.

days. He then bitterly attacked Carey because he "did not have the issues or the organizational strength or the other economic factors that are necessary to lead a successful strike," and for not accepting a company truce proposal.[10]

Strong back-to-work movements soon developed in many areas. Decertification petitions were filed by employees in Bucyrus, Ohio, and Burlington, Vermont, and threatened elsewhere. At Carey's request, GE dropped its retraining proposal. What apparently motivated Carey was the fact that he had bitterly attacked this proposal as misrepresented, whereas Jandreau had praised it as just what Schenectady needed. Carey also refused the company offer to make the wage increase effective the previous week so that Schenectady unionists lost the increase for one week.

GE likewise agreed to arbitrate the cases of individual union members who had been disciplined or discharged for alleged misconduct, including violence, during the strike. Since the contract was not in effect, GE had no contractual obligation to do this. The strike was called off after three weeks.

Although the company literally had the IUE on the ropes, it made no attempt, as John Fanning, member of the NLRB noted, to wring additional concessions from the union "despite the strength of its position."[11] On the contrary, at some risk to itself, it did not require the IUE to obtain new checkoff cards (and thereby risk resignations from an unhappy membership); it included in the contract, locations where decertification petitions had been filed; and it reinstated the agreement in a manner to ensure a contract bar for the IUE against rival union raiding.

The IUE, after suffering what *The New York Times* termed "the worst setback any union has received in a nationwide strike since World War II,"[12] sought solace by asking the NLRB to find that GE had "refused to bargain in good faith." Although the NLRB had rejected identical IUE complaints in 1954 and 1958, this time the general counsel made the charge his own and won a trial examiner's recommendation that GE had indeed violated the Taft-Hartley Act. How could a company be so indicted *after* concluding three-year agreements with more than 100 unions which guaranteed the union members substantial wage and benefit improvements; *after* having its

[10] *Local 301 News* (October 21, 1960), p. 1; *Schenectady Gazette* (October 17, 1960), p. 1.
[11] In a speech at Providence College, Providence, Rhode Island, December 13, 1960.
[12] A. H. Raskin, "GE's Labor Formula," *New York Times* (October 25, 1960).

plant struck by a union whose president declared he "owed" the company a strike before a single issue was on the bargaining table; and *after* having confirmed and supported the status of the striking union following the strike's collapse? This decision has implications for management far beyond the outcome of this case, which will undoubtedly be litigated through the courts during the next few years.

TRIAL EXAMINER'S REPORT

The charge of the IUE, as supported by the trial examiner, is basically that the company's communications program was aimed at undermining the union, because the basic role of communications is to persuade employees to induce union officials to accept company bargaining proposals "in derogation of the status of the union as a bargaining agent, and in order to undermine the union." Here is what the trial examiner found:

That GE came to the bargaining table with an "inference" of a fixed position and mind, if not a detailed offer, already worked out long in advance.

That the company's whole conduct at the bargaining table was a pretext merely to justify its communications activities, which were in effect a way of individual bargaining with individual employees.

That the company further tried to undermine the union by bargaining with local unions, and by urging union members, who were being asked by their unions to authorize strikes, to seek secret ballot votes.

That company concessions at the bargaining table were minimal and dictated by nonbargaining or ulterior motives.

That the company's willingness to conclude the strike without forcing punitive concessions on the IUE was merely further proof that the company refused to bargain in good faith until the union was on its knees, and then it acted as it did merely to prove that it "did right voluntarily."

In addition, the charge contained several specific items alleging refusal to provide information to the union, unlawful discharge of employees at one plant, and refusal to bargain over specific issues.

Just try to follow the trial examiner's reasoning. He found that:

GE was not seeking to get rid of the IUE as a bargaining agent.

GE was willing and even anxious to sign a new agreement at all times.

GE did not engage in individual bargaining as such.

GE's conduct at the bargaining table was not unlawful.

GE's communications to its employees constituted legally protected activity.

But to combine all these legalities created an illegality!

This is the position the trial examiner left himself in when he stated that GE's communications forced the company to freeze its position at the bargaining table, and "to shift the scene of the bargaining to the plants." In other words, "communication necessarily leads [GE] to support that position at the bargaining table, that [it] can't possibly change now under any circumstances, because . . . to change now would weaken . . . this communications effort that [it is] directing at the employees."[13]

Concessions and Bargaining

To construct his theory of the illegality resulting from a series of legal acts, the trial examiner first sought to show that GE arbitrarily "froze" its stance into an "inflexible" position. This ran counter to the fact that GE first put a substantial offer on the bargaining table, and then proposed numerous changes thereof after the initial offer was made.[14] The trial examiner ignored the fact that the offer was, in itself, a significant bargaining concession, and then maintained that the flexibility demonstrated by proposed modifications of the offer was really "inflexibility" because any change "was motivated by GE's gauge of employee sentiment at the plants and not by the desires of the bargaining agent," or by "employee sentiment and the request of unions other than the IUE." As to the concessions made "after the IUE had been forced to capitulate," they were admittedly "several" but "insignificant," or made by the company then because the company could do so without being open to a charge that it "had been forced to yield by reason of a strike or threat of a strike."[15]

In actual fact, the changes made in the original offer (particularly in regard to the holiday-vacation option, the insurance program, and the retraining program) were made in response to specific bargaining suggestions by top IUE negotiators as the record showed and as the chairman of the IUE–GE Conference Board testified in the NLRB hearings.[16] Moreover, if GE had not made final concessions to end

13 *Trial Examiner's Report* (see footnote 1), pp. 10, 103.
14 General Electric, by actual count, made 23 changes in its initial offer after the offer was first made to the IUE on August 30, 1962; see General Electric's *Brief (Respondents Brief for Trial Examiner*, Part I, pp. 68–72), for a listing thereof.
15 NLRB Case No. 2-CA—7581 *et al., Trial Examiner's Report* (1963), pp. 37–38, 51–53, 92.
16 See the testimony of John Callahan, second only to Carey on the union negotiating committee, *Transcript*, pp. 2401, 2404. See also the remarks of Leo Jandreau, president of IUE's largest local, and a member of the negotiating committee, in *Negotiating Minutes*, September 1, 1960, p. 29; September 7, 1960, p. 40; and remarks of union committeemen and benefits consultant in *Negotiating Minutes*, September 1, 1960, p. 19; September 26, 1960, pp. 22–23; September 29, 1960, pp. 9–12.

the strike, would the trial examiner have concluded that such "intransigeance" was not also an indication of a refusal to bargain in good faith? "Lack of concessions" was the skeleton on which the trial examiner hung his whole theory. Instead of weighing each action taken by GE and then determining whether GE bargaining policy or the individual action was unlawful, the examiner appears to have decided rather quickly that the alleged "firm offer" stand was unlawful, and to have extended the same decision to other company actions—communications, uniform application of policy, and so on—which, taken by themselves, could not be stretched into an unlawful construction. This is a departure from usual NLRB practice and appears to run counter to recent NLRB decisions,[17] as well as to a 1953 case in which the courts overturned a similar theory constructed by the same trial examiner and accepted by the NLRB.[18] But it appears to have been adopted here as a means of attacking GE communications which are specifically protected under the Taft-Hartley Act.

The trial examiner's reasoning in this case points up the need to protect collective bargaining from the steady encroachments of the NLRB, and to return the NLRB to its originally conceived role, that of determining, peacefully, representation disputes and proscribing discrimination relating thereto. Congress moved in this direction in 1947, by providing in Section 8(d) of the Taft-Hartley Act that the obligation to bargain "does not compel either party to agree to a proposal or require the invoking of a concession," but as many commentators have noted, the NLRB still uses the absence of a concession as evidence for a finding of "bad faith."[19]

As a result, many scholars of the law are convinced that the best way to safeguard free collective bargaining is to delete the refusal to bargain Sections 8a(5) and 8b(3) entirely from the law, and to confine the activities of the NLRB entirely, as expressed by Professor William Gomberg, a veteran of 20 years in the labor movement, to:

"1. The promulgation of rules and procedures for holding representation elections.

"2. Formulating adequate remedies for those workers who are the vic-

---

17 Cf. *Matter of Philip Carey Mfg. Co.*, 140 NLRB #90 (1963); *Matter of Bethlehem Steel Company* (Shipbuilding Division), 133 NLRB 1400 (1962); and Brief of NLRB before Second Court of Appeals in *Bethlehem* case.

18 *Texas Foundries* v. *National Labor Relations Board*, 211 F. 2d, 291 (1954).

19 For a discussion of the NLRB's intrusion into the collective bargaining process, see Herbert R. Northrup and Gordon F. Bloom, *Government and Labor* (Homewood, Illinois: Richard D. Irwin, Inc., 1963), pp. 111–25.

tims of discriminatory discharge or layoff prompted either by union or employer."[20]

Professor George W. Taylor, whose views on collective bargaining are excerpted at great length in the *General Counsel's Brief* in this case, has long believed that Sections 8a(5) and 8b(3) have no place in the Taft-Hartley Act, unless possibly applied only to the initial contract bargaining between the parties.[21]

If such reform is not accomplished, the NLRB will continue to be used as, in Gomberg's words, "a whipping boy for the frustration of a party to the bargain who refuses to face the consequences of overplaying his hand and then goes running to papa government."[22]

Right to Communicate

Having found that GE took a "fixed position," the trial examiner then argued (p. 96) that GE's communications were part of the illegal pattern because their "very massiveness showed that GE was trying to undermine the union by dealing with the union through the employees instead of the employees through the union." Moreover, in order to protect its communications, GE had to maintain its fixed position and, therefore, it further acted "in bad faith."

Noteworthy are the limits which such an oblique attack would place on the right to communicate—a right that presumably is protected by the First Amendment to the Constitution, and that Congress further sought to protect in Section 8(c) of the Taft-Hartley Act:

"The expression of any views, argument, or opinion, or the dissemination thereof, whether in written, printed, graphics, or visual form, shall not constitute or be evidence of an unfair labor practice under any of the provisions of this Act, if such expression contains no threat of reprisal or force or promise of benefit."

Under this doctrine the union would be free to communicate at will—but the company's views would be stifled. The trial examiner concluded that this was a minor factor because the IUE could not afford to communicate like GE—however, he refused to accept a company exhibit which showed that an average employee represented

---

[20] "Government Participation in Union Representation and Collective Bargaining," *Labor Law Journal,* XIII (November 1962), pp. 946–47.
[21] Taylor's views have been expressed personally to me. See *The Public Interest in Collective Bargaining* (New York: Committee for Economic Development, 1961), pp. 81–82; Taylor was on the independent study group which made the CED study.
[22] Gomberg, *op. cit.,* p. 944. The fact that Carey has announced that he will file another NLRB charge if GE bargains as it usually does illustrates Gomberg's point.

by the IUE received two IUE communications to every three of GE. Yet he himself, as the *Trial Examiner's Report* shows (p. 23, note 20), stated that IUE publications were "but a small fraction of the tremendous volume of literature GE put out at the same plants"—a statement not based on anything in evidence or set forth in the record.

The trial examiner also found that GE communications urging employees to seek a democratic vote on whether or not to strike were unfair and unwarranted interferences in union affairs, despite the importance of the outcome to the company. He stated (p. 97) that GE interjected "itself into an area, recognized by law to be exclusively one for internal union regulation, and of no legitimate employer concern." In support of his position, he cited the case of the *Wooster Division of Borg-Warner Corp.*[23] Here, however, the courts merely held that the company could not *insist* on a democratic vote. GE did not insist; it asked employees to seek a democratic vote and made no contract demand in regard to this suggestion.

In general, then, the trial examiner accepted the position of the general counsel, that is, "that there are limits to communications by an employer with its employees, particularly immediately prior to and during the course of collective bargaining negotiations."[24] But this is, of course, precisely the time the employer most needs to communicate; also it is when communications should be of most value to employees, and when the absence of employer communications gives the union maximum unrestricted access to union goals, whether they are in the union members' best interests or not. In a very real sense, therefore, what is at stake in the GE case is not only the right of a company to communicate; it is also the right of employees to evaluate the views of *both* management and union officials before making decisions which affect not only their livelihoods but also those of many others in the community.

Inherent also in the idea that the employer should not communicate is the view that employees are not sufficiently intelligent or educated to understand the issues, and therefore the union officials must do their thinking for them. As the general counsel stated, ". . . you are giving the employees all of these arguments which they may or may not be in a position to evaluate, but in any event *it is the union's job to do the evaluating.*"[25]

23 13 NLRB 1288, affd., 356 U.S. 342 (1958).
24 *General Counsel's Brief*, p. 261; *Trial Examiner's Report, op. cit.*, pp. 85–104.
25 *General Counsel's Brief, op. cit.*, p. 9907; see also *General Counsel's Reply Brief*, pp. 13–14, and *Trial Examiner's Report, op. cit.*, pp. 93–95.

The other findings and recommendations of the trial examiner follow from his conclusion that GE's communications were at the heart of his novel bad faith doctrine. Thus, these communications were evidence that GE favored local IUE unions at the expense of the national union, and that it did not accord the IUE proper status as the representative of the largest group of employees. The last is a concept which would apparently have GE employees treated better if they are represented by the IUE than if represented by another union, or if unrepresented. The fact that this would leave GE open to "whipsawing" or even a charge by another union that GE was unfairly discriminating against the IUE's members was brushed aside in the *Trial Examiner's Report* (p. 91) as "procedural difficulties."

Proposed Order

On the basis of the trial examiner's findings, the strike, which the trial examiner himself conceded (p. 17, note 15) that Carey said he "owed" GE long before anything was on the bargaining table, would be converted into an unfair labor practice strike caused by the company. GE would then be required to reinstate with back pay any of the 20 strikers who were replaced in the Augusta, Georgia, plant and who had not since been returned to work. Also, it would have to post notices stating that it would not refuse to bargain nationally with the IUE and would not "interfere with, restrain, or coerce employees in the exercise of their right to self-organization and collective bargaining through representatives of their own choosing."

This, on its face, is a standard, perfunctory NLRB order. However, since the novel refusal-to-bargain theory developed by the trial examiner is based almost wholly on GE communications, it follows that the aim of this offer is to force GE to abandon its communications. For the only way in which this order can be enforced, in the light of the trial examiner's findings, is to forbid GE to communicate, "particularly immediately prior to and during the course of collective bargaining negotiations." Meanwhile, the IUE and Carey are apparently free to communicate at will and as truculently as they desire.

EVALUATIONS AND APPLICATIONS

Apart from the question of NLRB doctrine, how should Boulwarism be considered as a management policy of employee relations and in what manner is it applicable to other companies? Let us look into this question.

Cynicism?

In an article widely and often quoted by IUE publications, the late Professor Benjamin M. Selekman termed General Electric's labor policy "an outstanding example of cynicism."[26] He based his evidence on the claim that Boulwarism "denies workers adequate and competent representation . . . that it deprives a human institution of the opportunity to grow in maturity and responsibility."

Selekman believed that unions would continue to grow in size, power, and respectability, a fact which is not clearly demonstrated by developments since 1958. He also thought that the way to industrial peace and social gain was to permit unions a strong voice in what many believe to be managerial prerogatives.

Basically, however, Selekman was a victim of his own system. His deep personal convictions about GE's policy stemmed from his belief that the only sound union-management relationships were fully cooperative ones in which the company in effect "built up" the union leadership. GE obviously did not do this. To Selekman, therefore, GE's approach took the wrong road. Instead of questioning the capacity of his theoretical structure to encompass the General Electric approach, Selekman attacked the morality of the approach.

However, even if judgment is to be made on the subjective and tenuous grounds of morality (which is not the point at stake) instead of on the basic economic grounds where the employment relationship belongs, General Electric and Boulware stand up fairly well. Is it morally superior, for example, to make a deal with union leaders rather than to let the rank and file know openly what the issues are and precisely what is on the bargaining table? Is it morally superior to build up the prestige of a union leader by pretending to acquiesce to strike threats or implied threats and to improve for public consumption a contract by an amount which management all the while thought proper instead of putting a complete, or thought to be complete, package on the table right from the start? How many companies really believe as much in democratic unionism as GE, whose entire communications posture is based on the belief that union members will make the right decision if they have the facts? Is GE's position on compulsory union membership less moral than the position of companies which have granted the union shop?

These and other such questions are personal, moral judgments which different men may well answer in different terms, or judge by

---

[26] "Cynicism and Managerial Morality," *Harvard Business Review* (September–October 1958), p. 64.

different criteria. To call one approach "cynical" or "moral" is only to make a subjective pronouncement. Neither the Selekman system nor the General Electric approach, nor any other for that matter, provides *the* "right" or sole answer to the difficult relations tasks of industry.

It is worthy of note, too, that the concern voiced in many quarters about failure of various industrial relations systems to solve questions peacefully, and in the public interest, has not been directed at GE. No long strikes, inconvenience of the public, interruption of defense work, or underpayment of employees has, or can be, charged to Boulwarism.

One-Sided Bargaining?

Professor Albert A. Blum concluded, without citing his evidence, that GE's bargaining was merely the issuances of "ultimatums."[27] The brief discussion here, it is hoped, will assist in demolishing this myth, often propagated by GE's well-intentioned but uninformed well-wishers and potential emulators. The fact that GE's offer is made in a package, instead of piecemeal, has not hindered GE from being at least as responsive to employee desires (as expressed by the unions with which it bargains) as are companies which follow more traditional approaches. Nor, as noted earlier, has GE's approach hindered it from altering offers once made, offering early negotiations, or, as in 1963, setting up pre-negotiation study committees. The fact is that the public image of Boulwarism is a lot "tougher" than is warranted by the careful approach of the high-caliber negotiators who handle General Electric's employee relations.

Application of Boulwarism

The employee relations policy pursued by a company depends on many factors—its products, type of labor, market position, the period of the business cycle, and so on. General Electric's Boulwarism is peculiarly its own. Its diversification and lack of plant interdependence give it strength; its long record of fair dealing has added employee support; and its conscious philosophy of employee relations innovation has added verve.

---

[27] "Collective Bargaining—Ritual or Reality?" *Harvard Business Review* (November–December 1961), p. 68. Professor Blum also blamed the 156-day Westinghouse strike of 1955 on the union's frustration with Boulwarism. Again his evidence for this remarkable statement was not presented.

The employer who would emulate General Electric would be well advised to study the record carefully. Is he prepared to make an investment in the face of a direct union challenge when the program is in its infancy? Does he have the resources, financial and mental, to stand up to a union challenge, and then possibly be hauled before the NLRB in order to provide the union with a political scapegoat? Is he willing to make the investment in communications, in talent, and otherwise be willing to provide the "tempting dish" to go with the strong words?

Such an employer contemplating a GE policy might well study GE communications in Utica, New York, where the IAM is the bargaining agent; or at Evendale, Ohio, where both UAW and IAM have bargaining rights; or at Lexington, Kentucky, where the IBEW represents employees. This is, of course, if James B. Carey's IUE does not represent his employees. For Carey is *sui generis*. For all his shortcomings, he is an artful communicator who never loses an opportunity to attack GE or to push his own point of view. Much of the volume of GE communications and a good deal of their strident tone are aimed at redressing the balance caused by Carey's almost continual bombardment.

At the non-IUE locations, which bargain on a local basis, the observer can study effective communications involving a more normal relationship. This is an area in which the average company can learn much from General Electric. The *right* of employees to know is exceeded only by their *need* to know, if our system is to survive. Management has a real need to communicate, and employees are generally receptive. How the communications are handled depends on the size of the company, the nature of its management, the management's ability to communicate by various alternative means, and a host of other factors. But, above all, communications must be truthful and continuous, if they are to be successful in maintaining credibility and an audience.

Another principle which General Electric has made clear is the need to put the same kind of effort in employee relations which a company puts in its other functions. The personnel or industrial relations department and function must be given the same status as other key functional areas. Employee relations is a full-time, year-round job requiring constant training, effort, research, and capability. The company which believes that employee problems will solve themselves or that labor negotiations can be ignored, except around contract reopening time, will find itself on the defensive and unable to handle problems. There is an employee relations aspect to all business decision-making which must be met, and which can be ignored only at the peril of the company's profit and success.

Nor can the employee relations aspects of business decision-making be accomplished merely by "building up" or supporting a few union officials. The recent rash of rank-and-file rejection of agreements reached with national union negotiators—such as occurred in the Boeing and Goodyear negotiations this year [1963]—illustrates the danger of such an approach. Employees have an interest and want a voice in their terms and conditions of employment.

CONCLUSION

Inherent in the Boulware approach is the program of having the company take the lead in the bargaining negotiations in laying a package on the table that becomes the basis for final settlement. This effectively puts the offensive in the company's hands. It gives the company something to sell in its communications. But, to be successful, the package must be carefully researched, artfully timed, and responsive to employee needs. Furthermore, union demands must be fully discussed and explained. Moreover, if conditions change, as in 1954, the company must have the courage to offer a new package; and it is obvious that adjustments, rearrangements, and, where appropriate, improvements in the package must be bargained.

Finally, those who would emulate the Boulware approach should realize that it was born out of the needs of a particular company with a long history of "doing right" in employee relations, that it has been developed, refined, and practiced by a highly qualified staff for a period of 16 years, and that it has had complete backing from the company's top executives. One does not arrive at GE's position overnight, or without investment. But the principles of communication, careful research, marketing, and an employee relations emphasis in all decision making, are all valid contributions to employee relations if they are understood and administered with due regard to company environment, capacity, and potential by a qualified staff with full top-management backing.

[In a decision released on December 16, 1964, the National Labor Relations Board, by a majority vote, adopted the trial examiner's ruling as well as his suggested remedy, which included an order to the General Electric Company to stop refusing to bargain in good faith with the union, to furnish certain cost data sought by the union, and to offer reinstatment to 18 employees who were replaced at one plant during the 1960 strike. The Board's decision has been appealed to a Federal district court.

On part of the decision the Board was unanimous, and on other parts one or two of the five Board members dissented. All five members agreed that General Electric violated the Taft-Hartley Act (a) by failing during the contract negotiations in 1960 to furnish certain information requested by the union and (b) by attempting to deal separately with local unions on matters that are properly the subject of national negotiations with the IUE, thus attempting to bypass the national bargaining representative.

With two members dissenting, the Board found that GE violated the Act by presenting its personal accident insurance proposal to the union on a "take-it-or-leave-it" basis.

One member dissented and another expressed some reservations on the finding that GE's overall approach to and conduct of negotiations amounted to a refusal to bargain in good faith. This overall approach and conduct included entering into negotiations "with a take-it-or-leave-it attitude," mounting an elaborate campaign of communications (by leaflets, recordings run in the plant, plant newspapers, phone calls, radio messages, personal letters, and other means) which appealed directly to union members over the heads of union officials and allegedly was "for the purpose of disparaging and discrediting the union in the eyes of its employee constituents." The majority said that "the employer's statutory obligation is to deal with the employees through the union, and not the union through the employees" and that the company "regards itself as a sort of administrative body which has the unilateral responsibility for determining wages and working conditions for employees, and it regards the union's role as merely that of a kind of adviser for an interested group—the employees." The company "consciously placed itself in a position where it could not give unfettered consideration to the merits of any proposals the union might offer." Such conduct, the Board majority said, "devitalizes negotiations and collective bargaining and robs them of their commonly accepted meaning."

This decision with respect to bad-faith bargaining raises the basic issue of the extent to which the Federal Government should be involved in regulating the methods and techniques of collective bargaining and judging whether and when employers and unions have or have not been bargaining in good faith. *Ed.*]

Management Paternalism and
Collective Bargaining

ALBERT A. BLUM

The image of a business operation as made up of one big family with the executives (not the owners—those nameless stockholders) as the composite parent and the workers as the children has had difficulty in completely disappearing from the American scene. True, the rather naive paternalism of the nineteenth century store merchant is no longer with us.[1]

"The store must be open from 6:00 A.M. to 9:00 P.M. the year round.

"Store must be swept; counters, base shelves and showcases dusted; lamps trimmed, filled, and chimneys cleaned; pens made; doors and windows opened; a pail of water, also a bucket of coal brought in before breakfast (if there is time to do so) and attend to customers who call.

"Store must not be opened on the Sabbath unless necessary, and then for only a few minutes.

"The employee who is in the habit of smoking Spanish cigars, being shaved at the barber's, going to dances and other places of amusement will surely give his employer reasons to be suspicious of his integrity and honesty.

"Each employee must not pay less than $5.00 per year to the church and must attend Sunday School regularly.

"Men employees are given one evening a week for courting, and two if they go to prayer meeting.

Taken from Personnel Administration, *XXVI (January–February 1963), pp. 37–41. Reprinted with the permission of the author and the publisher. Albert A. Blum is Associate Professor in the Social Science Department and assistant to the Director of the School of Labor and Industrial Relations at Michigan State University. He has worked as a labor relations writer for the National Industrial Conference Board.*

[1] Cited in George G. Kirstein, *Stores and Unions* (New York: Fairchild Publications, 1950), p. 5.

"After 14 hours of work in the store, the leisure hours should be spent mostly in reading."

True, the pious and self-righteous feelings of a Judge Baer are not common today among industrial relations executives.[2]

"The rights and interests of the laboring men will be protected and cared for—not by the labor agitators but by the Christian men to whom God in His infinite wisdom has given control of the property interests of this country."

But does this mean that paternalism is dead in American industry? Is it not still a common feeling among some executives that management and workers are a part of one big family, all working toward common goals, with papa (management) knowing what is best for the boys and girls (the workers) and therefore providing it for them? If he does not, the villain (the union) on the corner will lead the children down the unhappy path towards juvenile delinquency. Even if the manager does not view a union as a gang, he often still feels that they strike a discordant note in the happy home. Once there, unrest develops. A peer group outside the home becomes more important to the children than the parents; the father's powers are challenged; the child begins to think his goals are not synonymous with those of the parents (he may even want his allowance raised); and, perhaps worst of all, he wants to have his voice heard in how the home should be run. Collective bargaining thus takes the place of unilateral decision-making.

An example of this trend is described by Professor Chris Argyris of Yale. "Corporations," reports the industrial sociologist, "require employees, especially at the lower levels, to be dependent upon others and submissive to them." A sociologist of the family could have written the same sentence with only a few changes. And Argyris describes what happened to one firm that had the philosophy of " 'taking care of the workers' and protecting them from stresses, strains, and pressures." This company had to make some cuts in labor costs. The executives did not know how to institute the changes and became aggressive; the employees had not learned how to accept them, and, instead joined a militant union. Both groups because of paternalism, had not grown up.[3]

Thus, although it may be true that overt statements by management in which a paternalistic philosophy is expressed may be rare, I

[2] Cited in Joseph G. Rayback, *A History of American Labor* (New York: The Macmillan Company, 1959), p. 211.
[3] Chris Argyris, "A New Era in Personnel Relations," *Dun's Review and Modern Industry* (June 1962).

would suggest that it is behind a good many of the personnel practices of management. In particular, I would suggest that behind the view that company executives should by themselves develop personnel policies and in back of the concept of industrial relations that has been called Boulwarism there plays a persistent theme of paternalism.

PATERNALISM IN PERSONNEL POLICIES

Let us first look at the philosophy behind personnel policies. One of the leading spokesmen of personnel policies, S. Avery Raube, Director of the Division of Personnel Administration of the National Industrial Conference Board, states that they are "expression of the company beliefs. They stem from and express the company's creed, its philosophy, its intent. And when carefully formulated and courageously administered, they provide the base for management by principle as contrasted with management by expediency." He and his associate, Geneva Seybold, offer seven criteria for personnel policies:[4]

(1) "A policy is a statement of a company's intent or goal, based on philosophy or belief, that serves as a guide to individual action; (2) Policies are in writing; (3) Policies are stated in broad terms; (4) Policies are inviolate, insofar as this is within the power of management; (5) Policy formulation requires an unusually high level of thinking and contemplation; (6) Policies are approved by the highest authority in the organization; and (7) Policies are long-range, long-term."

Those firms that develop personnel policies are often quite conscious of the needs of their employees and want to satisfy them. But note steps 4 and 5. Who develops these policies which all personnel in a company are to follow: top management. Are the workers or their representatives to be called in to discuss these rules that are to be inviolate and will have so great an impact on their lives? No—only the top executives who believe they know what is best for the employees and for the company. If these are to be inviolate, and if the workers protest (for example, through their union) then under the philosophy, management should hold firm and fight to the bitter end.

Take, for example, the issue of a union shop. A firm's top management may believe, and so state in its personnel policies, that it

---

4 "Statements of Personnel Policy," *Studies in Personnel Policy, No. 169,* National Industrial Conference Board, New York.

does not believe its workers should have a union shop. But if the workers do so desire, and the firm still insists, the only alternative is futile collective bargaining and a bitter strike. This, in and of itself, may not be bad but the company executives frequently delude themselves into believing that the workers really do not want this union shop, or something else that the executives think is not good for them (particularly after they have gone through the trouble and expense of deciding what is good for them) and that it is only the foreign union who is pushing for this or that demand. This frequent delusion lasts despite the length of time and often the feeling with which the workers hit the bricks.[5]

While studying the personnel policies of one firm, I had one such experience. Its executives were sincerely convinced that the international union with which it had to deal was forcing a pattern of excessive fringe benefits on it. The firm consequently launched an expensive public relations program among its workers, attacking the supplements-to-wages package. When I reported that the workers did not appear to have been convinced by the advertisements and literature since the union held out and eventually won the package pattern, management argued that its workers actually had agreed with the company's policies, but that the union had forced the settlement on employees. The executives were sure they knew what their workers had wanted (one can, of course, wonder if management had been so positive why it had spent so much money on a public relations program), but they never explained by what process they had become that sure that they, not the union, knew their workers' wishes. My only evidence that the workers supported the union was objective— namely, they had stayed out on strike until the fringes were won. The evidence offered by management was subjective—as a good parent is often aware what his child wants (or is it what the parent feels he ought to want) or needs?

Personnel policy formulation consequently strikes me as often being a modern and sophisticated form of paternalism. An equally sophisticated and modern form is Boulwarism. Whether General Electric in fact does or does not practice what has been called Boulwarism need not detain us here. What is important is the philosophy of industrial relations that has been named after the former vice

<hr />

[5] For a further discussion of personnel policies, see James J. Bambrick, "Guidelines for Developing Workable Personnel Policies," *Personnel* (September–October 1961), pp. 69–76; and the author's "Personnel Policy and the Worker," *IUD Digest* (Winter 1961), pp. 120–128.

president of the largest firm in the electrical industry, Lemuel Boulware. Those personnel administrators who believe in Boulwarism have, as I have written elsewhere, had this dream.[6]

We are Lemuel Boulware, they dream, and we can bypass the union. We will enter union negotiations with an offer—one which we have arrived at after careful study. We will not really bargain with the union, for, like Boulware, we know that ours is the *best* offer that the company can make. If the union representatives disagree, it is because they are uninformed, unrealistic, or just rabble rousers. We the managers know truth; and if the union will not accept our proposals, the workers can go out on strike. In the interim the company will try to convince the workers that management, not the union, is correct.

I would suggest that the effect of going into collective bargaining with such an attitude is that it implies that management knows what is good for the workers. It does not matter whether these followers of Boulwarism do, in fact, make good offers. My concern is that the workers or their representatives have no real say about the proposed agreement, the terms of which have already been decided upon by management.

PATERNALISM BY UNION LEADERS, TOO

Now let me make the following point quite clear. I am under no illusion concerning unions. Many union leaders do act as if they know the desires of their members without ever having tried to find out what they are, and then relate these wishes to the realities of the industry with which they deal. Many of them practice their own form of paternalism that I find abhorrent.[7] Many of them often do not express the wishes of their members. But, and this is a most important *but,* the goal of unions *is to express this view.* Is this the same goal of managers who want to develop personnel policies or to practice Boulwarism? It is not. Their goals should be to help produce worthwhile items or services that can be sold at a profit. These are not the same as the unions' aims (if for no other reason, the items and services sold differ) although they may often mesh. If we believe they are the same, then, it would follow logically that executives could run for office in the union and give it funds (which is illegal)

---

[6] "Collective Bargaining, Ritual or Reality?" *Harvard Business Review* (November–December 1961), p. 68.

[7] See, for example, Edwin C. Pendleton, *Reversal of Roles—The Case of Paternalism in Hawaiian Labor-Management Relations,* University of Hawaii Industrial Relations Center (1962).

and that we can practice codetermination with union officials on the firm's executive board. It is doubtful that either suggestion would be happily received by management, or for that matter, by unions.

To conclude, the goals of labor and management, though often the same, are also often quite different. For one to speak for the other is a form of modern paternalism in which one side takes on the role of parent and the other of child. What I would suggest is that industrial relations ought to be considered as a relationship between representatives of two groups of mature people who differ because they are the mouthpieces of persons having somewhat different goals. An acceptance of this concept may not lead to industrial peace, but it may help both sides grow up.

The Case for Decentralized
Collective Bargaining

GEORGE W. BROOKS

It is assumed by many that unions influence the structure of collective bargaining. While this may be true, all the evidence I have
found suggests a reverse relationship. So I shall turn my attention to
the ways in which the structure of bargaining molds and influences
unions.

The basic terms need brief definition. The term "structure of collective bargaining" may have various meanings. In general, I understand it to mean the way in which bargaining is practiced: who takes
part, where the decisions are made, what plants and employees are
covered, and so on. The structure necessarily rests upon the bargaining unit and upon the organization of the industry. The bargaining
unit has become increasingly subject to governmental regulations,
in the form of decisions of the National Labor Relations Board. But
the unit, in turn, depends also on the way industry is organized and
operates. That organization depends partly upon the extent of the
market for the goods or services involved. These are basic, underlying
conditions that impose a fundamental character on the structure of
collective bargaining and on union organization and structure. The

*This article under the title, "Unions and the Structure of Collective Bargaining," is
reprinted from Arnold R. Weber (ed.),* The Structure of Collective Bargaining:
Problems and Perspectives *(New York: The Free Press of Glencoe, 1961), pp. 123–
40. Reprinted with the permission of The Free Press of Glencoe. Copyright © 1961
by The Graduate School of Business, The University of Chicago. George W. Brooks
is a professor at the New York State School of Industrial and Labor Relations. When
this article was written he had for many years been Director of the Research and
Education Department of the International Brotherhood of Pulp, Sulphite, and Paper
Mill Workers,* AFL–CIO.

survival of any union depends largely upon its capacity to adapt itself to these conditions.

Let me illustrate briefly with reference to the International Association of Machinists. When the IAM is bargaining for construction trade mechanics, the IAM is itself organized to operate in a local market industry, with a high degree of local autonomy and the other characteristics of local market bargaining. But when the IAM is bargaining for employees in a large aircraft plant, the structure of both the union and the bargaining are quite different. The same patterns of difference are found in all those long-established AFL unions that operate in part as craft unions in local-market industries and in part as industrial unions in national-market industries.

I believe that the single most important characteristic of collective bargaining structure is the location of decision-making authority. It is my thesis that over the past twenty years, decision-making in manufacturing industries has been largely transferred from the members of the union and the local union leadership to the national leadership of the union. This effect upon the unions has a correlative movement in management itself—in the growing centralization of decisions about labor-management relations, which are moving away from the plant manager and his supervisory employees and toward the industrial relations specialists, particularly those at the central offices of the large corporations.

The dangers arising from these developments are twofold. The first is the withering of the local union and the fading of vitality and energy within the union movement. The second is the risk that the centralized structure will, under pressures of various kinds, ultimately collapse and require authoritarian governmental action on a large scale.

I have never presented an argument with less hope of success. My position is certain to be repugnant to the only people who will hear it, the professional, full-time practitioners in the field of industrial relations—industrial relations and personnel officers, union leaders, and teachers who are part-time arbitrators.

I take it for granted that it is not necessary to argue the *desirability* of leaving in local hands the maximum amount of self-determination —at least, the maximum amount consistent with other established objectives. I recognize that to state it in this way is to beg the question. But it needs to be restated that there is no basis for opposition to local self-determination *as such*. Many people, within the union movement and outside, express some regret about the decline of local decision-making. On the other hand many of the paid experts who work in industry and with unions reveal a genuine belief in their own superior capacity to make the decisions for employees. Unfortunately many people confuse technical skill and competence with the capacity to adjust the myriad differences and conflicts among people who work together and to arrive at rules and agreements that have the advantage, at least, of common consent.

There is general agreement that bigness and complexity in modern industry have created strong drives toward the centralization of authority in management. Union response (cause and effect are, of course, not clear) has been to centralize union operations and restrict the area of decision-making available to local unions. This in turn has resulted in a substantial shift of authority and power to a relatively small group in the union and in a consequent decay in the vitality and significance of local union activity.

I do not think there are many people, in theory at least, who welcome the decline of local decision-making; but neither are there very many, in or out of the unions, who feel that it is worth trying to do very much about. The prevailing view is that since we are not prepared to give up any part of the material abundance that depends upon the bigness and complexity of modern industry, we will have to accept, however reluctantly, the steady centralization of decision-making both in the union and in the collective bargaining process itself.

It is my view that this fatalism is itself our principal problem. I do not believe that the decline of local unions is due wholly, or even mainly, to inexorable economic and social forces, but rather to two other things: first, to the more or less deliberate adoption of a degree of centralism in industrial relations that is *not* necessary to the survival of modern industry or collective bargaining; second, to a failure to seize the opportunities to maximize local self-determination that are available within the existing collective bargaining structure. In short, I believe that to a large extent we *can* have our cake and eat it too, and my subsequent discussion is concerned with the steps that might usefully be taken in that direction.

In its simplest terms, I would favor plant-centered unionism. I would like to see the maximum amount of collective bargaining— both negotiations and grievances—handled and decided by local management and local union leadership on a face-to-face basis. With numerous qualifications for particular industries, particular unions, and particular localities, it seems to me that this is the goal most worth pursuing, and that it is a much more concrete and realizable goal than "democracy" or "participation."

ELIMINATING COMPETITION FROM LABOR RELATIONS

The first major step toward this goal would require a large injection of the competitive spirit into industrial relations. This requires first that we demolish the widespread uncritical belief in the value of uniformity and conformity in collective bargaining.

It must be acknowledged that uniformity and pattern bargaining have *some* value. A large proportion of collective bargaining agreements are settled each year on the basis of what somebody else has done. This contributes to industrial peace, in the simplest sense of the term. It may reduce the number of times that established labor-management relationships will be put to the test of a strike or lockout. It is also true that the enlargement of the bargaining unit has made contributions in the same direction. Local disagreements, many of which might have resulted in interruptions of work, have been submerged in the larger settlement; generally speaking, workers who receive increases in their income through collective bargaining accept the general settlement as the best that could be gotten, even if their peculiar grievances went unattended.

This framework is not friendly to the competitive spirit, and it is therefore not surprising to find that more and more industrial relations executives appear to have accepted the time-honored union aim to "take wages out of competition." The preseason meeting of industrial relations and personnel executives has become commonplace, and union after union has testified that it is becoming more and more difficult to bargain settlements that differ even in a small degree from the bargain that has been made with "the competition." The sense of unity among employers grows apace.

Recently, a remarkable strike occurred in Washington, D.C. involving the seven principal food chains. Six of the chains, including Safeway and A&P, were party to multicompany agreements with both the Retail Clerks and the Meat Cutters. But the Meat Cutters had a separate agreement with the Giant Food Stores, a relatively new and aggressive chain centered in the metropolitan Washington area. The strike that was finally called against the six chains did not involve Giant directly, because the Giant contract terminated at a later date and involved a different local. Giant therefore had the right to operate, but decided to close its stores anyway. It announced publicly that its reason for doing so was, according to the *Washington Post,* that "a strike against one was a strike against all." Mr. Damzansky, attorney-negotiator for the companies, said that the reason for closing Giant was "to preserve the integrity of the bargaining unit," which had a somewhat peculiar sound in view of the fact that this was the first year the chains had negotiated together and that Giant was not directly involved. He was also reported to have said on another occasion that "an injury to one is an injury to all." What is he doing with this kind of union talk?

Surely it would be consistent with everything we believe about the American free enterprise tradition for Giant to have treated the strike as a happy windfall and to have taken advantage of the situation to sell enormous quantities of goods at unreduced prices. Since the seven chains sell about 75 percent of all the meat and groceries sold in the Washington metropolitan area, this would seem to those of us who are still innocent like a major opportunity to pick up a little business —some of it permanently—from those competitors who had been less fortunate or less skillful in their industrial relations.

Another example of the same thing is the pooling of strike risks by the airline companies. It seems fairly obvious that some of the airline companies have been more successful in their labor relations than others and thus have avoided costly interruptions of service. But they apparently felt that they should not take competitive advantage of this particular superiority. They therefore worked out an arrangement whereby the airlines that operate while others are on strike turn over some of their gain (not illegitimate gain, certainly!) to their less skillful competitors. For the purposes of industrial relations, they refuse to regard each other as competitors. Why?

Actions of this kind ought to make us very uneasy. Most companies expect to reap the full benefit of any special advantage they may have over their competitors—an aggressive sales organization, greater productive efficiency, a superior research department, and so on. But this is not the case in industrial relations. All that an industrial relations or personnel officer is expected to do, apparently, is to find out what everybody else is doing. The elaboration of this process into a profession is one of the more remarkable accomplishments of the twentieth century.

A great deal can be accomplished in industrial relations through the competitive process. Traditionally when a company finds itself at a disadvantage because of some major inefficiency in its organization, it corrects the problem or perishes. If it is a labor problem in an organized plant, the company presses the union to go along with the necessary changes.

Let me cite only one illustration. From its outset the Southern pulp and paper industry, including newsprint, operated on a seven-day basis. In eastern Canada and northern New England, the major newsprint producing area of the continent, the six-day week predominated and for the most part still does—the Catholic religious scruple being somewhat less flexible than the Methodist and Baptist. A few years ago the Great Northern Paper Company, the principal producer of newsprint in the northeastern United States, decided that shutting down the plant every week was too great a competitive burden. It therefore presented to the union a proposal for continuous operation, and set the stage for what was perhaps the most interesting and fruitful negotiations in fifty years of continuous bargaining history. In order to get union acceptance of continuous operation, the company made very substantial adjustments in rates for skilled workers in order to conform with higher rates in the South, raised the base rate substantially, and made other significant concessions. However, the greatest gain that year was made by the company, a fact that is generally known and causes no dissatisfaction. Most union members will show a vital interest in the economic success of the company in which they work, if they can perceive it.

But there appears to be a growing reluctance to deal with industrial relations problems through the competititve process. The work rules discussion in the 1959 steel negotiations was completely baffling to outsiders. The companies asserted that the work rules were costing them large sums annually. It was also agreed that the severity of the problem varies greatly from company to company and even from plant to plant. Some companies reportedly did not have the problem at all. But in that case, why does not each company meet the union for the discussion of its own specific problems, relying upon the self-interest of the members to provide the necessary will for the union to settle? The answer to this apparently simple question seems to lie in the passionate commitment of the steel companies and the steel union to industry-wide bargaining.

It is a concomitant of his dislike for competition that in established collective bargaining relationships the industrial relations executive would like to see his union negotiator equally free from the pressures of competition. The best labor leader, he usually feels, is the labor leader who can "stand up to the membership" or who is "not swayed too much by local pressures" or who "can see the industry's point of view." He wants "responsibility" in his union leader, which may be defined as the antonym of "responsiveness." This kind of "responsibility" can obviously be achieved only by a man who is relatively free from competitive pressures. Stability in industrial relations depends upon stability within the union leadership. In the case of a union leader this means protection from rank-and-file revolt and from rival union attacks. The risk of these unpleasant events can be greatly reduced by the development of large-scale bargaining units, long-term contracts, tight NLRB restrictions on rival union petitions, and numerous other institutions that management is able and willing to influence.

The union leadership naturally welcome this support. They believe in stability, too. The competitive spirit nowadays has little place *within* any union and has dwindling significance in interunion relations. The merger and the no-raid pact have abundantly fulfilled the expectations of their sponsors so far as the elimination of rival unionism is concerned. It is now proposed to enforce "final and binding" arbitration of disputes between affiliates of all kinds. And to close the last frontier of rival unionism, a significant number of unions have subscribed to the Industrial Union Department's Union Code of Organizing Practice, which prohibits, in campaigns to organize new plants, nasty statements about rival affiliates. One affiliate may not say of another that it is a "company union" or that it is "Communistic" or that it makes backdoor agreements or that it charges excessive dues. Note that this is not a prohibition against libel; these things may not be said, whether or not they are believed to be true.

In these and many other ways competition is suppressed by unions, by management, and by both of them together in collective bargaining. The total effect, and cumulatively it is very great, is to limit severely the freedom of choice of employees. If they work under a large multiplant contract, their voice in the collective bargaining process will be slight or absent; even if they work under a single-plant agreement, the effect of pattern bargaining and the removal of the representative of the international union from effective local control are likely to leave them without fruitful recourse. If they become sufficiently dissatisfied, they may attempt to persuade their fellows to withdraw from the union, but they will find that most of the unions they regard as "legitimate" are committed to refrain from "raiding," no matter how flagrant the failure of representation may seem to be. Even if there were no other factors in the situation, this decline in the competitive spirit would seriously limit local self-determination. Self-determination means discussion and decision on reasonable alternatives; to prevent the presentation of alternatives is to starve self-determination.

MARKET-WIDE BARGAINING

The second development limiting local self-determination should perhaps be regarded only as the most successful model of the first. This is the steady growth of market-wide bargaining. I use this term instead of "industry-wide bargaining" because it applies no less to the Washington food chains than to the steel industry. It is, briefly, the inclusion in one collective bargaining negotiation of all the enterprises that can be said to compete effectually with each other. The steel strike [1959] cast a long and ominous shadow over the future of collective bargaining by showing that when collective bargaining is "mature," when it reaches the point where the whole industry is prepared to negotiate with the only significant union in the field and make one national bargain, then the result may not be collective bargaining at all in the sense to which we have become accustomed. When the whole market is involved in a strike, two things happen that alter the fundamental character of collective bargaining. First, the employer is free from economic pressures in their traditional form. Second, the public is so injured in real or fancied ways that the settlement of the strike becomes a political rather than an economic problem.

What we are in for was bluntly stated by Adlai Stevenson in an address before the Institute of Life Insurance in New York on December 9, 1959. Mr. Stevenson suggested that we need a new law that would give greatly expanded powers to the President, including the power to take the dispute entirely out of the hands of the parties, and that would "require in one form or another that production be continued while the dispute was resolved by process of reason rather than by subjecting the economy to grievous injury."

He then added:

It was one thing to expect the public to accept the results of collective bargaining when that result represented the "decentralized decision-making" of a thousand different sets of negotiations. But with the development of industry-wide bargaining, as we have it now, decisions affecting the entire economy are made by a small group of men sitting at a single table, and the public has no alternative to accepting those decisions . . . it will be said that this proposal involves the denial of the rights of labor and management to strike and to shut down the basic industry. It seems to me that this, too, is a legitimate and necessary implication of the decision to resort to industry-wide bargaining. The greater the power, the larger the responsibility. When the public is denied alternative sources of supply, it is entitled to demand that the supply not be shut off.

Chairman Leedom of the National Labor Relations Board has said much the same thing. In the presence of industry-wide bargaining, he believes that collective bargaining must be "supplemented" to avoid work stoppages that create substantial inconvenience or hardship.

I do not see any way to prevent a steady drift of opinion in this direction if market-wide bargaining continues to expand. And even without the threat of compulsory arbitration, market-wide bargaining has other great hazards for the labor movement in terms of the slow strangulation of local initiative. The relationship between multiplant bargaining and local decision-making was set forth with startling clarity in an NLRB decision involving RCA and the International Brotherhood of Electrical Workers.

The IBEW had been bargaining agent under a nine-plant agreement for many years, when the United Electrical, Radio and Machine Workers filed a petition for a single plant of the group. The IBEW argued that the multiplant agreement was a bar to any election in a single plant. The Board ordered an election at the plant, because it found that the agreement covering the nine plants was "a mere framework for local contracts that contained the essentials of working agreements such as wages, seniority provisions, and the like."

At first blush, this may seem like a victory for local self-determination, in the sense that not only was a large amount of discretion retained in the local union, but in addition at least some disgruntled employees had an opportunity to urge a change through the election machinery of the NRLB. But consider the almost certain effect of the decision. On the basis of a reasonable assumption that RCA and the IBEW wished to continue the existing relationship, it will be easy to remedy the defect by simply withdrawing from the locals (using the decision of the Board as the persuader) all significant decision-making authority.

In the pulp and paper industry we have both kinds of bargaining —some relatively large multiplant agreements, in one case covering virtually an entire region, and also a number of single-plant or few-plant bargaining agreements.[1] There seems to be very little difference in the substantive results of the bargaining between the one type of agreement and the other. Other factors, such as geography and profitability, seem to have a much larger influence.

But there is a definite and direct correlation between the size of the bargain—that is, the number and dispersal of the plants covered —and the amount of local initiative and activity. The enlargement of the bargaining unit, particularly as we approach market-wide proportions, *always* reduces the amount of local self-determination.

---

1 [In 1964, the West Coast locals of the Pulp Workers and the Paper Makers, which for three decades had been under a market-wide bargaining system covering the whole region, voted in an NLRB election to abandon those two unions and to become an independent organization. Following this, the first significant strikes occurred in the history of the West Coast branch of the pulp and paper industry. *Ed.*]

Therefore, I think we ought to abandon market-wide bargaining as a union goal. This may seem like a reversal of long-established union policy, and to some extent it is. But I think it is justified and necessiated by the changes that have taken place in the general economic and political situation. During the Lewis period of the CIO the NLRB policy of granting multiplant and in some cases market-wide units was intimately tied up with the fundamental aims of the CIO. It was a defense against both the recalcitrant employer and the craft unions, and the fact that a company had the right to withdraw from a multicompany agreement, while the union did not, was not regarded as a serious matter. In steel, autos, longshoring, West Coast paper, and many other industries, the establishment of exclusive representation on a multiplant basis well served the aims of the industrial unions.

But times have changed, and the acceptance of unionism in some major industries, the merger, the no-raid pact, and parallel developments have reduced the organizational need for these large protected units. Meanwhile, the considerations that I have mentioned urging against industry-wide bargaining become more and more important.

There is, of course, no universal prescription. There are industries in which regional or market-wide bargaining serves to establish a stable *market* even more than a stable collective bargaining relationship. One might be rash to seek the abolition of market-wide bargaining in the needle trades. Even here, however, perhaps we were more dazzled than we should have been by the pioneering successes of the needle trade unions during the twenties, when other unions were doing badly. For it cannot be denied that in the needle trades, as elsewhere, the development of market-wide bargaining and the accompanying centralization of authority have had profound effects upon both the degree and kind of local self-determination.

INCREASING CENTRALIZATION OF DECISIONS

The third development undermining local decision-making is the centralization of collective bargaining negotiations and administration. This is again closely related to the other two. But even assuming that nothing could be done about restoring competition to collective bargaining or giving up market-wide bargaining, there still is in my opinion a great deal of room for the encouragement of local self-determination.

No one could respectably argue that the general wage bargain in major manufacturing corporations can or should be decentralized

In many industries the terms of the bargain must be settled in large multiplant (not necessarily multicompany) contracts, and the patterns thereby established will be applied to numerous other companies.

But having done this much, must we also work out the *details* of the bargain centrally, including each and every adjustment? Is it necessary for these decisions to be systematized into mysterious processes like job analysis, where they can be handled only by "experts"? Why does it seem so impossible to restrict the central collective bargaining negotiations to the essentials—for example, the total amount of money that will be added to payrolls—and leave the details to local choice and decision? I know that what I suggest imposes a larger task upon management, especially local management; but this seems a small price to pay for restoring to local officers and members some voice in their own affairs. It might not be a bad idea to do the same for local management. I recognize that most industrial relations executives, as well as most union leaders, will regard this suggestion with horror, but I think that if we are seriously concerned about preserving some vitality in local unions covered by multiplant agreements, this is exactly what we are going to have to do.

What we mean by local self-determination inevitably means differentiation. It is this that apparently offers the greatest obstacle to making a change. There is a profound reluctance on the part of both union and management leadership to recognize that the employees in Jonesboro might very well want to put their wage increase into a pension plan, while the employees at Smithville might regard such a suggestion with abhorrence. Management in large companies more and more insists upon uniform labor relations policies, as if there were intrinsic virtue in uniformity. But why is "consistency" important for the host of details of personnel management, such as the number of days that an employee must be at work before a holiday in order to qualify for holiday pay? Or what virtue is there in consistency from one plant to another with respect to the treatment of production employees who are promoted to management and wish to retain seniority rights within the production and maintenance group? Yet the Vice-President for Industrial Relations steadily presses for such consistency, always at the cost of depriving the local plant management and supervisory staff of the right to make their own decisions—decisions that might reasonably vary widely from one place to another.

If a large company imposes uniform policies and centralized decisions, the local union representatives at Plant X cannot come to any agreement with the local management because the dispute may involve an issue on which the New York or Chicago industrial relations officer wants to insure uniformity from one part of the country to another. If the problem in Plant X causes sufficient trouble, the end result may be that the international officer will have a telephone conversation with the New York or Chicago industrial relations officer and their decision will bc imposed upon the local people, even though it may not be acceptable either to the foremen in the plant who have to live with the decision or to the local union members. This unwritten step in the grievance procedure has become so important that in many places the steps set forth in the agreement have become mere formalities.

In the handling of certain subjects centralization has become a mania. Pensions, health and welfare plans, and arbitration are examples of this. An illustration: the Owens-Illinois Glass Company has recently become a paper company, by virtue of its merger with National Container Corporation. National had a pension plan covering most of its plants, but it had separate pension plans in at least one other plant. Ever since the merger Owens-Illinois has been pressing the unions vigorously to drop the National Container plan and the others and adopt instead the plan in effect in the glass plants. Why? The Owens-Illinois Glass plan is not superior to the National plan and is distinctly less favorable for higher-paid employees. But the company pursues its objective unrelentingly, as though the only important consideration in the discussions were to have one single plan for the entire corporation.

Because we have no stake in the glass plants, the union resists. But generally speaking the union leadership is as much on the side of centralization as the companies. The leadership of national unions eagerly embraces company-wide or regional "systems" for wage determination, pension administration, health and welfare plans, and even permanent arbitrators. Numerous centralized arrangements of this type have become deeply embedded in the collective bargaining process.

Pensions are widely regarded as the ultimate case for uniformity and central administration. This is argued largely on grounds of the advantage of central administration, particularly in the investment of funds. But this is an argument without merit except to the central administrator. It is perfectly possible to secure the advantages of expert investment counseling and other technical services without removing from local management and local unions the right to decide such questions as whether retirement shall be compulsory, whether past service shall be pensioned at the same rate as future service, whether past service shall be amortized promptly or slowly, and so on.

To some extent this centralization is applauded by the whole intellectual community that lives upon the industrial relations process. Lawyers, economists, actuaries, pension consultants, and many others regularly substitute their judgment and preferences for the judgment and feelings of the parties, thus speeding the process of centralization. The negotiation of pensions and health and welfare plans illustrates the point. Some of the techniques of pensions and group insurance are admittedly technical. To some extent employers have an interest in keeping these subjects technical and mysterious to the average employee, since it is much easier to make decisions favorable to the employers if the employees do not fully understand the issues at stake. But even employers are often mystified by the subject matter, and they turn over to hired experts decisions that in any other context they would never consider making unilaterally. When the union finally catches up with the problem, as it does sooner or later, it does not direct its efforts to removing the mystery; it employs its own experts, and all is lost.

Pension bargaining, like any other bargaining, encompasses a wide range of conflicts, not only between employees and employers. There are also conflicts of interest among the employees—between the older and the younger, for example. The careful disclosure of these conflicts, in such a form that working men can comprehend them adequately in order to express their choices, is not an easy task. The pension consultant too often prefers to make the decisions and then persuade the parties that the decisions are "to their best interests," rather than put himself in the position of a technical expert who elucidates or explains the meaning of terms, so that others can make the decisions.

I have the impression that in the steel industry, negotiations on pensions and health and welfare are conducted primarily by "experts," and that even high officials in the union and companies have little role to play, although they may be present and take some part in discussion. Furthermore, using experts to do the negotiating means that negotiations will be long, drawn-out affairs, dependent upon the availability of the experts.

Consider the ultimate in this development. We shall, on the one hand, have a small group of union leaders, surrounded by a retinue of experts on various subjects. They, and they only, will be masters of the details of the labor agreement—the wage structure, pensions, health and welfare, and numerous other so-called technical matters.

Even with respect to relatively simple matters such as holidays, vacations, or premium pay, the expert will become indispensable to the administrative process because of his familiarity with precedent throughout the company (and other companies!) established by agreement, company policy, or arbitrators' decisions. Even in these simple matters, therefore, the local union leader's role will be extremely limited and probably confined to mere "processing," as it is called. And after they have secured a clutch on the problem, is it ever likely that the experts can be made to let go? It is a poor expert indeed who, having once been consulted, cannot mystify his subject sufficiently to make himself forever indispensable.

On the other hand we shall have a large, faceless and voiceless mass of union members who will be asked only, in return for benefits conferred, to pay their dues and be ready to strike when advised to do so. But if they decide to strike, it will not because they understand the issues or the stakes, but because they have "faith" in the leadership. This is a prime example of what Bertrand Russell calls "priestly power" and is a most dangerous situation. This is not to say that union members ought not to have faith in their leaders, but rather that their faith ought to be firmly based upon an understanding of the course of action the leadership is advocating. Any other kind of relation between leader and member lends itself all too easily to manipulation, so that consent, which is the heart of collective bargaining, is achieved by manipulation instead of by conviction.

Union and management leadership both seem to welcome these developments, and perhaps it would be irrational to expect either group to regret a course of events that so greatly enhances their prestige and authority. A Princeton study of centralization and decentralization indicated that while most companies take a little time out each week to praise decentralization, very few of them actually practice it. Among those who did make some efforts to decentralize, it was least practiced and least desired in the field of industrial relations. Management has elaborate rationalizations about this, resting mainly on the fact that they must deal with "national" unions.

If centralism offered some significant advantages, it would be easier to accept the horrifying consequences in terms of the loss of local initiative and decision-making. But where are the advantages? Has any company-wide system of job evaluation ever produced a wage structure "better" in any sense than is produced by old-fashioned, unscientific higgling and haggling? The job analysis system is likely to be more "uniform" to be sure. But why are we so certain that this is an advantage? Is it not likely, in fact, that the very lack of uniformity, and greater flexibility, are the strongest arguments in favor of plant-by-plant bargaining?

One is obliged to conclude that the reason we have so much centralization is not that there is any significant gain in terms of employee benefits, but only because of the advantages to union and management leadership. The principal advantage is that it insulates the leadership from local pressures. No union or management spokesman can be blamed for seeking the protection of such insulation, but how do they get the tolerance of the rest of the community?

This is not wholly a rhetorical question. Part of the answer is certainly to be found in the fact that almost the whole intellectual community in the field is concerned with the justification of stability and its handmaidens, centralism and expertness. Hardly a murmur can be heard against the growing menace of arbitration, with its formalities, spurious judicial atmosphere, and phony reliance upon precedent. No one appears to be even mildly shocked by the tendency of arbitrators to quote each other, even from other agreements and other industries. In a recent case the arbitrator (a lawyer) noted plaintively that the parties "hadn't cited any cases" and was obviously disappointed when both sides disavowed any intention of doing so.

In the case of management the end sought and largely attained through centralization is a certain freedom from friction in the plant. No one would argue that this is an improper objective for an industrial relations executive to seek. No one can blame him for not wanting to go through rival union elections, changes of local and national officers, and so on. But the rest of us should remind ourselves that these so-called "frictions" are the very heart of useful collective bargaining. They are the devices by which members give voice to their dissatisfactions—dissatisfactions that cannot be suppressed over too long a period of time without serious consequences to industry. They may stay relatively dormant during long periods of "prosperity" and annual wage increases, but even in this kind of situation, not forever.

Initiative and decision-making by local management and unions are not things that we can continue to take for granted. These are not great slumbering forces, ready to spring into action at the moment of necessity. Local leaders must *practice* taking the initiative and making decisions, or they eventually lose the capacity to do so. Our task is not to protect the right to dissent, but to create the opportunities for dissent. During the thirties and early forties the opportunity was present, more or less, for most employees in most plants. In the last fifteen years we have steadily withdrawn the opportunity, through the devices I have mentioned, with a huge assist from the government. It is worth repeating familiar facts to remind ourselves how important, and in many ways unique, are the federal labor relations law and the decisions of the National Labor Relations Board.

EFFECTS OF THE LAW

The structure of collective bargaining, as noted earlier, rests in large part upon the bargaining unit, which may be one plant, a part of a plant, or a number of plants owned by one or more employers. The most significant influence upon bargaining units in American industry during the past two decades has been the body of decisions of the National Labor Relations Board. Too little attention has been given to these decisions and their effects upon collective bargaining and the freedom of employees to choose their collective bargaining representatives. Most bargaining units represent what most union leaders and most management want. But when the Labor Board certifies those units as "appropriate," it affects *all* management and *all* workers who are in roughly the same circumstances.

There are three principles that give the unit rulings overwhelming importance. The first is the rule of exclusive representation—namely, that a union representing workers in a bargaining unit represents *all* the workers, whether or not they are members of the union. The second is the principle of "majority rule," which means that all the employees in a unit are bound by the decision or choice of the majority. Finally, there is the rule of the Board that the electoral unit for purposes of the NLRB election, and the bargaining unit for purposes of negotiations, are the same.

When the Labor Board decided that an established multi-employer bargaining agreement precluded an election for employees of one company or one plant, the Board was saying that it would not permit the employees of that company or plant, who might overwhelmingly prefer to change their bargaining representative, to separate themselves from the larger group. The Board could just as easily have decided that the employees in one plant had a right to change their bargaining representative, although the conduct of bargaining would continue to be done for all the plants at one time, with more than the one union or groups of unions taking part. Instead, the Board chose to favor the incumbent union in the interest of stability of bargaining, and against the interest of a free choice of bargaining representative.

The unit rulings are only part of the mechanism with which the

Labor Board influences the structure of bargaining. In addition there are the growing restrictions imposed by the Board on change of representation, through the contract bar rules that determine when during the life of an existing agreement any rival union petitions may be filed. There is also a growing body of regulations that make it illegal to attack certified units. The net effect of all these restrictions is to strengthen the centralizing tendencies and to reduce the area of employee choice. In addition the pressures toward centralization are reinforced by the new federal law, the Labor Management Reporting and Disclosure Act.

CONCLUSION

One of the silliest notions abroad is that local union officers can somehow make up for their frustrations in collective bargaining by expanding their activities into other fields. Everything in the history of trade unionism cries out against such a notion. A union is only what it is in collective bargaining, and no grafting of extracurricular functions onto the union structure will make very much difference one way or the other. If therefore we seek to do something about restoring initiative and decision-making to local bodies, it is to the structure of collective bargaining that we must turn.

The choice before us is quite clear. We can continue in the direction in which we are now moving: toward a tightly controlled relationship between union, management, and the employees, probably with a good deal of collusion and manipulation through strongly fortified central leaderships, steadily enlarging collective bargaining units, and, inevitably, some form of compulsory arbitration.

Or, we can reconcile ourselves to more "friction" in the plant, more contested elections for union representatives, more face-to-face bargaining by management and local men who are actually engaged in the productive process, fewer experts and the special protection they provide, more time spent in actual discussion of plant problems, and, in the long run, a local leadership that knows how to lead. The latter course will, in my opinion, also produce a more enduring stability.

[The growing significance of Brooks' analysis became apparent in 1964 with local union revolts and rank-and-file dissatisfaction in industries such as autos and steel. For a discussion of the issue from a different viewpoint see A. H. Raskin, "Rumbles from the Rank and File," *The Reporter,* XXXII (January 28, 1965), pp. 27–30. *Ed.*]

Transportation's Labor Difficulties

EDWARD B. SHILS

There are simply too many labor organizations competing with one another in the railroad, airline, and maritime industries. Labor unrest and crippling strikes have forced the public to suffer many inconveniences, while business in general and shippers in particular have been hit hard.

The multiplicity of unions and their day-to-day jurisdictional rivalries have especially hurt carriers. It has prevented them from taking complete advantage of improvements in technology designed to increase customer service and to improve the return on investment to management and the stockholders.

Every airline, railroad, or steamship company executive involved in labor relations with the many fragmented unions in these industries realizes the seriousness of the situation which confronts his company. To be in the transportation business today is almost like being in a "cold" war—or in a "hot" war, as in the case of the New York harbor situation, where 3,000 tugboat operators went on strike in February [1964].

What does the average business executive know of the nation's transportation problems? Does he realize that they affect his business stability as well as the image of American business in foreign lands? Christmas 1963 almost brought the pullman activities of our railroads to a halt when it appeared that there would be a concerted walkout at that time. The same situation was true in the airlines, when it looked as though United Air Lines would stop operating during the holiday period because of a machinists strike.

Taken from Harvard Business Review, XLII *(May–June 1964), pp. 84–98. Only the first half of the article is reprinted here. Reprinted with the permission of the author and the publisher. Edward B. Shils is Associate Professor of Industry in the Wharton School of Finance and Commerce at the University of Pennsylvania.*

The average businessman in America must take a hard look at the problem. He must recognize the inherent danger in the present turmoil and strife glutting our transportation arteries. If he does not, he may awaken some morning to find all company shipments blocked, with no air, rail, maritime, or trucking facilities available. [The trucking industry is not discussed in this article; it is treated in Raskin's article in Part IV.]

Presidential appointments of labor relations experts to special government panels create optimism—but this is always followed by disappointment and requests for funds for additional studies. The business community appears to be confronted by insoluble, almost chaotic, transportation problems. Since companies depend increasingly on communications and transport, they are becoming more and more susceptible to transportation interruptions—to the point that bankruptcies and insolvencies can and do result. Look at our recent record:

In 1961 and 1962 the national maritime strike and the West Coast maritime strike cost the nation three quarters of a billion dollars.[1] In April 1962 the West Coast was nearing a state of economic paralysis, and Hawaii began to fear imminent starvation. Transportation to seaports became jammed, and rail cars en route to warehouses and ports piled up. Secondary effects soon became evident in every other mode of industrial transportation. Millions of tons of United States food consigned to foreign ports began to spoil. In large cities, where the inhabitants depend on shipped-in fruit and vegetables, prices rose as supplies dwindled.

In December 1962 and January 1963, a dock workers strike paralyzed the East and Gulf coasts of the United States. At one point, 14,000 rail cars filled with grain for export elevators were immobilized near the docks in the New York area. The strike of the East Coast longshoremen cost the United States $1 billion as well as contributing to an unfavorable trade balance for January 1963. During this strike, carpet makers ran short of jute. Sugar refineries closed for want of raw materials. Garment factories had to close for lack of required fibers. Exporters throughout the world who shipped goods to the United States in December 1962 found these products piled up on docks or in the holds of ships. Several exporters went bankrupt as did some U.S. distributors of these products.

It is high time that the American businessman realizes that in planning his own business future he cannot ignore the threatening

[1] [The exact loss of Gross National Product from a strike is very difficult to estimate. Ed.]

influence of labor-management problems in the transportation industry on his company's destiny. . . .

This article seeks to help such executives by making clear the extent to which union fractionalization is the cause of transportation's labor crisis. . . .

UNION FRAGMENTATION

Business executives have only to realize the extent to which fractionalization of unions exists to agree that it alone presents a significant barrier to effective collective bargaining. In fact, this may well be the key to the whole problem. Let us begin by getting the facts about its extent.

EXHIBIT I. OPERATING AND NONOPERATING UNIONS INVOLVED
IN RAILROAD LABOR RELATIONS
(*As of June 30, 1962*)

A. *The Operating Brotherhoods* (5)

BLE	Brotherhood of Locomotive Engineers (represents engineers in road and train service)
BLF&E	Brotherhood of Locomotive Firemen and Enginemen (represents firemen and helpers on road and yard service)
ORCB	Order of Railway Conductors (represents conductors and assistant conductors)
BRT	Brotherhood of Railroad Trainmen (represents road, train, baggagemen, brakemen, and yard foremen)
SUNA	Switchmen's Union of North America [not one of the big 4; represents yard conductors (foremen), yard brakemen (helpers), and switchtenders; employees only in yard service]

B. *The Nonoperating Unions* (25)

ARSA	American Railway Supervisors Association
ATDA	American Train Dispatchers Association
BB	International Brotherhood of Boilermakers, Iron Ship Builders, Blacksmiths, Forgers and Helpers
BMW	Brotherhood of Maintenance of Way Employees
BRC	Brotherhood of Railway & Steamship Clerks, Freight Handlers, Express & Station Employees
BRCA	Brotherhood of Railway Carmen of America
BRS	Brotherhood of Railroad Signalmen

EXHIBIT I. (*Cont.*)

BSCP	Brotherhood of Sleeping-Car Porters
DC&RRFWU	Dining Car & Railroad Food Workers Union
HRE	Hotel & Restaurant Employees & Bartenders International Union
IAM	International Association of Machinists
IARE	International Association of Railway Employees
IBEW	International Brotherhood of Electrical Workers
IBFO	International Brotherhood of Firemen and Oilers
LU	Local Union
MMS	International Union of Mine, Mill and Smelter Workers
ORT	The Order of Railroad Telegraphers
RED	Railway Employees Department, AFL-CIO
RYA	Railroad Yardmasters of America
RYNA	Railroad Yardmasters of North America
SA	System Association, Committee or Individual
SMWIA	Sheet Metal Workers International Association
URRWA	Transport Workers Union of America, Railroad Division
UMW	United Mine Workers of America, District 50
UTSE	United Transport Service Employes

C. *Marine Unions in Railroading* (15)

BRC	Brotherhood of Railway & Steamship Clerks, Freight Handlers, Express & Station Employees
GLLO	Great Lakes Licensed Officers' Organization
HRE	Hotel & Restaurant Employees & Bartenders International Union
IBL	International Brotherhood of Longshoremen
ILA	International Longshoremen's Association
IOE	International Union of Operating Engineers
IUP	Inlandboatmen's Union of the Pacific
MEBA	National Marine Engineers Beneficial Association
MMP	International Organization of Masters, Mates and Pilots
NMU	National Maritime Union of America
ORT	The Order of Railroad Telegraphers
RMU	Railroad Marine Union
SIU	Seafarers International Union of North America
TWU	Transport Workers Union of America, Railroad Division
UMW	United Mine Workers of America, District 50

SOURCE: *28th Annual Report of the National Mediation Board* (Washington, Government Printing Office, 1962), pp. 88–96.

In Railroads

EXHIBIT I indicates the scope of craft union representation in the railroad industry. The operating workers are divided into 5 unions known as the operating brotherhoods. With the exception of the Brotherhood of Locomotive Engineers, these unions are unaffiliated with the AFL-CIO and are independent, autonomous organizations.

In addition to these brotherhoods, the exhibit shows 25 other labor organizations which represent nonoperating workers on the railroads. These craft unions are generally affiliated with the AFL-CIO and traditionally represent the same kinds of workers in other industries.

EXHIBIT I also shows the 15 marine unions which represent deck and engine room workers, officers, bridgemen, cooks, waiters, chefs, and the like, on riverboats, tugs, rail ferries, and so on, some of which come under the control of railroads. Only 5 of these craft unions are likewise found in the list of nonoperating employees. The balance are primarily important maritime unions which, when engaged in shipping or longshore activities, come under the jurisdiction of the Taft-Hartley Act.

All in all, railroads must deal with a total of 40 different unions and brotherhoods. It is no surprise to find that the labor relations of the industry are not designed for stability. Let us take just one carrier, the Baltimore and Ohio Railroad Company, and look at its actual bargaining situation:

The Baltimore and Ohio bargains with 17 rail unions (some represent more than one classification of employee) and 5 marine unions. As for rail unions, it negotiates with the BLE (engineers); BLF&E (firemen); BRT (brakemen and baggagemen); ORCB (conductors); BRT (yard foremen); RYA (yard masters); BRC (clerical); BMW (maintenance); ORT (telegraphers); ATDA (dispatchers); IAM (machinists); BB (blacksmiths); SMWIA (sheet metal workers); IBEW (electrical workers); BRCA (coach cleaners); IBFO (powerhouse employees); BRS (signalmen); RED (mechanical foremen); BRT (stewards); and UTSE (cooks and waiters).

The Baltimore and Ohio also bargains with these 5 marine unions: MMP (licensed deck employees and float watchmen, bridgemen, etc.); TWU (licensed and unlicensed enginemen); SIU (unlicensed deck employees); ILA (captains, lighters, and grainboats); and IOE (hoisting engineers).[2]

2 *28th Annual Report of the National Mediation Board* (Washington: Government Printing Office, 1962), pp. 88–96.

In Airlines

As of June 30, 1962, 28 airlines operating in the United States had a total of 286 collective bargaining agreements on file with the National Mediation Board, which administers collective bargaining in airlines under the Railway Labor Act. There were 14 unions involved, representing various crafts and classes and constituting the

EXHIBIT II. CRAFT UNIONS IN THE AIRLINE INDUSTRY
(As of June 30, 1962)

Designation	Airline Labor Union
ALEA	Air Line Employees Association
ALCEA	Air Line Communication Employees Association
ALDA	Air Line Dispatchers Association
ALPA	Air Line Pilots Association, International
ALSSA	Air Line Stewards & Stewardesses Association, International
APA	Allied Pilots Association*
ATDA	Air Transport Dispatchers Association
BRC	Brotherhood of Railway & Steamship Clerks, Freight Handlers, Express & Station Employees
CWA	Communications Workers of America
FEIA	Flight Engineers International Association
IAM	International Association of Machinists
IBT	International Brotherhood of Teamsters, Chauffeurs, Warehousemen & Helpers of America
IGFA	International Guild of Flight Attendants
TWU	Transport Workers Union of America, Airline Division
UAW	International Union, United Automobile, Aircraft, Agricultural Implement Workers of America

* Since July 1963.
SOURCE: *28th Annual Report of the National Mediation Board* (Washington: Government Printing Office, 1962), p. 96.

fragmented picture which makes collective bargaining so difficult in the airline industry. Then, last year, an election at American Airlines resulted in an insurgent pilots' group, the Allied Pilots' Association, taking over from ALPA; so now there are 15 union groups.

EXHIBIT II provides the names and symbols for these volatile union groups. Here, in the number of different unions with which a particular airline must bargain, lies the explanation of why a walkout by a single craft union—even a small one—can close down an entire airline. Consider:

Trans World Airlines, Inc., bargains with ALPA (pilots); FEIA (flight engineers); TWU (navigators); ALDA (dispatchers); ALSSA (stewardesses and pursers); ALEA (radio operators); IAM (mechanics); and IAM (clerks, stock, stores, fleet, and passenger service employees).

Pan American World Airways, Inc. bargains with ALPA (pilots); FEIA (flight engineers); ALDA (dispatchers); TWU (stewardesses and pursers); TWU (mechanics); BRC (clerks, office, stores, fleet, and passenger service); and IBT (stock and stores employees).

These two airlines have many similar international responsibilities, yet their labor situations do differ. Both have ALPA (pilots), FEIA (flight engineers), and ALDA (dispatchers). Trans World Airlines employs navigators (TWU), while Pan American does not. Pan American contracts with TWU for stewardesses and pursers, while Trans World Airlines contracts with ALSSA for the same classes of personnel. Trans World Airlines has a contract with ALEA (radio operators), while Pan American does not. Pan American's passenger service personnel are with BRC, while IAM represents employees with similar duties at Trans World Airlines. Finally, IBT covers stock clerks at Pan American, while IAM covers these employees at Trans World Airlines. Other airlines have similar variations.

In the 1962 fiscal year, 6,630 airline employees were involved in 37 representation disputes under the Railway Labor Act as amended. The previous year, 8,607 airline employees had been involved in 30 disputes. For two years in a row (1961 and 1962) more airline employees were involved in representation disputes than were railroad employees.

All in all, in fiscal 1962, 91 cases were disposed of under the act, of which there were 37 involving representation, 53 mediations, and 1 interpretation. Whereas most of the representation problems centered about stewardesses, mechanics, and dispatchers, the heavy mediation work was with pilots and mechanics. Details are presented in EXHIBIT III.

In Shipping

The labor relations picture in the maritime industry possesses elements which are archaic. Bitter interunion rivalries exist resulting from wounds left by unsuccessful organizing campaigns and jurisdictional disputes of long ago. Furthermore, the personal ambitions of leaders such as Joseph Curran (NMU), Paul Hall (SIU), Harry Bridges (ILWU), and Thomas W. Gleason (ILA) contribute much to conflict and disorganization. The scope of craft union representation

EXHIBIT III. NUMBERS AND TYPES OF CASES DISPOSED
OF IN FISCAL 1962
(By employee craft)

	All types of cases	Repre- senta- tion cases	Media- tion cases	Inter- preta- tion cases
Combined airline	3	3	0	0
Mechanics	22	4	18	0
Radio & teletype operators	1	0	1	0
Clerical, office, stores, fleet & passenger service	10	3	6	1
Stewards, steward- esses, flight pursers	22	18	4	0
Pilots	18	0	18	0
Dispatchers	5	4	1	0
Mechanical foremen	2	2	0	0
Meteorologists	0	0	0	0
Flight engineers	4	1	3	0
Miscellaneous airline	4	2	2	0
Total	91	37	53	1

SOURCE: 28th Annual Report of the National Mediation Board (Washington: Government Printing Office, 1962), p. 81.

is indicated in EXHIBIT IV. Employer groups are also greatly fragmented for economic reasons and tend to further complicate the picture.

Certain craft unions historically have been in ideological conflict with each other. The terms "Communist" and "radical" have not been used with restraint in describing certain maritime leaders and organizations. Of major importance to the two principal chiefs, Curran and Hall, however, is how to divide and control in their respective orbits a declining number of jobs in the maritime industry. It is for this reason that both the SIU and NMU coalitions are in agreement on the importance of organizing the 600-odd American-owned, "foreign flag" vessels now registered principally in Liberia, Panama, and Honduras and employing alien crews, whose wages are about one quarter of those paid on United States flag vessels.

A decision of the United States Supreme Court on February 18, 1963, overruled prior findings of the National Labor Relations Board and denied to American maritime unions the right to organize the crews of foreign flagships merely because the vessels are American-owned or engaged extensively in United States trade. Though the

EXHIBIT IV. UNIONS INVOLVED IN MARITIME LABOR RELATIONS
(*As of June 30, 1963*)

Designation	Maritime Labor Union
AMMSOA	American Merchant Marine Staff Officers Association (purser department on the Atlantic Coast)
ARA	American Radio Association (ship radio officers on the Atlantic, Gulf, and Pacific coasts)
BMO	Brotherhood of Marine Officers (deck and engineering officers on the Atlantic Coast)
ILA	International Longshoremen's Association (dock workers on the Gulf and East coasts and Great Lakes)
ILWU	International Longshoremen's and Warehousemen's Union (dock workers on the West Coast)
MEBA	National Marine Engineers Beneficial Association (engineering officers on the Atlantic, Gulf, and Pacific coasts)
MCS	Marine, Cooks, and Stewards Association (stewards and so forth on the West Coast)
MFOW	Pacific Coast Marine Firemen, Oilers, Watertenders and Wipers Association (represents several departments, including stewards on the West Coast)
MFU	Marine Firemen's Union (West Coast)
MMP	International Organization of Masters, Mates and Pilots (masters and deck officers on the Atlantic, Pacific, and Gulf coasts)
NMU	National Maritime Union of America (unlicensed personnel of the deck, engine, and stewards' departments, primarily on the Atlantic and Gulf coasts)
ROU	Radio Officers Union of the Commercial Telegraphers Union (ship radio officers on the Atlantic, Gulf, and Pacific coasts)
SIU	Seafarers International Union of North America (unlicensed personnel of the deck, engine, and stewards' departments on the Atlantic, Gulf, and Pacific coasts)
SOA	Staff Officers' Association of America (pursers on the Atlantic and Gulf coasts)
SUP	Seamen's Union of the Pacific (unlicensed personnel in the deck, engine, and stewards' departments on the West Coast—affiliate of SIU)
UMD	United Marine Division of the National Maritime Union (tugboat crews primarily on the East Coast)

SOURCE: Files and records and special releases of the U.S. Maritime Administration.

Supreme Court decision was a blow to the cause of the seafaring unions, NMU President Joseph Curran indicated that his union would keep on with attempts to organize these vessels. In all probability, there will be a step-up in the turbulence of organizing efforts without the "calm" induced these past three years by National Labor Relations Board decisions "in storage," awaiting a review by the federal courts.

The problem of divisiveness is nearly as bad in the employer bargaining groups. This stems from the fact that only part (about one third) of the United States flag fleet is subsidized. (During the 1961 strike, 46% of the seamen involved were on subsidized vessels. A great many additional unsubsidized vessels, however, were to be found in the Pacific fleet with contracts which did not expire until 1962.) The unsubsidized employers claim that the subsidized employers give in easily to union demands and then pass on "most of the increases to the government." These charges were made in both the 1961 and the 1962 maritime strikes.

EXHIBIT V indicates how difficult it must be for the U.S. Department of Labor to approach labor-management relations in the maritime industry on an integrated basis. Six employer bargaining groups had to be consulted on three different coasts during the national 1961 maritime strike. Each group had a somewhat different economic self-interest, depending on subsidization, type of cargo, geography, and so on.

EXHIBIT V. AN ESTIMATE OF LICENSED AND UNLICENSED PERSONNEL BY EMPLOYER BARGAINING GROUP IN THE JUNE 1961 NATIONAL MARITIME STRIKE

Employer group	On subsidized ships	On un-subsidized ships	Total
Pacific Maritime Association (mostly dry cargo)	4,000	4,600	8,600
Harrison group (dry cargo and tankers, Gulf and some Atlantic)	1,000	7,000	8,000
American Merchant Marine Institute (dry cargo, East and Gulf)	14,950	3,000	17,950
Tanker Labor Service Committee	—	7,100	7,100
Collier Owners Association	—	900	900
Aluminum Corporation of America	—	600	600
Total personnel	19,950	23,200	43,150

SOURCE: Data derived from NMU files and information received from U.S. Department of Labor officials.

For example, in the 1961 strike the Pacific Maritime Association complicated the entire series of settlements by giving in on the foreign flag issue to the MEBA (engineers). The fact that this employers' group had no foreign flag vessels under its ownership or control influenced the decision. This served to "whipsaw" the other employer groups.

The difficulty in the 1961 settlements was the competition of Hall (SIU) and Curran (NMU) for the MMP (masters and deck officers). First, the MMP was in the SIU, but just before the strike it associated itself with the NMU. This created ill-will and some internal dissension. When the American Merchant Marine Institute and the Tanker Labor Service Committee reached understandings with the NMU, the employers did not want to sign until similar agreements were reached with the ARA and the MMP.

At last the ARA did reach agreement with the two employer groups. The Institute came to an agreement with MMP as well, but the Tanker Labor Service Committee could not reach agreement with it. In the case of the Tankers, the MMP wanted a special type of agreement waiving general increases in favor of fringes and changes in the working rules. One of these was a demand for no less than four mates on a tanker. This one request would have cost more than the entire NMU package. To reach a settlement, the Harrison group of employers finally settled with the ARA and the MEBA by following the NMU pattern.

EXHIBIT VI shows the comparative strength of the NMU vessels over the SIU during the 1961 strike. Note that Curran's major strength was on the scheduled United States flag liners, which are subsidized (80% or more of the operating differential subsidy received from the government goes toward achieving "parity" in wage costs with foreign operators). Hall's principal strength was on the unsubsidized vessels (tankers and tramps) flying the United States flag. These two union leaders made every effort in the 1961 national strike and in the 1962 West Coast strike to reach a competitive advantage over the other. Such rivalry makes it difficult to gain a national accord that is directed to the welfare of the United States and to the public.

Consider also the multiplicity of craft unions with which a shipping operator must bargain. In many cases these craft unions, all antagonistic to each other, are on board the same vessel. In EXHIBIT VII, three shipping companies—United States Lines Company, Veritas Steamship Company, and Union Sulphur and Oil Company—have been selected for illustrative purposes to denote the extent of fragmentation in each crew.

EXHIBIT VI. AN ESTIMATE OF LICENSED AND UNLICENSED PERSONNEL ON SHIPS IN THE JUNE 1961 NATIONAL MARITIME STRIKE

Union	On subsidized ships	On un- subsidized ships	Total
Seafarers International Union	3,900	8,900	12,800
National Maritime Union of America	12,100	8,000	20,100
International Organization of Masters, Mates & Pilots	1,600	2,700	4,300
National Marine Engineers Beneficial Association	2,000	3,000	5,000
Radio Officers Union of the Commercial Telegraphers Union	100	300	400
American Radio Association	250	300	550
Total	19,950	23,200	43,150

SOURCE: Data derived from NMU files and information received from U.S. Department of Labor officials.

EXHIBIT VII. BARGAINING PATTERNS IN THREE SHIPPING COMPANIES

(*As of June 30, 1962*)

Union	Type of crewmen

A. *United States Lines Company*

NMU	Unlicensed crew members
SOA	Staff officers
MMP	Deck officers
MEBA	Engineers
ROU	Radio officers

B. *Veritas Steamship Company*

SIU	Unlicensed crew members
MMP	Deck officers
MEBA	Engineers
ROU	Radio officers

C. *Union Sulphur and Oil Company*

SUP	Unlicensed crew members (affiliate of SIU)
MFOW	Unlicensed engineers
MCS	Stewards
MMP	Deck officers
ARA	Radio officers
MEBA	Licensed engineers

SOURCE: Data secured from U.S. Maritime Administration, Washington, D.C.

Deepening Morass

Thus we can see that the nation's serious state of industrial unrest is due in considerable part to the heavily fractionalized nature of the bargaining units in railroads, airlines, and shipping. In railroads and airlines, the influence of the Railway Labor Act contributes to the continued emphasis on "craft" and "class." Workers in the railroad industry were among the earliest organizers of strong craft unions; and, as might have been expected, this history led to an acceptance of the craft principle in the Railway Labor Act of 1926. Labor organization in the airlines came into being in the 1930's, and in 1936 the Railway Labor Act of 1926 was further amended to include airlines. . . .

As we have just seen, fragmentation in the maritime industry stemmed from historical conflict of the AFL and the CIO seafarer unions. Labor's divisiveness is further accentuated because bargaining takes place in widely separated areas and under much different conditions, and because contracts do not expire at the same time. . . .

All three industries are attempting to put into effect the fruits of a changing technology, but they find themselves blocked by the power tactics of the many craft unions who want to preserve their autonomous status. . . .

. . . Since 1947 the Taft-Hartley emergency disputes provisions have been employed 22 times in all industries covered by the act. Included were 8 cases involving the maritime industry, either merchant marine or longshoring. In only 6 of the 22 disputes where a board of inquiry was appointed and a Taft-Hartley injunction issued did a strike commence, recur, or run its full course, after all the procedures of the act were exhausted. This happened 6 times in the maritime industry; in other words, industry accounted for *all* of these unsuccessful outcomes—a record hard to beat.

PART VIII

PUBLIC POLICY
AND
LABOR RELATIONS LAW

INTRODUCTION

In a democracy the ideal is the maximum amount of personal freedom and self-government consistent with the protection of individual rights and the public interest. Companies and unions, however, constitute aggregations of economic power whose use (as in strikes and boycotts) can result in injury to persons, other firms, other unions, or the public at large. Governmental rules and action may, therefore, be necessary to protect citizens and businesses from the abuse of private power by managements and unions.

Yet, too much government control of unions, managements, and collective bargaining may stifle initiative and rob collective bargaining of its elements of flexibility and self-government. Too much government intervention in strikes may replace the process of mutual accommodation with reliance on governmental decisions. Thus, in the labor relations area, government needs to maintain a delicate balance among conflicting rights and should avoid encouraging either side to depend on the government for solving its problems.

The first two articles in this section deal with the art of government intervention in major labor disputes. Shultz ("Strikes: The Private Stake and the Public Interest") and Raskin ("The Government's Role When Bargaining Breaks Down") differ somewhat in their views on the subject. Both agree that there has been too much intervention by high Federal officials in recent years and that it is time for a new approach and, perhaps, some new measures. However, they disagree on the extent to which the public interest has been injured or imperiled in recent strikes, such as the East Coast longshore strike late in 1962, and the extent to which the public interest needs safeguarding by new measures. Raskin favors a clearer definition of Federal and municipal powers for dealing with strikes, and calls for strong action in some cases. He would give Boards of Inquiry in national emergency disputes the power to make recommendations and would even subject particular issues to compulsory arbitration following an eighty-day injunction, if that proved necessary in order to shield the public interest. Shultz, on the other hand, would not have the government become involved in so-called emergency disputes, except for mediation and perhaps very limited government operation of facilities to the extent absolutely necessary for reasons of health and safety or defense. Otherwise, he favors maximum freedom for strikes to perform their function of achieving self-settlement.

A strong plea for less government in industrial relations and more reliance on the slower but more effective method of working for a consensus is made by Dunlop ("Consensus and National Labor Policy"). In his opinion, industrial relations at the national level suffer from excessive legislation, litigation, formal awards, and public pronouncements. Industrial relations problems have become increasingly technical, he holds, and it is a mistake to regulate the details by highly partisan political decisions. Thus, the legislative framework and details are influenced, not by practitioners who confront problems in the work place, but by politicians without collective bargaining experience and under pressures from the top confederations (the AFL–CIO and the National Association of Manufacturers and the Chamber of Commerce). The management confederations especially take rigid positions, which do not reflect the consensus of industrial relations policies of American management. At that level, the atmosphere of politics and an air of unreality tend to prevail and hamper the development of a workable consensus by the parties directly concerned.

The point that Dunlop makes about partisan politics and excessive legalism is well illustrated by the two articles commenting on the policies of the National Labor Relations Board after the shift from Eisenhower to Kennedy-appointee domination. Lefkoe ("The NLRB's New, Rough Line") points out that the "Kennedy Board" has overruled precedents established by the "Eisenhower Board." It has handed down decisions (subject to court appeal) that add restrictions to employers' freedom of speech in connection with employee elections and that rule against a firm's closing a plant or dropping part of its business where the management's aim is considered to be avoidance of the requirement of "good faith" bargaining with a certified union. Apparently, Lefkoe favors the elimination of the Board's jurisdiction over complaints of unfair labor practice by providing direct action in the Federal courts in those cases—an invitation to encumber collective bargaining with further inexpert rule-making by large numbers of Federal courts.

On the basis of some of the same facts, Grodin ("The Kennedy Labor Board") comes to somewhat different conclusions. He points out that the "Eisenhower Board" readily reversed some of the positions established by the "Truman Board," and that the courts did not sustain certain views of the majority of the Eisenhower Board. The Kennedy Board has generally given more protection to the organization of labor, has been more prone to rule that employer and union communications aimed at influencing election results contravened the law, and has been more ready to accept picketing of unorganized businesses as aimed at advertising the existence of substandard labor conditions and, therefore, outside the law's restrictions on recognitional and organizational picketing.

The differences between the Eisenhower and Kennedy Boards may seem rather narrow and technical. However, they reflect differences in economic and industrial relations philosophy. The Eisenhower Board was more concerned with protecting management's rights and freedoms. The Kennedy Board has placed greater faith in collective bargaining and has been more willing to adapt its rulings to the changing realities of labor-management relationships. Neither, however, seems to have been very intent on restricting the role of government in industrial relations matters. As Dunlop explains, government regulation and litigation expand as attempts are made to plug unforeseen loopholes or to correct the unwanted consequences of judicial decisions.

Strikes: The Private Stake
and the Public Interest

GEORGE P. SHULTZ

It has been widely observed that Congressional approval of compulsory arbitration in the railroad industry marks a breakdown of private bargaining, and may well lead to compulsory arbitration for a wide range of vital industries.

This is a tragic half-truth.

The misunderstanding of what has taken place on the railroads and in other cases of intense government intervention may well lead to a drastic and, I believe, undesirable shift toward compulsion in our system of industrial relations. But this will not reflect a breakdown of private bargaining.

There has been no real private bargaining on the railroads for decades. What has failed is government-dominated bargaining. Ironically, when this much-government system finally failed completely, the answer was more government—in the form of compulsory arbitration—rather than less. And the irony is the more striking since free and more-nearly-private bargaining is, by and large, working well.

My purpose here is to convince you that a free and private system of industrial relations is far superior to a government-dominated one; and that this alternative is really available, despite the many and serious steps taken in the other direction during the past few years. To do so, I know, I must face up directly to the questions raised for the community by strikes, especially strikes involving large numbers of people or strategically placed workers. I must present a way of dealing with major labor disputes that you judge to be a workable,

This article appeared as Selected Papers No. 8 of the Chicago Graduate School of Business, 1963. Reprinted with the permission of the publisher. George P. Shultz is Dean of the Graduate School of Business at the University of Chicago.

practical way. No doubt government has important responsibilities which will tax its capacities in this area, but its role must not be the dominant one toward which it now seems headed.

My theme will be developed through discussion of the following points: (1) Some general comments about labor policy and current labor relations problems. (2) Examination of the role of conflict in labor relations and of objectives, private and public, other than simply labor peace. (3) Analysis of why the present course of developments is wrong. (4) Advocacy of a different course—one more consistent, I think, with the values of free institutions operating in a market economy.

GENERAL COMMENTS

Possible approaches to labor policy can be classified broadly into two types. The first, and most tempting to many people, is direct and solution-oriented. Its apparent simplicity is attractive. If we do not like strikes, outlaw them. If we don't like featherbedding, prohibit it. If we think wage rates are too low, raise them by action of the government; or if they are rising too fast, establish guides to control the rise. The emphasis here is always on meeting a pressing problem with a direct solution—or at least what may appear to be a solution. This approach can be summarized by the old saying, "There ought to be a law."

The other approach looks at the structure and processes from which solutions emerge, rather than at any individual result. When results in general are unsatisfactory, it asks what kind of process is producing them; and it leads to suggestions for changing the process, thus affecting results—but indirectly. I find it hard, by way of a process-oriented example, to accept an arrangement that involves the payment of unemployment compensation to strikers, as in New York or on the railroads.

On the whole, an approach that emphasizes processes seems to me preferable to one that goes directly to a particular result. This in part is a practical judgment about what is most likely to work. But it also is a statement of ideological preference—a preference for arrangements that allow freedom of action for companies, unions, and collective bargaining arrangements, and is in tune with the objectives of a society with at least major emphasis on individual and organizational liberty.

My second general comment is made in the interests of realism. In the field of labor relations policy, as in many others, there is hardly ever a course of action that is all gain. We are constantly engaged in weighing and balancing costs *versus* gains. We are always saying, "Yes, it would be nice to have a little more of this; but if we have more of this, we must be reconciled to a little less of something else which is also desirable, or which someone else may want."

By way of example: Both labor and management people could doubtless agree that you can find some uneconomic work practices, in some industries, if you look hard enough. I think it is very unlikely, however, if you want to get rid of some of these practices, that it will be done unless companies—and in some cases the public—are willing to pay the price in terms of a little conflict. There may be a gain; but there is also a cost. If you are not willing to put up with any conflict, you are not going to get many of these gains.

Or, in a completely different type of example: The National Labor Relations Board has recently been struggling with the problem of how long a contract should bar an election to determine the representation wishes of workers. I believe they have now settled on three years; but at any rate, it is quite apparent that the longer the period you allow, the more you are putting emphasis on the goal of stability in labor-management relations. You are saying, "Let a situation settle down a bit; let people work together and give them time to see what they can do."

At the same time, you are paying a price. The price is that there will be some workers who are dissatisfied with the labor-management relationship, and they are not able to change it. You are telling them they can't do it. In that sense you are paying a price in terms of some loss of individual liberties.

So the point here is that we frustrate and delude ourselves in this field if we seek something that is perfect in the sense of being a costless solution. There are no costless solutions.

Now finally, insofar as general comments are concerned, it seems clear that some very sharp changes are taking place in the kinds of jobs which must be performed to put out today's and tomorrow's production. We do not, in my view anyway, have any crisis on our hands; indeed, I get a little tired of all the talk about a crisis in collective bargaining. But there is a transformation under way, and it produces great stress for many bargainers.

THE ROLE OF CONFLICT

It has been said that "job-security" now outweighs "wages" in importance as an issue for collective bargaining. Certainly, all the well-publicized recent disputes—railroad, newspaper, longshore— revolve around the issue of jobs; or perhaps more accurately, around the jobs that used to be there but may now be on the way out. So like it or not, we will have to struggle in labor relations with all the stresses and strains that inevitably accompany important changes in the structure of jobs. No one should be surprised if these stresses occasionally break into the open.

So much emphasis has been placed in recent years on the public interest in labor peace that other important goals in labor relations— goals in which there is also a private stake and a public interest— have been almost totally obscured. Let us take a look at the role of conflict in attaining these goals. In doing so, we need not get in the position of advocating strikes, of condoning the purely destructive conflict that you see occasionally, or of denigrating in any way the importance of knowing how to resolve differences without strikes. Much has been learned in this area over the past three decades and many interesting and novel experiments are now under way. All these are to be applauded and encouraged, but not to the point where we become Pollyannaish about labor relationships.

First of all, we must acknowledge that conflict, of which the strike is but one example, is a widely used method for producing generally desirable results for our society. We use it in the academic com- munity, where much is made of the idea that a clash of views, a back- and-forth exchange, will yield illumination on the subject at hand. We have organized our economy on the basis of freedom to enter new businesses, to innovate, to engage in competition for markets. Let there be many companies in the field and let them fight with each other so that the consumer gets better products and lower prices. Some people get hurt by these processes; . . . they can on occasion be rough. But, by and large, they are productive.

By the same token, in the field of industrial relations the possibility of challenge and response, from a base of some power on both sides, can be constructive. It provides an opportunity for people who have different backgrounds and orientations to bring out and represent their interests forcefully. Such representation can be productive, but it cannot take place if we do not allow for the possibility of a clash in views and the likelihood of an occasional explosion.

Second, we must all realize,whether as members of "the public" or in our private capacities, that we have a tremendous stake and a great interest in the vitality of private parties and private processes. If you have a management that is moribund and is not doing anything, or if you have a union that is lazy and is not representing its workers

464 PUBLIC POLICY AND LABOR RELATIONS LAW

adequately, you really do not have a healthy situation at all. We want, instead, companies and unions who are alert, energetic, driving—who are analyzing their interests and representing them vigorously. So we have a great stake, as the public, in having private parties who are vital in this sense. And if, because of our abhorrence of strikes, we take action that in effect takes the play away from private parties, we will sap their vitality, and wind up with a peaceful, stagnant inefficiency on both sides.

A good case in point is the railroads, where the government-dominated system of collective bargaining, at least until very recently, has fairly well sapped the vitality of the processes involved and has left the situation much worse than it otherwise might be. When it takes six years to settle a simple grievance, you surely have a bad situation.

LET PARTIES BE RESPONSIBLE

Third, in this effort to suggest that the public has a stake in strikes other than only to get them settled, I offer you the great importance of having private parties *be* responsible, *feel* responsible and *take responsibility* for the results of their efforts. Whatever settlement is reached—good, bad, or indifferent—somehow it must be their own settlement. It is the settlement of the people who have worked it out, not somebody else's doing. "If we're responsible for it, we've got to make it work; it's our baby." It seems to me that the public has a great interest in seeing this kind of attitude develop.

Finally, we must recognize that some strikes are simply part of the price we pay for free collective bargaining. If you tell people they are not allowed to strike or, in the case of management, take a strike, then they are simply not free to pursue their interests as they see those interests. It is just one of the costs that goes with the gain of having a free system. This is a very simple—sometimes a very harsh—but surely a most important point.

Now, I am not saying that the public does not have a stake in damping conflict as much as possible; in making it orderly; in seeing it channeled to some degree; in doing all kinds of things to pound a little sense into the people concerned and make them see just what is coming before they get involved in overt conflict.

But on the other hand, there are these other private stakes and public interests which are important but which hardly ever are mentioned. They get completely obscured by this great emphasis upon peace and tranquility on the labor scene.

Of course, the greater the costs of labor-management conflict, the less happy we are to pay them. This point, then, is of great importance: The price we are paying for free bargaining in this country is an exceedingly small one, and we should not be reluctant to pay it.

We are all familiar with the statistics; by this time perhaps we all tend to dismiss them. But you just cannot get away from the fact that the volume of strike activity, of overt conflict, is very, very small. It runs in the neighborhood of less than one-fifth of one per cent of man days worked lost through strikes each year. It is down at that low level right along. So we are not dealing these days with a situation in which somehow conflict has gotten all out of bounds and is all around us. It isn't. It may seem to be, but on a statistical basis, it isn't.

Moreover, I will assert that there are very seldom times when strikes pose genuine threats to the health or safety of the community, or even to the operation of the economy. The resiliency of the economy, its ability to adapt and insulate itself from these things, is really very remarkable and should not be underrated. According to elaborate reports of people who have studied big strikes, the supposed dire effects from the impact of a strike are very hard to find.

THE LONGSHORE CASE

Now, perhaps you will say that the recent longshore strike, in which a Taft-Hartley injunction was used, is a case against me. That may be, but I think it is worth noting that the President sought and got an injunction against such a strike on the grounds that, if the strike were permitted to occur, it would create a national emergency. But after the injunction expired, a strike did run for over one month and what did people talk about? All I read about in the *Wall Street Journal* was the bananas; you are not going to get bananas, they are doubling in price. My, oh my, should we throw away our freedoms for a hand of bananas? Just for fun, one morning in New York after the strike had been on some weeks, I ordered bananas with my shredded wheat to see if they would come. The waiter didn't even give me an argument, he brought the bananas. Or *a* banana, I should say. Maybe he only had one. This is not to deny the genuine economic hardship and public inconvenience that can be caused by a prolonged strike on the docks or in some other industries. But the allegations of hardship need the closest scrutiny, and the true costs must be balanced against the price of intervention.

It should be further noted that, in the face of this crisis, the Senator Morse Board was appointed and was able to bring about a settlement under threat of Congressional involvement. The wage package was certainly steep and the settlement made little contribution to resolution of the basic issues of efficiency of operation and job security. I would rather have seen the parties fight it out.

So, in summary, my point is that the public has vital interests in allowing people freedom to strike—or take a strike—if they want to, and if these interests are disregarded, the system of industrial relations is going to change very drastically.

Furthermore, in taking this position, at least in this day and age, we are really not taking such a terrible risk, because the volume and the impact of strikes are not nearly so great as alleged. Most goods and services turn out to have fairly close substitutes, which, indeed, is one reason for prompt settlement of most disputes. Or, alternatively, inventories may provide a considerable hedge against the impact of a strike. There are problems, of course, but they are far overrated, and the health and safety aspects are usually not present.

A DANGEROUS COURSE

The present course of national policy has seemed, at least until very recently, to be: Intervene early; intervene with preconceptions of what the right answer is; and intervene frequently, over a wide scale, with high officials. And now the picture is further complicated by the fact that Congress, albeit reluctantly, is in the act.

I do not think that is a considered policy, but is just what has happened. That is in a sense the effective policy we have, and it has been born out of all sorts of frustrations, out of all sorts of problems arising from the structure and issues of collective bargaining.

Let us make the following points about this course:

This is an instance, to use the economists' terminology, where supply creates its own demand. As my colleague, Robert Livernash, put it: "If the President hangs out his shingle, he'll get all the business." People will come to a high official if he is willing to have them. So what we see as a result is a lot of pressure for intervention, from whichever party thinks it has more to gain. And there is also a lot of pressure for high-level attention. Who can be satisfied with just a plain old Federal mediator? Who's he? Or even the director of the Federal Mediation and Conciliation Service. It is getting to the point where you are not a big boy any more unless you have the Secretary of Labor involved. One thing leads to another in a cumulative process that is difficult to reverse.

Furthermore, when these high-level procedures are used with great frequency (and no doubt you have to use them sometimes), they completely lose their impact. Somebody who is very high up should be saved. He should not be running around, doing this, that, and the other thing with all kinds of disputes that everybody and his brother get into. Regardless of how much and how genuinely he wants to be helpful, he just cannot, because it depreciates the currency, so to speak.

POTENTIAL FOR FAILURE

This process also demands solutions, as in the case of the Morse Board. If you are going to take the intervention route, then you have to provide the answer. If parties feel they are not getting what they want through bargaining, they are certainly going to find out what the government's answer is and try to use that leverage as much as possible. We are all familiar with this process. And it can ruin private bargaining because it forces each party to hold back any concessions that might normally be made. Anything you concede will be held against you in the next higher round of discussions. This is precisely what has happened on the railroads, where the one thing everyone agrees on is that there has been little real bargaining until recently.

Finally, this course has in it a very, very great potential for failure. We are going to run into situations, right along the line, where all these procedures are going to be indulged in, and where one party or the other—management in some cases, union in others—will say: "With all due respect to you, Mr. President, or to your Board, I just don't agree with you, and I'm standing on my position."

When that happens—and it already has on at least one occasion—the gauntlet is down. That is a terrible situation for the President to be in. As President Kennedy said, in effect, in a television interview last Spring, commenting on the steel price conflict, "Well, what could I do, after all this had happened, there I was and I had been defied? I had to pull out all the stops."

The question one needs to ask is: Was it wise to get in that position in the first place? I ask this with respect not only to steel but to a whole range of cases. The potential for failure not only is great, it is absolutely certain that the high authority is going to be defied by the strong-minded groups we have in this country. And the results of failure of this kind of an approach drive you inevitably further into all sorts of relatively drastic types of solution that are not process-oriented but result-oriented. The big one that is always mentioned—everybody falls for it, I think—is compulsory arbitration. And now, as a friend of mine put it in discussing the railroads, "Here we is, damned if we ain't."

WHAT SHOULD BE DONE?

The implications of the present course are serious. We have gone quite a long way, and we ought to ask ourselves: Isn't it time for a fresh look? There are, of course, all sorts of places where blame can be put. But our problem, at least as I see it, is to say: "Where do we go from here? How do we rearrange things so that we can have a reasonable process of bargaining, and so that we don't get our high public officials involved in these impossible situations?"

Let me throw out a few ideas in the full realization that it is much easier to be critical than to be constructive.

First of all, as an administrative proposition, it seems very important somehow for the government to change its stance, to make a more considered assessment of the possible impact of strikes, and to help the public make such an assessment. The government seems now in the position of always playing up the possible damaging impact of a strike. I would like to see a shift to a stance in line with what the facts are, with the public being told, "All right, so there's a strike; there are still plenty of bananas. Relax, it isn't a crisis after all." Now, of course, a serious situation must be labelled as such; but it seems to me that the cry of an impending crisis comes all too quickly. And in this the press seems all too ready to cooperate. So my first point is to educate the public about what is really going on.

REFUSE TO GET INVOLVED

Second, it is very important for the high-level people to virtually refuse to get involved, and to say, "I've had it and I'm just not going to spend so much time on labor disputes any more." Let the top officials disengage themselves and try to get the problem pushed into an area where there are professional people who are supposed to spend all of their time doing this kind of thing. The mediation resources of the community are vast; and with leadership from a Mediation Service that is given a real chance, these resources can do a great deal.

My third point rests on a common analysis of the impact of major strikes. One almost always finds that the public health and safety aspect or defense aspect of the strike, when present, is a very small component of the total picture—involving the transportation of food from the Mainland to Hawaii, for instance, or the production of certain special types of defense steel.

So perhaps we can use an approach that has not been tried much but which would seem to offer real potential for protecting the public interest. We could have limited, continued operation, but still let most of the strike go on—an approach built on the possibility of partial operation of struck facilities. To be sure, there are all sorts of political difficulties, but the difficulties are worth facing up to.

Now some may say, "Partial operation—that's just strike breaking," or "This is just giving the employer a chance to divide the union against itself," or "giving the union a chance to divide the employers," by picking a little piece out of the total situation. After all, the industry wanted industry-wide bargaining for the sake of strength. The union wanted to have the industry sewed up for the sake of strength. So, some might argue, partial operation is simply a way of favoring somebody in their strategy.

I do not agree. Of course, if you let the union or the company call its shots on partial operation and have it done exactly the way either one wants, then partial operation could be manipulated in this way. But if you have your partial operations directed by a public official whose objective and legal responsibilities are purely and simply to get certain goods transported, or produced, in certain small quantities, then it seems to me the bargaining strategy argument really ought to fall by the wayside.

Finally, just to show you that I haven't lost my mind completely, let me assure you that I believe it is very important to encourage a wide variety of mediation approaches, private approaches. Private approaches have been producing and will produce good results. I hesitate to mention third parties, because that always seems to come with little grace from someone who acts occasionally in that capacity. But I'll mention it in part to say that, at least in my observation, some of the most effective third parties are drawn from unions or companies into some particular dispute. So it isn't always a so-called neutral. It may be that procedures which involve people with some standing from a company or from a union, in a private way and without commitment of all the superstructure of government, can produce a good result.

Together some of these things can help any administration give the public assurance that the government *is* doing something. It is trying to help get things settled; it is protecting the public interest in at least partial operation. Perhaps, if accompanied by sane and careful statements about the impact of a strike, these measures will diminish the pressure from the public somewhat and allow some of these less spectacular procedures to operate.

In any case, you can see that the cornerstones of my position are an assessment that the strike situation in this country does not present us with a crisis, that private processes can work well, but that private processes are doomed unless we develop more tolerance for at least a minimum level of conflict.

To be sure, there are costs as well as gains. But for my part, freedom and the vitality of private parties and private processes are worth the cost.

The Government's Role
When Bargaining Breaks Down

A. H. RASKIN

Faith in the effectiveness of collective bargaining as an instrument for protecting the public interest has been severely shaken by the costly strikes on the New York newspapers and the Atlantic and Gulf docks. For week after ice-bound week, the inanimate state of the negotiations testified to the futility of warnings by the Federal, state, and city governments that both tie-ups were becoming "intolerable." The non-bargainers seemed thoroughly unimpressed by the argument that the public's stake in the reopening of the waterfront or in the free flow of news transcended any interest of their own.

As a result of these two wasting strikes and with more disruption threatening, notably on the railroads and in the aerospace industry, the Eighty-eighth Congress is apt to give priority attention to a search for ways to limit strikes in key industries—a subject the Kennedy administration had hoped to avoid meeting head-on during this session [1963]. The problem will be to devise legislation that can provide an acceptable balance between the country's need for improved safeguards and the right of unions and employers to the maximum exercise of economic freedom. Unfortunately, any legislation passed in a crisis atmosphere is apt to be more responsive to the urge to "do something" than to the desirability of doing something that makes sense. And yet when things are quiet enough on the labor front to permit an objective appraisal of this most complex of economic issues, neither the White House nor Congress is eager to take new action.

Taken from The Reporter, *XXVIII (January 31, 1963), pp. 27–31. Reprinted with the permission of the publisher. Copyright © 1963 by The Reporter Magazine Company. A. H. Raskin is a member of the Editorial Board of the* New York Times.

MR. GOLDBERG'S SHOES

Before Mr. Kennedy moved into the White House, he emphasized his determination to overhaul the Federal machinery for dealing with major strikes. He even listed a variety of new weapons he felt the President ought to have, from fact-finding to Federal seizure of struck industries. His first Secretary of Labor, Arthur Goldberg, was equally convinced of the need for changes in the national-emergency provisions of the Taft-Hartley Act. The drafting of specific recommendations for a new strike law was among the first projects completed by the President's Advisory Committee on Labor-Management Policy, of which Goldberg was chairman.

But the President never sent any of the proposals—his own or the committee's—to Congress. The principal reason was that Goldberg's unique blend of audacity, resourcefulness, and energy proved so effective in averting large-scale explosions on the industrial front that improvisation was considered a wiser course than a venture into the morass of Congressional hearings and debate. In the administration's first year, time lost through strikes dropped to the lowest level since the Second World War, and the figure for 1962 was only a little higher.

Moreover, in the one area in which Congressional pressure became intense, Goldberg succeeded in winning labor-management agreement to a no-strike pledge without the necessity for any new legislation. This was in the missile field, where a disturbing increase in wildcat stoppages by construction unions had provoked demands for a legal ban by Senator McClellan and other critics of union abuses. The strike toll has been cut sharply in the year and a half since the policing of disputes at missile bases was turned over to a special arbitration panel made up of union, employer, and public representatives.

However, by the time the President moved Goldberg to the Supreme Court [August 1962], his magic wand seemed to have lost some of its power. He was finding it increasingly difficult to buy time when unions set strike deadlines or walked out in disputes over the effects of automation on working conditions and job security. His freewheeling technique failed to prevent a strike at the Chicago & North Western Railway, and the only deterrent to a new eruption of labor trouble in the airlines after more than a year on a sputtering fuze was the fact that the flight engineers had become so expendable in jet cockpits they could no longer conduct a crippling strike.

The new Secretary of Labor, W. Willard Wirtz, made it plain from his first day in office that he did not consider it any proper part of his job to mediate strikes. That is the mission of the theoretically autonomous Federal Mediation and Conciliation Service, and the Secretary felt that he would only detract from the service's usefulness if he involved the authority of his office in every labor dispute that came along. Wirtz feels that he ought to focus his attention on the overriding problems of full employment and adjustment to changing technology in the expectation that progress in finding satisfactory answers to these problems will do more than anything else to ease the sense of job insecurity that is the basic cause of most current strikes. Despite all the wrangling about money, anxiety about automation underlay both the dock and the newspaper strikes.

The new Secretary's hopes for a respite from strike-patrol duty lasted no longer than his opening press conference. He has been personally involved ever since—usually at the President's express order—in strikes in railroads, companies manufacturing missiles and spacecraft, the waterfront, and the New York newspapers. He has worked just as hard and just as imaginatively as his predecessor, but this sort of extra-legal improvisation in peacetime labor relations inevitably produces diminishing returns. The decline in the effectiveness of top-level intervention, already apparent before Goldberg's departure from the scene, becomes increasingly evident with each new application.

The choice now is to stop intervening or to get a new law. Otherwise, a series of failures will undermine the prestige of both the President and the Secretary. A close look at the dock and newspaper strikes demonstrates the urgency of the need for a clear definition of both the scope and the limit of Federal action. It also demonstrates how difficult it will be to formulate legislation that will give suitable weight to the often conflicting considerations of public responsibility and private freedom.

A TALE OF TWO UNIONS

The unions involved in the two disputes are as different as the nature of the crises they precipitated by going on strike. The International Longshoremen's Association, which has make-or-break power over all the ports from Maine to Texas, was expelled from the old American Federation of Labor ten years ago on charges of racket domination. It did not get back into full good standing in the merged labor movement until December, 1961, and even now the Waterfront Commission of New York Harbor is perennially at war with the ILA on the ground that underworld elements still have power in its affairs.

In the old days, waterfront strikes used to be settled by under-the-table payments to union officials. The ILA now seeks to demonstrate its purity as a reformed champion of the workingman by super-militancy in holding out for big gains at the bargaining table and by resisting the introduction of more efficient loading equipment to re-place antiquated manpower practices. A bistate compact passed in 1953 by New York and New Jersey and approved by Congress sub-jects the ILA's officers and members to more rigorous controls than any other American union. Yet none of these restraints has been any more successful at keeping the ILA in check than have the combined assaults of White House and Congressional critics on James Hoffa and his Teamsters.

The union that called the New York newspaper strike—Big Six of the International Typographical Union—is one of the country's old-est, cleanest, and most democratic. No breath of scandal or of author-itarianism has ever touched it. The strike that shut the metropolitan dailies was the first it had called against them in eighty years. In contrast to the ILA, where rank-and-file influence has always been notable by its absence, Big Six and its parent union carry membership debate over the formulation of policy to a length that has made the ITU the only American union with a permanent two-party system. The knowledge that a strong opposition is always ready to make political capital of any rank-and-file grievance is no stimulus to reasonableness at the bargaining table. The party in control must regard each new contract as its platform for the next election. If the members are dissatisfied, they can always vote in a new administra-tion.

Yet this very emphasis on the vigorous and autonomous exercise of internal democracy—one of the central goals Congress endeavored to establish for all labor in the Landrum-Griffin bill of 1959—is in large part responsible for the printers' unwillingness to accept the notion that their own economic interests ought to be tempered by concern for the public interest. The ITU opposes all forms of arbitra-tion, fact-finding, or other "encroachments" on its autonomy by either the government or the AFL–CIO. It is as rigidly committed to the idea that no outsider can tell it what to do as the most dedicated exponent of rugged individualism in the Union League Club.

So strong is the ITU attachment to this view that it sought unilater-ally to force repeal of the Taft-Hartley Act by refusing to sign any contracts with employers after its passage in 1947. This policy led to a crushing defeat for the union in its disastrous twenty-two-month strike against the Chicago newspapers. Even though repeal of Taft-Hartley stood at the top of the AFL's legislative program in that period, its executive council regarded the ITU tactics as suicidal and refused even to vote moral support to the Chicago adventure. But the go-it-alone spirit of the printers remains undimmed.

Bertram A. Powers, president of Big Six, told Secretary Wirtz that he regarded any form of government-imposed fact-finding studies as a camouflage for compulsory arbitration, the most hated of all terms in ITU's lexicon. He said he would not co-operate even if the panel of peacemakers consisted of George Meany, Walter P. Reuther, and Harry Van Arsdale, Jr., head of the New York AFL–CIO, whose local electricians' union contributed $10,000 to the Big Six strike fund.

But with negotiations deadlocked and all other channels apparently closed, Wirtz joined with Governor Rockefeller and Mayor Wagner in naming three distinguished jurists to a specially created Board of Public Accountability, charged with the responsibility of finding out why the strike had dragged on for more than a month and whether both sides were sufficiently mindful of the public interest. Powers promptly announced that he would boycott the proceedings and told a rally of sympathetic unionists that the extinction of labor's freedom in the Soviet Union had been carried out under a similar cloak of necessity to protect the common welfare.

The real trouble, it quickly developed, was not that the board had Khrushchev-like power but that it had none at all in the one area that was important—namely, providing some worthwhile help toward settling the strike. The judges put practically all the blame for the tie-up on Powers, an outcome that simply provided ammunition for his stock argument that no union should ever trust government intervention because it always comes in on the side of the boss. If the panel had been empowered to make settlement recommendations, the public and, more especially, the other newspaper unions would have had an impartial standard on which to base pressures for an agreement. Unfortunately, the board was categorically prohibited by the terms of its charter from making such recommendations. Thus, what might have been a useful new mechanism for bringing the public interest into focus became instead a mere finger-pointing exercise that did more harm than good.

WET AND INTRACTABLE

Precisely the same hostility toward government intervention was adopted by the ILA when the government vainly attempted to induce it to postpone its strike to permit a fact-finding review of the key issues. The President personally telephoned Thomas W. Gleason, the dock union's executive vice-president, at his home to ask his cooperation in a ninety-day delay. The call came through while Gleason was in the shower; and since it took some time to convince the union chief that the caller was not some prankster impersonating Vaughn Meader impersonating the President, the conversation did not even begin very auspiciously. It ended with Gleason offering to bring a three-man committee to Washington or Palm Beach to explain why the ILA did not believe it could hold off any longer after it had fulfilled all the legal requirements by complying with an eighty-day no-strike injunction under Taft-Hartley.

Mr. Kennedy, not interested in excuses, rang off and the strike rang on. Gleason blithely predicted that employer resistance would collapse in four days and that the longshoremen would win everything they wanted. When they didn't get a quick agreement on their terms, he accused the government of being in league with the shipping companies and went so far as to claim that its interference was as vicious as anything the Gestapo had done.

Again the fact proved the reverse of the bombast. In the fourth week of the tie-up, with Congressional clamor for rigid strike curbs mounting, the President named a decidedly pro-labor board to propose peace terms. It was obviously a final effort to check the legislative drive—and to do it on terms that seemed likely to give the balky ILA a bigger wage package than the administration's own guide lines would justify. In the present bargain-basement atmosphere surrounding government intervention, obstructiveness brings rewards rather than penalties.

What of the "emergencies" created by the hostility of these two dissimilar organizations to the efforts of government to help both sides reach a settlement? In the case of the dock union, the peril to the national health and safety of a prolonged shutdown was clear enough. The last three Presidents of the United States have so regularly certified to the Federal courts that a two-coast strike jeopardizes the country's interests (and have been sustained by the courts in that judgment) that an injunction has now become little more than a formality in the negotiating process.

This means no one really starts bargaining until after the no-strike order has been signed. What is worse, during the eighty-day truce, the Presidential board of inquiry is prohibited by law from making specific recommendations for breaking the deadlock in negotiations. Thus the cooling-off period runs out with no movement by either side, no informed suggestions as to what might represent an equitable settlement, and no further legal possibilities open to the President.

And, it might be added, with no diminution of the national emergency cited by the courts in ordering that there be no strike because it would put the country in danger.

What constitutes an emergency is, of course, a matter that varies from industry to industry and from strike to strike. Nothing shows this more clearly than the experience in steel, where a tradition of formal and informal government intervention has become firmly established. The diverse standards that have been applied to justify a particular form of intervention or to delay intervention make it obvious that a strike becomes an emergency when the President says it is—even if his determination or nondetermination is prompted by political rather than economic reasons.

To be sure, on the waterfront the threat to the national interest is much less obscure than it might be in other key industries. The high priority the President and Congress accorded to passage of the Trade Expansion Act last year was the best testimonial to the importance of uninterrupted movement of imports and exports in our harbors. That is why the settlement of labor disputes on the docks must be swift and sure.

PRESSURE ON THE PRESS

In a newspaper strike, even when the press of the nation's biggest city is blacked out, the nature of the emergency is not so readily apparent. Of course, many aspects of the metropolitan economy suffer—but the impact is not calamitous in the way that an extended work stoppage in foreign commerce can be. The real damage is to the community's awareness of what is going on in the world, the nation, the state, and the city. But just how big an emergency is this?

Is it enough to say, as everyone from the President on down does in other connections, that a vigilant press is an indispensable support and protector of freedom—and that to be vigilant it must be publishing? How much importance should we ascribe to that curious grayness which comes over the city when all there is to read is some other city's dailies, the sad feeling of emptiness with which we note even the lack of the familiar journalistic inanities when they are not around to pique our wrath or derision? Most pertinent of all, can a valid contribution be made to strengthening one freedom, the public's right to know and the press's right to publish, by abridging another freedom, the right of newspaper unions and publishers to make their own economic decisions, no matter how blunderingly they go about it?

My own reluctant conclusion, after weary weeks of the frustration of the New York strike, is that both the nature of the enterprise and of its function in a democracy rule out the use of Federal compulsion to keep newspapers printing, just as they would make it unthinkable to use compulsion to tell the newspapers what to print. This does not mean, however, that the government must stand on the sidelines while the presses rust away.

The most fruitful approach, it appears to me, is the establishment by municipal law in each city of a procedure through which the mayor could impanel a version of the Board of Public Accountability, made up of prominent citizens representing various segments of the community. However, the New York experience demonstrates the futility of such boards if they lack any power to suggest an equitable formula for resolving the strike issues. The board should have authority to subpoena reluctant union or management witnesses through the issuance of public show-cause orders—a recourse that would probably rarely require invocation once the board's legal foundation was established.

The panel's task would be to let the city know what the strike was about and also how it felt it could be settled most fairly. From there on, it would be up to the force of public opinion to compel progress at the negotiating table. No coercive power should rest with the board or the mayor, except to mobilize civic pressure and disseminate the report itself in a city lacking the best method of distribution, the local newspapers.

GRADUATED DETERRENCE

In situations where a strike produces greater dangers and stresses, such as the waterfront, stronger action is necessary. Apart from the dock strike, the most imminent such test now on the horizon is the prospective showdown in the long wrangle over featherbedding and the modernization of archaic work rules on the nation's railroads. The dispute will go next to the Supreme Court. From there it will probably go to a Presidential emergency board under the Railway Labor Act, but there is no basis for optimism that it will not result in a new strike sometime next summer. Once again the White House will find itself with no further legal devices available unless Congress supplies some new ones in the interim.[1]

The administration's reluctance to open the whole question of new strike legislation was made manifest by the President's total omission

1 [President Johnson, with expert assistance, mediated the issues not covered in the compulsory arbitration law. *Ed.*]

of the subject from his State of the Union message. His appointment of the stopgap fact-finding board in the dock strike was further evidence that he would like the whole subject to be buried for this session. However, the newspaper and dock strikes plus the threat of other big strikes in the transportation and aerospace fields are likely to force his hand. If the administration is obliged to act, it will be inclined to scrap the present national-emergency clause in favor of one that would put many more weapons in the President's arsenal. Instead of having no choice except an eighty-day injunction, the President would be free to choose any of these courses: demand a postponement without a court order; establish a fact-finding board that would have power to make recommendations or not make them as the President desired; seize a struck plant or industry, with an option to keep the profits or turn them back at the end of the take-over; get an injunction; or do nothing at all. The definition of what constitutes a national emergency would also be redrawn to give the Chief Executive broader discretion than he now has to decide when the nation's welfare was menaced.

The purpose of this imposing array of powers is to keep both labor and management guessing about which device the President will use if they fail to come up with an agreement by themselves. The thought is that this uncertainty will compel them to bargain more earnestly for fear that the White House will choose the instrument least favorable to the side it considers the more derelict in meeting its public responsibilities. While this flexibility is obviously preferable to the present complete dependence on the injunction, the danger it raises is that most of the bargaining will be done with the government on what device to use rather than between the parties on achieving a direct settlement. The more powerful the political connections of one side or the other, the more the multiplication of alternatives is likely to become a diversionary factor at the bargaining table instead of a goad.

A preferable revision, in my opinion, would be one that would retain the present eighty-day cooling-off period when the President felt the situation was serious enough to require intervention. The board of inquiry should have the authority to make settlement proposals if its mediation efforts during the first month or six weeks of the armistice prove ineffective. The proposals would not be legally binding on either side, but any points they could not agree on in bargaining before the eighty-day deadline would then be subject to mandatory arbitration. To argue that a tightly drawn arbitration law is unneeded because the country has survived lots of strikes without bleeding to death is no more persuasive than to contend that we can afford wars because we have never yet had one that blew up the world. Arbitration is a necessary shield for the public where private responsibility breaks down.

Ideally, nothing would ever have to go to arbitration. But this is an illusory expectation in a period when workers of all sorts are worried about losing their jobs to machines and when the solutions to technological problems worked out in collective bargaining are always experimental and usually inadequate. The very extent to which automation has created problems of retraining and re-employment that necessitate new relationships between government, management, and labor dramatizes the urgency for the overhauling of both our bargaining machinery and our laws to deal with bargaining breakdowns that cut off vital services.

HOW NOT TO MAKE NEW LAWS

The common attitude voiced by the leaders of the otherwise dissimilar dock and printers' unions, that government must stay out of any direct involvement in the negotiating process no matter what its public impact, is as out of tune with majority thinking in American labor as it is with the realities of the new industrial revolution. Joseph A. Beirne, president of the Communications Workers of America and a national vice-president of the AFL–CIO, is more representative of the emerging labor view when he says that the nation is moving toward a state-guided economy that will require a vastly greater measure of restraint and co-operation by both unions and management.

He is not at all unhappy about the prospect. On the contrary, as head of the union that represents most employees of the Bell Telephone system, he believes that the government has both a right and a duty to use an evenhanded process, short of compulsory arbitration, to achieve a fair industrial peace. He preaches restraint and co-operation as the surest way for unions and employers to discharge their obligation to the public without inviting shackling legislation.

That this type of thinking may be more welcome to employees in automated industries than the rewarmed hate-the-boss slogans of the 1930's or the posting of keep-out signs against government is indicated by the overwhelming support the Beirne union has just received from its members in the installation department of Western Electric. They repelled an attempted raid by Hoffa and his Teamsters by a margin of nearly 3-1 in an NLRB election.

Other big unions and their employers are demonstrating originality and enterprise in modernizing their bargaining structures to deal with the challenge of automation. Outside experts have helped Kaiser Steel and the United Steelworkers devise a formula for giving workers a tangible stake in increased productivity. U.S. Industries, Inc., has put a royalty on the automated equipment it makes to finance a foundation it operates jointly with the International Association of Machinists. The job of the foundation will be to seek durable solutions to the unemployment problems produced by the company's machines.

All these are signs that the state of labor-management relations is not so benighted as residents of New York and many other cities may have concluded from the recent history of labor-management relations at the newspapers and on the piers.

Crisis strikes are vestigial elements in industrial relations. Their frequency will diminish as automation renders more industries invulnerable to interruption by strikes, as more third-party machinery is perfected for taking the dynamite out of contract negotiations, and as we ease workers' fears of displacement by doing a better job of creating national full employment. But the community cannot afford to remain undefended while we strive for this millennial era of industrial harmony. The real victim of the crisis strike is the public, not the economic warriors.

Congress has a crucial job to do in reformulating our laws to deal with emergencies that result from such impasses. So have state and local governments. But rushing ahead in a spirit of vindictive rage or desperately clutching at this proposal or that as a magic formula is apt to produce both a bad law and an even greater sense of letdown than that which now depresses many citizens. Any serious effort to prevent labor crises in the United States must begin with the understanding that the over-all problems are too serious and complex to be dealt with in the haste of a crisis.

Consensus and National Labor Policy

JOHN T. DUNLOP

The theme of these remarks is that our national industrial relations system suffers from excessive legislation, litigation, formal awards and public pronouncements; that the principal carriers of this disease are politicians, and that the imperative need is to alter drastically our methods of policy formation to place much greater reliance upon the development of consensus.

Professor William Ernest Hocking defined the politician as the "man who deliberately faces both the certainty that men must live together, and the endless uncertainty on what terms they can live together, and who takes on himself the task of proposing the terms, and so of transforming the unsuccessful human group into the successful group." In proposing the changing terms on which government agencies, managements and unions shall live together in an industrial relations system our politicians have fallen far short of Professor Hocking's standards. Contrary to the wisdom of antiquity, they have separated legislation and a philosophy of collective bargaining; contrary to Holmes they have exalted a kind of legal logic over experience; they have reflected little understanding of the practical work level in an industrial society, and they have imposed rules rather than first develop a consensus among those to be affected. These same habits have characterized to a large degree the confederation levels of management and labor; thus, formalism, litigation and unreality pervade the national industrial relations system.

Collective bargaining, in the sense of the relationships between management and unions at the work place, enterprise or industry, is

Taken from Proceedings of the Thirteenth Annual Meeting of the Industrial Relations Research Association, *December 1960 (Madison, Wisconsin: 1961), pp. 2–15. Reprinted with the permission of the author and the publisher. John T. Dunlop is Professor of Economics at Harvard University.*

not the topic today, However, I wish to pause long enough on collective bargaining to express the judgment that I do not agree that the country faces a crisis in collective bargaining or that "something is seriously awry in the system of collective bargaining," at least as collective bargaining has been used to refer to the negotiation and administration of agreements. Rather, the overwhelming evidence is that on balance relationships never were better as judged by such standard as grievance handling, discipline, arbitration, wage structure administration, wildcat strikes, or violence. It is true that in some industries the environment has become tougher affecting the bargaining, but that is the function of collective bargaining. It is also true that new problems are emerging which may require a new form of relationship—the conference method—among labor, management, and even government. The need for these new forms of relationships in the decade ahead does not mean that collective bargaining has failed; indeed, these new conferences are often being created by traditional collective bargaining.

This discussion of national labor policy is divided into three sections which consider in turn the formation of national labor policy by government, the decisions of the labor movement at the federation level, and finally the policymaking of the confederation level of management.

THE FEDERAL GOVERNMENT

The management of American industrial enterprises prior to the Wagner Act, by and large, simply refused to recognize labor organizations. There were notable exceptions as where craftsmen were exceptionally strong, or where the social pressures of isolated communities or groups of workers were particularly intense or where some enterprises for financial reasons or through the idealistic conviction of a few managers accepted collective bargaining. But the expanding mass production industries were overwhelmingly anti-union.

On three occasions, as Professor Slichter pointed out, a major effort was made to persuade American managers voluntarily to adopt a labor policy of recognition of trade unions and the acceptance of collective bargaining. On each occasion the attempt failed miserably. The first attempt at the turn of the century was under the leadership of the National Civic Federation, Mark Hanna, and other business leaders. The second attempt was made by President Wilson through the Industrial Conference to perpetuate principles of labor-management relations temporarily accepted or imposed during World War I.

The third attempt was made through section 7a of the NIRA which proclaimed the rights of collective bargaining and sought to pledge employers to non-interference in the exercise by workers of self-organization.

The failure to persuade American managers without the compulsions of law to recognize labor unions is in marked contrast to the Scandinavian and British experience. In Denmark the September Agreement, made between the central confederation of employers and unions, following the great lockout of 1899, shaped fundamentally the patterns of industrial relations to follow. It provided for mutual recognition and acknowledged the right of strike and lockout after appropriate notice and votes. It recognized the employer's "right to direct and distribute the work and to use what labor may in his judgment be suitable . . ." In Sweden the 1906 "December Compromise" between the confederation levels of employers and unions recognized the full freedom of employers to hire and fire organized and unorganized workers and in exchange recognized the full freedom of workers to organize and provided for redress in case of discipline for exercising this right. In Great Britain the gradual development of its industrial relations system is well characterized by Allan Flanders: "Collective bargaining is for us essentially a voluntary process. . . . The process itself is not normally enforced or regulated by law. . . ."

While there was very considerable industrial conflict and political struggle for a period in Scandinavia and in Great Britain over the status of labor organizations, in the end the right to organize and to engage in bargaining, as well as the procedures and arrangements for bargaining, were evolved gradually by custom or by explicit agreement between organized managements and unions. They were not imposed by law.

In the early 1930's it might have appeared that the United States was headed in the general direction pioneered by Britain and Scandinavia with the lag of a generation to which our British cousins have been prone to point. The greater size of our country, the lesser cohesiveness of our managers, the lesser class consciousness of our workers, the lesser role of export markets, and the later industrialization and greater significance of agriculture combine to explain the lag.

The Norris–LaGuardia Act of 1932 only sought to remove the most serious obstacles which had been developed by the courts to labor organization and to the use of economic weapons in organizing and in bargaining with employers. This statute accorded with the dominant view of labor leaders that they only desired the government and courts to be "neutral"; they did not seek active intervention of the government in their behalf.

The Railway Labor Act of 1926 was in the same mold; it was largely shaped by the joint action of the carriers and the labor organizations. The significant fact is that the establishment of a collective bargaining relationship between the parties and the procedures for dealing with each other were mutually determined. They had the experience of together shaping the framework of their relations and an active joint role in defining the activity of governmental agencies. This experience provides the basis for further joint activity, and when politicians deprive labor and management of this experience they eliminate a sense of responsibility for the operation of a statute and deprive the parties of a basis for further cooperation.

The Wagner Act was to constitute a major change in the development of public policy, although it was probably not so intended. On the face of it, the statute did not seem complex. It was designed simply to require employers to recognize and to bargain with labor unions where the employees desired a union. It compelled managements to do what they had resisted doing under voluntary persuasion. However, the Wagner Act was to constitute a major fork in the road of labor policy, not merely on account of what it provided, but as a consequence of the inherent implications of the legislative approach in the absence of mutual sanctions for the statute. The signs on the road necessarily pointed to the Taft-Hartley law, the Landrum-Griffin Act, and beyond because of the way in which the policies were determined under the conditions of the times.

It is not necessary here to sketch the inevitable administrative, legislative, judicial, and political steps by which the nation moved from the Wagner Act to Taft-Hartley and then to Landrum-Griffin, nor to outline the steps that are yet to come down this fork in the road. The present state of determination of governmental industrial relations policy can be briefly summarized in seven paragraphs as follows:

(1) The legislative framework of collective bargaining is now regulated by a highly partisan political process. Thus, the Democratic Platform for 1960 promised the "repeal of the anti-labor excesses which have been written into our labor laws," and it accused the Republican administration of establishing a "national anti-labor policy." The Republicans pledged "diligent administration of the existing statutes with recommendations for improvements or to remove inequities."

(2) The responsibility of organized management and labor in shaping the legislative framework and in the administration of the statutes is virtually nil; it is confined to making formal and highly extreme public statements. The politicians have been poor mediators.

(3) The national policy encourages litigation rather than settlement. Litigation fosters unreality in the extreme. It takes a great deal of time; cases are decided years after issues are raised, violating the first principle of industrial relations. The proceedings are highly technical, lawyers are involved in game playing rather than in the process of practical accommodation of the parties and dispute settlement.

(4) The legislative framework is more and more technical and detailed. The point has been reached where general provisions no longer make sense in many industries and we have started in the direction of special provisions for particular industries, as Title VII of the 1959 Act indicates. Fewer and fewer members of the Congress can be equipped to understand the technical issues, and language is necessarily written hastily in late sessions and conference committees by staff lawyers far from the bargaining process. Formal compromises in words assure unending litigation.

(5) It should be recognized as a first principle that no set of men is smart enought to write words through which others cannot find holes when the stakes are high. Thus, the secondary boycott provisions of Taft-Hartley helped to create hot-cargo clauses which in turn led to new provisions in Title VII of the 1959 Act which in turn are leading to new clauses which may well lead to another decade of litigation and then further legislation. The game playing of the income tax law is not suitable to collective bargaining, the practical necessities of labor-management relations, and the imperatives of the times which require increased cooperation and productivity.

(6) The long-term legislative framework of collective bargaining has been excessively influenced by short-term influences. The depression shaped the Wagner Act; the post-war inflation and wave of strikes influenced decisively the Taft-Hartley law; and the McClellan Committee largely determined the 1959 law. The compulsions of the immediate are hardly the most appropriate in which to set the framework in which managements and labor organizations shall live for a generation. The long view has been lacking.

(7) In a democratic and pluralistic society the government is seeking to impose on parties to collective bargaining by statute and administrative rulings a set of standards of conduct which in many respects is highly unrealistic. To remove the parties from any significant responsibility for the formation and administration of policy is

destructive of the character of our society, leads to impractical and unreal policies and to mass evasion and disrespect. Such is the state of government labor policy.

I pause to urge that the most significant research contribution that can [be made] to government labor policy is to show how it actually operates. We need less analysis of the law and the cases and much research on the experience at the work place. We need to report and to analyze what actually happens in industrial relations after the NLRB, the courts or arbitrators issue decisions and how the parties use the existence of the law. We need a greater sense of the limitations of pieces of paper.

It is unrealistic to expect any substantial turning back on the present road to government policy, but it should be possible to resolve to proceed no further down the present course. The legislative and administrative framework of collective bargaining should be changed only after extensive consultation and mediation through neutral or government experts with organized management and labor. Labor-management legislation must be a matter of consensus to be effective. The parties should bear a measure of direct responsibility for policy rather than leaving both sides free to criticize legislation as biased and impractical and then devote their full energies and imagination to circumventing the law. A major role should even be evolved for the parties in the administration of the present statutes and to reduce formal litigation. Without the consensus of the parties there can only be further litigation and political legislation. No matter how long it takes, patient mediation and the development of a consensus among top labor and management (with public and government experts) is essential to any solution to the present policy gap.

THE LABOR MOVEMENT

The short road to merger, to use Mr. Meany's phrase, involved putting the many unresolved problems among international unions, including their relations to a single trade union center, in the hands of the merged federation with the hope that the divisive issues could be gradually resolved. The architects of the merger rejected what Mr. Meany has called the method of perfection, which would have resolved these issues in advance of merger on the grounds this road would have taken too long even if it could have led eventually to merger.

By August 1959 it was evident that the many hard problems had not obligingly drifted away, and the Executive Council appointed a special committee to study seven areas of internal disputes. They were listed as follows:

1. The No-Raid clause in the constitution.
2. The agreement between the Industrial Union Department and the Building Trades Department.
3. The dispute between the Metal Trades Department and the Industrial Union Department.
4. The matter of boycotts.
5. The transfer to national and international affiliates of directly affiliated local unions.
6. Organizing ethics in competitive organizing campaigns.
7. Anti-contracting out provisions in trade union contracts.

The Committee was charged with the responsibility of recommending procedures for "an early and conclusive disposition of such types of disputes." The San Francisco convention in September 1959 did adopt the recommendation of the Committee that it should develop a detailed plan, to be approved at a special convention, to resolve all these types of disputes, "embodying final and binding arbitration as the terminal point in such disputes." A qualification was added that ". . . such arbitration shall be limited to the settlement of disputes only and shall not include the determination of the work or trade jurisdiction of affiliates." The promise of San Francisco was widely hailed, but by the Miami meeting of the Executive Council in February 1960 this approach to internal problems appeared to have been abandoned, and thus far there has been no detailed plan nor special convention.

The fundamental defects of the proposed arbitration approach need to be stated. There can be nothing but respect for the willingness to give up autonomy and sovereignty to the extent proposed by arbitration, but the approach is impractical. So wide a range of problems as organizing ethics, boycotts, and work assignment disputes cannot readily be encompassed in a single machinery. The qualification in the resolution on jurisdiction is a reminder how far apart are those who still think in terms of "exclusive jurisdiction," the cornerstone of the AFL constitution, and those who exalt the "collective bargaining relationship," the central concept in the constitution of the merged federation. In the building trades–industrial union disputes there are more interests than the two groups of unions involved; neither contractors nor industrial plants will permit unions to arbitrate their economic destiny. No private disputes settlement can long endure when the governmental machinery yields opposite results and protects a violator of a private plan. There can be no effective enforcement machinery, and the federation has no effective sanctions except to encourage withdrawal of the strong. These difficulties are significant, but they do not go to the heart of the problem. Arbitration was to be invoked as a way to solve problems which do not lend themselves well to stipulated issues. There must be a meeting of minds, and agreement, a consensus, on the issues listed. Arbitration cannot be a substitute for agreement-making in the areas of such disputes. The short road to merger was taken on the presumption that a number of mergers would follow among competing international unions and that many bilateral jurisdictional agreements among disputing unions would be negotiated. Arbitration cannot achieve these results, nor can it be a substitute for consent. No set of words quickly contrived can substitute for the meeting of minds that comes from extended conferences or the good faith that must be built gradually from particular cases. There may have been a short road to merger, but there is only a long road to consensus.

There is relatively little working contact, except through the head of the Federation, between the presidents of the former CIO industrial unions and the building trades and craft unions. They often do not speak the same language; they have very different concepts of jurisdiction; they have different traditions and views of the union label; they use staff assistants in quite different ways; they do not often meet. This sort of gap which magnifies the substantive issues cannot be bridged by formal arbitration. Agreement-making among international unions is a long and slow process; it is hard and detailed work in which persistence and imagination are major tools. An illustration is afforded in the relations between the Iron Workers and the Glaziers. Their 1957 jurisdictional agreement needed to be modernized for a variety of reasons, including the position of the glazing contractors. It took at least 15 sessions and 30 days of meetings this year [1960], not to mention many other conferences with each group, to achieve the revision. In some cases more than seven years have been spent in mediating some agreements, as that between the United Association [of Plumbers] and the Sheet Metal Workers on air conditioning and kitchen equipment. The results cannot be achieved in a single session or in three or four a year. Moreover, relationships must be kept attuned to new problems, both internal and substantive.

The arbitration decisions under the no-raiding agreement and the CIO organizational dispute plan and the recommendations under Article III, Sec. 4 of the constitution, pursuant to the February 1958 action of the Executive Council, have resolved a number of particular cases. The powers of these umpires are very narrowly circumscribed, and they have increasingly confronted compliance problems; these plans have not been administered so as to achieve agreement over the underlying issues.

Let it be clear that I have not said there is no place for a neutral in helping to settle these disputes, nor that orderly procedures are not required. But my experience and conviction is strongly that the arbitration process, particularly of the more formal type, has relatively little to contribute to the development of consensus and working relations within the federation.

MANAGEMENT

In his presidential address to this association two years ago, Professor Bakke said: "It is not an exaggeration to say that when collective bargaining became a part of operations of a company, managerial methods underwent a revolution greater than would have been the case if those companies had been nationalized. . . ." There have been enormous transformations in industrial management in the past generation, and along with modern technology and business schools, the rise of unionism in large scale industry has been a decisive factor creating the changes.

There have been two principal developments in industrial management related to the rise of unionism: (a) the emergence of a specialized staff solely concerned with labor relations problems, and (b) the adoption of explicit policies designed to lay down lines of action in the wide range of questions—such as discipline, transfers and promotions, compensation, and grievance procedures—that arise under collective bargaining. Large-scale managements quickly learned that they needed full time staffs to follow industrial relations developments and to engage in collective bargaining and grievance handling with union representatives who devoted full time to this specialty. Managements have been slower to learn that long-run policies and explicit administrative procedures are essential to industrial relations, that improvising and expediency may avoid an untimely strike, but they tend to lead to lack of control over costs and to whipsaw-tactics and pressure on the part of the union.

But a specialized industrial relations staff and policies are not the real source of the transformation in management. It is rather the grappling with the problems that then arise in coordinating the new staff with other policies. There is hardly an internal managerial relationship, horizontally or vertically, that is left intact, and there is scarcely a policy that is not re-examined under the impact of this new institution, literally within the cell walls of the enterprise.

It is well known that there is no uniform relation today between line and staff in industrial enterprises. In some cases the line administers all labor relations policies and the staff is purely advisory in the classical textbook fashion, while in other instances the staff has operating responsibility for all labor relations decisions including incentive rates, transfers, and all grievances. The Brookings study by Professors Slichter, Healy and Livernash concludes, on the basis of their extensive field work, that line and staff coordination, cooperation, teamwork, or mutual help is indispensable to successful industrial relations. All practitioners of industrial relations have seen instances when conflicts and frictions between line and staff at the plant level over the setting of incentive rates, the extent to which foremen may work, the application of discipline standards, or the conflicts between plant levels and the home office have been the source of many grievances and have encouraged union pressures to force a problem to the most favorable point, from its point of view, in the management hierarchy. There is no mechanistic solution to the line-staff problems within management; there must be coordination and consensus to achieve economic objectives and stable relations with a union.

The transformation in substantive decision-making is no less significant than the changes in the internal structure of management. Industrial relations policies are highly interdependent with the full range of other decisions as the following questions indicate. Shall the company make a concession in a wildcat strike to furnish orders for an important customer? What margin in capacity and in inventories shall the company establish in view of its labor relations? What shall the company say to prospective investors about labor costs and efficiency since unions and employees also have ears? What shall the company say in its public relations program about its contract differences with the union? These questions indicate that industrial relations issues ramify throughout the full range of managerial decisions. Industrial relations policies affect all other policies. Despite the reserve power to make decisions at the very top—to resolve conflict among various subordinate staffs—final decisions within the enterprise typically involve a consensus.

These adjustments in business structure and policies have tended to produce an improvement in management organization, superior in the sense that it tends to operate by reference to policies, it is less addicted to slogans and platitudes, it is more adaptable and geared to change in market conditions and to changes in the community, it recognizes that internally and externally persuasion is more effective in the long run than the mere assertion of rights, and it places top priority in management upon coordination and organization building and executive development. The unions have played no small role in the vast improvement in enterprise management in the United States. But it is still true as Professor Slichter said that "By and large, the top executives of American enterprises have rather limited familiarity with problems of industrial relations. . . . Progress is being made. . . . Nevertheless, this interest is far less than it should be in view of the enormous possibilities of saving capital expenditures simply by improving employee-management relations."

These developments within the industrial enterprise are to be contrasted sharply with what has been happening at the confederation level of American management—the National Association of Manufacturers and the Chamber of Commerce. In referring specifically to the policy statements of the N.A.M. issued in 1903, 1936 and 1955, Professors Douglass V. Brown and Charles A. Myers at the annual meetings in 1956 said that one would be tempted to conclude ". . . that changes, if any, in philosophy toward unionism had been relatively minor." They observed that ". . . it is still the fashion, as it was thirty or more years ago, to concede that employees have the right to organize or not to organize. It is still the fashion, as it was earlier, to deny opposition to unions as such; only 'bad unions,' 'labor monopolies,' or 'unions that abuse their power' are formally beyond the pale. It is still the fashion to insist that unions be held legally responsible for their actions." What was true in 1956 is still true of the 1960 edition of the N.A.M.'s *Industry Believes*.

How is one to account for the contrast between the adaptability of management in enterprises and its intransigence at the confederation level? The contrast is the more striking when it is reported that over half the directorate of the N.A.M. come from companies with collective bargaining agreements. Perhaps the explanation lies partly in the fact governments are not the only organizations which have both state departments and war departments. Perhaps, the posture has been frozen for many years and an older era is perpetuated. Perhaps these confederations attract as active members managements militant in their concern to stop the spread of unionism. These factors may play a role, but there are more fundamental reasons.

The pronouncements of the N.A.M. and Chamber are slogans; they never have to confront the reality of the industrial work place; the consequences of the statements of policy are in the political sphere rather than measured in production and in costs. They resemble the initial demands of one party in collective bargaining rather than a negotiated settlement or a realistic compromise. The are on a par with many resolutions for legislation passed at AFL–CIO conventions. If the confederation level of American management were engaged in collective bargaining, as the SAF in Sweden, the actions of American enterprise management and policy pronouncements of the N.A.M. and Chamber might be more consonant. No enterprise is bound by the pronouncements, and so no one has to take their consequences in the practical sphere of the management of a work force.

These pronouncements do not represent the best practice of American management, nor even the average among larger industrial enterprises; rather, they are formal positions oriented toward political activity. By the practice of enterprise management in the United States, these pronouncements do not reflect any consensus of industrial relations policies. They do not even represent the self-interest of management. For instance, the call for the repeal of the Davis-Bacon Act, confined solely to the construction industry, does not have the support of a single national association of contractors.

The industrial relations system of the United States suffers from the unreality of the confederation level of management. The vigor, imagination and leadership of the enterprise level has no counterpart at the confederation level. I venture the view that until the confederation level of management is transformed, to reflect more faithfully the experience of industrial enterprises, management as a whole will not exercise its potential role in the industrial relations policies of the community, and the government will continue to extend further its role in the regulation of labor-management relations. Industrial management at the enterprise level in the past decade has shown itself well capable to develop policies to protect its competitive positions and to enhance efficiency within the framework of collective bargaining. There is every reason to expect that it could do as well at the confederation level. The first requirement to achieve a national labor policy by consent is to transform the confederation level of management to reflect more faithfully the experience of enterprise management.

THE ALTERNATIVE OF CONSENSUS

The theme of the preceding three sections has been that our national industrial relations system suffers from seeking solutions to problems in terms of legislation and litigation, formal arbitration, and public pronouncements. This malady alike afflicts national governmental policy, the labor federation, and the confederation level of management. The common difficulty in its essence is a failure to develop a consensus within government, the labor movement, or management. The consequence is resort to partisan legislation and litigation and the ascendency of the politicians in national industrial relations policy. An alternative policy is reliance, to a greater degree, upon the development of consensus.

Greater reliance upon consensus is particularly appropriate since the range of industrial relations problems has become increasingly technical, and uniform rules across wide reaches of the economy are impractical in many cases. Moreover, in our society rules and policies which have been formulated by those directly affected are likely to receive greater respect and compliance than when imposed by fiat. The rapidly changing circumstances of technology and markets require greater reliance on consensus since those most directly affected are more sensitive to such change, and adaptation can be more gradual than that imposed belatedly from without. Consensus develops habits of mind which encourage continuing adaptation to new circumstances.

The method of consensus is admittedly difficult to apply; it is so much easier simply to pass another law, or issue another decision or another resolution. The achievement of consensus is often a frustrating process since it must triumph over inertia, suspicion, and the warpath. It is slow to build. But it is clearly the most satisfying and enduring solution to problems. It always has significant by-products in improved understanding in many other spheres than those related to the consensus.

The most fundamental feature of consensus building is that it requires or creates leadership devoted to mediating among followers, a leadership which seeks to explain problems and sell solutions rather than merely to impose a solution by sheer power or to rail against a decision from without.

An industrial society requires a considerably greater measure of consensus on industrial relations problems than we have. The present course is set toward an unending sequence of legislative regulation, litigation, and political pronouncement. The community has a right to expect more from organized labor, confederation levels of management, and government agencies. Indeed, a shift in the method of national policymaking in the industrial relations area is required if labor and management are to make their potential contributions to the larger problems facing the community. The place to begin is to resolve that the method of consensus will be used internally in reaching decisions within the federation and confederation levels of management and in the formulation and administration of governmental policies. This is the fundamental challenge—in my view—of the next four or ten years in industrial relations in the United States.

The NLRB's New, Rough Line

M. R. LEFKOE

The National Labor Relations Board was not designed to win a popularity contest among businessmen. In the past several years, however, criticism of the board has become particularly bitter in and out of the business community. In a series of cases involving picketing, secondary boycotts, and free speech on the part of employers, the board is overturning sound precedents. More important, many businessmen believe that the present NLRB's avowed attempt to assume a policy-making role is infringing on the normal responsibilities and rights of management.

Businessmen are not alone in their disapproval. Theophil C. Kammholz, a former NLRB general counsel, joined the growing attacks on the board from the legal profession in a recent address before the American Management Association: "[The] Labor Board has changed the law governing employer-union relations in nearly 100 distinct areas—and more often than not with *ex post facto* decisions condemning and penalizing employers for acts perfectly legal when undertaken."

Congressmen have added to the drumfire of criticism. Last year Representative Robert P. Griffin (Republican, Michigan), co-author of the Landrum-Griffin Act of 1959, censured the board for its recent pattern of decisions, which, in his words, "gives rise to a serious concern that the policies laid down by Congress . . . are being distorted and frustrated, to say the very least." And several months ago Representative Phil M. Landrum (Democrat, Georgia) introduced a bill that would severely limit the power of the NLRB by turning most of its judicial authority over to the federal courts.

Taken from Fortune, *CXVIII* (*November 1963*), *pp. 164–66, 172, 176, 178. Reprinted with the permission of the author and the publisher. M. R. Lefkoe is president of Lefkoe Consulting, Inc., which provides consulting services to business firms and trade associations.*

While this idea is not new, its revival bespeaks a widespread dissatisfaction with the administration of current labor law. As is well known, the foundation of this law was laid down in the Wagner Act of 1935, which, in seeking to promote collective bargaining, decreed that an employer must recognize a union once an election has shown that it represents a bare majority of his employees in an "appropriate" bargaining unit. It also set forth a long list of so-called "unfair labor practices" on the part of employers. The NLRB was created with the dual function of supervising union representation elections and of hearing cases involving charges of such unfair practices.

Through the Taft-Hartley Act of 1947, Congress sought to redress the balance between unions and employers. It emphasized the basic freedom of employees to join or not to join unions, and spelled out a list of "unfair labor practices" applicable to unions. Despite these changes, the McClellan investigation, starting in 1957, revealed widespread union abuses and paved the way for the Landrum-Griffin Act, which sought to close loopholes in the existing law and reaffirmed the rights of employees, employers, and the general public. It left the discretionary power of the NLRB largely untouched.

The exercise of that power has, of course, always depended to no little degree on the personalities of the board, which is made up of five men, each appointed for a five-year term. In the last year of the Eisenhower Administration, under the chairmanship of Boyd Leedom, the board consisted of a majority of Republican appointees, although it was not necessarily considered "conservative" in its interpretations of highly complex law. Now while Leedom remains, the four other members of the board are Kennedy appointees or reappointees and this has meant a further change in general outlook. Gerald Brown, an early Kennedy appointee, has emphasized that the board should proceed on a "case by case" basis and should not be bound by "mechanical rules." Chairman Frank McCulloch for his part has professed some astonishment at the rising tide of public criticism of the NLRB, pointing out that such criticism involves relatively few cases out of the many handled. Nevertheless, even he has conceded that in certain "bellwether situations" the board has taken positions that "invite and should receive public discussion."

This is something of an understatement from the point of view of the critics. Admittedly, the board handles a tremendous volume of business—some 1,223 contested cases in fiscal 1963. But this scarcely alters the impact that a few cases are having on law and on business generally. Says Kenneth C. McGuiness, a labor-relations attorney and former acting general counsel of the board, in his new book, *The New Frontier NLRB:* "Irrespective of one's philosophy and predilections . . . the new board's divided opinions provide an impressive basis for the conclusion that the Kennedy majority is undermining the purpose of the statute, frustrating the intent of Congress, and demoralizing the major areas of labor-management relations. These are strong words but . . . the cases speak for themselves."

ANY GOOD BOYCOTT?

These cases, as noted, cover a wide territory involving the thorny questions of secondary boycotts, so-called "blackmail picketing," and, more seriously, what management deems infringements of its right to speak plainly to employees on economic matters and to make independent decisions (such as going out of business). With respect to secondary boycotts, the late Senator Taft once remarked that he had never discovered anyone who could distinguish between a "good" boycott and a "bad" one. And both Taft-Hartley and Landrum-Griffin threw up specific provisions aimed at (1) limiting labor disputes to the primary parties involved, and (2) preventing unions from coercing neutral parties into refusing to do business with, or handle the goods of, an employer with whom a union might be having an altercation. The nefarious practices of the Teamsters Union were on the mind of the legislators, especially after the McClellan investigation.

Yet a number of recent decisions by the NLRB have made businessmen wonder whether they are really safe from the secondary-boycott technique. One group of cases has had the effect of reversing an NLRB precedent that had stood for over eight years. This was set in the Washington Coca-Cola case when the board held it unlawful for a union to engage in "common situs" picketing (i.e., picketing at a site of more than one employer) so long as the employer with whom the union is having a dispute has his own place of business. Though some circuit courts did not uphold the board's reasoning, the Coca-Cola precedent received congressional approval in the legislative history of the Landrum-Griffin Act.

Despite this congressional intent, the new board has been extremely tolerant of "common situs" picketing. In the case of Plauche Electric Inc., an electrical contractor, the board allowed the Electrical Workers Union to picket a construction site where another company was also at work. In the case of Houston Armored Car Co., the United Plant Guard Workers followed the company's trucks along their routes and picketed some sixty-nine customers. When the com-

pany charged a secondary boycott, the new board ruled that the
union's action was permissible since it was conducted only so long as
a truck stayed at the address of a customer. The effect of such picketing, however, was just what Congress had tried to prohibit—namely,
union pressure on a neutral firm. And as Congressman Landrum
remarked, the new finding "should prove a special boon to Mr.
Hoffa."

Much more baffling is the case of the Middle South Broadcasting
Co., which owned a radio station, WOGA, in Chattanooga, Tennes-
see. In the course of a dispute with this station, the Radio and Television Engineers Union not only picketed WOGA's main office, but
also picketed outside the showroom of an automobile dealer from
which a WOGA program was being broadcast and distributed handbills to WOGA's advertisers and the public. In the course of NLRB
hearings the union admitted that its efforts were designed to encourage business firms to divert business to unionized stations. In its final
decision the board held that the picketing was justified on the theory
that the dealer's showroom had temporarily become WOGA's place
of business. It also justified the handbills under the "publicity proviso" of the law affecting secondary boycotts. This proviso states that
a union is within its rights in publicizing the fact that "a product or
products are produced by an employer with whom the labor organization has a primary dispute and are distributed by another employer."

To make the publicity proviso apply in this case, the majority of
the board had to argue that WOGA was in fact helping to produce a
"product"—namely, automobiles—which the automobile dealer was
distributing. In his dissent, Philip Ray Rodgers, then a member of the
board, stated: "I have no doubt that this finding will come as something of a surprise not only to WOGA, but to General Motors, Ford,
Chrysler, and other automobile manufacturers . . . It would seem
that the majority is here holding that a union may . . . handbill any
business establishment that has any commercial relationships, however remote, with any employer of any character with which the
union may have a dispute. Thus that which Congress prescribed as a
limitation takes on the aspects of a license."

THE POWER TO BLACKMAIL

License appears also to have crept into the board's interpretation of
the law as it affects many other areas, including so-called "blackmail
picketing." This phrase refers to a situation in which a union attempts

to bulldoze an employer into recognizing it even when his employees have shown no strong predilection for such recognition. One clear aim of the Landrum-Griffin Act was to prevent this kind of picketing where the employees of a company are already represented by another union, or where they have turned down a union through a valid NLRB election, or where the union has failed to file a petition for an election within thirty days of the time the picketing occurs. This last prohibition, however, is hedged with another "publicity" provision, which in effect states that picketing may be justified if the purpose is truthfully to advise the public that the employer does not have a contract with a labor organization—unless an effect of such picketing is to stop the pickup or delivery of goods.

The board's interpretation of this provision, plus other loopholes in the law itself, has let a lot of blackmail picketing go forward. In the case of Barker Brothers, which runs a group of stores in Los Angeles, the Retail Clerks Union made a number of overtures to management demanding recognition. The company refused on the grounds that the union had shown insufficient evidence to demonstrate that it really represented a majority of the employees, and the union later withdrew its claims. At the same time, however, the union began picketing Barker stores with signs requesting the public not to patronize the company because it was "nonunion." Subsequently Barker filed unfair-labor-practice charges against the union, pointing out that it had not petitioned for an election within thirty days as the law required.

The majority of the board threw out the complaint on the ground that the union's action was excused by the publicity proviso of the law. Once more members Leedom and Rodgers wrote a scorching dissent. They pointed out that one of the objectives of the picketing was recognition, which in itself made the publicity proviso inapplicable. They also pointed out that the picket signs were not truthful because in fact some of Barker's employees were unionized. Finally they stressed that the picketing had resulted in stoppages and work delays that clearly had interfered with the delivery of goods. It was their final judgment that the Barker decision "completes the virtual nullification of the congressional purpose" in enacting the provision.

FREEDOM OF SPEECH

Such nullification currently concerns both Congressmen and corporation lawyers, not only in highly technical cases involving secondary boycotts and picketing, but in a wide range of other areas—including union violence. By far the most important areas in controversy, however, concern free speech and the limits of collective bargaining itself. In the years following passage of the Wagner Act the NLRB adopted a policy that practically prevented employers from giving their side of the case to their employees when a union sought recognition or was engaged in bargaining. Taft-Hartley sought to remedy this situation by guaranteeing free speech to management so long as its statements contained "no threat of reprisal or force or promise of benefit." The Kennedy board has tended to interpret this exception very broadly. For instance, member Brown has said that "the question upon which each case should turn is whether when viewed in proper context, the employer's words, *even if couched in terms of a 'prediction'* or statement of legal position, render employee free choice impossible." (Italics added.)

Working within this kind of broad interpretation, the board as a matter of fact has in many cases applied the law in a way that businessmen feel leaves them gagged. In the case of Somismo Inc., a TV-cabinet manufacturer, the employer made a speech in which he stated that the promises of the union that was seeking recognition were "ridiculous" and predicted that if the union gained recognition and pressed its economic demands there would be a strike, adding, "use your own judgment." When the union lost the election by a narrow margin and petitioned the NLRB, the board held that the employer's speech implied the threat that he would go out of business if he had to deal with the union, and concluded that "such conduct interfered with the employees' freedom of choice." The union was then granted a new election, which it lost. In the case of Haynes Stellite, a division of Union Carbide Corp., the company told its employees during regularly scheduled meetings held before a United Steelworkers election that "we are the sole source of supply at present for some of our customers. We have been told that we would not continue to be the sole source of supply if we become unionized, due to the ever present possibility of a work stoppage." When the union lost the election it filed unfair-labor-practice charges. The board decided in favor of the union, holding that the company had "materially misrepresented" the facts when it stated that "some" customers would seek other suppliers when "only one" customer had said this. Leedom dissented on the grounds that no impropriety had been proved. And subsequently the Sixth Circuit Court unanimously reversed the board's decision, holding that the statement of the company under all the circumstances was fully protected by the free-speech provision of present law.

The issue of free speech on the part of the employer is also involved in a critical case now pending against General Electric.[1] In this case one of the board's trial examiners, citing previous NLRB rulings, held that the company had refused to bargain in good faith with the International Electrical Workers during negotiations back in 1960, when the union initiated a three-week strike. In his interim report the examiner noted that the company had criticized various actions of union leaders, and he called in question G.E.'s long-standing policy of communicating directly with its employees and promptly explaining to them the terms of its contract proposal to the union. This, in the view of the examiner, seemed to imply refusal to bargain in good faith. General Electric promptly appealed the case to the NLRB, which may not render its decision until next year. In doing so, G.E. based its position squarely on the First Amendment, and its vice president, Virgil Day, stated that the recommendations of the trial examiner "attempt to judge General Electric's 1960 bargaining conduct by a set of new and vaguely formulated standards which violate the basic rights of free speech and free collective bargaining, and, in our opinion, disregard the clear teachings of the U.S. Supreme Court."

WHAT ARE THE LIMITS?

Whatever the final outcome of the G.E. case, it has increased the worry of buinessmen not only as regards their rights of free speech but as regards the limits of collective bargaining itself, which were also at issue. Present law clearly requires such bargaining concerning rates of pay and hours of employment. It also stipulates that firms must bargain with duly certified unions concerning "other terms and conditions of employment." Under broad interpretation this could affect just about every kind of managerial decision, and some of the board's interpretations have been very flexible indeed. Sometimes it has charged bad faith when a company simply tried to narrow the issues during the course of collective bargaining. In other cases it has condemned companies for making what appear to be perfectly legitimate management decisions without long discussion with the union.

As an example of the first kind of case, consider that of General Tire & Rubber Co., which in 1960 held long negotiating sessions with the Operating Engineers. In the course of negotiations the company, through a series of compromises and agreements, reduced the list of the union's "must" demands from seventy-nine to twenty-six items. At a final meeting General Tire offered to compromise nine more issues, but thereafter negotiations broke down and the union lodged a

1 [Discussed above in the article on Boulwarism by Herbert Northrup. *Ed.*]

complaint with the NLRB on the grounds that the company was refusing to bargain in "good faith." In 1962 the board found for the union, holding that despite long negotiations the company had no real intention of concluding an agreement. It cited as evidence for this view the fact that General Tire had refused to accept any limitation on subcontracting and had also refused a union offer to make concessions in return for a checkoff of dues. This kind of reasoning seems to disregard the position taken by the Supreme Court, which has held that present labor law "does not compel either party to agree to a proposal or require the making of a concession."

More direct infringements of management's freedom of action in conducting a business are contained in a number of other recent cases. Back in 1954 the Eighth Circuit Court of Appeals held in its New Madrid decision that an employer has "the absolute right at all times to close permanently and go out of business . . . for whatever reason he may choose, whether union animosity or anything else . . . No one can be required to stay in private business." This would seem to be sensible doctrine in an enterprise economy, but the NLRB seems to question it. Some years ago the Darlington Manufacturing Co., a textile mill, was successfully organized by the Textile Workers Union. Shortly after the union won the election, Darlington's president recommended to his board of directors that the plant be closed down. There were many cogent economic reasons for doing so that had nothing to do with unionization, but the union charged an unfair labor practice.

In a decision finally rendered in 1962 the NLRB held that in closing down Darlington had "destroyed the possibility of collective bargaining." It further stressed that the major stockholders of Darlington were also the major stockholders in a larger textile combine, Deering, Milliken & Co. And on the basis of this "connection" the board ordered Deering, Milliken to pay back wages to some 500 Darlington employees who had lost their jobs. The implications of this kind of decision are that going out of business can, under current labor law, be even more hazardous than keeping a plant open.

FREEDOM TO CONTRACT

Still more disturbing to businessmen was another board ruling in the case of Town & Country Manufacturing Co., producer of house trailers, whose delivery drivers were organized by the General Drivers, Chauffeurs and Helpers Union. Both before and after the union organizing drive, the company encountered difficulties with the Inter-

state Commerce Commission about deliveries of its products to customers, and finally decided to discontinue its own delivery system and
to use commercial trucks hired under ICC permits. This satisfied the
ICC but enraged the union, which appealed to the NLRB. The board
decided that the company's unilateral action was designed to undermine the union and constituted a refusal to bargain; it ordered the
company to reinstate its delivery department and give its drivers back
pay. It held that the company's action "even if it was taken to avoid
violations of ICC regulations or because of economic considerations,
constituted an unlawful refusal to bargain for we believe that [the
employer] was under a statutory obligation to bargain as to its decision to subcontract."

Having made this decision, the board reopened and overturned a
previous case against Fibreboard Co. Once again, board member
Rodgers registered a dissent that sums up the misgivings of many
businessmen in this whole field. Said Rodgers: "If this ruling of the
majority stands, it is difficult to foresee any economic action which
management will be free to take of its own volition and in its own
vital interest (whether it be the discontinuance of an unprofitable
line, the closing of an unnecessary facility, or the abandonment of an
outmoded procedure) which would not be the subject of *mandatory*
bargaining . . . The subjecting of such management decisions as
this to the ambit of the Board's processes, and particularly to the
mandatory bargaining requirement, simply means that short of complete union agreement, any action taken by management must hereafter be taken at its peril."

The above cases are by no means the only ones that have caused
concern to many businessmen, but they are a fair sample. As pointed
out earlier, they certainly do not imply that the Board always holds
against management, and were labor relations a kind of ball game the
actual box score of cases won by labor and won by management
would not look so bad for industry. What critics rightly fear, however, is that new and important precedents are being set that will
steadily enlarge the already enormous power of the unions. Board
member Brown holds that the purpose of labor law is "in essence the
encouragement of collective bargaining as the democratic method of
solving labor problems." But it is all too easy under this formulation
to make collective bargaining an end in itself rather than one possible
means of protecting individual rights and fostering industrial relations.

It can be argued that if these ends are really to be achieved we
must make far-reaching changes in the content of labor law itself,

quite aside from its administration. From the Clayton Act, which largely exempted unions from antitrust prosecution, through the passage of the Norris-LaGuardia Act in 1932, unions have been given ever greater privileges and exemptions by government, and the Wagner Act simply carried on this trend. From this point of view, Taft-Hartley and Landrum-Griffin were at best palliatives and more far-reaching reforms are called for that would directly cut down on union power. Such reforms would aim at withdrawing the excessive power that government itself has given to unions.

RULE OF LAW

But quite aside from this kind of fundamental reform, there is reason to ask whether the NLRB needs all the discretionary authority it now possesses. Long before the "Kennedy Board" hove on the scene it was notable that NLRB decisions shifted with every change in its personnel. As Kenneth McGuiness has said: "The questions raised by the Kennedy Board's conception of its function are distinguishable from historical problems of the NLRB only in degree . . . Stated another way, the new Board's conduct has demonstrated more clearly than ever before the necessity for some revision in the system of enforcing our basic labor law."

One revision might be to allow the Board to go on deciding cases of union representation, but to clip its wings as regards cases involving "unfair labor practices." As matters stand, the Board passes on these in the first instance though they can eventually be appealed to the courts, a process that involves long delay. In 1961 members of the Labor Law Section of the American Bar Association gave substantial support to a proposal that unfair-labor-practice cases go to the courts directly. Representative Landrum is now pushing for such reform in Congress on the grounds that "cases involving unfair labor practices are private lawsuits—nothing more." It follows that such cases should never have been handed over to the NLRB in the first place.

The Landrum proposal would be a step, though only a step, in remedying a situation that is proving increasingly onerous to businessmen. It also points in the right general direction. The U.S. already has far too much administrative law and has paid a heavy price for weakening and short-circuiting judicial process. To give the courts initial jurisdiction over major labor disputes might have its inconveniences. But it would further the objective of promoting a government of law rather than of men.

The Kennedy Labor Board

JOSEPH GRODIN

Labor relations law has never been noted for its stability. From the period of the early English Combination Acts to the days of the Wagner, Taft-Hartley, and the Landrum-Griffin Acts, changing social conditions and political climates have produced fluctuations in legislation which are bewildering to lawyer and layman alike. Courts, too, have felt the impact of whatever it is that makes for judicial change, and their decisions on such matters as antitrust laws and unions, or picketing and free speech, or federal pre-emption have displayed variations inclined to make attorneys who deal in less dynamic parts of the law sigh in sympathy.

Consequently, it ought to come as no surprise that the National Labor Relations Board, which administers rather broadly drafted legislation in this highly sensitive area, should likewise react to changing conditions and attitudes; nor, in view of the fact that the members of the Board are appointed by the President for terms of only five years, should it be surprising that the pattern of its decisions will to some extent reflect the policies of a particular administration. Often the pattern is blurred by the impact of court decisions which require, or may be argued to require, modification of Board precedent; and it is further blurred by the rather frequent refusal of Board members to follow party lines. Nevertheless, the pattern is undeniably there and recognized by every labor law practitioner and student.

CHANGING CHARACTER OF THE BOARD

Thus the Board which, after March 2, 1954, included a majority of Eisenhower appointees, is commonly referred to as the Eisenhower

Taken from Industrial Relations, *III (February 1964), pp. 33–45. Reprinted with the permission of the publisher. Joseph Grodin is an assistant professor at Hastings College of Law and a member of a law firm in San Francisco.*

Board, and there is little doubt that it departed substantially from the precedents established by its predecessor, the Truman Board. It is reasonably clear, moreover, that the pattern of departure reflected certain policy judgments: for example, that employers should be allowed greater latitude in opposing union organization, particularly in the area of "free speech"; that government should interfere less in the bargaining process; that statutory prohibitions against union economic action should be strictly interpreted; and that craft unions should be allowed greater opportunity to represent employees previously represented in over-all industrial units.[1] While it would be inaccurate and unfair to characterize its decisions broadly as pro-employer or anti-CIO, few would dispute the proposition that they tended to create a more favorable legal climate for employers and a more restrictive one for unions, particularly (in unit decisions) for unions of an industrial type.

The Kennedy Board came into being in the spring of 1961, with the appointment of Frank A. McCulloch as Board Chairman, and Gerald A. Brown as Member, replacing two Eisenhower appointees. These two appointments would not have been sufficient to create a new majority had it not been for the fact that Board Member John H. Fanning (a Democrat) had been a frequent dissenter since his appointment by Eisenhower in 1957 and displayed greater affinity with the policies of McCulloch and Brown than with those of his Republican colleagues, Philip Ray Rodgers and Boyd Leedom. Thus, Board decisions became characterized (as they were during the early years of the Eisenhower Administration) by a frequent 3–2 split, with McCulloch, Brown, and Fanning on one side and Rodgers and Leedom on the other. President Kennedy reappointed Member Fanning to an additional term in 1962, so that the 3–2 composition of the Board remained unchanged until the appointment of Howard Jenkins to replace Rodgers in August 1963. It is still too early to tell how this new appointment will affect the voting. Of course, the 3–2 split is by no means uniform. The overwhelming majority of decisions are unanimous, and in several important cases the Board has divided in other directions.[2] Nevertheless, the split is typical in cases overruling or distinguishing Eisenhower Board precedents, and it provides a valuable clue to the policy patterns of the new Board.

Chairman McCulloch has suggested that the distinctive feature of the new Board "lies in a sincere attempt to substitute a pragmatic, ad

---

[1] See Brinker, *Member Murdock Dissenting,* 7 LAB. L.J. 671 (1956).
[2] For example, *Miranda Fuel,* 140 NLRB No. 7 (1962), one of the most far-reaching and radical decisions of recent years (holding that violation by a union of its duty of fair representation constitutes an unfair labor practice) was the product of a Rodgers-Leedom-Brown majority, McCulloch and Fanning in dissent.

hoc technique for the previous too-frequent applications of per se doctrines,"[3] and there is a good deal of merit in his observation. The Eisenhower Board had been criticized by the courts for establishing rules of conduct, violations of which they regarded as per se violations of the Act.[4] The new Board has sought to avoid that pitfall. And it has, in many cases, justified its departure from precedent on the basis of changing conditions or the unique character of particular situations.

Yet the policies of the new Board are not fully described by calling them pragmatic, for the goals of the Act are not so well defined, nor the impact of particular decisions so easily predictable, that reasonable people applying a pragmatic philosophy would necessarily reach the same conclusions. Interests must be weighed and balanced, and value judgments must be made. Insofar as the new Board has departed from precedent, its decisions reflect judgments with respect to goals and methods (and, indeed, with respect to the desirability of adhering to precedent itself) which spring from the outlooks and philosophies of particular members.

By way of illustrating the kinds of policy determinations called for in administration of the Act, we will examine briefly the Kennedy Board's decisions in three legal areas bearing upon the establishment of the collective bargaining relationship: (1) unit determinations, (2) electioneering, and (3) recognitional and organizational picketing. It is my thesis that these decisions reflect a general policy of giving greater protection and impetus than did the Eisenhower Board to the creation of bargaining relationships, with the likely effect of stimulating collective bargaining in relatively unorganized areas. This is not to say that the Kennedy Board is uniformly prounion, any more than the Eisenhower Board was uniformly proemployer. To the contrary, there are many areas in which Kennedy Board decisions have been strongly criticized by unions. For example, the Board has given the hot-cargo provisions of the Act a restrictive interpretation;[5] it has

---

3 Speech at 8th Annual Joint Industrial Relations Conference, Michigan State University, April 19, 1962 (49 LRRM 74).

4 For example, *Local 357, International Brotherhood of Teamsters v. NLRB*, 365 U.S. 667, (1961) (reversing the "Mountain Pacific" hiring hall doctrine).

5 For example, the Board holds that, while a union may by agreement lawfully prohibit subcontracting altogether, it may not, even to protect its work standards, limit subcontracting to employers who pay union scale. *Falstaff Brewing Corp.*, 144 NLRB No. 22 (1963) (Member Brown dissenting); and that, while the Act allows hot-cargo agreements confined to job-site work in the construction industry, a union may not picket to obtain or enforce such an agreement. For example, *Stockton Plumbing Co.*, 144 NLRB No. 3 (1963). One federal circuit court has registered disagreement with the latter view. *Construction Laborers Union v. NLRB*, 54 LRRM 2246 (9th Cir., Sept. 26, 1963).

granted greater leeway to employers in the use of lockouts as defensive weapons;[6] and it has held, contrary to one circuit court of appeals, that consumer picketing of a neutral employer is unlawful under the secondary boycott provisions of the Act.[7] These, too, involve mixed questions of law and policy (and it would be an interesting endeavour to ascertain and reconcile the policy assumptions implicit in these various determinations, but that is beyond the scope of this article).[8]

UNIT DETERMINATIONS

When the Board is called upon to conduct an election, it must determine "in each case" whether the unit of employees sought by the petitioner is "appropriate" for the purposes of collective bargaining, "in order to assure to employees the fullest freedom in exercising the rights guaranteed by [the] Act."[9] Except for a few restrictions,[10] the Act provides no further criteria for such a determination. Consequently, over the years the Board has developed its own criteria— for example, prior bargaining history, the desires of the employees, extent of organization, the skills of the employees, whether they are separately or commonly supervised, and so forth. In addition to these general criteria, however, it has developed "rules," more or less automatic, for unit placement in certain industries or of certain types of employees. These rules provide a certain amount of stability and predictability, but at the occasional expense of ignoring factual differences in situations.

It is in regard to these rules that the ad hoc approach of the Kennedy Board is most apparent. In cases involving the inclusion or exclusion from the bargaining unit of particular groups of employees, the Board has declined to follow many of the rules established by the Eisenhower Board, or even the Truman and Roosevelt Boards, and has insisted on application of general criteria on a case-by-case basis.

For example, a rule of long standing decreed that "technical" employees (those with considerable technical skills, but not "professional" within the meaning of the Act) would not be included in an

[6] For example, *Building Contractors Assoc. of Rockford, Inc.*, 138 NLRB No. 143 (1962).

[7] See *Fruit and Vegetable Packers v. NLRB*, 308 F.2d 311 (D.C. Cir., 1962).

[8] I suggest that a close relationship can be found between the Board's policies and the recommendations contained in the Pucinski and Kerr committee reports.

[9] LMRA, Sec. 9(b).

[10] For example, a restriction on including professional employees in a nonprofessional unit without their consent or including guards in a unit of other employees (Sec. 9(b)).

over-all production and maintenance unit, if any party objects.[11] In the context of an ever-increasing number of automation-created white-collar jobs and the traditional resistance of such employees to unionization, such a rule may have had the effect of forestalling representation. In any event, the new Board has reversed the rule, stating that henceforth unit placement of technical employees will be a "pragmatic judgment," based on usual placement criteria.[12]

Similarly, and in the face of vigorous dissent, the Democratic majority has reversed the Eisenhower Board's rule that a unit of truck drivers may automatically be severed from an industrial unit if any union desires to sever them[13] and will automatically be included if no union desires to represent them separately.[14] Again, the Board says it will look to usual placement factors in each case.

Through the ad hoc process, however, run threads of policy. The new Board appears less willing than its predecessor to allow severance of craft or departmental units from previously established industrial units.[15] On the other hand, when it comes to establishment of new collective bargaining relationships, the Board appears to be less concerned with establishing "ideal" units, and more concerned with encouraging collective bargaining by allowing smaller units in which there is some chance of a representative being selected. For example, prior Board policy decreed that in the event of dispute as to unit placement the only appropriate unit for a retail department store chain was a unit which included: (1) all stores within the employer's administrative unit or geographical division, and also, (2) all selling and nonselling employees. The new Board in 1962 reversed the first rule on the ground that "too frequently it has operated to impede the exercise by employees . . . of their rights to self-organization";[16] and more recently it reversed the second rule as well, allowing a unit of restaurant employees within a department store where no union sought a broader unit.[17]

The Eisenhower members dissented from these rulings on the ground (among others) that the majority was giving "controlling"

---

[11] Litton Industries of Maryland, 125 NLRB 722 (1959).
[12] Sheffield Corporation, 134 NLRB 1001 (1961).
[13] Kalamazoo Paper Box Company, 136 NLRB 134 (1962).
[14] E. H. Koester Bakery Co., 136 NLRB 1006 (1962).
[15] For example, American Hard Rubber Co., 142 NLRB 116 (1963) refusing to allow severance of employees classified as pipefitters, electricians, etc., on the ground they were not "true craftsmen." Rodgers and Leedom dissented, claiming the majority was failing to follow the American Potash rules of craft severance established by the Eisenhower Board, 107 NLRB 1418 (1954).
[16] Sav-On Drugs, Inc., 138 NLRB 1032 (1962).
[17] F. W. Woolworth Co., 144 NLRB 35 (1963).

weight to the union's extent of organization—something which has been prohibited by the Act since 1947.[18] Whether the dissenters are right depends upon the meaning of "controlling." If it means that the Board may not establish an arbitrary unit solely on the ground that the union has not succeeded in organizing further, then the dissenters are probably wrong; for in each of the cases the majority relied upon other factors to establish the alternative appropriateness of the smaller unit. There is little doubt, however, that the majority is more inclined to allow small units than the Eisenhower Board, with the obvious result of encouraging collective bargaining relationships.

ELECTIONEERING CASES

One of the most significant developments under the Kennedy Board, and one that again implies judgments based on policy, is an increased tendency to set aside election results on the ground that particular employer or union communications have interfered with the "laboratory conditions" requisite to free expression of choice.

Section 8(c) of the Act, the so-called free speech provision added in 1947, forbids the Board from holding any expression of "views, argument or opinion" to constitute or be evidence of an unfair labor practice, "if such expression contains no threat of reprisal or force or promise of benefit." The Truman Board, in what is known as the *General Shoe* doctrine, took the position that Section 8(c) was applicable only to unfair labor practice cases, and did not preclude the Board from overturning an election on the basis of speech which, though protected by Section 8(c) from being held to constitute or be evidence of an unfair labor practice, interfered with a free election. The Eisenhower Board, though not expressly overruling *General Shoe,* appeared to apply the protection of Section 8(c) to representation cases as well.[19] Indeed, in some cases it declined to overturn an election even on the basis of speech which, unprotected by Section 8(c), might have been the basis for an unfair labor practice charge.[20] But most significantly, legal doctrine aside, the Eisenhower Board tended, at least in the absence of strong evidence of coercive context, to allow wide scope to pre-election speeches which foreboded an implacable employer position in bargaining or the probability of strikes, loss of business, or plant removal if the union won the

---

[18] LMRA Sec. 9(c)(5).
[19] For example, *American Laundry Machinery Co.,* 107 NLRB 511 (1953).
[20] For example, *National Furniture Manufacturing Co., Inc.,* 106 NLRB 1300 (1953.)

election, so long as the speeches were phrased in terms of "predictions," "expressions of opinion," or "statements of legal position," rather than threats. The new Board has diverged widely from that point of view. In a series of cases it has taken the position that: (1) Section 8(c) is not applicable to representation proceedings, (2) speech which constitutes an unfair labor practice is a fortiori coercive in an election context, and (3) the Board will not be bound by phraseology, but will look to "the economic realities of the employer-employee relationship and . . . set aside an election where we find that the employer's conduct has resulted in substantial interference with the election, regardless of the form in which the statement was made."[21]

On its face, the Board's statement of departure appears to be but another example of rebellion against per se, mechanical rules; but in application, it is something more. It is undoubtedly true that the new Board is more willing to view communication in its total context, but its evaluation of that context—of the "economic realities of the employer-employee relationship"—necessarily implies policy judgments and assumptions of fact which may go beyond the evidence in a particular case. A good illustration is the *Lord Baltimore Press* case,[22] in which an employer, about one week before the election, sent his employees a letter which began by stating that the union "wants to control your future and destroy a relationship which had been a benefit to you and your Company." The letter went on to say that the union is a small one, composed mainly of employees in the commercial printing industry; that it withdrew from the AFL–CIO rather than abide by the no-raid pact; that it was really out to protect the interests of its members in the lithographic printing industry by attempting to impose working conditions in that industry upon the "noncomparable" folding box industry (in which the employer participated) and that such standards would be "uneconomic and noncompetitive" in the latter industry. The letter went on to state that if the employer were forced out of offset [printing], "your jobs would be eliminated," and that if the union attempted to impose such noncompetitive standards, the company would have "no choice but to resist," and the union would have "no choice but to either agree or force you out on strike." Finally, the letter indicated that the employer felt the Board-determined unit was legally inappropriate and that he intended to test the propriety of the unit in court by refusing to bargain, which test is characterized as a "time consuming process

---

21 *Dal-Tex Optical Co.*, 137 NLRB 189 (1962).
22 142 NLRB 40 (1963).

which might take several years from the date of the election." The letter concluded with the statement, "The best way to not only prevent this situation from occurring, but also prevent the union from attempting to use you for its own selfish interests is to vote 'NO' when you cast your secret ballot on November 2."

A majority of the three-man Board panel decided that this letter, standing alone, was sufficient basis for setting the election aside. "Its entire truth," the majority said, "achieved by the careful juxtaposition of foreboding possibilities, is to impress upon the employees the futility of choosing the Petitioner." Even if the employer's legal position were defensible, viewed in the context of the entire letter, it was a "statement of legal position as a threat to use the delaying processes of the law to the fullest extent possible in order to thwart the policies of the Act we enforce. Such conduct, combined with the fear of economic loss that must flow from the Employer's predictions of its reaction to the Petitioner's unknown demands must be held to have destroyed the laboratory conditions we seek to maintain and, consequently, to have prevented the employees' free choice."

Member Rodgers, dissenting, found the letter to contain nothing more than "frank and forthright statements," including a "bona fide" statement of intent to adhere to a "plausible" legal position. Moreover, he accuses the majority of failing to adhere to its own principle, that is, of viewing the speech in its context of a four-week election campaign, with "ample time for the Petitioner to answer and counteract whatever influence it might have had."

Clearly, the difference between the majority and Member Rodgers involves more than the issue of looking behind words; it involves a judgment as to what factors have to be looked at and how they are to be weighed. Board Member Brown made this clear in a speech before the Labor Law Section of the Texas State Bar, in which he said that the process is one of balancing the rights of free speech against employee freedom of choice, and that "over the years the Board has tipped the balance in favor of one right or the other, depending on the views of the Members at the time." Brown's views, and one may assume they are shared in large measure by the other majority members, give substantial weight to the following factors:

1. An employer has the edge over a union in pre-election persuasiveness, because "the employer is known to the employees, controls their jobs and income, and has the power effectively to express his displeasure."

2. According to studies, employees often develop a "deference pattern toward their employer, which causes them to respond to his

suggestions because they are in the habit of responding to his direction."

3. The degree to which an employer's speech will have coercive effect may depend upon the degree of sophistication of the employees, which in turn may depend upon the location of the plant and the prior experience of the employees with labor organizations.

4. Decisions of the Eisenhower Board had been criticized by such groups as the Pucinski Committee and the Independent Labor Study Group headed by Clark Kerr for not giving sufficient weight to the preceding factors.

"Because of its concern about the merit of these criticisms," Brown said, "the Board has re-examined and will continue to re-examine many of the criteria which have been applied." In light of these policy assumptions, the *Lord Baltimore Press* case may indicate that the Kennedy Board is not as concerned with the intent or spirit (whether good or bad) behind a particular communication as it is with the probable consequences of the communication itself—that it is not so important whether a particular statement is *intended* as a threat, as whether it is likely to be *interpreted* (reasonably) as a threat by the employees.

Further evidence of the Board's policies in this area is found in cases dealing with misrepresentations of fact made during the course of an election campaign. Pointing to what it regards as an "increasing tendency for parties to an election deliberately to time the distribution of propaganda literature making new and powerful points so close to the election that the other parties will be unable to make effective answers,"[23] the majority has stated that it will overturn an election where one of the parties engages in "misrepresentation or other similar campaign trickery, which involves a substantial departure from the truth, at a time which prevents the other party or parties from making an effective reply, so that the misrepresentation, *whether deliberate or not,* may reasonably be expected to have a significant impact on the election." In ascertaining whether misrepresentation carries a "significant impact," the majority says it will consider whether: it relates to an important or unimportant matter; it was so extreme "as to put the employees on notice of its lack of truth under the particular circumstances so that they could not reasonably have relied on the assertion"; the employees possessed "independent knowledge with which to evaluate the statements"; the party making the statement possessed "intimate knowledge of the

23 *Trane Company,* 137 NLRB 1506 (1962).

subject matter so that the employees sought to be persuaded may be expected to attach added significance to its assertion."[24]

Although the doctrine of misrepresentation existed during the Eisenhower Board regime, it was not so clearly defined, nor did it appear to apply to unintentional misrepresentations. The Kennedy Board's position that misrepresentations need not be deliberate is further evidence that the Board is primarily concerned with consequences of communication.

Similar policies underlie the Kennedy Board's limited revival of the old "captive audience" doctrine of the Truman Board—that an employer may commit an unfair labor practice if, during the course of an election campaign, he makes an antiunion speech (even though noncoercive) on company time and premises without allowing the union equal opportunity to reply.[25] The Board has limited the doctrine, at least so far, to a situation in which the employer maintains a broad nonsolicitation rule, which forbids employees from soliciting other employees for union membership while they are off-duty (say, during the lunch hour), but still on company premises.[26] Such a rule is lawful in some industries, such as department stores, but the Board's theory is that such a rule combined with a captive audience speech creates a "glaring imbalance in opportunities for organizational communication." (As the dissenting Eisenhower members rather enthusiastically point out, this doctrine embodies a per se approach to the extent of saying that a union's actual opportunities for communication off the job will not be evaluated on a case-by-case basis.)

RECOGNITIONAL AND ORGANIZATIONAL PICKETING

The third area we shall consider involves questions of statutory interpretation more directly than the two previous topics, but here as well policy considerations are evident.

Section 8(b) (7) of the Act prohibits an uncertified union from picketing for "an object" of forcing or requiring recognition or organization in three situations: (A) where the employer has lawfully recognized another union and a question concerning representation cannot appropriately be raised; (B) where a valid election has been conducted within the preceding 12 months; or (C) where picketing is

---

24 *Hollywood Ceramics Co.*, 140 NLRB 36 (1962).
25 *Bonwit Teller*, 96 NLRB 608 (1951).
26 *May Department Stores Co.*, 136 NLRB 797 (1962).

continued without a petition for election being filed within "a reasonable period of time not to exceed thirty days." In the latter situation, where a petition has been filed, the Board is directed to hold an
expedited election, without the necessity of a hearing. A proviso to
subparagraph (C) permits picketing or other publicity "for the purpose of truthfully advising the public . . . that an employer does
not employ members of, or have a contract with, a labor organization," so long as the picketing does not have "an effect" of inducing
employees of other employers not to cross the picket line.

The McCulloch-Brown-Fanning majority has rendered interpretations of these provisions which differ widely and significantly from
those of Rodgers and Leedom and from those of the Eisenhower
Board. Indeed, the divergence from the old Board was dramatically
emphasized when the new Board granted motions for reconsideration
in a series of 8(b) (7) cases and issued new and, to a considerable
degree, conflicting decisions.[27] The Kennedy Board's most significant
interpretation of Section 8(b) (7), in terms of practical consequences, is that the Section does not apply at all to standards picketing, i.e., picketing for the purpose of protesting and eliminating substandard wages or working conditions. The Eisenhower Board had
held (in the context of an alleged jurisdictional dispute, but the same
principle is applicable to Section 8[b] [7]) that picketing to protest
an employer's wage rates necessarily involves a claim for recognition,
but the new Board says that the objective of eliminating substandard
conditions "could be achieved without the employer either bargaining
with or recognizing the union."[28]

The Kennedy Board's position on standards picketing has many
practical consequences. A union faced with an employer who provides less than prevailing wages, fringe benefits, or working conditions (whether he has a contract with another union or no union at
all), may wish it could organize the employees, or obtain a contract,
or even force the employer off the job he is working on. But if it is
unable to accomplish these goals, whether because of legal or economic obstacles, it almost always has a secondary interest in protecting its membership from competition by employers whose labor costs
are below its own standards. Under the new Board's rules, if the
union is careful to use the proper language in approaching the employer and in its picket signs and other communications, it is free to
protect these standards by picketing, free of the limitations of Section
8(b) (7)—that is to say, without regard to how recently an election

27 See *Blinne Construction Co.*, 135 NLRB 121 (1962).
28 *Claude Everett Construction Co.*, 136 NLRB 321 (1962).

has been held, or whether another union has been recognized, or how long the picketing continues. If this interpretation allows some unions to evade the strictures of Section 8(b) (7) by concealing an active recognitional or organizational object, a contrary interpretation would preclude unions from picketing even when their purpose is, in fact, just to protect standards.

EVALUATION

Hopefully, the foregoing brief examination of Board decisions in select areas will serve to illustrate that policy determinations are inevitable in administration of the Act and cannot be avoided without drastic alteration of the institutional framework in which the Act is administered. It would be possible, perhaps, for Congress to be so specific in its statutory language that the area for policy determination would be narrowed considerably, but at the expense of a degree of rigidity and inflexibility hardly appropriate to such a rapidly changing area as labor relations. It might also be possible to isolate policy determinations from political change somewhat by adopting longer terms for Board members or by vesting decision powers in permanently appointed trial examiners or labor courts. But such alternatives would simply perpetuate over a longer period of time, and with concomitant inflexibility, the policies of particular appointees. Moreover, they leave out of account the desirability of allowing changes in public opinion to be reflected in policy determinations of the Labor Board, subject, of course, to review by the courts.

Board member Leedom has argued[29] that his colleagues should refrain from following their own views to the extent of overruling precedent, except where changing conditions dictate a different result. His argument for stare decisis in Board decisions is based on three considerations. First, he suggests that Board members should have the "humility" to recognize that long-established rules may embody great wisdom. In fact, he puts the argument a bit more strongly: ". . . the fact that a rule of law is well-established and strongly entrenched is persuasive evidence that the rule is correct."

Whatever the merits of such an argument generally (the fact that a rule of law has existed for a long time is equally consistent with the hypothesis that the rule was established and maintained by people with different policy outlooks or who ignored changes in circumstance), it casts little light in the context of Board law, considering

[29] Speech to Labor Law Section of the Illinois Bar Assoc., Jan. 19, 1962, reported at 49 LRRM 85.

that the Board is less than 30 years old and that many of the rules being reversed today were themselves established only a few years ago through reversal of prior precedent.

Second, Leedom contends that stare decisis in Board decisions is necessary to maintain public confidence in the Board itself—that "sharp reversals of Board decisions and policy, and especially those taking place soon after changes in Board membership, serve to foster the idea that Board decisions . . . are like a restricted railroad ticket, good for this day and train only."

Leaving aside the aptness of the metaphor, if it is true that Board decisions must of necessity depend on value judgments, it would seem that the public has a right to know that fact. For Board members to refrain from reversing judgments of which they disapprove, whether soon after a change in Board membership or later, for the purpose of giving the public an illusion of stability, is itself a difficult policy to defend.

Leedom's third point is a more substantial one—that stare decisis is desirable because it affords predictability. Without question it is of value that parties be able to predict Board decisions so they can guide their conduct accordingly. But the problem is more complex. In the first place, adherence to precedent will produce predictability only to the extent that the principle adhered to itself provides a basis for prediction. For example, the Eisenhower Board rules on unit placement in particular industries produced a high degree of predictability, whereas the Kennedy Board's decision to throw out such per se rules and treat each situation on a case-by-case basis provides very little, and it will provide no more no matter how long it is adhered to. The question in such a case is not one of stare decisis, but of the rule itself—whether it should give greater weight to predictability or to the unique factors of each individual situation. In some areas—such as employer discrimination—such a choice is available to a much lesser extent, because of the necessary emphasis on the facts of each case.

Assuming a rule to provide some predictability, whether it should be changed to another rule (which, let us assume, will then provide equal predictability until it is changed) involves, obviously, the desirability of the new rule and also an evaluation of the impact of the change on those who relied on the old rule. For example, in the unit cases discussed above, it is hardly likely that any of the parties involved would have acted in reliance on prior decisions to the point where reversal of those decisions would have resulted in significant injury to their interests. Similarly, the direction of a new election is in most situations not an inequitable remedy for election interference, even if the conduct complained of resulted from reliance on prior decisions. On the other hand, there are situations where reliance on a reversed principle may result in serious detriment—for example, in the contracting out of work—and in such situations establishment of a new rule may work a hardship.

It must be borne in mind, however, that the predictions of the aware labor law counsellor will take into account not merely the decisions of record but the tendencies and policies evidenced by those decisions and by other facts he can gather about the members of the Board. On the basis of such factors he may be able to make reasonably safe predictions, even to the extent of anticipating reversal of prior decisions, and in such manner the adverse impact of change can be lessened. Thus, the very fact that Board decisions imply policy judgments, and that such judgments vary from administration to administration with the composition of the Board, is itself a predictive tool. It would be a foolhardly counsellor indeed who, the next time a Republican is elected President, failed to advise his clients as to the likely effect of new Board appointments upon existing law.

PART IX

MANPOWER PLANNING

INTRODUCTION

A significant development in recent years has been national planning for the training and use of labor resources. Analyses have indicated that investment in education and other preparation for a work career pays off for the individual and for the nation. The same may be true of manpower programs for vocational testing, guidance, and placement of unemployed workers and of new entrants into the labor force.

High levels of unemployment and significant changes in industry (including automation) have stimulated thinking about manpower problems. One result has been the growing emphasis upon manpower planning and upon the critical analyses of different instruments for aiding in such planning.

An introduction to this subject area is provided by Brandes' article on "Manpower Planning and the 'Drop-out Problem.'" He outlines the steps already taken, places the program in proper perspective, and makes some realistic observations on educational requirements for different kinds of jobs.

President Johnson's 1964 Manpower Report shows how broad-gauge and long-range the national planning for full and effective use of human resources should be. His "active manpower policy" is not very clearly defined as stated in the Report. Indeed, the President's Report, in stating what needs to be done and legislative proposals, may seem to imply more logic, coordination, and accomplishment than is actually the case. One reason for the new piece of machinery announced in the Report, namely, the President's Committee on Manpower, is to highlight manpower considerations and to help integrate the manpower aspects of independent Federal programs.

The Clark Subcommittee Report provides a critical survey of the whole manpower field. The excerpts selected from the majority statement cover the main issues. A basic issue is the roles of deficient demand and structural changes in unemployment since 1957. (This issue is also discussed in Sultan and Prasow's article on "The Skill Impact of Automation" in Part VI.) The Clark Report suggests better integration of programs for increasing demand and programs for manpower preparation and mobility, pointing out that the Council of Economic Advisers is deficient in the area of manpower analysis and policy.

Another issue is the important role of the Federal-State employment service. Should it just provide a job exchange, or should it be a community and national manpower agency, conducting aptitude and performance tests, engaging in career counseling, and developing skill and job information and analyses, including projections of occupational needs and supplies for the use of workers, employers, and educators?

A third issue is whether workers are receiving the proper kinds of preparation through the retraining programs (under the Manpower Development and Training Act and the Area Redevelopment Act) and through the vocational education programs in the high schools. In many instances, insufficient attention is given to future job requirements and opportunities and to the employment effects of automation in deciding what the training shall be. Sultan and Prasow comment extensively on this aspect. The Clark Report complains that too few high school students are enrolled in vocational training for occupations where employment opportunities are expanding, and that there ought to be a closer tie-up between manpower and educational policies.

Furthermore, the Clark Subcommittee points out that proper training soon pays for itself from the extra earnings of trainees, which also increase tax revenue and reduce unemployment compensation and relief costs. It is evident that manpower programs need to be guided by more adequate analyses of costs and benefits, both to the individual and to society, than have hitherto been available. For such analyses, goals would need to be clearly defined, so that measures of success and standards of efficiency of operation could be satisfactorily established. Also, such cost-benefit analyses would raise interesting questions concerning the type and incidence of financing for particular programs.

In the manpower area, the Federal Government has embarked on a challenging venture with far-reaching implications. Because the program involves the vital interests of millions of persons in a democracy, the government must operate through information, advice, and persuasion. With the long lead time required for some careers, skillful analysis and long-range planning on a local and national basis are necessary. The returns from theoretical and empirical research in this field promise to be high in terms of national income and personal satisfaction and welfare.

Manpower Planning and
the "Drop-out Problem"

ELY M. BRANDES

James Dierke, an assistant school superintendent in San Francisco, recently came forth with an unusual proposal for dealing with the problem of school dropouts. He suggested that all high-school students be given duly certified diplomas, regardless of whether they had passed their examinations or not. Dierke was willing to grant that there might be some merit in letting the diplomas so issued be annotated to indicate whether the recipient had mastered the arts of reading and writing, but he deplored any further certification of scholastic achievement.

This modest proposal, it should be noted, came in response to a complaint by the San Francisco welfare department that the school system's failure to graduate enough students was the immediate cause of the dropout problem. What Dierke was saying with his wry reply, then, was simply that if we have created a society in which the very possibility of any individual's economic usefulness requires his possession of a high-school diploma, the obvious solution is to degrade the diploma to the level of a birth certificate, presented amid appropriate commencement ceremonies some eighteen years after the fact.

How serious or even real is the problem of high-school dropouts? For more than a year the nation's publications have been filled with articles and reports about this social problem of teen-agers who are unwilling or unable to complete their high-school courses. The articles are full of facts and figures—all undoubtedly valid—detailing

Taken from The Reporter, *XXX (March 26, 1964), pp. 17–19. Reprinted with the permission of the author and the publisher. Copyright © 1964 by The Reporter Magazine Company. Ely M. Brandes is an economist with the Stanford Research Institute at Menlo Park.*

the present plight of these young people in finding employment and forecasting an even dimmer future. President Johnson's annual Manpower Report, which was sent to Congress just a few days ago, states that ". . . nearly a million young people are leaving our educational system each year before completing even elementary or secondary school." The report also points out that "Two-thirds of the unemployed have less than a high-school education. One of every twelve workers with only elementary school is unemployed, compared with only one of seventy college graduates."

And yet there is a strange air of unreality about this problem of the dropouts, or at least about the way it has been defined, if one considers that fifty years ago the vast majority of our youngsters left school without obtaining a high-school diploma. Has our economy changed to such an extent that we can no longer utilize janitors, hospital attendants, truck drivers, gardeners, waitresses, and many other workers in the service trades, unless they are high-school graduates? True, some jobs that were once rated as unskilled now require, for instance, the ability to read and write and to do simple arithmetic, but on the whole technology has affected these jobs primarily by making them less burdensome. Generally they are no more complex now than they were ten or even fifty years ago, although the proportions have changed: fifty years ago one job in eight was unskilled; today the ratio is one in twenty. Technology has definitely not eliminated these jobs, nor is it apt to do so in the foreseeable future. The service industries, in fact, have provided the greater part of all new jobs in our economy since the end of the war.

The dropout problem was not created by the inability of nongraduates to perform the more or less menial tasks in society. The problem exists because employers will not hire dropouts even for low-grade service jobs if they can possibly avoid doing so.

This is not to say that this normal screening process would not have occurred if the term "dropout" had never gained currency and that many of the same youngsters would have been jobless anyway. But without our penchant for categorization and problem-making, they might have escaped the additional burden of being branded as members of a separate clan of pariahs.

The dropout problem, which has occupied so much of the time and attention of our public officials in recent months, must be seen in its proper perspective as one aspect of a far larger program, that of "manpower planning," on which the Federal government formally embarked in 1962. The Manpower Development and Training Act passed in that year attracted interest primarily because of its training provisions. The public had become aware of "structural unemploy-ment," of workers whose skills had become obsolescent through au-tomation, and the act promised specific relief in the form of retraining programs. In fact, this measure was primarily regarded as a compan-ion piece to the Area Redevelopment Act, and both were designed to give immediate assistance to distressed areas.

But that portion of the Manpower Act which dealt with "develop-ment" focuses not on the present but on the future; its avowed pur-pose, in the words of the first Manpower Report submitted to Con-gress by President Kennedy last March, is "to anticipate and prepare to meet the country's future manpower requirements." The report further stated that the "Act represents a mandate to the Department of Labor for new dimensions of leadership and action in strengthen-ing the nation's human resources." President Johnson's second an-nual Manpower Report states the same problem in almost identical language.

This program represents a remarkable new Federal venture. Though similar to previous governmental programs in the field of education and employment, it goes far beyond them in scope and intent. For the first time, the Federal government assumes, through this act, a continuing responsibility for defining the nation's man-power goals and requirements and for initiating policies to meet them. In oversimplified terms, the Federal government has set itself the task of forecasting the number of square, round, and odd-shaped holes that will be open in the future; and it will also seek to supply the necessary pegs in the required numbers.

The entire concept of manpower planning is a relatively new one. It had its origin in the Second World War, and the problems that fostered its growth then were highly practical: the armed forces, faced with an influx of millions of men, wanted to base their gigantic task of personnel assignment on something better than pure chance. This first experiment in the efficient use of our human resources was not entirely successful, as anyone who had even a passing acquaint-ance with the services during this period can attest. But even the failures were instructive.

The new science got a second and even greater boost during the 1950's, when the economists discovered and nearly appropriated it. The occasion of this rediscovery was our involvement with foreign aid, more specifically our concern with the economic problems of underdeveloped countries.

Until then most economists had tended to ignore the qualitative aspects of a labor force and concentrated primarily on measuring its actual or potential size. Even advanced economic models of national economies considered the qualitative aspects of a labor force as fixed, with no speculation about the changes in output that might be affected by an upgrading of that labor force. And it was shown that there can be a crucial labor shortage even in the midst of poverty and distress.

While most of the original work was done for underdeveloped countries, this new knowledge also found quick application in this country. The plight of the depressed areas and the issue of "structural" unemployment, both of which arose during the late 1950's, were recognized as being basically of a manpower nature, problems of individuals whose economic skills—if they had any—were unsuited for their environment. Measures designed to stimulate total demand and increase our economic growth rate would not necessarily benefit those unfortunate individuals whom progress had somehow passed by. In this context, training or retraining of the affected individuals, if at all possible, appears a more practical way of dealing with the problem. And the Manpower Development and Training Act provides for such training.

OPPORTUNITY: THE BASIC TOOL

But Congress did not wish to stop with remedial actions designed to alleviate current problems; it wanted to plan their future elimination as well. Out of this desire came the development portion of the act. And Congress, unlike the general public, did not underestimate the importance of this long-range portion of the act. A great part of the testimony offered before the Senate subcommittee on Employment and Manpower concerned the desirability of manpower planning. Practically all the experts who appeared before the committee agreed that such planning was necessary. They emphasized that the basic changes in our economy, notably automation, which had produced the problem of workers unfit for present employment opportunities, would not only continue but would accelerate. And manpower planning, they felt, was the only answer.

The experts recommended indirect methods rather than frontal attacks. The G.I. Bill of Rights, whose ostensible purpose was to reward a generation of veterans for service to their country, was in fact a manpower measure by indirection. Another was the soil-bank plan, which paid farmers to keep land out of cultivation and thus reduced the demand for agricultural labor; this in turn increased our industrial labor supply, particularly in the South.

Unfortunately, no brilliant new plans were incorporated into the act, and the development portion of the final manpower bill is devoid of any specific measures. It simply entrusts the Department of Labor with the primary job of manpower planning and requires the President to submit an annual Manpower Report to the Congress.

The first Manpower Report, submitted by President Kennedy a year ago, is in many ways a remarkable document. The actual Presidential report occupies only a few pages in a very hefty book. Yet for all its brevity the report managed to make nearly all the good points that can be made on this subject. The Federal government, Kennedy wrote, has a long tradition   stretching from the Northwest Ordinance of 1787, to the Morrill Act which set aside Federal land for use by "land grant" colleges, to the G.I. Bill of Rights—of actions and programs designed to enlarge people's opportunities for education and training and thus enhance their economic usefulness. Providing opportunity is the basic tool of a free government in this field. Recent events, the late President continued, have made our present arsenal of tools inadequate for the task.

Mr. Kennedy was careful to point up the effectiveness of indirection in manpower policy, and suggested that many parts of his legislative program were really manpower measures. The tax bill and the Civil Rights bill could make contributions in this field that would be on equal footing with the more direct programs, such as the Youth Employment Act and aid to higher education. He also called for a greater willingness to experiment in this field.

The need for further experimenting will doubtless increase, as President Johnson's second annual Manpower Report makes clear. It is also worth noting that the importance and scope of the program has become such that the Manpower Report itself has now become the fourth major executive proposal of the legislative year (after the State of the Union Message, the Budget Message, and the Economic Report).

In his report, President Johnson initiated two major administrative actions. The first is a study of the impact of automation and technological change on workers, unions, and firms, to be conducted by the President's Advisory Committee on Labor-Management Policy. The second is the establishment of a President's Committee on Manpower to appraise, among other matters, the present and future labor-force requirement of the national economy.

The basic method by which the government's fantastically complicated planning effort is to be accomplished is to provide information that might guide young people in their selection of careers. In other words, to accomplish our goal of producing the right numbers of engineers, physicians, or teachers, we have to know first how many of these we shall need and when.

The Department of Labor is candid enough to admit that we do not have accurate information on this point. But the department is pretty sure that the increased demand will be for technically trained people; and to qualify our young people for these jobs, at least potentially, it is considered essential to keep them in school, certainly through the twelfth grade. And here, as the Labor Department begins to view with alarm, we are once more back with the dropout problem. "The country," according to one gloomy official statement, "simply cannot afford to go on permitting thirty or forty per cent of its young people to drop out of school before graduation."

A CONFUSION OF OBJECTIVES

All this sounds eminently logical. But is it really? During the decade from 1965 to 1975, an average of about 3.8 million Americans will turn eighteen each year, as against only about 2.5 million during the 1950's. No matter how rapidly our demand for technically trained people is likely to grow, it could easily be filled by the sheer increase in numbers without any change in the proportion of high-school or college graduates. So the present rate of dropouts is not in itself apt to keep us from having all the engineers we need or from attaining whatever heights of technical training we might aspire to.

The dropouts must therefore be undesirable for other reasons. What it really boils down to is that their presence is inconsistent with our view of a free society that provides opportunity for all. Furthermore, given the present rate of unemployment, we would rather keep youngsters out of the labor market as long as possible anyway. But granting all this, can we solve the problem simply by issuing a lot of dire warnings to teen-agers that a life of economic uselessness awaits them unless they mend their ways? Unfortunately, this is precisely the method we seem to be following. All across the country, special groups have been formed to assist and counsel high-school students. These groups will undoubtedly be able to point to many individual success stories, thereby aggravating the difficulties of the millions who are not—and cannot be—so fortunate.

Thus the origin of this problem can really be traced to a confusion of objectives. A measure primarily designed to provide our nation with more skilled workers suddenly became a program to eradicate ignorance.

The primary danger of our present approach to the dropout problem is that in seeking to reduce its size we are hardening its core. Problems associated with failures cannot be measured solely by counting the afflicted. In dealing or trying to deal with the problem of the dropouts, we are still planning in the dark—partly because we lack sufficient information, but largely because of a tendency to go on approaching the problem as a purely economic one, without giving adequate attention to the social and moral considerations. Put in the simplest terms, we have not yet found a way of raising the quality of our labor force without branding those who are bound to be left behind as pariahs.

President Johnson's Manpower Report, 1964

To the Congress of the United States:

This nation is prosperous, strong, materially richer than any in history—largely because of the knowledge, skills, competence, and creativity of our people.

But we are short of our potential. Many of our people do not adequately participate in the national well-being. Much of our human capability is not developed or used.

Moreover, our economy is changing markedly, in ways which call for new and better training, skill and adaptability.

The new tax cut will stimulate demand and provide impetus to further economic growth. But it will not directly solve such problems as inadequate worker skills and hard-core unemployment.

We cannot therefore rest content with our forward momentum or with our already considerable adaptability.

We must focus on how far we can go—and how better to get there—rather than on how far we have come.

We must raise our sights—and strive to realize each person's highest productive and earning capability. We must seek to develop more completely our people's talents and to employ those talents fully—to fulfill the rich promise of technological advance and to enable all to share in its benefits.

There must, in brief, be an active manpower policy—to complement our new national attack on poverty.

Not all dimensions or details of the active manpower policy can now be formulated, but broad directions are clear. We know that:

Taken from Manpower Report of the President and a Report on Manpower Requirements, Resources, Utilization, and Training by the United States Department of Labor, *transmitted to the Congress March 1964 (Washington, D.C.: U.S. Government Printing Office, 1964), pp. XI–XIX.*

—This cannot be a responsibility of the Federal government alone. Business, labor, and all private groups and institutions, along with State and local governments, all have vital roles to play.

The Federal government can provide leadership, information, and other assistance, but fundamentally it is action carried forward in each community that will decide how well we achieve national objectives.

—This is a long-range task, requiring more than onetime or short-run efforts. Immediate action is necessary on certain evident needs, but we must move ahead also to gauge needs of the future and to undertake longer-run development programs.

In many respects, analysis of manpower needs is still in an early stage of development. We will have much to discover and apply as we proceed.

—We are not starting from scratch, however. We have been steadily raising our educational and skill qualifications through a vast range of activities. Important new efforts initiated in the last several years can help further to upgrade abilities and expand employment.

—No narrow approach will suffice. Manpower policy must blend and coordinate its efforts with other forces shaping manpower resources and needs—including educational, economic, scientific, health, social welfare, and other basic policies.

Underlying all efforts is a need to appraise total national manpower requirements and prospects as an essential basis for achieving full development and use of our human resources.

WHERE WE STAND

The past year was one of excellent economic growth. As my economic report noted in detail, national output, income, profits, and employment each moved up substantially to record heights.

The gross national product was boosted by $30 billion so that it now is more than $600 billion a year. Average factory pay for those employed has been raised to over $100 a week. Profits rose very substantially.

And employment was increased by almost a million, going over the 70-million mark for the first time in peak months of the year.

But unemployment persisted grimly despite 1963's strong economic advance. Overcoming that unemployment is the greatest immediate manpower challenge before us—and the new tax cut is a long step toward meeting that challenge.

Other major challenges on the path to full and creative use of our human resources are posed by our labor force growth and by the problems which technological adjustment raises for many individuals.

Unemployment imposes hardships on individuals and inflicts economic loss on the Nation. In 1963, high rates of unemployment also increased racial tension, aggravated difficulties in labor relations in major industries, and heightened doubts among many workers about automation's benefits.

In the average week in 1963

—4.2 million Americans seeking work were unemployed. This was 5.7 percent of our labor force, an unemployment rate over twice that of most industrialized countries.

—another 2.6 million persons seeking full-time work were employed only part time. And additional heavy underemployment existed among our farm workers.

Such a waste of our human resources and loss of potential production cannot be tolerated.

Unemployment did not improve in step with the strong economic advance in 1963 because our labor force grew more rapidly than in earlier years, at the same time that new technology was raising productivity and changing demand for skills.

Even greater economic growth is therefore necessary—and we must develop also specific measures expressly aimed at special problems which block employment of many of the jobless.

The accompanying report of the Secretary of Labor describes in detail recent manpower trends and the current picture—including the features which characterize our unemployment. I want to stress these major developments.

The labor force expanded by 1.1 million last year and annual increases are expected to be even greater in the future. The largest increases are occurring among those under age 25 and among married women.

—Last year's labor force growth was nearly a third more than the annual average increase of the previous 5 years. As we look ahead, annual growth in the latter years of the 1960's is likely to step up to over 1.4 million, a third larger than last year and nearly twice the number of additional workers we had to absorb annually in the preceding half decade.

—Far more young persons are seeking work than ever before as the postwar babies reach working age. The youngsters turning age 18 next year will number a million more than this year.

—Large numbers of married women, seeking to increase family income, to provide better opportunities for their children, and to enrich their own and the national life, are also entering the work force.

Productivity and demand shifts, meanwhile, are changing our requirements for workers.

—Manpower needs are shrinking in declining industries and in those where new machines and methods are replacing workers faster than new jobs are being created by new demand. Agriculture, whose employment declined a quarter of a million last year, rail transport, mining and some manufacturing industries continue to release workers into the pool of jobseekers.

—But more manpower, with skills not always possessed by displaced workers or by new entrants into the labor force, is required by other industries. In 1963 four-fifths of the new increase in jobs was in service, trade, and State and local government activities.

—Occupationally, unskilled jobs are declining in importance. Demand is expanding most in professional and technical, clerical, and service occupations. Requirements for education and training for employment are increasing steadily.

—Yet nearly a million young people are leaving our educational system each year before completing even elementary or secondary school. Each year more than 100,000 high school graduates with high aptitudes and interest in college fail to continue their education because of financial inability. And about 40 percent of all students who go on to college withdraw before completion of a 4-year program.

Imbalances flowing from these trends require our attention. Current and prospective shortages of needed skills must be better identified if we are to prevent any drag on our economic growth—and to help in providing young people and displaced workers with the education and training needed to benefit from opportunities in expanding fields.

The major losers in the shifting patterns of manpower supply and demand are the young, the undereducated and unskilled, the laid-off older workers with outmoded skills, and the unemployed caught in communities where the economic base has deteriorated.

—Among youth, unemployment went up in 1963 as fast as the increase in teenage labor force. Employment of teenagers did not increase at all, so that the first surge of rising growth in our resources of young manpower was translated into greater unemployment. Almost one teenager in six who seeks work today can find no one to employ him.

—Two-thirds of the unemployed have less than a high school education. One of every twelve workers with only elementary schooling is unemployed, compared with only 1 of 70 college graduates.

—Nonwhite workers, with limited opportunities to acquire skills and further hampered by discrimination in getting employment, suffer more than twice the rate of joblessness of white workers.

—Unemployed workers over age 45 remain out of work far longer than those who are younger. Some who suffer continued frustration in job hunting stop searching for work—they involuntarily "retire" and no longer appear in the unemployment count.

—Heavy concentrations of unemployment and underemployment plague many areas. Some communities in Kentucky, West Virginia, and other States in the Appalachian region and in the upper Great Lakes area have as many as a fourth or more of their employable people idle. The central parts of many of our larger cities are similarly afflicted.

ACTIVE MANPOWER POLICY

For manpower policy to succeed in meeting these challenges, we must have

—new awareness that effective action requires attention in such broad interrelated fields as education, monetary and fiscal and other economic policy, science and technology, defense, and social welfare.

—new willingness to experiment with fresh approaches and put resulting knowledge to practical use.

—new efforts to anticipate and prepare for future requirements.

—new institutions to coordinate separate activities as part of a considered overall policy.

These new attitudes and efforts must be geared to three fundamental goals:

The first is to develop the abilities of our people.

Another is to create jobs to make the most of those abilities.

The third is to link the first two, to match people and jobs.

Develop Abilities

Many forces influence human ability, but an active policy of manpower development must be concerned principally with (a) education at all levels, (b) training in occupational skills for youth, the employed, and the unemployed, and (c) rehabilitation and other development aid for those handicapped by physical, mental, cultural, or other disadvantages.

(a) Education must provide, as a basic part of its human development responsibility, the preparation needed for effective participation in our economic life.

But the education and related counseling of many of our people have not prepared them adequately to qualify for today's jobs, to absorb skill training, or to capitalize on new opportunities. And our systems of higher education are not providing the quantity and caliber of persons we seek for many high-level occupations necessary for national innovation and growth.

We must provide *elementary and secondary education of high quality for all our citizens,* to serve as a foundation for training and further learning. Such education increasingly has become a minimum requirement for effective activity and contribution in an advancing industrial economy. A modern program of vocational education also must be built to provide vocational skills for many who will not seek higher education.

We must provide *broad opportunity for education beyond high school.* A sound college education or junior college or technical school preparation is necessary for a rapidly growing proportion of occupations.

We must provide *increased opportunity for education at the postgraduate level.* The increasing complexity of many technical and managerial occupations makes education beyond college essential. Moreover, to foster the leadership resources of the Nation, we must augment the supply of qualified teachers and stimulate the creative talent of our managers, scientists, engineers, educators, and other strategic professional personnel.

We must provide *extensive programs of adult education.* Two aspects are critical: Undereducated adults must be helped to gain literacy and basic education, without which all employment opportunity is limited. And adults who have received a diploma must be encouraged and given opportunity to update and broaden their learning.

(b) Training is necessary to provide specific job skills. Reliance wholly on casual experience, even for lower skill jobs, often means less than achievable competence.

A new study by the Department of Labor finds, however, that all our public and private schools, industry, and the Armed Forces combined have provided some formal occupational training to only about half of American workers.

To make the Nation's manpower more adaptable and productive, and to overcome skill shortages which impede growth, we must encourage and expand

—*training programs for the employed,* to improve existing skills and develop needed new ones,

—*training or retraining for the unemployed,* to equip them for employment, and

—*apprenticeship programs* to provide the needed supply of proficient, highly skilled craftsmen.

(c) Rehabilitation and other special development techniques can enhance the productive potential of people beyond the reach of usual education and training programs.

Many persons on our welfare rolls or regarded as "unemployable" can be helped to rise to positive participation in the economy.

We must extend those rehabilitation, counseling, and related services which experimentation has demonstrated can build the hope, self-respect, motivation, and productive ability needed for self-betterment for many of our disadvantaged—the chronically dependent, the socially hostile, the mentally retarded, the physically handicapped, the emotionally disturbed, and the children being reared in deprived circumstances.

On each of these basic ability-development fronts, we have initiated new and promising steps in the last 3 years.

It is now our responsibility to carry through these new efforts, with needed resources and resourcefulness, to reap their full potential.

Thus, on education, the landmark Federal legislation of last year is enabling us to

—expand and modernize vocational and technical education.

—provide Federal financial assistance for construction of higher education facilities.

—enlarge aid for medical and dental education.

—increase student support programs in several vital fields.

On training, we can under recent Federal legislation

—provide new training and retraining programs for the unemployed.

—make available literacy training for the undereducated jobless who need it as a prerequisite for occupational retraining.

On related rehabilitation activities, we have begun to

—launch new programs to aid the mentally ill and retarded.

—encourage new emphasis on rehabilitation and work training for persons on public assistance.

—experiment with new means of aiding actual or potential juvenile delinquents.

—undertake demonstration programs under the Manpower Act to mobilize community agencies and to develop new techniques to improve employability of disadvantaged persons who need more than normal job training.

In addition, early this year I ordered the start of a Manpower Conservation Program to aid the extraordinarily large proportion of our youth—one-third of all our young men—found unqualified to serve the Nation in the Armed Forces.

Most of these rejectees will be rejected in the employment world as well if they are not helped to overcome their limitations while still young.

The effort to help them develop their potential—part of our attack on the poverty which cripples too many of our people—is already underway.

Specifically, I have directed that all new selective service registrants who are out of school and otherwise available for service be examined as soon as possible.

Those young men found unable to meet military service standards because of educational deficiencies are to be referred to local offices of the public employment service so that they may take advantage of guidance, training, and rehabilitation services to overcome those deficiencies. Those who fail on physical grounds will be referred to sources of assistance on their health needs.

Create Jobs

To employ all our manpower resources, our economy must generate sufficient new jobs for

—the unemployed,

—the rising number of newcomers to the labor force.

—those displaced by machines, by changing technology, or by declines in individual industries or areas, and

—those outside the labor force who want to work as opportunities become available.

For those already employed, we want to open better opportunities to put to use talents and abilities not fully utilized in present employment.

Total employment has been growing, but not at the pace required by these needs.

This means that our monetary, fiscal, and other economic policies must stimulate greater job growth in the years ahead.

It means that we must improve existing institutions, private and public, to help in many ways to realize the potential for greater employment in urban development, housing, transportation, recreation and other services sought and needed by our growing population.

It means that we must do more to translate advances in science and technology into additional job opportunities providing services and new products either unknown or not feasible before.

It means also that we must try to identify needed relatively unskilled work—and to inaugurate programs to have that work performed by long-term unemployed workers and by inexperienced youth as a steppingstone to better employment.

We have been moving in these directions. Three efforts warrant note here:

—Already this year we have taken a major economic step to greater employment. The newly enacted tax cut will provide needed stimulus to employment expansion the rest of this year and in the years ahead.

—Area redevelopment efforts are helping to develop jobs in high-unemployment urban and rural communities.

—And programs to develop abilities are creating new jobs which awaited the development of qualified workers. In particular, we have begun to recognize that availability of highly talented scientific and managerial manpower stimulates the innovation and provides the leadership which spur the development of new jobs.

Help Match People and Jobs

Beyond upgrading of human abilities, there is vast need for improvement in other ways of bringing and keeping together workers and jobs. We must improve many activities which, while neither new nor dramatic, are nevertheless essential for the needs of many of our people and our economy in this increasingly complex age. Critical among these are:

PREPARATION FOR CHANGE. By increasing efforts to look ahead and prepare for likely technological or economic change, management and unions can ease displacement problems and meet new manpower requirements more effectively. This is elementary, yet we have not done as much or as well as we could. Improved government assistance of the types cited below can contribute materially to such efforts.

INFORMATION. Supplying of information on occupational requirements and manpower resources is a fundamental aid. Particularly necessary is improved information on current job vacancies, on emerging occupational opportunities, and on availability of qualified workers. Projections of probable need in particular occupations are an essential guide for education, training, and other policies aimed at developing the right skills at the right time in the right place.

COUNSELING. Youth and adult workers should have ready access to competent counseling to help them match their aptitudes and occupational preferences with opportunities for education, training, and employment.

PLACEMENT SERVICES. To fill jobs better and more quickly, we also must expand and make more resourceful the public employment services available to workers and employers for recruiting, testing, guidance, and adapting of jobs to fit abilities—on an interarea and national as well as local basis.

MOBILITY. Beyond these services, additional aid is desirable to help workers or industry relocate to overcome geographic separation of workers and jobs—and to help migrants, particularly those from rural to urban areas, adjust to new work life in a different environment.

Progress is being developed on these varied needs in many ways:

—Management and labor increasingly are exploring and adopting additional means of easing worker adjustment difficulties stemming from technological change.

—Research on manpower needs is being expanded, notably under the Manpower Act, to develop new knowledge and techniques to improve our programs.

—Committees of distinguished private and public representatives have conducted special reviews of problems involving major groups: youth, women, minority workers, older workers, and scientific and engineering personnel.

—Experiments to aid mobility of unemployed workers are being initiated under a 1963 amendment to the Manpower Act.

—A Manpower Administration has been established in the Department of Labor to lead and coordinate many activities.

—A high-level government committee has been designated to review and coordinate economic effects of our defense programs. It will help us act to minimize potential manpower disturbances which might result from changes in the level and pattern of defense spending.

We must also be concerned with

LABOR STANDARDS. Our work force must be assured of reasonable protection and income maintenance through minimum wage, unemployment benefit, safety, child labor, and other basic labor standards programs.

ELIMINATION OF DISCRIMINATION. We must guarantee that no individual is barred from access to employment opportunity, or to the education and training necessary to prepare for it, because of race, national origin, age, sex, or other characteristics unrelated to ability.

To meet these objectives, in recent months

—the Equal Pay Act was enacted to prohibit sex discrimination in payment of wages.

—a new approach to industry's participation in a voluntary program was developed by the President's Committee on Equal Employment Opportunity to provide greater employment opportunities to members of minority groups.

—a new Executive order was issued, prohibiting Federal contractors and subcontractors from setting maximum age limits for most jobs, to provide equal employment opportunity for older persons.

—new apprenticeship regulations were adopted by the Secretary of Labor to promote equal opportunity in apprenticeship programs.

FEDERAL GOVERNMENT AS AN EMPLOYER

As the Nation's largest single employer of manpower, the Federal Government should set an example of effective manpower development and utilization. Much is being done, and more will be done, to accomplish this. Among the major activities:

—Training and career development programs have been instituted to obtain maximum contributions from employees in all occupations. Special stress is being put on more effective use of high-talent personnel, including scientists, engineers, managers, and other professional manpower.

—Action is being taken to insure fair-employment opportunities in the Federal service. Particular attention is being given to provide opportunities for groups that traditionally have not done as well as others in the American economy: women, members of minority groups, handicapped workers, and older workers.

—Adjustment programs have been developed to minimize adverse effects on employees of increasing use of automation and of shifts in government programs. To effect needed reductions in personnel, emphasis is given to attrition and to transfer and retraining to meet needs of displaced employees.

—Better estimates of the government's future manpower requirements are being developed. These will aid in carrying forward training and fair employment opportunity programs.

—Recruitment by Federal departments and agencies at the college level is being better coordinated. And high-potential young persons with less than college-level training are being sought out and employed for Federal jobs as supervisors, aides, and technicians.

NEXT STEPS

An active manpower policy must also focus on needed additional measures. And it must provide new mechanisms to assess and to correlate all our efforts bearing on the Nation's manpower resources and needs.

Legislative Action

The Congress already has before it a range of proposals, some first presented in earlier years and several newly presented this year, which are necessary in shaping an active manpower policy. These are the major proposals:

1. Youth unemployment must not be allowed to grow unchecked. The rapid surge of new young workers and their rising unemployment rates require immediately additional means to develop and employ many who will not be aided by other available programs.

President Kennedy's proposed youth employment programs can help meet this urgent need, and I urge the Congress to act favorably on these programs as part of the war against poverty.

2. Poverty must be attacked through new and intensive combinations of varied Federal, State, and local government and private programs. My message on poverty outlines the concentrated efforts I propose.

3. Education must be strengthened. Pending legislation and the budget requests I have presented spell out the diverse efforts needed.

Let us not shortchange our future. Our people's abilities in the years to come patently depend heavily on the scope and wisdom of our educational investment today.

Elementary and secondary education improvement is particularly vital. No youth should reach working age without at least a sound basic education with which to build employable skills. Expansion of technical and adult education is another imperative.

We must also, as an urgent long-term investment in fostering leadership, better our programs of assistance for higher education. Needs are mounting for top talent in key scientific, professional, and managerial fields. Only by increasing the number of the most highly trained and competent individuals will it be possible adequately to design the programs, build the institutions, and teach the leaders of tomorrow.

4. Areas of high unemployment must be revitalized. I have requested additional funds to continue and expand the valuable assistance provided under the Area Redevelopment Act.

For the largest and most poverty-stricken region, the Appalachian area stretching over 10 States, I am asking the Nation to embark on a farsighted task. I am requesting Federal assistance for a comprehensive program to develop human and natural resources and eradicate the hunger, disease, ignorance, and hopelessness which afflict much of this part of America.

5. Overtime work must be examined critically to determine if it is feasible to convert regular and substantial overtime hours into new jobs.

I have recommended legislation under which tripartite committees will determine whether higher overtime penalty rates in specific industries could increase employment without unduly increasing costs. The legislation would authorize increased penalty rates where this is found to be so.

6. Racial discrimination must be eliminated. Programs to help economically depressed members of racial minority groups gain new skills will benefit little if employment opportunity is still blocked by discrimination.

I strongly urge adoption of the civil rights legislation recommended by this Administration, including requirements for Federal fair-employment practices applicable to both employers and unions, to help assure all Americans the right and opportunity to earn a decent living.

7. Unemployment insurance must be extended and its benefits increased. Nearly half the unemployed are receiving no unemployment benefits at all because of coverage restrictions or qualifying requirements or because duration of benefits is too brief.

The legislation I have recommended to remedy these inadequacies will improve financial security for the jobless and economic and social stability for the economy.

8. Protection of the Fair Labor Standards Act must be extended. To provide new or improved protection for over 2.6 million workers, I have recommended extension of

—minimum wage and overtime protection to 735,000 workers in hotel, motel, restaurant, laundry, dry cleaning, agricultural, processing, and logging industries.

—new or improved overtime protection to 1.9 million workers in the agricultural handling and processing, transportation, and gasoline services industries.

Administrative Action

Many other necessary actions which can be carried forward under existing statutory authority require additional funds as set forth in my budget requests.

I want to note particularly that strengthening of the Federal-State employment service system's vital job market information, counseling, placement and related services is one basic need for which I have requested increased funds.

I am also proceeding on two new major administrative actions.

One is to develop needed perspective on automation. I have asked my tripartite Advisory Committee on Labor-Management Policy to undertake a study of the impact of automation and technological change on workers, unions, and firms, and of the problems of adjustment arising from such change.

I have asked the Committee to focus on what is being done and can be done by management and labor to meet displacement effects.

It is my hope and expectation that the Committee's report on what the private economy is and can be doing—and the recommendations it may make for needed supplementary government measures—will provide valuable guidance to overcoming any potential adverse effects while capitalizing on the benefits of automation.

In addition, I believe it is also desirable either through legislative or administrative action to establish a special high-level commission to conduct a broader evaluation of our technological course and the means of channeling progress toward meeting our society's unfilled needs.

The other action is to start a continuing top-level assessment of the relation of the government's programs and our country's manpower assets and needs.

I regard this as necessary to help us analyze and determine national programs from a human resources standpoint.

Congressional support for such action is already well reflected in the

—Manpower Development and Training Act's call for the Federal Government "to appraise the manpower requirements and resources of the Nation," and the

—Employment Act's mandate "to promote maximum employment, production, and purchasing power."

I am establishing for this purpose a President's Committee on Manpower, which will include the principal Federal executives administering programs which significantly affect our manpower, under the chairmanship of the Secretary of Labor.

The Committee will assist in appraising

—the implications of major government programs and policies for our national manpower needs and resources,

—the interrelation of government programs to manpower requirements of other sectors of the economy, and

—the present and prospective manpower resources and requirements of the Nation.

Only through such considered appraisal and the development of improved techniques and data for current and long-range manpower assessment can we arm ourselves with adequate information and sound linking of separate programs—elements essential for full effectiveness in carrying forward an active manpower policy.

CONCLUSION

A fundamental objective of this Nation is to assure all Americans full and fair opportunity to develop and apply their maximum productive and earning potential. But progress toward that objective can too easily falter in competition with other concerns.

I have here urged several programs as parts of an active policy for full development and use of our manpower resources. I have set forth earlier a related program for a concentrated attack on poverty.

These programs will take hold and succeed only when we become determined that nothing is to take priority over people.

We have the ideas and ideals to reach our objective. We must now crystallize into action the sense of overriding commitment that nobody is to be passed by.

What is at stake is whether a free democratic economy can attain well-being for the less fortunate as well as the more fortunate of its people—and whether it can make population growth and technological advance fruitful for all rather than fateful for some.

It is up to us. Our action or inaction toward realizing the full potential of our human resources is a major factor in determining whether we will strengthen justice, security, and freedom at home— and enhance America's ability to set a proud example for all the world.

A Comprehensive Employment
and Manpower Policy

CLARK SUBCOMMITTEE

THE MANPOWER REVOLUTION

The labor markets of the United States have been plagued since 1953 with a persistent upward trend in unemployment which has averaged above 6 percent for the [period of 1958–64]. Despite a high level of personal income and above average rates of economic expansion, unemployment remained above 5.5 percent during all of 1963. This unemployment has been concentrated among youth for whom the rate tends to be triple the national average, minority groups whose unemployment experience is double the average, older workers, the uneducated and unskilled, and among certain economically depressed geographical areas.

The subcommittee believes that this persistently high level of unemployment is but one symptom of a pervasive and far-reaching Manpower Revolution which has been underway at an accelerating rate at least throughout the years since World War II. Symptoms of this "revolution" are underemployment, part-time employment, withdrawal from the labor force of those who would prefer participation, rural and urban poverty, a cycle of dependency among those who, generation after generation, find no way to break into the mainstream of economic life, growing pressures upon an educational system already inadequate to its tasks, and persistent shortages of the skilled,

Excerpts from a Report of the Subcommittee on Employment and Manpower of the Committee on Labor and Public Welfare, United States Senate, entitled Toward Full Employment: Proposals for a Comprehensive Employment and Manpower Policy in the United States, *Committee Print, 88th Congress, 2nd session (Washington: U.S. Government Printing Office, 1964).*

technical, scientific, and highly educated manpower so important to economic and social progress.

This Manpower Revolution, like the industrial revolution from which it sprang, holds great promise for the creation of a better society if properly understood and dealt with. But it also contains the seeds of economic and social disaster if left to itself without any attempt at human guidance and control.

The Impact of Technological Change

The Manpower Revolution, like the industrial revolution, is first and foremost the product of technological change. The nature of this change, however, is little understood, even by those who have had most to do with it.

In part, this lack of understanding stems from a confusion of tongues—a failure to define terms and a tendency to lump all technological developments under one increasingly meaningless term: automation. A paucity of statistical data and a tendency to ignore that which does not square with cherished preconceptions is also to some extent responsible. A final element has been the natural tendency of every expert to examine only his own part of the elephant. It has been the task of the subcommittee to distill from the combined wisdom of its witnesses and the relevant literature and data examined by the members and staff, its own estimate of the present impact and future prospects of technological change. . . .

The Labor Force: Its Size and Composition

Higher postwar rates of productivity increase and dynamic technological developments occurred simultaneously with unprecedented growth in the size and changing composition of the labor force. The postwar baby boom and its implication for population growth were obvious throughout the years immediately following World War II. . . .

GROWTH PATTERNS OF THE SIXTIES

The 1950–60 expansion of the labor force far exceeded that of any previous decade. However, the increase projected for the 1960's is 12.6 million, or more than half again as large as that experienced over the preceding 10 years. Young people (ages 14 to 24) are expected to increase their number in the labor force by 6.2 million, or a rise 1.7 times as great as over the previous decade. But this is only the net increase for the age group as a whole. Actually, some 26 million young people will seek their first jobs during the 1960's. The impact is accelerating. By 1970, the annual influx is expected to reach 3 million—compared with 2.6 million this year and 2.1 million in 1960.

As of early 1964 the implications of this influx have been well publicized and widely discussed. The imperative need to bring public resources to bear on the youth employment problem is undeniable. However, the justifiable attention given to this important component of the work force should not overshadow the importance of another relatively sharp shift in composition. Due to both aging of persons in the labor force, and the entrance or reentrance of adult women, the 45 to 64 year age group will again increase by 5 million to a total of 29.1 million and by 1970 will account for more than a third of the labor force. This [is] nearly as great as the upward shift for older workers during the 1950's. Workers in this preretirement age group with inadequate education or training, or lacking adequate resources for mobility, face serious readjustment problems when confronted with job elimination caused by technological change, industry relocations, or sudden changes in demand. In short, workers in this group may be especially vulnerable to displacement of one kind or another which results in prolonged joblessness. Currently it has a disproportionately high representation among those who have been unsuccessfully seeking work for 6 months or longer—especially for men, who outnumber women workers by 2 to 1 in this age group.

JOB OPPORTUNITIES AND LABOR FORCE GROWTH

Labor force projections are estimates of the number of people who will be seeking employment at a future date. This depends not only upon population growth, the school leaving and retirement age, and similar considerations, but upon the availability of job opportunities. Because of the slower rate of economic growth during the late 1950's and subsequent unemployment, the size of the labor force has already fallen behind projections made during that period.

If job growth steps up, so will expansion of the labor force as more people are attracted by the increased opportunities. If job opportunities are not available fewer women will work, more older workers will retire involuntarily, youth will remain idle and not seek nonexistent work though not in school, many nonwhite workers will exist without seeking gainful employment.

For these reasons unemployment totals now underestimate the extent to which manpower resources are being wasted. This undetermined number is the great imponderable of future labor force growth but it is generally assumed that another 800,000 to 1,500,000 persons would enter the labor force if job opportunities were more readily available.

EDUCATIONAL ATTAINMENT

In addition to size and composition, there is concern as to whether the educational attainment of the labor force is keeping pace with changing occupational requirements. Modern technological change demands a generally higher level of educational attainment, not only for the mastery of specific skills, but also because a sound basic education is a necessity if retraining is required at a later date.

Nearly 9 million young workers have entered this labor force in the first 4 years of the decade and another 17 million will seek their first jobs in the next 6 years. Over the decade as a whole it is expected that 3 out of every 10 youngsters in this group will have less than a high school education. Only a little more than a fourth will enter college. Thus roughly three out of four young labor force entrants during the 1960's will have high school educations at most. Among the fourth who enter college, there are a substantial number of women who will leave the labor force at least temporarily to raise families.

Many older workers are handicapped by the fact that their education was inadequate or is presently out-of-date when they come to seek new jobs. A public education system to which older workers can return to upgrade their skills does not yet exist in the United States. In 1960, nearly three-fifths of the adult population (those 25 years of age and older) had less than a high school education. In some States, the adult population with less than a high school education exceeds 70 percent, and in only eight States was the percentage slightly below half of the population. . . .

The Causes of Unemployment

The high unemployment rates of the past few years have occasioned a debate within the economics profession which was reflected in testimony before the subcommittee. On one side are those who find the primary cause of unemployment in slow growth and the solution in economic expansion. The other group of debaters find the major explanation in certain transformations which have occurred in the supply of and the demand for labor and stress measures for matching demand with supply as the more potent cure.

THE DEFICIENCY OF AGGREGATE DEMAND

The expansionist school of thought, with the Council of Economic Advisers as its leading advocates, attributes the persistently high unemployment level primarily to a slow rate of economic growth resulting from a deficiency of aggregate demand for goods and services. The majority of this school advocate the position of the Council that tax reduction should be the primary tool of employment policy at the moment. Though some speeches of Council members have seemed to reject the structural explanation entirely, the considered opinion of the CEA appears to be that the 1964 tax cut can eventually reduce the unemployment level to 4 percent of the labor force with no other assistance. At 4 percent, bottlenecks in skilled labor, middle-level manpower and professional personnel will manifest themselves, in the Council's view, retarding growth and generating wage-price pressures at various points in the economy. To go beyond 4 percent, advocated by the Council only as an interim goal, will require improved education, training and retraining, and other structural measures.

Among those who stress the need for economic growth are a few who are pessimistic about the effectiveness of the tax cut as a solution to unemployment. It is their belief, first, that the CEA tends to underestimate the magnitude of unemployment and the likelihood of acceleration in the rate of output per man-hour as output rises. The CEA recognizes the existence of persons outside the labor force who have ceased looking for work because of discouragement but who would enter the labor force if jobs were available. The CEA estimates this group at 800,000 while the estimates of others range up to 1,500,-000.

Those who accuse the Council of setting its sights too low also count among the unemployed the full-time equivalent of those working part time for economic reasons and also those underemployed in such industries as agriculture who would move to more productive employment if it was available. It is also their view that productivity is being restrained because industrial plants are operating below their most efficient levels of production. They would expect productivity to accelerate as output rose. Secondly, this subdivision of the expansionist school holds that demand for goods and services is so near to satiation that it is impossible for the private market sector of our affluent economy to absorb an output increase sufficient to reduce unemployment substantially. In their estimate, only the low-income fifth of the population and the public sector of the economy offer sufficient outlets for the productive efforts of the potential labor force. The fact that the needs of the poor and the many unmet demands for public services and facilities hold higher priority than the demands of the marketplace in the value structures of this group of economists no doubt plays a role in their economic judgments.

STRUCTURAL UNEMPLOYMENT

Those who find the major explanations of unemployment in structural factors are primarily labor economists. Concerned professionally with efficient functioning of labor markets, they tend to focus on the development of skills and the placement of individual jobseekers rather than aggregates of spending and employment. The majority of this school maintain that increased aggregate demand is a necessary but not sufficient condition for reaching either the CEA's 4-percent unemployment target or their own preferred 3 percent. The pessimism of this group concerning the aggregate demand route to high employment has four bases. They argue that: (1) The concentration of unemployment among the young, the unskilled, minority groups, and depressed geographical areas is not easily attackable by increased general demand. (2) Their estimate of the numbers of potential members of the labor force who have withdrawn or not entered because of lack of employment opportunity exceeds that of the Council. (3) As the level of demand increases, changes in consumption patterns and technology will create a radically different demand for labor than in past high employment periods. Therefore, increased demand will put added pressure on skills already in short supply rather than employing the unemployed. (4) Technological change is replacing manpower to the extent that much higher levels of demand will be necessary to create the same number of jobs as in the past.

The structural school of thought, too, has its hyperenthusiasts. These are not labor economists but fiscal conservatives who as an alternative to expansionary policies argue that a job is available for every unemployed person if only he had the requisite skill or would move to the appropriate locale. Among them are those who derogate the character, trainability, and will to succeed of the hard-core unemployed. Advocacy of the structural explanation does not necessarily entail support of structural legislation among this group. . . .

Shortages of High-Talent Manpower

An anomaly of the manpower revolution is the concurrence of unemployment and unfulfilled demands for labor. We have no satisfactory measure of job vacancies and only vague ideas of the meaning of labor shortages. But by no measure would the number of job vacancies approach the numbers of the unemployed. Witnesses before the subcommittee disagreed as to whether there is really a general shortage of technical and scientific manpower. They were agreed that shortages do exist in a number of specific job categories. The near full employment of college graduates and the fierce competition for qualified graduate students in the natural and physical sciences demonstrate the ability of the economy to absorb many more of the highly educated. In fact, there is reason to believe that the supply of manpower of this type to some degree creates both its own demand and demand for supporting skills. The fact that one-fourth of all those working as engineers do not hold a college degree is evidence that the supply has been short enough to foster considerable upgrading. The lists of shortage occupations circulated among the State employment services and want ads seeking skilled craftsmen, white-collar workers, and engineers in nearly every large city reinforce testimony that unemployment is, in part, a problem of the wrong skills in the wrong places. The rapid growth in the number of jobs requiring substantial preparation and the disappearance of unskilled ones also suggests that the shortage problem may get worse as the level of demand increases.

TOWARD A COMPREHENSIVE EMPLOYMENT AND MANPOWER POLICY

Responsibility for employment and manpower decisions in the United States is widely dispersed. Employment relationships are predominantly private. Therefore, the primary manpower agencies are private employers, labor organizations, families, and individuals. The level of employment is determined in general by private consumption and investment decisions. The development of manpower resources, in the main, is the responsibility of individuals, families, employers, local school districts, and private and State universities.

But the Federal Government can and does play a significant complementary role. The Federal Government itself is the direct employer of 2.4 million persons (4.1 million including military personnel) and employs indirectly, through contractors and suppliers, 4 million more. Through the Employment Act of 1946, the Federal Government accepted the responsibility for maintaining employment, private and public, at high levels. The monetary and taxation policies of the National Government profoundly affect private economic activity and, thereby, employment. A wide range of Federal expenditure programs, direct and indirect, affect the economies and employment levels of all parts of the country. Federal funds and policies play an increasingly significant role in education and training. The federally financed public employment services are the most important supplement to the efforts of employers and individual workers to match job openings with available manpower. In a sense, Federal policies and programs act as a catalyst to private, State, and local efforts. Their effectiveness can make the difference between a slow-moving or even stagnant economy and a dynamic, progressive one.

The ability of the Nation to adjust to and exploit the full potential of its growing labor force and dramatically improving technology will depend in large measure upon the effectiveness of these programs and policies. . . .

Testimony before the subcommittee by public and private officials from Sweden and testimony on the methods of other countries by U.S. observers furnished insights into the possibilities of positive, carefully coordinated employment and manpower policies. Countries such as Sweden, France, West Germany, and Japan have, by aggressive monetary, taxation and expenditure policies maintained a high level of production and unemployment levels below 2 percent by U.S. definitions. Sweden, in particular, by carefully integrating manpower policy with employment policy, has avoided having high levels of demand side-tracked into unacceptably high inflationary pressures rather than employment.

Though cultures, traditions, and economic factors vary, making it undesirable if not impossible to simply adopt institutions from other economies, the United States can learn much from these experiences. One lesson is that policy measures which set overall goals and determine overall rates of employment growth and price stability without involving Government in the market process may result in more rather than less economic freedom. Once assured of full employment and production, labor organizations and private firms have been less given to restrictive practices or monopolistic tendencies in their own defense and have therefore required a lesser degree of Government control.

The United States is perhaps not ready for the sophisticated indicative planning typical of France or the tripartite economic coordination of the Swedish Labor Market Board. However, the establishment of overall economic goals and projections have been advocated in this country at least since 1945 with little effect. The "national production and employment budget" advocated in the Full Employment Act of 1945 and adopted by the U.S. Senate in that year was such a device. Though the provision was dropped from the act by the House and the conference committee, there is nothing in the Employment Act of 1946 to discourage the procedure. The risks and difficulties of economic forecasting are recognized. Projections can be accurate only within a range. Timetables must be of a general order. Public officials may be understandably reluctant to risk their reputations in such a hazardous enterprise. Yet goals never established are never attained.

With nearly two decades of additional U.S. experience and the contrasting European example of the postwar period, the value of establishing short and longer run economic goals is evident. A certain level of unemployment is inevitable and necessary in a free, dynamic economy as economic and technological forces change and individuals exercise their freedom of occupational choice. Considering past experience and present international example, 3 percent unemployment is a reasonably attainable level given adequate employment and manpower policies. Since a certain amount of time is necessary to absorb increased expenditures and for new programs to gain momentum and since our labor force is expanding so rapidly, 1968 appears to be the earliest reasonable date for attainment of 3 percent unemployment. . . .

The Integration of Employment and Manpower Policy

For too long, the level of employment, development of skills, and the matching of men and jobs have been considered as separate problems. One of the major findings of the subcommittee's investigations has been that manpower development and area redevelopment programs cannot be successful without adequate economic growth and job creation. Conversely, the jobs created are unlikely to fit the unemployed portions of the labor force without conscious training efforts. Job openings and idle manpower will not automatically find each other without effective placement mechanisms. Yet no common meeting ground for consideration of employment and manpower policies as integral parts of economic policy exists in the United States today.

The demand side of the equation, employment policy, was the subject of the Employment Act of 1946. The Council of Economic Advisers was established to assist the President in the formulation of employment policy with the Economic Report as the organ of transmittal to the Congress and the country. The Manpower Development and Training Act places the Secretary of Labor in a like position on the supply side as the President's adviser on manpower policy. For supply considerations, the Manpower Report is the communications instrument.

The problems of coordination on the supply or manpower side have been stressed. Those on the demand or employment side between the Council of Economic Advisers, Federal Reserve Board, and other agencies are less complex but still difficult. The problem of coordinating the Federal Reserve Board's absorption with price stability and balance-of-payments problems with the employment goals advocated by this report merits particular attention. In addition, a better method of integrating employment and manpower considerations as a part of overall economic policymaking is a high priority need. By the very nature of their responsibilities, the members, staff, and consultants of the Council of Economic Advisers over the years have been primarily fiscal, monetary, and business cycle experts. The staff usually includes one labor economist with responsibility for the entire range of wage-price, collective bargaining, and manpower issues. But the overall focus is on the level of aggregate demand for goods and services rather than people. The Labor Department on the other hand, though it has on its staff national income analysts, is primarily manpower and labor market oriented. The "expansionists versus structuralists" argument alluded to earlier is to some degree a manifestation of this specialization. In the same fashion, other Government agencies have their own specialized viewpoints on economic policy. This is as it should be. Each agency must be expected to develop its own expertise as it faces its own responsibilities. The problem is to find some means of bringing about joint consideration and integration of employment and manpower policies.

The development of mechanisms to integrate employment and manpower policy is an administrative function within the responsibilities of the Executive. Legislation is not required but the subcommittee may be of some service in pointing out a number of alternatives which have been suggested by witnesses or which occur to subcommittee members. The most frequent proposals have been the following: (1) Appointment of a Council of Manpower Advisers on a level equal to the Council of Economic Advisers; (2) appointment of a manpower expert as one of the three members of the Council of Economic Advisers; (3) a special assistant to the President for Manpower who, acting as the President's deputy would coordinate manpower efforts and acting on the same level as the CEA assure consideration of manpower issues in connection with overall economic policymaking; (4) a national council for economic affairs similar to the National Security Council with representation from all relevant departments aided by an executive director and a competent staff; and (5) coordination of all economic policy by the Bureau of the Budget. The subcommittee does not consider itself entitled nor competent to recommend one of these or other alternatives but does strongly believe that some such mechanism is needed. The President's Committee on Manpower, though it includes most of the officials necessary for joint consideration of overall economic policy, will apparently be charged with only manpower responsibilities. With experience and experimentation, however, it could become the first step toward the needed employment and manpower policymaking machinery. . . .

Developing Our Manpower for Full Employment

An increasing dilemma of recent years has been the concurrence of willing but idle manpower and vacant jobs. No one knows how many job vacancies exist which cannot be filled for lack of skills but the inverse correlation of education and unemployment is indicative. Trends in job creation suggest continued expansion of employment in occupations requiring extensive education and training and decline in employment opportunities for the unskilled. There is, in fact, some reason to fear that accomplishment of the full employment goal through expansion of aggregate demand might be thwarted by bottlenecks in the skilled and highly trained manpower such economic growth might require.

A truly free economy will offer freedom of occupational choice as well as freedom for investors and consumers. Freedom of occupational choice is often a hollow freedom without the opportunity to fully develop potential skills and to have a choice of alternative employment opportunities for those skills. Failure to develop skill potential not only threatens the individual with decreased employment opportunities but lessens his income and job satisfaction. The economy as well as the individual has a substantial interest in manpower development. Increased productivity of the individual adds to the goods and services available to society and speeds the growth and economic power of the Nation. Shortages of highly skilled personnel and educated manpower can slow growth rates and reduce national strength. Careful studies at numerous universities have demonstrated repeatedly that the economic return to investment in human resources far exceeds returns to investment in capital equipment. The Nation can ill afford failure to exploit the promising investment opportunities of manpower development. . . .

The Manpower Orientation of Education

The American people have always placed heavier responsibilities upon their educational system than they have been willing to financially support. At the close of the 1950's, the Soviet "sputnik" and the superior growth rate of most Western European nations generated a great deal of criticism of American education for its alleged failure to provide the Nation with an adequate supply of scientific and technical manpower. "Identification of the gifted" and "the pursuit of excellence" became the watchcries. More recently, as the inverse relationship between education and unemployment became more apparent, American education found itself accused of a bias in favor of higher education and against vocational training. Education for employment became an alternative slogan.

This lack of orientation among critics, which is also a reflection of debates current among professional educators, may be one of education's major shortcomings. The manpower role of education cannot be appraised without making explicit the orientation of the appraisers.

It is important to separate, in concept at least, education from training for specific skills or occupations. The primary responsibility of the educational system is to teach people to think, not to prepare them for employment. Nevertheless, though the development of manpower resources is a secondary goal of education, the role of education is fundamental to full employment in an increasingly complex technological society. The goal of education should be to develop within each individual the ability to think logically and plan rationally, to understand himself in relationship to his environment and to accumulate those basic intellectual tools necessary to a productive and meaningful life.

For many of the unskilled tasks of another generation which required primarily physical strength or manual dexterity, education was largely irrelevant to jobseeking. These tasks, however, have been the ones most susceptible to mechanization. Machines have been replacing the physical efforts of human beings for centuries but at an accelerating pace in recent decades. Many simple, repetitive mental tasks requiring comparatively little education are now shifting into the realm of the computer. Man's superiority over the machine lies in his imagination, his rationality, and his emotional sensitivity, all in part products of education.

In practice, separation of education from training is difficult. The basic intellectual tools provided by formal education have become the prerequisites of successful training. Many have direct employment application. At the elementary and high school level, however, the general principle is clear. The time has arrived in our complex world when the elementary and high schools have all they can do to inculcate in the student rationality, creativity, and the fundamental skills and knowledge necessary for communication and computation. A sound basic high school education for everyone capable of assimilating it should be a minimal goal. Some courses of general value also have direct employment application—typing, for example. Training for specific occupations should to the extent feasible be postsecondary through higher, vocational, or technical education, through apprenticeship, and through on-the-job training. In recognition of the need for specialized training beyond high school, free public education should soon include at least vocational schools, technical schools, junior or community colleges, and the first 2 years of college so that up to 14 years of education and training is available at public expense.

Vocational and Technical Education

Of the approximately 12 million full-time high school students in 1960, only 1.7 were enrolled in federally supported vocational classes. An additional undertermined number were registered in nonfederally supported commercial courses. If it could be assumed that the majority of the remainder would either continue on to college or acquire skills through vocational, technical, apprenticeship, or on-the-job training following high school, the small proportion of high school students involved in vocational training would not be disturbing. At present trends, however, approximately two-fifths of youngsters now in the fifth grade will not graduate from high school. Only half of those who do will enter college and the dropout rate there will be an additional 50 percent. Less than 20 percent of present-day youth will graduate from college. Two-thirds will receive no formal education or training of any kind beyond high school. Yet only 2 million persons are involved in postsecondary vocational education, mostly on a part-time basis.

The quality of vocational education has been as disturbing as the quantity. Only a small proportion of the secondary school students taking vocational courses have been enrolled in occupations where employment opportunities are expanding. As a result of the structure of Federal vocational education legislation, an inordinate emphasis has been put on home economics and agriculture. The former has done more to prepare for marriage than employment. The total amount spent on the latter has not been excessive, even considering that only 1 of 10 rural youths are expected to remain on farms. As an ordering of priorities, however, the stress has been unrealistic.

It was these facts and the obvious correlation between skill training and employment which led to passage of the Morse-Perkins Vocational Education Act of 1963. A panel of consultants on vocational education had recommended Federal expenditures of $400 million a year for vocational education. The Morse-Perkins Act increases authorizations from the present $55 million level to $225 million a year by 1967. While the increase is significant, need for the higher amount is evident. The act also broadened the occupational structure of Federal support and made other needed reforms representing the first important breakthrough in vocational education in many years.

As long as substantial numbers fail to complete high school or receive no post-secondary-school skill training, vocational training at the high school level will be needed. The goal should be, as stated above, however, to extend free public education to up to 2 years beyond high school and place skill training in a postsecondary atmosphere. In doing so, technical schools, junior colleges, or community colleges which mingle vocational training and basic education should be the focus. The tendency for vocational schools which have traditionally concentrated solely on nontheoretical skill training to become technical schools providing basic educational, scientific, and theoretical subjects as well, is already apparent.

The postsecondary 2-year institution is also an answer to the high college dropout rate. The availability of a community college within commuting distance of every student encourages postsecondary skill training, offers the technical training programs for which 4 years of college are unnecessary, allows the college student to obtain his first 2 years nearer home and serves as a facility for adult education, all at a substantial saving in costs to the student and resources to the community. Accomplishment of the goal of 14 years of free public education and lifetime educational opportunities will require a vast expansion of the community college system. . . .

Apprenticeship and On-The-Job Training

Training on the job has the advantage of furnishing employment, income, experience in the workplace, and the availability of equipment and instruction. It has the added advantage of direct attachment to the source of labor demand whereas institutional courses often train to meet demands existing at or before the commencement rather than after the completion of the training. Actually, the amount of training given on the job today exceeds all other forms of training. Even the college graduate receives his specialized skills, in effect, on the job, as either the medical student or the U.S. Senator can testify.

The amount of informal on-the-job training is unknown but is probably not large enough considering the advantages of this type of training. The number of people trained through formal apprenticeship is far short of need.[1] Small employers and those in industries where employment relationships are casual are reluctant to spend time, effort, and money on training when the benefits may accrue to the whole industry rather than the individual employer. Apprenticeship training requires expansion, not so much to increase the quantity as the quality of skilled craftsmen. Only a small percentage of today's craftsmen were formally trained through apprenticeship and a high percentage of these have been promoted to supervisory positions. Some of the rest have been trained in vocational schools or the armed services. The majority have "picked up the trade" in a hit-and-miss fashion. The cost to the economy is less than adequate competence and to the individual is an unnecessarily high incidence of unemployment. A few of the crafts in the construction industry have done a commendable job of apprentice training. The printing industry also trains substantial numbers of apprentices. Even in these cases the numbers are not adequate to assure that fully trained and competent replacements are available for present craftsmen. Outside these industries relatively little apprenticeship exists.

The costs of vocational education are almost entirely borne by the public while the costs of apprenticeship and on-the-job training are borne entirely by the employer. The result is a discrimination in favor of institutional training which justifies greater public support of training in the employer's establishment. . . .

Adult Education

Over 23 million Americans 18 years of age and older have completed less than 8 years of schooling. Eight million adults 25 and over have completed less than 5 years. At least the latter and many of the former are likely to be, for all practical purposes, illiterate. Those

---

[1] Apprenticeship differs from on-the-job training in general in that it is longer, usually at least 2 years, trains skilled craftsmen and usually includes related classroom instruction.

who have not completed high school are only 46 percent of the total labor force; yet they account for 64 percent of the unemployed. Sixty-two percent of the jobless fathers of children receiving aid to dependent children have no education beyond elementary school. Forty-five percent of all families with less than $2,000 annual income have a family head with less than an eighth-grade education. The link between lack of education and the over $4.5 billion now spent annually on welfare payments to 7.25 million persons is beyond dispute.

Yet, of 15,200 school systems studied by the Office of Education, only 4,840 reported any type of adult education programs. Only 160, or 3.3 percent, offered any instruction whatsoever in adult basic education. Of 23 million educationally deprived adults, only 47,500 were being taught basic literacy skills and only 1.1 percent of the limited number of adult education courses offer such training. For the older worker who was deprived of educational opportunity in his youth, the Nation as a whole simply has no educational system. By way of contrast, the city of Los Angeles operates 27 adult schools with 100 branches and 66,000 currently enrolled students. In 1963, these schools issued 2,130 high school diplomas, nearly a thousand of them to dropouts of the Los Angeles school system.

Beyond the problem of remedying deficiencies in the past education of adults lies the need for continual upgrading of skills and refreshing of education to meet the exigencies of changing employing trends and the demands of a more complex world. It has been suggested that education must become a lifetime effort, but this goal cannot be realized unless the facilities are available. The amendments adding provisions for basic education and literacy training to the Manpower Development and Training Act passed by Congress in 1963 have transformed that act from a limited program applicable primarily to the best trained and most employable among the unemployed to an effective weapon against hard-core unemployment. As educational requirements rise in the labor market, even those with high school educations and beyond find themselves in need of further education or refresher courses if they are to avoid displacement and extensive unemployment. Availability of instruction, not motivation, appears to be the major obstacle to adult education. . . .

Retraining the Unemployed: The Manpower Development and Training Act and Area Redevelopment Act

The retraining provisions of the Area Redevelopment Act passed in 1961 and the Manpower Development and Training Act of 1962 were new departures in the manpower policies of the Federal Government. The former has had the longer experience but is limited to a maximum of 16 weeks of training allowances in areas of high chronic unemployment. The start of the latter was delayed until September of 1962, waiting for an appropriation. Therefore, only a little over 1 year of experience is available for appraisal.

THE INITIAL EXPERIENCE

During the first 15 months, approximately 100,000 persons were approved for training programs under the Manpower Development and Training Act. By September 1963, 17,700 had completed institutional training compared to 500 who had completed on-the-job training. Of these, approximately 70 percent had been placed, 60 percent of them in training-related jobs. The average cost per trainee for institutional training was about $1,500 with nearly one-fifth going for administrative expenses and the balance divided approximately equally between training costs and subsistence allowances. The training allowances have ranged from $23 to $43 a week and have averaged $35.

The Manpower Development and Training Act training courses which have a legal maximum of 52 weeks of training allowances have averaged 23 weeks. About one-fourth of the courses have been 44 weeks or more in length. Four-fifths of the latter were for skilled and technical occupations.

Slightly over 6,000 trainees had been approved for the Manpower Development and Training Act on-the-job training courses through November 1963. The average course was 16 weeks in length and the estimated average cost per trainee was about $400. The shorter Area Redevelopment Act courses for which 28,000 trainees have been approved have averaged 11 weeks for an average cost of $700 per trainee.

Every State has participated in one or both of the retraining programs. Of the approximately 450 occupations for which training projects have been approved, half of the total trainees were enrolled in 5: stenography, machine operation, nursing, automobile repair, and welding. Others have ranged from computer programing to service station attendants. A number of the programs have been highly imaginative, including courses for farm equipment operation and repair in several States to give employment stability to migratory workers, special courses for Indian electronic solderers and wirers, Alaskan electronics technicians, and sewage plant technicians. Where the numbers of a particular occupation needed in a locality were insufficient to justify a class, trainees have been gathered together from a number of States and then returned to employment in their home location. Multioccupational courses have been developed which allowed several hundred trainees to be selected for a number of occupations. These were given preliminary training jointly before splitting into occupational groups for completion.

Particularly heartening have been the 28 demonstration projects which have focused on hard-core unemployed with special problems such as school dropouts, older workers of low educational attainment, welfare recipients, the physically and mentally handicapped, migrant farmworkers and even soon-to-be released young prisoners. For most of these, the established training techniques of the vocational schools were not adaptable and the Office of Manpower, Automation, and Training and the State affiliates of the U.S. Employment Service have developed specialized programs and facilities to meet the needs. Experience with those of the 30,000 persons approved for these demonstration projects who have received counseling, testing, or training has given substantial evidence that very few are without the potential to make a positive contribution to society if their capabilities are developed. Experience under the vocational rehabilitation program noted above indicates, and future studies will likely prove that Manpower Development and Training Act training costs will be returned in a relatively short time by the employees' extra earnings, increased tax revenues, and reduced unemployment insurance and welfare costs.

AREA REDEVELOPMENT ACT TRAINING ROLE

The Area Redevelopment Act training program is a more limited one in size and scope but it fills a specific need. Since Manpower Development and Training Act funds are limited relative to retraining needs, there might be an understandable tendency to concentrate on retraining in the more prosperous areas where employment opportunities are more plentiful. Thus, the depressed areas might suffer relative to others. The Area Redevelopment Act training funds are limited to areas of substantial and persistent unemployment. Thus the program concentrates on the areas that need it most and can prepare trained workers for the attraction of new firms and the expansion of existing business. The existence of two programs also expands somewhat the limited funds available. The Manpower Development and Training Act program will require State matching funds in the near future.

Since the depressed areas, because of their special financial problems will require continued 100-percent Federal financing, it is important that the two training programs should continue.

TRAINEE CHARACTERISTICS

The training provisions of the Area Redevelopment Act and the Manpower Development and Training Act have been generally successful but a number of problems have developed. The proportion of long-term unemployed among Manpower Development and Training Act trainees has been greater than that among the unemployed as a whole. The proportion of nonwhites among Manpower Development and Training Act trainees has corresponded closely to their proportion among all unemployed. However, the poorly educated and older workers have been seriously underrepresented. Sixty percent of Manpower Development and Training Act trainees have been high school graduates compared to a little over one-third among the unemployed. Only 3 percent of trainees had less than an elementary school education compared to 20 percent of the unemployed. Only one of nine Manpower Development and Training Act trainees was over 45 years of age but nearly one-quarter of the unemployed were in that age group.

This apparently excessive selectivity has been in part due to the lack of trainability among the trainees and in part deliberate. Only one of six screened has been enrolled in a training course. Many have been without the basic literacy skills deemed necessary for training by orthodox techniques. For the rest, since the training opportunities were limited, the most capable were accepted first. The 1963 amendment allowing an additional 20 weeks for basic education should offer a partial solution to this problem but deliberate attempts must be made to reach these hard-core unemployed groups.

Originally, the Manpower Development and Training Act was intended to focus on retraining the experienced worker whose skills had been made obsolete by technological change. The inordinately high rate of unemployment among youth has made the need for some reorientation in favor of youth evident. The fact that the program did not get up a full head of steam until late in 1962 because of the delayed appropriation and the time required thereafter to organize the program, meant that the States had no opportunity to evaluate the program before the biennial meetings of many of the State legislatures in early 1963 had adjourned. Both of these obvious deficiencies were remedied in the 1963 act by lowering the entrance age and required labor market experience, increasing the proportion of funds allocable to youth, and delaying State matching requirements. Training allowances which were tied to the level of unemployment compensation proved too low, particularly for those with families who were tempted to drop out of the longer training programs to take temporary employment. The 1963 amendments made allowances for part-time work by trainees and authorized a special bonus of up to $10 a week on the basis of need but this will doubtless prove inadequate as well.

AVAILABILITY OF FACILITIES

The meager vocational education facilities available in most areas and the complete lack of such facilities in others have been an obstacle to the retraining programs. Much of what has been available has been deficient in quality and the entire vocational education plant of the country is already overburdened with students in the regular programs. Vocational educators have made tremendous efforts to adjust their programs to the new load but facilities can stretch only so far. The increase in resources made available by the Morse-Perkins Act will be a boon to the retraining effort as well as to regular vocational education.

The retraining program has failed to take as much advantage of the vocational education program as it might. Often the number of unemployed or the number of job openings has been insufficient to justify establishment of a full Manpower Development and Training Act course. At times, special Manpower Development and Training Act courses have been established when existing vocational courses could have supplied the need. A program for supplementing the project orientation of Manpower Development and Training Act to date with referral of individual trainees to ongoing programs is at present being implemented.

ON-THE-JOB TRAINING

The single greatest disappointment under Manpower Development and Training Act is the failure of on-the-job training to assume the major role expected by the authors of the act. On-the-job training has the advantage of furnishing employment (often permanent), income, and actual work experience without the burden of furnishing and constantly updating equipment and finding skilled instructors.

The slow start of on-the-job training under Manpower Development and Training Act is attributable to several factors. Institutional facilities were immediately available through public channels. On-the-job training programs required promotional efforts to gain employer cooperation. Careful planning was necessary to assure an addition to existing training rather than a shouldering of the expense of employers' existing training efforts. Finally, the Manpower Development and Training Act program was added to the existing responsibilities of the Bureau of Apprenticeship and Training with only a minor addition to the Washington staff and budget and no addition to the field staff. In order to prevent excessive administrative costs per trainee under the resulting budget constraints, on-the-job training courses were initially limited to a minimum of 10 trainees. Approval of all on-the-job training courses has been centralized in Washington to prevent feared abuses, [thus] further slowing the development of the program. Efforts are being made to eliminate all of these obstacles and it is to be hoped that on-the-job training will play a larger role in future retraining efforts.

ADMINISTRATIVE PROBLEMS

State and local vocational education authorities complain of what they consider undue redtape and excessive centralization in administration of the retraining programs. Federal responsibilities under the program are highly diverse. Labor Department responsibilities are divided among three bureaus and the technical aspects of training are under the jurisdiction of the Department of Health, Education, and Welfare. Manpower Development and Training Act courses are normally approved at the regional level, while OJT and ARA courses must come to Washington for final approval. Relationships between all of the Federal agencies involved have not been as cooperative nor the lines of authority as clear as they might have been. State vocational educators believe greater authority for developing training courses should be placed in their hands. Considerable progress has been made in working out differences and shortening timelags, but further improvements are needed, not the least of which is greater cooperation among the Federal agencies, as well as among the State and local authorities involved. Title I of the Manpower Development and Training Act places the primary responsibility for the formulation and administration of manpower policy upon the Secretary of Labor. Good progress has been made considering the brief time period involved but better coordination will be needed for complete fulfillment of the responsibility.

FUTURE OF MANPOWER DEVELOPMENT AND TRAINING ACT

The Manpower Development and Training Act is making a substantial contribution to the development of manpower resources through the preparation of the unemployed to fill available job openings, but its resources have been insufficient to make more than a dent in the training needs. The majority of the 4 million unemployed could doubtless profit from some degree of retraining. The Swedish Labor Market Board has established as its goal a retraining effort of 1 percent of the labor force each year. This proportion, which would mean 700,000 trainees each year if applied to the U.S. labor force, would not be excessive in relation to need.

The role of the Manpower Development and Training Act at present is a broad one. Years of neglect accompanied by rapid change have created a backlog of the untrained, the poorly educated, and those with obsolete skills. The elimination of this backlog would take years, even if the educational and training system were made adequate to supply skills and the flexible base for retraining to each new entrant to the labor force. Most skill training will always be furnished by the employer on the job. The regular educational system, including vocational, technical, and adult education, should be the major institutional reliance for skill acquirement. This is necessary, both because the marginal costs of training one more worker in an ongoing program are low and because training and retraining should be undertaken in anticipation of threatening unemployment or to make possible occupational advancement rather than after unemployment strikes.

In the long run the focus of the Manpower Development and Training Act program should increasingly be upon research, demonstration projects, and specialized attacks on the toughest manpower problems—those not amenable to more general programs. . . .

Matching Men and Jobs in a Changing Labor Market

A level of demand adequate for full employment and a well educated and highly trained labor force would not by themselves supply the complete answer to employment and manpower problems. There is no automatic process by which job vacancies and available workers are matched. Neither the employer nor the potential employee may know of the other's existence or demand and supply may exist in geographical separation. Recruitment and job search will tend toward successful placement but considerable time may elapse with consequent loss of income and waste of manpower. In a dynamic economy with a high turnover of jobs and workers, unemployment may remain excessively high simply for such frictional reasons.

A number of institutions, both private and public, have developed to facilitate the recruitment and placement process, either by furnishing labor market information or bringing employers and potential employees into direct contact. The U.S. Employment Service and its affiliated State agencies is the primary source of public labor market services. The efforts of the public employment service are supplemented by the statistical information services of the Labor Department and the specialized services of such agencies as Vocational Rehabilitation and Public Assistance in the Department of Health, Education, and Welfare and the Bureau of Indian Affairs in the Department of the Interior. In addition, private employment services are active in a number of communities.

1. The U. S. Employment Service

Officials of the U.S. Employment Service must consider themselves the prime example of those who are "damned if they do and damned if they don't." The agency has been frequently criticized for playing a too small role in the labor market and has been recently attacked by the private, fee-charging employment agencies for an alleged attempt to monopolize placement. As the "front line" of public attempts to match men and jobs, the interest in public employment service operation is justified but the criticisms are probably not.

PLACEMENT ROLE

The placement role of the employment service is a relatively small but key one.[2] An estimated 16 percent of the hirings by employers in 1960 involved the services of one or more of the 1,900 State employment offices affiliated with USES. By way of contrast, it is estimated that 36 percent of placements came about by direct contact between employer and job applicant, 23 percent through relatives and friends, and 11 percent through newspaper ads. Private employment agencies officiated at only 4 percent of such man-job marriages, usually finding jobs for highly trained job seekers at one end of the spectrum and domestic servants at the other. Miscellaneous means accounted for the remaining 10 percent. The recruitment and job search process will always remain predominantly private and in-

---

[2] The role of the employment service is, of course, broader than placement alone. In addition to many other services to employees, job applicants and other members of the labor force, the employment service furnishes a number of important employer services. Among these are labor market information, wage surveys, job analysis, testing services, and recruitment. Services to the employer, of course, encourage use of the public employment service as a source of labor.

formal. Even in the more highly organized Swedish labor market, no more than 25 percent of the hiring in the nation occurs through use of the services of the public employment service.

The percent of all hires represented by employment service placements (or "penetration rate" as it is called by employment service personnel) varies widely by industry and occupation. In manufacturing, the penetration rate is estimated at 30 percent. In all industries 30 percent of the unskilled workers found their jobs through the employment service, compared to 14 percent of clerical and sales people hired, 13 percent of the service workers, 11 percent of the semiskilled workers, 10 percent of the professional and managerial, and 8 percent of the skilled workers.

THE "NEW" EMPLOYMENT SERVICE

Throughout most of the decade of the 1950's the employment service called attention to emerging manpower problems and to its own inability to keep operations abreast of these due to limited funds. The inability to meet all demands had an impact on the quality of the services which were provided, since efforts were made to meet the needs of as many people as possible. As a result, Secretary of Labor James Mitchell in October 1958 expressed his concern to State agency administrators and employment service directors. The employment service sought the advice of academic consultants and their recommendations, as well as those of the Senate's Special Committee on Unemployment Problems which reported in March 1960, served as the basis for a program undertaken by the U.S. Employment Service to give the public employment service system in this country a new image.

Substantial improvements have been made. The funds appropriated to the employment services increased from $90 million in 1961 to $145 million by 1963. Even at that, employment service resources were less in relation to the size of the labor force in 1963 than in 1948. Yet nonagricultural placements rose from 5.2 million in 1958 to 6.6 million in 1963. Instead of giving initial counseling interviews to 8.6 percent of job applicants as in 1958, 11 percent were counseled in 1963. The percent of those counseled given general aptitude tests rose from 48 to 62 percent. In 1958, the employment services furnished employment counseling and placement services on a formal agreement basis to jobseeking high school graduates in only one-third of the Nation's high schools. The services were provided in over one-half of the high schools in 1962. Unemployment insurance and employment placement functions were separated in most of the large metropolitan areas, sometimes into separate buildings, in an attempt to dispel the "unemployment office" reflection.

With all of these improvements, it is doubtful that the penetration rate has improved substantially. By its very nature, the employment service will always be faced with the hardest-to-place workers and the hardest-to-fill jobs. This very fact increases the importance of the public employment service since these are the very situations where the most manpower is wasted, the frictional portions of unemployment statistics rise, and output is restricted by labor shortages.

CRITICISM BY PRIVATE EMPLOYMENT AGENCIES

The attacks by private fee-charging agencies have resulted from the actual and potential competition of the public agencies. The private services do not object to the gathering of labor market information and other nonplacement functions of the public employment service. They do argue that the public service should restrict itself to servicing unemployed workers and, by implication, primarily those who are unemployment compensation recipients. The fee-charging agencies particularly resent public efforts in the professional placement field.

Private agency charges that the USES was concentrating on finding new jobs for already employed workers were erroneous. A followup study revealed that 97 percent of those placed in the survey month were unemployed. At the same time, the public employment service cannot and should not be restricted to placing the unemployed. An employment service which cannot service the already employed cannot effectively service the unemployed. The employer's concern is to recruit competent employees, not to take the unemployed off the labor market. Many employers already tend to suspect the quality of employment service referrals. If the employment service were limited to the placing of the unemployed, employers would be convinced that only the less desirable employees were available from that source and fewer job orders would be forthcoming. This, in part, is the significance of the professional placement service efforts of the employment service. Employers who find higher quality manpower through this source are encouraged to seek all levels of skills through the employment service.

From the standpoint of efficient utilization of manpower, it is also important to place an already employed worker in a job for which he is better suited as well as to bring an unemployed person into employment. In fact, the upgrading process then makes room at the bottom for the unemployed. For those who operate in a regional or nationwide labor market, it is also important from an efficiency standpoint to know of alternative opportunities or needed manpower elsewhere. It is at this point that the professional placement efforts of the employment service become especially important.

LISTING JOB VACANCIES

Theoretical discussions of a perfect labor market always assume perfect knowledge of alternative employment opportunities. Only the public employment service offers any hope of even the slightest movement in this direction. The private agencies are naturally interested primarily in placement to earn their fee. Only a public agency will be concerned with anything as broad as overall efficiency in the utilization of manpower resources.

It is this concern for increasing the information available to those who are attempting to find the best outlets for their skills and abilities which has led labor market experts to dream of full listing of all job openings with the public employment service. Employer reluctance to do so probably arises from fears that requirements to accept employment service referrals would follow but this need not be the case. The employer could be left to choose freely among job applicants but knowledge and opportunity would be open to all.

Serious efforts to make full listing of job openings compulsory have not been contemplated, both out of respect for traditional values and because no such program could be successful without voluntary cooperation. Two routes are open, however. Government agencies and Government contractors whose costs are reimbursable by the Government could be required to list openings. Experience rating provisions governing unemployment insurance rates could be adjusted to encourage voluntary listing. Experience ratings were designed to encourage stable employment patterns and reduce drains on unemployment insurance funds. Full listing of all vacancies would likely lead to even greater savings. Also, in the interest of more widespread information, employment services should increase advertising expenditures from [the] present one-third of 1 percent of the total USES budget.

THE NEEDS OF THE FUTURE

The role of the public employment service in the labor market is likely to take on new significance with impending developments. The cancellation of the Dyna-Soar project, the closing of the Studebaker plant, the cutbacks in nuclear warhead production, and forthcoming military base closures are all indications that a particularly difficult period of employment adjustment may be impending. The participation of the employment service in vocational education must be increased to assure training in harmony with labor market need. Greater stress is needed in economic development efforts upon labor market information, the types of labor available, and the type of industry to be attracted to employ local manpower.

New attention for the problems of poverty, school dropouts, and hard-core unemployed can also be expected to increase employment service burdens. Up until now, the unemployed served by the employment services have been generally those who have taken the initiative to go to the local employment office, about 30 percent of them as unemployment insurance claimants. The school dropout has rarely learned jobhunting techniques. The hard-core unemployed and poverty-stricken may have, through discouragement, withdrawn from active job search. It may well be necessary for the Employment Service to seek out these disadvantaged persons rather than wait to be approached by them. Many of these disadvantaged persons will be identified by the Selective Service under the manpower conservation program and referred to the Employment Service. Once contacted, these persons will require more intensive services—more frequent counseling at greater depth, group guidance in how to function in the labor market, followup efforts to assist the newly placed employee to remain employed and preventative efforts to identify and assist occupations and employees vulnerable to unemployment. All of these diagnostic, remedial, and preventative efforts will increase the costs per placement but they are a necessary part of any attack on poverty and hard-core unemployment.

At this point, valuable lessons can be learned from the experience of the vocational rehabilitation program in which the Employment Service has played an important role. By massing effort, resources, and facilities on the particular problems of individual handicapped persons, near miracles have been worked in the preparation for and placement of the seriously handicapped in productive employment. Lack of education, skill or other obstacle to employment is no less of a handicap. The vocational rehabilitation program has been spending an average of $1,000 a year for each individual rehabilitated. Yet the expenditure has proven to be an investment soon returned in reduced welfare expenditures and augmented tax revenues. About $25 is spent on the average Employment Service placement. A greater expenditure of resources in a concentrated attack on the individual problems of the hard-core unemployed would pay equal dividends.

The major requirement is increased numbers of better trained and more competent employment counselors within the Employment Service. Recruitment of such personnel would require raising the minimum qualifications for counselors and recognizing the inadequacy of their current classifications. State salary structures are often too low to attract professionally trained talent. Employers and Government agencies often recruit candidates for counseling and other professional positions on a regional or national basis. In the competition to attract competent staff, States with low salary structures are at a distinct disadvantage. Federal legislation may be necessary to permit supplementation of salaries in such States for professional classifications in short supply.

Federal standards should be imposed in this and other areas to assure adequate policies among the now widely varying States. The State employment services are financed 100 percent with Federal funds; yet little is presently done to require compliance with national policies or standards. . . .

2. Labor Mobility

The labor force in the United States is the most mobile geographically of any industrial country. Nevertheless, the average worker is still very reluctant to leave familiar surroundings even for improved employment opportunities. There are certain social values in the stability of familiar environments and high costs in social and political disorganization accompanying high mobility rates. Nevertheless, unemployed workers and job openings will often fail to match geographically just as they do occupationally. Communities decline and die as others prosper and grow. While efforts are necessary to encourage job expansion in areas of labor surplus, some workers will find their opportunities improved by movement to a new location. As long as unemployment is general, relocation of surplus labor will be resisted both by businessmen at the point of origin who object to the loss of customers and workers in the community of destination who resent increased job competition. Relocation of surplus labor will never be an important program numerically but freedom of occupational choice has its geographical as well as industrial dimension.

The first requirement is that knowledge of alternative job opportunities be available. Thorough, rapid, and widespread dissemination of timely information on job opportunities and worker qualifications among employment offices, interstate and intrastate, and from the employment offices to the unemployed can make possible more intelligent job choices. The rudiments of such a program exist and research is continuing. To become fully effective it needs access to modern methods of data storage and retrieval and more rapid expansion into a nationwide communications network.

Secondly, most unemployed workers do not have geographical freedom of occupational choice because their financial resources are inadequate. The costs of leaving a home, moving a family to another area, and meeting living expenses until a steady income is attained are formidable to one who has been unemployed for some time. The 1963 amendments to the Manpower Development and Training Act authorized the Secretary of Labor to spend up to $4 million in experimentation and demonstration projects to test the feasibility of relocation allowances. Unfortunately, the act does not encourage experimentation in providing the personal services necessary to successful relocation. . . .

3. Manpower Research and Statistical Needs

The subcommittee did not undertake an appraisal of the expanded research efforts fostered by the Manpower Development and Training Act or the various statistical data available for guidance on manpower policy. Nevertheless, a few areas where expanded research and more statistical information would be of assistance in the making of employment and manpower policy became apparent to us during our studies. We note them as suggestions to the relevant agencies and to interested researchers.

The subcommittee is particularly impressed with the need for more information concerning the nature, pace, and present and prospective impact of technological change. No aspect of the manpower situation has been the subject of more discussion in recent years but the absence of factual data has made most of the discussion inconclusive. Overall information on output per man and per man-hour is reasonably adequate for manufacturing as a whole and probably for agriculture. Productivity data for public employment is nonexistent (and perhaps nonproducible), the little data available for construction appears misleading and the data for service sectors of the economy needs improvement.

The greatest lack is in industry and occupational detail. Productivity data for the economy as a whole or for major sectors supplies evidence only of job creation needs. An understanding of the individual impact and the problems of adjustment to technological change depends upon the availability of information by occupation and by industry.

From the policy point of view the future impact of technological change is even more important than the present. The spectacular nature of some speculations concerning the future of automation and cybernation and the sanguine nature of other forecasts have been noted. Actually, there appears to be little dependable information concerning the pervasiveness and rate of introduction and potential applications of various technological developments.

Any reasonably dependable forecasts of the employment impact of technological change will depend upon constant industry by industry assessment of impending changes and future developments. The cooperation of business firms in the oft-suggested technological clearinghouse would give public policymakers both advance warning of impending job displacements and insights into longer range developments. The Department of Labor has begun a program to assess technological changes by industry. Its augmentation and analysis of the resulting data would be an important aid to policymaking.

The complement to a better understanding of the nature and pace of modern technology is a continuous appraisal of the changing occupational structure of employment. Which jobs are most vulnerable to technological change? How many are employed in vulnerable jobs? What are their personal characteristics? What are the likely adjustment problems, considering these characteristics? What is the geographical location of the vulnerable jobs and the likely community impact? What has been the process of adjustment to past technological change? What lessons can past experience provide for the future?

The existing occupational classification system also needs reexamination to give it more functional meaning. The present classifications are unduly broad and contain jobs too diverse in content for meaningful analysis.

Finally, the possibilities for applying computer technology to manpower research and policymaking should be examined. Testimony extolling the versatility, speed, and capacity of modern data processing equipment and computers was impressive. Is the "information revolution" being applied to manpower research? Can the very devices which are playing an important role in present changes in manpower requirements contribute to the solution of manpower problems by adding the accessibility and analysis of manpower data?

PART X

CASES

Case studies taken from actual experience in industry present the realities of collective bargaining in action. They indicate the complexities of the real world of industrial relations, where personal, institutional, historical, cultural, and economic factors vary enormously. As in courts of law, the challenge to the student is to analyze and weigh the various factors or considerations and to arrive at a decision based on evidence and valid reasoning. Samuel Butler once observed that "life is the art of drawing sufficient conclusions from insufficient premises."

The following four case studies can be used in pairs. The first two raise questions of management's rights and skill in handling particular situations. The second pair deal with two separate subjects (job evaluation and wage incentives) in the same company.

It may be helpful to state some of the issues in each case, and to suggest a few pointers or hints for the third and fourth cases.

The Bethlehem Shipyard case raises the following sorts of questions:

1. Was the management seeking unfairly to use the union stewards as a means of changing the agreement instead of formally negotiating such a change with the union?

2. Was the management under obligation to notify directly all the employees of the action it would take to enforce this rule and not to use the union shop stewards for publicizing its instructions and achieving compliance with its rules?

3. Can employees, especially shop stewards, be permitted to refuse to obey management instructions while declining to challenge the validity of those instructions under the grievance procedure established for that purpose?

4. Do union officials have an obligation to act responsibly and to see to it that the provisions of an agreement are respected and complied with, including use of the grievance procedure to process alleged violations of the agreement?

5. How should the arbitrator have reasoned and ruled in this case?

The Chrysler case involves conflicting evidence as to the attitude of the men, which the arbitrator concluded was not necessary to resolve in order to decide the case. Some of the issues raised by the Chrysler case are:

1. If management has reason to believe that the presence of a particular employee in the plant will lead to serious trouble (including interference with production and possible personal injury and property damage), does it have the right to send that employee home without pay under a clause in an agreement giving the company exclusive right to manage the plant and direct the work force?

2. Is the company justified by the unusual circumstances in this case in deviating from its normal practice of disciplining those employees who refuse to work or who threaten to make trouble?

3. If the employee or the union steward appear to accept management's decision without protest at the time that an alleged violation of an agreement occurs, does such acquiescence preclude subsequent processing of that grievance against the company?

With respect to the third and fourth cases involving the Sedgewick-Cole Corporation, well-supported, written answers to the following questions might be prepared:

1. Why did the Craftown local reject job evaluation and the Kingsville local accept it?

2. Why did the Craftown management have so much trouble with wage incentives? What could it have done to remedy some of its troubles with incentive wages?

It is desirable to analyze the job evaluation case separately and to avoid any mixing of the two cases. With respect to the job evaluation case, there were significant differences between the two plants with respect to past experience, union leadership, and the way job evaluation was introduced. Note the following facts: (a) Until Tedrick joined the management, he was on the executive board of the national union and had been primarily responsible for organizing the rubber plants in the Craftown (population, 125,000) area, whereas in the smaller plant in Kingsville (population, 2,000,000), Morgan had only been a former president of the local union and was a member of its executive board just before he shifted to management. (b) Skilled craftsmen dislike division of the occupation into A and B classes, and such division worked out differently for the current and former union officials at the Craftown and the Kingsville plants. (c) For historical reasons, the use of "red circle" rates raised fears for union security in Craftown. (d) The Kingsville local was anxious to eliminate wage inequity grievances.

The fourth case on wage incentives concerns the Craftown plant only. The main opposition came from the "C" inspectors. What historical and job security factors influenced their opposition? Did the management and the consultant do a good job of communication and selling of the program to the necessary groups? Were the incentive wages and the production standards properly established to avoid charges of wage inequity?

In these cases there is no single, correct answer. The "right" answer is the one that is most convincing to a thoughtful and perceptive class.

1

Bethlehem Shipyard Case

COMPANY: Bethlehem Steel Company
UNION: Industrial Union of Marine and Shipbuilding Workers of America, Local 13 (CIO)

This grievance, filed in Step No. 2 on July 12, 1949, reads as follows:

The Union claims that Nick Parascondole DP 73, George Porkorny DP 196, Joseph Ryan DQ 10, William Capper DS 92, James McGrath DAJ 286, and Robert Lenihan DEA 180, were unjustly suspended in violation of Sec. 5 of Article 3 & of Article XIX, Sec. 4.

The Union asks that these men be compensated for all time lost due to this suspension and that the notation of said suspension be removed from their employment records.

FACTS OF CASE

The Union claims that the six employees mentioned in the grievance were unjustly suspended for five days on July 6, 1949. Five of the employees suspended were shop stewards in different departments; the sixth, William Capper, was a shop committeeman.

Tardiness after Lunch

Article IV (Hours of Work) of the agreement between the parties, as supplemented by Appendix 2, provides that the lunch hour on the first shift shall be from 12 noon to 12:30 P.M. For some time prior

---

Taken from Labor Arbitration Reports, *XV (Washington: Bureau of National Affairs), pp. 749–51. Reprinted with the permission of the publisher.*

to the events hereinafter related, employees were not required to be on their jobs at the conclusion of the lunch hour at 12:30 P.M. and were considered late only if they were not inside the gate by 12:30 P.M. The 27th Street Yard covers a large area, and a walk of several minutes is often required of employees after entering the gate to reach their places of work. At the end of June, 1949, the Company, believing that an existing rule required employees to be back on their jobs at 12:30 P.M. and not merely inside the gate, decided to take steps to cure what it says was laxity on the part of employees in returning to their jobs. At a grievance meeting on June 28, 1949, Mr. Starick, Assistant to the Manager at the Yard, and Mr. Minihan, Management's Representative at the Yard, discussed the matter informally with the Grievance Committee and asked that it cooperate to see that the men were back on their jobs at 12:30 P.M. The Union Committee was noncommittal.

On July 1, 1949, the Company called a meeting of the day shift shop stewards and the Grievance Committee, which meeting the President of the Local Union, who was not employed at this Yard, also attended. It explained its economic and competitive position in the shipbuilding field, stated that it was receiving complaints from customers, and asked that the shop stewards cooperate to see that the men were back on their jobs at 12:30 P.M. It also asked the shop stewards themselves to observe the rule. The shop stewards were noncommittal, and asked the Company to post a notice to that effect. There was also some argument about whether the lunch hour should be lengthened. The same day the Company called a meeting of the second shift shop stewards for the same purpose, at which it was met with a similar reaction on the part of the stewards.

Observation of Tardy Employees

The largest job in the Yard at the time was a repair job on a vessel known as the *S.S. Ferguson,* which was located about 350 feet from the gate. Beginning on June 28, 1949, the Company kept a record of the employees working on that vessel who returned to their jobs after 12:30 P.M. For that purpose it stationed various of its supervisors at points between the gate and this vessel each day from June 28 to July 6, inclusive. The supervisors noted the employees who returned after 12:30 P.M. These records indicate that on June 28, June 30, and July 6, a substantial number of employees were late, while on the other three days only a few of the employees were late, the Company's request having some effect. The six employees here involved were late on all of the six days, with the exception of Mr. Lenihan, who was not working on June 28, and June 29 and June 30, but who was late on July 5 and July 6, and Mr. Capper, who was late on five of the six days. It also appeared that on July 5 and July 6, 1949, these employees were among the last, if not the last, to enter the Yard at the conclusion of the lunch hour. The testimony also indicated that each of these employees was spoken to by one of his supervisors prior to July 6, 1949, and was personally requested to be back on his job at 12:30 P.M. Several of these employees admittedly refused to do so, stating that the Company was attempting to change the agreement, and to shorten the agreed upon lunch hour. One or two of them replied also that they or the men were "looking for a show down."

On the afternoon of July 6, these employees were called to the office of Mr. Starick. Mr. Starick again asked for their cooperation in getting the men back on their jobs at 12:30 P.M. and also asked that they themselves comply with the rule. He called their attention to the fact that they had been repeatedly late. They were again noncommittal and, at the conclusion of the hearing, Mr. Starick informed them that they were all suspended for a period of five days. It is the validity of this suspension which is here in question.

Late that afternoon of July 6, 1949 a meeting was held with Mr. Crane, assistant manager of the Yard. At the meeting Mr. Crane offered to lift the suspensions if the men involved would agree to attempt to persuade other employees to be back on their jobs at 12:30 P.M. and do so themselves. He was told they "couldn't do it."

It also appeared at the hearing that the rule which the Company was endeavoring to enforce was not in writing, and, if it existed, had not been enforced for many years; certainly not during the life of the current agreement. The weight of the evidence as to custom and practice was that in this and other yards in the New York area employees have been considered late only if they have not passed through the gate by the stipulated end of the lunch hour.

Position of the Union

It is the Union's basic position that the Company violated Section 4 of Article XIX and Section 5 of Article III of the agreement. It contends that (1) the employees were discriminated against for union activity, in that the Company selected Union representatives to discipline from among all of the employees who were not back on their jobs at 12:30 P.M.; (2) there has been and is no rule requiring employees to be back on their jobs at 12:30 P.M., and the Company was in fact attempting to institute a new rule, which new rule was in violation of the agreement; (3) the custom and practice for many years in this Yard and other Yards has been that employees are not considered late if they are inside the gate at 12:30 P.M.; (4) the Company has not, for as long as memory serves, disciplined any employee for violating any so-called rule, and the rule has not been publicized to the employees in the Yard, orally or in writing; (5) no employee may be disciplined for doing something which he has a right to do under the agreement. It argues also that the reason these employees were suspended was that they would not undertake, as Union representatives, to "police" the rule for the Company.

Position of the Company

The Company contends that (1) the employees here involved were instructed to be back on their jobs at 12:30 P.M. and were properly disciplined for violation of such instruction; (2) there was no discriminination because of union activities, since the men involved were the most consistent violators of the rule; (3) as Union officers they should be held to a higher standard of conduct and responsibility than other employees; (4) the disciplinary action taken was justifiable alone on the basis of the conduct of the employees in flaunting the authority of the Company. It argues that the Umpire need not, and should not, decide the question of whether, under the agreement, employees are required to be back on their jobs at 12:30 P.M. It states that, if this question is gone into, the conduct of employees in the past in returning late from lunch was not a custom and practice specifically approved or accepted by the Company but rather, to the extent that it was engaged in, was a violation of the agreement and rule suffered or endured by the Company.

2

Chrysler Case

COMPANY: Chrysler Corporation
UNION: United Automobile, Aircraft, and Agricultural Implement Workers of America

The grievance read:

Protest against sending employee home without cause.

The Union requests that employee X—, badge #181-446, Classification #1010, seniority 7-18-46, be reimbursed for time lost on Wednesday, March 5, 1952, when this employee was sent home by the Corporation without cause at 8:30 A.M.

The Union requests that this employee be paid at his regular rate for the full eight hours, from 7:00 A.M. to 3:30 P.M. on that date.

UNION'S STATEMENT

The Union Statement of Facts reads:

The involved employee, X—, started to work on Tuesday, March 4, 1952, at 7:00 A.M. Because of an article in the Detroit *Times* stating that his name was brought up in a meeting of the Un-American Activities Committee there was quite a bit of unrest in the shop.

It was agreed to by the Union that the Company should give this man a pass out of the plant on March 4th. X— and another employee Y—, went over to the Local 7 office and made statements to the Local Union President Tony Cassara and the Plant Shop Committee Chairman Jesse Cundiff. Y—'s statement reads as follows:

Taken from Labor Arbitration Reports, *XIX* (*Washington: Bureau of National Affairs*), *pp. 408–12. Reprinted with permission of the publisher.*

"I am not a member of the Communist Party and have not been since 1946."

He was asked to sign an affidavit that he was not now a Communist, which he did. He was told to report for work the next morning, which he did and had no more trouble.

X— was asked whether he was a Communist and his statement is as follows:

"No, I am not a Communist or never was a Communist or sympathizer. I have a son fighting the Communists in Korea right now."

X— signed a statement to that effect and was told to report for work the next morning as was Y—.

The night before the Executive Board of Local 7 had met on this question and also on Y—'s problem. They agreed that there should be no trouble among the employees regarding these employees working and the enclosed leaflet was distributed at the plant gates on the morning of March 5, 1952, stating the Union's position very clearly on this matter. These leaflets were accepted by the employees as they went in to work, and there were no protests registered against the leaflets or about those two employees working.

When X— started to work at 7:00 A.M. Wednesday, March 5th, the foreman did not like it and went among the employees showing them the article from the Detroit *Times*. But the Union representatives were there to see that X— was permitted to work without a demonstration from the workers on the line.

When the foreman saw that the work was moving along as usual, he was stumped. Mr. Jacks, X—'s immediate foreman, went over to X— and requested that he accompany him to the office. At this point, Chief Stewart Scott asked Foreman Jacks what the trouble was. Foreman Jacks answered him that he had a right to take an employee to the office if he wished to do so and could keep him there all day.

Jesse Cundiff, the Plant Shop Committee Chairman, W. Felske, a Committeeman, and Joe Meader, a Skilled Trades Committeeman, went to the office shortly thereafter and saw that the Company was going to send X— home and they protested to General Superintendent Dobson. Dobson told the foreman to go out in the department and make a survey of the people to see if they would work with X—. The foreman then told Dobson that the employees did not want to work with X—; and Dobson sent X— home, over the protest of the union and X—.

Therefore, the Union is asking that X— be paid 6½ hours' pay because the Company improperly penalized him.

COPY OF LEAFLET

The Union submitted the following copy of the leaflet distributed at plant gates on the morning of March 5, 1952:

TO ALL LOCAL 7 MEMBERS: IMPORTANT!

The organic structure of our Union is based on the Constitution of the United States. We are against dictatorship because we believe in the protection of the right of every citizen according to the law. If anyone is proven of conspiring against our country we have courts of law to handle them. And if the courts fail, then it is the constitutional right and the duty of our Union to cope with any conspirators against our Union.

A statement was issued by the International Union, UAW–CIO and reads as follows:

"The UAW–CIO is opposed to violence in any form that attempts to substitute for democratic processes. Violent action that deprives individuals of their democratic rights is the weapon of the totalitarians themselves. It is not a weapon of democracy.

"We cannot defeat the communists or the adherents of any other form of totalitarianism by falling into the trap of using their own tactics.

"The democracy of our Union and our nation is strong enough to bring to justice any person who gives reason to believe that he is engaging in subversive activities or is otherwise engaging in conduct detrimental to the best interest of our Union.

"We urge that the officers of all Local Unions convey this message to our members and take every precaution to see that such incidents do not occur. The best way to safeguard our Union and our democratic rights is to see to it that we ourselves observe all democratic procedures.

"Signed:

Walter P. Reuther, President
Emil Mazey, Secretary-Treasurer
Richard Gosser, Vice-President
John W. Livingston, Vice-President"

AS YOU CAN SEE, BROTHERS AND SISTERS, WE HAVE A PROCEDURE TO FOLLOW AND WE ASK YOU TO FOLLOW IT.

DON'T LISTEN TO FOMENTERS OF DISSENSION. THEY MAY BE PAID TO SPLIT OUR RANKS AND WEAKEN OUR UNION.

DON'T FORGET THAT THE ULTRA ANTI-LABOR REACTIONARIES LOVE
TO SEE OUR UNION TORN APART.
LET'S ALL FOLLOW DEMOCRATIC PROCEDURE.

Officers, Executive Board Members,
Shop Committee and Chief Stewards
Local 7, UAW–CIO

ND:GO

liu72cio

STATEMENT OF UNION OFFICERS

Statement dated March 5, 1952 signed by H. Scott, Chief Steward;
Jesse Cundiff, Chairman Plant Committee; Walter Felske, Plant Committeeman; Joe Meader, Plant Committeeman:

The four of us went into Dobson's office when Jacks brought X— in.
At this time we told Dobson to what extent we went to see that X—
would be treated fairly, and the people on the line were working when
X— was taken off the line.

We the Union representatives, protested vigorously against sending this
man home but Management would give us no reason for their action.
They just kept saying the people don't want to work with X—. We knew
this was not the fact because when the leadership of Local 7 passed out
the leaflet this morning, the people complimented us on the position we
were taking and saying it was the only fair position to undertake.

When Scott, the steward, went back to the department, the group that
works with X— stopped work and gathered around him and wanted to
walk out because Foreman Jacks would not let X— work. However, we
persuaded the employees to work and would settle this case through the
bargaining procedure.

STATEMENT OF GRIEVANT

Statement by X— dated March 5, 1952:

I was taken off my job by Foreman Jacks down to Mr. Dobson's
office.

The Union representatives were also present protesting my being sent
home.

I protested being sent home as I was doing my work as I always do it,
but they told me the other employees would not work with me.

This was not so, as all the employees were working when Mr. Jacks
took me to Dobson's office.

The Union said: there was much unrest all over the city at the time; in several plants employees had been thrown out; because of the feeling on Tuesday, March 4, 1952, the Union did agree to have X— and Y— brought out of the plant on that day so there would be no trouble; as shown in the statement both men were taken to the Union hall and questioned: Y— admitted that he had been a member of the Communist Party; X— stated he had never been a Communist and did not remember of ever attending any meeting having to do with communistic activities; it was not known how his name got in the paper; on Wednesday, March 5th, there was no trouble in the plant, the men, having received the leaflets, were working; Y— worked all day and was not molested; production quotas on that day were met, there being full production in X—'s department; the agitation against X— was started by supervision; this was local supervision, top management having nothing to do with it; in sending X— home the Company acted in a manner contrary to all past practice; in the past, the employees who objected to working with other employees were sent home; the Company always took the position that if employees did not want to work they should go home and if they did, they might be subject to discipline; it always has been the Union's position that the objectors should be sent home; there have been hundreds of instances involving objectors in the plants and, in each instance heretofore, the objectors, and not the person objected to, were the ones penalized; X—'s work was available; X— was willing to work, and his seniority entitled him to the work.

COMPANY'S STATEMENT

The statement on behalf of Chrysler Corporation read:

During the week of February 25, 1952, a Congressional Committee was in Detroit investigating "Un-American Activities." During these hearings, the newspapers reported that X—, an employee at the Chrysler–Jefferson Plant, had been named as a Communist.

On Monday, March 3, there were rumors to the effect that the employees in Department 181, Sheet Metal, would not work with Mr. X— the following day. On Tuesday, March 4, the rumors of the previous day proved true. The employees in Mr. X—'s group as well as the rest of Department 181 did not start work at 7:00 A.M.

The following Foreman's Reports cover this event as well as the activity on March 5:

"Foreman's Report, 3-4-52, 181-446 X—

"There was a work stoppage today because the men objected to working with a suspected Communist.

"When this man was removed from the plant by mutual agreement between himself, the Management and the Union, the men resumed work normally without any loss in production on metal finishing of C52 and C54 front fenders.

"/s/W. Maki
Foreman Dept. 181"

"Foreman's Report, March 4, 1952, 181-446, X—

"This employee's name appeared in a local newspaper as a known Communist, the result of the Un-American Activities Committee's investigation.

"On Tuesday, March 4, employees of this department refused to work as long as this employee was in this plant. He was given a pass and sent home at 8:46 A.M.

"/s/K. Hess
Gen. Foreman Dept. 181"

"Foreman's Report 3-5-52, 181-446, X—

"A majority of the men refused to start working this morning because they suspected one of their fellow workers of being a Communist.

"When this man was removed from the plant by his own consent, the men started doing their work normally without any loss in production on metal finishing of C52 and C54 front fenders.

"/s/W. Maki
Foreman Dept. 181"

At the Appeal Board step the Union members of the Board claimed that the employees on March 5, 1952, in Department 181 were willing to work with Mr. X— but that Supervision sent him home contrary to his wishes. Upon checking this point again with the Supervision of Department 181, the Corporation Appeal Board members found the Union's statement in conflict with the facts. Both Messrs. Maki and Hess stated that:

"September 22, 1952, 181-446, X—

"The Un-American Activities Committee under Senator Estes Kefauver named X— as a Communist.

"This information appeared in the local newspaper over the weekend of March 1st and 2nd, 1952.

"On Monday, March 3rd, there was a considerable amount of discussion among the men as to whether or not they would work with a Communist. By Tuesday morning, March 4th, the men had decided that they would not work with a Communist and refused to work with X—

"When X— was removed from the plant by mutual agreement between himself, the Union and the Management, the men started working normally without any loss in production on metal finish of C-52 and C-54 front fender.

"On Wednesday morning, March 5th, the men again refused to start working with X—.

"Being his foreman, I asked him to go into the office where we could discuss the matter with higher supervision.

"It was quite evident and clear to X— by this time that the men would not work with him because they were fairly sure he was a Communist. He readily agreed to leave the plant and was given a pass about 8:30 A.M.

"He went to the Union Hall in connection with the matter and did not return to work until Monday, March 10th, 1952.

>   "/s/W. Maki
>   Foreman, Dept. 181"

"September 22, 1952 181-446, X—

"This employee's name appeared in a local newspaper as a known Communist. The results of the Un-American Activities Committees investigation.

"On Tuesday, March 4th, employees of this department refused to work as long as X— was in this plant.

"This employee was sent home at 8:46 A.M. on March 4th, by mutual agreement between the Union and Management.

"X— reported for work on Wednesday, March 5th, and again employees of this department refused to work with this employee in the plant.

"Foreman W. Maki, approached this employee about going home till this issue was settled. Employee X— readily agreed that he would go home rather than cause more trouble. He was then sent home after conferring with higher management.

>   "/s/K. Hess
>   General Foreman"

In addition, Foreman Maki stated that on March 5, 1952 the employees under his supervision did not start to work at 7:00 A.M., which is their regular starting time. Upon making an inquiry as to the reason for their behavior, some of the employees expressed sentiments which were to the effect that they would not work with a Communist. Mr. Maki remembers Mr. E. Steele, Badge No. 181-805 and F. Cynawa, Badge No. 181-468 stating that they were pretty well convinced that X— was a Communist. Another employee, C. Kenyon, Badge No. 181-532 said he had buddies in Korea fighting the Communists so why should he work with them. An employee who was scheduled to enter Military Service, P. White, Badge No. 181-294, said that he was not going to work with a Communist.

Foreman Maki at approximately 7:30 A.M., when it was apparent that the employees in the Department were not going to begin work, requested Mr. X— to come with him to the Department Office. Mr. X— accompanied Foreman Maki to the office without any protests being made. Upon entering the office, Mr. Dobson, Assistant General Superintendent, told X— to sit down and wait while he discussed this matter with his superiors. Foreman Maki upon returning to his work group found all of the employees working as well as the remainder of Department 181.

After conferring with General Superintendent Hillburg, who in turn talked with Plant Management and Labor Relations, Mr. Dobson informed Mr. X— that he thought the best thing to do, so as not to cause any more trouble, was for Mr. X— to leave the Plant. Mr. X— did not object. Foreman Maki states that when he gave Mr. X— his pass to leave, he seemed anxious to leave the premises and made no objection whatsoever to being sent home.

Both Foreman Maki, and General Foreman Hess stated that prior to the start of the first shift on March 5, 1952, their attention was called to an effigy of X— hanging in the washroom of Department 181, Bay 86, wherein they found a pair of stuffed coveralls with a rope around the dummy's neck which was hanging from an over-head pipe. Mr. Hess stated that he ordered the dummy taken down, which was done. Foreman Maki states that a large white chalk arrow had been drawn on the floor pointing to X—'s work bench with the inscription, "Get rid of that Damn Communist." The night before X—'s work bench had been painted red sometime during the second shift. It was immediately painted green again upon orders from supervision prior to the start of the first shift.

In view of these facts Plant Management, after full consideration and because of the delicate situation sent Mr. X —home at approximately 8:30 A.M. He was escorted from the Plant by Plant Protection as a precaution from possible violence.

The following day, March 6, Mr. X— did not report for work

but later in the day Union representatives (Messrs. Felske and Cassara) requested a two-week leave of absence for Mr. X— which was granted by Mr. Horton, Labor Relations Supervisor. On March 7, Mr. Cassara, President of Local 7 called Mr. Horton and told him that Mr. X— would like to come to work Monday, March 10, at which time Mr. Horton agreed to cancel his leave of absence. Mr. Cassara assured Mr. Horton that there would be no more trouble since X— had signed a Non-Communist affidavit at the Local Union Hall. Mr. X— returned to work without any further incident on March 10, 1952.

The fact that the Union requested a leave of absence after Mr. X— was sent home on the 5th lends further evidence to the fact that not only employees in his own work group but the majority of the employees in Department 181 refused to work with X— at that time. In order to avoid any further incidents or possible violence the plant management, after careful consideration of all the factors involved, decided that the best thing to do was to send Mr. X— home on March 5, 1952. Certainly their decision was a reasonable one in view of all the circumstances involved in this case. This they did without further incidents occurring.

This grievance should be dismissed.

The company said: Jacks was with Maki at the time X— was asked to go to the office; it has referred to Maki rather than to Jacks because it was Maki who had done the talking; although newspaper articles were in the plant, local supervision did not go among the men talking about X— or displaying the article having to do with him; there was no production loss because the time when the people were not working was of short duration and, apparently, production was made up by the workers; there was dissension in the plant; this was evidenced not only by the remarks of employees mentioned in the statement but by the issuance by the Union of the leaflets; X— was sent home not as a penalty to him, but to protect him against possible injury and to prevent further trouble in the plant; the situation was an emergency and the Company acted properly; under Article I, Section 2, this being the management's right clause, the Union recognized that the Company has exclusive right to manage the plant and direct its plants and working forces; its actions regarding X— were taken under, and in accordance with these rights; while in other instances, objectors, rather than employees with whom they refused to work, have been sent home, this situation, with the Communist issue involved, was different and called for the handling given.

3

Job Evaluation at
Sedgewick-Cole Corporation

I

The Sedgewick-Cole Corporation, a major manufacturer of floor coverings, operated two plants, one at Craftown, and the other, about 60 miles away, at Kingsville. In anticipation of extensive demand for a new product, NuCrest, as well as for its regular products, the company initiated plans for improvements and new equipment to cost $5,250,000. While the proposed improvements were being effected, the Craftown local of the United Rubber Workers (CIO) entered a grievance regarding a job-evaluation plan that its membership had rejected but that the Kingsville membership had accepted.

II

The company was organized in 1930 to continue businesses formerly conducted independently by the Sedgewick Company at Craftown and the Cole Company at Kingsville. During the depression of the 1930's, the company suffered substantial losses, reduced wages, and abandoned an incentive system installed at Craftown in 1928 which had promised substantial benefits for all.

In 1937 some Craftown employees requested the Rubber Workers to organize the plant. A few months later the company recognized the Craftown local and granted an increase of five cents an hour. The

This and the next case are from B. M. Selekman, S. K. Selekman, and L. Fuller, Problems in Labor Relations, 2nd ed. (New York: McGraw-Hill, 1958), pp. 81–92 and 93–104. Reprinted with the permission of the President and Fellows of Harvard College.

Craftown local then organized the Kingsville workers, and the two locals formed a joint committee that negotiated a company-wide agreement, effective February 15, 1938. Less than a month later, management, citing losses, announced a five-cent hourly wage reduction. When negotiations failed, the Craftown employees struck and the Kingsville men walked out to support Craftown. The strike lasted one day, work being resumed after joint agreement to choose a fact-finding board consisting of two union, one company, and two federal representatives. This board did not find the reduction justified, and the company withdrew it. However, the board did report as follows:

The company has inadequate reserves to weather even a short depression, and it has not been able to raise capital necessary to keep equipment abreast of competition. Wage rates have averaged less than in competitors' plants, but Sedgewick-Cole gets less production per man-hour than its competitors.

The contract negotiated in 1939 provided for a union shop and for a substantial number of upward adjustments in rates to go into effect at both plants. No horizontal increase in hourly base rates was granted. The union based demands for rate revisions upon the company's past practice of setting rates in haphazard fashion upon what were believed to be "going community rates," or upon the whims of supervisors, particularly with respect to new jobs.

During 1938, financial conditions had improved sufficiently to permit installation of new equipment, which had changed jobs throughout the plants. In anticipation of grievances resulting from production changes, the following clause was written into the 1939 contract:

All special grievances concerning a speed-up, slow-down, or other serious matter shall be deemed of emergency nature and the usual procedure on grievances shall be dispensed with. These matters will be handled immediately through the shop committee and the management.

Grievances regarding wage inequities increased sharply during 1939. The contract negotiated in 1940 ran for three years, providing for reopenings on wages only. Because grievances had involved wage rates so extensively, this contract provided:

ARTICLE 4, SECTION 2, PARAGRAPH "d"

In any case where a speed-up occurs, through increasing speed of present equipment or revamping of same, whereby the company's costs are lowered and maintained for a period of 90 days, the employees affected will receive a fair share in the savings involved, such share to be distributed at the discretion of company and union officials.

This clause, however, proved unsatisfactory since the "share in the savings" was based not upon greater effort but upon improvement in equipment. Only those employees working in departments where such improvements were made enjoyed increased pay. Such increases, in turn, gave rise to a multitude of inequity grievances in other departments.

III

After the 1940 contract had been signed, the company offered the position of personnel director to Albert C. Tedrick, treasurer of the Craftown local, editor of its paper, and member of the international's executive board. As one of the organizers of his local, Tedrick had been active in the formulation of union policy, and had always served as chief union spokesman in negotiations. After serious consideration, Mr. Tedrick accepted the company's offer.

Shortly thereafter, Mr. Tedrick enrolled in evening courses to study job evaluation and incentive systems. Upon completion of his course, he was convinced that solution of the company's wage problems lay first in effecting a sound job-evaluation program, and then in building a well-conceived incentive system. His first objective was to dispel any suspicion that his program would be similar to the previous incentive plan at Craftown. Accordingly, Mr. Tedrick began informally to suggest to union officials at weekly grievance meetings the merits of job evaluation.

During the war, operations differed radically from regular work, and the "haggle" system of rate setting continued. Repeatedly, wage rates were submitted to arbitration. To reduce arbitration, the parties concluded a new agreement providing: "In the event new equipment is installed for any operations, rates for jobs on same will be settled by mutual agreement." Wage rates continued, however, to be arbitrated rather than settled by mutual agreement.

IV

In their postwar contract, the union and the management agreed, with the assistance of a federal conciliator, to include the following clause:

ARTICLE 4, SECTION 2, PARAGRAPH "c"

The company will undertake a job evaluation study with a view of eliminating intraplant inequities. The job evaluation and wage adjustment is to be subject to the mutual agreement of both parties with the provision that any disputes thereunder will be subject to impartial arbitration by an arbitrator to be selected by the parties. In the event new equipment is installed for any operation, rates for jobs on same will be decided by a mutually satisfactory job analysis and evaluation.

A joint job-evaluation committee composed of two union and two company representatives from each plant was formed, and a former federal conciliator was retained by the company as consultant. Within four months this committee had completed a job-evaluation manual and had agreed on evaluation for all jobs.

The locals in Kingsville and in Craftown, however, rejected the plan. At the time, wage-increase demands of 30%, equivalent to about 33 cents per hour, were pending.

Two months later the contract was extended for another year, by a joint stipulation which provided as follows:

JOINT STIPULATION

There is to be inserted in place of Article 4, Section 2, Paragraph "d" a paragraph calling for the development of an incentive plan to be worked out between a union committee and a company committee with the usual arbitration clause. The company agrees immediately to increase by 15 cents hourly wage rates applicable to all members of the union alike.

Under this extended contract, the job-evaluation committee at Craftown applied job-evaluation standards despite the previous vote of rejection, to establish rates for 16 new jobs and to review one old job. Vincent Rosetti, president of the Craftown local, signed acceptance stipulations for the union. Four months after the extension of the contract, Mr. Rosetti refused to sign any other acceptance stipulations or to accept new rates thenceforth set by the evaluation unless they were higher than the prevailing base rate.

Three months later, a consultant engaged to install an incentive system under the terms of the joint stipulation also reviewed the evaluation plan. He recommended that higher credits be allocated to physical effort, which the union had protested as "rated too low." Union leaders thereupon agreed to present the revised evaluation plan to their members. The revised plan was approved by the Kingsville local, but Craftown again voted rejection.

Notified of these votes, Mr. Tedrick informed union officials that notwithstanding rejection at Craftown, evaluation would be used in setting rates on new jobs. Before such rates were applied, however, union representatives on the job-evaluation committee would be invited to check them, and disagreements would be submitted to arbitration.

During the next month, accordingly, union representatives on the Craftown committee reviewed one job and approved evaluations on five new jobs. James O'Hara, vice president, and William Phillips, secretary, did not sign acceptance stipulations on these rates. Mr. Tedrick nevertheless put them into effect.

V

Four weeks later, Mr. Tedrick received the following grievance at Craftown:

After investigating the plastic tile job we feel that since the job formerly had three men and now has two, the job has been revamped and speeded up in more ways than one, so that production has been doubled without any chance for the men to gain a fair share of the profits such as in our Contract (Article 4, Section 2, paragraph "d"). We must ask to arbitrate this case since company refuses to compensate these men accordingly.

Mr. Tedrick replied immediately as follows:

We assume the job in question is the pressing of Nu-Crest tile by the double platen process instead of on single platen presses with a crew of two men, each of whom worked about half their time due to the heats.[1] This job is one on which the company cannot make any great profit and therefore there is no share in the profits to be considered.

We will gladly re-evaluate the job according to Article 4, Section 2, paragraph "c" and if additional wages are agreed upon, we will pay same. Our job analyst has prepared his analysis for discussion by the job evaluation committee. We are willing to meet at any time.

Furthermore, our joint stipulation calls for the elimination of Article 4, Section 2, paragraph "d" and in its place we are to substitute a wage incentive clause; therefore, the clause you refer to is no longer a part of our agreement. We will agree to have the job time studied and determine a rate of pay. To do this, this job would first be evaluated.

We suggest that the company-union job evaluation committee set a rate; if no agreement can be reached, submit the question to arbitration.

[1] A platen is a flat molding plate which holds the tile during the application of heat and pressure. The time period during which the tile is under pressure is referred to as a "heat."

We do not intend to set any rates by guesswork, nor pay increases unless justified by systematic methods. The present process of curing Nu-Crest tile is a temporary expedient to get this product on the market and will be discarded when multiplatened presses are installed.

The outcome of this grievance, Mr. Tedrick believed, would be crucial in establishing job evaluation as the method of determining new rates. Otherwise, the haggle system would inevitably return and wage inequities would continue a serious problem.

Five months prior to the filing of this grievance, the company had notified the union that press crews would be reduced from three to two men, and that twelve men thus released would be transferred elsewhere. A better product could be turned out if molds were left longer in the presses and the number of heats reduced. If the union opposed this change, the company warned it might be necessary to lay off all 36 men until new presses were installed. The union responded that the men would not comply and requested that action be withheld until the officers explained the situation to them. The company agreed but added that, in the event the union did not cooperate, the company would request arbitration. Within a few days, crews were reduced. A multipress had been ordered a week before the union filed the above grievance.

Two weeks after receipt of the grievance, Mr. Tedrick informed the union that the company had evaluated the disputed jobs, that the results indicated that the jobs were overpaid, but that, in spite of that, the rates would not be reduced. The union requested arbitration and the following submission was jointly drawn up:

Are the employees pressing Nu-Crest entitled to a rate adjustment as the union contends, pursuant to Article 4, Section 2, paragraph "d" or pursuant to paragraph "c" of the same article, as the company contends?

The union supported its claim to a "share in the savings" by three major arguments:

1. The company changed the one-platen process to a two-platen process, increasing output. Article 4, Section 2, paragraph "d" applies.

2. This is not a new job, nor is new equipment used.

3. The local has twice rejected job evaluation. Therefore, Article 4, Section 2, paragraph "c" cannot apply.

The company supported its position that the new rates be determined by job evaluation on four main grounds:

1. The job is a new operation, and even if it were not, it is subject, as are all jobs, to the job evaluation provided for in the contract.

2. The union accepted job evaluation as proved by acceptance stipulations signed by Mr. Rosetti on a reviewed old job and 16 new jobs.

3. One old job was reviewed and 5 new jobs were approved by the joint evaluation committee, and made effective.

4. Article 4, Section 2, paragraph "c" does not require complete mutual agreement for it provides for arbitration of disputes.

In his first finding the arbitrator stated, "The contract does not clearly express the method to be followed. The arbitrator urges the parties to expedite the conclusion of job evaluation for more harmonious relationships." Both the union and management thereupon requested the arbitrator to render a decision. Since both parties preferred an award, he ruled that the job was subject to evaluation.

Mr. Tedrick believed that through arbitration he had accomplished at Craftown the long-sought objective which had been impeded by the negative votes of the Craftown local union. Following the arbitration, Mr. Tedrick discussed the case with a friend who was interested in union-management cooperation. He invited him to interview the principal individuals who had been concerned with the job-evaluation program. Several of the the interviews follow.

INTERVIEWS AT THE CRAFTOWN PLANT

James O'Hara, President of the Craftown Local

(Mr. O'Hara was a mechanic.)

O'HARA: I can talk my head off but it does no good. The company cooperates, the union agrees, and we tell the men, but they don't pay any attention.

INTERVIEWER: How did the evaluation program start?

O'HARA: We were in negotiations, getting no place. The company wanted to give only certain departments increases. The union couldn't go that. After the federal conciliator came, he told us about evaluation. He had been here many times before and helped us, so we formed a joint job evaluation committee. However, most of the men in the shop didn't want anything to do with it. Some sections were for it because management had sold the gang leader. If they sold him, the gang went along.

When the consultant came to our department he evaluated the jobs, determined the requirements for an "A" mechanic, and decided that four men were to get "A" ratings. After that, we had a meeting to decide who would get these four "A" jobs. I was the representative for the mechanical department. The foreman picked out four men he thought qualified. I asked about men I had in mind. But the foreman didn't agree with me.

Today I do one job and one of these "A" men does another, and tomorrow he does the thing I did yesterday and I do the thing he did. You can't say his job is harder than mine and so [slowly and with emphasis] the foreman was evaluating the men, not the jobs. That's just the foreman picking out his favorites and "mechanical" voted in a block against the job evaluation proposal.

Take that one department [inspection department]. They were all against it, even some who would have gotten 10 cents more per hour.[2] They were afraid of cuts. Let me give you an example. Suppose I'm getting $1.35 an hour and you're working as my helper. Well, *my job* is evaluated down to $1.30, but *I* would still get $1.35 [as a "red-circle" rate]. Now you were making $1.20 and are evaluated up to $1.28. When you are promoted to my job on another machine, when there is an opening, you would only get $1.30! You see, you'd only get a 2-cent raise instead of a 15-cent raise! You'd be doing the same work as I am and I'd be getting $1.35 on the next machine, and the union always stands for "equal work, equal pay."

INTERVIEWER: Were there many of these "cuts"?

O'HARA: No. That's the strange thing. Most of the jobs, 60 per cent of them, were to get better rates. The men are beginning to realize now how much money was involved.

INTERVIEWER: You have evaluation on new jobs, don't you?

O'HARA: That's reasonable. They used to give you whatever they wanted to. It's their right to set rates on new jobs, and we'd rather have a fair method so we see why a job is rated so much.

INTERVIEWER: Why did Kingsville accept evaluation when you turned it down?

O'HARA: They don't have that inspection department down there or things would be different. The committee tried to do a job in selling evaluation here, but the men just yelled, "We don't want no part of it." When we are introduced at Kingsville as officers from Craftown, everyone applauds. When we introduce a Kingsville officer here, the fellows boo and someone shouts, "Go on home." The Kingsville company was always good to work for, even before the two plants consolidated. Kingsville as a city has fewer problems. Take the Craftown plant of the Crocker Company. There isn't a company in America which is more antiunion. Our union had an "in" there once but that company beat it down.

---

[2] Most references to inspection at Craftown in plant interviews indicated its widely held reputation as a "trouble spot."

Edward Diffin, Former Vice President of the Craftown Local

(Mr. Diffin, an older employee, was a mechanic.
At one time he had been a railroad employee.)

DIFFIN: When the union was formed, I was very active. Some wanted a one-man union; they thought officers should run everything. I thought each department ought to have its own union committee. When the others did not agree, I got out. Too many unions have been destroyed because of fights between officers.

History proved I was right. We had a one-man union. When that one man went over to management, it hurt the union. Al Tedrick knew everything about the union and everyone in it, so management got along O.K. It's just like a dictatorship: when the leader dies, the country has no leader. In a democracy a great man like Roosevelt can die and the people can continue because they all have had a part in the show. When Al did go over on the other side, the boys did not like it. If you fight alongside someone and then find, all of a sudden, without warning, that he is on the other side, you naturally don't like it.

Al has brains and plenty on the ball politically. He can put an idea across if he wants to. Our fellows can hardly read or write, so what we need is an educated person to negotiate for us. It takes a liar to catch a liar, and a robber to catch a robber.

INTERVIEWER: Could you tell me something about the evaluation plan?

DIFFIN: It would have split the men and the union apart. When a fellow would be promoted he might not get the same rate if the job had been lowered by evaluation. Then fellows would be getting different pay for the same work and start fighting. The union would be split. It's happened at the Crocker Company. That company got the AFL and the CIO unions fighting each other. Now they don't have either union.

Stanley Gardner, Organizer of the Craftown Local

(Stanley Gardner, 60 years old, worked in the
blacksmith shop in the mechanical department.)

GARDNER: I organized this union. We were getting the lowest wages around and the efficiency engineers had been in with time watches and had done a job on us. That's when I got the union. Then I went to Kingsville and they signed up.

A lot of foremen used to be union members. If any of them want to, they can come back to the union. Any guy who moves up [pauses]—well, almost any of them—can come back. Mr. Tedrick used to be in the union. He had his chance and ran the whole show once, but he left. He and Rosetti were real thick, but Rosetti isn't nearly as smart as Al is.

INTERVIEWER: Can you tell me anything about evaluation?

GARDNER: I was against evaluation. Our foreman had his nose in it all the way while our mechanical department representative just sat and didn't say anything. The foreman picked out his fair-haired boys for favors rendered.

INTERVIEWER: Were any departments for it?

GARDNER: Sure, the print room. The gang leader got sold. In the print room all the boys are Italians. Most guys who work here only went to the third grade. We've got a League of Nations here. Over in the presses there are Italians, Hungarians, Poles, Serbs, a little of everything. We have some colored workers, and there are a few women.

Vincent Rosetti, Former President of the Craftown Local

(Mr. Rosetti, worker in the pipe shop, was union
president when votes were taken on the evaluation
program.)

ROSSETTI: What do you want? Who sent you?

INTERVIEWER: I am studying your labor problems. No one sent me.

ROSETTI: You aren't a snoop? Someone didn't send you?

INTERVIEWER: No.

ROSETTI: I thought someone was getting information through the back door. You are not a snoop?

INTERVIEWER: No. That is not playing the game.

ROSETTI: O.K., if you aren't a spy, we get along pretty good. At one time the company used to be lousy on wages. Then we got the organization and they couldn't push us around any more.

INTERVIEWER: You were union president when they voted on evaluation?

ROSETTI: Yes, but we didn't go for that. The company was going to get the cream and give the men skimmed milk. We say "equal work, equal pay." How were they going to evaluate guys in the pipe department? We all work on the same pipes. The company said no one would be cut—that the evaluated pay, if lower, would apply only to new men. Who the devil did they think the new men were going to be? Paper boys they dragged in off the street? The new man was going to be the guy who had worked here nine years, and who had earned a promotion. There weren't going to be new men because the union wouldn't stand for it. But they thought we were dumb.

[After the interview.]

O'HARA: Rosetti and Tedrick used to be union leaders. They lived on the same street. Their wives knew each other; the kids played together. They don't go together since Tedrick moved.

William Phillips, Secretary of the Craftown Local

(Mr. William Phillips worked in the pattern department.)

PHILLIPS: We were in on evaluation from the very first. We talked with the men, got their ideas. From my work on the committee I learned more about the plant than any single foreman. If we had proposed the evaluation, we could have sold it. But because the company proposed it, the men didn't want it.

INTERVIEWER: Why did they oppose it?

PHILLIPS: Oh, they never say *why*. They just yell it down. It was a case of a vocal minority. All the people who wanted evaluation and would have gotten increases didn't bother to vote. Of course, all the minority voted. We put in a rule that any member missing three meetings would be fined, but it doesn't help. It was too bad that Pat Kelly died; he would have been the difference. We seldom elect a president for more than one term, but he was always re-elected.

INTERVIEWER: How did evaluation ever start in the first place?

PHILLIPS: It was Tedrick's idea. He studied about it. Then he started talking and it seemed like a good idea to Kelly.

The trouble goes back more than 15 years. Wages were low and many days there wasn't any work. Men thought there was favoritism shown in who got to work. That's all changed now, but the inspectors never changed. They don't trust anybody. They were even against the union at first. Now they are against the company.

They didn't like it when Al Tedrick changed over. At the time, he was representing the union in negotiations. The company wanted a three-year contract. When we had a meeting, it was clear nobody wanted it. Tedrick sold it to the members. It turned out to be a good thing. Wages were frozen so we could not have gotten increases anyway. But it wasn't more than six months later that Tedrick became personnel manager.

Things that happened since haven't helped. Things have tightened up a lot in the last few years. There is more discipline. Also, to get a foreman they used to promote one of the men. Lately they have gone outside. I don't resent it, though it happened in my department. The people they bring in don't know anything. That's half the trouble in inspection, too; the foreman is weak.

INTERVIEWS AT THE KINGSVILLE PLANT

Elder Morgan, Personnel Manager at Kingsville

MORGAN: I was the first union president here. For a depression period things weren't too bad here. We had a few men who wanted to remain outside the union. We thought we would have better union members in the long run if we didn't force the issue. I was president for four years when I told the boys, "You've got a fine contract, a strong union, and a cooperative company." I explained I would rather step aside for someone else. I agreed to continue on the executive board and they saw my point. Soon I was offered the job as personnel manager to work under Albert Tedrick.

I knew the only way was to let the boys decide. I told them I wouldn't accept unless they felt I was acting in good faith. I said if I did take the job, I would represent the company with my full energy. They answered, "Go ahead and take that job, Elder. We don't expect any favors."

At first a few were skeptical. I insisted that workers handle problems through their union representatives and that foremen handle their own problems on the floor. I would not discuss a problem unless it had been first discussed with them. I told the foremen when they did not feel qualified to decide, they should come to me.

INTERVIEWER: What about your relationship here?

MORGAN: We have less than a dozen grievances every year, not more than six in writing. Since the union came we have had only one stoppage and one arbitration. We are proud of the record, and I keep reminding the union about their part in it. Now they remind me about *their* record and how it is *my* responsibility to live up to it!

INTERVIEWER: How is the job evaluation working out?

MORGAN: We feel it is working well. The saturation department took a beating because a number of men had their jobs evaluated lower there. However, Carl Wilson explained it to them in terms of the best interests of all workers in the plant. Of course, the men turned it down on the first vote. They were probably waiting to see if they could get a better deal. It may be they were waiting on Craftown to accept.

INTERVIEWER: Do you have regular grievance meetings?

MORGAN: No, we meet as soon as the grievance comes up. Many times I get an idea of what's troubling the men from Carl Wilson, for I often have a beer with him on the way home. We have no groups in our plant. Of course, we have good union officers here. Occasionally they make a mistake, but so do we. Several months ago they brought a grievance. We fought it hard and they fought it harder. To continue might have thrown us back in building good feelings, so we gave in.

Josiah Blakely, President of the Kingsville Local

(Mr. Blakely, 65 years of age, was a class A machinist.)

BLAKELY: We have an excellent relationship. The union is very proud of it. We try to remind the management what a good record we have so we can make them proud of it, too. We have never had a strike here, not one of our own. Craftown got into trouble once and spoiled our record.

Since I have been president we have had only two grievances where the vice president in charge of operations was called in. Do you know what he did once? Management was on one side of the table and we were on the other, and after we presented our case, even before management answered, the vice president got up and said, "Boys, I like to be on the right side so I am going to move my chair over and argue with you." You see our company believes in unions and in paying good wages.

INTERVIEWER: How long have you been president?

BLAKELY: I have been re-elected seven times. Of course, I was thrown out of office once. A new fellow—a loud mouth—told the boys what he would do if he was president. He won, but when he learned the men didn't want to shake the buildings down, he quit. The real function of a trade union is to work so that both the company and the workers prosper. When we negotiate it might be possible to get a 50-cent increase, but there wouldn't be any jobs next year after we put the company out of business. People used to look down on union members, but they don't any more. They are looking to us to do a good job.

INTERVIEWER: Didn't you reject job evaluation the first time?

BLAKELY: Well, we may have waited for Craftown to make up their minds.

Carl Wilson, Secretary of the Kingsville Local

(In the opinion of both company and union officials at the
Craftown and Kingsville plants, Mr. Wilson was "the real
leader of the Kingsville union.")

WILSON: We needed a systematic method to develop a wage structure. Management, failing to educate foremen, permitted them to be sole judges of wage increases. Their favoritism and lack of knowledge gave the union an effective means of increasing wage rates by claiming B's wage was too low in relation to A, A's wage having been improperly set by management itself. As soon as management conceded, C, D, E, and F immediately had complaints with regard to their pay. By playing the wage inequity game we sowed seeds of multiple grievances throughout the union. That is why the union accepted job evaluation.

INTERVIEWER: What was the program of installing evaluation?

WILSON: We kept the membership informed why evaluation was necessary. We indicated the substantial advances it would mean in total payroll. We called in the man who had complaints, explained the system, and had him evaluate his own job. As a rule he evaluated himself too low, in which case the committee's evaluation prevailed.

The engineer hired by the company to assist us was not a production man. We had to do a great deal toward assisting him. Yet his problem was common to any man who might have come in from the outside.

INTERVIEWER: Why did Kingsville accept job evaluation when Craftown turned it down?

WILSON: People will tell you Craftown is different from Kingsville. I cannot agree. People everywhere are pretty much the same. First, the Craftown union does not do a good educational job, and second, Craftown officers have abdicated their position of leadership. They listen too much to various opinions and express their own ideas too little, and the result is chaotic thinking.

It was unfortunate that Pat Kelly, the Craftown union president, died. Jim O'Hara, who succeeded him, was new and uncertain about the program. Craftown did not explain the system as well to their membership. If we had their inspection department here, we would be much firmer. We would have been glad to have their criticisms, but we would not permit them to shout us down. The union hasn't done an education job at Craftown. That is in part due to management.

4

Incentive Wages at
Sedgewick-Cole Corporation

I

The Sedgewick-Cole Corporation considered it necessary to offset wage increases through increased productivity to maintain its competitive position. Some 17 months after authorization to develop an incentive system had been incorporated into the union agreement, Mr. Tedrick, company personnel director, met with the union officers of the Craftown local, United Rubber Workers (cio), and filed the following grievance:

A definite effort is being made by certain groups of employees to control to a predetermined number of units the production in the inspection department. One has only to look at the level of production on the "C" inspection to feel certain these crews are not making a reasonable effort to attain and maintain the production as agreed upon.

In view of the union's repeated assurance that they will not approve *any* control of production we request some reason for the actions of these inspection crews. We can see no reason for them to refuse to make some incentive on the present standard. The whole group is determined to sabotage the agreement between the company and the union. Will you kindly reply to this grievance in writing at your earliest convenience?

II

The contractual provision empowering the development of an incentive system read:

There is to be inserted in place of paragraph "d"[1] a paragraph calling for the development of an incentive plan to be worked out between a

1 The superseded paragraph "d" had provided: "In any case where a speed-up occurs, through increasing speed of present equipment or revamping of same, whereby

union committee and a company committee with the usual arbitration clause.

Thereupon the company had hired D. K. Coates as consultant to develop the plan. Within 9 months he had a group of incentive rates and standards ready to install. The union requested a delay until the completion of contract negotiations, which were to open the next month. Without citing any specific objections, they said they wished to review the situation.

During the new negotiations, in addition to the pattern agreed to by basic industry, the company offered an *additional* increase of 6 cents per hour if the union would accept the proposed production norms. Although management estimated that only 40% of the work force could increase their output, Mr. Tedrick did not consider it feasible to limit the additional 6 cents to them. The union negotiators rejected this offer, reporting that an informal membership survey indicated the offer inadequate, inasmuch as proposed norms would necessitate a 15% increase in output.

After two months of discussion, the union finally agreed to consider the proposal if the additional increase were to be 10 rather than 6 cents. The company offered 7 cents. The union amended its counterproposal to 9 cents. Both parties agreed on 8 cents, and the incentive joint stipulation was incorporated into the new contract.

III

With this agreement, the company put into immediate effect production standards for all direct-production workers. For those operations which he had time-studied, Mr. Coates first determined the rate of output reasonably to be expected of the normal operator working under the inducement of the incentive wage. He then established as the production "standard" a level of output 30% less than the output expected of the normal operator. Thus management anticipated that most operators would produce 30% over standard, and earn 30% over the base rate, which included all increases granted at the most recent negotiations. For operations not yet time-studied, management established a temporary estimated standard equal to the average of the past performance of the department increased by 15%. Starting from this estimated standard, the company would give pay increases

the company's costs are lowered and maintained for a period of 90 days, the employees affected will receive a fair share in the savings involved, such share to be distributed at the discretion of company and union officials."

directly proportional to increases in production. For a few departments in which the nature of the process allowed no decrease in production time, the management established a temporary standard which, when increased by 30%, would equal the prior production rate. Thus such workers would receive a 30% bonus for the same amount of work which they had previously performed. By whichever one of the three methods the standard was established, management expected each worker to earn 15% over his base rate to justify the extra 8-cent increase it had granted.

Reviewing subsequent developments, Mr. Tedrick recalled that many workers, especially inspectors, did not like the new system. "One inspector who had griped for years clammed up. Another announced, 'I know when I'm licked. I quit.' He had been with us 20 years. Another inspector asked, 'Why should we speed up just to give the mechanics a raise? Give it all to us, and we'll do the job.' The inspection department was in a state of internal warfare over acceptance of incentives."

IV

Several days after incentives were installed, Craftown averaged but 68% of the new standard, while the company's other plant at Kingsville was averaging 90%. The Craftown plant manager told Mr. Tedrick that the situation would improve with time. Nevertheless, Mr. Tedrick decided to talk with the men.

Mr. Tedrick selected the pulling-out department as the first for such a conference. This small department, always cooperative, and working under a foreman considered firm but fair, was producing 70% of standard. Accompanied by the union vice president, a "quiet, stable" production worker, Mr. Tedrick spoke to the workers. Mr. Tedrick told them they were "laying down on the job" and if they didn't attain standard within one day, every one of them would lose his 8-cent increase. He said, "This is an ultimatum."

One man answered, "This isn't what the union told us." The union vice president interjected with: "You didn't understand. Mr. Tedrick is right."

Output in the pulling-out department reached standard within 4 hours after Mr. Tedrick's talk. The talk was repeated the next day in the inspection department with similar results on all inspection tables except those assigned to "C" inspection. Output there continued at exactly the same level registered before the installation of incentives. It remained exactly the same each day. Often the inspectors did nothing for the last 30 minutes of each shift if they had already reached their daily level. After three months, Mr. Tedrick entered the grievance set forth above and stated, "If no action is taken, the company will be compelled to eliminate employees willfully holding up any jobs."

V

After receiving the company's grievance, the union announced that a union time-study engineer would make independent studies. After six weeks, the union engineer submitted his report objecting to methods the company had employed in establishing standards for the inspectors. The company restudied the operation and reaffirmed its standard fair. The union requested arbitration.

Two months later the standard developed by the company was upheld in arbitration. Pending this arbitration, problems had continued to arise. Interviews held during this same period appear below.

Four days following the arbitration, the Craftown inspectors held a departmental meeting at the union office. Following this meeting, the department committeeman advised the foreman that the men felt they had no obligation to produce any more than the standard. Mr. Tedrick immediately informed the union officers that control of production was continuing, and unless they corrected the situation within two days, the company would take drastic action.

VI

Two days later Mr. Tedrick filed another grievance against the Craftown union:

After six months' discussion, negotiation, and finally arbitration, a standard of production is established for "C" inspection. Employees are refusing to make more than standard. This refusal is a violation of our agreement. Unless these crews decidedly improve by tomorrow, it will be necessary to dismiss those controlling production. The reluctance of the union to control the actions of its members will be taken up as a separate grievance.

The following morning Mr. Tedrick read this latest grievance to all inspectors in the presence of local union officers and the international representative. The following discussion took place:

INTERNATIONAL REPRESENTATIVE (u): We want the names of those employees who supposedly are controlling production.

TEDRICK (m): Henry Perry and Thomas Dowler are among those present whom we accuse. However, we will discipline any other employees whom supervision names.

INTERNATIONAL REPRESENTATIVE (u): How are the union officers to know what employees are controlling production?

TEDRICK (m): The union was given ample time to make their own investigation.

COMMITTEEMAN (u): If the company is making a charge, it should point out the offenders. The company is all wrong in making its charge against Perry and Dowler. They should not be held responsible for the poor production of an entire crew. They have never been given a fair standard to shoot at.

TEDRICK (m): This morning Perry's table did not work for 22 minutes with no apparent reason. If Perry, as inspector, had ordered another roll to be placed on the table for inspection and the men refused, then it would be up to supervision to take action.

COMMITTEEMAN (u): Does a man have to make over standard?

TEDRICK (m): Yes.

COMMITTEEMAN (u): If production does not increase tomorrow, will Perry and Dowler be accused of controlled production?

TEDRICK (m): Yes, and any others inspection supervision accuses. Dismissals will be made. I suggest this department meet with your international representative to discuss this matter before it becomes necessary for the company to take final action.

The next day production was 10% above standard on the "C" inspection tables. Eleven days later, output was 34% above standard, having increased a little each day. Thus increased productivity had been achieved in the inspection department 11 months after the incentive stipulation was incorporated in the contract, and 14 months after the first incentive standards had been formulated.

INTERVIEWS

James O'Hara, President of the Craftown Local

O'HARA: Some of the boys are pushing for more production under the incentive. They argue, each blaming the other if they don't make the bonus. We are in for trouble.

INTERVIEWER: How did the incentive come in?

O'HARA: The inspectors didn't want it. They fought hard, but everyone got an eight-cent increase. The inspectors said, "It stinks." It was discussed, and finally voted in. The inspectors were very mad.

Yet I know inspectors right now who are doing all right. They make the bonus. They wouldn't talk against it any more, but they couldn't say anything for it.

INTERVIEWER: What about the inspection department?

O'HARA: When I first came, they were the biggest department. They always demanded things and got it. Almost everyone was in inspection then. Of course it's smaller now, but they still have over 100 men. They always got their own way before—special privileges. They always voted in a bloc. They never elected any officers, but what they were against didn't go through. They are breaking up now though. This incentive is splitting them. There are only three tables which aren't doing anything, and I know they could.

The consulting engineer has taken months to put in this incentive system. He is a "blow-hard." He is doing his best to drag his job out to last as long as it can. I'll bet the company is paying him plenty. No wonder the company can't afford to give us a wage increase.

The fellows are anxious to get the incentive set up. The maintenance men can't get anything until the whole system is in operation. Half the trouble we have—all these grievances—could be eliminated if incentives had been put in faster. Grievance meetings are costly. The arbitration on the incentive will cost us at least $100. We are a small union. I'm going to have to do something to get this thing hurried up.

William Phillips, Secretary of the Craftown Local

PHILLIPS: The inspection department has never been for the incentive. The only word for them is "aginners." They are "agin" everything. The incentive arbitration will be their last chance to save face.

If the standard is put down where the inspectors think it ought to be, they might make it. They never have tried to make it. They could if they wanted to. Some inspectors were doing all right and the others got mad at them.

INTERVIEWER: How did the incentive get started?

PHILLIPS: No one wanted it at first. It was forced down our throats. The men needed more money with prices going up. The company offered eight cents more if the incentive plan was accepted, and the men wanted money. They accepted it to get money but lots of them think it's glorified piecework. The inspectors didn't want the indirect men to share. The company shifted men around in inspection and the men against the incentive didn't like that.

Two "C" Inspectors, Perry and Dowler

DOWLER [to interviewer]: I don't know anything to tell you. [Perry leaves his work place and joins discussion.] Perry, I was saying I don't know about things that go on here. You tell him what he wants to know.

PERRY: I don't know that we are going to have much time to talk. They complain we don't make the standard so we had probably better get on the job.

INTERVIEWER: I don't want to interfere with your work, Mr. Perry; in fact, I would be very interested in seeing what you do. Would you mind if I just watched?

PERRY: It is not interesting and there is nothing to it. I don't think you'd learn much. Besides we are about through for the day.

[The time was 2:30. The shift was scheduled to go off duty at 3:00. At the time there was no indication of any work.]

INTERVIEWER: You think the incentive standard is too high?

PERRY: We can work as hard as a man can and still not make it. There is no use to try.

INTERVIEWER: How are they doing on the other inspection tables?

PERRY: Not very good.

DOWLER [to Perry]: I thought they were making around 20% bonus.

PERRY: No, nothing like that. I don't know what *they* do. Did you want to know anything else?

INTERVIEWER: You were here when they proposed evaluation?

PERRY: Yes.

DOWLER [interrupting]: I don't know anything about that.

INTERVIEWER: Could you tell me how you felt about that?

PERRY: I don't remember anything about it. Is there anything else you want to know?

INTERVIEWER: No, but if you don't mind, I would like to come down again.

PERRY: You can come but you won't find out anything. The arbitrator came down, but he didn't find out much.

Herbert Furst, Inspector

INTERVIEWER [to William Phillips, Craftown secretary]: There must be some inspector who likes to talk.

PHILLIPS: Herb Furst loves to talk; in fact, if he gets started you can't stop him. He is on a crew that isn't trying to make standard. Here he is. Herb, tell this man about the incentive.

FURST: We always turned out 106 pieces a day. The company brought in engineers who timed us and set a standard of 123. I don't know how they ever got that number. We complained and they admitted they were wrong because they changed the standard to 121. But that was no change and there is absolutely no use in trying to make 121. It is just a way to get old quick.

PHILLIPS: I am going to walk down here where I can't hear in case you want to talk confidentially.

FURST: That is about all I know anyway. Stay, Phillips. Don't go walking away or the fellows will think something is funny.

INTERVIEWER: You were speaking about the incentive plan.

FURST: I was saying there is no use to even try it. Some of the boys are making bonus. We feel sure that their standards have been set differently, so just because they make them is no reason why we should make them. Say, I can't talk to you any longer. The boys are wondering what I am saying to you. They won't like it at all, so I'd better get over there and explain it to them. You know how it is, don't you? We work in teams.

Peter De Lucca, a "D" Inspector

INTERVIEWER: How is the incentive working out on your table?

DE LUCCA: We are making 30% bonus. Of course, I have a young crew. The men who have worked here 15 years and always work the same way don't like incentives. They find it difficult to change. The foremen say they have to make the incentive, so a lot would rather shut up and try it instead of finding another job.

INTERVIEWER: Do the men have to change the way they do their jobs?

DE LUCCA: No, but now they work faster and steadier. They can't talk as they used to. The younger ones can change, but it's not easy on the others. There are some who don't want to try to make the incentive, but most of them could if they tried.

Vincent Rosetti, Former President of the Craftown Local

INTERVIEWER: What do the men think about the incentive system, Mr. Rosetti?

ROSETTI: Some are doing all right; some are too lazy. We had these time-study men once before, and the boys went along. After a few months under the old incentive we got production up and were making some money. Then the company said, "Fine, boys. We see what you can do. Just keep on and we'll pay you less than we ever did." Out went the bonus, and if you didn't keep up the pace, they got rid of you.

INTERVIEWER: How is it going now?

ROSETTI: They can't get away with that now. But they're playing games all right. They told the indirect men like us in the pipe department, "You'll get in on this bonus, so vote with us." We sold the thing to the membership, and now we would be better off without it. They were to build a common fund to be divided among all the indirect men. The production men on incentive were to get 30% bonus. We were to get one-half of what the production men got. So if the whole plant made 30%, we would get 15%. We didn't expect to get anything the first week because it wouldn't be much, but the company was to build up this fund and distribute it in 90 days.

INTERVIEWER: The stipulation provided that indirect men would participate 90 days after the incentive was installed?

ROSETTI: That was it, and it's not been 90 days either. Hell no. It's been 7 months, and what have we gotten? Nothing. The company is getting fat by keeping all our money for themselves.

INTERVIEWER: How do the production men feel about the indirect men sharing in the bonus?

ROSETTI: That makes me so damn mad. [Rosetti becomes excited.] That's what the production men say. They are dumb—just plain ignorant. They don't understand a thing. They would like to hog it all themselves. Where in hell do they think my pay has been coming from all along? Out of production, hasn't it? We are all on the same production wheel, and as the wheel turns, we all move together. Just let them have a breakdown. We'll take our good old time to fix it up and see how much incentive they make then. They're going to have to learn the hard way. They can't make more than 30% incentive anyway, and what's left over they would rather give to the company. At least, with the indirect men sharing, we get some of it instead of the company keeping it all.

Edward Diffin, Mechanic and Former Vice President
of the Craftown Local

DIFFIN: An incentive is a speed-up system. That's all it is. The boys wanted money and the only way to get it was to agree to incentives. The membership didn't want anything to do with it. We turned it down several times.

INTERVIEWER: You voted on it?

DIFFIN: The only way it passed was the print department all voted for it. The company got the votes where the standards were set so low it was easy to make the standard. The standards were set loose in some departments to get votes.

INTERVIEWER: Why were the inspectors against it?

DIFFIN: They were afraid of working themselves out of a job. You can only print so much linoleum on the machines. What will happen if the inspectors speed up and finish ahead of the machines? Print machines can't turn out more just because the inspectors hurry. Someone will have to be laid off.

The company says they need incentives for more production. What they need is foremanship. If you have good foremen, you don't need incentives. But they won't have good foremen if they keep bringing them in from outside.

D. K. Coates, Consultant

COATES: The time watch will soon be a thing of the past. It won't be long until we have only synthetic standards. After we develop curves for all factors we will have a scientific basis for establishing incentives.

INTERVIEWER: I am interested in problems you encounter which affect the attitudes of workers or relations with the union.

COATES: We emphasize that. The first thing I did here was to give a training course for supervisors. It is important we educate management first, so we always give a course. The thing wrong with incentive installations that have soured is there are no human relations. We do a constant selling job, especially to top management.

Let's look at the course outline. [Coates reads the course outline.]

1. Rules for straight thinking.
2. Progress and people.
3. Does the existing distribution of income tend to promote or retard progress?
4. Are we merely machine tenders?
5. Does the machine throw men out of work?
6. The industrial accountant and the need for incentives.
7. Types of averages.
8. Time-study techniques, including
   a. The Bedaux system

    b. History of time and motion
    c. Types of charts
9. Motion study.
    a. Twenty rules or principles of human motion
    b. Standard therbligs

The course was made especially for this plant. You will notice each page has the name Sedgewick-Cole in the corner. At the beginning, we state the basis for the course. [Coates reads from his lecture notes.]

This course will reaffirm the high purpose and the important responsibilities which beset the industrial engineer. Time and motion study is the one common denominator for the measurement of endeavor on a factual basis.

One of the first things we must consider are the human motors—people —and the things that affect them. What is wrong with people? There are two outstanding things that are wrong. They are that it is human nature (1) to resist the new, and (2) to resent criticism. Like the parachute, the mind functions only when open.

We teach 23 workable rules of human relations. [Mr. Coates reads the following 11.]

1. Indirectly introduce the new idea so that the person accepts it as his own. (Sell 'em; don't tell 'em.)
2. Show respect for the other person's opinions. Never tell him he is wrong.
3. To get the best of an argument, avoid it. Nobody ever wins.
4. Try to see things from the other person's point of view.
5. Praise every suggestion or improvement, no matter how small.
6. Give the person a fine reputation to live up to.
7. Never accept a challenge.
8. Call attention to people's mistakes indirectly.
9. Make sure you pronounce and write his name correctly.
10. Remember we are all egotists, more or less.
11. Smile. Less effort required than to frown.

INTERVIEWER: I have a good idea of the training you give.

COATES: This course gets us rolling. Then we start taking times. We didn't analyze plant layout or methods prior to making our time study here because there wasn't enough time. The company was anxious to have the system installed.

INTERVIEWER: What do you do in a department before you use the stop watch?

COATES: We send a notice to the vice president in charge of operations, the plant manager, the director of personnel, and the foreman. When we go into the department, we tell the men to go on just as usual.

INTERVIEWER: Have you had any problems?

COATES: In one department they were not making standard. I had the foreman come up to my office and asked him what was wrong. I told him his poor performance was a reflection on his ability. One of the problems is the failure of foremen to back up the standard. Of course a foreman won't have his department make 200% because it means something is wrong with the standard, and if he used his head he will peg his production at 130%.

INDEX

A NOTE ON THE TYPE

The text of this book was set on the Linotype in a face called TIMES ROMAN, designed by Stanley Morison for The Times (London), and first introduced by that newspaper in 1932.

Among typographers and designers of the twentieth century, Stanley Morison has been a strong forming influence, as typographical advisor to the English Monotype Corporation, as a director of two distinguished English publishing houses, and as a writer of sensibility, erudition, and keen practical sense.